CITY POLITICS
Private Power and Public Policy
Fourth Edition

DENNIS R. JUDD
University of Illinois at Chicago

TODD SWANSTROM
Saint Louis University

PEARSON
Longman

New York San Francisco Boston
London Toronto Sydney Tokyo Singapore Madrid
Mexico City Munich Paris Cape Town Hong Kong Montreal

Vice President and Publisher: Priscilla McGeehon
Executive Editor: Eric Stano
Senior Marketing Manager: Megan Galvin-Fak
Managing Editor: Valerie Zaborski
Project Coordination, Text Design, and Electronic Page Makeup: Electronic Publishing
    Services Inc., NYC
Cover Designer/Manager: John Callahan
Cover Image: Courtesy of Getty Images, Jacobs Stock Photography
Manufacturing Buyer: Lucy Hebard
Printer and Binder: Courier Corporation-Stoughton
Cover Printer: Coral Graphic Services, Inc.

Library of Congress Cataloging-in-Publication Data

Judd, Dennis R.
    City politics : private power and public policy / Dennis R. Judd, Todd Swanstrom.--
4th ed.
        p.   cm.
    Includes bibliographical references and index.
    ISBN 0-321-12971-7
    1. Municipal government--United States. 2. Urban policy--United States. 3. United
States--Economic policy. 4. Sociology, Urban--United States. I. Swanstrom, Todd. II.
Title.

    JS331.J78 2003
    320.8'5'0973--dc21

                                                2003049796

Please visit our website at http://www.ablongman.com

ISBN 0-321-12971-7

 3 4 5 6 7 8 9   BKM BKM   0 9 8 7 6 5 4

CONTENTS

PREFACE

This fourth edition of *City Politics* has been comprehensively revised to take into account the historic changes that are occurring in America's metropolitan areas. Two recent developments have now become clear: Central cities are reviving, and the suburbs are becoming opened to groups of all income and ethnic characteristics. The divided metropolis of the twentieth century, which pitted cities against suburbs and whites against blacks, has been replaced by the multiethnic metropolis. This is a result of the recent period of intense immigration from all over the world. The question posed at many places in this text is whether the multiethnic metropolis will continue to be characterized by segregation and the proliferation of enclaves, as the divided metropolis was, or whether it will take on a new form.

New research has been incorporated throughout the book so that it may serve as a scholarly reference work—as it has in the past—as well as a textbook accessible to students at all levels. *City Politics* should be useful to advanced scholars and graduate students as well as students taking their first courses in urban politics, urban sociology, urban planning, urban geography, or urban history. It is not easy to write a book intended to accomplish such diverse goals. To do so, we not only attempt to synthesize the findings in the vast secondary literature of urban politics, we also rely on our own original research. To make the complex scholarship of the field accessible to students, we build the book around a clear, coherent narrative. As far as possible, each chapter picks up where the previous one left off, so the reader can gain an understanding of how urban politics has unfolded during more than two hundred years of the nation's history.

Scholars and students will find their own research opportunities enriched by several new features incorporated into this edition:

- Comprehensive revisions of all chapters in order to achieve thematic clarity and incorporate recent research;
- The systematic incorporation of data from the 2000 census and updated statistics from other sources as well;
- Extensive recent research on the new immigration, with a special emphasis on understanding how multiethnic cities and suburbs differ from those of the past;
- A revised analysis of minority mayors and the new generation of conservative mayors;

- An expanded and updated discussion of the revitalization of central cities, including a new discussion of the impact of globalization and the rise of the New Economy;
- An expanded and updated discussion of urban tourism;
- A new discussion of urban finance, with an emphasis on intergovernmental relations and the creation of special authorities;
- An outtake section in each chapter that highlights the chapter theme.

We are pleased to able to thank, in print, the following reviewers who made insightful comments and suggestions: Andrew Aoki, Augsburg College; Mark D. Brewer, Colby College; and Jon R. Taylor, University of St. Thomas. These scholars did a wonderful job of identifying gaps in our argument and calling our attention to new research directions. Dennis Judd would like to particularly thank his graduate assistant, Daniel Bliss, for his very able research assistance, as well as for his patience when things would be lost that he had already provided. Eric Stano, our very experienced and well-seasoned editor at Longman Publishers, helped keep the book on track in ways both honest and devious as need be. But we thank him anyway.

Dennis R. Judd
Todd Swanstrom

THE POLITICS
OF AMERICAN CITIES:
AN INTRODUCTION

GROWTH, GOVERNANCE, SECESSION

City politics in the United States arises from the intersection of governmental power and private resources. Despite the importance of government in people's lives, the public sector has not eclipsed the authority of businesses and private individuals to make society's most critical decisions involving jobs, land use, and investment. City governments influence, but they do not control, the voluntary actions and decisions that, taken together, determine the material well-being, the social character, and the quality of life of an urban community.

Throughout America's national history, the most fundamental goal of its cities has generally been *local economic growth*. Founded originally as centers of trade and commerce, the nation's cities and towns came into being as places where people could make money. This was true for the oldest colonial cities and for cities on the frontier. The movement west across the continent placed towns at the leading edge of territorial expansion:

> America was settled as a long, thin line of urban places, scattering outward and west-ward from the Atlantic seaboard. The popular imagination has it that farmers came first and villages later. The historian's truth is that villages and towns came first, pulling farmers along to settle the land around and between urban settlements.[1]

Each town was its own capitalist system in miniature, held together by the independent actions of individuals in search of profit and fortune. The restless search for wealth encouraged the formation of what urban historian Sam Bass Warner called a national "culture of privatism," which stressed individual efforts and aspirations over collective or public purposes: "[The] local politics of American cities have depended for their actors, and for a good deal of their subject matter, on the changing focus of men's private economic activities."[2]

The culture of privatism nurtured a profound distrust of government, an attitude expressed in Thomas Jefferson's injunction that the best government is that which governs least. The limited-government ideal was founded on the assumption that freedom would be preserved not primarily by government but by its absence. Considering how strong this cultural imperative has been, it might seem strange that, over time, the responsibilities of governments at all levels in the United States have expanded remarkably. This expansion has occurred for two principal reasons: The powers of local government have been used to promote economic growth, and local governments have also been involved in the task of *governance*.

Although American cities often seem preoccupied with promoting prosperity, they are not plutocracies, with political power simply handed over to wealthy elites. American city governments are run according to rules that reflect a long tradition of local democracy that cuts against the grain of the culture of privatism.[3] Alongside individual rights is the right of cities to self-rule based on democratic principles.[4] City charters and the formal rules of city politics emphasize votes, not money. Just as the currency of the economic marketplace is money, votes are the currency of the political system. To assemble a winning electoral coalition, politicians must spread the benefits of city government broadly enough to gain a minimum level of satisfaction from a variety of political interests and groups.

City governments are mechanisms for arbitrating among the groups and factions that make up the local polity, a task that is as difficult today as it ever was in the past. Democratic procedures invest those who govern with the legitimacy to act in the name of citizens collectively. Governmental authority springs from the right to "make and apply decisions that are binding upon any and all segments of society."[5] At the same time that city officials must satisfy investors, they must also satisfy voters. City officials can preserve their claim to authority only as long as they seem sufficiently responsive to a large enough proportion of the urban population.

In the United States, most metropolitan areas comprise an incredible number of separate governments. Because of this extreme pattern of fragmentation, citizens have the option of moving to another city rather than engaging in the messy process of political bargaining and compromise. Escape is an option that has often been exercised. Urban residents have always tended to move into different neighborhoods, but in recent decades they have increasingly sorted themselves into enclaves that mirror the racial, ethnic, and class divisions of American society. This *politics of secession* from the larger urban community has become a defining feature of American urban politics.

The imperative of growth, the logic of governance, and the politics of secession are themes that recur throughout America's urban history. These three forces generate the tensions that make the study of urban politics so fascinating. Urban leaders in all historical periods have tried to balance the demands that local government promote economic prosperity and at the same time respond to many political claims. This balancing act became much more difficult in the twentieth century, when urban areas became more fragmented and citizens became more mobile and therefore able to leave if they were dissatisfied. Metropolitan fragmentation and its consequences are likely to be the most challenging problems of America's cities and urban areas in the twenty-first century.

THE POLITICS OF GROWTH

The imperative of growth has been a constant in the history of urban politics in America. The founders of cities and the business owners who made their money in them recognized that in order to ensure their mutual success, they had to take steps to promote their city or region. In nineteenth-century America, boosters went to some pains to advertise their city's natural advantages—a harbor or strategic location on a river, for example, or proximity to rich farming and mining areas. They boasted about local culture—music societies, libraries, and universities. And they went further than boasting; they used the powers of city governments to promote local prosperity. These entrepreneurs were aware that they were participating in a race that some cities would win and others would lose. As the city went, so went their own prospects. Municipalities were corporations that could be used to help finance a variety of local undertakings, from subscriptions in railroad stock to improvements in harbors and docks.

Over time, American cities were transformed from centers of trade to centers of production. The economic transformation brought about by the factory system in the nineteenth century depended on cities. Energy, raw materials, and labor converged at the wharves, factories, and the downtowns of cities, and these cities sent forth to the world an amazing variety of goods such as finished steel, farm implements, packaged meat, and clothes. Cities still play that role. Today, it is in the largest cities that businesses have the best chance of assembling teams of computer experts, corporate lawyers, fashion models and fashion designers, or advertising executives. It is not surprising that the media and publishing industry is centered in midtown Manhattan or that financial services and investment companies have clustered around the commodities exchange in Chicago.

It is tempting to think that the economic vitality that makes cities work occurs only through market forces, that somehow cities became trade centers in one era and locations for computers and media in another solely because entrepreneurs happened to locate in one city, but not another, for their own unpredictable reasons. This has never been the case. Ironically, an important reason why the public powers of American cities expanded was that local entrepreneurs wanted some protection from the unpredictability of the marketplace. Businesses whose fortunes are tied to local prosperity are rarely willing to trust to chance. Thus, they lobby cities to pursue policies that favor growth, such as lower taxes and subsidies to business investors. In the 1980s, gleaming office towers, luxury hotels, and tourism and entertainment facilities sprang up in central cities all across the nation, and much of this activity could be tied to public leadership and public subsidies. It may sometimes appear that all politics revolves around efforts to regenerate the local economy. Cities and special authorities provide subsidies and incur long-term debt to, for example, build new sports stadiums and convention centers, to restore waterfronts and historic buildings. In these and countless other ways cities today use their public powers and resources to promote local economic prosperity.

The only reason that such efforts often generate controversy is that they do not benefit everyone equally. For renters and low-income residents, a booming economy with rising land values may put affordable housing out of reach. Growth in the downtown corporate and financial sector may create a lot of high-paying jobs for educated (and mostly suburban) professionals but leave many central-city residents unemployed. A downtown that encroaches on nearby neighborhoods may benefit the businesses located in the new office towers but compromise the quality of life for nearby residents. Residents who do not care about sports may resent helping to pay for a new football stadium. Different perspectives such as these explain why there is a politics of growth at all.

THE POLITICS OF GOVERNANCE

Until the mid-nineteenth century, most political authority was held by men of social standing or wealth. In the cities, "leadership fell to those who exercised economic leadership. All leadership, political, social, economic, tended to collect in the same set of hands."[6] Business owners, professionals, and aristocrats ran municipal affairs without challenge, deriving their authority from their social standing. Obviously, the governance of cities is much more complicated today, for two reasons: Cities have taken on greater responsibilities, and many groups attempt to influence what cities do with those responsibilities.

The powers and responsibilities of cities have grown over time in response not only to the social and physical problems of the urban environment but also because of the demands of urban residents. The services and the infrastructure of American cities can be traced to the nineteenth century. As cities grew, sometimes exploding within a few years from small settlements to densely packed industrial cities teeming with immigrants, citizens saw that they were powerless to correct or to escape from collective problems such as crime, fire, and disease. Cities today provide a remarkable array of services. They build and maintain a public infrastructure—roads, bridges, sewer lines, sewage treatment plants, water mains, parks, zoos, hospitals, and sometimes even universities. They provide police and fire protection. They collect garbage (or pay someone who does). They run public health services that inspect restaurants, vaccinate children, and test for the HIV (AIDS) virus. Through city zoning ordinances, they influence the location of homes, factories, office buildings, restaurants, and parking lots. Through local building codes, they regulate such matters as plumbing, wiring, building materials, the height of structures, and architectural styles. Cities poison rats and sometimes try to scare away pigeons. These public activities and more are essential to the safety and well-being of all city residents. Without them, life in most cities would quickly become not only dangerous but intolerable.

But just what should cities do, and who should benefit from their activities? These questions take on a sense of urgency because the demands and needs of different groups differ sharply. The needs of one group—say, business—cannot always win because so many other groups make political claims. In a democratic system, politicians must spread the rewards of public policies around in order to construct governing coalitions. If only a few benefit from the activities of government, opposition will arise, and political leaders may find themselves replaced. If enough people begin to feel that their interests or needs are ignored, two things may happen: Other politicians may step into the fray and depose those in office, or unrest and even violence may erupt as an expression of pent-up grievances.

The fundamental logic of governance requires cities to arbitrate among contending political interests, and although those interests have changed over time, there are constants, too. American cities have always experienced ethnic, racial, and neighborhood rivalries. During the nineteenth century and the early twentieth century, cities attracted waves of immigrants, first from England, Ireland, and Germany, then from Italy and eastern Europe. In the twentieth century they received millions of new migrants, this time blacks from the South and destitute whites from rural pockets of poverty, plus Mexicans escaping violence and poverty in their own country. In recent decades they have attracted new waves of immigrants from all over the world. These movements have made cities culturally and socially dynamic places, but they have also meant that the politics of cities generally has been contentious.

THE POLITICS OF SECESSION

The deep cultural and political divisions that have so often been on display in America's cities have made them objects of suspicion. The habit of equating cities with a breakdown of the social fabric is as old as the nation. Only a few years after the Constitution was ratified, Thomas Jefferson wrote, "I view great cities as pestilential to the morals, the health, and the liberties of man."[7] In the 1970s, John V. Lindsay, the former mayor of New York, observed that "in the American psychology, the city has been a basically suspect institution."[8] These attitudes have persisted despite the fact that, according to the 2000 census, 80 percent of Americans now live in metropolitan areas.[9] But it is unclear what it means to observe that America is an urban nation. Residents of Phoenix or Dallas may feel they have little in common with residents of New York City or Boston, and the residents of the suburbs of all of these cities may feel only distantly related to their central cities, or to one another. The segregation and fragmentation of America's urban regions helps perpetuate an atmosphere of fear and suspicion.

Because America is a land of immigrants, it has sometimes been said that Americans have a tendency to pick up and move whenever they feel dissatisfied. First was the move to America, and then—or so goes the standard narrative—came the move to the frontier. The story of westward expansion fills the history books, but there was another important movement as well. In nineteenth-century cities, the wealthy and the middle class began a restless flight from the densely crowded neighborhoods close to the waterfront. The development of new forms of transportation, first the streetcar and then the automobile, enabled the well-to-do to move farther and farther from the inconvenience and problems of the congested city. In the last few decades, an increasing proportion of affluent urban dwellers has withdrawn into defended enclaves made up of people much like themselves. This politics of secession became the defining feature of urban America in the second half of the twentieth century.

In the late nineteenth century, people who migrated to the urban fringe formed separate suburban governments. This process continued all through the twentieth century, so that now metropolitan areas comprise literally hundreds of governmental jurisdictions. There is, however, a pattern to this arrangement. Typically, older central cities are encircled by a ring of autonomous suburbs and edge cities, and, almost always, a high proportion of affluent white families reside in the suburbs.

By 2002, there were 87,900 governments in the United States. In addition to the federal government and the fifty states, there were 38,971 local governments: 3,034 counties and 35,937 subcounty governments, including 19,431 municipalities and 16,506 townships. The remainder, which comprises over one-half of the total, are special-purpose local governments, including 13,522 school districts and 35,356 special districts.[10] Special districts and authorities set up with taxing and spending powers that serve special purposes, such as running toll bridges or building sewer systems, are the fastest-growing types of local government in the United States. Many of the services previously supplied by city governments are now provided by special districts, which are run more like private corporations than governments.[11] These districts are so numerous and they overlap so haphazardly that most surburbanites know nothing about them, at least until the tax bill arrives.

The politics of secession undermines the politics of bargaining and compromise that characterizes the governance of cities; indeed, secession becomes a substitute for governance. The politics of secession accentuates rather than moderates racial and class differences. Those who lack the resources to move to desirable suburbs or gated communities are forced to live in jurisdictions where the needs are great but the resources to treat them are meager. Today, urban politics in the United States involves a struggle between separate places as much as a struggle between groups and individuals within places.

INTERWEAVING THE THEMES

The imperative of growth, the logic of governance, and the politics of secession generate the tensions that make the study of urban politics compelling. Urban leaders in all historical periods have tried to promote local economic prosperity, but they have had to do so within the constraints of democratic processes with many claimants, and against a background of racial, ethnic, and social divisions and animosities. The narrative of city politics in America is fascinating because it is woven from these strands.

NOTES

1. Lawrence J. R. Herson and John M. Bolland, *The Urban Web: Politics, Policy, and Theory* (Chicago: Nelson-Hall, 1990), p. 43.
2. Sam Bass Warner, Jr., *The Private City: Philadelphia in Three Periods of Its Growth* (Philadelphia: University of Pennsylvania Press, 1968), p. 4.
3. Robert Bellah et al., *Habits of the Heart: Individualism and Commitment in American Life* (Berkeley: University of California Press, 1985).
4. For a theoretical analysis of the popular democratic theory of American local government, see Anwar Syed, *The Political Theory of Local Government* (New York: Random House, 1966).
5. Eric Nordlinger, *On the Autonomy of the Democratic State* (Cambridge, Mass.: Harvard University Press, 1981).
6. Herson and Bolland, *The Urban Web*, p. 46.
7. Quoted in James A. Clapp, *The City: A Dictionary of Quotable Thoughts on Cities and Urban Life* (New Brunswick, N.J.: Center for Urban Policy Research, Rutgers University, 1984), pp. 128–129.
8. Quoted in ibid., p. 148.
9. U.S. Bureau of the Census, Census 2000 (http://www.census.gov/cens2000).
10. U.S. Bureau of the Census, Census of Governments, July 2002.
11. Nancy Burns, *The Formation of American Local Governments: Private Values in Public Institutions* (New York: Oxford University Press, 1994).

PART I

THE ENDURING
ISSUES IN AMERICAN
CITY POLITICS

The history of American urban politics reveals that the big issues have been around for a very long time. In its first century and a half, America evolved from a rural to an urban society and from a trading to an industrial economy, with all the attendant tensions and anxieties of these large-scale changes. Americans tended to cling to the notion that America was different because its citizens were close to the land. As Thomas Jefferson famously said, "I think our governments will remain virtuous for many centuries as long as they are chiefly agricultural; and this will be as long as there shall be vacant lands in any part of America. When they get piled upon one another in large cities as in Europe, they will be corrupt as in Europe."* And yet cities were, in fact, the engines of the nation's economic progress. Decade by decade, they grew at an astonishing rate because jobs and industry were located there; accordingly, they drew millions of newcomers. It was inevitable that cities would become the places where

*Quoted in James A. Clapp, *The City: A Dictionary of Quotable Thoughts on Cities and Urban Life* (New Brunswick, N.J.: Center for Urban Policy Research, Rutgers University, 1984), pp. 128–129.

9

monumental political battles were fought. As the chapters in this section show, those conflicts resonate with a contemporary ring.

As America became urban, its cities were transformed from relatively small, cohesive communities into chaotic industrial centers. As the responsibilities and resources of city governments grew, those governments became important political prizes in their own right. By the second half of the nineteenth century, the opportunities presented by growing public budgets and payrolls were seized by political leaders skilled at mobilizing the immigrant electorate. After the Civil War, a machine-style politics emerged. Though machines seemed to provide a political representation for some immigrant groups, they also tended to engage in corrupt election practices and often used the powers of city government to enrich themselves and their friends. Their style of politics affronted middle- and upper-class citizens, igniting a war for control of the cities that would last for decades.

The leaders of the municipal reform movement—one of the most influential reform movements in American history—argued that city government should be run just like a business; experts and administrators, they said, should replace politicians. In their view, the major objectives of city government should be to keep taxes as low as possible and to provide municipal services cheaply and efficiently. Such a definition of a city's purpose certainly seems plausible even in hindsight, but it is well to remember that it was also disingenuous because it served as a cover for a politics meant to reduce influence by immigrants and their leaders. Inevitably, reform undermined democratic processes in essential respects, which is why some reforms adopted a century ago have recently been challenged.

GROWTH AND GOVERNANCE: THE POLITICAL LEGACY OF AMERICA'S URBAN PAST

NATIONAL DEVELOPMENT AND THE CITIES

When the Constitution was ratified in 1789, the cities of the new nation were scattered along the coastline of a vast, mostly unexplored continent. Only five of these cities exceeded 10,000 in population. Over the course of the next century, the nation's social and economic development went hand in hand with the growth of cities. By the beginning of the twentieth century, a culture that had defined its character by reference to rural life and a western frontier had become urban and industrial.

Urbanization occurred at such an incredible pace and scale that it generated nearly irresolvable political and social tensions. The symbols and the reality of the industrial age—belching smokestacks, wave after wave of foreign immigrants, social disorder, and racial and ethnic strife—all were concentrated in the cities. The cities and the people who lived in them became the symbols of vast, disruptive economic and cultural changes. A distrust and fear of the cities became an enduring feature of American culture. The anti-urban attitudes formed in an earlier time helped to fuel the suburban boom in the second half of the twentieth century and energized the tendency toward a politics of secession in today's metropolitan regions.

The new industrial economy required a steady supply of cheap and plentiful labor. A flood of foreign immigration began to surge into the country in the 1840s, and it did not ebb until Congress passed legislation to curb it, in the 1920s. Most of the immigrants settled in crowded urban neighborhoods close to the factories. Right from the start there were tensions between the newcomers and those who thought of themselves (mistakenly) as native Americans, as dramatically portrayed in the 2002 film release *Gangs of New York*. Cultural and religious conflict became an everyday occurrence, and sometimes it escalated into violence. Successive waves of immigrants—poor, often illiterate, unfamiliar with the language and customs of their new country, and unaccustomed to city life—struggled to cope with miserable conditions in overcrowded slums. Those who had come to America earlier generally viewed the most recently arrived as not only inferior but as threatening and morally deficient.

The basic outlines of this historical narrative are relevant to the contemporary American city because in recent decades the cities once again became associated with images of poverty, crime, racial conflict, social disorder, and moral decline.[1] By the 1980s, a backlash against immigrants began to take the form of legislation to curb immigration and to reduce social spending on illegal immigrants, and laws requiring English only instruction in the schools. "Underclass" neighborhoods were targeted for intensified law enforcement. As in the past, immigrants and the poor served as lightning rods for other people's fears. Throughout much of the nineteenth century, the cultural representation of cities was remarkably similar to current media images of inner-city minority neighborhoods. To understand urban politics in the United States today, there is no better place to start than the cities of the past.

THE URBANIZATION OF AMERICA

In the nineteenth century, cities of the Western industrializing nations grew at a pace unprecedented in history. In 1800 London was the only city in the world to approach one million in population.[2] Paris ranked second among European cities with a population of 547,000. Just over 60,000 people lived in New York, which was the largest city in America by far. By 1900, eleven Western cities had topped the million-person mark; London had 6,586,000, Paris 2,714,000,[3] and New York 3,437,000. In England and Wales, the percentage of the population living in towns[4] and cities increased from 25 percent to 77 percent in the nineteenth century. Commenting on the growth of cities in 1895, the *Atlantic Monthly* noted: "The great fact in . . . social development . . . at the close of the nineteenth century is the tendency all over the world to concentrate in great cities. This tendency is seen everywhere."[5]

The experience in the United States was similar. As shown by the data in Table 2.1, from the first national census of 1790 to the census of 1920, the urban population (defined by the census bureau as people living in cities and towns of 2,500 or more) increased in most decades more than twice as fast as the U.S. population as a whole. The only significant exception to this trend showed up between 1810 and 1820, when homesteaders and farmers streamed across the Appalachian Mountains to settle the old Northwest (now western Pennsylvania, Ohio, and Indiana). But in subsequent decades, even the expanding frontier could not absorb enough people to keep America from becoming urban.

As late as the census of 1840, only one American in ten lived in cities and towns of 2,500 or more. In that decade, however, cities began growing at

Table 2.1 **The Pace of Urbanization in the United States, 1790–1920**

Year	Total Population	Percent Increase over Preceding Census	Urban Population	Percent Increase over Preceding Population	Percent of Total Population in Cities*
1790	3,929,214	—	201,655	—	5
1800	5,308,483	35	322,371	60	6
1810	7,239,881	36	525,459	63	7
1820	9,638,453	33	693,255	32	7
1830	12,866,020	33.5	1,127,247	63	9
1840	17,069,453	33	1,845,055	64	11
1850	23,191,876	36	3,543,716	92	15
1860	31,443,321	36	6,216,518	75	20
1870	39,818,449	27	9,902,361	59	26
1880	50,155,783	26	14,129,735	43	28
1890	62,947,714	25.5	22,106,265	56.5	35
1900	75,994,575	21	30,214,832	37	40
1910	91,972,266	21	42,064,001	39	46
1920	105,710,620	15	54,253,280	29	51

*Cities and town of 2,500 or more.

Source: U.S. Department of Commerce, Bureau of the Census, *Historical Statistics of the United States, Colonial Times to 1970,* pt. 1, Bicentennial ed. (Washington, D.C.: U.S. Government Printing Office, 1975), p. 8; U.S. Department of Commerce, Bureau of the Census, *1970 Census of Population,* vol. 1, *Characteristics of the Population,* pt. 1 (Washington, D.C.: U.S. Government Printing Office, 1973), p. 42.

breakneck speed. Foreign immigrants began pouring into the cities, and at the same time a steady migration from farms to cities began to transform the United States into an urban nation. By 1860, the census bureau classified almost 20 percent of the American population as urban, and by century's end the urban proportion had doubled again to almost 40 percent. When the 1920 census was taken, more than half—51 percent—of Americans lived in urban places. In less than a century, the United States had become more urban than rural.

Because of their importance as financial and commercial (and later as industrial) centers, the old cities on the eastern seaboard benefited from national development. New York maintained its supremacy as the hub of finance and trade. Its continued status as the nation's premier city was assured in 1825, the year the Erie Canal was completed. The canal linked the city directly to the Great Lakes, turning New York into a giant funnel gathering the resources of a vast continent into a worldwide trading system. After the Civil War, it consolidated its status when it became a great manufacturing city. Huge numbers of immigrants passed through New York, and many of them settled there. From a population of 369,000 in 1840, New York exploded to over 3.4 million by 1900—nearly a tenfold increase in sixty years! By 1920 it had become a leading global center of finance, trade, and manufacturing, and its population exceeded 5.6 million.

Despite its incredible growth, New York's share of the nation's urban population fell steadily throughout the nineteenth century. Hundreds of new towns and cities sprang up as the nation expanded westward, and these cities grew as fast or faster than New York—though none ever reached its size. In 1800, 18 percent of the nation's urban population lived in New York City, but by 1890 this proportion had fallen to 7 percent.[6] New York remained the largest city, but as the century progressed, other cities assumed prominent places in an increasingly integrated network of cities (see Table 2.2). As the continent filled in, interior towns popped up like mushrooms. St. Louis, the old French settlement where Lewis and Clark outfitted their expedition in 1805, exploded from a town of only 16,000 people in 1840 to a city of over 160,000 by 1860. In the same twenty years, Chicago changed even more, from a swampy frontier village of 4,500 to a city of more than 112,000. But this was only the beginning; by 1920, Chicago's population had soared to 2.7 million people. Smaller urban settlements dotted the landscape between the larger cities. In 1840, only twenty-five cities in the United States could claim 10,000 people or more, but by the turn of the century 465 cities had grown to that size, or larger.[7]

Until at least the middle of the nineteenth century, the settlements that sprang up along the leading edge of westward movement and that gradually filled in the interior served as trading and distribution centers. It did not take long until an urban hierarchy began to emerge. Cities located on rivers and waterways, such as St. Louis and New Orleans (on the Mississippi River), Chicago (at the foot of Lake Michigan), and Cincinnati (on the Ohio River), got a head start as major trading centers, transferring goods through the Great Lakes or the inland river system to the eastern seaboard cities, or directly to Europe.

After midcentury, a growing web of rail lines tied the older port cities with cities and towns in the interior. The biggest cities prospered because they attracted huge volumes of capital investment and cheap immigrant labor. Second-tier cities had more specialized economies, and they served as transfer points to the larger urban centers. The bottom of the hierarchy was composed of the multitude of small towns that shipped agricultural and extractive resources gathered from mines, forests, and farms to the larger cities, which entered them into international commerce or transformed them into manufactured goods. Without the network of cities, the nation could not have opened its frontier.

THE COMPETITION FOR URBAN GROWTH

From the very beginning, European settlement in North America was founded on town promotion and growth. The first colony, Jamestown, founded in 1607, was the risky venture of a group of English entrepreneurs who organized themselves into a joint stock company. Shares sold in London for about $62 in gold. If the colony was successful, investors hoped to make a profit on their investment.

Table 2.2 Population and Rate of Growth in Five Large Cities, 1820–1920[a]

	New York City[b]	Percent Increase	Chicago	Percent Increase	Philadelphia	Percent Increase	St. Louis	Percent Increase	Boston	Percent Increase	Percent Increase in U.S. Population
1820	137,388		—		63,802		4,598		43,298		
1830	220,471	60	—		80,462	26	5,847	27	61,392	42	33
1840	369,305	67	4,470		93,665	16	16,469	182	93,383	52	33
1850	660,803	79	29,963	570	121,376	30	77,860	373	136,881	47	36
1860	1,183,148	79	112,172	274	565,529	366	160,773	107	177,840	30	36
1870	1,546,293	31	298,977	167	674,022	19	310,864	93	250,526	41	27
1880	2,061,191	33	503,185	68	847,170	26	350,522	13	362,839	45	26
1890	2,507,474	22	1,099,850	119	1,046,964	24	451,770	29	448,477	24	26
1900	3,437,202	37	1,698,575	54	1,293,697	24	575,000	27	560,892	25	21
1910	4,766,883	39	2,185,283	29	1,549,008	20	687,029	20	670,585	20	21
1920	5,620,048	18	2,701,705	24	1,823,779	18	772,897	13	748,060	12	15

[a]These five cities were ranked as the five largest in the 1910 census.
[b]Using the consolidated borough boundaries of 1898.

Source: Glen E. Holt, personal files; U.S. Department of Commerce, Bureau of the Census, The Growth of Metropolitan Districts in the United States: 1900–1940, by Warren S. Thompson (Washington, D.C.: U.S. Government Printing Office, 1947); Blake McKelvey, American Urbanization: A Comparative History (Glenview, Ill.: Scott Foresman, 1973), pp. 24, 37, 73.

OUT TAKE

CITY-BUILDING HAS ALWAYS REQUIRED PUBLIC INVESTMENT

M unicipalities are corporations that can be used to used to promote collective purposes; one of the most important of these is economic prosperity. All through American history, civic leaders have used public resources to promote their cities' growth. Three periods of city-building illustrate the intimate connections between public investment, governmental powers, and the local economy. In the nineteenth century, the intense competition among cities ignited a "struggle for primacy and power" in which "like imperial states, cities carved out extensive dependencies, extended their influence over the economic and political life of the hinterland, and fought with contending places over strategic trade routes."[8] In an attempt to promote their own cities, civic boosters heavily subsidized private turnpike, canal, and railroad companies. The railroads received huge subsidies from the national and state governments, but cities contributed the most of all.

The second period of city-building occurred in the half-century from the 1870s to the 1930s, when cities made the transition from chaotic, disease-ridden places with dirt streets and open sewers to livable environments. By any standard, the scope of the physical reconstruction was breathtaking. Miles of underground pipes were laid to deliver water and to remove sewage. Streets were paved and then redesigned for the car and the truck. Rails and overhead wires, bridges and tunnels, and, in some cities, subway systems became the forerunners of integrated transportation systems. Within a few decades, monumental public works projects had transformed the physical environments of cities from coast to coast.

In recent decades, huge public subsidies have again been devoted to the rebuilding of the physical environment of center cities. As in the nineteenth century, civic boosters are motivated by the conviction that the fate of their cities hangs in the balance—that if they fail to build a stadium, a convention center, a downtown mall, or a cluster of high-rise office buildings, their city will wither away. Most supporters of public subsidies believe that the new projects are worthy of public support because they will help contribute to the local economy and therefore benefit everyone. But there is often vigorous disagreement about this assumption, just as there was in the nineteenth century. When municipal taxpayers foot the bill, the question will always be: Who benefits?

Though Jamestown failed, town promotion and civic boosterism became a way of life in the New World as cities competed for the settlers and investors who swept across the continent.

For much of the nineteenth century, an intense competition among cities was the mainspring of local politics. The fortunes of individual cities were only partially determined by locational advantages—what might be called "place luck." Instead, transportation connections—turnpikes, canals, and especially railroads—determined a city's destiny. Good links to the national transportation network could instantly secure a city's place by expanding its reach into the surrounding hinterland and tying it into national or international trade networks. Because such connections were so important, city governments provided expensive subsidies to the railroads in the form of free land and terminal facilities and stock purchases. The logic was simple: Rising real estate values were expected to provide more than enough additional revenues to pay off the debts. This logic did not always pan out, but any city that failed to make the effort to secure good railroad links would surely die on the vine. Railroad building intensified the competition. Before the railroads, corn could be transported by wagon only 125 miles and wheat, 250 miles before the cost made it unmarketable.[9] Beyond that distance, agricultural land was almost worthless for anything except subsistence farming because there was no way to get crops to market. Railroads opened up huge areas of farmland to commercial agriculture, which not only allowed the countryside to fill in but also resulted in soaring land values and population growth for the cities able to capture the increased trade in agricultural goods. Thus, rather than depending on luck and circumstance, civic leaders tried to shape patterns of trade and economic development. Local entrepreneurs were keenly aware that they were involved in a competition in which some cities would grow while others would stagnate or even die.

The building of the Erie Canal demonstrated that individual cities could gain substantial control over their own destiny. In 1817, after being prodded by the civic elite of New York City, the New York State legislature authorized money for the construction of a 364-mile waterway to connect the Hudson River with Lake Erie. When the canal opened in 1825, it became possible to ship huge volumes of agricultural and extractive goods from the continental interior through the Great Lakes to Buffalo, down the canal, and on to the port at New York, where they could be distributed along the eastern seaboard, used in factories, or shipped to Europe. Many producers and shippers abandoned the long, circuitous, and hazardous journey down the Ohio, Missouri, and Mississippi rivers to the port at New Orleans. New York's direct connection to the heartland via the canal quickly vaulted it past all the other eastern seaboard cities in population and volume of trade. By 1860, 62 percent of the nation's foreign trade passed through New York's harbor.[10]

The lesson was not lost on city boosters elsewhere. Civic leaders lobbied their state capitals for financial assistance to build canals. Pennsylvania, Maryland, Virginia, North Carolina, and South Carolina financed canal projects designed to cut through the Appalachians. Between 1824 and 1840, more than 3,000 miles of canals were constructed, most of them run by state governments.[11] About 30 percent of the costs were raised through private sources, but the capacity of the states to sell bonds was essential for these expensive undertakings.[12]

Canal building was so expensive, the engineering so complicated, and the natural barriers often so formidable that most cities could not hope to build them unless state legislatures helped out. But the railroads opened new opportunities. In the first decades of the nineteenth century, for the river towns like St. Louis, Pittsburgh, Cincinnati, and New Orleans, the steamboat had been "an enchanter's wand transforming an almost raw countryside of scattered farms and towns into a settled region of cultivated landscapes and burgeoning cities."[13] After midcentury, the railroads became the new enchanter's wand. The rail lines became the new rivers of commerce, capable of carrying huge volumes at amazing speed over long distances. A rail connection carried the promise of economic prosperity for a city. The railroads guaranteed that America's frontier would eventually vanish and that a network of cities, towns, and villages would spread over the entire continent.

In 1840, only 2,800 miles of track existed, most of it in the urban East. No connection reached even as far west as Pittsburgh. The early steam locomotives were hazardous contraptions, blowing up with a regularity that provoked opposition to their use in urban areas. Lacking the capital to take on bigger projects, railway companies built short lines. Because each company used its own particular gauge (width between the rails), at the end of each line goods had to be unloaded from one company's cars and put onto cars that fit the next company's rails. Even with these limitations, however, the early rail system was vastly superior to the only alternative, horse-drawn wooden wagons.

Rail lines were built at astonishing speed, and by the 1880s the adoption of standard gauge sizes made the system much more efficient. The rail network expanded from 9,021 miles of track in 1850 to 258,784 miles by the turn of the century.[14] In 1857, the newly consolidated Pennsylvania Railroad first connected Pittsburgh to Chicago. Three years later, eleven trunk lines ended in Chicago and twenty branch and feeder lines passed through it, making the city the nation's largest rail center terminus. By 1869 and with much fanfare, the symbolic Golden Spike was pounded in at Promontory Point, Utah. It completed the first cross-continental route by joining the Union Pacific line originating on the east coast to the Central Pacific line starting in San Francisco. Within a few years, the outline of the modern rail system was almost complete, a spider's web with strands reaching into every section of the country.

More miles of track were laid more quickly than in any other nation in the world. The main reason for this rapid growth was the huge public subsidies that were pumped into railroad building. Relying strictly on private investment, the railroads would have expanded much more slowly than they did. Until the 1890s, most private corporations lacked the ability to raise the huge amounts of capital that would later become routine for them. Public subsidies helped make the railroads "America's first big business,"[15] thus rendering the popular image of nineteenth-century America as the age of laissez-faire capitalism utterly false.[16]

In the Pacific Railways Acts of 1862 and 1864, the federal government gave massive amounts of land to railroads, which the companies sold to raise capital. The most generous subsidies, however, were provided by cities. Treasury secretary Albert Gallatin's 1808 plan for a federal system of transportation improvements failed to gain congressional approval because of regional rivalries.[17] Following President Andrew Jackson's veto of the Maysville Turnpike bill in 1830, transportation became viewed mainly as a state responsibility. States rushed into the vacuum and began feverishly subsidizing canals and railroads. The Panic of 1837 caused many states to lose money on their railroad investments, prompting what one historian called a "revulsion against internal improvements."[18] In the 1840s, many states wrote prohibitions against loaning money or buying stock in private corporations. Facing restrictions at the state level, railroad promoters quickly shifted their efforts to cities, which raced to outbid one another for railroad stock.

The anarchic competition imposed many costs, including overbuilding and redundancies that resulted in bond defaults and bankruptcies. Up to 1861, 25 to 30 percent of all direct investment in railroad building was supplied by state and local governments. The cities were the biggest spenders; they contributed an estimated $300 million in railroad subsidies, while the states spent $229 million and the federal government $65 million (the states would have spent more if some restrictions had not been put in place).[19] However, the state and federal subsidies were much larger than these figures might indicate, because they provided huge indirect subsidies in the form of land grants, which the railroads then converted to cash by selling the land to settlers. In the post–Civil War period, the railroads accumulated so much land that they sent agents to the Scandinavian countries, Germany, and elsewhere to recruit immigrants to buy and settle it. Partly because the railroads recruited heavily there (and also because of persistent hardships in their homeland), one-sixth of all Swedish citizens left for the United States in the last half of the nineteenth century, many of them settling in a broad swath of territory paralleling rail routes from the Great Lakes through the Dakotas and Montana.

Railroad owners became adept at playing cities against one another to secure the most lucrative subsidies. By the 1850s, cities along the eastern seaboard were floating bond issues so that they could invest in stock subscriptions, clear rights-of-way, and build terminal facilities—actions intended to ensure rail connections. The competition quickly spread west. In the 1860s, the business leaders of Kansas City, Kansas, sold bond issues to private investors, gave the proceeds to a railroad company, and persuaded Congress to approve a federal land grant to a railroad company. As a result of its success in this venture, Kansas City prospered while its nearby rival Leavenworth stagnated (today, Leavenworth is known mainly for its federal prison).[20] Denver's board of trade raised $280,000 to finance a 100-mile spur line to obtain access to the intercontinental track that ran through Cheyenne, Wyoming.[21] Some of Denver's businesses had already moved to Cheyenne in the expectation that its position astride the intercontinental line would make it the premier city of the Rocky Mountain West. The convergence of rail lines from all directions at Denver, however, secured its status as the dominant city of the Rocky Mountain region.

No city benefited from railroad building as dramatically as Chicago, whose phenomenal growth was founded on its access to agricultural and extractive products gathered from a vast region. Corn and grain, cattle and hogs, iron ore and coal poured into Chicago through the Great Lakes and over the rails. The city became a center for steel making, the manufacture of agricultural implements, tools, and machines, slaughtering and meat packing, and trade. By 1870, Chicago eclipsed St. Louis as the Midwest's premier city, a feat accomplished partly through the success of its local business community in securing railroad links. Chicago built its first railroad in 1852 and then helped finance feeder lines into the city. The city also invested in grain elevators, warehouses, switching yards, and stockyards. By contrast, for too long St. Louis's business community held fast to a faith that the steamboats would be enough to guarantee the city's continued prosperity. By the time St. Louis began seeking rail connections,

Chicago's advantage was overwhelming. Although Chicago also enjoyed the considerable advantage of being located on the Great Lakes and it was closer to the great farming regions of the Midwest than St. Louis, its aggressive leadership strongly reinforced its locational advantage.

For many years there was little conflict over the question of whether cities should go into debt to secure rail connections. When asked to vote for bond subscriptions and other subsidies, most urban voters supported railroad subsidy schemes. As long as everyone's attention was riveted on external threats to local prosperity, a politics of consensus tended to develop around the schemes to subsidize local prosperity: "Developmental policy was almost wholly a product of consensus-building among groups of merchant elites to support particular canal, turnpike, rail and other projects in response to merchant elites in nearby communities."[22] From 1866 to 1873, the legislatures of twenty-nine states granted over 800 authorizations for aid by local governments to railroad projects.[23] A study of governmental aid to railroads in New York found that no community ever voted against subscribing to railroad stock.[24] The votes were usually so lopsided as to be a foregone conclusion.[25]

For many cities, the fight for rail connections brought prosperity, but the overheated competition brought disaster to some. Railroad promoters played one town against another in search of better subsidies (a process akin to the competition today among state and local governments for footloose businesses such as sports franchises). The competition among cities was often so fierce that they often bid up the subsidies beyond what was economically rational; cities incurred huge debts on a hope and a promise. In New York State, for example, fifty towns bypassed by a major railroad joined in a $5.7 million stock subscription to the New York and Oswego Railroad. Zigzagging across the state to link the towns, the railroad went bankrupt shortly after completing the line in 1873 because the areas it served had too few people and products to sustain a healthy business. Most of the investments made by the towns were wiped out, with taxpayers left holding the bag.[26]

Then, as now, promoters exaggerated the positive effects expected of public subsidies, predicting rapid town growth, rising real estate values, and overflowing municipal treasuries. Profits on railroad stocks, they often promised, would eliminate the need for local taxes altogether. For most cities, however, "the direct effect on government finances was on the whole unfavorable."[27] Too many cities bought railroad stock that went bust, or the railroads brought far less prosperity than promised.

Many cities that had heavily invested in speculative railroad ventures found themselves dragged into fiscal crises. Although some cities defaulted on railroad debts in the 1860s, during the three-year economic depression that began in 1873 (which was itself partially brought on by the overbuilding of railroads and the overvaluing of railroad stock and local real estate), hundreds of towns and cities were forced into default. In 1873, an astounding $100 million to $150 million of municipal debt was involved in railroad bond defaults—one-fifth of all the municipal debt in the nation.[28]

Municipal defaults on railroad bonds and revelations of political corruption associated with railroad building affected politics at all levels. Citizens rebelled against paying back Eastern financiers for railroad bonds that had become worthless. In some cases the railroads had not even been built. When federal marshals came to towns to collect the debts, they were sometimes run off by shotgun-wielding mobs. Cries of debt repudiation filled the air, and some cities and states did manage to repudiate their debts.[29] From 1864 to 1888, the most common type of case before the U.S. Supreme Court involved railroad bonds.[30] Especially after 1872, many states adopted restrictions on local debt and limited the aid that could be given to private corporations.[31]

Financial and political abuses by railroad barons fueled a populist rebellion against big business that shook the national political system in the late nineteenth century.[32] In many smaller cities, consensus dissolved into conflict. In larger cities, however, the bonds of community had already become frayed. The twin processes of industrialization and immigration fragmented the cities into separate social, ethnic, and racial enclaves. Increasingly, the diverse groups clashed with one another for political control of the city.

THE BREAKDOWN OF COMMUNITY: INDUSTRIALIZATION

A statistical portrait of the frenetic growth of cities in the nineteenth century cannot adequately convey the social and political turmoil brought about by urbanization. In both Europe and the United States, urbanization on this scale was historic. Never before in world history had cities grown so large or so fast, and never before had such a high proportion of the population lived in cities. The urban historian Eric Lampard has said that "the period c. A.D. 1750–1850 [is] one of the crucial disjunctions in the history of human society. Whatever constraints had hitherto checked or moderated the growth and re-distribution of population were suddenly relaxed."[33] In the United States, the economic and technological changes brought about by industrialization signaled an abrupt break from the past. Cities changed from relatively compact communities held together by informal community norms to sprawling industrial cities characterized by social stratification and segregation, constant population change, and social and political conflict.

Before the age of industry and the railroad, trading cities sprang up along navigable waterways and harbors. The lifeblood of these cities flowed along the waterfront. Wharves and docks, warehouses, clerks' offices, banks, newspapers and printing establishments, taverns and breweries, and private homes all clustered close to the harbor or riverfront. Urban historians have labeled the mercantile city "the walking city" because the area of urban settlement was bounded by the distance that the inhabitants could walk within an hour or two. Typically, the city spread about two miles from the center, but the area of dense settlement was only a few blocks deep. The cost and inconvenience of hauling goods on horse-drawn wooden wagons guaranteed that cities would remain compact. For the same reason, settlements without access to water transportation could not amount to much. In the first decade of the nineteenth century, a ton of goods could be shipped all the way from Europe for the same amount that it cost to haul it nine miles over inland roads.[34] Inland cities without waterfronts could not conceivably compete with port and river cities as centers of trade.

The political systems of American cities became democratic only slowly. Property qualifications for voting began to be eased after 1776, and by 1850 almost all free white males were eligible to vote.[35] Until the 1820s, almost all mayors were appointed by governors or city councils. Beginning with Boston and St. Louis in 1822, charter revisions gradually transformed the office into a popularly elected post, and by 1840 this practice had become nearly universal.[36] The secret ballot and the private polling booth became the norm.[37]

Though democratic practices and norms began to spread, extreme social and economic inequality undermined their full implementation. The economy of the merchant cities revolved around trade and commerce: the importation and distribution of European goods; the regulation of docks and farmers' markets; the financing and insuring of ships and goods; and the printing of accounting ledgers, handbills, and newspapers. Educated aristocrats, importers, bankers, wholesalers, and shopkeepers were among a city's most prominent citizens. Craft workers and artisans engaged in services and small manufacturing were a notch down in the social hierarchy: shoemakers, hatters, bakers, carpenters, blacksmiths, potters, butchers, wheelwrights, saddle and harness makers, and shipwrights. At the bottom were sailors, domestic workers, servants, and the unskilled workers who moved goods from docks to warehouses. Overall, in colonial New England the inequality in wealth was about the same as in the slave-holding South.[38] At the time of the Revolution, about three out of four white persons in Pennsylvania, Maryland, and Virginia had come to America as indentured servants, and most of them remained at the bottom.[39]

The rigidly enforced class relationships were generally accepted by people at both ends of the spectrum. The small size of the merchant cities (so called because social, economic, and political affairs were dominated by the merchant class) moderated the effects of inequality by fostering "a sense of community identification similar to that of traditional societies."[40] Production was located mostly in small shops typically run by skilled artisans who employed one or two apprentices, who often lived on the premises. A close relationship and interdependence between employer and employee was common. People of all classes often lived within the same neighborhoods. Workers clustered together in shanties or back alleys, still within shouting distance of the better homes of wealthy merchants. In his study of colonial Philadelphia, Sam Bass Warner found that various occupational groups were highly segregated in 1774, but it was a proximate segregation: "It was the unity of everyday life, from tavern, to street, to workplace, to housing which held the town together in the eighteenth century."[41]

Class conflict was moderated by this proximity as well as a sense that everyone's welfare depended on the commercial success of the city. The merchant elites expected to run the city's affairs, and they did. With few exceptions, they held the mayor's office and dominated city councils without opposition.[42] Consistent with their view that the scope of local government should be limited, they spent very little on the poor or on public services for public health, sanitation, parks, and libraries. In 1810, prosperous New York City spent only $1 per capita on all public services combined.[43]

In the second half of the nineteenth century, the dislocations of rapid industrialization and urbanization transformed city politics. In 1850, not much more than 10 percent of all workers were engaged in manufacturing, and they produced less than 20 percent of the nation's economic output. But by 1870 industrial production exceeded the commercial and agricultural sectors in value added to the economy, and by the turn of the century manufacturing accounted for more than both sectors combined.[44]

Industrialization brought with it new extremes of inequality. The rapid growth of big corporations spawned a class of industrial magnates who flaunted their wealth by building mansions and estates, throwing lavish parties, and constructing monuments to themselves.[45] The number of poor people in the cities multiplied, prompting the rich to found charitable societies to deal with the "dangerous classes." Between these extremes, the number of people in middle-class occupations soared. Between 1870 and 1910, the number of clerical workers, salespersons, government employees, technicians, and salaried professionals multiplied 7.5 times, from 756,000 to 5,609,000.[46]

Industrialization removed economic production from small shops and homes and moved it into factories. Before the Civil War, manufacturing establishments rarely employed more than 50 workers, and even in large cities they ranged between 8 and 20 workers. In 1832, for example, the average-sized manufacturing establishment in Boston employed 8.5 workers.[47] In the years following the Civil War, manufacturing firms grew quickly in size. In agricultural implements and machinery, the number of employees per establishment increased from 7.5 in 1860 to 79 in 1910. In malt liquor breweries, the number of workers increased from 5 to 39, and in iron and steel establishments, from 54 to 426.[48]

Capital became concentrated in large firms. Limited-risk corporations[49] were relatively rare before the Civil War, but by the turn of the century there were 40,000 such firms, and though they amounted to only one-tenth of all companies, they produced 60 percent of value in manufacturing.[50] (Such corporations raised capital by selling stocks to investors who risked their investment but not their personal assets if the company failed.) In 1896, twelve firms were valued over $10 million, but by 1903 fifty firms were worth more than $50 million.[51] Several giant corporations formed between 1896 and 1905, including U.S. Steel, International Harvester, General Electric, and American Telephone and Telegraph, became models of the corporate form in the twentieth century.

In the small shops of the merchant cities, relations between owners and workers tended to be highly personal and informal. Within limits, artisans and craft workers chose their working hours and manner of production. By contrast, the relationships between factory owners and workers were impersonal, hierarchical, and rigid. Most workers did not even know the owner of the business that employed them. Machine-tooled, standardized parts replaced handcrafted goods. Standardized production began in 1798, when Eli Whitney designed a musket that was built and repaired with interchangeable parts. Before long, standardized components made it possible to make a variety of goods rapidly and cheaply, so that clocks, sewing machines, and farm machinery, for example, soon were assembled by factory workers rather than by craftsmen. Huge military orders during the Civil War led to mass-produced shoes and clothing. As a result of these new processes, work became regimented and closely monitored. Factory methods of production required specialized, repetitive work and a rigid distinction between management and workers.

THE BREAKDOWN OF COMMUNITY: TRANSPORTATION

Throughout the nineteenth century, city residents tried to escape the noise, congestion, and filth of the waterfront. A series of transportation improvements—most of them the products of the technological advances made possible by industrialization—allowed the cities to spread over larger areas. Class differences increasingly became expressed in segregated residential patterns. Immigrant working-class tenement slums crowded close to the downtown business districts or in bottomlands near the docks and factories. Middle-class neighborhoods tended to be located away from the crowded center. The wealthy claimed such exclusive areas as Park Avenue in New York and Beacon Hill in Boston, or lived on newly developed suburban estates.

When the omnibus was introduced to the streets of New York City in 1828, it represented a genuine breakthrough in urban transportation. The way that people commuted to work had changed little for hundreds of years. The wealthy owned or rented carriages; everyone else walked or, rarely, rode a horse. From the 1830s until the Civil War, dozens of omnibuses careened down the streets of all the major cities. Basically an enlarged version of the long-distance stagecoach, the omnibus was pulled by a team of two to four horses and typically carried up to a dozen people. Omnibuses were crowded and uncomfortable, cold in the winter, hot in the summer, and slow, barely moving faster than a person could walk. The coaches swayed and lurched over cobblestones and rutted unpaved streets.[52] A newspaper of the time complained that "during certain periods of the day or evening and always during inclement weather, passengers are packed in these vehicles, without regard to comfort or even decency."[53]

Nevertheless, those who could afford the fares—merchants, traders, lawyers, artisans, managers, junior partners—crowded into these crude conveyances. The omnibus ran on a fixed schedule and route, and picked up and dropped off passengers at frequent intervals. The fixed fare, typically a nickel, was a small fraction of the cost of renting a hackney coach. The omnibus was thus more convenient and less expensive than any alternative mode of traveling except walking. By encouraging in some urban residents the "riding habit,"[54] the omnibus signaled the beginning of the end of the walking city. For the first time, the workplace could be located at some distance from the home. American cities began to take on their present form, in which the center is abandoned by the affluent classes.

Other transportation innovations exerted a similar impact. Steam railroad lines, for example, were constructed in Boston in the late 1830s and in several other large cities over the next twenty years. Steam engines were suited for constant speed rather than for frequent stops and starts, they were expensive to build and operate, and they were fearfully loud and prone to blowing up. They did not therefore compete with omnibuses on crowded urban streets but instead facilitated the commute from the area of dense settlement in the city center to smaller towns and villages a few miles away. The 40- to 75-cent fares were out of reach of all but the wealthy (the average laborer made about $1.00 a day; sometimes skilled workers made as much as $2.00 a day).[55] Even so, by 1848 one-fifth of Boston's businessmen commuted daily by steam railway,[56] though in cities less hemmed in by water the proportion was much lower.

After 1852, with the development of a steel rail that could be laid level with the surface of the street, horse-drawn streetcars quickly replaced the omnibuses on main thoroughfares. Because they were pulled on rails rather than over potholed streets, the horsecars were able to carry twice as many passengers and travel almost twice as fast as the omnibuses. The lower cost of the horsecars "contributed to the development of the world's first integrated transportation systems."[57] In the bigger cities, the lines radiated from the center like spokes on a wheel. Because horsecars could travel 6 to 8 miles in an hour, middle-class residential settlements spread that far and more from the city center. (The rule of thumb, then as now, was that most people were willing to commute up to an hour, but not much more.) In addition, the horsecar lines sometimes extended well beyond built-up areas, serving hospitals, parks, cemeteries, and independent villages.[58] Wherever they reached, land speculators and builders bought up property in the expectation that development would follow and real estate values would rise.

In 1888, Frank Julian Sprague revolutionized urban transit when he installed the first electric streetcar system in Richmond, Virginia.[59] The motive force driving the electric streetcar came from a wheeled carriage that moved atop an overhead cable. This device trolled along the wires, pulling the car as it went. The "troller" gave the trolley car its name.[60]

Trolley cars had so many advantages over horsecars that despite the expense of installing overhead wires, traction companies and cities rushed to install them. In 1890, 60 percent of the nation's streetcars were still pulled by horses, but twelve years later the figure was less than 1 percent.[61] Trolleys traveled almost twice as fast as horsecars. Areas 6 to 8 miles from the city center could now be reached in half an hour, making it possible for people to live 10 miles or more from work. And electric streetcars were infinitely cleaner than the horsecars they replaced. City residents had always complained about "an atmosphere heavy with the odors of death and decay and animal filth and steaming nastiness."[62] The trolley allowed cities to remove thousands of horses, together with their tons of manure, from the streets.

The horse-drawn streetcars and then the electric trolleys facilitated a segmentation of activities within the cities. Until the 1870s, crowded financial and retailing districts were located close by and even mixed in with warehouses and factories.[63] In the last third of the nineteenth century, well-defined downtown shopping and financial districts became separated from industrial and warehouse areas. The middle class developed a new shopping habit, riding the streetcars downtown to shop in the new chain and department stores. The first chain retail company, the Great Atlantic and Pacific Tea Company, was organized in 1864, and in the 1870s the A&P stores expanded to several cities. Frank W. Woolworth opened his five-and-dime store in Lancaster, Pennsylvania, in 1879, and by the 1880s Woolworth's became a familiar marquee in downtown areas.[64] The middle-class habit of shopping in downtown stores for major purchases persisted right up until the end of the 1950s, by which time the streetcar system had been dismantled in most cities.[65]

While separate residential and business zones were evolving within the cities, new residential communities were springing up just beyond the city limits. Between 1890 and 1910, America experienced its first suburban boom. In most large metropolitan areas, suburban growth kept pace with the central cities in the 1890s, and after the turn of the century, in many urban areas the suburbs grew at a faster rate than the cities at the center. Chicago's population grew by 29 percent between 1900 and 1910, but the population of its suburbs increased by 88 percent. In the St. Louis, Philadelphia, Boston, Pittsburgh, and New York urban areas, suburban growth outpaced the central cities.[66]

The development of social and ethnic segregation between neighborhoods, cities, and suburbs eroded the sense of community. If the term had once evoked images of a diverse assortment of people rubbing shoulders in their daily lives, it increasingly came to mean a collection of people who were similar. The poor began to inhabit different neighborhoods than the middle class, who became, in turn, separated from the wealthy. Ethnic groups continued to mingle together to a high degree, though the Irish, Italians, and Jews began to claim their own turf. The sense of community of the merchant cities became a thing of the past, a nostalgic remembrance.

THE BREAKDOWN OF COMMUNITY: IMMIGRATION

Industrialization set off waves of foreign immigration and a restless internal population movement that eventually destroyed the informal community of the merchant cities. The industrial economy depended on a constantly expanding pool of cheap labor. Millions of foreign immigrants were pushed out of their homelands by war, civil unrest, and hardship and pulled to American shores by opportunity. They worked on the railroads, in meat packing, in steel making, in coal and lead mining, and in factories of every kind. Simultaneously, an unprecedented migration from farm to city was set in motion. Between 1830 and 1896, developments in farm machinery cut in half the average time and labor required to produce agricultural crops. During this period, for example, the time required to harvest wheat was reduced by 95 percent and labor costs for farming fell by one-fifth.[67] The new machinery drove up the capital investment required for starting and running a farm. Unemployed farm laborers and young people streamed into the cities.

Between 1820 and 1919, 33.5 million foreign immigrants arrived on American shores (see Table 2.3). Almost three-fourths of them, 24 million in all, settled in the cities. By 1870, more than half the population of at least twenty

Table 2.3 Decennial Immigration to the United States, 1820–1919

	1820–1829	1830–1839	1840–1849	1850–1859	1860–1869	1870–1879	1880–1889	1890–1899	1900–1909	1910–1919
Total in millions	0.1	0.5	1.4	2.7	2.1	2.7	5.2	3.7	8.2	6.3
Percentage of total from:										
Ireland	40.2	31.7	46.0	36.9	24.4	15.4	12.8	11.0	4.2	2.6
Germany	4.5	23.2	27.0	34.8	35.2	27.4	27.5	15.7	4.0	2.7
United Kingdom	19.5	13.8	15.3	13.5	14.9	21.1	15.5	8.9	5.7	5.8
Scandinavia	0.2	0.4	0.9	0.9	5.5	7.6	12.7	10.5	5.9	3.8
Canada	1.8	2.2	2.4	2.2	4.9	11.8	9.4	0.1	1.5	11.2
Russia					0.2	1.3	3.5	12.2	18.3	17.4
Austria-Hungary					0.2	2.2	6.0	14.5	24.4	18.2
Italy					0.5	1.7	5.1	16.3	23.5	19.4

Source: From N. Carpenter, "Immigrants and Their Children," *U.S. Bureau of the Census Monograph*, no. 7 (Washington, D.C.: U.S. Government Printing Office, 1927), pp. 324–325.

American cities were foreign-born or children of parents who had immigrated (see Table 2.4). The census of 1920 showed that almost half (48 percent) of the nation's entire urban population were first- or second-generation immigrants,[68] a result of the fact that in just the two decades between 1900 and 1920, 14.5 million immigrants entered the country.[69] The immigrant flood would have continued had Congress not enacted restrictive immigration laws in 1921 and 1924.

Immigrants passed through the port cities of the eastern seaboard, and many of them stayed in those cities and contributed to their phenomenal growth. From midcentury on, increasing numbers fanned out to the growing cities in the interior, went on to mining camps, or joined railroad construction

Table 2.4 **Proportion of Immigrant Population in Cities of 500,000 or More, 1870 and 1910**

		Percent Foreign-born	Percent Foreign-born or Native-born with At Least One Foreign Parent[a]
New York	1870	44	80
	1910	40	79
Chicago	1870	48	87
	1910	36	78
Philadelphia	1870	28	51
	1910	25	57
St. Louis	1870	36	65
	1910	18	54
Boston	1870	35	63
	1910	36	74
Cleveland	1870	42	75
	1910	35	75
Baltimore	1870	21	38
	1910	14	38
Pittsburgh	1870	32	58
	1910	26	62
Mean for all 8 cities	1870	40	72
(each counted equally)	1910	32	72

[a]Native-born with foreign parents is unavailable in the 1870 census. The figures for 1870 are estimated by adding 80 percent to the number of foreign-born. In all cases, this should yield a safely conservative estimate.

Source: U.S. Department of the Interior, Superintendent of Census, *The Ninth Census* (June 1, 1870), vol. 1, *Population and Social Statistics* (Washington, D.C.: U.S. Government Printing Office, 1872), p. 386; U.S. Department of Commerce, Bureau of the Census, *Thirteenth Census of the United States Taken in the Year 1910,* vol. 1, *Population 1910* (Washington, D.C.: U.S. Government Printing Office, 1913), p. 178.

gangs. Most of the immigrants, however, settled in cities. In 1920, more than 80 percent of the Italians, Irish, Russian, and Polish immigrants were urban, as were 75 percent of the immigrants from the United Kingdom.[70] A lesser proportion of German immigrants, about two-thirds, lived in towns and cities, reflecting the fact that in the middle decades of the century many of them had settled in rural areas of the Midwest. A smaller proportion of the Scandinavians settled in urban places than any other group. Many of them were lured into immigration by railroad agents sent to the Scandinavian countries in search of buyers for land secured through government land grants. Enough Scandinavians settled in rural areas in Wisconsin, Minnesota, the Dakotas, and throughout the Midwest that only 55 percent were classified as urban in the census of 1920.

Sixty percent of all the European immigrants between 1820 and 1919 flowed through New York harbor. Between the turn of the century and World War I, approximately two-thirds of all U.S.-bound immigrants were processed through New York's Ellis Island, making it (together with the Statue of Liberty) an enduring symbol of America's immigrant history. Though clustered in large numbers in a few northeastern and midwestern cities, immigrants spread out to all the cities that supplied industrial jobs. As shown in Table 2.4, by 1870 immigrants made up 40 percent, and immigrants and their American-born children accounted for at least 72 percent, of the populations of eight cities of more than 500,000 people. In New York City, first- and second-generation immigrants made up almost 80 percent of the population. In Chicago, an astounding 87 percent of the population was composed of the foreign-born and their American-born children. And the immigrants kept coming. Despite a huge migration from rural areas to the cities in the latter years of the nineteenth century, by 1910 the proportion of first- and second-generation foreign-born in most cities was about the same as it had been forty years before (see Table 2.4). By the census of 1920, just before Congress passed legislation restricting immigration, 58 percent of the population of all cities with over 100,000 people was first- or second-generation immigrant.[71]

The ethnic composition of the immigrant tide changed substantially over the decades. The data in Table 2.3 show that in the 1840s and 1850s, the Irish and Germans made up more than 70 percent of all immigrants. By the 1880s, however, their proportion had fallen to 40 percent, and after the turn of the century they accounted for only about 8 percent of all immigrants. Likewise, immigration from the United Kingdom declined decade by decade before plummeting after the turn of the century.

After the depression of 1873–1879, immigration reached floodtide proportions. It doubled from 2.7 million in the 1870s to 5.2 million in the 1880s. After falling slightly because of a major depression in the 1890s, the number of immigrants in the first decade of the twentieth century soared to the highest level in American history, to over 8 million. In the 1890s, Jews from Russia and Austria-Hungary, together with Catholics from Italy, made up 42 percent of immigrants, and their proportion of all immigrants rose to more than 60 percent from 1900 to 1920.

The Irish and then the Germans set off the first big surge of nineteenth-century immigration. Famine and disease pushed the Irish to American cities.

Irish peasants subsisted primarily on potatoes and vegetables grown on tiny, rocky plots of ground and in strips of soil along the roads, the only usable land not claimed by English landlords. When a potato blight swept through Europe in the 1840s, its effects were more devastating in Ireland than elsewhere. Between 1845 and the mid-1850s, up to a fourth of Ireland's peasants starved to death. Many of the survivors streamed into Liverpool and bought or bartered passage on ships heading for America.

As soon as they arrived, the Irish encountered intense hostility. Irish workers could rarely read or claim a skilled occupation. They took menial, temporary, low-paying jobs—moving goods on the waterfront, building streets and roads, working in slaughterhouses and packinghouses. Because of their poverty and their religion and perhaps their peasant origins as well, they became etched in the public mind as dangerous, alcoholic, criminal, and dirty. As portrayed in the 2002 film *Gangs of New York*, anti-Catholic and anti-Irish riots broke out from time to time. Irish churches, taverns, and neighborhoods were attacked by mobs whipped up by a rhetoric that spoke of "an invasion of venomous reptiles . . . , long-haired, wild-eyed, bad-smelling, atheistic, reckless foreign wretches."[72] Protestant Yankees were in a position to hire, promote, and fire. Even as late as the 1920s, want ads in Boston frequently added "Protestant" as a qualification for employment.[73] The Irish clustered on the lowest rungs of the social and economic ladder well into the twentieth century.

The Germans encountered far less antipathy. A large proportion of German immigrants were wealthy or from middle-class origins. They were escaping war and political turmoil, not poverty and starvation. They brought with them music and literary societies and a commitment to formal education. Although the Germans nominally faced a greater language barrier than did the Irish, the Irish brogue—and even more, the widely used Gaelic—sounded just as foreign to American ears as did the German language.

Important variations existed among the different immigrant groups as they strove to catch up to the native Yankee Protestants. In late nineteenth-century Boston, for example, an immigrant "pecking order favored some groups over others."[74] The Irish and Italians competed for the lowest wages and lowest-skill jobs. Only blacks were below them. German and recent British immigrants frequently entered middle-class occupations right away. A few with exceptional education or a needed skill achieved real success quickly. The Russian and Eastern European Jews, who came in the 1890s and later, placed emphasis on formal education and business. Though discrimination kept them out of corporations and larger business enterprises, they occupied their own niche as job brokers, middlemen, and shopkeepers.

The various immigrant groups crowded into densely packed communities near the waterfront and factories. In the 1840s and 1850s, real estate speculators and landlords shoehorned them into deteriorated houses and into attics and basements, into unused warehouses and factories. Housing was so scarce and rents so high that a large proportion of property owners made money by renting extra space in their own living quarters.[75] Narrow three- and four-story buildings divided into tiny living quarters sprang up in alleyways and on back lots.

On vacant lots and behind and between buildings, immigrants crowded into sheds and shanties.

In New York as early as the 1850s and in other cities somewhat later, the first tenement districts began to spread. With the middle class beginning to leave the city center, it became cost-efficient to raze older structures and replace them with buildings designed to crowd as many people as possible into the available space. The tenement—the name given to any low-cost multiple-family rental building—became a universal symbol for urban slums. Indeed, by the twentieth century, multistory buildings of any kind came to represent city living, and the suburbs became identified with freestanding houses and low-density subdivisions. The dumbbell—so named because of two 28-inch-wide air shafts that provided the only light and air to the interior rooms—became the most notorious tenement structure. Based on an award-winning 1879 design, the dumbbell maximized economic return but not ventilation and sanitation. Tenants on the upper floors would pitch their garbage down the shafts, where it was left to rot. On each floor, located next to the foul air shafts, were one or two public toilets and a sink. By 1893, 70 percent of the population of New York City lived in tenements, most of them dumbbells.[76]

The dense clustering of immigrants into slum districts led native-born Protestants to conclude that the immigrants were dangerous and morally deficient. In spite of the obvious problems caused by overcrowding, however, the clustering of the various immigrant groups into separate communities was crucially important for assimilating them into city life. For some groups, ethnic traditions and social and religious practices smoothed the transition to city life in America. Thus, although the Lower East Side of Manhattan became the most densely crowded residential district in any American city during the 1890s, its disease, death, crime, and alcoholism rates remained extremely low. The customs and lifestyles of the Eastern European Jews who settled there accounted for this anomaly. Jewish families insisted on personal cleanliness and careful preparation of food. By 1897, over half of New York's bathhouses were Jewish.[77] Jewish children were imbued with the idea that education was the sure road to success. Orthodox Jews did not tolerate heavy drinking, and suicide and crime were virtually nonexistent among Jewish youth. By contrast, rates of crime, alcoholism, and disease ran high in the Irish wards. The Irish tended to be the hardest hit by the periodic epidemics that swept through the cities. The Irish populations were virtually decimated, for example, by the yellow fever epidemics that swept Memphis in 1873 and 1878. No other group suffered as much.[78]

THE INCREASING IMPORTANCE OF MUNICIPAL SERVICES

All city residents, whether native-born or immigrant, rich or poor, were subjected to the dislocations arising from the frenetic pace of urban growth. For most city residents in the latter half of the nineteenth century, the conditions of urban life ranged from squalid to barely tolerable. Epidemics sometimes swept through the cities. Streets turned to seas of mud in winter and to dust bowls in summer, and in every season they were littered with refuse and piles of steaming horse manure. A Swedish novelist commented that Chicago in 1850 (when it still had only 30,000 people) was "one of the most miserable and ugly cities," where people had come "to trade, to make money, and not to live."[79]

Urban residents complained about the conditions of daily life, but there was no guiding philosophy about what municipal governments should do to improve them. The American Revolution was fought to throw off an oppressive imperial power. As a consequence, all governments became defined as potential threats to individual liberty. Alongside the suspicion of government was a tradition of privatism—the idea that progress came through individual, not collective, endeavors. As a consequence, though urban leaders could persuade their fellow citizens to use local government to support schemes to promote the local economy, it was much more difficult to persuade them to tax themselves to support municipal services.

In the compact merchant cities, most services were provided by volunteers. Volunteer night watchmen, for instance, tried to enforce the law; even in the larger cities (New York had 369,000 people by 1840), full-time, paid, uniformed police forces were rare until the mid-nineteenth century. Volunteer fire gangs answered the fire alarm. Individual property owners swept the streets and collected refuse. Even when city life became increasingly unpleasant, city residents were reluctant to acknowledge that municipal government might do better than the community's volunteer efforts.

Even in an atmosphere that denigrated governmental undertakings, the responsibilities of municipal governments vastly increased in the latter half of the nineteenth century. In New York City, for example, per capita city expenditures increased from $6.53 in 1850 to $27.31 in 1900.[80] During this half-century, cities spent more money and employed more people than either the state governments or the national government. When governmental spending was cataloged for the first time in the federal census of governments in 1902, it was found that local governments accounted for half of all governmental expenditures in the United States.[81]

At least three reasons explain why city governments took on new public responsibilities. First, new public services were provided in cases when urban residents of all classes felt threatened by imminent catastrophe or crisis. Second, local boosters assumed the lead in organizing public services when the absence of such services threatened local economic vitality. And third, by the late nineteenth century the growing middle class became intolerant of urban conditions that had previously been considered normal or inevitable.

In the absence of a positive philosophy about the responsibilities of government, urban services tended to be minimal. Essential as they were to basic health, water systems, for instance, were chronically inadequate. In the early nineteenth century, most city residents got their water from wells, and these were often contaminated by waste. As a result, outbreaks of contagious diseases occurred with regularity. In the summer of 1793, 10 percent of Philadelphia's population died from yellow fever.[82] The city's economy came to a standstill, and a third of the population and virtually all wealthy families fled for the summer months. Outbreaks of yellow fever or cholera occurred in Philadelphia, Baltimore, and New Haven in 1793; in New York City, Baltimore, and Norfolk, Virginia, in 1795; and in Newburyport, Massachusetts, Boston, and Charleston, South Carolina, the next year.[83] Nearly a dozen cities were hit in 1797; three-fourths of Philadelphia's population fled and 4,000 people died (about 7 percent of the population).[84]

The threat of contagion prompted cities to invest in waterworks, drain swamps, and regulate the keeping of animals and the dumping of refuse. Philadelphia was goaded by its epidemics to construct the first municipal waterworks in the nation's history. Begun in 1799 and operational by 1801, it piped water to the city from the upper Schuylkill River. Philadelphia's system was constantly improved by the merchant elites that ran the Watering Committee. By the 1840s, however, these elites began to withdraw from political activities, partly because competition for political office had become more intense. Without their guiding hand on the committee, the water supply system became less and less adequate.[85] Only slowly did the city take over the responsibilities of the Watering Committee.

New municipal services tended to lag behind the need for them because they always constituted a minimal response to a crisis; "municipal authorities, loath to increase taxes, usually shouldered new responsibilities only at the prod of grim necessity."[86] Devastating outbreaks of yellow fever, typhoid, and cholera periodically made their rounds, especially in the inland cities such as New Orleans and Memphis that lagged furthest behind in providing uncontaminated water. Several urban water systems were built in the 1850s, and by the Civil War seventy towns had waterworks, which were owned by eighty private companies.[87] Most people, however, had to fetch the water from street hydrants and hand pumps. Only wealthy people who could afford to pay for the service had water piped into their homes. In 1860, about one-tenth of Boston's residents had access to a bathtub, and only five percent of the homes had indoor water closets.[88]

Urban water supplies were polluted by human and animal waste. Sewage was generally not drained away from the cities but instead was collected in huge community cesspools, which had to be dug out frequently. Even when sewer pipes carried waste away from the city, the main result was merely to move the pollution somewhere else. Serious typhoid epidemics broke out in the cities along the Merrimac River in Massachusetts in the 1880s because residents were drinking water polluted by cities located upstream. Because of Boston's habit of dumping wastes directly into it, by 1877 Boston Harbor had become "one vast cesspool."[89] Until the 1920s, crowded residential districts were dotted with outdoor privies, and water bearing a burden of horse manure and other refuse flowed in open gutters along the edges of the streets. There were so many sources of contamination that only those cities that piped their water from isolated watersheds far away from urban settlement could avoid a contaminated water supply.

Ultimately, the water supply problem could be solved only through the development of adequate technology. Even Philadelphia's relatively sophisticated system delivered its water with only the heaviest silt filtered out.[90] Pumps frequently failed; in the winter, pipes froze. People found dirt, insects, and even small fish in their water. During the first decade of the twentieth century, when modern filtration techniques were developed, death rates in New York, Boston, Philadelphia, and New Orleans were cut by one-fifth.[91]

Epidemics also prompted cities to build sewers. In 1823, Boston began installing the nation's first sanitary sewers. Other large cities followed suit, but slowly. By 1857 New York City, with a population of nearly one million people, had built sewers under only one-fourth of its streets, and most of these were storm rather than sanitary sewers.[92] Taxpayers resisted the high cost of laying underground pipes and installing costly pumps. Though most of the big cities had constructed sewers by the 1870s, these were usually paid for by the property owners who subscribed, leaving vast areas—always the neighborhoods inhabited by the poor—without service.

In response to a crisis in public order, cities also began to finance and organize professional police forces. In the merchant cities of the early nineteenth century, social control had been based on face-to-face relations within the household and the community. Most cities remained "a community in which every citizen was closely bound to other members of the community by familial, recreational, economic, and social ties. The social hierarchy was clear; a series of institutions supported that hierarchy; and the community was so compact that it was difficult to escape the vigilance of the dominant class."[93] Accordingly, until at least midcentury the law was enforced in most cities by part-time or volunteer night watches and constables.

As cities grew in size and complexity, it became clear that informal community norms could not keep the peace. The constant influx of new immigrants provoked high levels of ethnic conflict, pushed up crime rates, and broke apart the bonds of community. For example, in the 1830s and 1840s, rioting directed against Irish immigrants and free blacks broke out regularly in Philadelphia. Almost all cities experienced rising levels of violence. In frontier cities, the connection between rapid population growth and social instability was especially obvious. In the early years, more than half the residents of San Francisco, St. Louis, and New Orleans were transients. A constant stream of river men, wagon drivers, and traders moved in and out of these cities. Saloons proliferated; gambling and prostitution flourished. In San Francisco during the gold rush years of the 1850s, violent crimes became such a fact of everyday life that merchants funded vigilante committees. The vigilantes soon organized their own crime rings and became almost as dangerous as the criminals they were supposed to catch.[94]

In 1845, Boston became the first city to provide uniforms for its officers. The same year, when its population numbered more than 400,000, New York replaced its force of part-time policemen with full-time officers. The police went about their jobs in street clothes, completely untrained and without supervision.[95] Eight years later, the city's police finally received uniforms and some modest training. Until the late 1830s, Philadelphia relied on posses, militia, and night watches to enforce the law. They worked parttime and did not wear uniforms.[96]

New York's police forces were in constant turmoil for many years. There was considerable resistance to the idea of creating a professional police force because the two political parties that contended for power in the city considered the police an important source of patronage. Following the 1857 mayoral election, the new mayor fired everyone on the police force and installed officers loyal to his own party. The former police officers refused to quit their jobs, and so for several months the city had two competing police forces. In June of that year, a full-scale riot broke out between the two groups.[97] Similar confusion repeated itself in 1868, when the newly elected Democratic governor removed all of the city's police commissioners because they were Republicans. The commissioners refused to vacate their offices. Finally, the state legislature resolved the dispute by assuming the power to appoint the police commissioners.

These events illustrate why it took so long to build modern, fully professionalized police forces. Many people feared that, as a quasi-military organization, the police might be used by one political faction against another. This fear was well founded. At least until the mid-twentieth century, police departments were prolific sources of patronage, and their political loyalties and political debts, as well as their ethnic prejudices, often affected their work. A presidential commission investigating the urban riots of the 1960s found that police conduct was the most common provocation for rioting.[98] And even today, police are often accused of biased enforcement of the law.

If it seems that crisis goaded governing elites into organizing and financing municipal services, this fact still begs an important question: What provoked a sense of crisis? Objective conditions, however dire, may be adjusted to, may be considered normal, or may seem beyond anyone's control. In the nineteenth century, urban leaders perceived that a crisis had arrived when the economic vitality and very existence of the cities they lived in seemed threatened. On the whole, civic elites and business leaders preferred to support public services rather than abandon the city.

Once provided, urban services became institutionalized; they quickly seemed normal and routine. This was especially the case with services such as water systems and fire departments that required the construction of permanent infrastructure and investment in expensive equipment. In this way, the responsibilities of city governments grew step by step. In the early nineteenth century, when confronted with a new problem, the cities' merchants, landowners, and other civic leaders would typically organize a committee to decide what to do. Over time, such informal arrangements gave way to services provided by full-time, paid employees. This is exactly what happened with Philadelphia's waterworks. At first, the Watering Committee raised money through private donations and individual subscriptions to the water service. Prominent merchants led the committee until 1837.[99] But in subsequent decades, the system expanded until it provided water to all citizens, and it became necessary to impose taxes to support it.

The origins of modern government bureaucracies can be found in the breakdown of informal community and recognition of the inadequacy of the informal committee system. Part-time politicians could not organize and supervise complex urban services. Increasingly, during the latter half of the nineteenth century, city services were provided by paid employees of city governments who were organized into bureaucratic hierarchies. As the scope of municipal services broadened, the number of paid city employees multiplied. Where volunteers once joined firehouse gangs and scavengers picked garbage off the streets, salaried, full-time employees took their place.

Milwaukee's volunteer fire department gave way to paid professionals in the 1850s, when new steam pumps proved too complicated for volunteers to maintain and operate.[100] Public works employees were hired to maintain the streets when it became too difficult to find volunteers for the task. In the same decade, the provision of health services became too complex for volunteers when the Milwaukee city council required vaccination for smallpox and when it provided funds to build a sewer system. Gradually, the day-to-day administration of services was put in the hands of salaried employees. "Politics became a full-time business and professionals moved in to make careers of public office."[101]

In the last three decades of the nineteenth century, a growing middle class began to demand integrated water and sewer systems,[102] and by the 1890s there was popular pressure to improve services of all kinds. From the 1850s to the 1870s, assistance to railroads had been the largest single cause of municipal debt. In striking contrast, during the last thirty years of the century, the cities went into debt mainly to finance the expansion of new services and to build infrastructure.[103] Compared to the merchant elites who had previously dominated city governments, the working-class professional politicians who ran urban machines had few qualms about increasing taxes to pay for city services. In fact, city contracts and patronage jobs provided the glue that held local political machines together. Cities ran up debts at a feverish pace to finance improved water systems, sewers, paved streets, parks, and other improvements.[104] Because of rising standards of public health, new technologies, even when very expensive, were quickly adopted. The creation of integrated sewerage systems is instructive. Systems of separate sanitary and storm sewers were not completed in most cities until very late in the nineteenth century. Laying sewer pipe was a huge public works project for any city. Nevertheless, the number of miles of sewer pipe laid increased fourfold from 1890 to 1909.[105]

By the turn of the century, American cities, in general, provided more and better services than European cities, with more miles of sewer and water mains, more miles of paved streets, more street lamps, better mass transportation, and more fire departments with better equipment.[106] Urban residents in the United States used more than twice as much water per capita as their counterparts in England and many times more than city dwellers in Germany.[107] This was no doubt due to the fact that flush toilets and bathtubs were far more widespread in American cities.[108] The cities also vastly expanded public health efforts. Using the new science of bacteriology, health inspectors examined children in schools, checked buildings for ventilation and faulty plumbing, and inspected food and milk.[109] Such public health measures, when combined with the completion of integrated sewer systems and installation of new water filtration technology, dramatically reduced typhoid mortality rates.[110] Overall death rates fell sharply in the big cities, by 20 percent or more in New York, Chicago, Cleveland, Buffalo, and other cities in the 1890s,[111] and just as sharply again in the first decade of the twentieth century.[112]

In many ways, the late nineteenth century was the golden age of American city-building. The massive investment in physical infrastructure placed city governments at the cutting edge of technology, resulting in such engineering marvels as the Brooklyn Bridge and New York's Croton aqueduct system, with its thousands of miles of pipes and reservoirs. The Parks Movement and the City Beautiful Movement, both supported by urban elites and the middle class, swept the country, resulting in new and improved parks, ponds, formal gardens, bandstands, ball fields, broad tree-lined avenues, and ornate public buildings. Urban residents came to expect a level of municipal services that was not conceivable in an earlier time. The squalor of the nineteenth-century industrial city began to yield to the relative safety, cleanliness, and health of the twentieth-century metropolis.

THE POLITICAL ISOLATION OF THE CITIES

During the colonial period, local governments were self-organized. Because they had existed before the states and the constitution, they exercised considerable powers; some ran municipal markets, regulated harbors, and regulated the prices of key goods and commodities. Because it does not mention cities, the Constitution did not change this fact. In his classic work, *Democracy in America* (1835), Alexis de Tocqueville emphasized that local governments in the United States were sovereign, and he compared them to independent nations: "Municipal independence is . . . a natural consequence of the principle of the sovereignty of the people in the United States: all the American republics recognize it more or less."[113] Even after the states asserted the right to oversee the affairs of cities in the nineteenth century, many articles, books, and court rulings made the case for the autonomy of local governments.[114]

Nevertheless, during the nineteenth century, court decisions consistently upheld the powers of the states to define the powers and obligations of local governments. In 1819, in the Dartmouth College case, the U.S. Supreme Court held that cities were created by the states and that their charters could therefore be amended or rescinded at will. (By contrast, private corporations were protected from interference by the constitutional provision against "impairing the obligation of contract.")[115] A second definitive case was handed down in 1868, when the chief justice of the Iowa Supreme Court, John F. Dillon, declared that states could rightfully exert total control over their cities, with no restrictions whatever:

> Municipal corporations owe their origin to, and derive their powers and rights wholly from, the legislature. It breathes into them the breath of life without which

they cannot exist. As it creates so it may destroy. . . . Unless there is some constitutional limitation on the right, the legislature might, by a single act, if we can suppose it capable of so great a folly and so great a wrong, sweep from existence all of the municipal corporations of the state, and the corporations could not prevent it. . . . They are, so to phrase it, the mere tenants at will of the legislature.[116]

Dillon was motivated by the fact that cities had been active in providing subsidies to railroads, and he reasoned that if they could help private corporations so directly, they could regulate them as well. Dillon's missionary zeal was also fired by a conviction that cities were governed by riffraff: "Men the best fitted by their intelligence, business experience, capacity and moral character, for local governors and counsellors are not always, it is feared—it might be added, are not generally—chosen."[117] His solution was for state governments and courts to supervise cities and strictly limit their powers. In 1872, Dillon published his *Treatise on the Law of Municipal Corporations.* Originally 800 pages long, by the time the fifth edition was published in 1911, it had grown to five thick volumes.[118] It became the bible on municipal law. By 1924, William Munro, the author of a leading textbook, *The Government of American Cities*, wrote that Dillon's rule was "so well recognized that it is not nowadays open to question."[119]

Inspired by a similar distrust of cities—or, rather, of immigrant voters—state legislators took steps to ensure that no matter how fast and big cities grew, their representatives to the state house would never be able to gain a majority of the votes in state legislatures. Most rural legislators would probably have agreed with the delegate to the New York state constitutional convention of 1894 who said, "the average citizen in the rural district is superior in intelligence, superior in morality, superior in self-government to the average citizen of the great cities."[120] A distrust of cities was hardly new. Decades earlier, Maine's constitutional convention of 1819 had established a ceiling on the number of representatives who could represent towns in the state legislature. In 1845, the Louisiana legislature limited New Orleans to 12.5 percent of the state's senators and 10 percent of the state's assemblymen. (The population of New Orleans then accounted for 20 percent of the state's total.[121]) By the end of the century, every state had ensured that no matter how large the cities became, representatives from rural legislative districts would continue to hold a controlling majority in state legislatures.

It mattered very much who controlled state legislatures. By the end of the nineteenth century, more people lived in the cities of some states than lived outside them. If their influence in state legislatures had grown in step with their populations, cities would have been able to secure state financial support for the expansion of city services. In fact, however, cities received practically no help at all. If urban voters had been able to gain more influence in state politics and in state governments, they also could have asserted a political voice in national politics. Rural elites firmly controlled the party caucuses that nominated governors, members of congress, senators, and presidents. Immigrants and labor unions had no effective means of influencing governmental policies at the state or national levels. The underrepresentation of the cities resulted in indifference to the problems faced by big cities in state legislatures, governors' offices, Congress, and the White House. Traffic congestion, slum housing, orphaned children, contagious diseases, poverty—none of these problems interested rural and small-town legislators or a Congress and president beholden to state party leaders who answered to rural constituents.

Underrepresentation of cities throughout the federal system exerted profound and enduring consequences, for it allowed governmental leaders at all levels to wash their hands of the devastating effects of industrialization and urbanization. In the late nineteenth century, powerful populist movements pushed for the recognition of the right of labor unions to organize. In the first twenty years of the twentieth century, reformers lobbied state legislatures to adopt universal health insurance, workers' compensation, and relief programs for widows, children, and the elderly. A groundswell of opposition to child labor swept the country; nevertheless, the federal government did not adopt child labor legislation until 1916, and it was struck down by the Supreme Court two years later.[122] Partially because urban residents had so little political voice, these and other reforms were delayed until the New Deal of the 1930s, and some reforms, such as national health care, have never been adopted.

The federal courts finally moved against legislative malapportionment in the 1960s, more than forty years after the 1920 census showed that a majority of Americans lived in urban places. In *Baker v. Carr* (1962), a group of Knoxville, Tennessee, residents challenged the fact that the Tennessee legislature had not been reapportioned since 1901.[123] Their lawyers argued that citizens living in urban areas were being deprived of "equal protection of the law," as guaranteed by the Fourteenth Amendment to the U.S. Constitution. The important court decision that decided this case, as well as others, came on June 15, 1964, when the U.S. Supreme Court, in *Reynolds v. Sims*, ruled that state legislative apportionments must follow a "one man, one vote" principle.[124] Within a few years, for the first time in the nation's history, state legislative and congressional districts were apportioned to give city residents equal representation.

The "one man, one vote" remedy came too late; by the time it was adopted, cities were losing population to the suburbs. The nation's population and therefore the balance of power in national politics were shifting to the suburbs and to the Sunbelt. If cities had gained equal representation in state legislatures and in Congress decades earlier, the influence of urban voters would have virtually guaranteed that they could have secured from the federal government as well as from many states funding for such urban priorities as mass transit, public housing, urban revitalization, and community health programs. Financial assistance for cities and for urban infrastructure would have been similar to the support provided to cities by European countries. But the American political system was biased against the urban electorate—a circumstance that arose because the people who lived in the cities of America had long been regarded as "strangers in the land."[125]

NOTES

1. Robert A. Beauregard, *Voices of Decline: The Postwar Fate of U.S. Cities* (New York: Blackwell, 1993).
2. London proper had 957,000, but the greater London area had 1,117,000 people.
3. Brian R. Mitchell, *European Historical Statistics, 1750–1970* (New York: Columbia University Press, 1975), p. 76.
4. Defined as settlements with at least 5,000 population.
5. "The Inevitability of City Growth," reprinted from *Atlantic Monthly,* April 1985, in *City Life, 1865 –1900: Views of Urban America,* ed. Ann Cook, Marilyn Gittell, and Herb Mack (New York: Praeger, 1973), p. 17.
6. Eric H. Monkkonen, *America Becomes Urban: The Development of U.S. Cities and Towns, 1780–1980* (Berkeley: University of California Press, 1988), p. 78.
7. U.S. Department of Commerce, Bureau of the Census, *Historical Statistics of the United States, Colonial Times to 1970,* pt. 1, Bicentennial ed. (Washington, D.C.: Government Printing Office, 1975), p. 11.
8. Richard C. Wade, *The Urban Frontier: Pioneer Life in Early Pittsburgh, Cincinnati, Lexington, Louisville, and St. Louis* (Chicago: University of Chicago Press, 1959), p. 103.
9. D. Philip Locklin, *Economics of Transportation,* 7th ed. (Homewood, Ill.: Irwin, 1972).
10. David M. Gordon, "Class Struggle and the Stages of American Urban Development," in *The Rise of the Sunbelt Cities,* ed. David C. Perry and Alfred J. Watkins (Beverly Hills, Calif.: Sage, 1977), p. 64.
11. George Rogers Taylor, *The Transportation Revolution, 1815–1860* (New York: Holt, Rinehart and Winston, 1951), p. 52.
12. Carter Goodrich, *Government Promotion of American Canals and Railroads, 1800–1890* (New York: Columbia University Press, 1960), pp. 266–267.
13. Wade, *The Urban Frontier,* p. 70.
14. U.S. Department of Commerce, *Historical Statistics of the United States, Colonial Times to 1970,* pt. 2, pp. 728, 731.
15. Alfred D. Chandler, *The Railroads: The Nation's First Big Business* (New York: Harcourt Brace Jovanovich, 1965).
16. Henry W. Broude, "The Role of the State in American Economic Development, 1820–1890," in *United States Economic History: Selected Readings,* ed. H. N. Scheiber (New York: Knopf, 1964).
17. Paul Kantor, *The Dependent City Revisited: The Political Economy of Urban Development and Social Policy* (Boulder, Colo.: Westview, 1995), p. 24.
18. Carter Goodrich, "The Revulsion Against Internal Improvements," *Journal of Economic History* 10, no. 2 (November 1950): 145–169.
19. David Chalmers, *Neither Socialism nor Monopoly* (Philadelphia: Lippincott, 1976), p. 4.
20. Blake McKelvey, *American Urbanization: A Comparative History* (Glenview, Ill.: Scott Foresman, 1973), pp. 25–26.
21. Ibid.
22. Paul Kantor with Stephen David, *The Dependent City: The Changing Political Economy of Urban America* (Glenview, Ill.: Scott, Foresman, 1987), pp. 499–500.
23. Goodrich, *Government Promotion,* p. 241. Goodrich estimates that until 1860 local governments provided 29 percent of total public subsidies (p. 268). The proportion of local contributions increased significantly after the Civil War. In his study of New York from 1826 to 1875, Harry Pierce concludes that three-quarters of the subsidy came from local governments and one-quarter from the state. See Harry H. Pierce, *The Railroads of New York: A Study of Government Aid, 1826–1875* (Cambridge, Mass.: Harvard University Press, 1953).
24. Ibid.

25. In 1849, for example, the voters of Cleveland approved a $100,000 subscription to stock in the Cleveland and Pittsburgh Railroad by a vote of 1,157 to 27. Despite the enthusiasm of the voters, the stock never paid any dividends and eventually sold at far below par. Charles C. Williamson, *The Finances of Cleveland* (New York: Columbia University Press, 1907), pp. 218–220.

26. Goodrich, *Government Promotion*, p. 42.

27. Ibid., p. 272. One study gave the following figures for New York: "Only 52 of the 297 municipalities that bought stock in a railroad disposed of their securities at par or better, 162 held stock with no market value." (Pierce, *The Railroads of New York*), p. 273.

28. A. M. Hillhouse, *Municipal Bonds: A Century of Experience* (Englewood Cliffs, N.J.: Prentice-Hall, 1936), p. 39.

29. Goodrich, *Government Promotion*, pp. 268–271. Repudiation goes beyond default, which is simply a failure to pay the debt on time. Repudiation declares an unwillingness to ever repay the debt.

30. Alberta M. Sbragia, *Debt Wish: Entrepreneurial Cities, U.S. Federalism and Economic Development* (Pittsburgh: University of Pittsburgh Press, 1996), p. 91.

31. Goodrich, "Revulsion Against Internal Improvements"; see also Sbragia, *Debt Wish*, chap. 5.

32. Lawrence Goodwyn, *The Populist Movement* (New York: Oxford University Press, 1978).

33. Eric Lampard, "Historical Aspects of Urbanization," in *The Study of Urbanization*, ed. Philip M. Hauser and Leo F. Schnore (New York: Wiley, 1965), p. 523.

34. Allan R. Pred, *The Spatial Dynamics of Urban-Industrial Growth, 1800–1914* (Cambridge, Mass.: MIT Press, 1966), p. 103.

35. Donald S. Lutz, *Popular Consent and Popular Control: Whig Political Theory in the Early State Constitutions* (Baton Rouge: Louisiana State University Press, 1980), p. 105; Advisory Commission on Intergovernmental Relations, *Citizen Participation in the American Federal System* (Washington, D.C.: U.S. Government Printing Office, 1979), p. 41.

36. William Bennett Munro, *Municipal Government and Administration* (New York: Macmillan, 1923), p. 94.

37. Lee Benson, *The Concept of Jacksonian Democracy* (Princeton, N.J.: Princeton University Press, 1961).

38. Edwin J. Perkins, *The Economy of Colonial America* (New York: Columbia University Press, 1980), p. 157.

39. Philip Foner, *History of the Labor Movement in the United States* (New York: International, 1975), pp. 13–18.

40. Howard P. Chudacoff, *The Evolution of American Urban Society* (Englewood Cliffs, N.J.: Prentice-Hall, 1975), p. 26.

41. Sam Bass Warner, Jr., *The Private City: Philadelphia in Three Periods of Its Growth* (Philadelphia: University of Pennsylvania Press, 1968), p. 21.

42. Kantor, *The Dependent City*, p. 22.

43. Ibid., p. 33.

44. Pred, *The Spatial Dynamics*, p. 16.

45. The skyscraper boom on Fifth Avenue between 1900 and 1915 was largely fueled by the desire of rich individuals to outdo one another in pretentious architecture. See Seymour I. Toll, *Zoned American* (New York: Grossman, 1969), chap. 2.

46. Samuel P. Hays, *The Response to Industrialism, 1885–1914* (Chicago: University of Chicago Press, 1957), p. 73.

47. Ibid., p. 170.

48. Ibid., pp. 68–69.

49. Chartered by the states, limited-risk corporations allowed the selling of shares to investors whose liability in case of corporate failure was limited to their direct investment. In partnerships, the partners were liable for all debts incurred by the company, and these could easily exceed the partners' own assets. The corporate form of business

organization thus made it easier to raise capital, for investors risked less than in other forms of business investment.

50. U.S. Department of the Interior, Census Office, *Census Reports of 1900*, vol. 7, Manufacturers, pt. 1: "United States by Industries" (Washington, D.C.: U.S. Government Printing Office, 1902), pp. 503–509.

51. William Miller, "American Historians and the Business Elite," *Journal of Economic History* 9 (1949): 184–208.

52. Kenneth Jackson, *Crabgrass Frontier: The Suburbanization of the United States* (New York: Oxford University Press, 1985), p. 35.

53. George Rogers Taylor, "Building an Intra-Urban Transportation System," in *The Urbanization of America: An Historical Anthology*, ed. Allen M. Wakstein (Boston: Houghton Mifflin, 1970), p. 137.

54. Glen E. Holt, "The Changing Perception of Urban Pathology: An Essay on the Development of Mass Transit in the United States," in *Cities in American History*, ed. Kenneth T. Jackson and Stanley K. Schultz (New York: Knopf, 1972), p. 327.

55. Taylor, "Building an Intra-Urban Transportation System," p. 139.

56. C. G. Kennedy, "Commuter Services in the Boston Area, 1835–1860," *Business History Review* 26 (1962): 277–287.

57. Jackson, *Crabgrass Frontier*, p. 41.

58. David Ward, *Cities and Immigrants: A Geography of Change in Nineteenth-Century America* (New York: Oxford University, Press, 1971), p. 4.

59. Jackson, *Crabgrass Frontier*, p. 108.

60. Ibid.

61. Gary A. Tobin, "Suburbanization and the Development of Motor Transportation: Transportation and Technology and the Suburbanization Process," in *The Changing Face of the Suburbs*, ed. Barry Schwartz (Chicago: University of Chicago Press, 1975), p. 99.

62. "The Smell of Cincinnati," *Enquirer* (Richmond, Va.), November 15, 1874, in *City Life*, ed. Cook, Gittell, and Mack, p. 143.

63. Ward, *Cities and Immigrants*, chap. 3.

64. Blake McKelvey, *The Urbanization of America, 1860–1915* (New Brunswick, N.J.: Rutgers University Press, 1963), p. 54.

65. For an excellent history of America's downtowns, see Robert M. Fogelson, *Downtown: Its Rise and Fall, 1880–1950* (New Haven: Yale University Press, 2001).

66. U.S. Bureau of the Census, *The Growth of Metropolitan Districts in the United States: 1900–1940*, by Warren S. Thompson (Washington, D.C.: U.S. Government Printing office, 1947).

67. Hays, *The Response to Industrialism*, p. 14.

68. Ward, *Cities and Immigrants*, p. 52.

69. Thomas Monroe Pitkin, *Keepers of the Gate: A History of Ellis Island* (New York: New York University Press, 1975), p. ix.

70. Ward, *Cities and Immigrants*, p. 56.

71. Ibid., p. 52.

72. John Higham, *Strangers in the Land: Patterns of American Nativism, 1860–1925* (New Brunswick, N.J.: Rutgers University Press, 1955), pp. 54–55.

73. Stephen Thernstrom, *The Other Bostonians: Poverty and Progress in the American Metropolis, 1880–1970* (Cambridge, Mass.: Harvard University Press, 1973), p. 160.

74. Ibid.

75. Charles N. Glaab and A. Theodore Brown, *A History of Urban America* (New York: Macmillan, 1967), p. 160.

76. Gwendolyn Wright, *Building the American Dream: A Social History of Housing in America* (Cambridge, Mass.: MIT Press, 1983), p. 123. Dumbbell waiters are rope-pulley devices used to move small items up and down a shaft in multi-story buildings.

77. Moses Rischin, *The Promised City: New York's Jews, 1870–1914* (Cambridge, Mass.: Harvard University Press, 1962), p. 87.
78. Gerald M. Caters, Jr., "Yellow Fever in Memphis in the 1870s," in *The City in American Life, From Colonial Times to the Present*, ed. Paul Kramer and Frederick L. Holborn (New York: Capricorn Books, 1970), pp. 180–185.
79. Glaab and Brown, *A History of Urban America*, p. 86.
80. Ibid., p. 180.
81. Terrence J. MacDonald and Sally K. Ward, eds., *The Politics of Urban Fiscal Policy* (Beverly Hills, Calif.: Sage, 1984), p. 14.
82. Nelson M. Blake, *Water for the Cities: A History of the Urban Water Supply Problem in the United States* (Syracuse, N.Y.: Syracuse University Press, 1956), p. 6.
83. Ibid., pp. 102–103.
84. Ibid., p. 6.
85. Warner, *The Private City*, pp. 107–109.
86. Arthur N. Schlesinger, "A Panoramic View: The City in American Life," in *The City in American Life*, ed. Kramer and Holborn, p. 23.
87. McKelvey, *The Urbanization of America*, p. 13.
88. Edgar W. Martin, *The Standard of Living in 1860* (Chicago: University of Chicago Press, 1942), pp. 44–47, 89–112.
89. McKelvey, *The Urbanization of America*, p. 90.
90. Ibid., p. 13.
91. Ibid., p. 90.
92. McKelvey, *American Urbanization*, p. 44.
93. Stephen Thernstrom, *Poverty and Progress: Social Mobility in a Nineteenth-Century City* (Cambridge, Mass.: Harvard University Press, 1964), p. 39.
94. Fred M. Wirt, *Power in the City* (Berkeley: University of California Press, 1974), p. 110.
95. James F. Richardson, "To Control the City: The New York Police in Historical Perspective," in *Cities in American History*, ed. Kenneth T. Jackson and Stanley K. Schultz (New York: Knopf, 1972), pp. 272–289.
96. Warner, *The Private City*, chap. 7.
97. Richardson, "To Control the City," p. 278.
98. *Report of the National Advisory Commission on Civil Disorders* (New York: Bantam Books, 1968).
99. Warner, *The Private City*.
100. Bayrd Still, *Milwaukee: The History of a City* (Madison: State Historical Society of Wisconsin, 1984), chap. 10.
101. Warner, *The Private City*, p. 86.
102. Sbragia, *Debt Wish*, p. 76.
103. Ibid.
104. Ibid.
105. Ibid.
106. Jon Teaford, *The Unheralded Triumph: City Government in America, 1870–1900* (Baltimore: Johns Hopkins University Press, 1984), chap. 8.
107. Ibid., p. 222.
108. Ibid., p. 221.
109. Ibid., p. 247.
110. Stanley K. Schultz, *Constructing Urban Culture: American Cities and City Planning, 1800–1920* (Philadelphia: Temple University Press, 1989), p. 174.
111. Ibid., p. 246.
112. McKelvey, *The Urbanization of America*, p. 90.
113. Alexis de Tocqueville, *Democracy in America*, vol. 1 (New York: Shocken Books, 1961), p. 60.

114. For citations, see Gerald Frug, "The City as a Legal Concept," *Harvard Law Review* 93, no. 6 (April 1980): 1113–1117.

115. See *Dartmouth College v. Woodward*, 4 Wheat. 518 (1819).

116. *City of Clinton v. Cedar Rapids and Missouri River Railroad Co.*, 24 Iowa 455–475 (1868).

117. Schultz, *Constructing Urban Culture*, p. 73.

118. Ibid., p. 69.

119. William Munro, *The Government of the American Cities*, 3rd ed. (New York: Macmillan, 1924), p. 53.

120. Mark I. Gelfand, *A Nation of Cities: The Federal Government and Urban America, 1933–1965* (New York: Oxford University Press, 1975), p. 11.

121. Ibid.

122. *Hammer v. Dagenhart et al.*, 247 U.S. 251 (1918).

123. *Baker v. Carr*, 369 U.S. 189 (1962).

124. *Reynolds v. Sims*, 377 U.S. 533 (1964). "One man, one vote" was the term used in the court's decision.

125. Higham, *Strangers in the Land*.

CHAPTER
3

PARTY MACHINES AND
THE IMMIGRANTS

MACHINES AND MACHINE-STYLE POLITICS

The image of the rotund, cigar-smoking machine politician handing out buckets of coal to poor widows and cutting deals in smoke-filled rooms in the back of taverns holds an almost sacred place in the lore of American politics. Though machine-style politics exists throughout the world, the city-based party machine that appealed for votes strictly on the basis of ethnic solidarity and individual service to constituents was unique to the United States. Americans have long romanticized and abhorred the machines in equal measure. President Theodore Roosevelt caught this mood when he observed in his autobiography, "A leader is necessary; but his opponents always call him a boss. An organization is necessary; but the men in opposition always call it a machine."[1]

Some degree of machine-style politics—a style that relies on material incentives to nurture loyalty—is almost always present in every political system. A clique of silver-haired "suits" who help their favored developers obtain zoning variances for a suburban mall are acting as much like machine politicians as a ward boss who helps a constituent deal with a rat inspector in a downtown apartment building. In politics, material incentives come in many forms: a patronage job, a government contract, a zoning variance, a fixed parking ticket, an expedited business license. Claims to lofty ideals are often little more than fig leaves covering naked self-interest.

For this reason, something more than machine-style politics is necessary if we are to accurately apply the term *machine* to a political organization.[2] A machine is a hierarchical organization controlled by a single leader, a "boss," or by a tightly organized clique. In some local governments a hierarchical structure centralizes power into one or a few pairs of hands. A full-fledged political machine is characterized by both machine-style politics and a well-defined hierarchy of command, coordination, and control.

A majority of America's big industrial cities once were governed by machines. Between 1870 and 1945, seventeen of the nation's thirty cities with populations of more than 500,000 had boss rule and a disciplined, hierarchical party organization at some point.[3] In most of these cities, factional machine-style politics existed for some time before the actual machines emerged. With only two or three exceptions in the big cities, the classic machines flowered in the last years of the nineteenth century and the first few years of the twentieth century. Boss rule peaked sometime in the 1920s. In 1932, the year that Democratic candidate Franklin D. Roosevelt won the presidency, ten of America's thirty biggest cities were ruled by machine bosses. Today, the urban political machine is pretty much extinct. The death of Chicago boss Richard J. Daley in 1976 marked the end of the era of the classic party machines, which relied on patronage and material incentives to keep their organizations intact.[4]

Despite the demise of the machines, any comprehensive discussion of city politics in America must take them into account because their previous existence still reverberates within the political system. "Machine politics" is still occasionally used as an epithet hurled against political opponents. Early in the twentieth century, the machines became the object of a furious campaign designed to clean up politics and reduce the influence of immigrant voters. But were the attacks on the machines justified? It is useful to consider whether machine-style governance might help deliver important benefits to ethnic and racial groups even in today's cities.[5]

THE ORIGINS OF MACHINE POLITICS

The rise of the machines was made possible by the confluence of two factors: the emergence of a mass electorate, and industrialization.[6] When the Constitution was ratified in 1789, only about 5 percent of adult white males were eligible to vote, but by the presidential election of 1840, 80 percent of adult white males went to the polls, the highest rate in any major democracy.[7] The spread of universal male suffrage coincided with the explosive growth of cities. From the 1830s to the 1920s, more than 30 million immigrants came to the United States, most of them pouring into the cities. As soon as they were citizens, if they were male, they could vote. A new breed of enterprising politician took advantage of this circumstance.

The mass electorate could be mobilized on the basis of feelings of ethnic solidarity and the promise of material rewards. Politicians who managed to gain control of local government commanded important resources that could be distributed to their loyal supporters. Between 1870 and 1900, municipal workforces grew even faster than the population of cities.[8] During this period, local governments spent more money than either the federal government or the state governments.[9] The fiscal resources and the powers of city governments were prizes worth pursuing.

In most large American cities, a "friends and neighbors" or "local followings" style of politics evolved that reflected the decentralized nature of their political systems. Aldermen were elected from wards, and because these electoral units were quite small, politicians were able to enter politics by taking advantage of their social connections. No one benefited from this arrangement more than pub owners. Saloons were central to the day-to-day life in working-class wards and, more than any other institution, they served as neighborhood centers. Especially in Irish neighborhoods, pub owners were considered reliable sources of information and advice. The density of pubs in immigrant neighborhoods was astonishing. In 1915, for example, there was a saloon for every 515 residents in New York, and the ratio was greater in Chicago, with a saloon for every 335 persons, and in San Francisco, with a saloon for every 218 residents.[10] In working-class districts, the ratio in most cities was at least one pub for every fifty males.[11] In late nineteenth-century Chicago, half the city's total population entered a saloon every day.[12] A large proportion of machine politicians got their start as pub owners. Of New York City's twenty-four aldermen in 1890, eleven were pub owners. Pub owners made up a third of Milwaukee's city councilmen in 1902 and a third of Detroit's aldermen at the turn of the century.[13]

Party machines combined two seemingly incompatible qualities: the absence of formal rules, and a disciplined organization. Machine politicians were not "hired" into party organizations, and they did not have a job description. Their ability to deliver votes and their skill at forging alliances with other politicians determined their standing in the organization. Normally, a machine politician started at the bottom and worked his way up. Precinct captains, who were responsible for getting out the vote in the smallest and most basic political unit of the city, knew each voter personally, often as a friend and neighbor. To secure a following at this level, a politician had to be known not only as a person involved in politics but as someone who participated in local community life. Politicians climbed the political ladder only if they demonstrated that they could reliably deliver the vote. If they did, the next rung they reached for was alderman.

Most machine politicians came from backgrounds that offended silk-stocking elements. Schooled in rough-and-tumble political competition, they generally were men of incredible energy, quick temper, and rough manners. At the least, they loved what they were doing; they felt no alienation from their job. Politics was everything the machine politicians knew and did—it was their social life, their profession, their first love. They pursued political power, not social standing.[14] George Washington Plunkitt, a sachem in the Tammany Hall organization in New York, advised against what he called the "dangers of the dress suit in politics." "Live like your neighbors," Plunkitt admonished aspiring politicians, "even if you have the means to live better. Make the poorest man in your district feel that he is your equal, or even a bit superior to you."[15]

Disciplined political organizations emerged when skillful leaders succeeded in persuading other politicians that everyone would benefit if they cooperated. When this happened, a military-style hierarchy evolved, with those lower in the organization waiting for their chance to move up. This structure was once described by Frank Hague, the Jersey City boss, to columnist Joseph Alsop, who wrote, "He [Hague] was talking in the dining room of one of the local hotels. He took the squares on the tablecloth to illustrate precincts and wards, tracing them out with his finger, and he explained the feudal system of American politics, whereby the precinct captain is governed by a ward lieutenant, the lieutenant by a ward leader, and each ward leader by the boss."[16]

As shown in Figure 3.1, precincts and precinct captains constituted the foundation of the machine organization. The typical precinct had 400 to 600 voters and precinct captains were expected to know most of them by name. Thirty to forty precincts were generally included within a ward. The captains of the precincts were chosen by and worked for the ward's alderman. The alderman served as the chair of the ward's party committee, unless he selected a committeeman to supervise the precinct captains on his behalf. Finally, the aldermen reported to the machine boss, who was usually but not always the mayor.

The whole structure held together because everyone gained by cooperating in what was, in essence, a "system of organized bribery."[17] Bosses and individual aldermen had at their disposal patronage jobs in police, fire, sanitation, and streets departments—and sometimes even in private industry. Construction projects, such as levee construction or road building, could give a boss control over hundreds of permanent and temporary jobs. Precinct captains usually held low-level jobs arranged through the machine, perhaps serving as supervisors on street crews. Ward committeemen generally were rewarded with higher-paying

Figure 3.1 **The Organization of Machine Politics**

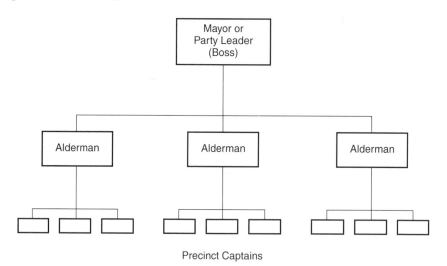

Precinct Captains

The organization of local political machines, or parties, parallels the formal structures of government but is also separate from them. Like the mayor, the party leader or boss controls the entire city, or perhaps county. The alderman represents a ward in the city council or board of aldermen. The alderman may or may not serve as ward leader of the party. Each ward consists of many precincts or election districts. Precinct captains are responsible for delivering the vote in their precinct.

In principle, power flows from the bottom up: Precinct captains elect the ward leaders, and the ward leaders elect the party boss. In fact, power flows from the top.

administrative positions in city government. Aldermen and other elected officials typically owned lucrative insurance companies, ran their own construction
firms, or owned saloons. The most menial jobs were passed along to some of the
loyal voters who turned out faithfully on election day.

An understanding of the patronage ladder can be gained by examining the
machine of Richard J. Daley, mayor of Chicago from 1953 until his death in 1976.
In the early 1970s, the Cook County Central Committee (which contains Chicago)
had about 30,000 positions available for distribution. Most of these jobs were
unskilled; 8,000 were available through Chicago's departments and commissions,
including street cleaners, park supervisors, and the like. [18] The jobs ranged from
$3,600-a-year elevator operators and $6,000-a-year stenographers to $25,000-a-
year department directors (in the early 1970s, a skilled factory worker in a union
plant made approximately $9,000 per year). Individual ward committeemen con-
trolled as many as 2,000 jobs. (Richard J. Daley had begun his career as committeeman of his ward.) There were (and still are) fifty wards in the city of Chicago, with
an average of 500 to 600 jobs available in each of them in the 1970s.[19]

The number of jobs available for distribution by individual precinct captains
and ward committeemen was determined by the election-day result. A precinct
captain in Chicago was expected to know all the voters in the precinct and to be
known by them. "When a man is given a precinct, it is his to cover, and it is up to
him to produce for the party. If he cannot produce for the party, he cannot
expect to be rewarded by the party. 'Let's put it this way,' [one alderman said] 'if
your boss has a salesman who can't deliver, who can't sell his product, wouldn't
he put in someone else who can?'"[20]

Alderman Vito Marzullo was a successful salesman for the Chicago organization. Every week he scheduled a formal audience with his constituents.
Flanked on each side by a precinct captain, he heard their complaints:

> A precinct captain ushered in a black husband and wife. "We got a letter here from
> the city," the man said. "They want to charge us twenty dollars for rodent control in
> our building." "Give me the letter, I'll look into it," Marzullo replied. The captain
> spoke up. "Your daughter didn't vote on November fifth. Look into it. The alderman
> is running again in February. Any help we can get, we can use."[21]

In the course of hearing his constituents, Marzullo exclaimed, "Some of those
liberal independents in the city council, they can't get a dog out of a dog pound
with a ten-dollar bill. Who's next?" Marzullo then arranged to have a traffic
ticket fixed, agreed to recommend someone for a job at an electric company,
refused to donate money to the Illinois Right to Life Committee ("Nothing
doing.... I don't want to get into any of those controversies. People for it and
people against it."), agreed to try to find a job for an unemployed truck driver,
and gave $50 to a welfare mother. Responding to several more requests, he
offered to "see what I can do."[22]

During the Daley years, the Chicago machine was structured like a political pyramid. Committeemen and the aldermen directed the captains of the
precincts within their wards; in turn, they reported to the Cook County Central Committee. Although most of the city machines at the turn of the century
were similarly organized, some were directed from the top with an iron hand,

as in Daley's Chicago, while others were little more than loose confederations of politicians. However tightly run the individual machines were, they all showed these qualities: They were rooted in neighborhoods, and they were held together by a combination of material incentives and ethnic and community attachments.

Being close to constituents did not mean the machines were democratic, however. Though all machines provided something to their supporters, many of them engaged in corrupt practices that undermined elections, such as vote-buying and even intimidation of voters. Machine politicians often enriched themselves by taking bribes and making back-room deals. Positive assessments of the machines have relied upon three major claims: that the machines (1) centralized power and "got the job done," (2) served as vehicles of upward mobility for immigrants, and (3) helped assimilate the immigrants into American life. In the next three sections, we examine these claims.

DID MACHINES "GET THE JOB DONE"?

It has often been asserted that political machines arose in the late nineteenth century to fill a void left by the absence of effective local governments. City governments were characterized by an extreme, often chaotic division of responsibilities among a multitude of separate officials, boards, and departments. The mayor generally wielded little authority. The city council or board of aldermen typically controlled the budget and made most decisions. Day-to-day administrative responsibilities were generally assumed by committees whose members were appointed by the city council, or sometimes by the mayor, state legislature, governor, or other state or local officials. When committee or board members were elected by the voters, a long list of names on the ballot made it impossible to know anything about the candidates (like today, when judges are elected). Edward Sait wrote in 1933 that "when the people or particular groups among them demanded positive action, no one had adequate authority to act. The machine provided an antidote."[23] In other words, machines were necessary if anything were to get done.

If it is true that machines arose mainly to fill a void left by disorganized and inefficient government, then we would expect to find that machines prospered especially in cities where governments were the most fragmented. This is not the case, however. In the big cities, municipal reformers achieved their aim of concentrating more power in the hands of mayors and civil service administrators in the late nineteenth century and early twentieth centuries. Centralized party machines emerged at about the same time that the institutions of local government were being reformed.[24]

It turns out that it was easier to build disciplined organizations where local government had been streamlined and reformed than where government was fragmented and chaotic. In 1913, for example, reformers in Jersey City, New Jersey, persuaded the voters to fuse legislative and executive functions into one five-member commission. When the machine mayor, Frank Hague, gained

MACHINES HAD TWO SIDES

The careers of two machine politicians, James and Tom Pendergast of Kansas City, Missouri, illustrate both the positive and the negative sides of machine politics.[25]

In 1876, James Pendergast, an Irishman with a short, thick neck and massive arms and shoulders, moved to Kansas City. Just twenty years old and with only a few dollars in his pocket, he rented a room in the West Bottoms ward, an industrial section on the floodplain of the Missouri River. The residents of West Bottoms worked in the meat packinghouses, machine shops, railroad yards, factories, and warehouses of the area. Blacks, Irish, Germans, and rural migrants lived in crowded four- and five-story tenements and tiny shanties. Overlooking this squalid area of dirt streets and open sewers was Quality Hill, from which the wealthy elite presided over the town. Pendergast held jobs in the packinghouses and in an iron foundry until 1881, when he used racetrack winnings to buy a hotel and a saloon. He named the saloon Climax in honor of his lucky horse.

Three factors contributed to Pendergast's success in First Ward (West Bottoms) politics. First, he was Irish, like the majority of his constituents. Second, most of the politicians of the First Ward made their money from gambling, prostitution, and liquor, and Pendergast's new business made him a member of this group. Third, as a successful saloonkeeper, Pendergast was in a position to meet the people of his ward. By staying out of factional fights within his ward's Democratic party and simultaneously making himself a trusted friend of politicians and ward residents, he soon found himself being promoted for an alderman's seat, which he won in 1892.

During his first term, Pendergast established himself as a champion of the working class by successfully fighting against salary reductions for firefighters, securing a city park in the West Bottoms, and opposing an attempt to move a fire station out of the ward. He won support from reformers by favoring lower telephone rates and by proposing an improved garbage collection system. Within his ward, he served his constituents. On payday, he cashed payroll checks and settled credit agreements; he posted bonds for men who had been arrested for gambling. His generosity cost money, but his business flourished: "Men learned that he had an interest in humanity outside of business and that he could be trusted, and they returned the favor by patronizing his saloon and giving him their confidence."[26] Thus, Pendergast's politics and his everyday life became one and the same. It even seemed that politics was merely an extension of his personality rather than a calculated activity:

> He had a big heart, was charitable and liberal, . . . no deserving man, woman or child that appealed to "Jim" Pendergast went away empty handed, and this is saying a great deal, as he was continually giving aid and help to the poor and unfortunate. . . . Grocers, butchers, bakers and coal men had unlimited orders to see that there was no suffering among the poor of the West Bottoms, and to send the bills to "Jim" Pendergast.[27]

In 1892, Pendergast opened another saloon in the Second Ward, located in the city's North End. In that saloon he employed twenty-two men to run gambling tables, and in his West Bottoms ward he continued to employ a large gambling staff. Gambling was run on a large scale in Kansas City. Opening his own operations in the North End enabled Pendergast to form close relationships with the

(continued on next page)

politicians of that ward, and he soon became as influential in the Second Ward as he was in the First. He was able to secure police protection for gambling and liquor operations by paying off police officers and by influencing the choice of a police chief in 1895.

Pendergast's political influence began to spread, especially when he extended the legendary generosity he had long shown to his West Bottoms constituents to the politicians and citizens of the Second Ward:

> The North Siders went to Pendergast for more than jobs. They went to him when they were in trouble and needed someone to soften the stern hand of justice. Many of them got fuel and other supplies from his precinct captains when they were down and out. Others ate his turkey and trimmings at the free Christmas dinners, . . . beginning with fifty guests and growing into the hundreds as the number of drifters increased year after year.[28]

In 1900, Pendergast ran the city's Democratic Party convention and personally selected the mayoral candidate. In return, the newly elected mayor gave Pendergast control over hundreds of patronage jobs and appointed Pendergast's brother, Tom, to the position of superintendent of streets. More than 200 men were employed by the streets department, which placed orders for gravel and cement with suppliers and contractors loyal to the machine. James Pendergast also gained control over positions in the fire department and also named the city's deputy license inspector, an important job because saloons and other business establishments needed licenses to operate. Finally, and perhaps most important of all, by 1902 he had named 123 of the 173 patrolmen on the police force. In sum, he leveraged his ability to control politics in two wards into alliances with men who benefited from knowing him. Thus, although he never was mayor, he soon became Kansas City's most powerful politician.

Like the party machines in other cities, the Pendergast machine operated on the basis of mutually beneficial relationships. The boss distributed material rewards and expected loyalty in return. Some machine politicians made this relationship explicit, but the most effective ones never had to. After helping their constituents with problems such as paying the rent or dealing with the police, a machine politician could advise them to "vote your conscience." A politician could get a lot of mileage out of only a modest amount of help; the word spread. James Pendergast expressed the principle in this way: "I've been called a boss. All there is to it is having friends, doing things for people, and then later on they'll do things for you."[29] Pendergast's ward always elected him by at least a 3-to-1 margin, and without discernible vote fraud. It never occurred to him that he would need to steal an election.

The contrast to his brother Tom could not have been more stark. Tom, who inherited the Kansas City Democratic organization after James died, regularly resorted to a mixture of fraud and coercion. In the summer of 1914, Tom Pendergast's organization "used money, repeat voters, and toughs to produce North Side majorities" to gain approval of a proposed railway franchise.[30] Machine workers distributed liquor and money in black and Italian neighborhoods. They "paid men to vote under assumed names; and election judges who questioned some of those dragged off the streets and out of flop houses to vote were intimidated and abused, both verbally and physically."[31] On election day in 1934, four persons were killed by thugs. Two years later, an attempted assassination and massive voter fraud led to an investigation that eventually resulted in 259 convictions for election fraud and criminal behavior.

James Pendergast succeeded in politics because he went out of his way to ascertain the needs of his constituents. By all accounts, he had an engaging personality and was attentive to his constituents. By building a powerful political organization, he was able to provide them with jobs and other benefits. However, when his brother, Tom, took over the organization, corruption and intimidation became the order of the day. The story of the two Pendergasts highlights the main question about the classic party machines: Were they vehicles for democracy, or were they inherently flawed by their concentration of power in few hands?

control of the city commission, he was able to accomplish something he had not been able to do before: consolidate his power over a faction-ridden Democratic Party and become the uncontested boss of Jersey City.[32]

There is no evidence that machines accomplished more than nonmachine governments. A study of cities from 1890 to 1940 found no difference between machine and nonmachine cities in the overall level of public expenditures.[33] In the late nineteenth and early twentieth centuries, all big cities spent huge gobs of money on infrastructure—they paved streets, installed water and sewer lines, laid trolley tracks, strung electric power lines, built harbors, and constructed parks and public buildings. Even cities with factionalized politics, such as Los Angeles, made huge investments in infrastructure.[34] The political support for reducing disease rates through better water and sewer services, for better roads and public transit, for new public utilities and better parks was sufficiently strong that these services were bound to expand, however badly the government of a city was organized.[35] In any case, most urban infrastructure was built through specialized bureaucracies, not by party politics.

Often enough, corruption canceled out any benefits that might have accrued from the informal centralization of power. Corruption could make the price of "getting the job done" astonishingly high. Probably the most notoriously corrupt machine in American history was led by William Marcy "Boss" Tweed, who ran the infamous Tweed Ring in New York City from 1868 to 1871. In three years, Tweed diverted $30 million to $100 million of public funds to himself and his cronies. Under his regime, the machine's traditional take of 10 percent on construction contracts ratcheted upward. A courthouse project originally estimated to cost $250,000 ended up costing taxpayers $14 million. At least 90 percent of this cost overrun went to pay payoffs, bribes, and fake contracts.[36] Tweed's rule has been called the politics of "rapacious individualism" because everyone in the machine seemed to be after personal wealth. Because Tweed was not able to count on the loyalty of his fellow politicians, he was forced to buy it directly, and therefore his authority was fragile and short-lived.[37] In 1869 and 1870, the city's debt increased from $36 million to $97 million. By 1871, when Tweed was arrested, the city was bankrupt.

Machines bosses frequently resorted to corruption to build and maintain their organizations. Machine politicians were in a position to use the powers of cities to help businesses make money; in return, bribes were there for the taking.

Cities awarded multiyear contracts for streetcar operations and utility services (such as electricity, gas, and telephone). Cities issued tavern and liquor licenses and regulated gambling and prostitution (or had the option of looking the other way when they were illegal). They engaged in a continuous stream of public works projects, including the building of roads, bridges, public buildings, sewer and water systems, streetlights, and parks. There was money to be made on both sides of these transactions.

Control over the police force opened an avenue for bribes to Abraham Reuf's regime, which ruled San Francisco just after the turn of the century.[38] Soon after his handpicked candidate for mayor entered city hall in October 1901 (Reuf himself was an attorney who never held public office), Reuf let it be known that the city's laws against prostitution would be strictly enforced. He advised the brothel owners that it would be wise to have an attorney—himself—who could effectively represent their interests. The owners agreed to pay him a fourth of their profits, half of which Reuf shared with the mayor. This arrangement allowed the brothels to continue their operations without fear of prosecution. Reuf also "advised" saloons in the red-light district to pay premium prices for a low-quality whiskey supplied by one of Reuf's legal clients. In return, the saloon owners were protected from police raids.

In 1905, for an annual retainer of $5,000, Reuf became the attorney for the French Restaurant Keeper's Association of San Francisco. The restaurant owners had decided to retain Reuf after the city's police commissioners revoked the liquor license of one of their establishments. On behalf of his new clients, Reuf persuaded the mayor to remove one of the commissioners and replace him with someone sympathetic to the owners, thus ensuring renewal for all of the restaurants' liquor licenses.

Almost everywhere, machines forged alliances with illicit business owners. The relationship benefited both parties: The businesses were free to operate without having to worry about the law, and the politicians could count on a steady flow of bribes. One of the reasons that machines flourished in the 1920s is that the national prohibition of liquor sales opened unprecedented opportunities for selling police protection to speakeasies and bootleggers.

But machines took bribes from legitimate enterprises as well. Like other cities of the late nineteenth century, San Francisco invested huge resources in a variety of new municipal services, and businessmen competed viciously for the contracts. The mayor, the city council, or a utilities commission could, in a single stroke of a pen, enrich a business owner by awarding a contract to build electric trolley lines, install streetlights, supply gas, or install telephones. The temptation to make decisions secretly in smoky rooms was overwhelming. The chairman of the public utilities committee of the San Francisco Board of Supervisors reminded a group of businessmen in January 1906:

> It must be borne in mind that without the city fathers there can be no public service corporations. The street cars cannot run, lights cannot be furnished, telephones cannot exist. And all the public service corporations want to understand that we, the city fathers, enjoy the best of health and that we are not in business for our health. The question at this banquet board is: "How much money is in it for us?"[39]

There seemed to be plenty of money for everyone. When two telephone companies submitted competing bids to supply service to the citizens of San Francisco, Reuf collected a $1,200 monthly "attorney's fee" from one company while secretly accepting a $125,000 bribe from the other. Reuf persuaded the Board of Supervisors to award the contract to the company that paid the biggest bribe. Keeping $63,000 for himself, he used a loyalty test to distribute the remainder of the $125,000 to the individual supervisors: $6,000 each to those who had taken no independent bribes (showing they were not trying to compete with Reuf), $3,500 to those voting correctly despite bribes to do the opposite, and nothing to those who did not cooperate.

Reuf's position as the power behind the mayor's throne ended when he was indicted and tried for corruption. His downfall was precipitated by too much success. After seeing how lucrative politics in the city could be, other members of the city administration struck out on their own in search of bribes, and before long the feeding frenzy attracted attention.

Although most machines were less reckless than Reuf's, virtually all of them engaged in graft. The temptation was enormous. The machines governed the cities during a period of explosive growth in population, services, and construction. Even if the politicians tried to be honest, business tycoons eager to expand their empires were eager to spread their money around to get what they wanted. They found it convenient to work with bosses who could make decisions expeditiously behind the scenes. Big business paid bigger bribes than anyone else. As a result, companies were able to negotiate monopoly contracts on favorable terms. The franchises typically were granted for periods of fifty to a hundred years, and some specified no terminal dates at all.[40] In the 1880s and 1890s, national financial syndicates made millions of dollars by gaining control of street railway franchises. In 1890 there were thirty-nine street railway companies in Philadelphia, nineteen in New York City, twenty-four in Pittsburgh, nineteen in St. Louis, and sixteen in San Francisco.[41] By the turn of the century, only one or two major street railway companies operated in most cities.

It needs to be said that then, as now, corruption was not confined to machines—it was virtually everywhere. In any case, the extent and style of corruption varied from one machine to the next, as did the apparent benefits. During the 1930s, Boss George Cox was credited with bringing "positive and moderate reform government to Cincinnati."[42] In the years when Richard J. Daley was boss (1953–1976), Chicago was known as "the city that works." Daley was popular with voters because they felt he was responsible for the efficient delivery of city services, and there is no evidence he ever took money for himself.[43]

WERE MACHINES VEHICLES OF UPWARD MOBILITY?

An influential scholar has argued that the machines succeeded partly because they provided "alternative channels of social mobility for those otherwise excluded from the more conventional avenues of 'advancement.'"[44] In the nineteenth century, many employers refused to hire the Irish; "Irish need not apply" was written on many an employment notice. Local politics was "like a rope dangling down the formidable slope of the socioeconomic system" which poor immigrants could use to pull themselves up.[45]

There is ample evidence to support the thesis that machines aided the upward mobility of immigrants. Though surely this is not a typical example, politics was pivotal to the rise of the Kennedy clan in Boston from poverty to wealth and national power. President John F. Kennedy's grandfather on his mother's side, John "Honey Fitz" Fitzgerald, rose from a ward heeler running errands for an alderman to the office of mayor of Boston. Kennedy's grandfather on his father's side was a respected ward politician and saloonkeeper whose contacts helped the early career of the president's millionaire father, Joseph P. Kennedy, who made a fortune in bootleg liquor.[46]

The thesis that the machines aided the upward mobility of immigrants is based on the notion that machines had to work tirelessly to incorporate new groups of voters into their coalitions by offering them jobs and other favors. In their early years, machine politicians typically worked hard to attract voters so they could gain access to the patronage jobs in city government.[47] Once they had built a winning coalition, however, machine politicians often became complacent. They continued to reward their loyal supporters but stopped reaching out to new groups.

Most of the big city machines built in the nineteenth century were dominated by Irish politicians, and they stayed that way for a long time. In a study of six machines, Steven Erie concluded that they were consistently biased in favor of Irish constituents. Machine leaders "turned their backs on later-arriving immigrants."[48] Between 1900 and 1930, for example, the machines in New York City, Jersey City, and Albany, New York, added nearly 100,000 municipal jobs. Close to two-thirds of the new jobs went to Irish people, even though they made up only about one-third of the population in these cities. The Irish were especially careful to maintain their control over police forces. As late as 1970, for instance, 65 percent of police officers in Albany were of Irish descent, even though no more than 25 percent of the city's population could trace their ancestry to Ireland.[49]

Later-arriving immigrants to American cities found themselves shut out of the benefits of machine rule. In New York City, for example, the machine organization called Tammany Hall was run by and for the Irish. Though Jews and Italians represented 43 percent of New York's population by 1920, only 15 percent of the city's aldermen and assemblymen were Jewish and only 3 percent were Italian in 1921.[50] Fiorello LaGuardia, who was elected mayor in 1933, was able to smash the Tammany machine by assembling a coalition of disgruntled Jews, Italians, and other excluded groups. LaGuardia was a master at ethnic politics, perhaps because, "half Jewish and half Italian, married first to a Catholic and then to a Lutheran of German descent, himself a Mason and an Episcopalian, he was practically a balanced ticket all by himself."[51]

It perhaps goes without saying that blacks were excluded from virtually all urban machines. In some cities, "submachines" run by black bosses eventually were built, but they were subordinate in every way to the white machine bosses.[52] In Chicago, William Dawson, who was a congressman from 1942 until his death in 1970, ran a submachine in the South Side ghetto, but he was kept on a short leash by white politicians. Dawson reliably delivered huge pluralities for machine candidates from the black wards, but black voters received relatively little in return.[53] Throughout Chicago's history, weak and inexperienced black politicians who accepted a devil's bargain were recruited into the machine: In exchange for a few favors, they delivered the vote and kept a more militant black leadership from emerging.[54] The legacy of such practices was still apparent in the Daley years. Though blacks made up 40 percent of Chicago's population in 1970, they held only 20 percent of the government jobs in the city, and most of those jobs were the least desirable.[55] A study of a typical ward in Chicago in the 1970s found that the machine consistently overrewarded middle-class voters and underrewarded loyal working-class voters.[56]

The Chicago machine was finally challenged by disaffected groups. In 1983, a charismatic black politician, Harold Washington, assembled a coalition of poor people, blacks, Hispanics, and white liberals to defeat the machine's mayoral candidate.[57] But the victory was short-lived. After Washington suffered an unexpected heart attack in his office in 1987, Richard M. Daley, Richard J.'s son, won the mayor's race in 1989 by successfully reassembling the remnants of his father's organization and forging alliances with African American and Latino politicians.

It made perfect sense for machine politicians to keep their coalitions from expanding any more than necessary.[58] The more ethnic groups joined together in a coalition, the greater the interethnic squabbles over the distribution of patronage and the thinner the distribution of rewards. As a consequence, "once minimal winning coalitions had been constructed, the machines had little incentive to naturalize, register, and mobilize the votes of later ethnic arrivals."[59] For entrenched machines, expanding the electoral base past the coalition needed for winning just complicated things.

Even for the Irish, who benefited most from machine rule, the machines did not generally provide many opportunities for upward mobility. Though city governments grew rapidly in the late nineteenth century, the number of public jobs was pitifully small compared to the jobs available in the private economy. In 1900, Tammany's vaunted patronage army made up 5 percent of New York City's workforce. It is true that from 1900 to 1920 local governments grew so fast that public employment accounted for 20 percent of all urban job growth.[60] But for most people, including immigrants, private industry rather than patronage provided the best opportunities for upward mobility.

Though for decades the Irish laid claim to a disproportionate share of the jobs in city government, it took a long time for them to catch up to other ethnic groups in the broader economy. Scandinavians, Germans, and Jews, for example, participated relatively little in machine politics. Yet they assimilated into the American middle class faster than the Irish, who achieved economic parity with these groups only in the 1960s and 1970s. Ironically, the preoccupation of the Irish with public-sector employment may have slowed their entry into middle-class occupations. Especially at the bottom of the patronage ladder, jobs were deliberately kept low-paying in order to maximize the number that politicians could distribute. Most patronage jobs were blue collar, and they were distributed not to further the upward mobility of immigrants but to maintain machine organizations.

DID THE MACHINES HELP IMMIGRANTS ASSIMILATE?

Though the machines did not appreciably contribute to the economic success or upward mobility of their constituents, they nevertheless were instrumental in assimilating millions of impoverished immigrants into a culture that was generally fearful of and hostile to every new immigrant group. The machines helped create a sense of community and belonging for the immigrants. Machine organizations organized picnics, patriotic gatherings (always Fourth of July celebrations), baseball teams, choirs, and youth clubs. Machines were important community institutions, the Democratic Club being a place where men played cards and checkers or just talked.[61]

With the material resources at their disposal already devoted to their core constituency, machine politicians learned to satisfy immigrants who arrived later with largely symbolic benefits. In New York City, Tammany leader "Big Tim" Sullivan, an Irishman, ruled the Lower East Side even though as early as 1910 it was 85 percent Jewish and Italian. He retained the loyalty of his constituents by doing favors:

> He and his Irish lieutenants distributed coal, food, and rent money to needy Jews and Italians on the Lower East Side. Tammany's police department opened up station houses as temporary shelters for the homeless. Sullivan expedited business licenses for ethnic shopkeepers and pushcart peddlers. He shamelessly "recognized" the new immigrants with symbolic gestures and donned a yarmulke to solicit Jewish votes. Sullivan solicited Italian votes by sponsoring legislation to make Columbus Day a holiday.[62]

Many immigrants felt like outsiders in the dominant Protestant and middle-class culture of the United States. One of the secrets of the machines' appeal was that they tolerated the immigrants' "strange" practices and defended them from the dominant culture.[63] This was a benefit that machine politicians could deliver at little cost. Though working-class communities in American cities were not economically independent, they were, to a remarkable degree, socially independent. Immigrants built their own churches, mutual aid societies, and clubs for drinking and gambling. Machine politicians supported such activities because they could use them for campaigning and political organizing.[64]

Machine politicians appealed to and were supported by immigrant voters because they represented the possibility of success in this strange new country. Almost all machine politicians came from lower-class, immigrant origins. One study of twenty bosses found that fifteen were first- or second-generation immigrants, thirteen had never finished grammar school, and most had gone into politics at a young age, serving as messenger or detail boys at rallies and meetings.[65] Machine leaders, therefore, become symbols of success. Immigrants may not have read the Horatio Alger stories, but in machine bosses they could see men who had risen out of poverty. Aspiring politicians often accepted this interpretation of themselves, too; they viewed themselves as examples of what could be done with hard work and a little luck along the way. These real-world symbols of upward mobility were sources of pride and hope for the masses of immigrants who lived and worked under incredibly difficult conditions. However, symbol exceeded substance, especially for later-arriving southern and eastern European immigrants. Irish politicians would shrewdly pick a handful of men from other immigrant groups and place them on the ballot to demonstrate their generosity. Meanwhile, the bread-and-butter patronage stayed home.

The immigrants paid a high price for assimilation on these terms. Machines never attempted to address the collective aspirations of ethnic groups. The immigrants were encouraged to "cast their ballots on the basis of ethnicity rather than policy considerations."[66] Immigrants gave their votes to party politicians not as an act of consciousness about group goals but because it was easy to do and plausible alternatives were rare. The vote was a minimal commitment by the immigrant but a sufficient one for the machine. Commensurate with the level of commitment, constituents could hardly expect miracles in return.

The operating principles and structures of the urban machines ensured that the politicians who ran them steered clear of ideological battles. To deal with constituents' requests effectively, machine politicians had to learn the art of manipulating power within the framework of the existing political system. A special premium was placed on effective pragmatism, the ability to pull strings to get things done. Idealism was scorned. If a constituent came to complain about a building inspector, the politician's job was to make things nice with the inspector. Changing the building code was irrelevant and even counter-productive, because it might reduce the need for the politician's services.

Machines were hostile to political movements that tried to reform the system because such movements threatened their control of the immigrant vote. Until the 1930s, most machines vigorously opposed labor unions. In the first years of the twentieth century, Irish machine politicians ordered the police to attack labor organizers in Lawrence, Massachusetts, and in New York City.[67] In Pittsburgh's 1919 steel strike, the machine likewise ordered police to harass strikers.[68] After Franklin D. Roosevelt's landslide victory in the presidential election of 1932, some of the big-city machines formed alliances with the moderate trade unions, but the relationship was never easy to maintain. The machines expected the unions to respect their turf by focusing mainly on state and national politics and on labor-business relations.

On balance, the immigrants' potential as a political force was stunted by the machines. Working-class immigrants desperately needed reforms such as widows' pensions, better working conditions, laws regulating hours and wages (especially for women and children), and workers' compensation. On occasion, machine politicians supported these reforms as well as the regulation of utilities, the legal recognition of labor unions, and the regulation of insurance companies.[69] But this kind of selective and often half-hearted support for some reform measures did not exactly transform machine politicians into crusading reformers. Machine politicians were willing to offer support for selected pieces of reform legislation at the state level if it made them look good, but they never became active advocates of reform. Machine politicians could be quite capricious, for immediate political circumstances always took precedence over principle.

Machine politicians rarely considered how things could be changed. They often referred to reformers as "goody-goodies" or "goo-goos" who presumably were in politics for a few thrills. ("Goo-goo" was derived from "good government," often the reformers' rallying cry.) Much of this disdain was rooted in the social differences between upper-class reformers and the less educated immigrant politicians. The result was an excessive respect for the pragmatic fix.

THE SOCIAL REFORM ALTERNATIVE

Defenders of political machines have argued that there were few alternatives to the machines' style of politics, that in the face of the vast economic and political resources held by corporations and wealthy elites, machine politicians milked the system on behalf of their constituents as effectively as they could, and that to criticize them is to engage in wishful thinking about what might have been.

However, a look at the political movements of the time shows that practical alternatives did exist. In the first two decades of the twentieth century, social reformers won elections in cities all across the country. The social reformers were intent on improving the quality of life for immigrants and workers, and they campaigned for support from both working-class immigrant and middle-class voters.[70] Mayors Tom L. Johnson of Cleveland, Ohio (1901–1909), Samuel "Golden Rule" Jones of Toledo, Ohio (1897–1903), and Brand Whitlock of Toledo (1906–1913) all won election by fighting against high streetcar and utility rates and for fair taxation and better social services. Their campaigns became models for like-minded reformers elsewhere. Reform-oriented mayors in Jersey City, Philadelphia, and Cincinnati, for example, attempted to increase municipal revenue by raising taxes for businesses and wealthy property owners and by renegotiating streetcar and utility franchises. Machine politicians and the business community bitterly fought reform in these cities, just as they had a few years earlier in Cleveland and Toledo.[71]

The career of Hazen S. Pingree, who served as Detroit's mayor from 1890 to 1898, revealed the enormous possibilities of reform. Born in Maine to a poor farmer and itinerant cobbler, Pingree did not seem destined to become a political reformer. After fighting in the Civil War, Pingree moved to Detroit, where he worked as a leather cutter in a shoe factory. After a few years, he and a partner pooled their savings to purchase the outdated factory. By modernizing the machinery and producing a new line of shoes that fit current fashions, Pingree became independently wealthy. He was picked as the Republican candidate for mayor in 1889, largely because he was the only member of the exclusive Michigan Club who could be persuaded by its members to run. The businessmen who controlled Republican politics trusted him, as a member of the club, to advocate a program of low taxes and a minimal number of municipal services. In any case, few of them imagined he would win, and they had grown used to working with the Irish-dominated Democratic machine.

But unlike the typical business candidate, Pingree campaigned in the ethnic wards, and in fact kicked off his campaign by drinking whiskey in an Irish saloon. Pingree was a big hit with German and Polish voters, who had long been ignored by the Irish politicians. He called attention to the corruption of the machine and advocated an eight-hour workday for city employees. His willingness to seek the ethnic vote was the foundation on which he built his subsequent political success.

Pingree's programs, and the strategies he used to implement them, reveal how much could have been accomplished in other cities. When Pingree took over city hall, Detroit had one of the worst street systems in the nation. Many of the streets were made of wooden blocks, which caught fire in the summer and sank into the mire in the winter. The paved streets were pocked with ruts and potholes. Pingree quickly realized that collusion between paving contractors and machine politicians was at the heart of the street problem. He launched an aggressive campaign against this arrangement, appealing to his business supporters by pointing out that the prosperity of the city depended on good streets. His insistent efforts led the city council to adopt strict paving specifications for the city, and as a result, by 1895 Detroit had one of the best street systems in the United States.

It was not long before Pingree understood that the local business establishment was as much a problem as was the machine. He challenged the high fare charged for a ferry ride across the Detroit River to Belle Isle Park. The company dropped its rate from 10 cents to 5 cents after the mayor threatened to revoke its franchise or put into operation a municipal ferry service. Pingree also found that private companies had located along the Detroit River waterfront, often on municipal property, which choked off public access to water and recreation. He soon opened up waterfront areas for public use.

Above all, it was Pingree's fight with the Detroit City Railway Company that turned him into a true social reformer willing to use public authority to curb private power to benefit the city as a whole. At a time when streetcar companies in other cities were converting from horses to electric power, Detroit's company refused to make the change. In April 1891, the company's employees went on strike, presenting a perfect opportunity for Pingree to begin a battle for modernization and lower fares. The three-day strike culminated in a riot in which workers and citizens tore up the tracks, stoned the streetcars, and drove off the horses. Pingree ignored the company's request to call in the state militia and instead took the position that privately owned public services were "the chief source of corruption in city governments."[72] Pingree's stance initiated a protracted, bitter fight to regulate the streetcars. This conflict vaulted him to national prominence.

Many business leaders had supported the strike, feeling that the street railway was so badly run that it was hurting local business. The business community was mainly interested in more reliable service, but Pingree pressed further, pressing for lower fares and municipal ownership. Such a position ran afoul of business leaders when the company passed into the hands of an eastern business mogul. The new owner's first action was to pack the company's board of directors with prominent business leaders from Detroit. The company then demanded that the city negotiate a more favorable franchise. Pingree countered with a lawsuit meant to terminate the existing company in favor of municipal ownership. At that point, the company bought Pingree's own attorney away from him and proceeded to offer bribes to city council members, including a $75,000 bribe to Pingree himself. The Preston National Bank dropped Pingree from its board of directors; he lost his family pew in the Baptist church; he and his friends were shunned in public. For Pingree, the lesson he learned in all this was that business supported reform only on its own terms. And he also began to form his own analysis about what was wrong with America's cities.

In 1891, Pingree began attacking the tax privileges of the city's corporations. The railroad, he observed, owned more than one-fifth of the property value in the city but paid no taxes at all because of the tax-free status granted to it by the state legislature. Shipping companies, docks and warehouses, and other businesses escaped local taxation by claiming that their principal places of business existed outside the city. The city's biggest employer, the Michigan-Peninsula Car Company, paid only nominal taxes. Although he was unsuccessful in equalizing the tax burden, Pingree was able to modify some of its worst features, especially the practice of assessing, for tax purposes, real estate owned by wealthy people at rates far below value. Pingree earned the special enmity of the city's elite by successfully campaigning for a personal property tax on home furnishings, art objects, and other luxury items.

On April 1, 1895, Detroit began operating a municipal electric plant to supply power for its streetlights. This ended a five-year running battle between Pingree and the private lighting company. Pingree had used two issues to win his battle. His main argument against the private control of electricity was that it cost too much. Pingree gathered voluminous information to show that Detroit's service was more expensive and less reliable than service in other cities. Despite the merits of his case he would have lost, but a scandal tipped the scales in his favor. In April 1892, Pingree walked into a city council meeting waving a roll of bills and dramatically accused the Detroit Electric Light and Power Company of bribing council members. The mayor had been sure to pack the room with his working-class supporters. With Pingree's followers whipped into a dangerous mood, the council members hastily capitulated.

Pingree used similar tactics in his fights with the gas and telephone interests. To force the Detroit Gas Company to lower its rates for natural gas, he initiated a campaign to inform the public about the high price of Detroit's gas. When his attempt to force lower prices stalled in the courts, he got the public works board to deny permits to excavate streets for the purpose of laying gas lines. When the gas company attempted to excavate anyway, Pingree saw to it that the owners were arrested. "Possession is a great point," argued Pingree. "Let them get their gas systems connected and then they could float their $8,000,000 of stock in New York City and become too powerful for the city to control. Detroit would be helpless in the hands of corporations as never before in her history."[73]

Pingree continued his battle, encouraging users not to pay their gas bills. As public resistance against the Detroit Gas Company mounted, investors' confidence in the company plummeted, initiating a plunge in the company's stock values. Even after Southern Pacific Railroad magnate Samuel Huntington became the company's principal investor, stock prices continued to fall, and

Huntington negotiated an agreement to lower the price of gas from $1.50 per cubic foot to $0.80.

In his fourth term, Pingree took on the Bell Telephone Company. Again, the issue was high prices and inadequate service. This time he helped organize a competing phone company that charged less than half Bell's rate. The new Detroit Telephone Company soon attracted twice as many customers as Bell. In response, Bell initiated a rate war and began to improve its equipment and service. By 1900, when Michigan Bell bought out Detroit Telephone, Detroit had the lowest telephone rates and the most extensive residential use among large American cities.

No other mayor in America accomplished such a broad program of social reform. During his last two terms, Pingree traveled around the country making speeches and gathering information. He wrote prolifically. He inspired reformers elsewhere, and his national prominence helped him bring reform to his own city. After winning four terms as the mayor of Detroit, Pingree went on to serve two terms as the governor of Michigan, where he continued to fight for reform.

Pingree recognized the necessity of building a broad-based political coalition. He so assiduously courted ethnic voters that by his fourth term he had even won the dependable Irish away from the Democratic machine. In effect, Pingree pieced together his own machine, filling patronage jobs with his own supporters and firing his opponents. However, "he absolutely refused to tolerate dishonesty or theft."[74] Unlike Detroit's machine politicians, who regularly exploited ethnic hostilities to win votes in their wards, Pingree tried to unify working-class Poles, Germans, Irish, and the middle class. In short, he was aware that to accomplish reform it was necessary to "recruit a coalition of power sufficient for his purpose."[75] A great many political machines had likewise constructed powerful electoral coalitions, but the politicians who built them were more interested in furthering their own careers than in making the economic and political system more just.

MACHINE POLITICS IN TODAY'S CITIES

Cities are once again magnets for millions of immigrants and minorities. In this context, an intriguing question arises: Would recent immigrants and ethnic and racial minorities benefit if they built political machines much like those that ruled a century ago?

The urban machines brokered a deal in which poor immigrants and economic elites each gave up something and got something in return. Business elites ceded control over local governments to working-class ethnic politicians who controlled armies of patronage workers, supported in part by income from bribes and contributions paid by the wealthy. In return, machine politicians essentially promised to leave business alone. In effect, each side struck a bargain by recognizing a sharp separation between the market and the public sphere. This compromise was important in managing the tension between capitalism, with its attendant inequalities, and popular democracy.[76]

Machine politicians and their ethnic supporters gave up a great deal and got little in return. Rather than passing out favors and low-paying jobs, machine politicians could have emulated Pingree by attacking the practices that inflated the cost of urban services and infrastructure. They could have forged alliances with labor unions to pursue programs designed to modify dangerous working conditions, long hours, child labor, and low pay. Instead, the machines discouraged immigrants from organizing around their common interests.

There is reason to believe that today's city residents can expect even less from any machines that might arise. The machines prospered in rapidly growing industrial cities that required massive expenditures on roads, bridges, sewers, streetcar systems, schools, and parks.[77] The resulting government jobs, contracts, and franchises were traded for the political support necessary to maintain the party organizations. Like the industrial city a century ago, contemporary cities still hold large numbers of needy people. A potential electoral base exists to support machine organizations.

But it would be extremely difficult for today's politicians to assemble the patronage and other material rewards necessary to build and maintain machine organizations. City services are now administered through civil-service bureaucracies, and merit employment systems have been put in place so that patronage can no longer be regularly delivered on the basis of personal or political relationships. Even under Richard J. Daley's machine, decisions on the distribution of city services in Chicago during the 1970s relied heavily on "technical-rational criteria" that were "largely devoid of explicit political content."[78]

The urban machines that endured beyond the 1920s relied heavily on relationships forged with national politicians and federal aid for their survival.[79] After the New Deal, many machines skillfully used federal programs to expand their resource base.[80] But those days have passed. After the late 1970s, the federal government sharply cut grants to cities. In addition, the exodus of industry and the middle class to the suburbs has deprived the cities of critical tax sources and borrowing power.[81] The largest public projects are now administered through special authorities that are separate from municipal government.[82]

All this does not necessarily mean that the political control of cities is "a hollow prize."[83] Minority mayors can implement important policies to advance the interests of their constituents. For example, affirmative-action hiring and city residency requirements for city jobs favor city minority residents over nonminority workers who live in the suburbs—and who often take the lion's share of central city jobs. Minority contractor set-asides help ensure that a percentage of jobs on public projects go to minorities.[84] City agencies can be made to be more sensitive to poor and minority constituents. When Harold Washington served as Chicago's mayor from 1983 to 1987, capital improvement programs were put in place in neighborhoods; special loan programs provided capital for businesses owned by minorities and women; the city made a commitment to purchase 25 percent of its services from minority-owned and women-owned businesses; and job training programs were funded for unemployed people.[85]

City governments make decisions and command resources critical to the well-being of city residents. City politics, however, will not likely proceed again on the basis of direct trade-offs and favors exchanged for the vote. The Chicago machine led by Richard M. Daley—the son of a legendary machine boss, Richard J. Daley—may be the only party machine left operating today in a big city. Chicago has a "rubber stamp" city council that invariably endorses Mayor Daley's proposals; even on controversial issues, few aldermen dare to vote no.[86] Nevertheless, the machine run by the younger Daley is very different from his father's. Although the Daley organization still calls upon precinct captains to manage their precincts and to deliver the vote, patronage is no longer what it used to be. Court decrees from the 1980s ended most blue-collar patronage jobs. A new kind of white-collar patronage is now distributed to lawyers, brokers, financial consultants, advertising and public relations firms, and lobbyists. Reflecting the shape of a new globalized economy, the most important sources of campaign contributions are the financial services sector, the construction industry (including its unions), law firms, the tourism and hospitality sector, and downtown corporations.[87] Campaign contributions from aldermen and other politicians and governmental employees loyal to the mayor amount to less than 2 percent of Daley's financial support. The big volumes of money required for Daley's campaigns go more to media advertising aimed at higher-income voters who have moved into gentrified neighborhoods than to grass-roots campaigning.

Media-centered campaigns have replaced door-to-door and face-to-face campaigns at all levels of the American political system. National issues such an abortion rights, gay rights, and social-welfare spending have also become important in local politics almost everywhere.[88] Because voters care about many national issues, it is difficult to imagine how an old-style party machine oriented to ethnic voters or to a politics of immediate material rewards would now emerge in any city.

NOTES

1. As quoted in Edward McChesney Sait, "Political Machines," in *Encyclopedia of the Social Sciences*, ed. Edwin R. A. Seligman (New York: Macmillan, 1933), p. 657. We will use the terms *machine* and *boss*, but in doing so we are not implying any moral judgment.
2. Raymond Wolfinger, "Why Political Machines Have Not Withered Away and Other Revisionist Thoughts," in *Readings in Urban Politics: Past, Present, and Future*, ed. Harlan Hahn and Charles H. Levine (New York: Longman, 1984), p. 79. Wolfinger makes the distinction that we draw here between machine politics and a centralized machine. See also Roger W. Lotchin, "Power and Policy: American City Politics Between the Two World Wars," in *Ethnics, Machines, and the American Urban Future*, ed. Scott Greer (Cambridge, Mass.: Schenkman, 1981), p. 9.
3. M. Craig Brown and Charles N. Halaby, "Machine Politics in America, 1870–1945," *Journal of Interdisciplinary History* 17, no. 3 (Winter 1987): 598. In order to qualify as a dominant political machine, a machine-style party had to control both the executive and the legislative branches of the city for an uninterrupted series of three elections.
4. One of the last classic machines, the O'Connell machine in Albany, New York, lost its grip in the 1980s. See Todd Swanstrom and Sharon Ward, "Albany's O'Connell Organization: The Survival of an Entrenched Machine" (paper delivered at the American Political Science Association Convention, Chicago, September 1987). In Chicago, Richard M. Daley, the son of Richard J., still presides over a disciplined machine, but it relies on well-funded media campaigns and a high level of amenities and services rather than on patronage and

spoils for its support. For a comprehensive history of machine politics in Chicago, see Dick Simpson, *Rogues, Rebels, and Rubber Stamps: The Politics of the Chicago City Council, 1863 to the Present* (Boulder, Colo.: Westview Press, 2001).

5. For the definitive treatment of this question, see Steven P. Erie, *Rainbow's End: Irish-Americans and the Dilemmas of Urban Machine Politics, 1840–1985* (Berkeley: University of California Press, 1988). President Lyndon Johnson's National Advisory Commission on Civil Disorders linked the 1960s urban riots to the "demise of the historic urban political machines." *Report of the National Advisory Commission on Civil Disorders* (New York: Bantam Books, 1968), p. 287.

6. Amy Bridges, *A City in the Republic* (Cambridge, U.K.: Cambridge University Press, 1984), p. 8.

7. William N. Chambers, "Party Development and the American Mainstream," in *The American Party System: Stages of Political Development*, 2nd ed., ed. William Nisbet Chambers and Walter Dean Burnham (New York: Oxford University Press, 1975), p. 12.

8. Alan DiGaetano, "The Rise and Development of Urban Political Machines," *Urban Affairs Quarterly* 24, no. 2 (December 1988): 247, table 3. For more information on the expansion of city governments in the late nineteenth century, see Jon C. Teaford, *The Unheralded Triumph: City Government in America, 1870–1900* (Baltimore: Johns Hopkins University Press, 1984); Eric H. Monkkonen, *America Becomes Urban: The Development of U.S. Cities and Towns, 1780–1980* (Berkeley: University of California Press, 1988).

9. Terrence J. McDonald and Sally K. Ward, eds., *The Politics of Urban Fiscal Policy*, (Beverly Hills, Calif.: Sage, 1984), Introduction, p. 14.

10. Jon M. Kingsdale, "The 'Poor Man's Club': Social Functions of the Urban Working-Class Saloon," in *The Making of Urban America*, ed. Raymond A. Mohl (Wilmington, Del.: Scholarly Resources, 1988), p. 123.

11. Ibid.

12. Ibid.

13. Ibid., p. 130.

14. "He [the boss] does not seek social honor; the 'professional' is despised in 'respectable society.' He seeks power alone, power as a source of money, but also power for power's sake." Max Weber, "Politics as a Vocation," in *From Max Weber: Essays in Sociology*, ed. H. H. Gerth and C. Wright Mills (New York: Oxford University Press, 1946), p. 109.

15. William L. Riordan, *Plunkitt of Tammany Hall* (New York: Dutton, 1963), p. 50.

16. Quoted in Dayton McKean, *The Boss* (Boston: Houghton Mifflin, 1940), p. 132.

17. Edward C. Banfield and James Q. Wilson, *City Politics* (New York: Vintage Books, 1963), p. 125.

18. Milton Rakove, *Don't Make No Waves . . . Don't Back No Losers: An Insider's Analysis of the Daley Machine* (Bloomington: Indiana University Press, 1975). The following material on Daley's machine is drawn from Rakove.

19. Ibid., pp. 114–115.

20. Ibid., p. 115.

21. Ibid., p. 120.

22. Ibid., p. 122.

23. Sait, "Political Machines," p. 658. See also Robert M. Merton, *Social Theory and Social Structure* (New York: Free Press, 1949), pp. 126–127. For decades, Merton's functional analysis of political machines was widely accepted, but it has been seriously challenged in recent years. See Erie, *Rainbow's End;* DiGaetano, "The Rise and Development of Urban Political Machines"; M. Craig Brown and Charles N. Halaby, "Functional Sociology, Urban History, and the Urban Political Machine: The Outlines and Foundations of Machine Politics, 1870–1945" (Albany: Department of Sociology, State University of New York at Albany, n.d.).

24. DiGaetano, "The Rise and Development of Urban Political Machines," pp. 257–262. See also M. Craig Brown and Charles N. Halaby, "Bosses, Reform, and the Socioeconomic Bases of Urban Expenditure, 1890–1940," in *The Politics of Urban Fiscal Policy*, ed. Terrence S. McDonald and Sally K. Ward (Beverly Hills, Calif.: Sage), p. 90.

25. The information presented here on the Pendergast machine comes from Lyle W. Dorsett, *The Pendergast Machine* (New York: Oxford University Press, 1968). Only direct quotations from Dorsett are cited by page in subsequent notes.
26. Ibid., p. 14.
27. Ibid., p. 21.
28. Ibid., p. 41.
29. Ibid., p. 26.
30. Ibid., p. 59.
31. Ibid., p. 60.
32. DiGaetano, "The Rise and Development of Urban Political Machines," p. 261. Urban politics is often portrayed as a morality play in which reformers are pitted against machine politicians. In fact, machines often used reforms to consolidate their power and put reformers on the ballot in order to legitimate their rule. On the other side, reformers often created their own type of political machines. For a critique of the dichotomy between bosses and reformers, see David P. Thelen, "Urban Politics: Beyond Bosses and Reformers," *Reviews in American History* 7 (September 1979): 406–412. For an example of a reformer who created a new type of political machine, see Robert Caro's masterful biography of Robert Moses, *The Power Broker: Robert Moses and the Fall of New York* (New York: Vintage Books, 1974).
33. Brown and Halaby, "Bosses, Reform, and the Socioeconomic Bases of Urban Expenditure, 1890–1940," p. 87. Interestingly, the authors found that machine cities, after reform—such as the establishment of a city manager form of government—spent more than other cities (p. 89).
34. Lotchin, "Power and Policy," p. 11.
35. Stanley K. Schultz, *Constructing Urban Culture: American Cities and City Planning, 1800–1920* (Philadelphia: Temple University Press, 1989).
36. There are many sources of information on the Tweed Ring. The two books used here are Alexander Callow, Jr., *The Tweed Ring* (New York: Oxford University Press, 1966), and Seymour J. Mandelbaum, *Boss Tweed's New York* (New York: Wiley, 1965). For a provocative, yet ultimately unpersuasive, defense of Tweed, see Leo Hershkowitz, *Tweed's New York: Another Look* (Garden City, N.Y.: Anchor Books, 1977).
37. Martin Shefter, "The Emergence of the Political Machine: An Alternative View," in *Theoretical Perspectives on Urban Politics,* ed. Willis D. Hawley et al. (Englewood Cliffs, N.J.: Prentice-Hall, 1976), p. 21.
38. The information presented here on Abraham Reuf's machine is taken from Walter Bean, *Boss Reuf's San Francisco* (Berkeley: University of California Press, 1952; reprinted 1972). Only direct quotations from Bean are cited by page in subsequent notes.
39. Ibid., pp. 93–94.
40. Paul Kantor, with Stephen David, *The Dependent City: The Changing Political Economy of Urban America* (Glenview, Ill.: Scott Foresman, 1988), p. 104.
41. Ernest S. Griffith, *A History of American City Government: The Conspicuous Failure, 1870–1900* (New York: Praeger, 1974), p. 183.
42. Zane Miller, *The Urbanization of Modern America: A Brief History* (New York: Harcourt Brace Jovanovich, 1973), p. 121.
43. Ester R. Fuchs and Robert Y. Shapiro, "Government Performance as a Basis for Machine Support," *Urban Affairs Quarterly* 18, no. 4 (June 1983): 537–550.
44. Merton, *Social Theory and Social Structure,* p. 130.
45. Robert A. Dahl, *Who Governs? Democracy and Power in an American City* (New Haven, Conn.: Yale University Press, 1961), p. 34.
46. See Doris Kearns Goodwin, *The Fitzgeralds and the Kennedys: An American Saga* (New York: Simon and Schuster, 1987).
47. The discussion of mobilizing versus entrenched machines relies heavily on Erie's "life cycle" theory of political machines in *Rainbow's End.*

48. Erie, *Rainbow's End*, p. 69.

49. Terry Nichols Clark, "The Irish Ethic and the Spirit of Patronage," *Ethnicity* 2 (1975): 341–342.

50. Martin Shefter, "Political Incorporation and the Extrusion of the Left: Party Politics and Social Forces in New York City," in *Studies in American Political Development*, vol. 1, ed. Karen Orren and Stephen Skowronek (New Haven, Conn.: Yale University Press, 1986), p. 55.

51. Caro, *The Power Broker*, p. 354.

52. For a useful review of the relationships between African Americans and political machines, see Hanes Walton, Jr., *Black Politics: A Theoretical and Structural Analysis* (Philadelphia: Lippincott, 1972), chap. 4.

53. William J. Grimshaw, *Bitter Fruit: Black Politics and the Chicago Machine, 1931–1991* (Chicago: University of Chicago Press, 1992).

54. Ibid.

55. Erie, *Rainbow's End*, p. 165.

56. Thomas M. Guterbock, *Machine Politics in Transition: Party and Community in Chicago* (Chicago: University of Chicago Press, 1980).

57. See Paul Kleppner, *Chicago Divided: The Making of a Black Mayor* (DeKalb: Northern Illinois University Press, 1985).

58. Michael Johnston, "Patrons and Clients, Jobs and Machines: A Case Study of the Uses of Patronage," *American Political Science Review* 73, no. 2 (June 1979): 385–398.

59. Erie, *Rainbow's End*, p. 218.

60. Ibid., pp. 48, 242.

61. For a discussion of the role of political clubs in the evolution of Tammany Hall, see Shefter, "The Emergence of the Political Machine," p. 35.

62. Erie, *Rainbow's End*, pp. 102–103.

63. Kenneth D. Wald argues that ethnics supported machines not so much in response to socioeconomic disadvantage but out of an awareness of their social marginality and in the belief that machines would defend them from external pressures; see his "The Electoral Base of Political Machines: A Deviant Case Analysis," *Urban Affairs Quarterly* 16, no. 1 (September 1980): 3–29.

64. It would be misleading to say that such practices simply reflected the desires of poor immigrants. Irish family life was disrupted by the easy availability of illicit entertainment. Catholic priests and a significant proportion of the immigrant population opposed vice activities.

65. Harold Zink, *City Bosses in the United States* (Durham, N.C.: Duke University Press, 1930).

66. Wolfinger, "Why Political Machines Have Not Withered Away," p. 70.

67. Allan Rosenbaum, "Machine Politics: Class Interest and the Urban Poor," paper delivered at the annual meeting of the American Political Science Association (September 4–8, 1973), pp. 25–26.

68. Ibid., p. 26.

69. John D. Buenker, *Urban Liberalism and Progressive Reform* (New York: Scribner, 1973). Joseph J. Huthmacher also provides evidence of machine legislators' support for reform; see his "Urban Liberalism and the Age of Reform," *Mississippi Valley Historical Review* 44 (September 1962): 231–241.

70. For the distinction between social and structural reformers, see Melvin G. Holli, *Reform in Detroit: Hazen S. Pingree and Urban Politics* (New York: Oxford University Press, 1969), chap. 8. We discuss the social reformers in this chapter; in the next chapter we discuss the structural reformers.

71. Martin J. Schiesl, *The Politics of Efficiency: Municipal Administration and Reform in America, 1880–1920* (Berkeley: University of California Press, 1977), pp. 80 ff.

72. Quoted in Holli, *Reform in Detroit*, p. 42.

73. Quoted in ibid., p. 92.

74. Ibid., p. 195.

75. Peter Marris and Martin Rein, *Dilemmas of Social Reform* (New York: Atherton Press, 1967), p. 7.

76. Kantor, *The Dependent City*, pp. 117–118. Machine politicians appealed to voters on the basis of where they lived (their ethnic identification), not on the basis of where they worked (their class identification). Thus machine politics confirmed the "city trenches" that have divided the American political landscape into community politics and workplace politics and blunted political action by the working class. See Ira Katznelson, *City Trenches: Urban Politics and the Patterning of Class in the United States* (New York: Pantheon, 1981).

77. See James C. Scott, "Corruption, Machine Politics, and Political Change," *American Political Science Review* 63 (December 1969): 1142–1158; Clarence N. Stone, Robert K. Whelan, and William J. Murin, *Urban Policy and Politics in a Bureaucratic Age*, 2nd ed. (Englewood Cliffs, N.J.: Prentice-Hall, 1986), chap. 7.

78. Kenneth R. Mladenka, "The Urban Bureaucracy and the Chicago Political Machine: Who Gets What and the Limits to Political Control," in *Readings in Urban Politics: Past, Present, and Future*, ed. Harlan Hahn and Charles H. Levine (New York: Longman, 1984), p. 114. A later study of Chicago found that the local party structure did influence the provision of one service: building code enforcement. See Bryan D. Jones, "Party and Bureaucracy: The Influence of Intermediary Groups on Urban Public Service Delivery," *American Political Science Review* 75, no. 3 (September 1981): 688–700.

79. Erie, *Rainbow's End.*

80. By ending the dependence of the urban poor on political machines for favors, many argued, the rise of the New Deal welfare state undermined political machines. See Rexford Tugwell, *The Brain Trust* (New York: Viking, 1968), pp. 366–371. Historical research has shown, however, that many machines were able to use the welfare state to strengthen their organizations. See Bruce M. Stave, *The New Deal and the Last Hurrah: Pittsburgh Machine Politics* (Pittsburgh: University of Pittsburgh Press, 1970); Lyle W. Dorsett, *Franklin D. Roosevelt and the City Bosses* (Port Washington, N.Y.: Kennikat Press, 1977); Wolfinger, "Why Political Machines Have Not Withered Away," pp. 85–88; Erie, *Rainbow's End.*

81. Lotchin, "Power and Policy," p. 17.

82. Dennis R. Judd and Dick Simpson, "Tourism and the New Urban Politics: Restructuring Regimes, Reconstructing the Local State," *American Behavioral Scientist* Vol. 46, no. 8 (April 2003).

83. H. Paul Friesema, "Black Control of Central Cities: The Hollow Prize," *Journal of the American Institute of Planners* 35 (March 1969): 75.

84. Melvin G. Holli and Paul M. Green, *Bashing Chicago Traditions: Harold Washington's Last Campaign* (Grand Rapids, Mich.: Eerdmans, 1989), p. 120.

85. Dennis R. Judd and Randy L. Ready, "Entrepreneurial Cities and the New Policies of Economic Development," in *Reagan and the Cities*, ed. George E. Peterson and Carol W. Lewis (Washington, D.C.: Urban Institute Press, 1986), pp. 232–233.

86. Simpson, *Rogues, Rebels, and Rubber Stamps*, p. 280.

87. Ibid.

88. Elaine Sharp, (ed.), *Culture Wars and Urban Politics* (Lawrence: University Press of Kansas, 1999).

CHAPTER
4

THE REFORM
CRUSADES

THE MOTIVE FOR REFORM

In 1902, George Washington Plunkitt of Tammany Hall pontificated that reformers "were mornin' glories—looked lovely in the mornin' and withered up in a short time, while the regular machines went on flourishin' forever, like fine old oaks."[1] At the time Plunkitt delivered himself of that poetic homily, he was essentially correct. Through the last quarter of the nineteenth century, reform movements sprang up in cities all across the country. The reformers aimed to dismantle the party organizations that thrived on immigrant votes, but these movements tended to be short-lived, exactly as Plunkitt observed. Reformers were often successful in persuading state legislatures to take budgeting and the administration of some services out of the hands of aldermen and city councils and put them under the control of boards dominated by a "better class" of people. They were not able, however, to undercut the electoral influence of immigrants. Aldermen elected from individual wards still decided such matters as streetcar and utility franchises, construction contracts, and the provision of city services. Plenty of patronage jobs and money, the lifeblood of machine politics, were bound up in these decisions.

To many middle- and upper-class Americans, cities seemed to be in the hands of criminals who plundered the public purse for personal gain. Although reformers in Cleveland, New York, Chicago, and other cities sometimes did throw machine politicians out of office and succeeded in getting some of them prosecuted in the courts for corruption, the offending politicians were easily replaced by men cut from the same cloth. Commenting on this fact of life, Englishman James Bryce expressed the view that "the government of cities is the one conspicuous failure of the United States."[2] Many middle- and upper-class voters shared his opinion. As stated at the time in a pro-reform textbook on municipal government:

> The privilege seeker has pervaded our political life. For his own profit he has willfully befouled the sources of political power. Politics, which should offer a career inspiring to the noblest thoughts and calling for the most patriotic efforts of which man is capable, he has . . . transformed into a series of sordid transactions between those who buy and those who sell governmental action.[3]

70

The widespread concern about political corruption in the cities was closely connected to a rising fear of foreign immigrants—the so-called Great Unwashed. The reaction against immigrants had been building for a long time. As early as 1851, an article in the *Massachusetts Teacher* asked:

> The constantly increasing influx of foreigners . . . continues to be a cause of serious alarm to the most intelligent of our people. What will be the ultimate effect of this vast and unexampled immigration. . . ? Will it, like the muddy Missouri, as it pours its waters into the clear Mississippi and contaminates the whole united mass, spread ignorance and vice, crime and disease, through our native population?[4]

Protestants descended from the older immigrant groups were scandalized when they observed Irish and German immigrants drinking beer on Sundays and by lurid newspaper accounts of prostitution, gambling, and public drunkenness in the immigrant wards. Protestant moralists secured city and state statutes abolishing prostitution, gambling, and Sunday liquor sales. To teach immigrant children middle-class versions of dress, speech, manners, and discipline, reformers passed laws requiring school attendance and raised the upper age limit for mandatory schooling. Truant officers were hired to search for wayward youth.

The vicious reaction against immigrants aggravated class, racial, and religious tensions. Immigrants were compared to the Goths and Vandals who invaded the Roman Empire in the second century A.D. In his book, *Our Country*, the Reverend Josiah Strong accused the immigrants of defiling the Sabbath, spreading illiteracy and crime, and corrupting American culture and morals. Gathered into the cities, he said, the immigrants provided "a very paradise for demagogues" who ruled by manipulating the "appetites and prejudices" of the rabble.[5]

The spatial segregation of social classes within the cities exacerbated middle- and upper-class fears about the immigrants. By the turn of the century, all large cities contained overcrowded immigrant ghettos near the waterfronts and factories, with middle- and upper-class neighborhoods located farther from the urban center. Jobs were still concentrated in downtown districts, so affluent city residents could hardly escape seeing, on their way to work and to shop, the drab tenements, dirty streets, and littered alleys where the immigrants lived.

Most reformers were members of the upper class or exceptionally well-educated members of the middle class. The reforms they advocated were designed to enhance the influence of the "better classes" and to undercut the immigrants' electoral influence in city politics. Where they were successful, they fundamentally changed the way local political systems operated. Some of the reforms undermined democratic governance, a legacy that has come under challenge in recent decades.

THE REFORM ENVIRONMENT

The municipal reform movement was energized by the reform impulse that swept the country in the first decades of the twentieth century. Several developments ushered in the so-called Progressive Era. Excesses of wealth existed side by side with the grinding poverty of the immigrant wards. Newly developed mass media brought a heightened awareness about these conditions to upper-class and educated middle-class readers. By the turn of the century, falling paper prices and technical advances in rapid printing made it possible to produce high-quality mass-circulation newspapers and magazines. During the 1890s, newspaper circulation doubled and then tripled. A multitude of new periodicals appeared. All that was required to develop a mass audience was a way to popularize the press. Muckraking was such a technique. Crusading journalists investigated and reported "inside stories" exposing organized vice and the corruption of the urban machines. They also wrote about pervasive corruption in the national government, big business, the stock market, and the drug and meatpacking industries.

Beginning with its September 1902 issue, *McClure's* magazine printed a series of seven articles by Lincoln Steffens, that told lurid stories of municipal corruption in the nation's big cities. In October, *McClure's* carried an article by Ida Tarbell exposing corporate corruption and profiteering by John D. Rockefeller's Standard Oil Company. The stories were an instant success, revealing an insatiable appetite in the public for sensational accounts of wrongdoing in business and government. A new mass-circulation formula was discovered. Over the next few years, *Munsey's, Everybody's, Success, Collier's, Saturday Evening Post, Ladies' Home Journal, Hampton's, Pearson's, Cosmopolitan,* and dozens of daily newspapers carried stories that appealed to the popular feeling that political, economic, and social institutions had become corrupt. Big business was accused of producing unsafe and shoddy goods, fixing prices, and crushing competition. There were exposés of fraudulent practices in banking; heart-rending accounts of women and children working at long, tedious, and dangerous jobs in factories and sweatshops; stories about urban poverty, prostitution, white slavery, and business-government collusion to protect vice.

An outpouring of popular books played on the same themes. In 1904, Steffens published his *McClure's* articles together in a best-selling book, *The Shame of the Cities*. Other popular titles included *The Greatest Trust in the World,* an exposé of price-fixing and collusion in the steel industry; *The Story of Life Insurance;* and *The Treason of the Senate,* which detailed systematic bribery of U.S. senators. Several important novelists entered the field. In *An American Tragedy,* Theodore Dreiser described the corrupting influence of greed on a self-made small-town boy. Dreiser's *Sister Carrie* and David Graham Phillip's *Susan Lenox* both played on the theme of how the impersonal forces of urban life victimized young women. In *The Financier,* Dreiser's theme was the ruthless drive for power and wealth, using the Chicago streetcar magnate Charles Yerkes as his model. Upton Sinclair's *The Jungle* dealt with a Lithuanian immigrant's fight to survive in a corrupt and chaotic Chicago. Beaten down by destitution and poverty, eventually his wife becomes a prostitute, his children die, and he becomes a socialist revolutionary. By vividly portraying the nauseating conditions in Chicago's meatpacking industry (with rats, feces, and spoiled meat being swept into sausage vats, for example), Sinclair catalyzed a national crusade that resulted in congressional legislation creating the U.S. Food and Drug Administration in

1905. The literature produced by the muckrakers—an epithet applied to them in 1906 by President Theodore Roosevelt, referring to a character in John Bunyan's 1645 book *Pilgrim's Progress* who was too busy raking muck to look up and see the stars—was influential in building popular interest in reform. Although the details of reform were often dull and unexciting to the average citizen, the muckrakers' stories provided a feeling of drama and urgency.

This environment spawned the formation of organizations dedicated to the goals of regulating business practices, improving working conditions, imposing standards on the professions, and reforming government. Business leaders organized the National Civic Federation in 1900. By advocating workers' compensation and other minor social insurance schemes, the founders of the federation hoped to undermine more militant demands being put forth by union organizers.[6] The National Child Labor Committee was organized in 1904 to fight for child labor legislation. In 1910, the National Housing Association brought together housing reform groups from many cities to agitate for building codes. A large number of public officials' associations and municipal research bureaus came into existence specifically to promote municipal reform: the National Association of Port Authorities, the Municipal Finance Officers Association, the American Association of Park Superintendents, the Conference of City Managers, the National Short Ballot Association.

Though government corruption had provoked campaigns to "throw the rascals out" in a few cities during the 1870s and 1880s, the issues had usually been local and the remedies specific to an immediate situation. Several developments in the 1890s transformed reform into a national movement aimed at promoting systematic change in local government structures. In response to widespread government corruption, citizens' groups sprang up all across the country to lobby for improved public services and honesty in government. The problems faced by the reformers varied little from one city to another. Like-minded reformers from different cities soon began to exchange advice and information about their efforts. These informational networks subsequently led to the formation of national reform organizations.

In 1894, delegates to the First Annual Conference for Good City Government met in Philadelphia to found the first national municipal reform organization, the National Municipal League. The delegates to the conference were united in the belief that democratic institutions in the cities had been corrupted by machine politicians and their immigrant constituents. There was, however, little agreement about the measures that could be taken to change this condition. "We are not unlike patients assembled in a hospital," one of the participants put it, "examining together and describing to each other our sore places."[7] After the formation of the National Municipal League, the nationalization of reform proceeded quickly. Within two years, 180 local chapters were affiliated with the league and, by the turn of the century, all large cities had member organizations. In their yearly meetings, reformers from all over the country got a chance to compare notes. By its November 1899 meeting, the members of the National Municipal League reached agreement on a model municipal charter containing the elements making up the reformers' ideal of "good government." The charter was meant to serve as a blueprint for bringing fundamental change to local government.

To abolish the machines, the model charter recommended that ward elections be abandoned in favor of at-large elections, so that all city council members would represent the entire city rather than each alderman or council members representing a single ward. It also recommended that nonpartisan elections replace the party label on election ballots. It urged reformers to fight for civil service appointment procedures, so that party officials would not be able to use public jobs for patronage. The league also said that local elections should be held in different years than national and state elections, so that the national political parties would find it more difficult to influence local affairs.[8]

All of these measures were designed to undermine the basic foundation of machine politics: the political party. But in addition to eliminating the machines, the reformers wanted to reorganize local government. The league's model charter recommended that a small, unicameral city council replace the bicameral councils then existing in most cities (many city governments had been modeled on the national government, with its two legislative chambers). In addition, it encouraged reformers to lobby for new city charters that would give the mayor the power to appoint top administrators and to veto legislation. The assumption behind this reform—called "strong mayor government" —was that with authority centralized in the hands of the mayor, voters would be able to hold the mayor accountable for the city's overall governance. At the same time, the reformers thought that this change might help end the style of politics in which city council members or aldermen made deals with one another behind the scenes. Finally, the league urged city reformers to seek so-called home rule charters from their state legislatures, reasoning that this reform would free cities from state party leaders and reduce meddling by state legislatures in local affairs.

The municipal reformers shared the conviction that it was their responsibility to educate and instruct the public about the principle of what they called good government. They placed their faith in rule by educated upper- and middle-class Americans and, increasingly, in administration by trained administrators and professionals. In this way, the municipal reform movement began to build a style of government by bureaucracy that many Americans complain about today.

THE CAMPAIGNS AGAINST MACHINE RULE

The urban machines and their immigrant constituents were the reformers' principal targets. In their zeal to undermine the machines, some reformers went so far as to question the wisdom of universal suffrage, using the argument that immigrants were too ignorant and illiterate to vote intelligently. There was some support for this view among the reform ranks. The Tilden Commission,

OUT TAKE

MUNICIPAL REFORM WAS BIASED

The municipal reforms of the early nineteenth century were designed to undercut the electoral influence of the working class and immigrants. Most of the prominent reformers of the Progressive Era were upper-class people,[9] and many, in fact, were wealthy industrialists, with names like McCormack, du Pont, Pinchot, Morgenthau, and Dodge. Most of them had a college education in a day when this fact marked a select social stratum; even more telling, most of the women and social workers had gone to college. The expectation that new forms of government would result in the election of a "better" class of citizens, meaning businessmen and their favored candidates, was usually fulfilled, and this fact explains why business leaders were at the forefront of the municipal reform movement.[10]

The New York City Bureau of Municipal Research, founded in 1906, was initially financed by Andrew Carnegie and John D. Rockefeller.[11] The U.S. Chamber of Commerce provided office space and paid the executive secretary of the City Managers Association for several years.[12] Civic clubs and voters' leagues generally contained names from elite social directories, and the professionals involved in reform tended to be the most prestigious members of their professions.

Machine politicians, ethnic voters, and working-class groups usually opposed reform proposals because they correctly perceived that these were designed make it more difficult for working-class candidates to win public office.[13] Because immigrants accounted for a disproportionate share of the working class and poor within cities, both class and ethnicity were important factors determining attitudes toward reform.[14] In the big cities, coalitions of immigrants and working-class groups were generally successful in opposing key features of the reform agenda. In smaller cities and cities outside the northern industrial belt, however, immigrants and working-class groups were generally outvoted. A dramatic illustration of the effects of reform occurred in the 1938 municipal elections in Jackson, Michigan. The local chamber of commerce persuaded voters to approve a council-manager charter with at-large elections. After the charter was adopted, the new slate of candidates sponsored by the chamber swept into office. The new mayor and council members celebrated with a reception in the Masonic hall (the Masons were an anti-Catholic organization) and, once in power, dismissed most of the Roman Catholic city employees.[15]

The two-sided nature of reform makes most people ambivalent about its effects. On the one hand, it helped reduce widespread corruption in city politics. On the other, it made cities less democratic and city government more bureaucratic. But whatever one's judgment about reform, it is important to recognize that it involved a battle over the most essential question in politics: "Who governs?"

---

appointed by the New York legislature to investigate the Tweed Ring scandals in New York City, recommended in 1878 that suffrage be restricted to those who owned property.[16] The commission's report was reprinted in an 1899 issue of *Municipal Affairs,* the National Municipal League's magazine, and was read with approval by those reformers who shared the view that an ignorant electorate accounted for the city's problems. The rationale for disenfranchising the immigrants was stated by the first president of Cornell University, Andrew D. White, who wrote in an 1890 issue of *Forum* that:

> A city is a corporation; . . . as a city it has nothing whatever to do with general political interests. . . . The questions in a city are not political questions. . . . The work of a city being the creation and control of the city property, it should logically be managed as a piece of property by those who have created it, who have a title to it, or a real substantial part in it, . . . [and not by] a crowd of illiterate peasants, freshly raked in from the Irish bogs, or Bohemian mines, or Italian robber nests.[17]

Although taking the vote away from immigrants appealed to some reformers, it was hardly feasible to attempt such a drastic remedy. To wage an all-out campaign on this issue would surely have invited a negative reaction even from groups that supported reform causes. From the constitutional period until the Jacksonian voting reforms of the 1820s and 1830s, most states had restricted the vote to owners of property. The abolishion of these restrictions had been hailed as a triumph for popular democracy. It seemed unlikely that property qualifications could ever again be attached to the vote. The 1912 charter of Phoenix, Arizona, restricted voting in municipal elections to taxpayers, but the state courts invalidated this restriction as unconstitutional.[18] Even before Phoenix's attempt, it was clear that the reformers would have to find less direct methods to reduce the influence of immigrant voters.

Most reformers did not oppose voting participation by immigrants per se. They were convinced that the real problem with elections was that they were run in a corrupt fashion by machine politicians who victimized their immigrant constituents. On this score, they were not entirely wrong: Without doubt, municipal elections were chaotic and corrupt, conducted in the absence of well-established rules and regulations. Because the political parties were considered private organizations, their nominating procedures were not regulated at all. To select candidates for public office, political parties held city conventions or ward caucuses according to their own changeable rules, often on short notice and at locations known only to insiders. It was not unusual for caucuses to be held in the back rooms of saloons owned by ward bosses. According to one scholar,

> This was the period of massive voting frauds. In the elections of 1868 and 1872, 8 percent more people voted in New York state than were registered. In 1910, when the New York City vote was challenged and recounted, half of the votes were found to be fraudulent. In New Jersey, the stuffing of ballot boxes was so common that the state legislature replaced the wooden boxes with glass ballot jars. In Pennsylvania and Michigan, gangs of thugs moved from polling place to polling place beating up the opposition and voting at will. Fictitious and repeat voters, false counting, and stuffed ballot boxes were such regular features of city elections that voting statistics from this period are suspect.[19]

A Philadelphia politician once boasted that the signers of the Declaration of Independence were machine loyalists: "'These men,' he said, 'the fathers of American liberty, voted down here once.' 'And,' he added with a sly grin, 'they vote here yet.'"[20]

Politicians sometimes completed the ballot for voters or accompanied them into the voting booth. "Farmer Jones," a member of the Chicago machine in the 1890s, revealed to an inquiring reformer how he guaranteed voter loyalty:

> [The reformer asked,] "When you got the polling stations in your hands, what did you do?"
> "Voted our men, of course."
> "And the negroes, how did they vote?"
> "They voted as they ought to have voted. They had to."
> " . . . how could you compel those people to vote against their will?"
> "They understood, and besides," said he, "there was not a man voted in that booth that I did not know how he voted before he put the paper in the judges' hands."[21]

Buying the vote was the most direct and effective means of guaranteeing election-day results. The 1896 election in the First Ward of Chicago was conducted thus:

> The bars were open all night and the brothels were jammed. By ten o'clock the next morning, though, the saloons were shut down, not in concession to the reformers, but because many of the bartenders and owners were needed to staff the First Ward field organization. The Bath, Hinky Dink and their aides ran busily from polling place to polling place, silver bulging in their pockets into which they dug frequently and deeply. The effort was not in vain, and the outcome was gratifying.[22]

Not content with mere fraud, machine politicians sometimes resorted to intimidation and violence. The Chicago ward boss John Powers threatened voters and told business owners that they would lose their business licenses unless they supported him in his 1898 campaign for alderman.[23] "Hinky Dink" Kenna and "Bathhouse John" Coughlin of Chicago's First Ward defended their loyal constituents but routinely harassed opponents. During the 1920s, organized crime and machine politics in Chicago became closely connected. Gangland hits were visited on meddling politicians who stood outside the inner circle of men controlling and protecting illegal liquor, speakeasies, prostitution, and gambling.

Ed Crump, the boss of Memphis, Tennessee, won his first mayoral election in 1909 by watching the polls himself. He personally stopped the use of marked ballots by a machine organization he was opposing, in one case by hitting a voter in the face.[24] In Pittsburgh's state and city elections of 1933, the Democrats and Republicans—both rightly fearing fraud by the other party—mobilized opposing armies of poll watchers. The state police were called in to keep the peace, and lawyers and judges stood by to provide quick court action.[25]

In the late 1890s, reformers introduced several measures to reduce election fraud. The key reforms included:

- *Voter registration and literacy requirements.* These requirements reduced repeat voting and stopped the practice of importing voters for an election. By 1920, almost all states had imposed registration laws.
- *Australian ballot.* This was a ballot that could be marked only by the voter and cast in secrecy. Before its introduction in the 1880s, ballots were printed by the parties and often marked and placed in a ballot box in front of observers. They were even handed already marked to voters. Use of the Australian ballot became universal after the turn of the century.

- *Nonpartisan elections.* Reformers fought hard to remove party labels of any kind from many state, and most municipal, election ballots. Where they succeeded, voters had only one clue as to how they should vote: the printed name of the individual candidate.

Though these reforms helped clean up elections, they also had the effect of reducing voting participation by immigrants and less educated voters. Twenty-five percent of the white males of voting age in the United States in 1900 were first-generation immigrants, and two-thirds of them had come from non–English-speaking countries. In the cities, the proportion of foreign-born immigrants was much higher—typically more than two-thirds of the voters in the big cities. Illiterate voters often asked for help in reading and filling out the ballot, or asked for a pre-marked one. When they showed up at the polling place, no one questioned their right to vote. After reforms were adopted, they had to register to vote in writing, often months before an election. And when they went to the polling station, they now faced an election judge, a secret voting booth, and a printed ballot they could not read. Machine politicians were frequently able to get around the problems of the secret ballot by controlling polling places, but these actions exposed them to the possibility of criminal prosecution.

Large numbers of voters were effectively disenfranchised by reforms adopted in the cities that lacked machine organizations, where there were no precinct captains and ward committeemen to help voters register or look over a sample ballot. In the South, there was an explicitly racist motive for adopting the Australian ballot, as made clear by a Democratic campaign song popular in Arkansas in 1892:

> *The Australian Ballot works like a charm,*
> *It makes them think and scratch,*
> *And when a Negro gets a ballot*
> *He has certainly got his match.*

Illiteracy among southern white males varied between 8 percent and 19 percent; for black males it varied between 39 percent and 61 percent. Thus, because a voter had to read it and fill it out without assistance, the Australian ballot drastically reduced voting by both blacks and poor whites. Some states also imposed poll taxes and literacy tests to make sure that blacks could not vote. When such measures did not work well enough in deterring blacks from voting, Ku Klux Klan violence was brought to bear.

By 1905, voter registration laws had been placed on the books in most of the states.[26] Between 1905 and 1920, states and localities set up election boards, made it illegal to vote more than once, and tried to define the legitimate uses of campaign funds. Although enforcement of these laws was uneven, especially in the cities—the machines continued to control prosecutors and the courts in many places—the existence of new laws provided the basis for investigations and prosecutions when the middle- and upper-class public became disturbed about corruption.

Once electoral reform was adopted, the reformers focused their attention on the machine organizations. It was obvious that machine politicians derived their strength from the ethnic neighborhoods and that the machines greatly benefited from the immigrants' ability to identify a party label on the election ballot. By voting a straight party ticket, the voter did not have to read the candidates' names. To make it harder for the voters to support machine candidates in this way, the reformers fought hard for two reforms—nonpartisan ballots and at-large elections.

Municipal reformers agreed that party labels encouraged bloc voting and blind loyalty to a political organization. They wanted a more "rational," educated voter who could "accumulate and carry in his head the brief list of personal preferences and do without the guidance of party names and symbols on the ballot."[27] The reformers asserted that it was the responsibility of citizens to educate themselves and to vote for the best candidates strictly on their merits, not on the basis of party loyalty or ethnic solidarity.

The proposal to remove the party label from election ballots reflected the reformers' conviction that an overall public interest overrode the preferences of particular ethnic groups. Reformers generally agreed on the principle that public services should be provided as cheaply and efficiently as possible, and that this required cities to be run by educated professionals. Just as business firms produce a product as cheaply and efficiently as possible, cities should—and could—do the same. Party symbols created the impression of political differences when, according to the reformers, everyone had the same fundamental interest. Voters were supposed to ask only one question: Which candidate is most qualified to help the city provide services at lowest cost? Brand Whitlock, the famous reform mayor of Toledo, Ohio, observed:

> It seems almost incredible now that men's minds were ever so clouded, strange that they did not earlier discover how absurd was a system which, in order to enable them the more readily to subjugate themselves, actually printed little woodcuts of birds—roosters and eagles—at the heads of the tickets, so that they might the more easily and readily recognize their masters and deliver their suffrages over to them.[28]

Just as the reformers intended, the nonpartisan ballot made it harder for immigrants to vote as a bloc. Reading their alderman's printed name could be hard for illiterate voters. Recognizing the party symbol on the ballot was infinitely easier than reading the names of candidates.

Nonpartisan elections favored educated voters and were biased against working-class candidates as well. The party organization supplied campaign money and workers and freed working-class candidates from the necessity of holding a normal job, which would have denied them time to participate in politics. Few politicians in the cities could have started or stayed in politics without a party organization's help. Party organizations pooled resources and built cooperative relationships among politicians; without them, people of wealth and social standing tended to hold an overwhelming advantage. This result was, in fact, the objective of the nonpartisanship crusade—to make politics once again a calling appropriate to the educated and cultured classes.[29]

The proposal to replace wards with at-large elections was designed to break the link between neighborhoods and machine politicians. Andrew White complained that "wards largely controlled by thieves and robbers can send thieves and robbers" into public office, and "the vote of a single tenement house, managed by a professional politician, will neutralize the vote of an entire street of well-to-do citizens."[30] The remedy was to require every candidate for the city council or board of aldermen to seek the votes of all city residents. By constituting the entire city as the one and only election district, no particular neighborhood or ethnic group could elect a candidate. Gone would be the politics of trade-offs, logrolling, and compromise among legislators representing their own neighborhoods, ethnic groups, and wards. "Special interest" politics would supposedly give way to "public interest" politics. To the reformers, honest politics was virtually impossible as long as elections were decided by wards:

> For decades the election of councils by wards had superimposed a network of search for parochial favors, of units devoted to partisan spoils, and of catering to ethnic groups that time and again had either defeated comprehensive city programs or loaded them with irrelevant spoils and ill-conceived ward projects. The ward and precinct were the heart of machine control, and the councils so elected were usually also infested with corruption, however acceptable the councilors may have been to the voters of their wards.[31]

Small wards potentially gave even relatively small ethnic and racial groups leverage at the ballot box. Lithuanian voters, for example, might be able to send a Lithuanian alderman to the city council, even if they constituted a tiny proportion of a city's total population. Small wards multiplied the points of access through which groups and individuals could influence public officials. Citywide, at-large elections exerted an opposite effect. If the city is one big electoral district, candidates representing ethnic and racial groups clustered in specific neighborhoods are handicapped; in order to be elected, they are forced to appeal to a variety of groups distributed over many neighborhoods. Because campaigns covering a city are costly and time-consuming, wealthier candidates have a built-in advantage. In such a system, personal wealth and social status become the ingredients of political success. These effects were well known to reformers, which explains why the National Municipal League's model city charter of 1899 recommended at-large elections and nonpartisan ballots. Every subsequent model charter of the League contained these two features, and over the years the League compiled annual statistics to track the adoption of these reforms across the nation.

Civil-service hiring systems constituted the last big plank in the reform platform. Reformers considered civil service crucial because it was aimed at the machines' practice of rewarding loyal supporters with patronage jobs. Under civil-service reform, written and oral civil-service examinations were to become the sole basis for hiring municipal employees, and a system of tenure and seniority was supposed to make employees safe from political firings. Without patronage, the machine would quickly wither away.

Within the first two decades of the twentieth century, nonpartisan, at-large elections and civil service reforms were implemented in cities from coast to coast. Reformers were least successful in the big industrial cities with large numbers of immigrant voters. In smaller cities, however, and in the newer cities in the West and Southwest, working-class voters tended to be outnumbered, discouraged from voting, or divided along ethnic lines. As a consequence, when reform proposals were put before the voters, they usually passed. Though there was widespread recognition that some reforms effectively disenfranchised the immigrant and working-class electorate, the aggressive campaigns sponsored by the National Municipal League persuaded local voters to pass reform measures. When local electorates balked, the reformers were able to bypass them altogether in some states by persuading state legislatures to abolish ward elections and require non-partisan elections, civil service, and other reforms for all cities in the state.

Campaigns to adopt nonpartisan, at-large elections and civil service were energized by a melodramatic rhetoric that recounted lurid episodes of corruption. Such stories could just as well be, and often were, imported from cities hundreds of miles away. In this fashion, reformers were able to persuade voters to adopt reform in cities where machines had never existed. Reformers constantly made machines into a bogeyman that was hiding just around the corner, ready to pounce at the first opportunity.[32] In smaller towns and cities, where machines did not exist, reform was sold as a way to streamline government and make it efficient. The residents of smaller cities viewed government as, at best, a necessary evil that should provide such essential public services as water, sewage disposal, streets, and perhaps libraries and community centers. "Consensus" politics—which tended to ignore the ethnic and racial minorities that might be present—characterized politics in small towns then as it often does now.

The electoral rules preferred by the municipal reformers are much in evidence in contemporary cities. Before 1910, nonpartisan elections were almost unknown. By 1929, they were utilized in 57 percent of the cities with populations of more than 30,000.[33] By the 1960s, many states required their cities to use nonpartisan elections; these included Minnesota, California, Alaska, and most of the western states. In ten more states, nonpartisan ballots were used in 90 percent or more of the cities (the exceptions usually being cities above a specified size). In the West, 94 percent of cities used nonpartisan elections. The eastern seaboard was the only region of the country where more cities used partisan than nonpartisan elections. Among the nation's cities with over 500,000 people today, 85 percent use partisan elections. Reforms generally go together; most cities with nonpartisan elections use at-large rather than district or ward elections.

Reformed electoral systems were originally designed to reduce influence by working-class ethnic voters, and there is plenty of evidence that reform accomplished its purpose. Before the adoption of nonpartisan and at-large elections, working-class candidates, some of them socialists, were elected to city offices in dozens of cities.[34] At-large elections made it much more difficult for these kinds of candidates to win. In the 1909 elections in Dayton, Ohio, socialists elected two aldermen and three assessors from wards. Because they only received 25 percent of the citywide vote, without the ward system these candidates could not have won. Before the 1913 election, Dayton implemented citywide elections and abolished ward boundaries. In 1913, the socialists received 35 percent of the popular vote and, in 1917, 44 percent, but because all candidates were elected at-large, in neither year were the socialists able to elect a single candidate. Similarly, in 1911, Pittsburgh adopted at-large elections, with the result that upper-class business leaders and professionals pushed lower- and middle-class groups out of their previous places on the city council and the school board.[35]

St. Louis provides an excellent example of these two electoral systems at work. The members of the city's Board of Aldermen are elected to office through partisan elections in each of the city's twenty-eight wards (see Figure 4.1). In a city that was 41 percent African American in 1970, race had become a contested terrain. Because of St. Louis's ward system, ten blacks were elected to the city's

Figure 4.1   **Racial Composition of Municipal Wards in the City of St. Louis, 1977**

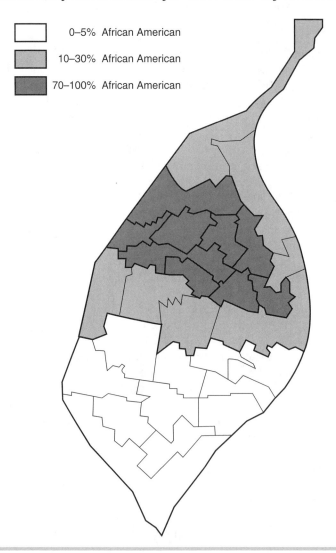

0–5% African American

10–30% African American

70–100% African American

Board of Aldermen in the 1977 municipal elections (and eleven by 2000). All of them represented predominantly African American wards located in the northern half of the city. On the other hand, all of the eighteen majority-white wards elected white aldermen. (As in many cities, *alderman* is an official term in the St. Louis city charter and does not refer exclusively to males.)

Because all school board candidates must run at-large, the composition of the school board was entirely different. In the 1977 election, in a city where 70 percent of the public school enrollment was African American, not a single black candidate was elected to the school board. All five of the seats on the ballot went to white, middle-class candidates because the three African American candidates were rejected by white voters.

The St. Louis case illustrates the effects of at-large elections on racial and ethnic minorities. In the late 1970s, the highly concentrated African American minority was excluded from effective participation in the governing of the local schools, even though more than two-thirds of the students in the city school system were African American. The ward representation used to elect aldermen, in contrast, ensured that blacks would be represented in city hall.

The combination of nonpartisan and at-large elections was adopted in virtually all cities throughout the Southwest. Partially as a result, a style of politics evolved that was tilted heavily in favor of business elites. Most cities provide a minimal level of services to citizens, but they are extremely active in promoting economic development. "Frugality, efficiency, and professionalism in public administration" have always been the themes guiding government in southwestern cities, but frugality has rarely been applied to what business has wanted government to do.[36] For decades, legions of bureaucrats and professionals have found employment in special districts and authorities devoted to developing land, providing water, dredging harbors, supplying electricity, and lobbying the federal government so that business could grow.[37] Until the 1960s, candidates for public office tended to be selected by business groups. In effect, these groups constituted a kind of political machine that controlled local politics. Turnout for elections tended to be low—much lower, in fact, than for elections in the industrial cities of the North.[38] This state of affairs began to change in the 1960s, only when civil rights and neighborhood groups mobilized in several Sunbelt cities to challenge the business-dominated regimes.

"EFFICIENCY AND ECONOMY" IN MUNICIPAL AFFAIRS

In the early years of the municipal reform movement, "efficiency and economy" became the code words for good government. When Theodore Roosevelt addressed the delegates to the First Annual Conference for Good City Government in 1894, he urged them to go beyond their moral outrage at the way things were being run to find ways of streamlining and improving government: "There are two gospels I always want to preach to reformers. . . . The first is the gospel of morality; the next is the gospel of efficiency. . . . I don't think I have to tell you to be upright, but I do think I have to tell you to be practical and efficient."[39] Actually, it is doubtful that the reformers needed such advice. Municipal reformers were hard at work searching for guidelines that would show them how to govern cities. If they succeeded at "kicking the rascals out," they needed to know what to do with their inheritance.

The extreme disorganization of city governments gave the reformers a big target to aim at. All through the nineteenth century, cities had tended to add new responsibilities and services piecemeal, one at a time. By the late century, every city had a multitude of independent boards and commissions administering water, police, health, and other services. No organization charts existed, so it would have been impossible to make sense of how an individual city ran. This state of affairs was a perfect recipe for corruption. Typically, a city was governed by a board of aldermen or a city council, with each alderman representing a separate ward. A politics of trade-offs, logrolling, and partisan wrangling could, and often did, result in a free-for-all, with each alderman looking for a way to trade his vote for some personal favor. Individual aldermen often sold their votes to paving contractors, restaurant or brothel owners, or utility companies in exchange for contracts, licenses, and franchises. Aldermen also got in the habit of filling the multitude of independent committees, boards, and commissions with their political cronies, who also took bribes when the opportunity arose.

The widespread graft and corruption incensed civic and business elites and middle- and upper-class voters, but what was to be done? One remedy was to approach state legislators with requests for special legislation designed to enhance the power of mayors and curtail the powers of aldermanic councils. In contrast to the aldermen, mayors tended to come from prominent, even upper-class, backgrounds. Rather than running for election in only one ward, they were required to win citywide elections, and thus they were forced to appeal to a broad cross section of the urban electorate. Campaigns covering an entire city were expensive, and in the late nineteenth century candidates for mayor paid most of their own campaign costs.[40] What was an advantage, even a requirement, for an alderman—to come from the neighborhood, meet people in saloons and beer halls, speak the language of immigrants, accentuate ethnic identity, be one of the people—became a liability for someone running for citywide office.

State legislatures intervened to take budgetary and supervisory authority from elected councils and to give these powers to mayors or to full-time boards and commissions that were independent of aldermen. In 1891, the Indiana legislature gave the Indianapolis comptroller the authority to draft the budget; the council could lower but could not increase appropriations. New charters gave the mayors of Cleveland and Indianapolis the authority to remove executive officials, a feature that was also adopted in new charters approved in other states: New Orleans in 1896 and Baltimore in 1898.[41] In 1892, New York's legislature mandated a Board of Estimate and Apportionment, modeled on New York City's, for all cities over 50,000 in population. In the 1870s and 1880s, state legislative committees assumed financial or administrative control of the police departments of Detroit, Baltimore, Boston, St. Louis, Kansas City, and New York. In other states, commissions or boards were created to take over functions such as public parks, education, libraries, health, and public works.

Reformers became accustomed to trying to persuade legislatures to pass special legislation favoring their cause. Legislatures became, in effect, referees among the contending interests that were trying to control city politics. Even if they had wanted to, state legislatures could not have stayed aloof from the political battles occurring in the cities. Local governments provided key public services, and representatives to state legislatures answered to local constituents; therefore, local and state affairs were closely entwined: "The ordinary work of state politics was local affairs, and an ordinary branch of local government was the state legislature."[42] Most legislators were not inclined to interfere actively in issues arising from local governments outside their legislative districts. In a sample drawn from a large number of states, two scholars have shown that "Virtually all bills affecting big cities were introduced by representatives from those cities."[43] Non-local representatives "routinely deferred to local governments."[44] Therefore, the important question became: Who spoke for local governments?

Ordinarily, the big-city representatives to the state legislature came from the upper strata of society. Whereas aldermen and city council members came from and represented neighborhoods, the members of boards and commissions often were "bastions of the city's elite."[45] They were businessmen, bankers, lawyers, and other men of professional and social standing. The men of wealth and social prestige, who had deserted electoral politics in the industrial city, now found a new niche. They refused to run for office against the new breed of immigrant saloonkeepers and party loyalists. Instead, they were appointed by governors, legislative committees, and mayors to sit on boards and commissions. These boards were "protected from popular control, insulated from the undue influence of the city's aldermen, and dominated by those perched proudly on the top rung of the urban social ladder."[46]

But this method of reform was flawed. Even if the reformers managed to persuade state legislatures to reform city government by special legislation, this piecemeal approach caused as many problems as it solved. If anything, city government was becoming even more disorganized. The various boards and commissions often went their separate ways, and political appointment by a mayor, governor, or even legislative committee was not a guarantee of good government. What the reformers needed was a consistent, comprehensive approach.

By the late 1890s, the municipal reformers managed to develop a theory of governance. The reformers held that there was a public interest that could be defined objectively and that, if implemented, would benefit all citizens equally. As they defined it, the public interest could be satisfied by observing four sacred principles: (1) there must be strict budgetary controls to ensure that taxes would be kept as low as possible and public services delivered at the lowest possible cost; (2) the day-to-day administration of city government should be strictly separated from "politics"; (3) experts with training, experience, and ability should run city services; and (4) government should be run like a business and the principles of scientific management, then being applied in business organizations, should also be applied to government.

The reformers derived their ideas about how to run government from the scientific management movement that swept the country in the first two decades of the twentieth century. As businesses became larger, accountants, engineers, and corporate managers were busily inventing the structure of the modern corporation. What emerged from this search for efficiency was a quasi-military model of hierarchical administrative control.

In 1911, Frederick Winslow Taylor became world famous with the publication of his book, *The Principles of Scientific Management*.[47] Basically, Taylor wanted to apply military discipline and hierarchy to the factory. He said that the movements of individual workers could be studied in order to discover how to organize work tasks to achieve the maximum output with a minimum expenditure of each worker's energy. Taylor promised that his efficiency principles would bring progress, prosperity, and happiness to society by increasing material wealth to all. By applying the new science of management, Taylor said, it would be possible to achieve harmony and cooperation between owners and workers because both had the same interest in maximizing output. There was even a spiritual side; principles of efficiency would allow each man to develop "his greatest efficiency and prosperity."[48] The essence of the Taylor catechism was that "In the past, the man has been first; in the future the system must be first."[49]

Taylor and his disciples spread an urgent message: "Soldiering" (slow work) and inefficiency should be stamped out both at work and at home. Popular magazines featured articles on efficient housework—describing, for instance, how a housewife could sequence her daily chores and arrange appliances and furniture so as to minimize wasted movement while doing household work. The efficiency movement quickly achieved the status of a secular religion; its gospel of progress through efficiency swept the country.

To its advocates, scientific management seemed to be a bloodless revolution, a perfect solution to hostile employer-worker relations, disastrous economic panics, and poverty and want. Efficiency societies sprang up in cities all over the country, and efficiency experts were in demand as speakers.[50] Taylor's disciples invaded the factories to implement the gospel of efficiency. They also applied the principles of scientific management to the governmental realm. Efficiency and scientific management—"business methods"—soon became the model for municipal reform. The appropriateness of efficiency principles to government seemed obvious to the reformers: "The rising prestige of technicians in industry and the increasing demand for new public works and municipal services strengthened the desire for more technical efficiency in local government."[51]

In 1912, Henry Brueré, the first director of the privately funded New York Bureau of Municipal Research, published a book applying efficiency principles to municipal management.[52] Brueré took the position that much of the mismanagement in New York City "formerly attributed to official corruption and to popular indifference was really due to official and popular ignorance of . . . orderly and scientific procedures."[53] What these procedures amounted to were elaborate accounting and reporting devices designed to codify the responsibilities of city officials, the actions taken by them to carry out their duties, the costs of equipment and personnel, and other details. Brueré invented a scoring system whereby the efficiency of cities could allegedly be rated and compared. Cities were to be rated on the basis of such items as: "Is a record kept of all city property?" "How often are the treasurer's books audited?" "Twenty questions on the protection of milk supply." "Is the location of houses of prostitution known and recorded?"[54] In all, Brueré and his aides used a list of 1,300 standardized questions to rate cities from the "worst governed" to the "best."

In 1913, Brueré was given the opportunity to make New York City efficient. In November of that year, John Purroy Mitchell, one of Brueré's closest confidants, was elected New York's mayor. Mitchell appointed Brueré to the office of city chamberlain (the mayor's policy adviser). Brueré immediately launched an attack on Tammany Hall's patronage system. He managed to push through the first large civil-service system in the nation. It was explicitly designed as a Taylorite approach to municipal reform.

Brueré assigned the task of designing the details of the civil-service system to Robert Moses, a young staff member at the New York Bureau of Municipal Research. Moses carried out his assignment with the enthusiasm of a Taylorite zealot. He proposed a system in which all municipal employees would be closely and constantly observed at work by trained efficiency experts who would rate each worker's efficiency according to an elaborate mathematical formula. Various functions and responsibilities of each employee were codified and "given a precise mathematical grade. These grades would . . . be used as a basis for salary increase and promotion."[55] To implement his system, Moses instructed his assistants to draw up rating forms, which he then distributed to supervisors. The idea was that each day, the supervisors would hand a score-card to each employee with the employee's mathematical rating. City workers would be paid, promoted, or fired on the basis of the ratings.

Such a system, if implemented, would have fallen of its own weight. There was no way to ensure objective ratings. The amount of time required to rate employees would have resulted in a truly enormous civil-service administrative staff. Instead of spending the prodigious amounts of money required to hire hundreds of specially trained supervisors, Moses tried to rely on existing city employees. The 50,000 city employees steadfastly refused to use the reporting forms, objecting that the system was hopelessly time-consuming and unwieldy, and arbitrary and capricious to boot.

The civil-service reform attempted during Mitchell's mayoral tenure illuminates the values, assumptions, and foibles of the municipal reformers. As Taylor had put it, "The natural laziness in men is serious, but by far the greatest evil from which both workmen and employers are suffering is the systematic soldiering which is almost universal."[56] Reformers were taking on the formidable task of remaking human beings. Such an ambition could only be based on a distrust of people as they were. The human element was lacking. Mayor Mitchell, while trying to reorganize city departments and implement civil-service procedures, tried to reduce all "unnecessary" programs and expenditures. He instituted cutbacks in school expenditures, asked teachers to work without salaries in the summers, tried to close down special schools for the retarded, and reduced park and recreational expenditures.[57]

New York's civil-service proposals proved too draconian even for most reformers. Suitably modified, however, the reform agenda made sense. There was little doubt that more careful administration and well-trained city workers could save money and result in better service besides. Cities across the country adopted civil-service systems but omitted New York City's elaborate reporting system. Not only the cities but the federal government and the states entered the field. President Taft appointed a Commission on Economy and Efficiency, and President Wilson later created the Bureau of Efficiency. Between 1911 and 1917, sixteen states established efficiency commissions. These commissions generally recommended streamlining budgeting procedures, centralizing more power in the governor, consolidating state agencies, and establishing civil service.[58]

THE BUSINESS MODEL

With efficiency and scientific management supplying the rationale, it was pre-dictable that the organization of municipal government would be compared with the structure of private business. Reformers pointed out that municipal govern-ments, unlike business firms, were not organized to maximize efficiency. A his-tory of reform sympathetic with this view described the problem in these terms: "The reformers, who tried to get good men into office, found . . . that, even if they elected a mayor or council, they were intolerably handicapped by the existing systems of municipal government. [Due to] the principles of separation of pow-ers and of checks and balances . . . there was no single elective official or govern-ing body that could be held responsible for effecting reform."[59] Reformers claimed that the "weak mayor" form of government, which existed in most cities, left too much authority in the hands of a multitude of politicians—aldermen or council members well as specialized boards and commissions. No one person could be held accountable for overall governmental policy. The reformers used organizational charts like the one shown in Figure 4.2 to demonstrate this fact.

Figure 4.2   **Weak Mayor Government**

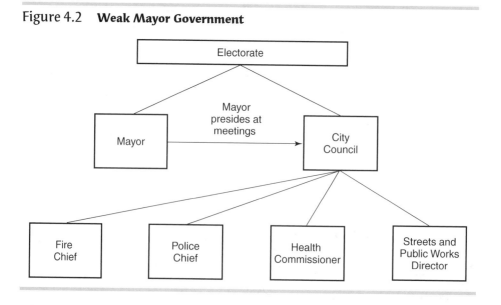

It was supposed that businesses, in contrast, operated efficiently because there was clear separation between policy making, which was located in a board of directors, and day-to-day administration, which was left in the hands of professional executive officers. Applied to cities, this model would still leave policy making to elected officials, who represented their constituents, just as a board of directors in a business presumably represents the interests of the stockholders. The policies, however, would be implemented by administrators, the equivalent of the professional executive officers, applying "scientific" principles of cost accounting and personnel management.

The business model required a strong executive with sufficient authority to run the company. Applying this principle to city government, reformers sought charter reforms to reduce the number of elected officials and to expand the mayor's power to appoint most city officials and to veto legislation passed by the council. The mayor would preside at the top of a hierarchical chain of command with clear lines of authority and accountability. As recommended by the National Municipal League in 1899, the "weak mayor" was to be replaced by a "strong mayor" form of government, as represented in Figure 4.3. The league's model city charter also recommended a small city council of five to nine members elected at large, together with a strong mayor with broad appointive and veto powers. In the first decade of the twentieth century, municipal research bureaus began to design organization charts in order to promote governmental reorganization along these lines.

Now that the reformers felt confident they knew what to do if they gained control of cities, they attempted to persuade state legislatures to grant them broad "home rule" charters. In contrast to the latter decades of the nineteenth century, when municipal reformers often went to state legislatures to request

Figure 4.3   **Strong Mayor Government**

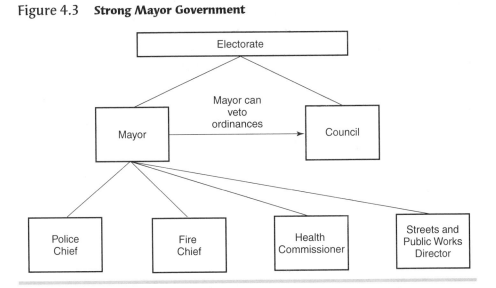

special legislation to bypass elected officials, they now wanted cities to possess full authority to set their own tax rates and decide how and where to provide services. They argued that trained administrators should replace elected and appointed boards and commissions. At its state constitutional convention in 1875, Missouri became the first state to write a general home rule charter for its cities, though the legislature retained control of St. Louis's police budget. Ultimate legal power was still held by the state, but Missouri's cities would not have to seek approval for their every action, as long as they stayed within their broad charter powers. Cities could hire new sanitation workers and firefighters, for example, or build a new street without consulting the legislature. The general charter spelled out the range of services to be provided, not such details as salary levels, the location of fire-houses and streets, and the number of city employees. The home rule movement, pushed hard by the National Municipal League and other organizations, spread to other states. By 1925, fourteen states had granted home rule charters to their cities, and today virtually all cities are governed by such charters.

COMMISSION AND MANAGER GOVERNMENT

Galveston, Texas, set up the first municipal government derived explicitly from the business model. In 1894, Galveston's business and professional leaders organized a campaign to elect business leaders to the city government. The following year, a coalition of city council members and business leaders secured a charter amendment from the Texas legislature that replaced ward with at-large elections, but the reform did not result in the sweeping changes its sponsors had hoped for. Over the next few years, some business leaders were elected to the city council, but they continued to be outvoted by a nonbusiness faction.[60]

An emergency provided the pretext for business and corporate leaders to decisively assert themselves. On September 8, 1900, hurricane-driven waves breached the seawall protecting Galveston, and the inrushing sea washed over the town, killing 6,000 of the town's 37,000 residents. Half of the property in the city was destroyed. To rebuild the city, prominent business leaders organized the Deepwater Committee and set out to gain control of local government. If "a municipality is largely a business corporation,"[61] as reformers maintained, it follows that it should be run as such, with the voters being viewed as stockholders and a board of directors responsible to the stockholders. On this principle, the Deepwater Committee drafted an outline of a commission form of government and asked the state legislature to approve it. It was promptly enacted.

The Galveston Plan created a five-member commission that exercised the legislative powers previously assigned to the city council as well as the administrative authority normally assigned to professional supervisors. Each of the commissioners headed a separate department of government. Such a concentration of authority seemed appropriate in an emergency. Initially, the commission was even given jurisdiction over criminal and civil law enforcement in the city, though this power was subsequently struck down by a state court. Even without this power, however, the commission exercised sweeping authority. Behind the leadership of five aggressive businessmen, Galveston initiated a vigorous rebuilding program and, in the process, reduced its debts and restored and, improved public services.

The success of Galveston's commission form of government captured national attention. Commission government spread like wildfire. Its appeal was obvious: It seemed to streamline government; it held the potential for attracting business and civic leaders back into active government service; and it was a straightforward plan around which reformers could rally in challenging machine politics and the urban party bosses. Galveston's performance so impressed business leaders in other Texas cities that they pressed the Texas legislature to allow them to install commission government. By 1907, seven major cities in the state had imitated Galveston's charter, including Houston, Dallas, and Fort Worth.

In 1908, voters in Des Moines, Iowa, approved a charter that became a model for reformers around the country. Besides a five-member commission, Des Moines adopted the initiative, referendum, and recall; nonpartisan and at-large elections; and a civil service system. This package of items, labeled the Des Moines Plan by reformers, caught on rapidly. Commission government was adopted by 23 cities in 1909 and by 66 cities in 1910.[62] By September 1915, at least 465 cities were governed by a commission, and by 1920, about 20 percent of all cities with populations of more than 5,000 had adopted it.[63] During these years, a few states made commission government compulsory for their cities, and in most states it became an option for cities that wanted to adopt it.

Reformers promoted the Des Moines Plan as a cure-all, sure to bring less taxation, more efficient public services, and a "better class of men" to government. In city after city, it was promoted as a means of making government more businesslike. Accordingly, chambers of commerce and other organized business groups became the strongest backers. The Commercial Club succeeded in pushing through Des Moines's new charter in 1907, though, interestingly, the first commissioners voted into office represented a working-class slate—much to the dismay of the business group.[64] In Pennsylvania, the Pittsburgh Chamber of Commerce organized a statewide convention of business organizations with the purpose of persuading the state legislature to require cities above a minimum size to adopt commission government. The coalition of bankers, merchants, and manufacturers secured the legislation in 1913.[65] The pattern was similar elsewhere: Business leaders were trying to transform government into a businesslike operation.

Commission government was not, however, without its problems. To its critics, its worst feature was that it did not fit the business model faithfully enough. A commission was not truly like a board of directors because commissioners engaged in both policy making and administration. Because each of the commissioners headed a separate department, leadership was fragmented, with the commissioners often refusing to cooperate with one another. Sometimes they built personal empires by adroitly handing out jobs and contracts. It was hard for the mayor to prevent such practices because all the commissioners were "first among equals." This feature was the chief complaint of the secretary of the National Short Ballot Association, Richard S. Childs. Noting that commission government was "an accident, not a plan" (referring to the Galveston emergency that brought it into being), he addressed the problem of having five coequal executives: "The theory that the commission as a whole controlled its members in their departmental activities became neglected—the commission could not discipline a recalcitrant member."[66] Commonly, Childs asserted, commissioners would ignore one another's performance ("You attend to your department and quit criticizing mine") or exchange favors and support ("I'll vote for your appropriation if you'll vote for mine").[67] It sometimes seemed like a replay of machine politics.

Municipal reformers responded to these complaints with a new idea. This time, they wanted to place all administrative authority in the hands of a single appointed, trained administrator—a city manager. According to this plan, the mayor and the city council would be responsible for making policy, but a professional city manager specifically trained for the job would be responsible for coordinating all administrative functions. "The reform leaders realized that technical ability could not be expected of elected officials, and they hoped that a strong mayor could appoint trained technicians and administrators as department heads."[68] The city manager was to supervise day-to-day administration, thus bringing to local government administrative unity, expertise, clear accountability, and formal training in management.[69]

This time, the reformers intended to get the business model right. In 1913 the National Municipal League issued a report (written by Childs) recommending that commission government be abandoned in favor of the city manager plan. Only six years later, in 1919, the League amended its model charter to recommend city manager government. Because of its persuasive logic and "pure" business analogy, the city manager structure quickly replaced commission government. By the 1920s, the commission form was regarded as a failed experiment.

Between 1908 and 1912, several midwestern cities hired city managers. The idea caught on in earnest when Dayton, Ohio, changed its city charter, though the ward system remained. As in Galveston, an emergency served as the catalyst for a new government form. In 1913, John H. Patterson, president of the National Cash Register Company, persuaded the Dayton Chamber of Commerce to draft a new city charter. The chamber established the Bureau of Municipal Research to promote the idea, and the Committee of One Hundred, a group funded by the business community, sponsored a slate of candidates for city office who were pledged to changing the city charter. By organizing a well-run campaign ward by ward, the business slate put several Republican candidates on the city council, but they still were outnumbered by Democratic machine politicians. Charter reform seemed to be stymied. Two months later, however, the Miami River flooded the town, and the municipal government was slow in organizing emergency services. Patterson turned his factory into a shelter for flood victims. Overnight, he became the town's leading citizen. When requested by local business leaders, the state governor appointed Patterson to head a new charter reform commission. The commission successfully persuaded the voters to adopt its recommended charter.[70]

The results were spectacular. The new government improved public services, retired most of the city debt, instituted new budget-making procedures, enforced a uniform eight-hour day for city employees, and established civil service. The

Dayton Plan soon became the nation's most popular "good reform" reform model. Though rarely instituted in the big industrial cities, it became common in smaller cities around the country. In the five years before 1918, 87 cities adopted manager charters, and 153 did so between 1918 and 1923. During the next five years, 84 more cities were added to the list.[71]

The commission and then the manager plans became popular because they seemed able to fulfill the reformers' desire to find an objective, nonpolitical, efficient way to run government. Analogies to business organizations almost always supplied the principal supporting arguments for reform. The *Dallas News* promoted the manager plan in 1930 by asking, "Why not run Dallas itself on a business schedule by business methods under businessmen? . . . The city manager plan is after all only a business management plan. The city manager is the executive of a corporation under a board of directors. Dallas is the corporation. It is as simple as that. Vote for it."[72]

Despite such references to the business model, in fact the city manager reform was political. It was intended not merely to achieve efficient government but also to ensure the election of a different class of people who would insulate government from the influence of the Great Unwashed. By putting business leaders in charge of local government, reformers were able to ensure that cities would not try to take on social responsibilities. A delegate to the 1913 meeting of the League of Kansas Municipalities, after listening to his colleagues orate about the necessity of treating the city as a business, protested that "a city is more than a business corporation" and that "good health is more important than a low tax rate."[73] The vast social chasm dividing municipal reformers from the rest of the urban populace, however, made such utterances anathema to most reformers.

Reformers made ambitious claims about the efficiencies to be realized by adopting businesslike models of government. But there is evidence that these claims were overblown. The adoption of city manager government had little, if any, effect on the level of city expenditures.[74] In the end, it was more important to reformers to reduce the political influence of immigrants than to alter the policies that cities implemented.

DID REFORM KILL THE MACHINES?

It has often been assumed that the party machines died out because the reformers were successful in changing the rules of the game under which local politics was conducted. A large number of machines had short lives, only a decade or so, before they went into slow decline or the machine politicians suddenly lost their grip on elective offices. Between 1909 and 1918, machines fell apart in Dayton, Ohio; Detroit and Grand Rapids, Michigan; Los Angeles; Portland, Oregon; Milwaukee; Minneapolis; San Francisco; and Seattle. In each case, a variety of reforms was put through; in each case, civil-service systems changed hiring rules.[75] Most of the machines that survived this era of reform died by the mid-1950s, if not before, including New York's Tammany Hall. By World War II, it would have been impossible to find a city left completely untouched by reform: Voter registration was universal and civil-service hiring was nearly so; at-large, nonpartisan elections were used in most cities. Even in the big industrial cities, where reform was generally less successful, election rules were at least partially reformed. Boston, New Orleans, and Pittsburgh had switched to at-large elections; Memphis and Detroit had adopted both at-large and nonpartisan elections. Denver, New Orleans, Philadelphia, Cleveland, and Pittsburgh also became nonpartisan before World War II.[76]

Nevertheless, these reforms did not lead inexorably to the demise of the machines and, therefore, they did not immediately or invariably restructure politics so that ethnic voters lost influence. "The adoption of structural reform was not sufficient to eliminate or preclude the appearance of machine politics."[77] Machines were often adept at adjusting to the new rules and institutions. In fifteen cities, they actually seem to have been helped by the reformers' centralization of power in the hands of mayors or city managers.[78] The reformers accomplished their goal of making someone accountable to voters, but the voters did not always use their power as the reformers hoped. After the adoption of city manager government in Cleveland in the 1920s, the city's machine was able to appoint a party hack as manager because it still controlled the city council, which was elected by wards.[79] Richard J. Daley built his powerful machine in Chicago, beginning with his election in 1953, despite the fact that the city's elections were nonpartisan and the vast majority of its employees were civil service.

The machines died, in most cases, because they were unable to adapt to the large-scale population and economic transformations that were changing the cities. Two developments were particularly important. First, the immigrant base of the machines began to erode. After the turn of the century, Irish and German immigration dropped sharply; the bulk of new immigrants came from Italy and Eastern Europe. The Irish and, secondarily, the Germans had been the mainstay groups for most machines, and, as their numbers declined, machines found that their support gradually eroded. In Boston, for example, the Irish and Germans accounted for 32 percent of ethnics in 1890 but only 20 percent by 1930; in New York City, their share of the total ethnic population fell even more. In New York City, Fiorello LaGuardia put together a coalition of Italian and Jewish voters to defeat Tammany Hall's candidate in 1933. James Michael Curley, Boston's longtime boss, lasted longer than most other bosses but was finally defeated for reelection in 1949.[80]

The second devastating blow to the machines occurred when their immigrant constituents began to move up the economic ladder. As the immigrants joined the ranks of the middle class, the petty favors and patronage offered by the machines carried less weight, both in material and symbolic terms. After World War II, the immigrants and the children of immigrants joined the mass movement to the suburbs. Precinct captains saw their constituents moving out of the city, and sometimes they moved, too. Machines were not generally successful in reaching out to immigrants or to blacks and poor whites who moved into the cities during and after World War II.[81]

After the war, a new generation of politicians came to power by mobilizing the business community, labor, and the middle class behind programs of urban revitalization. In this cause they were helped by the federal government, which supplied the funds for public housing and slum clearance programs. Richard J. Daley rebuilt the Chicago machine by adding the middle class, business, and African Americans to the machine's base in the old immigrant neighborhoods. Daley aggressively sought federal funds for the city. Few machine leaders in other cities, however, had the vision or the political ability to follow his example.

THE REFORM LEGACY AND THE POLITICS OF REPRESENTATION

Interest in election rules at all levels of government has been rekindled in recent decades because of clear evidence that racial and ethnic minorities were consistently underrepresented in the American political system. For two decades, battles were fought in the federal courts challenging electoral rules on the ground that they violated the Fourteenth Amendment guarantees of equal protection of the laws for all citizens. Groups such as the National Association of Colored People (NAACP) and the United Latin American Citizens challenged the at-large elections systems of local governments and the boundaries of state legislative and congressional districts, claiming that they were drawn to minimize the chances of minority candidates. The courts have sometimes upheld challenges to at-large elections but struck down the drawing of legislative boundaries expressly to increase minority representation (a practice known as *racial gerrymandering*)[82] of legislative districts. The intensity of the battles fought in and out of the courts serves as a reminder that the rules of representation are still as crucial as they were during the reform crusades one hundred years ago.

Research has consistently shown that at-large elections result in the underrepresentation of racial and ethnic minorities.[83] In response to the accumulating evidence and over the strenuous objections of the Reagan Administration, in 1982 Congress amended the 1965 Voting Rights Act to make it easier for minorities to challenge local election practices. Congress passed the amendments, contained in Section 2 of the new act, in reaction to a 1980 U.S. Supreme Court decision that required litigants to demonstrate an *intent* to discriminate before an election rule could be declared invalid.[84] In Section 2, Congress specified that challenges to local election rules could meet a much easier standard than before: They would be considered illegal if they merely had the *effect* of underrepresenting minorities in elected positions.

On June 30, 1986, the Supreme Court handed down a landmark decision, *Thornburg v. Gingles,* interpreting the 1982 amendments.[85] This case came to the Court after the U.S. Justice Department brought suit against the state of North Carolina, arguing that several multimember state legislative districts in North Carolina violated the voting rights of blacks because in those districts white candidates invariably won all seats.[86] The Court ordered North Carolina to create single-member districts and laid down standards for deciding when at-large and multimember district systems would be considered suspect: (1) when litigants could show that it would be possible to create at least one single-member electoral district that would give a minority group an electoral majority; (2) when it could also be demonstrated that the minority group seeking more representation was politically cohesive; and (3) when it could be shown that whites had previously voted as a bloc to prevent minority candidates from being elected.[87]

At-large district systems have since been successfully challenged throughout the United States. In 1986, after finding that at-large elections made it impossible for African American candidates to win, a federal court ordered several Alabama counties to institute single-member districts for electing county commissioners.[88] In a 1987 lawsuit filed against the city of Springfield, Illinois, a federal judge ordered the city to expand the number of electoral districts from five to ten. Because only 10.8 percent of the city's population was African American, the expansion to ten districts was necessary if any one of them was to contain a majority of black voters.[89] (Interestingly, a different federal judge did not require this solution in a similar suit against the Springfield Park District.[90]) In the same year, the city of Danville, Illinois, expanded its city council to fourteen members elected from seven wards after a federal judge threw out its previous system in which a three-member commission and a mayor were all elected at large.[91]

The numerous court decisions arising from the 1982 amendments to the Voting Rights Act produced an extraordinary amount of confusion about local election rules. All through the 1980s and into the 1990s, court decisions called into question the electoral systems of hundreds of cities, counties, townships, and special districts. To preempt court action, some local governments voluntarily redrew district and ward boundaries to facilitate minority representation. Frequently, this required devising districts with tortuously meandering boundaries.[92] The attempt to redraw boundaries, however, is not a solution available to every city and may, in fact, be available only to those whose minority populations live in rather segregated circumstances rather than in several distinct but unconnected neighborhoods, because in segregated cities it is easier to draw boundaries that seem coherent. In a series of decisions beginning in 1993, the U.S. Supreme Court invalidated congressional district boundaries that did not meet standards of "compactness, contiguity, and respect for political subdivisions."[93]

Though the courts seem to be enforcing this standard quite strictly, it does not necessarily signal an end to all redistricting meant to achieve representation by particular racial or ethnic groups.[94] One way to meet the court's standards would be to increase the number of legislative districts to ensure that even somewhat small neighborhoods containing a large proportion of minorities would make up most of a compact legislative district. For several years, it was unclear whether there was some upper limit to the number of districts that a local government might have to draw to achieve the equitable representation of minorities. By 1987, however, it seemed likely (despite the city of Springfield case) that, under normal circumstances, the number of districts already existing would be left alone.[95]

Another question that arose was whether the entire minority population or the voting-age minority population would be counted in the districts drawn to give minorities better representation. Most courts decided that a majority voting-age population was required.[96] Could two or more minority groups be combined to constitute a district if the combined minorities would make up the majority of voters in a district? Only, the courts have said, if it could be shown that the groups were politically cohesive—and research makes it clear, for example, that blacks and Latinos do not generally vote similarly.[97]

Proponents of the principle that electoral districts should be drawn so as to maximize the representation of ethnic and racial minorities also took their fight to the state and federal levels. In 1991, minority representation was at the forefront of the political infighting over congressional reapportionment required as a result of the decennial census of 1990. Because state legislatures approve the boundaries for congressional districts, party control at the state level was crucial. In 1990, there were thirty-seven blacks and Latinos in Congress. As a result of redistricting in 1992, nineteen additional blacks and Latinos were elected to Congress. In many states, it was Republicans, working with the Congressional Black Caucus, who promoted the formation of districts safe for minority candidates. This move increased the number of minorities in Congress, but by locating minorities into fewer districts, it reduced the number of districts favorable for white Democratic candidates.[98]

In June 1991, the Supreme Court ruled that judicial elections in Louisiana and Texas violated the 1982 Voting Rights Act because at-large election districts diluted the electoral strength of minorities. A flurry of lawsuits followed that challenged election procedures for state and local judges. Traditionally, nearly all state and local judges have been elected at large—that is, multiple positions were filled in each electoral district. This perhaps explains why, as of 1985, only 3.8 percent of judges in state courts were African American and only 1.2 percent were Latino.[99]

The court challenges resulted in an ongoing revolution in local electoral practices. In 1981, 66.5 percent of cities used at-large electoral systems. By 1986, in a space of only five years, the proportion had fallen to 60.4 percent.[100] This revolution was energized by research demonstrating that changing from at-large to district elections did, as anticipated, improve the representation of blacks and Latinos.[101] Cities almost everywhere came under pressure to institute a ward system or to redraw existing ward and district boundaries. In 1991, for example, African American leaders in St. Louis threatened to go to court to force a redrawing of the boundaries of the city's twenty-eight wards. At the time, eleven of the twenty-eight aldermen were African American, but a new ward map would have made it mathematically possible to give half of the wards a majority of African American voters.[102]

Court cases in the 1990s made most racial gerrymandering illegal, and erased the nearly automatic presumption against at-large elections. In *Shaw v. Reno* (1993), the U.S. Supreme Court ruled that a very oddly shaped district in North Carolina was gerrymandered, calling such districts "political apartheid."

Speaking for the majority, Sandra Day O'Connor wrote that "when a district obviously is created solely to effectuate the perceived common interests of one racial group, elected officials are more likely to believe that their primary obligation is to represent only the members of that group, rather than the constituency as a whole."[103] The Court left the door open for modest attempts to take race into account in redistricting by declaring that race could not be the "predominant factor" in drawing district boundaries, and in 1996 it declared that each case would be decided on its own merits and that minority districting might be permissible if the boundaries were sufficiently compact and coherent.[104] These rulings had the effect of discouraging the drawing of tortured boundaries but otherwise did not change the status quo greatly.

After the municipal reforms of the Progressive Era, it took more than half a century for questions about representation and local democracy to resurface as a political issue. The years since the Voting Rights Act of 1965 may be properly regarded, therefore, as the first reform period since the Progressive Era aimed specifically at local electoral politics. This latter period of reform focused on undoing some key reforms of that period precisely because they had placed roadblocks in the way of equitable representation. The new era of reform has increased representation for African Americans and for Latinos. It has also resulted in increases in the volume of state aid received by state legislative districts that were reapportioned by court order because they were underrepresented in state legislatures.[105] In politics, the rules of the game matter, which is why they are the object of bitter contention.

NOTES

1. William L. Riordon, *Plunkitt of Tammany Hall* (New York: Dutton, 1963), p. 17.
2. James Bryce, *The American Commonwealth,* 3rd ed., vol. 1 (New York: Macmillan, 1924), p. 642.
3. H. E. Deming, *The Government of American Cities: A Program of Democracy* (London and New York: Putnam, 1909), p. 194
4. Quoted in Michael B. Katz, *School Reform: Past and Present* (Boston: Little, Brown, 1971).
5. Josiah Strong, *Our Country,* ed. Jurgen Herbst (Cambridge, Mass.: Belknap Press, Harvard University Press, 1963; first published in 1886), p. 55.
6. James Weinstein, *The Corporate Ideal in the Liberal State, 1900–1918* (Boston: Beacon Press, 1968).
7. Melvin G. Holli, "Urban Reform in the Progressive Era," in *The Progressive Era,* ed. Louis L. Gould (Syracuse, N.Y.: Syracuse University Press, 1974), p. 137.
8. Frank Mann Stewart, *A Half Century of Municipal Reform: The History of the National Municipal League* (Berkeley: University of California Press, 1950), chap. 1.
9. George Mowry, *The Era of Theodore Roosevelt, 1900–1912* (New York: Harper and Row, 1958), p. 86. Mowry claims the reformers represented the "solid middle class," but his own data belie this classification.
10. Weinstein, *The Corporate Ideal,* pp. 103–105; Harold A. Stone, Don K. Price, Kathryn H. Stone, *City Manager Government in the United States: A Review After Twenty-Five Years* (Chicago: Public Administration Service, 1940), pp. 32–50.
11.   Samuel P. Hays, "The Politics of Reform in Municipal Government in the Progressive Era," in *Social Change and Urban Politics: Readings,* ed. Daniel N. Gordon (Englewood Cliffs, N.J.: Prentice-Hall, 1973), p.111.

12. Ernest S. Griffith, *A History of American City Government, 1900–1920* (New York: Praeger, 1974) p. 167.
13. Weinstein, *The Corporate Ideal*, pp. 106–109.
14. Kenneth Finegold, *Experts and Politicians: Reform Challenges to Machine Politics in New York, Cleveland, and Chicago* (Princeton, N.J.: Princeton University Press, 1995), p. 175.
15. Stone, Price, and Stone, *City Manager Government*, pp. 35–36. Several other case studies in this book reveal a similar bias.
16. Samuel Haber, *Efficiency and Uplift: Scientific Management in the Progressive Era, 1890–1920* (Chicago: University of Chicago Press, 1964), p. 99.
17. Andrew D. White, "City Affairs Are Not Political," originally titled "The Government of American Cities," *Forum*, December 1890, pp. 213–216; reprinted in Dennis Judd and Paul Kantor, eds., *The Politics of Urban America*, 2nd ed. (New York: Addison Wesley Longman, 2002).
18. Amy Bridges, "Winning the West to Municipal Reform," *Urban Affairs Quarterly* 27, no. 4 (June 1992): 511.
19. Arthur T. Hadley, *The Empty Polling Booth* (Englewood Cliffs, N.J.: Prentice-Hall, 1978), p. 61.
20. Alexander B. Callow, Jr., ed., *The City Boss in America* (New York: Oxford University Press, 1976), p. 158.
21. William T. Stead, *If Christ Came to Chicago* (Chicago: Laird and Lee, 1894), pp. 56–57.
22. Lloyd Wendt and Herman Kogan, *Bosses in Lusty Chicago* (Bloomington: Indiana University Press, 1967): p. 169.
23. Allan F. Davis, *Spearheads for Reform* (New York: Oxford University Press, 1967), pp. 156–162.
24. William D. Miller, *Mr. Crump of Memphis* (Baton Rouge: Louisiana State University Press, 1964), p. 74.
25. Bruce M. Stave, *The New Deal and the Last Hurrah: Pittsburgh Machine Politics* (Pittsburgh: University of Pittsburgh Press, 1970), p. 77.
26. Griffith, *A History of American City Government*, p. 71.
27. Richard S. Childs, *Civic Victories: The Story of an Unfinished Revolution* (New York: Harper and Brothers, 1952), p. 299. In this passage, Childs was referring to the short ballot reform in conjunction with nonpartisanship. The short ballot reformers felt there should be fewer elected officials so voters would not be confused and elected officials would be held accountable to voters.
28. Edward C. Banfield, ed., *Urban Government: A Reader in Administration and Politics* (New York: Free Press, 1969), p. 275. Selection from Brand Whitlock, *Forty Years of It*, preface by Allen White (New York and London: Appleton, 1925; first published 1914).
29. Haber, *Efficiency and Uplift*, pp. 99–101.
30. White, "City Affairs Are Not Political," pp. 213–216.
31. Griffith, *A History of American City Government*, p. 130.
32. Amy Bridges, *Morning Glories: Municipal Reform in the Southwest* (Princeton, N.J.: Princeton University Press, 1997), chap. 8.
33. Willis D. Hawley, *Nonpartisan Elections and the Case for Party Politics* (New York: Wiley, 1973), p. 14. Subsequent information on the use of nonpartisan elections is from Hawley, pp. 15–18.
34. Weinstein, *The Corporate Ideal*, p. 109. Subsequent information on the Dayton election is from Weinstein.
35. Hays, "The Politics of Reform," pp. 107–127.
36. Bridges, *Morning Glories*, p. 146.
37. Ibid., chap. 7.
38. Ibid., pp. 144–145.
39. Quoted in Holli, "Urban Reform in the Progressive Era," p. 144.
40. Ibid., p. 47.

41. Ibid., p. 45.
42. Nancy Burns and Gerald Gamm, "Creatures of the State: State Politics and Local Government 1871-1921," *Urban Affairs Review* 33 no. 1, (September 1997): 90.
43. Ibid., p. 86.
44. Scott Allard, Nancy Burns, and Gerald Gamm, "Representing Urban Interests: The Local Politics of State Legislatures," *Studies in American Political Development*, vol. 12, p. 294; see also Nancy Burns, Laura Evans, Gerald Gamm, and Corrine McGonnaughy, "The Local Politics of State Legislatures," paper delivered at the Annual Meetings of the Midwest Political Science Association, April 25, 2002.
45. Allard, Burns, and Gamm, "Representing Urban Interests," p. 68.
46. Ibid., p. 76.
47. Frederick Winslow Taylor, *The Principles of Scientific Management* (New York: Harper and Brothers, 1919; first published 1911).
48. Ibid., p. 140.
49. Ibid., p. 7.
50. Haber, *Efficiency and Uplift*, p. 56.
51. Stone, Price, and Stone, *City Manager Government*, p. 5.
52. Henry Brueré, *The New City Government: A Discussion of Municipal Administration Based on a Survey of Ten Commission-Governed Cities* (Englewood Cliffs, N.J.: Prentice-Hall, 1912).
53. Ibid., p. v.
54. Ibid., pp. 27–29.
55. Robert A. Caro, *The Power Broker: Robert Moses and the Fall of New York* (New York: Oxford University Press, 1969), p. 75.
56. Taylor, *The Principles of Scientific Management*, p. 20.
57. Melvin B. Holli, *Reform in Detroit: Hazen S. Pingree and Urban Politics* (New York: Oxford University Press, 1969), p. 167.
58. Haber, *Efficiency and Uplift*, p. 115.
59. Stone, Price, and Stone, *City Manager Government*, p. 4.
60. Martin J. Schiesl, *The Politics of Municipal Reform: Municipal Administration and Reform in America, 1880–1920* (Berkeley: University of California Press, 1977), pp. 134–135.
61. Quoted in Weinstein, *The Corporate Ideal*, p. 96.
62. Clinton R. Woodruff, ed., *City Government by Commission* (Englewood Cliffs, N.J.: Prentice-Hall, 1911), pp. 293–294.
63. Childs, *Civic Victories*, p. 138.
64. Hays, "The Politics of Reform," p. 116.
65. Weinstein, *The Corporate Ideal*, p. 99.
66. Childs, *Civic Victories*, p. 137.
67. Ibid.
68. Stone, Price, and Stone, *City Manager Government*, p. 5.
69. Griffith, *A History of American City Government*, p. 167.
70. Ibid., p. 166; Schiesl, *The Politics of Municipal Reform*, pp. 175–176.
71. Weinstein, *The Corporate Ideal*, pp. 115–116.
72. Quoted in Stone, Price, and Stone, *City Manager Government*, p. 27.
73. Quoted in Weinstein, *The Corporate Ideal*, pp. 106, 107.
74. Anirudh V. S. Ruhil, "Structural Change and Fiscal Flows: A Framework for Analyzing the Effects of Urban Events," *Urban Affairs Review* 38, no. 3 (January 2003): 396–416.
75. Alan DiGaetano, "Urban Political Reform: Did It Kill the Machine?" *Journal of Urban History* 18, no.1 (November 1991): 37–67.
76. Ibid.
77. Ibid.
78. Ibid.
79. Ibid, p. 67.

80. Ibid.
81. Steven P. Erie, *Rainbow's End: Irish-Americans and the Dilemmas of Urban Machine Politics, 1840–1985* (Berkeley: University of California Press, 1988).
82. Shafritz, Jay M., *The Dorsey Dictionary of American Government and Politics* (Dorsey Press, 1988), pp. 244–246. A legislative district is considered gerrymandered when it is drawn with tortuously meandering boundaries as a means of advancing the interests of a party or group. The term comes from a district drawn in Massachussetts in 1811 and signed into law by Governor Elbridge Gerry.
83. Robert L. Lineberry and Edmond P. Fowler, "Reformism and Public Policies in American Cities," *American Political Science Review* 61 (September 1967): pp. 701–716; Chandler Davidson and George Korbel, "At-Large Elections and Minority Group Representation: A Reexamination of Historical and Contemporary Evidence," *Journal of Politics* 43 (November 1981): 982–1005; Jerry L. Polinard, Robert D. Wrinkle, and Thomàs Longoria Jr., "The Impact of District Elections on the Mexican American Community: The Electoral Perspective," *Social Science Quarterly* 71, no. 3 (September 1991): 608–614; Richard L. Engstrom and Michael D. McDonald, "The Effect of At-Large Versus District Elections on Racial Representation in U.S. Municipalities," in *Electoral Laws and Their Political Consequences*, eds. Bernard Grofman and Arend Liphart (New York: Agathon, 1986), pp. 203–225; W. E. Lyons and Malcolm E. Jewell, "Minority Representation and the Drawing of City Council Districts," *Urban Affairs Quarterly* 23 (1988): 432–447; Delbert Taebel, "Minority Representation on City Councils: The Impact of Structure on Blacks and Hispanics," *Social Science Quarterly* 59 (1982): 729–736; Jeffrey S. Zax, "Election Methods, Black and Hispanic City Council Membership," *Social Science Quarterly* 71 (1990): 339–355.
84. *City of Mobile v. Bolden*, 446 U.S. 55 (1980).
85. *Thornburg v. Gingles*, 106 S.Ct. 2752 (1986).
86. A multimember legislative district is just like an at-large system that covers an entire city. All candidates for city council seats must run in the same district; by contrast, in a ward system, a single alderman or council member represents each ward.
87. C. Robert Heath, "*Thornburg v. Gingles:* The Unresolved Issues," *National Civic Review* 79, no. 1 (January–February 1990): 50–71.
88. *Dillard v. Crenshaw County*, 649 F.Supp. at 289 (C.O. Ala. 1986).
89. *McNeal v. Springfield*, 658 F.Supp. at 1015, 1022 (C.D. Ill. 1987).
90. *McNeal v. Springfield Park District*, 851 F.2d at 937 (7th Cir. 1988).
91. *Derrickson v. City of Danville*, 87–2007 (C.D. Ill. 1987).
92. Joseph F. Zimmerman, "Alternative Local Electoral Systems," *National Civic Review* 79, no. 1 (January–February 1990): 23–36.
93. The quotation is from *Shaw v. Reno* 509 U.S. 630 (1993), commonly known as Shaw I. Other cases are *Miller v. Johnson*, 63 U.S.L.W. 4726 (1995); *Shaw v. Hunt*, 64 U.S.L.W. 4437 (known as Shaw II), *King vs. Illinois Board of Elections*, 65 U.S.L.W. 3353 (1996); *Abrams v. Johnson*, 65 U.S.L.W. 4478.
94. Carmen Cirincione, Thomas Darling, and Timothy O'Rourke, "Does the Supreme Court Have It Right?" Paper delivered at the 1997 Annual Meeting of the American Political Science Association, Washington, D.C., August 28–31, 1997.
95. Heath, "*Thornburg v. Gingles*," pp. 51–53.
96. Ibid., pp. 54–55.
97. Ibid., pp. 55–59; Charles S. Bullock III, "Symbolics or Substance: A Critique of the At-Large Election Controversy," *State and Local Government Review* 21, no. 3 (Fall 1989): 91–99.
98. Edward Blum and Roger Clegg, "The GOP's 2002 Racial Redistricting Dilemma,' *Weekly Standard*, October 17, 1992; www.ceousa.org/html/redistarticle1.htm.
99. Scott Armstrong, "Minorities Seek More Clout on the Bench," *Christian Science Monitor*, October 1, 1991, pp. 1–2.

100. International City Management Association, *Baseline Data Report: Municipal Election Processes: The Impact on Minority Representation* 19, no. 6 (November–December 1987): 3–4.

101. Ibid., pp. 6–9; Polinard, Wrinkle, and Longoria, "The Impact of District Elections," pp. 608–614.

102. Tim O'Neil, "Blacks Want Half of City's Wards in Redistricting," *St. Louis Post-Dispatch,* June 8, 1991, p. 3A.

103. *Shaw v. Reno* 92 357 (1993). In 1996 the Court rejected a somewhat redrawn 12th congressional district in North Carolina yet again.

104. *Miller v. Johnson* 515 US 900 (94 631), 1995; *Bush v. Vera* 571 US 900 (94 805), 1996.

105. Stephen Ansolabehere, Alan Gerber, and James Snyder, "Equal Votes, Equal Money: Court-Order Redistricting and Public Expenditures in the American States," *American Political Science Review* 96, no. 4 (December 2002): 767–777.

PART II

NATIONAL POLITICS AND THE CITIES

For most of the twentieth century, the fate of American cities was closely tied to the politics of the nation. When central cities began to exhibit problems of poverty, racial segregation, and physical decline, political leaders at all levels of government were alarmed, and they were convinced that action was needed. For a half century, from the 1930s through the 1970s, national policy and resources were focused on solving the problems of cities. Ultimately, however, the federal government withdrew. The chapters that make up Part 2 trace this long trajectory of concern followed by indifference.

The evolution of American national politics cannot be understood without taking into account the politics of its cities and urban areas. In the twentieth century, the contest between the Democrats and the Republicans was often decided by city voters. Cities came of age in the nation's politics in the 1930s, when the urban electorate became pivotal partners in President Franklin Delano Roosevelt's New Deal coalition. For several decades, cities derived considerable benefit from the political alliances that urban politicians forged with Democrats in Congress and the White House. After World War II, several national initiatives influenced urban development. Public housing and urban renewal were meant to help the cities, but their effects were often more negative than positive; the razing of urban neighborhoods did not bring the expected benefit of inner-city revitalization. Federal policies canceled one another out. At the same time that the national government was trying to help the cities, federally insured loans for homeowners and a federally subsidized freeway system accelerated a massive middle-class flight from the central cities to the suburbs. By the mid-1960s, central cities had become ringed by miles of suburbs, building the foundation for the metropolitan fragmentation that came to define twentieth-century urban America.

White flight to the suburbs created deep racial divisions. In the 1960s and 1970s, Congress enacted legislation designed to help the cities, with mixed results. Beginning in 1980, the national government began to withdraw—in large part because central-city voters no longer played a decisive role in national politics. The rapid growth of the Sunbelt changed the national political balance, so that neither the Democrats nor the Republicans derived political benefit by paying attention to the problems of cities. This has forced urban leaders to place a high priority on using their own resources to stimulate local economic vitality.

CHAPTER 5

THE NEW DEAL COALITION AND THE CITIES

THE CHANGING POLITICAL BALANCE

In 1912, a Harvard political scientist wrote that "before many years have passed, the urban population of the United States will have gained numerical mastery."[1] His judgment was based on a simple calculation of demographic change. Though an increasing number of people were beginning to move from the cities to the suburbs in the early years of the twentieth century, the volume of migration to the cities still vastly exceeded the population growth in the suburbs.[2] In the thirty years from 1890 to 1920, more than 18 million immigrants poured into America's cities. These new immigrants came mainly from Italy, Poland, Russia, Greece, and Eastern Europe. They were overwhelmingly Roman Catholic and Jewish. They made up the preponderance of the workforces in the iron and steel, meatpacking, mining, and textile industries. Few spoke English when they arrived, and many were illiterate even in their own language. To Americans who were the descendants of earlier immigrants, the immigrants and the cities they poured into seemed almost like alien islands floating in the midst of a sea of white Protestants. A nativist reaction aimed at the new immigrants became a potent political force.

The reaction against the immigrants ultimately failed to keep the cities and the people who lived within them from gaining a voice in national politics. In the election of 1928, the ethnic groups that were clustered in the inner-city immigrant wards began to identify with the national Democratic Party. In that year, the Democrats selected an Irish Catholic from New York City, Alfred E. Smith, as their presidential candidate. He lost, but he won a majority of votes in the twelve largest cities. With Franklin D. Roosevelt's landslide victory in the presidential election of 1932, voters in the industrial cities became crucial to the electoral prospects of the Democratic Party. The nation's eleven largest cities provided 27 percent of the popular vote in 1932 and a commanding majority in several of the industrial states with the largest numbers of electoral college votes.[3] For the first time in the nation's history, the politicians representing urban voters began to wield influence in national politics. Their influence would fundamentally shape American politics for decades.

THE POLITICAL ISOLATION OF THE CITIES

Before the 1930s, neither the Republicans nor the Democrats paid much attention to the cities. The national party organizations did not care much about urban voters because they did not have to. Following the Civil War, each of the parties appealed to separate sectional interests. The Republicans, the triumphant party of Abraham Lincoln, emerged from the war as the dominant national party controlling Congress and the presidency. Between 1860 and 1928, the Republicans won fourteen of eighteen presidential contests and controlled both houses of Congress the majority of the time. Representing eastern

---

OUT TAKE

CITY VOTERS BECAME IMPORTANT TO THE DEMOCRATIC PARTY

From the perspective of the early twenty-first century, it may be difficult to recall a time when strong political support existed for programs to help the cities. But the explanation is straightforward: For half a century, voters who lived in cities played a pivotal role in presidential elections, and their votes were the key to Democratic majorities in Congress. Attention to the problems of the cities was guaranteed when both of the national political parties began to win or lose elections on the basis of urban votes.[4]

The alliance that provided the foundation for the Democratic Party's ascendancy became known as the New Deal coalition, which was made up two wings, the urban North and the solid South. Voters in the cities learned to vote Democratic because of the programs that were enacted during the New Deal years. For the first time in the nation's history, federal agencies were granted powers to regulate the economy and to assist citizens during times of need. Urban working-class people were benefited by labor legislation such as Section 7a of the National Industrial Recovery Act and the Wagner Labor Act, which implemented workers' compensation for death or injury, safety and workplace regulations, and the right of workers to organize unions. As a result, craft and industrial unions became reliably Democratic voters. The black electorate also became important to the party. Even in the 1930s, long before civil rights legislation was possible, the Roosevelt Administration took steps to ensure that blacks received some appointments to federal posts and a share of the benefits from job and relief programs.

From the Roosevelt presidency until its decline and collapse in the 1980s, the New Deal coalition provided the foundation for the Democratic Party's electoral success in Congress and in presidential elections. Modern American liberalism, as expressed in the New Deal programs of the 1930s and the Great Society programs of the 1960s, can be traced to the mobilization of the urban electorate in the 1930s.

financial, industrial, and commercial interests, they enacted high tariffs on foreign imports, gave land to the railroads for westward expansion, and financed canal and river improvements. Republicans opposed taxes on business, encouraged private exploitation (mineral, grazing, homesteading) of federal lands in the West, used federal troops to quell strikes, and generally promoted a laissez-faire ideology protecting business from regulation.

The Republican Party was also popular in the middle- and working-class electorates in the North because of the outcome of the Civil War and because it presided during a period of general economic expansion tied closely to frontier development and industrial growth. In the prairie states and in the West, "cattle barons, lumber kings, the mineral exploiters, the land speculators, and the humble homesteaders"[5] identified their prospects with the party. By identifying with the ideas of competitive individualism, the Republicans appealed to all those elements that hankered after the "main chance": "Thanks to a deep-rooted American ideology of individual enterprise, even the small farmers generally remained faithful to the party. . . . They, too, were entrepreneurs, after a fashion."[6] The Republicans' business philosophy fit well with the post–Civil War climate that stressed the exploitation of natural resources and the glorification of unfettered individual enterprise.

In the years after the Civil War, the Democrats became the party of protest. Southerners joined with a loose coalition of groups opposed to economic domination by eastern banks and corporations, the railroads, and "big money." The worst problem with the Democrats' coalition was its fragility, for its major issues arose from the insecurities of small farmers about credit and prices, the bitterness of the South, and the tensions between business and labor. The party prospered during hard times but lost support when the economy improved. Its only secure base was in the South, where the Republican Party—the party of Lincoln, the Great Emancipator—was virtually absent.

In the presidential race of 1896, near the end of a three-year economic depression, the Democrats campaigned on a program advocating government intervention to protect the common man against the so-called money interests symbolized by the industrial magnates Andrew Mellon, Andrew Carnegie, James Fisk, and J. P. Morgan. With William Jennings Bryan of Nebraska as its presidential candidate, the party advocated lower tariffs as a means of forcing industrial enterprises to lower prices to compete with foreign producers. Bryan called for a paper currency backed by silver as well as by gold. Such a move would have increased the amount of money in circulation because silver was much more readily available than gold. The resulting inflation would have helped heavily indebted small business owners and farmers. The Democrats also proposed a graduated federal income tax, government takeover of land grants previously ceded to railroads, and public ownership of telegraphs and telephones. The Democrats lost the election mainly because these positions failed to appeal to workers in the cities, who felt that high tariffs protected their jobs by reducing imports.

Between the elections of 1896 and 1932, several issues helped broaden the Democrats' electoral base. In 1900, Bryan was once again named as the Democratic

Party's candidate. This time he fashioned an appeal specifically designed to build support among the urban working class. He assailed trusts and monopolies, claiming that they were crowding out smaller businesses and entrepreneurs. He urged the direct election of senators (who were, at that time, selected by state legislatures), opposed the use of federal troops and injunctions to break strikes, and advocated the establishment of a Department of Labor. Bryan saw the possibility of forging a coalition of western farmers, southerners, and industrial labor against big business's control of the nation's money supply, credit, and economic policies. Later, the American Federation of Labor (AFL) endorsed Bryan when he ran for the third time as the Democrats' choice in 1908.

In 1912, the Democrats won the presidency for the first time in the twentieth century. President Woodrow Wilson immediately pushed a distinctively Democratic legislative agenda. The Underwood-Simmons Act lowered tariffs for the first time since 1857 and put wool, lumber, paper, wood pulp, steel rails, and sugar on a free trade list. The prices of these commodities dropped sharply. A graduated income tax was adopted, shifting federal revenues from reliance on excise taxes and tariffs, which consumers paid in higher prices, to direct taxation on earnings. The Federal Reserve Act of 1913 reformed the banking system. It spread the money supply more evenly across the nation by establishing a dozen regional banks to receive federal deposits, and it increased the money supply by the issuance of notes that did not have to be backed by full value in gold reserves. The Clayton Act and the Federal Trade Act outlawed some unfair business practices (such as price fixing), established boards for voluntary mediation between management and labor, created an eight-hour workday for railroad workers, and provided federal administrative assistance to states and companies to set up workers' compensation programs. The Federal Farm Loan Act extended a very limited amount of credit to farmers. Additionally, the Wilson administration sponsored child labor laws and laws to limit women's work hours, exempted labor unions from antitrust legislation, and encouraged employers to negotiate with organized labor.

Despite these programs, ethnic voters in the cities did not immediately rally to the Democratic banner. About half of the urban party machines were Republican, but whatever their partisan affiliation, machine leaders were not well connected to the national or even the state party organizations. In most states, party leaders came out of the governor's mansion and state legislature, and these tended to be dominated by rural, not city, interests. Machine politicians had gotten into politics through their local precincts and wards, and they paid little attention to national candidates and issues. Theirs was a politics of ethnicity and trade-offs, not of abstract principles. The machines were strictly local organizations, a product of the segregation of ethnic voters from the rest of American society.

There was little pay or respect for urban ethnic politicians who were elected to the state legislature. It was often a kiss of political death to be sent away to small upstate or downstate towns like Albany, New York, or Springfield, Illinois, away from friends, family, and the local community. When the machine organization Tammany Hall sent Al Smith to the state legislature at the age of thirty, he had scarcely been outside New York City. He felt exiled:

> Al Smith went to Albany unprepared to be legislator—or even to sleep away from home. . . . [O]vercome by the intricacies of the legislative process, he sat day after day in the high-ceilinged chamber in silence.
>
>   As he sat there staring down at the desk, a page boy would deposit another pile of bills on it. The wording was difficult enough for the expert. It might have been designed to mock a man whose schooling had ended in the eighth grade, who had never liked to read even the simple books of childhood, who, he had once said, had in his entire life read only one book cover to cover: *The Life of John L. Sullivan.*[7]

Before Al Smith, no Tammany politician had ever done much in Albany.

Urban ethnic voters, too, were motivated by their personal loyalties and by their pocketbooks more than by political issues. When precinct captains took them to the polls, they voted for the local party organization, not for a cause. What in their background would excite them about national issues and candidates—tariff policy, child labor legislation, William Jennings Bryan, Woodrow Wilson? The upshot was that although many cities were dominated by powerful party machines, the leaders of these organizations and their loyal constituents had only occasionally become important in gubernatorial contests and had hardly figured at all in presidential contests.

Though President Wilson sponsored several programs in response to demands made by labor unions during World War I, and though Bryan had campaigned for a Labor Department and for laws against strike injunctions in the presidential elections of 1896 and 1900, the national Democratic Party had not transformed itself into anything resembling an urban working-class party. Far from it. Its center of gravity was still found in the South and on the farm. When the urban wing of the party began to grow in strength, a potentially devastating split developed between the cities and the party's southern wing. By the 1920s, the party was bitterly divided.

THE NEW URBAN CONSCIOUSNESS

The cleavages within the Democratic Party mirrored the urban-rural conflicts that obsessed the nation. Rural Democrats feared that the urban wing of their party might someday command a voting majority in national conventions. A similar concern preyed on the minds of native Protestants. What would happen to political and religious traditions if the barbarous hordes from Europe took over? The ever-present nineteenth-century nervousness about the "strangers in the land" escalated into a national phobia in the twentieth century. The rise of the cities in national politics began when nativist Protestant elements launched a national assault on the city machines and their immigrant constituents. In doing so, they created issues that an urban electorate could easily understand.

Prohibition constituted a direct assault on the immigrants. Proposed to the states by Congress in 1917 and ratified in 1919, the Eighteenth Amendment prohibited the sale and distribution of alcoholic beverages. Small-town Methodists and Baptists—joined in their crusade by upper- and middle-class Protestants in the cities and in the new suburbs—said they wanted to reduce poverty, improve workers' efficiency and family life, and end immorality and crime by forcing the immigrants to abstain from alcohol. Prohibition became the most compelling political issue of the 1920s, for it represented a frontal assault upon the cultural values and customs of the immigrants:

> [Drinking] was associated with the saloonkeepers who ran the city machines and who used the votes of the whiskey-loving immigrant . . . with the German brewers and their "disloyal" compatriots who drank beer and ale. . . . The cities, which resisted the idea that "thou shalt not" was the fundamental precept of living, were always hostile to prohibition. The prohibitionists, in turn, regarded the city as their chief enemy, and prohibitionism and a pervasive antiurbanism went hand-in-hand.[8]

To rural and urban Protestants, the sins of liquor were indistinguishable from the sins of the immigrants. Southern and western newspapers reflexively connected crime, national origin, and liquor. When it was not legitimate to attack foreigners directly, it was easy to attack them through the surrogate liquor issue, allowing "prohibition partisans to talk about morality when in reality they were worried about cultural dominance and political supremacy."[9]

Prohibition was intimately connected to religious conflict. To Protestant Americans, the Roman Catholic Church was evil incarnate. It signified ostentatious authority—the robes, the ceremony, and the architecture of Catholic cathedrals bespeaking a menace to the simplicity and informality of small-town life. Like the right-wing groups of the 1950s obsessed by the idea that an international Communist conspiracy was poised to subvert the American system, religious fundamentalists of the early twentieth century were convinced that the Roman Catholic Church was intent on subverting civil authority around the world.

Feeding on such fears, the Ku Klux Klan attracted millions of members. Revived in Atlanta in 1915, for a few years the Klan enjoyed spectacular growth in both the North and the South. Klan membership skyrocketed in California, Oregon, Indiana, Illinois, Ohio, Oklahoma, Texas, Arkansas, and throughout the South. At its peak in 1924, 40 percent of the Klan's membership resided in Ohio, Indiana, and Illinois. Half of its membership was located in cities of more than 50,000, with chapters of hundreds of members in such cities as Chicago, Detroit, Indianapolis, Pittsburgh, Baltimore, and Buffalo.[10] The Klan was a powerful political force until at least the mid-1920s. It helped elect a member of the Senate; governors in Georgia, Alabama, Oregon, and California; and seventy-five members of the House of Representatives.

Though the Klan found its strongest support among lower-middle-class fundamentalist Christians, its basic message reached a broad audience. In 1916, Madison Grant, curator of New York City's Museum of National History, published a book entitled *The Passing of the Great Race,* in which he worried that Aryans might someday be overwhelmed by dark-skinned races. His book was elevated to the status of a scientific work, along with Lothrop Stoddard's *The Rising Tide of Color Against the White World-Supremacy* (1921).

Congress responded to the rising xenophobia with the Emergency Quota Act of 1921 and the National Origins Act of 1924. Both laws drew support from intellectuals, labor leaders, rural people from all sections of the country, and anxious middle-class suburbanites. The Emergency Quota Act reaffirmed the total exclusion of Asians and established a national origins quota of 3 percent of each nationality's proportion of the U.S. population as recorded in the 1910 census. The law succeeded in cutting immigration from 805,228 in 1920 to 309,556 in 1921–1922.[11] Three years later, the National Origins Act reduced the origins quota to 2 percent and established the 1890 census as the new baseline. By changing the baseline census used for calculating the percentage of each ethnic group allowed into the country, Congress was able to sharply reduce the numbers for nationality groups that had flooded in after 1890. Italian immigration was reduced by 90 percent; British and Irish immigration, by contrast, declined by just 19 percent.[12] The total number of immigrants fell drastically, from 357,803 in 1923–1924 to 164,667 in 1924–1925.

In debates on these two bills, members of Congress reviled the foreign-born of the cities in language not unlike that found in Ku Klux Klan pamphlets. This assault helped make immigrants aware of how deeply national politics could affect them, and in the 1920s they began to express their new understanding. Before long, it became apparent that they "were not going to support candidates who wanted them to stop drinking, Protestantize their schools, or tell them as often as possible that they were inferior."[13]

THE URBAN WING OF THE DEMOCRATIC PARTY

The prosperity of the 1920s came as a serious blow to the Democratic Party because the party's coalition had long been held together mainly with the glue of shared grievances. The party was composed of an unlikely combination of urban ethnics; western farmers and prohibitionists; and southern, racist, religious fundamentalists. The fragile nature of this alliance was revealed by the 1924 Democratic convention, held in Madison Square Garden in New York City. The Democrats treated the first radio audience of a national convention to a futile, sixteen-day, 103-ballot marathon. The galleries booed the speeches of Southerners and Westerners, especially when William Jennings Bryan asked the convention to reject a proposed resolution condemning the Ku Klux Klan by name. The resolution to condemn the Klan brought forth such heated oratory that police were brought onto the convention floor in case a free-for-all broke out. Delegates shouted at and cursed one another. When the final vote on the resolution to condemn the Klan was taken, it lost by one vote, 542 $3/_{20}$ to 541 $3/_{20}$. Demands for a recount were drowned out when the band struck up "Marching Through Georgia," which incited the southern delegates to paroxysms of anger. After sixteen days, the convention finally nominated a presidential candidate almost nobody wanted.

The delegates from the towns and farms of the South and West were disoriented and frightened by the crowds and the din of New York City. They found New Yorkers unfriendly and rude, and the city seemed all too easy to get lost in. Delegates who "wandered downtown to Fourteenth Street to gawk at Tammany

Hall with its ancient Indian above the door reacted as if they expected to see an ogre come popping out. Almost all delegates were dismayed by the New York traffic, the noise and hustle."[14] Their antagonism toward the city was reaffirmed every day the convention dragged on through the muggy July heat. Small-town reporters filled their hometown newspapers with vivid accounts of the horrors of the city.[15]

Despite these divisions, only four years later the Democrats named Al Smith, the four-term governor of New York, as their presidential candidate. Smith represented everything that was anathema to the city haters. He was a self-made Catholic member of the nation's most notorious machine, Tammany Hall. He said "foist" instead of "first" and wore a brown derby, which only accentuated his bulbous nose and ruddy complexion. He proudly reminisced about his past: swimming in the East River and working at the Fulton Fish Market as an errand boy. Considering the divisive conflicts within the party, how could he have been nominated? Once he was nominated, why did the party not simply come apart?

The southern and western factions had little choice but to stay within the fold. In spite of their differences, the Democrats had come to share, however crudely, a class interest. The party had symbolically become—mostly by default because the Republicans took an uncompromising pro-business stand—the "little man's" party. Those who opposed Republican policies could never hope to have a voice in national politics unless they aligned with the Democrats.

The time was ripe for compromise. Few Democrats thought that Smith could win, but no candidate was available who was capable of bridging the gap between the factions. Smith had acquired broader political support than anyone else. As the four-term governor of New York, he had gained national prominence as a progressive leader who had created state parks and beaches, sponsored workers' safety legislation, and financed public improvements throughout the state. He had reorganized state government, making New York the model for progressives who believed in efficiency principles. Admired by progressives for his record as governor and supported by Democratic organizations with ethnic constituencies, his nomination could be denied by rural delegates, but only at the cost of another fiasco like 1924—multiple ballots and a guaranteed loss for the presidential nominee. There was even reason to believe that Smith might have a chance. In his victorious gubernatorial run in 1924, he had received 100,000 more votes than the losing Democratic presidential ticket in New York.

In 1928, the Democrats gave the nomination to Al Smith. Though he lost the election, his candidacy marked the beginning of the party's political ascendancy in the big cities. The election of 1928 marked a significant change in the attitude of the urban masses. Both in 1920 and 1924, the twelve largest cities in the United States had, taken together, given a decisive majority to the Republicans; now the tables were turned, and the Democrats came out ahead. As later elections were to prove, this marked the beginning of a long-term trend in which voters in the cities cast most of their ballots for Democrats.[16]

For the Roman Catholic ethnics in the cities, Smith's campaign sharpened their perception of the national issues of Prohibition, ethnicity, and religion.

Table 5.1 **The Revolt of the City: Voting in the Twelve Largest Cities**

Year	Net Party Plurality
1920	1,540,000 Republican
1924	1,308,000 Republican
1928	210,000 Democratic
1932	1,791,000 Democratic
1936	3,479,000 Democratic
1940	2,112,000 Democratic
1944	2,230,000 Democratic
1948	1,481,000 Democratic

The cities in this table include New York, Chicago, Philadelphia, Pittsburgh, Detroit, Cleveland, Baltimore, St. Louis, Boston, San Francisco, Milwaukee, and Los Angeles.

Source: Reprinted from the table on page 49 in *The Future of American Politics,* 3rd revised edition, by Samuel Lubell. ©1951, 1952, 1956, 1965 by Samuel Lubell. Reprinted by permission of Harper & Row Publishers, Inc.

Smith campaigned with his brown derby and his theme song, "The Sidewalks of New York." Protestants shuddered at the idea of a Catholic in the White House. Smith's equivocal stand on Prohibition made drink the main issue of the campaign. Blue-blood upper-class Protestants found him beneath them. The campaign highlighted the issues of race, religion, culture, and social class so clearly that never again would the ethnics be unmindful of their stake in national politics.

The election of 1928 brought a Democratic electoral plurality to the cities of the nation (see Table 5.1). Since then, the major cities have normally voted heavily Democratic, and until the 1980s they were a mainstay of the Democratic Party's electoral strength. Al Smith's candidacy broke new ground in establishing a role for the cities in national politics. What cemented the relationship between the cities and the Democratic Party was the Great Depression and Franklin Delano Roosevelt's New Deal.

THE DEPRESSION AND THE CITIES

The Great Depression came as a shock to Americans and to their public leaders. The 1920s had been a decade of prosperity and optimism, especially for the rapidly growing middle class. Business leaders and politicians promoted the idea that the potential for sustained economic growth was limitless. A strong undertow of poverty ran below the surface, in the immigrant slums and on farms alike, but on the surface the signs of prosperity prevailed. It was an age that extolled mass consumption and complacency. The discontent of the industrial age seemed long past.

The symbolic beginning of the Great Depression occurred on October 24, 1929. On that day—Black Thursday—disorder, panic, and confusion reigned on the New York Stock Exchange. Stock prices virtually collapsed. For several months prices had sagged, then rallied, then sagged again, with each trough lower than the previous one and each peak less convincing. When the bottom fell out, "the Market . . . degenerated into a wild, mad scramble to sell, . . . the Market . . . surrendered to blind, relentless fear."[17] In one morning, eleven well-known speculators committed suicide. From Wall Street the economic catastrophe rippled outward, with consequences that would fundamentally reshape American politics.

Over the next three years, the nation sank steadily deeper into economic stagnation. In the spring of 1929, the unemployment rate stood at 3.2 percent. Within a few months, the number of unemployed exceeded 4 million, representing 8.7 percent of the labor force.[18] By 1932, 24 percent of all workers—more than 12 million in all—could not find jobs. In the depths of the depression, during the spring of 1933, the number of unemployed reached 13 million workers, fully one-fourth of the labor force.[19]

The depression dragged on for a decade. Unemployment levels remained above 20 percent in both 1934 and 1935 and dropped below 15 percent only in 1937. Most of those who managed to find work made less than before. From 1929 to 1933, the average income of workers fell by 42.5 percent.[20] Weekly wages dropped from an average of $28 in 1929 to $17 by 1934, and workers faced the ever-present threat of layoffs. Many jobs were reduced from full-time to part-time status, and employers cut wages and hours to meet payrolls. For example, the payroll of the nation's largest steel company, U.S. Steel, was cut in half from 1929 to 1933, and in 1933 it had no full-time workers at all.[21] Steel mills operated at only 12 percent of capacity by 1932.[22]

The productive capacity of business seemed irreparably damaged. In the three years following the stock market collapse, national income fell by 44.5 percent. By the summer of 1932, stocks had fallen 83 percent below their value in September 1929.[23] By the end of 1932, 5,096 commercial banks had failed. Farm income declined from $7 billion in 1929 to $2.5 billion in 1932.[24] For many farmers whose incomes had been sharply dropping throughout the 1920s, the depression was the final blow.

The statistics only hinted at the extent of human suffering. Between one million and two million men rode the rails and gathered in hobo jungles or camped in thickets and railroad cars. Others lived in "Hoovervilles," clusters of cardboard, scrap wood, and scrap metal shacks in empty lots and city parks. Those who had been chronically poor in the 1920s were now hungry and destitute. They stood in bread lines, ate from garbage cans, or went begging from door to door. One-quarter of all homeowners lost their homes in 1932, and more than 1,000 mortgages a day were foreclosed in the first half of 1933.[25] By March 1933, when Franklin D. Roosevelt was inaugurated as president, 9 million savings accounts had been lost.[26]

Never before had the nation faced an economic catastrophe of this magnitude, nor was there a tradition of federal government assistance for the unemployed and destitute.[27] Unemployment and poverty were certainly not new. In the period from 1897 to 1926, unemployment levels in four major industries fluctuated around the 10 percent level,[28] and poverty was a chronic condition of industrialization and immigration. What made this depression unique was its depth, persistence, and broad reach. In earlier depressions, including the panics of the 1870s and 1890s, production and employment declined much less severely, and the recovery began within a year or two.[29] The depression of the 1930s lasted for over a decade, it touched all classes, and its effects were felt by people at all income levels. The measure of the crisis of the 1930s was not just unemployment and poverty but also the breakdown of economic institutions.

No one knew how to respond. President Herbert Hoover firmly resisted intervention by the federal government and instead launched two national drives to encourage private relief. Late in 1930, he appointed the President's Emergency Committee for Employment. Its main task was to encourage state and local committees to expedite public construction and to coordinate the public and private giving of relief. In August 1931, he formed the President's Organization on Unemployment Relief, whose job was to help organize private unemployment committees in states and communities.

Despite Hoover's undying opposition to federal assistance, two major programs were funded during his administration. First, the Federal Home Loan Bank Act supplied capital advances to a small number of mortgage institutions so that they could forbear rather than foreclose on mortgages in default. A few banks were saved by this program. Second, the Emergency Relief and Construction Act extended $300 million in loans to state and local governments so that they could continue to provide relief to indigent people.

Hoover was hardly alone in opposing aggressive federal action. Until 1932, most governors took a "we'll do it ourselves" attitude toward solving unemployment and its associated problems.[30] Two governors refused to work with the President's Organization on Unemployment Relief, even though federal funds were not involved.[31] The officials of financially strapped local governments were also skeptical of federal aid. In July 1931, the socialist mayor of Milwaukee wrote to the mayors of the largest one hundred cities asking them to come to a conference to discuss a joint request for a national relief program. He got no response at all from several of the major cities, and several mayors criticized the idea, arguing that federal aid would constitute "an invasion of community rights."[32]

In the 1932 campaign, the Democrats accused Hoover of doing too much rather than too little. Their nominee, Roosevelt, promised to balance the budget while accusing Hoover of having presided over "the greatest spending administration in peace times in all our history."[33] It was apparent that the weight of the past lay heavily on both political parties. Against a cultural tradition that extolled individualism and free enterprise, there was great reluctance to expand the powers of government—especially the federal government—to meet the crisis. Nevertheless, when Roosevelt was inaugurated on March 4, 1933, he set in motion a concentrated period of reform that vastly increased the powers of the federal government in areas of business regulation, farm policy, and social insurance. Why did Roosevelt break so thoroughly from tradition?

Roosevelt's change of heart was motivated by the overwhelming sense of crisis that ushered him into the White House. Between his election in November and his inauguration in March, the nation passed through the worst months of the depression.[34] The economy teetered on the brink of utter collapse. In February 1933, some of the nation's biggest banks failed; "People stood in long queues with satchels and paper bags to take gold and currency away from the banks to store in mattresses and old shoe boxes. It seemed safer to put one's life's savings in the attic than to trust the financial institutions in the country."[35] Roosevelt wondered if there would be anything left to salvage by the time he assumed office. By inauguration day, thirty-eight states had closed their banks, and on that day the governors of New York and Illinois closed the nation's biggest banks.[36] The New York Stock Exchange stopped trading. The Kansas City and Chicago Boards of Trade closed their doors; "In the once-busy grain pits of Chicago, in the canyons of Wall Street, all was silent."[37]

It was also one of the harshest winters on record. In desperation, people overran relief offices and rioted at bank closings. Relief marchers invaded state legislative chambers. Farmers tried to stop foreclosure proceedings and blockaded roads. Amid marches, riots, arrests, and jailings, politicians feared a revolution.

The first one hundred days of Roosevelt's administration were characterized by unceasing activity.[38] On March 9, Roosevelt signed the Emergency Banking Act. The act extended financial assistance to bankers so they could reopen their doors and gave the government authority to reorganize banks and to control bank credit policies. It received a unanimous vote from a panicked Congress, sight unseen. A flurry of legislation followed: the Civilian Conservation Corps (March 31), the Agricultural Adjustment Act and the Federal Emergency Relief Act (May 12), the Tennessee Valley Authority (May 18), the Federal "Truth in Securities" Act (May 27), the Home Owners' Loan Act (June 13), the National Industrial Recovery Act (June 16), and more than a score of other bills.

Most of the legislative onslaught was designed to stimulate, regulate, and stabilize the most important economic institutions of the economy. But the benefits filtered down. After the Emergency Banking Act was passed, depositors gained confidence and redeposited their savings. Under the National Housing Act (adopted in 1934), home buyers could secure long-term mortgages from banks whose loans were guaranteed by the federal government. Foreclosures on farms and homes were sharply reduced when the government, through the Farm Credit Administration and Home Owners' Loan Corporation, agreed to buy up defaulted mortgages. New Deal programs affected many people's lives by salvaging their savings, houses, and farms. Nevertheless, the New Deal's attempts to reform the economy were designed more to bring stability to financial institutions than to fight poverty and destitution. Home lending and farm credit programs primarily helped the nation's important economic institutions and secondarily aided the heavily mortgaged middle class.

The other side of the New Deal included its public works and relief programs, which assisted millions of unemployed and penniless people. These programs vastly broadened the Democratic Party's electoral coalition by bringing into the fold the same elements that had identified with Al Smith. For millions of families, the New Deal meant the difference between hunger and having food, between unemployment and finding a job. Between 1933 and 1937, the federal government administered public works programs for several million people and supplied direct relief to millions more. The earliest of the public works programs was the Civilian Conservation Corps (CCC), established on March 31, 1933. In all, more than 2.5 million boys and young men were employed by the CCC. In 1935 alone, 500,000 men were living in CCC camps. They planted trees, built dams, fought fires, stocked fish, built lookout towers, dug ditches and canals, strung telephone lines, and built and improved bridges, roads, and trails. Their contribution to conservation was enormous; the CCC was responsible for more than half of all the forest planted in the United States up to the 1960s.[39]

The Civil Works Administration (CWA) was much larger and broader in scope. Established in November 1933, it employed 4.1 million by the third week of January 1934.[40] In a few months, it employed almost a third of the unemployed labor force. Although the CWA lasted for less than a year—Roosevelt ended it in the spring of 1934 because he thought it was too costly—it enabled many families to survive the bitter winter of 1934. The CWA was "immensely popular—with merchants, with local officials, and with workers," and its demise was resisted in Congress.[41] The Public Works Administration (PWA) enjoyed a longer run, and its impact was more lasting. In six years, from 1933 to 1939, the PWA built 70 percent of the new school buildings in the nation and 35 percent of the hospitals and public health facilities.[42]

The Federal Emergency Relief Act (FERA), signed into law on May 12, 1933, was never as popular as public works legislation, for it undercut the cherished principles of work and independence by making relief money directly available to the destitute. Roosevelt himself viewed the Federal Emergency Relief Administration with distaste, thinking it would sap the moral strength of the poor. Though Roosevelt constantly sought ways to cut its budget and though its benefit levels were extraordinarily low, it was mandated by the want and the civil disorder that prevailed in Roosevelt's first term. In the winter of 1934, 20 million people received FERA funds.[43]

The FERA was treated as an embarrassing necessity. The government's response was understood to be an emergency measure, comparable to helping victims of catastrophes such as floods, earthquakes, and tornadoes. Congressional debate on the FERA received little coverage by the media. When the act was passed on May 9, 1933, the *New York Times* mentioned it on page 3 only in a column listing legislation passed by Congress. When it was signed by President Roosevelt on May 12, it made page 21 of the *Times,* but only in reference to the appointment of the administrator. In a culture that extolled individualism, competition, and hard work, people were uncomfortable with the idea of relief.

Roosevelt often expressed doubts about relief and public works programs. He preferred economic recovery to government spending. But his response to the economic emergency broadened the base of the Democratic Party. Public works and relief created a loyal following among middle- and working-class people who were benefited. By the 1936 election, and for decades thereafter, voting in small towns split between the Republicans on the "right" side of the tracks and the working class and poor on the other. The most reliable new

Democratic following, however, could be found in the cities. Urban ethnics, especially if they were union members, learned to vote Democratic. The loyalty of black voters to the Republican Party was broken by New Deal programs. Before the 1936 election, a prominent black publisher counseled, "My friends, go turn Lincoln's picture to the wall. That debt has been paid in full."[44] In that election blacks gave Roosevelt 75 percent of their votes, and they have voted heavily for the Democrats ever since.

The Great Depression revolutionized the group composition of the party system in the United States. In addition to their traditional base in the South, the Democrats now claimed solid support among workers, blacks, and the poor in the northern cities, where large numbers of the working class and the poor were concentrated. Additionally, so many people benefited through New Deal programs that the electoral coalition supporting the party broadened sufficiently to ensure that the Democrats would become the ascendant national party for some time. In 1936, the Gallup poll found that 59 percent of farmers favored Roosevelt (Agricultural Adjustment Act, Farm Credit Administration, Farm Mortgage Corporation, abolition of the gold standard); 61 percent of white-collar workers (bank regulation, Federal Housing Administration, savings deposit insurance); 80 percent of organized labor (government recognition of collective bargaining, unemployment insurance, work relief); and 68 percent of people under age twenty-five (Civilian Conservation Corps, National Youth Administration). Among lower-income groups, 76 percent favored Roosevelt, compared with 60 percent of the middle class.[45] By contrast, upper-income groups identified overwhelmingly with the Republican Party, and they do to this day.

THE CITIES IN THE INTERGOVERNMENTAL SYSTEM

The depression years marked a turning point in American politics. Presidential candidates and a large number of senators and House members knew that they needed to campaign for the votes of people living in cities. To secure the votes of urban ethnics, they supported the New Deal's initiatives. These links were reinforced by another development: the forging of a direct relationship between the federal government and the cities. Three elements stand out as key factors in this development: (1) a fiscal and social crisis in the cities; (2) indifference by the states; and (3) the forging of an alliance among city officials for the purpose of securing a federal response to their problems.

Even before Roosevelt took office, the cities had exhausted their resources. In the 1920s, they had borrowed heavily to finance public improvements and capital construction. They were already seriously in debt when the onset of the depression confronted them with rising unemployment and poverty. Local officials could not avoid seeing the misery and want on their streets. Faced with a manifest emergency, they provided relief funds as rapidly as they could, but it was not enough. Municipal governments simply lacked the financial resources to cope with the emergency.

During the 1920s, counties and municipalities financed a multitude of new public improvement programs. The government activity represented a response to the automobile, to middle-class demands for improved public education, and to public demands for parks and recreational facilities. The auto imposed heavy new costs on local governments. Cities invested in traffic signals, police cars, garbage trucks, school buses, snowplows, roads, and bus and airline terminals. The cities increased spending for education, built new school buildings and public libraries, and invested heavily in improving parks and recreational facilities.

Local governments made heavier investments in these areas than did either the state or the federal governments. During the 1920s, counties and municipalities spent 55 percent to 60 percent of all public funds in the nation, and their total debts mounted to $9 billion.[46] From 1923 to 1927, while the states increased expenditures by 43 percent, spending by the largest 145 cities rose by 79 percent, and cities, of 100,000 or more increased their budgets by 82 percent.[47] In these latter cities expenditures for work relief and welfare shot up by 391 percent from 1923 to 1932; during the same period, states increased their relief and welfare budgets by only 63 percent. In the last year of the Hoover Administration, the thirteen cities with populations above 100,000 spent $53 million more than all the states combined for public welfare. Federal grants as a percentage of all public expenditures actually declined from 2 percent to 1.3 percent over the decade of the 1920s.[48] The thirteen biggest cities incurred 50 percent more debt in the 1920s, and many of them were hard-pressed, even at the beginning of the depression, to pay for government services and public improvements.[49]

The depression placed unprecedented responsibilities on city officials at the very time that fiscal resources were drying up. Cities could not expand tax revenues to keep pace with increased responsibilities. Two-thirds of the revenue for city budgets came from property taxes. As property values plummeted, property tax revenues fell by 20 percent from 1929 to 1933.[50] At the same time, the rate of tax delinquency increased from 10 percent to 26 percent in cities of over 50,000 in population.[51] Between 1931 and 1933, tax losses resulted in a reduction in the budgets of the largest thirteen cities from $1.8 to $1.6 billion.[52] State-imposed debt limitations did not allow cities to borrow for day-to-day services. Cities were allowed, in principle, to borrow for capital improvements, but this option soon evaporated. By 1932, because of their high debt loads, cities found it impossible to sell long-term bond issues to investors. In 1932 and 1933, many states and municipalities, including Mississippi, Montana, Buffalo, Philadelphia, Cleveland, and Toledo, were unable to market any bond issues at all.[53] Temporary loans with high interest rates replaced long-term notes.

When the cities financed public works programs to help the unemployed, their budgets quickly ran dry. Municipal governments lacked sufficient resources to treat the depression's symptoms, yet many mayors saw this as their principal mission. Detroit's experience revealed the impossibility of the task. In the fall of 1930, Frank Murphy won a surprise victory in a special mayoral election on a campaign promising unemployment relief.[54] His efforts to provide relief by expanding public jobs and welfare in Detroit attracted national attention. He appointed an unemployment committee, operated an employment bureau, sponsored public works projects, raised private donations for poor relief, and consulted with private firms about rehiring workers. Detroit did more than any other city for its unemployed, but its compassion was costly.

With over 40,000 families receiving relief and one-third of the work force unemployed, it was spending $2 million a month for relief in 1931, far more than second-place Boston.[55]

The burden soon brought financial disaster to the city, and by the spring of 1931, Detroit faced municipal bankruptcy. To avoid default on its debts and payroll, Murphy curtailed the city's health and recreational services and slashed the fire and police department budgets. Only an emergency bank loan allowed Murphy to meet the June 1931 payroll, but even this measure was insufficient. Under pressure from the New York banks that held most of Detroit's bonds, Murphy was forced to cut relief expenditures in half during 1932. Thousands of families were dropped from the relief rolls as it became obvious that Detroit could not single-handedly solve the local problems caused by a national economic calamity.

The mayors of other cities were learning the same lesson. Finally, their sense of desperation galvanized them to take action. In the spring of 1932, Murphy invited the mayors of the major cities to a conference. In June, representatives from twenty-nine cities met in Detroit with a single purpose in mind. Murphy stated the cities' case succinctly: "We have done everything humanly possible to do, and it has not been enough. The hour is at hand for the federal government to cooperate."[56] New York City's mayor likewise pleaded for assistance:

> The municipal government is the maternal, the intimate side of government; the side with heart. The Federal Government doesn't have to wander through darkened hallways of our hospitals, to witness the pain and suffering there. It doesn't have to stand in the bread lines, but the time has come when it must face the facts and its responsibility.
>
> We of the cities have diagnosed and thus far met the problem; but we have come to the end of our resources. It is now up to the Federal Government to assume its share. We can't cure conditions by ourselves.[57]

The mayors' demands for federal assistance marked a turning point. Historically, there had been no direct relationship between cities and the federal government. Many local officials felt it was illegitimate to ask the federal government for help, and others feared any aid, thinking it might cause their cities to lose their independence. Only a few months before, most of the mayors had declined to attend a similar mayors' conference suggested by the mayor of Milwaukee.[58] Desperation finally brought about a change of heart.

The situation was made worse by the fact that state governments refused to respond to the cities' plight. While municipal governments' expenditures for jobs and relief skyrocketed, the states sharply cut back. "As tax revenues dwindled and unemployment increased, economy in government became a magic word."[59] State officials were more concerned with balancing budgets than with alleviating human suffering. As state tax revenues declined, public works and construction programs were curtailed. In 1928, the states had spent $1.35 billion for public works projects, mainly in the form of road building, but this amount was reduced to $630 million by 1932 and to $290 million for the first eight months of 1933.[60] Because these budget cuts reduced public payrolls, they aggravated the unemployment crisis.

Per capita spending for highways and education fell only slightly from 1927 to 1932,[61] but in some states budgets were cut drastically. Tennessee, for example, failed to provide funds for its rural schools for much of 1931.[62] Beginning in 1932, several states slashed their budgets: Arizona by 35 percent; Texas, Illinois, and Vermont by 25 percent; South Carolina by 33 percent. State educational institutions, especially universities, were hard hit. During 1933, education budgets dropped by 40 percent in Maryland, 53 percent in Wyoming, and more than 30 percent in several other states.[63]

Relief spending by the states went up in the early years of the depression, from $1.00 per capita in 1927 to $3.50 four years later.[64] But the overall amount of welfare spending was small and failed to come close to what was needed. The overall statistics, in any case, masked a tremendous variation among the states. From mid-1931 to the end of 1932, welfare spending by the states increased from $500,000 to $100 million, but almost all of the money was provided by a few states, principally New York, New Jersey, and Pennsylvania. When the New Deal began, only eight states provided any money at all for relief.[65]

Local officials petitioned the states for help, and their pleas sounded increasingly desperate as the depression wore on.[66] Except for the very few states that provided relief payments to the unemployed, no response was forthcoming. State governments were slow to respond to the needs of their cities because their legislatures were controlled by rural representatives. In state after state, legislative districts were drawn up to ensure that rural counties would outvote cities in the state legislative chambers. In Georgia, each county was represented equally in the legislature, regardless of its population.[67] Louisiana likewise provided that each parish would have at least one representative in the state senate and house. Rhode Island applied this standard to each town.[68] Without exception, all the states made sure that representatives from rural areas would continue to hold legislative majorities, no matter how much a state's population became concentrated in the cities.

There were important political stakes in this pattern of underrepresentation. If cities were allowed to gain majorities in legislatures because of their growing populations, political alignments and party structures would fundamentally change. Incumbent rural legislators would lose their positions, and a shift in legislative power would inevitably result in new governmental policies. The persistent underrepresentation of urban areas resulted in indifference to urban problems. Traffic congestion, slums, inadequate park space, and smoke pollution did not interest rural and small-town legislators. Governors, too, tended to be insensitive to urban problems. Governors' and legislators' national conferences studiously ignored the depression. At the 1930 governors' conference in Salt Lake City, for example, the major topics of discussion included such items as the essentials of a model state constitution, the need for constitutional revisions, constitutional versus legislative home rule for cities, and the extent of legislative control of city governments.[69] The 1931 conference likewise ignored the economic crisis. In the face of such indifference, the cities had nowhere to go but to the federal government.

Urban leaders could not necessarily expect a favorable response from the federal government, either. Conditions in many rural areas were even worse than in the cities. There was grinding poverty in the Appalachian region and throughout the South; families lived in one-room hovels, children walked around with distended bellies caused by malnutrition, and some parents could not afford to clothe their children to send them to school. A drought from the Midwest to the Rockies turned much of the plains into a vast dust bowl; in the winter of 1934, New England's snow turned red from the huge billowing clouds of dust blowing from Texas, Kansas, and Oklahoma. Families left the ravaged land by the thousands. The experiences of those heading for California provided the grist for John Steinbeck's moving novel *The Grapes of Wrath*.

In addition to the compelling need in rural areas, Roosevelt and his advisers distrusted city politics and culture. Roosevelt's first public works program, the Civilian Conservation Corps, was based on his feeling that the moral character of unemployed youth in the cities would be improved by living in the country.[70] Roosevelt felt "small love for the city."[71] One of the president's closest advisers confessed that "since my graduate school days, I have always been able to excite myself more about the wrongs of farmers than those of urban workers."[72] In its first two years, the New Deal accomplished a comprehensive farm policy of guaranteed price supports, crop allotments to reduce supplies and increase prices, and federally guaranteed mortgages. By contrast, it produced its first program specifically for the cities, the Wagner-Steagall Housing Act, in 1937, and that program provided slum clearance and public housing on a very limited scale.

Despite the initial indifference to the plight of the cities, city officials were able to forge productive relationships with politicians and administrators in Washington, D.C. The New Deal's first relief and recovery programs were administered through the states, but federal programs were later enacted that put local officials in charge. The three largest public works programs—the Public Works Administration, Civilian Works Administration, and the Works Progress Administration—were administered by federal officials in cooperation with both state and local officials. The Federal Emergency Relief funds were channeled through the states, but local relief agencies actually administered the funds. In several cities, such as New York, Pittsburgh, and Kansas City, local Democratic machines found that the new federal resources allowed them to rebuild their strength.[73] Local officials found themselves testifying to congressional committees about programs that affected the cities. By 1934, a southern mayor observed, "Mayors are a familiar sight in Washington these days. Whether we like it or not, the destinies of our cities are clearly tied in with national politics."[74]

THE NEW DEAL LEGACY

The New Deal transformed American politics. Local officials learned to petition the federal government for help. This learning process took two forms. First, it became legitimate to seek federal assistance. Second, local officials formed an enduring urban lobby organized specifically to represent cities in the federal system. Through the United States Conference of Mayors (USCM), formed in 1932, mayors met annually to discuss their mutual problems. The USCM financed a permanent office in Washington to lobby for urban programs. Together with the International City Management Association (now the International City and County Management Association), the National Municipal League, the American Municipal League, and other organizations representing local public officials, cities developed the capacity to lobby federal administrators, Congress, and the White House.

The nation's first urban programs were implemented because of the new capacity to bring political pressure to bear on Washington. Through the 1937 Housing Act, the federal government undertook slum clearance and built public housing. In the late 1930s, federal policy makers expressed a concern about urban problems. The National Resources Committee, composed of federal administrators and experts appointed by the president, published a report in 1937 entitled *Our Cities: Their Role in the National Economy.*[75] The committee asserted that slums and urban blight threatened a hoped-for economic recovery and recommended federal action to improve the economic performance of cities. In 1941, the National Resources Planning Board prepared a report entitled *Action for Cities: A Guide for Community Planning.* The report recommended that cities devise local plans to combat blight and that the federal government pro-vide assistance for this purpose.[76] In 1944, a federally assisted highways bill was enacted; unlike previous highway legislation, this time the cities got their fair share of construction money. Five years later, in 1949, Congress passed a mas-sive program to build public housing and clear slums in the inner cities.

Between 1953 and 1961, when a Republican president, Dwight Eisenhower, served in the White House, urban interests were able to push through only one significant new program, the Interstate Highway Act of 1956, and only because nonurban interests wanted it too. From 1959 to 1961, President Eisenhower even eliminated public housing requests from the federal budget. But after the election of John F. Kennedy in 1960, the urban lobby found a receptive environment; it did not take long for them to exploit it. The New Deal experience had convinced city officials that they had a right to lobby for their interests in Washington.

NOTES

1. W. B. Munro, *The Government of American Cities* (New York: Macmillan, 1913), p. 27.
2. In the first significant suburban movement of the twentieth century, which lasted from the late 1890s to about 1914 (the outbreak of World War I), the rate of growth in the sub-urbs exceeded the rate of growth in many central cities, but the total population gains in those cities were much larger than the population gains in suburbs. Growth rates can be deceptive when expressed as percentage increases on a small original population base.
3. Samuel J. Eldersveld, "The Influence of Metropolitan Party Pluralities in Presidential Elections Since 1920: A Study of Twelve Key Cities," *American Political Science Review* 43, No. 6 (December 1949): 1200.
4. Francis E. Rourke, "Urbanism and the National Party Organizations," *Western Political Quarterly* 18 (March 1965): 150.
5. Wilfred E. Binkley, *American Political Parties: Their Natural History* (New York: Knopf, 1943), p. 285.
6. Ibid., pp. 285–286.

7. Robert A. Caro, *The Power Broker: Robert Moses and the Fall of New York* (New York: Knopf, 1974), pp. 118–119. John L. Sullivan was a well-known boxing champion.

8. William E. Leuchtenburg, *The Perils of Prosperity, 1914–1932* (Chicago: University of Chicago Press, 1958), pp. 213–214.

9. Robert K. Murray, *The 103rd Ballot: Democrats and the Disaster in Madison Square Garden* (New York: Harper and Row, 1976), p. 9.

10. Kenneth T. Jackson, *The Ku Klux Klan in the City, 1915–1930* (New York: Oxford University Press, 1967).

11. Murray, *The 103rd Ballot*, p. 7.

12. Ibid.

13. Kenneth Finegold, *Experts and Politicians: Reform Challenges to Machine Politics in New York, Cleveland, and Chicago* (Princeton, N.J.: Princeton University Press, 1995), p. 174.

14. Ibid., p. 103.

15. For good accounts of the 1924 convention, see Murray, *The 103rd Ballot*; Edmund A. Moore, *A Catholic Runs for President: The Campaign of 1928* (New York: Ronald Press, 1956); and Arthur M. Schlesinger Jr., *The Crisis of the Old Order, 1919–1933* (Boston: Houghton Mifflin, 1956).

16. John D. Hicks, *Republican Ascendancy, 1921–1933* (New York: Harper, 1960), p. 212.

17. John Kenneth Galbraith, *The Great Crash, 1929*, rev. ed. (Boston: Houghton Mifflin, 1979; first published 1961), p. 99.

18. Lester V. Chandler, *America's Greatest Depression, 1929–1941* (New York: HarperCollins, 1970), p. 5.

19. Ibid.

20. Ibid., p. 35.

21. William E. Leuchtenburg, *Franklin D. Roosevelt and the New Deal, 1932–1940* (New York: Harper and Row, 1963), p. 19.

22. Ibid., p. 1.

23. Chandler, *America's Greatest Depression*, p. 19.

24. Ibid., p. 57.

25. Arthur M. Schlesinger Jr., *The Coming of the New Deal* (Boston: Houghton Mifflin, 1957), p. 3.

26. Leuchtenburg, *Franklin D. Roosevelt*, p. 18.

27. Most relief was given by local public and private agencies. Though many states had programs for relief to designated categories of people—dependent children, the blind, and the disabled—few of these were actually funded.

28. Arthur E. Burns and Edward A. Williams, *Federal Work, Security, and Relief Programs* (New York: Da Capo Press, 1971), pp. 1–2; first published as *Research Monograph 24* (Washington, D.C.: Works Progress Administration, Division of Social Research, 1941).

29. James T. Patterson, *The New Deal and the States: Federalism in Transition* (Princeton, N.J.: Princeton University Press, 1969), p. 30.

30. Ibid., p. 15.

31. Ibid.

32. Mark I. Gelfand, *A Nation of Cities: The Federal Government and Urban America, 1933–1965*, Urban Life in America Series (New York: Oxford University Press, 1975), p. 35.

33. Leuchtenburg, *Franklin D. Roosevelt*, p. 11.

34. Inauguration day was changed to January by Amendment XX to the Constitution, ratified in 1933.

35. Leuchtenburg, *Franklin D. Roosevelt*, p. 39.

36. Ibid.

37. Ibid., p. 40.

38. For a thorough account of New Deal programs, see Burns and Williams, *Federal Work*.

39. Leuchtenburg, *Franklin D. Roosevelt*, p. 174.

40. Burns and Williams, *Federal Work*, pp. 29–36.

41. Leuchtenburg, *Franklin D. Roosevelt*, pp. 122–123.
42. Ibid., p. 133.
43. Josephine Chapin Brown, *Public Relief, 1929–1939* (New York: Holt, Rinehart and Winston, 1940), p. 249.
44. Quoted in Binkley, *American Political Parties*, p. 284.
45. Ibid., pp. 380–381.
46. Patterson, *The New Deal and the States*, p. 26.
47. Calculated from James A. Maxwell, *Federal Grants and the Business Cycle* (New York: National Bureau of Economic Research, 1952), p. 23, table 7.
48. Ibid.
49. Gelfand, *A Nation of Cities*, p. 49.
50. U.S. Department of Commerce, Bureau of the Census, *Historical Statistics on State and Local Government Revenues, 1902–1953* (Washington, D.C.: Government Printing Office, 1955), p. 12.
51. Maxwell, *Federal Grants and the Business Cycle*, p. 27, table 11.
52. Ibid., p. 24, table 8.
53. Ibid., p. 29.
54. Gelfand, *A Nation of Cities*, p. 31.
55. Ibid., p. 32.
56. Ibid., p. 36.
57. Ibid.
58. Ibid., p. 34.
59. Patterson, *The New Deal and the States*, p. 39.
60. Ibid., p. 40.
61. Ibid.
62. Ibid., p. 44.
63. Ibid., p. 47.
64. Ibid., p. 40.
65. Brown, *Public Relief*, pp. 72–96.
66. George C. S. Benson, *The New Centralization: A Study in Intergovernmental Relationships in the United States* (New York: Holt, Rinehart and Winston, 1941), pp. 104–105.
67. Robert G. Dixon, Jr., *Democratic Representation: Reapportionment in Law and Politics* (New York: Oxford University Press, 1968), p. 174.
68. Ibid., pp. 71–75, 80, 86–87.
69. Patterson, *The New Deal and the States*, p. 45.
70. Leuchtenburg, *Franklin D. Roosevelt*, p. 52.
71. Ibid., p. 136.
72. Guy Rexford Tugwell, quoted in ibid., p. 35.
73. Finegold, *Experts and Politicians*, p. 12; Bruce M. Stave, *The New Deal and the Last Hurrah: Pittsburgh Machine Politics* (Pittsburgh: University of Pittsburgh Press, 1970); Lyle W. Dorsett, *Franklin D. Roosevelt and the City Bosses* (Port Washington, N.Y.: Kennikat, 1977); Dorsett, *The Pendergast Machine* (New York: Oxford University Press, 1968).
74. Quoted in Gelfand, *A Nation of Cities*, p. 66.
75. U.S. Department of the Interior, National Resources Committee, Urbanism Committee, *Our Cities: Their Role in the National Economy* (Washington, D.C.: Government Printing Office, 1937).
76. Philip J. Funigiello, "City Planning in World War II: The Experience of the National Resources Planning Board," *Social Science Quarterly* 53 (June 1972): 91–104.

NATIONAL POLICY AND THE DIVIDED METROPOLIS

NATIONAL POLICIES AND URBAN DEVELOPMENT

By the end of World War II, there was a growing concern about the condition of the inner cities. The neglect of basic infrastructure brought about by the Great Depression and then by war could be seen in the decay of business districts, the dilapidation of older housing stock, and the tattered state of roads, bridges, parks, and urban amenities. These problems seemed all the more urgent because of overcrowding. The wartime boom had brought a crush of new residents to cities, but new housing was hard to find. At first, the new suburban subdivisions seemed like a welcome safety valve, but soon they were perceived as threats to the viability of the central cities. Too much seemed to be at stake to allow the older cities to continue an exorable slide into decay.

A broad coalition of leaders from both political parties supported ambitious urban renewal and housing legislation to renew the cities and provide housing for inner-city residents. Through the 1949 Housing Act and subsequent legislation, the federal programs made available massive volumes of public funding for America's cities. These programs also leveraged an astonishing volume of private investment—$35.8 billion by 1968.[1] The public housing program, also funded through the 1949 legislation, built much-needed housing in the cities, which poor blacks and whites alike applied for, though waiting lists were long.

But the promises of help for the inner cities and their residents turned out to be hollow. Even while urban renewal funds were being used to bulldoze neighborhoods and displace their residents, and while public housing projects became segregated ghettos, other federal programs were devoting even larger flows of funds to the building of suburban housing tracts and highways needed to take middle-class families to them. The opposing policies pursued by the federal government ended up promoting the segregation of inner-city black from suburban white and middle class from poor. The result was a disaster of tragic consequences and national proportions.

From the 1930s through much of the 1960s, the federal government helped finance a suburban housing boom that was effectively put off limits to blacks. Federal administrators worked hand in hand with local developers and financial institutions to enforce restrictive covenants that prohibited property from being sold to blacks, and they also made it virtually impossible for blacks to secure the federally subsidized mortgages that fueled the suburban boom. In the cities, nationally funded slum clearance and public housing policies sharply reduced the supply of housing available to African American homebuyers and renters. Because they were denied access to the suburbs, many low-income blacks were forced into the high-rise public housing projects being constructed through federal funding, and both low-income and middle-class blacks were forced into an intense competition for the older housing left available in urban neighborhoods. Though the federal government began to change policies in the 1960s, the changes were too little and too late. By then, the metropolitan pattern of rigid racial segregation was written in cement.

The extreme racial segregation that came to characterize America's urban areas was also encouraged by the federally assisted highway programs, which cut broad swaths through inner-city neighborhoods all through the 1950s and 1960s—the same decades when the suburbs were booming. The patterns of residential segregation that separated the central cities from the suburbs began to differentiate inner-ring suburbs from the newer subdivisions spreading inexorably outward. Initially, the federal government's policies were viewed as benign in their racial impact or as positively beneficial to poor and affluent, black and white alike. Over time, however, urban renewal and public housing— the two programs meant to help the cities and their residents—became thoroughly discredited. By contrast, the programs favoring the suburbs continued to operate, and in considerable measure they still contribute to the racially segregated residential patterns of today's urban areas.[2]

THE CONCERN ABOUT HOUSING AND SLUMS

The first positive federal response to the problems of urban America came in 1892, when Congress appropriated $20,000 to investigate slum conditions in cities with more than 200,000 people.[3] In his subsequent report to the Congress, the Commissioner of Labor noted, among other observations, that all of the nation's big cities contained block after block of rundown tenement districts that packed immigrants together into often unsafe and unsanitary conditions. The commissioner made much of the fact that these areas had a higher incidence of arrests and saloons than anywhere else in the country.

Federal assistance for the construction of urban housing can be traced to the entry of the United States into World War I. In 1918, Congress authorized direct federal loans to local realty companies.[4] At a cost of $69.3 million, eight hotels, nineteen dormitories, 1,100 apartment units, and approximately 9,000 houses were constructed to house wartime shipyard workers in twenty-seven cities and towns.[5] Later in the same year, Congress approved the nation's first public housing

OUT TAKE

SOME URBAN POLICIES REINFORCED DISCRIMINATION

I t is a tragic irony that the urban programs initiated after World War II contributed to one of the most enduring problems of American culture—racial segregation and discrimination. While urban renewal clearance programs bulldozed slum housing, public housing projects segregated blacks more than ever. Meanwhile, the white middle class was paid, in essence, to move to the suburbs, and their commute to their jobs in the center city was eased by expensive new freeway systems. The fact that national programs worked at cross-purposes for questionable results left a legacy of distrust that lingers to this day.

The federal programs that cleared slums in the cities and built miles of tract housing in the suburbs powerfully shaped metropolitan development. For decades, millions of white middle-class families were able to secure loans guaranteed by the federal government. It allowed them to move into new suburban developments, where housing values appreciated. For white middle-class America in the postwar period, the home became the principal source of capital worth and savings, money that could be invested in a child's education, in a bigger or newer house, or saved for retirement. Until the late 1940s, federal policy excluded African Americans from federal home loan programs, and it took until the late 1960s, when open-housing legislation was passed, for African American families to be able to fully enter the real estate market. If blacks had been able to buy homes wherever they wanted to much sooner, they also would have been able to invest in the future. Most African Americans were denied this crucial means of life savings and upward mobility.

Despite significant progress in breaking down racial barriers in recent decades, family wealth remains as one of the enduring differences between black and white American families. In 1995, the median net worth (assets minus debts) for white households was $49,030, compared to $7,073 for black households—a ratio of 1 to 7.[6] The median net financial assets (cash that is immediately available) in the early 1990s was $6,999 for white families but *zero* for black families.[7] This gap, which measures the ability of families to pass on life chances from generation to generation, was created in substantial measure by the federal government via its housing policies. Needless to say, it is unlikely that policies will soon be adopted to reverse the effects of these past policies.

program, designed to accommodate defense plant workers who needed housing near wartime factories. The U.S. Housing Corporation was created to manage the program. In the brief three months of the program's existence, the Housing Corporation built about 6,000 single-family dwellings, plus accommodations for 7,200 single men, on 140 project sites scattered around the country.[8] At the conclusion of the war, all of these federally owned housing units were sold to private owners, and the government removed itself from the housing business.

The next federal intervention into housing came during the Great Depression. Even after the prosperous twenties, all the nation's cities contained run-down business districts and residential slums. As the depression wore on, the situation deteriorated rapidly; landlords and owners invested little or no money in repairs and renovation, and the construction of new housing slowed to a crawl. The apparent solutions to the problems of housing and slums lay beyond the financial capacity of local governments. The slums that plagued the nation's cities slowly became defined as a national problem, and local officials and business elites who were concerned about deteriorating business and residential districts looked to the national government for help.

In 1932, the last year of Herbert Hoover's presidency, Congress created the Reconstruction Finance Corporation (RFC) and authorized it to extend loans to private developers for the construction of low-income housing in slum areas.[9] Only two projects were actually ever undertaken, with over 98 percent of the money spent in three slum blocks of Manhattan to construct Knickerbocker Village, with its 1,573 apartments.[10] This program had two contradictory purposes. On the one hand, it was supposed to help revive the construction industry; on the other hand, it was supposed to be a means of increasing the supply of low-income housing in New York. In the case of Knickerbocker Village, the first goal won out. Eighty-two percent of the slum families who initially moved into the apartments were soon forced to move back to the slums they had left because of the escalating rents charged by the owners.[11]

Franklin D. Roosevelt introduced a great number of national programs designed to stimulate the economy and end the depression. One of the first of these, the National Industrial Recovery Act of 1933, included a minor provision authorizing "construction, reconstruction, alteration, or repair, under public regulation or control, of low-rent housing and slum clearance projects."[12] The Housing Division of the Public Works Administration (PWA) was charged with implementing this provision. At first, the PWA tried to entice private developers into constructing low-income housing by offering them low-interest federal loans. This strategy conformed with one of the major purposes of the program, which was "to deal with the unemployment situation by giving employment to workers . . . [and] to demonstrate to private builders the practicability of large-scale community planning."[13] But contractors and home builders did not find low-interest loans sufficiently attractive, and only seven projects ever met specifications and were approved. As a result, the PWA decided to bypass the housing industry altogether and finance and construct its own federally owned housing. The U.S. Emergency Housing Corporation was created for this purpose in 1933, and it claimed the right of eminent domain to force the sale of slum property for clearance and construction.

Federal court decisions in Kentucky and Michigan stopped federal administrators from using eminent domain to take over slum land for clearance,[14] so they tried another tack. The Emergency Housing Corporation decided to make low-income housing grants to local public housing authorities. Local authorities could be chartered by the states, and previous court cases made it clear that the states could use eminent domain to accomplish a variety of public purposes. With the offer of federal money dangled before them, city officials lobbied their state legislatures to allow them to create local housing authorities to receive the funds. By the end of the PWA public housing program in 1937, twenty-nine states had passed enabling legislation allowing local governments to create and operate local public housing authorities, and forty-six local housing agencies had come into existence.[15] These authorities built almost 22,000 public low-income housing units in thirty-seven cities.[16]

For all the effort to get the PWA program off the ground, the eventual results were mixed. More low-income units were torn down through slum clearance than were ever built. Local public housing authorities were closely tied to the housing industry in their communities, with the result that a substantial proportion of PWA funds was used to help owners sell slum properties to local housing authorities at inflated prices.[17] These properties were then slated for clearance, even though no new housing units were planned to replace them. In all these respects, the PWA experience provided a warning for the future: Program goals were easily subverted if local communities were allowed to make all of the consequential decisions. Unfortunately, the warning was ignored.

The PWA experience provided the administrative model for future housing programs. It was accepted that if federal grants were made available for public housing in the future, local public housing agencies would become the recipients of the funds and federal agencies would not try to build public housing units themselves. The Public Housing Act of 1937 (also called the Wagner-Steagall Public Housing Act after the names of its legislative sponsors) succeeded the PWA program. The act adopted the principle that housing programs would be implemented through federal grants-in-aid to local housing authorities. Under the legislation, public housing would be built and administered by local agencies, not by the federal government, and private realtors and contractors would handle land sales and construction. Its stated purposes were:

> To provide financial assistance to the states and political subdivisions thereof for the elimination of unsafe and unsanitary housing conditions, for the eradication of slums, for the provision of decent, safe, and sanitary dwellings for families of low income and for the reduction of unemployment and the stimulation of business activity, to create a United States Housing Authority, and for other purposes.[18]

The Public Housing Act of 1937 was "designed to serve the needs of those of low income who otherwise would not be able to afford decent, safe, and sanitary dwellings."[19] However, the absence of substantial profits for realtors, builders, and banks for constructing public housing projects meant that they steadfastly opposed the program. As far as they were concerned, government-owned housing competed with the private housing market, and its only redeeming virtue was that public housing provided jobs in the construction industry. But this benefit failed to outweigh the unpopularity of providing housing subsidies to the bottom third of the population. As explained by the president of the National Association of Real Estate Boards, the housing industry's philosophy was that low-income housing should become available through a filter-down process:

> Housing should remain a matter of private enterprise and private ownership. It is contrary to the genius of the American people and the ideals they have established that government become landlord to its citizens. There is a sound logic in the continuance of the practice under which those who have the initiative and the will to save acquire better living facilities and yield their former quarters at modest rents to the group below.[20]

Senator Robert F. Wagner of New York, one of the cosponsors of the 1937 housing bill, defended the legislation by pointing out that it was not intended as a program that would interfere with the private housing market:

> The object of public housing in a nutshell, is not to invade the field of home building for the middle class or the well-to-do which has been the only profitable area for private enterprise in the past. Nor is it even to exclude private enterprise from major participation in a low-cost housing program. It is merely to supplement what private industry will do, by subsidies which will make up the difference between what the poor can afford to pay and what is necessary to assure decent living quarters.[21]

To make sure that middle-class families could not opt out of the private housing market by moving into public housing, the legislation contained specific limitations on the costs and quality of rental units and a restriction that occupancy be strictly limited to low-income families. A requirement was also added that the number of new housing units constructed could not exceed the number of slum dwellings torn down. [22]

The U.S. Housing Administration (USHA) was authorized by the 1937 act to extend low-interest loans to local public housing agencies. The loans could cover up to 100 percent of the cost of financing slum clearance and the construction of low-income housing units. The USHA was also authorized to make grants and annual subsidies to local housing agencies for the operation and maintenance of housing units after they were built. The USHA and its successor agencies, the Federal Public Housing Authority (1942 to 1946) and the Public Housing Administration (1946 to the present), completed a total of 169,451 low-income public housing units under the authority of the 1937 housing act.[23]

World War II was the third national emergency (the others were World War I and the depression) recognized by Congress as requiring the production of publicly built and financed housing. In addition to 50,000 units built during the war through the 1937 housing act authorizations, two million more housing units were provided through temporary and emergency programs to house workers who streamed into cities to take jobs in defense industry plants. Of these, around one million units were privately built with federal financial assistance.[24] Another million units were completed under programs that left ownership in the hands of the federal government. As soon as the war was over, these government-owned units were sold on the private market.

THE STRUGGLE OVER PUBLIC HOUSING

The concerns about inner-city slums that had been expressed in the depression years were voiced again following World War II. A broad coalition of interests pressed for congressional action. Local public officials and business leaders were alarmed by the condition of downtown business districts and nearby residential areas. Public housing administrators, labor unions, social workers, and liberal Democrats were concerned about the plight of the poor and argued that slum residents had a moral right to adequate housing. In addition, they said, slums bred disease, crime, and delinquency and were therefore detrimental to the moral fiber and social fabric of the city. It was noted, for example, that though Cleveland's slum areas contained only 3 percent of the city's population, they accounted for 8 percent of the juvenile delinquency arrests and 21 percent of the city's murders in 1932.[25] Improving the physical environment of slum residents, it was argued, was a good thing to do not only because it gave poor people immediate aid but also because it would help families and individuals living in the slums to begin improving their lives, thus lowering the level of social disorder.

Realtors, developers, financial institutions, and local business elites had their own reasons for favoring slum clearance. They were not concerned so much about the conditions of life for slum dwellers as for their own real estate investments. Dilapidated commercial and residential areas, they said, threatened the economic vitality of the central cities. They reasoned that falling rents and increasing vacancy rates formed a downward spiral with less and less maintenance in slum areas. The powerful U.S. Savings and Loan League voiced support for the redevelopment of blighted areas: "Our people have studied the problem of slum clearance for some years and agree that it is an appropriate field for public action . . . we think it appropriate for . . . land assembly [to proceed] in the slum areas of our cities."[26]

Even the National Association of Real Estate Boards (NAREB) favored urban redevelopment, as long as it was implemented through private developers and involved slum clearance but not public housing.[27] NAREB spearheaded the lobbying against federally subsidized public housing. Although its headquarters were in Chicago, NAREB maintained a well-staffed office in the nation's capital—known as the Realtors' Washington Office—from which it exerted pressure on Congress and federal administrators. The executive vice president of the association was Herbert U. Nelson, who was fond of calling his opponents communists and subversives. Throughout the 1940s, though NAREB and its allies promoted federally subsidized urban redevelopment, the issue remained subordinated to their venomous opposition to public housing programs. This unwavering opposition derived its force from Nelson's ideological stand against the evils of "socialism"—defined as publicly subsidized housing—and was supported by the real estate industry's interest in preventing government competition with private landlords.[28] The association pressed its opposition to public housing all across the country—on Capitol Hill, in state houses, in city halls, and in communities and neighborhoods. Between 1939 and 1949, it was instrumental in stalling congressional legislation. The furious hatred NAREB officials expressed about public housing led them to adamantly oppose the 1949 housing act, even though this legislation also made federal funds available for slum clearance, which NAREB favored.

The U.S. Savings and Loan League was the second most powerful housing industry group. In 1949, the league represented 3,700 associations, which included in their membership most of the nation's savings and loan institutions. These financial institutions issued long-term mortgage loans for the construction and purchase of homes. Although originally established to serve the working class as an alternative to conventional banking institutions, over the years savings and loan institutions acquired a middle- and upper-class bias in their policies. Like the realtors, the savings and loan industry opposed any governmental action that competed with privately owned housing.

The National Association of Home Builders (NAHB), which represented approximately 16,500 companies in 1949, weighed in and was joined by an array of industry, trade, and financial associations that also opposed public housing, including the U.S. Chamber of Commerce, the Mortgage Bankers Association of America, the Producers Council, the National Economic Council, and the National Association of Retail Lumber Dealers.[29]

Though a broad coalition of groups favored public housing, perhaps the most influential among them was the National Public Housing Conference. Formed during the early years of the depression, this group became a kind of brain trust for public housing policy. It had been largely responsible for the research and staff work that went into the 1937 housing act. Unlike the real estate lobbies, it was not a federation of local groups, nor was it a mass-based organization. It was an elite group of individuals interested in housing policy, and it included some of the more influential local housing administrators, government officials, and academic experts on housing problems and policies. The Public Housing Conference maintained close connections with the federal government's housing administrators and thus was able to partially offset the housing industry's opposition to public housing.

Organized labor provided decisive support for public housing. The American Federation of Labor and the Congress of Industrial Organizations maintained housing committees and participated in the Washington-based Labor Housing Conference. Of all the pro–public housing groups, only the unions carried the political clout attendant to mass-based organizations. Organized labor led the way in criticizing the real estate industry's redevelopment proposals. A booklet of the period published by the United Auto Workers accused realtors and developers of promoting their own narrow economic interests under the cover of slum clearance:

> Climbing on the "slum clearance" bandwagon, they [the real estate and building trade associations] are trying to hoodwink the public into buying city slum areas at a high price and turning such areas over to them at a fraction of such cost to the public. Not a word of "subsidy" here. Not a word of re-housing the families who now live in the slums.[30]

The National Association of Housing Officials (NAHO) also attacked the urban redevelopment proposal advocated by the real estate industry. This group was formed during the depression and was responsible for educating supporters of public housing through its publication, the *Journal of Housing*. Reflecting the basic values that drew the pro–public housing coalition together, NAHO insisted that the goal of providing adequate housing was far more important than urban economic development itself.

Local government officials and the organizations representing them were interested in federal subsidies in any form, and therefore they lobbied for both slum clearance and public housing. The U.S. Conference of Mayors, the National

League of Cities, and the American Municipal Association all lined up behind a program of federally subsidized development. They were instrumental in knitting together a coalition sufficiently broad that the legislation before Congress was not be sabotaged by bickering among the various groups.

Perhaps the best indicator of the unlikely nature of the political alliance that supported the 1949 housing act is to be found in its unofficial title—the Wagner-Ellender-Taft Act. The three senators whose names were identified with the legislation spanned the spectrum of American political philosophy. The conservative Republican presidential aspirant, Robert A. Taft of Ohio, the New Deal big-city liberal, Robert F. Wagner of New York, and the segregationist southern Democrat, Allen J. Ellender of Louisiana, united to see their bill through five rounds of hearings, four years of controversy, three redrafts, and two changes of leadership in Congress.

The housing bill was introduced in the Senate (S. 1592) in 1945 and approved there in April 1946, only to die in the House Banking and Currency Committee, where it was killed by "very potent private lobby groups" opposed to public housing.[31] The bill (now S. 866) again passed the Senate in April 1948, despite the fact that as a result of the 1946 elections the Republicans had become the majority party in that chamber. Again, the bill was killed in the House. The general elections of 1948 returned Democratic majorities to both houses of Congress. Finally, the Housing Act passed in the spring of 1949. Despite intensive lobbying efforts by the realtors and their allies, the public housing title was retained by a razor-thin five-vote margin, and the entire bill was then passed by a bipartisan majority of northern Democrats, urban Republicans, and a few southern Democrats.[32]

In the Housing Act of 1949, Congress declared a national commitment to rebuild the cities, eliminate slums and blight, and provide decent housing for the nation's citizens. The preamble to the act, titled a "Declaration of National Housing Policy," made a sweeping statement about the need for a housing program:

> The general welfare and security of the Nation and the health and living standards of its people require housing production and relating community development sufficient to remedy the serious housing shortage, eliminate substandard and other inadequate housing through the clearance of slums and blighted areas, and the realization as soon as feasible of the goal of a decent home and suitable living environment for every American family.[33]

The housing industry got most of what it wanted in the housing bill, but to win federal subsidies for slum clearance, it was forced to accept public housing. The housing bill received the endorsement of key business, real estate, and housing interests because of the key provisions that allowed local authorities to supervise and profit from redevelopment. Title I of the act empowered the Housing and Home Finance Agency (HHFA) to assist local efforts at blight and slum removal. Through this agency, the federal government offered grants-in-aid to help local urban renewal agencies absorb the cost of the write-down on land that had been cleared of slum buildings. The write-down was the difference between the local agency's cost of assembling and clearing the site and a negotiated below-market price subsequently paid for the land by private developers.

In addition to the money authorized for the write-down subsidies, HHFA was authorized to extend loans to local urban renewal or public housing agencies for land assembly and site clearance. The act gave private developers preference over local governments in redeveloping the clearance sites. Tenants and slum dwellers displaced by renewal programs were supposed to be supplied with "decent, safe and sanitary dwellings." The redevelopment effort was required to be "predominantly residential" in character. Amendments to the legislation, adopted in 1954, allowed communities to use 10 percent of project funds for nonresidential, commercial revitalization. In 1960, this proportion was raised to 30 percent.

Title III, Low-Rent Public Housing, authorized (but did not appropriate money for) the production of 810,000 government-subsidized housing units over the next six years. This amounted to 10 percent of the estimated national need for new low-cost dwellings. Occupancy preferences were given for veterans and families displaced by Title I (clearance) activities. Per-room and per-unit cost limitations were imposed to prevent "extravagance and unnecessary" amenities. Rent levels and tenant eligibility requirements were regulated to minimize competition with the private housing market and to ensure that public housing benefited only the neediest families.

URBAN RENEWAL AND ITS PROBLEMS

Local political and economic elites were far more concerned about the economic decline of central business districts (CBDs) than they were about slum residents. Business leaders and politicians were convinced that slums were responsible for the steady decline in downtown property values and retail activity. Right from the beginning, low-income housing was sacrificed to commercial development, a sacrifice made possible by the way federal administrators interpreted the legislation. Any renewal project that allocated 51 percent or more of its funds to housing was classified by federal administrators as a "100 percent housing" project. By applying such misleading definitions or by ignoring guidelines altogether, local authorities were able to allocate as much as two-thirds of their funds for commercial projects, despite the "predominantly residential" language contained in the legislation.

Public housing immediately ran into trouble. In the abstract, housing for low-income people might seem worthwhile, but few local politicians felt they could afford to tolerate it in their own neighborhoods. Site selection was of paramount concern, for example, to Chicago's politicians in the 1950s.[34] The Chicago experience was duplicated in cities across the country. Public housing was not supported by strong grassroots support in local communities; in contrast, local chapters of NAREB organized opposition to public housing projects in city after city. In vitriolic campaigns, the opponents of subsidized housing played on fears that public housing might be used to promote racial integration. Between 1949 and the end of 1952, public housing programs were rejected by referenda, many of them sponsored by local chapters of NAREB, in Akron,

Houston, Los Angeles, and almost forty other cities. Social and political realities at the local level made public housing a volatile issue. Local officials were acutely aware that "there could hardly be many votes to be gained in championing the cause—and perhaps a great many lost."[35]

By contrast, slum clearance and economic redevelopment added up to good politics. Seizing on redevelopment as a way to secure federal funds, enterprising mayors could simultaneously advance their political fortunes and improve the public image of the city. To implement big clearance and redevelopment projects, an alliance had to be forged between the mayor and other local officials on the one hand and the business community on the other. In most cities, the alliance was organized by corporate executives, but there were other crucial participants as well. Real estate and merchant interests in central business districts, metropolitan newspapers, and the construction trades unions lent their support. For many years, this political alliance constituted a "new convergence of power" that completely dominated the politics of most large cities.[36]

By the end of the 1950s, virtually every city in the United States had put together an urban renewal coalition. Richard J. Daley, first elected mayor of Chicago in 1953, rebuilt the Democratic machine in that city by aggressively launching the revitalization of Chicago's downtown Loop and lakefront. By contrast, Boston's machine met its demise at the hands of a political coalition dedicated to renewing the city. The candidate selected by the business-sponsored New Boston Committee defeated long-time machine boss James Michael Curley in the 1951 mayoral race, then backed the massive clearance of Boston's Italian West End and the construction of a large government center. Ultimately, Boston's renewal program took 10 percent of the city's land area.[37] In 1950, St. Louis's mayor, Joseph Darst, received widespread national publicity when his city became the nation's first to secure federal funding for a massive urban renewal program. Raymond Tucker, who replaced him in 1953, was even more aggressive in pushing clearance projects. A former St. Louis mayor recalled that renewal united political and business leaders behind a common cause:

> About a year ago, a group of distinguished citizens of our community were called into the Mayor's office and there charged by Mayor Darst with the responsibility of giving leadership to a program. . . . It was suggested that an urban redevelopment corporation be organized. There was much fine publicity on the part of the metropolitan press—they not only gave considerable space but they also subscribed to the extent of better than a quarter of a million dollars to the debentures and stock of that corporation. So, we salute the press on this occasion. I should add that many other fine business institutions, 69 in number, subscribed a total in excess of $2,000,000 toward the capital structure of the corporation. It is a distinguished list. There's the May Department Stores, Stix, Baer and Fuller, Scruggs, Vandervoort and Barney, the Anheuser Busch Company, Ely Walker Company, the Falstaff Company, the First National Bank, . . . and others.[38]

A similar alliance came together in New Haven, Connecticut, where the young Democrat Richard Lee hung his mayoral aspirations and his political future on the prospect of a successful urban redevelopment program. He won the 1952 election and several terms thereafter by leading a broad coalition that sponsored federally funded redevelopment. Lee's political capital derived from an alliance between government officials and local notables, particularly business leaders. It took shape in the formation of the Citizen's Action Committee (CAC), an advisory board required by the federal legislation, which included "businessmen concerned with traffic and retail sales, trade union leaders concerned with employment and local prosperity," and "political liberals concerned with slums, housing, and race relations." This group was characterized by Mayor Lee as the political alliance that ran New Haven. He described it as

> the biggest set of muscles in New Haven. . . . They're muscular because they control wealth, they're muscular because they control industries, represent banks. They're muscular because they head up labor. They're muscular because they represent the intellectual portions of the community. They're muscular because they're articulate, because they're respectable, because of their financial power, and because of the accumulation of prestige they have built up over the years as individuals in all kinds of causes.[39]

The programs financed by the 1949 housing act were perfect vehicles for mayors who wished to secure their personal political futures. Mayors and business leaders tended to share the view that the economic fortunes of their cities depended on the health of the central business district. The flight of the middle class to the suburbs was seriously undermining the economic viability of inner cities. Since the central business district was the center of activity where the local business establishment held heavy real estate and business investments, it was only logical that businesses would seek to protect their investments through revitalization of their immediate environment. The need for political visibility and campaign contributions from wealthy donors ensured that elected officials would favor downtown sites. Those areas were generally the oldest in the cities and were therefore easily designated as officially "blighted" by the local urban renewal authority, the first step in a process that led to condemning and clearing property.

The members of the renewal coalition needed one another. Local officials needed the investment capital and the public prestige the business community possessed. The business community in turn depended on the resources of the public sector. Governmental authority was a necessary ingredient for a successful redevelopment effort. Public authority was, in the first instance, called on to apply for federal funds through an officially constituted urban renewal agency. The government's power of eminent domain, which allowed it to condemn "blighted" property for a "higher" public use, was crucial for land assembly, because individual property owners could not otherwise be compelled to sell. Finally, the unique ability of local renewal agencies to receive the necessary write-down subsidies and loans from the federal government made local officials and agencies indispensable to business leaders who wanted urban redevelopment. "This strange coalition"[40] was thus a mutually reinforcing alliance of formidable power.

THE URBAN RENEWAL STEAMROLLER

As a result of their successful efforts to secure federal backing for urban renewal, the national political coalition that pushed the urban renewal program through Congress "engineered a massive allocation of private and social resources" in the cities.[41] The public funds invested in write-down subsidies and clearance leveraged investments by developers, corporations, and local businesses. By 1968, $35.8 billion had been committed by private institutions in 524 renewal projects across the nation.[42] From 1953 to 1986, when the last money left in the pipeline was finally exhausted, over $13 billion in direct federal spending had been committed to urban renewal.[43] In addition, the huge federal expenditures on the interstate highway program, funded through the National Defense Highway Act of 1956, provided hundreds of thousands of jobs and considerable profits to construction firms building highways through urban neighborhoods.

The clearance of neighborhoods associated with urban renewal and highway building soon ignited resistance and controversy. While business leaders talked glibly about benefiting all the residents of the city through the provision of jobs and increases in revenues, it was painfully apparent that viable neighborhoods were often destroyed in the process. In Boston, block after block of well-kept bungalows and row houses, grocery stores, barber shops, bakeries, and taverns—all the elements making up historic, safe, thriving Italian neighborhoods in Boston's West End—were leveled. *Blight* was such a loose term that it could be, and often was, applied even to healthy neighborhoods.[44] Because of this, a great deal of community protest was directed at the massive destruction of neighborhoods caused by urban renewal and highway construction projects. According to one scholar, "development issues . . . dominated the neighborhoods" in the 1950s and 1960s in the four cities he studied.[45]

Considering the intensity and frequency of protest, it seems surprising that neighborhoods won so few victories. The reason for this poor record was that the groups that opposed renewal were small and often divided from one another on the basis of race and ethnicity. Neighborhoods acted as interest groups protecting their own turf. The various neighborhoods were so diverse that it was difficult for them to form stable alliances with one another. As a consequence, the renewal coalition usually outlasted protests originating from a single neighborhood. By astutely selecting renewal and redevelopment sites, urban renewal administrators could pursue a politics of divide and conquer.

Atlanta provides an excellent example of this process. Beginning in 1952, Atlanta's Metropolitan Planning Commission became concerned about the movement of blacks into neighborhoods close to the central business district. In its report of that year, entitled *Up Ahead,* the commission maintained that "from the viewpoint of planning the wise thing is to find outlying areas to be developed for new colored housing." The commission recommended "public policies to reduce existing densities, wipe out blighted areas, improve the racial pattern of population distribution, and make the best possible use of central planned areas."[46] The actual goal, thinly disguised by this rhetoric, was to move blacks into areas farther from the downtown area and to secure land near the CBD for redevelopment.

Atlanta's organization of big corporations, the Central Atlanta Improvement Association, backed faithfully by the white-owned newspapers, energetically promoted clearance. Special care was taken to obtain the backing of the Chamber of Commerce, which represented smaller businesses. The Atlanta Real Estate Board was brought on board by promises that renewal would help maintain segregated housing patterns and that no public housing would be constructed on urban renewal land. Support from some leaders of the black community was obtained by promises to make land available for the construction of black housing subdivisions farther from the CBD and by a commitment to build single-family, owner-occupied housing for blacks, which was to be subsidized by federal funds available under Section 221 of the 1949 housing act. Years after the area was cleared, downtown Atlanta was still undergoing massive clearance and reconstruction, and the historic downtown had been almost entirely replaced by a huge enclosed mall called the Peachtree Center.

The local renewal coalitions born in the 1950s used their potent political muscle to crush opponents. Though almost any city could be used as an example, San Francisco's single-minded pursuit of downtown renewal is especially revealing.[47] In 1953, the San Francisco Board of Supervisors approved a plan to clear several blocks of land adjacent to the financial district and south of Market Street. This area, with its market stalls, narrow passageways, and constant bustling activity, concerned business and political leaders, who worried about the impact it might have on the future downtown, which they envisioned as an expanding agglomeration of corporate, cultural, and tourist facilities. By the late 1950s, a plan for redevelopment had taken shape. The city planned to build a huge sports arena and convention center on the site, to be named the Yerba Buena Center. It was thought that Yerba Buena would act as a magnet for the expansion of the city's financial center.

It was easy for the mayor and urban renewal administrators to build support for such a concept. San Francisco contained scores of corporate giants, including Standard Oil of California, Southern Pacific, Transamerica Corporation, Levi Strauss, Crown Zellerbach, Del Monte, Pacific Telephone and Telegraph, Bethlehem Steel, and Pacific Gas and Electric. Among the many financial institutions located in downtown San Francisco were Bank of America, Wells Fargo, Crocker National Bank, Bank of California, Aetna Life, John Hancock, and Hartford Insurance. During the 1960s, the buildings that housed these institutions changed San Francisco's skyline. Between 1960 and 1972, twenty-three high-rises were constructed in downtown San Francisco.[48]

The director of the San Francisco Redevelopment Agency, M. Justin Herman, became the "chief architect, major spokesman, and operations commander" for the massive renewal project. Under his leadership, the redevelopment agency hired several hundred professionals and dozens of consultants and applied for millions of dollars in federal urban renewal subsidies. Herman believed in his mission so zealously that he interpreted any criticism of his project as an attempt by parochial interests to stand in the way of progress. In 1970, he was quoted as saying, "This land is too valuable to permit poor people to park on it."[49] He was cited in a major publication in 1970 as "one of the men responsible for getting urban renewal" renamed "the federal bulldozer" and "Negro removal":

> He was absolutely confident that he was doing what the power structure wanted insofar as the poor and the minorities were concerned. That's why San Francisco has mostly luxury housing and business district projects—that's what white, middle-class planners and businessmen envision as ideal urban renewal. . . . Also, with Herman in control, San Francisco's renewal never got slowed down by all this citizen participation business that tormented other cities.[50]

Federal administrators turned a blind eye to the fact that the Yerba Buena Center project was being planned with no thought to building replacement housing for the people who lived in the clearance area. During the summer of 1969, the residents living in the proposed clearance area challenged the project in federal court, arguing that it violated the 1949 housing act's requirement that residents in clearance projects be relocated into safe and suitable housing. The judge who heard the case concluded that the secretary of the Department of Housing and Urban Development "had not been provided with any creditable evidence at all" in regard to the redevelopment agency's plan to relocate residents.[51] Temporarily stopped in its tracks, the redevelopment agency eventually agreed to increase the hotel tax in San Francisco in order to finance the construction of low-income housing for tenants who would be displaced by the Yerba Buena Center. Court battles over this plan, however, plus the escalating costs of the Center, eventually doomed it, and it was not built.

Justin Herman's attitudes toward the poor were generally shared by urban renewal administrators and their allies. In the core areas of the cities, poverty and race were inextricably linked; as a result, most urban renewal programs had racial (or racist) overtones. The blacks who moved to the cities in the twentieth century were housed in the most rundown areas of the inner cities. The oldest and most dilapidated housing was generally located near central business districts, which meant that black populations were frequently displaced by clearance projects. The "black residents of the inner cities [and] black businesses were among the prime victims of federally-sponsored urban renewal programs" referred to as "black removal."[52] The program was derisively referred to by critics as "Negro clearance," a phrase that derived from the fact that over three-fourths of the people displaced by urban renewal in the first eight years of the program were black.[53] Black tenants were forced into other parts of the city by clearance projects—usually to dilapidated housing in a slightly more distant slum, or to public housing constructed on cleared land still surrounded by slums. Economic and racial barriers left them no choice other than to move to another area much like the slum they left behind: "Given the realities of the low-income housing market . . . it is likely that, for many families, relocation [meant] no more than keeping one step ahead of the bulldozer."[54] Thus a new game was added to the harsh realities of urban life—"musical slums."

Not only were the poor displaced but they also were forced to pay higher rents when the supply of low-rent housing units dwindled. With only 5 percent of the new housing units within the economic reach of low-income families, there was a 90 percent decline in the supply of low-income housing within redevelopment areas during the first ten years of the program's operation.[55] Only $34.8 million of the urban renewal funds—less than 1 percent—was used for relocation assistance, placing a disproportionate share of the cost of the program on the slum residents who were forced to move.[56]

PUBLIC HOUSING: URBAN RENEWAL'S STEPCHILD

It was obvious to even the most ardent opponents of public housing that the families and individuals displaced by clearance would have to find new housing. The 1949 legislation required that people displaced by clearance be given priority in moving into public housing projects. Public housing was reluctantly accepted as a necessary evil by supporters of renewal, but this lukewarm support meant that over the years Congress appropriated far less money for low-cost housing than called for in the original legislation. By the end of 1961, clearance had eliminated 126,000 housing units. The 28,000 new units that replaced them could house less than one-fifth of the 113,000 families and 36,000 individuals who were displaced by clearance.[57] Most of the cleared land was slated for commercial uses rather than housing. Public housing accounted for only 6 percent of the construction started and only 1 percent of additional construction planned in urban renewal areas as of April 1, 1961.[58]

Their status as slum dwellers gave blacks "the dubious privilege of eligibility for public housing."[59] Nationwide, nonwhites accounted for 38 percent of all public housing tenants in 1952, but by 1961 this percentage had risen to 46 percent. In individual projects, segregation was the norm. Whites who were eligible for public housing or who had been victims of slum clearance had housing options in the private market that were unavailable to blacks. Blacks, therefore, tended to take over public housing in the cities by default—the supply of low-income housing units was shrinking—and, as a result of racial discrimination, they were also kept out of the neighborhoods they *could* afford.

Public housing never got over its stepchild status. In most European countries, housing constructed and administered by governments in the years following World War II was available to middle-class families as well as to the poor, and much of this housing was considered as good as or sometimes better than the housing available through the private market. As a consequence, there was widespread political support for a public role in housing.[60] In the United States, by contrast, public housing was regarded essentially as a welfare program, and therefore it was never politically popular.

Public housing "was born with profound defects, and the hostile environment in which it grew aggravated its congenital ailments."[61] Three nearly fatal restrictions were built into the program. The first, and perhaps most important, problem was that eligibility was restricted to those who could not afford any other kind of housing. The real estate lobby would have tolerated no other policy. The insidious result of such a policy was to concentrate those poor families together that, for whatever reasons, were unable to improve their circumstances. Tenants who got jobs and increased their incomes were evicted. Already, in the 1950s, the concentration of families in poverty meant that public housing projects were prone to high levels of violence and juvenile crime. Over the years, public housing tenants were increasingly made up of "broken families, dependent families, and welfare families."[62] If the families whose incomes went up had been able to stay in their apartments and pay higher rents, the tendency to worsening social pathologies might have been moderated,[63] and the rental income they paid would have helped make public housing more economically viable.

A second built-in flaw was related to the fact that public housing projects were almost always built on slum land that had been cleared for that purpose; almost never were they built outside ghetto areas or, heaven forbid, in the suburbs. This meant that nearly all projects were surrounded by slums, and most of these areas were inhabited by blacks. From the beginning, most public housing projects were segregated by explicit policy in all but a few northern states. A significant portion of the buildings were occupied by whites and were, for a time, considered desirable by young families headed by veterans, who received first priority.[64] But by the time President John F. Kennedy signed an executive order forbidding the racial segregation of public housing projects in 1962, it could have little practical effect, since by then the overwhelming majority of public housing tenants in large cities were African American anyway; white families found it easy to find other housing, while black families did not. Thus, public housing policy had the perverse effect of reinforcing and intensifying the racial segregation that already existed in the cities.

A third fundamental problem flowed from cost and design restrictions that guaranteed that most of the units would be undesirable, especially as they aged. Public housing served as a constant reminder to its tenants and to everyone else that this was a grudging welfare program. To save money on site preparation and construction costs, cities built clusters of high-density high-rise buildings. The African American writer James Baldwin might have been describing almost any of these projects when he referred to those in Harlem as "colorless, bleak, high and revolting."[65] Of course, big American and European cities are full of high-rises that command steep rents from affluent clientele, but such structures, especially when built cheaply, "were not suitable for poor people with big families."[66] It was difficult for parents to supervise children even when play facilities were available. The architecture was a virtual invitation to vandalism and crime; elevators were often broken and stuck, laundry rooms were many floors removed from tenants' apartments, dark hallways and stairwells were poorly lighted even bulbs were available.

The Cabrini-Green projects north of Chicago's Loop began as two- story brick row houses built to house war workers in World War II. All of the occupants were white. In 1958, these houses were replaced by fifteen high-rise buildings, and another eight were constructed in 1962. These nineteen-story rectangular monstrosities loomed over the surrounding neighborhoods. Almost all the tenants were black. The same situation existed in New York City, where public housing often rose to more than twenty stories. The Pruitt-Igoe project in St. Louis, completed between 1954 and 1959, was composed of 2,762 apartments in thirty-three eleven-story buildings on a 57-acre site. By the time the last building was completed, the project was already a community scandal.[67] By 1973, it had become an international symbol for the failure of American public housing. In that year, photographs that made *Life* magazine's "The Year in Review" showed the shocking spectacle of one of the buildings imploding from hundreds of charges of carefully placed dynamite. As a monument to a policy failure, the episode could hardly have been more dramatic and fitting: Explosives experts got the opportunity to hone their demolition skills on buildings that had been built, complete with awards to the architectural firm, just fifteen years before.

Perhaps the most unfortunate legacy from this period of public housing is that "the projects" became enduring symbols of racial segregation, crime, and poverty in the inner cities, and as such they obscured the fact that not all public housing was a failure. The two- and three-story townhouses constructed in the 1930s were often pleasant places with satisfied tenants. Townhouse projects built in the 1960s and after were often quite successful—but of course success rarely made the news.

THE LEGACY OF INNER-CITY PROGRAMS

By the early 1960s, there was widespread opposition to federally assisted urban renewal. Liberal critics viewed urban renewal as a "federally financed gimmick to provide relatively cheap land for a miscellany of profitable, prestigious [private] enterprises."[68] Conservatives were also appalled by the results of the program. At its inception and through its early years, business leaders and politicians expected a miraculous reversal of central-city decline. The optimism soon turned into frustration. Redevelopment took too long. By the late 1960s, it took an estimated four years to plan a clearance and renewal project and then an additional six years to complete it. Often, by the time a project was finished, the original plans had long been abandoned.[69] Blighted neighborhoods and slums grew faster than the renewal projects could eliminate them.

In 1965, rent supplement programs were enacted as an alternative to public housing for the poor. Through direct housing aid, the poor would presumably be able to choose their own housing on the private market. The Housing and Urban Development Act of 1968 required that a majority of housing units constructed on redevelopment sites be for low- and moderate-income families.[70] Such tinkering with the urban renewal and public housing programs was designed to provide more benefits for the poor. The improvements, in the end, were modest. Low-income housing continued to be replaced at far less than a one-to-one basis; indeed, only 51 percent of the new units built in urban renewal areas after 1968 were reserved for people of low or moderate incomes.[71]

Both public housing and urban renewal met their effective demise in the 1970s. The inability of either program to slow significantly the decay of the nation's inner cities weakened their bases of support. They had persisted in the face of bitter criticism because everyone felt that something should be done, but there was no agreement on what would work. In 1974, urban renewal was merged into the Community Development Block Grant program. Public housing was allowed to wither away during the Nixon administration, from 104,000 starts in 1970 to only 19,000 starts by 1974.[72] A few years later, it was essentially abandoned when the Reagan Administration eliminated low-income housing built by the government in favor of programs to subsidize landlords and a few experiments in housing vouchers.

The urban renewal and public housing programs inflamed racial tensions and helped shape contemporary attitudes and stereotypes about African Americans, who were forced to cluster in densely packed, run-down areas where rents were cheap. The families that were unable to move far enough away often found themselves facing the nightmare of the bulldozer all over again. Families that could qualify for public housing ended up living in neighborhoods that were as segregated as before. The intense segregation of blacks in poverty made it seem as if they were different from everyone else, as if somehow their isolation from the rest of urban society was natural and preordained.

By reducing the supply of inner-city housing, clearance projects increased the pressure on neighborhoods at the margins of ghetto areas, an effect that was enforced by policies that kept middle-income blacks from looking for homes in the suburbs. Because they were kept out of all other areas, middle-class blacks could find acceptable housing only on the fringes of the inner-city ghetto. The movement of a black family onto a block inhabited by whites became a symbol of neighborhood decline—and a self-fulfilling prophecy. Realtors eagerly exploited whites' fears. In a typical scenario, a realtor would sell a home to a black family, then send someone door-to-door or distribute leaflets to spread the word that the neighborhood was about to change. Then, in a practice that became known as block-busting, the realtor would offer to buy property from panicked whites at bargain-basement prices. When white families began to move, the realtor would advertise the for-sale properties in neighborhoods occupied by potential black buyers and sell the homes at inflated prices. In this way, the white middle class learned to associate the presence of blacks with residential decline.

NATIONAL POLICY AND THE SUBURBS

The migration of millions of white, affluent families from the central cities to low-density suburbs constitutes one of the "great population migrations in American history"[73] (another author used similar words to describe the post–World War II movement of blacks to northern cities[74]). A movement to the suburbs certainly would have occurred in twentieth-century America, with or without governmental policies to hurry the process along. The spilling across city boundaries was a logical extension of the outward push from the urban center that had begun with the nineteenth-century development of the omnibus and the horsecar. However, the suburban movement would have been far slower and more uneven if it had depended on the housing market alone. Without doubt, its pace was quickened, and its shape was substantially determined, by powerful national policies. From the 1930s through the 1960s, suburban development was accelerated by two programs: the Federal Housing Administration (FHA) loans established by the National Housing Act of 1934 and the Veterans Administration (VA) loans made available to returning GIs by the Serviceman's Readjustment Act of 1944. Millions of Americans were able to purchase their first suburban home because of the liberal financing features of the FHA and VA programs.

Until the depression of the 1930s, the government played little direct role in housing provision. The notable exception was the role of the courts in enforcing restrictive covenants on housing deeds, which restricted the sale of homes in many urban neighborhoods to whites only. There were also some minimal building codes and fire regulations imposed by a few big cities. The federal government was prompted to intervene in the nation's housing market because it constituted a significant sector of the national economy. Second only to agriculture as an employer, the housing industry experienced a sudden, devastating retrenchment in the late 1920s. Before the stock market crash of October 1929, 900,000 new housing units were being built each year. In 1934, only one-tenth of this number, 90,000 units, was constructed. Throughout the 1930s, housing starts lagged far behind the demand for new housing.[75] In Chicago, only 131 new housing units were constructed in all of 1933, compared with 18,837 in 1929 and 41,416 in 1926.[76] Across the nation, 63 percent of the workers in the housing industry were unemployed in 1933. The housing problem was exacerbated by foreclosures on millions of mortgages, which brought hardship both to the banks and to homeowners. The banks looked to the federal government for assistance.

The National Housing Act of 1934 created both the FHA and the Federal Savings and Loan Insurance Corporation (FSLIC). The FSLIC insured individual accounts up to $5,000 (this level has since risen in a series of steps to more than $100,000). It was hoped that such insurance would inspire confidence by potential savers and investors, so that people would put their savings into banks instead of under their mattresses. These savings accounts would enable savings and loan institutions to invest more capital in the floundering housing market.

By far, the most important provision of the 1934 housing act is Section 203, the basic home mortgage insurance program under which the bulk of FHA insurance has been written up to the present day. Fully 79 percent of all FHA-insured units from 1934 to 1975, about 9.5 million units representing a face value of more than $109 billion, were insured under Section 203.[77] The purpose of the program was to finance the acquisition of proposed, under construction, or existing one- to four-family units. The housing act provided for FHA insurance of 80 percent of the value of the property. (Through the Housing and Urban Development Act of 1974, this amount subsequently was increased to 97 percent of the first $25,000 and 80 percent of the remaining value, and since then the formula has been changed from time to time.) The low risk involved for the lending institution permits the borrower to pay a low down payment, with the remaining principal and interest spread over a period of up to thirty years.

Various groups viewed the 1934 housing act with totally different goals in mind. Title I of the act provided FHA insurance for loans used for "permanent repairs that add to the basic livability and usefulness of the property."[78] Social welfare liberals saw Title I as a means of eliminating substandard living conditions in the central cities by providing low-interest, low-risk loans. City officials hoped Title I would entice affluent people to stay within the city limits and remodel their homes rather than move to new homes in the suburbs. Downtown business interests had a different goal in mind; they favored Title I because they thought it could shore up the value of the central business districts. Most banks, savings and loan institutions, realtors, and contractors saw Section 203 as a way to finance new construction beyond the city. In lobbying for the housing act, they had agreed to Title I only as a compromise to facilitate quick congressional action.

Despite the impression one could derive from reading the legislation, new construction under FHA came to mean housing outside the cities. Very little money was ever appropriated to finance Title I repairs. Section 203, by contrast, was used to assist millions of people to move to the suburbs in the years after World War II. The VA loans had much the same impact as the FHA. Together with the FHA, the no-down-payment policy of the VA helped increase the federally insured share of the mortgage market from 15 percent in 1945 to 41 percent by 1954.[79]

Table 6.1 shows how much more difficult it was to buy a home before the FHA program. In the 1920s, down payments of 30 percent to 50 percent were standard, and savings and loan institutions normally allowed a maximum of eleven years for loans to be repaid. Banks were not so generous; six years was the norm, often with a balloon payment (the entire loan) due at the end. In the 1960s, conventional mortgage loans typically required 25 percent down and were amortized over a twenty-

Table 6.1 Relative Burden of Loan Terms, 1920s and 1960s[a]

Decade and Lender	Terms	Percent of Annual Income	
		Down Payment	Annual Payment
1920s			
Savings and loan association	60 percent of house value loaned for 11 years at 7 percent; fully amortized	100	20
Bank or insurance company	50 percent of house value loaned for 5 years at 6 percent; unamortized	125	7.5 plus 125 in 5th year
1960s			
Conventional lender	75 percent of house value loaned for 20 years at 7 percent; fully amortized	62.5	18
FHA	95 percent of house value loaned for 30 years at 7.5 percent; fully amortized	12.5	20

[a]For a house equal to approximately 2.5 times the purchaser's annual salary.

Source: Henry J. Aaron, *Shelter and Subsidies: Who Benefits from Federal Housing Policies,* Studies in Social Economics (Washington, D.C.: Brookings Institution, 1972), p. 77. Copyright © 1972 by the Brookings Institution. Reprinted by permission.

year period (since then, loans with 10 percent to 20 percent down became the norm, with amortization periods of thirty years). Under the FHA, a home buyer could get a thirty-year mortgage with only 5 percent down and could obtain a much larger loan. The VA allowed banks to finance a mortgage with no down payment at all.

The FHA loan guarantee program radically changed the home credit market. Between 1935 and 1974, more than three-fourths of the total FHA insured home mortgages financed new housing.[80] The proportion of all homes that were owner occupied increased from 43.6 percent in 1940 to 62.9 percent in 1970.[81] Table 6.2 shows how much the FHA and VA programs influenced the housing market. About one-third of all homes purchased in the 1950s were financed through the FHA or VA programs. The proportion of government-financed loans gradually declined after the 1950s, but they remained important to the housing market, especially during economic downturns. By 1972, however, the FHA had helped almost 11 million families become homeowners.[82] In 1984, the FHA/VA share of home loans fell below 10 percent for the first time since World War II, but it later rebounded to 25 percent by 1988 and was still at 15 percent in 1998. The fluctuations closely followed the state of the economy.

Almost all of the new homes bought with FHA/VA loans were built in the suburbs. Throughout the 1940s and 1950s, the FHA exhibited an overwhelming bias in favor of the suburbs; for instance, in its first twelve years it did not insure a single dwelling on Manhattan Island. In part, the FHA's suburban bias reflected a preference for less dense, single-family neighborhoods, as found in

Table 6.2 **Use of FHA- and VA-Insured Loans in the United States, 1950–1998**

Year	Percent of Private Housing Financed Through FHA or VA	Total Number of Single Family Housing Starts (in Thousands)
1950	35	1,952
1955	41	1,646
1960	26	1,274
1965	16	1,510
1970	37	1,434
1975	15	1,160
1980	24	1,292
1984	9	1,750
1988	25	1,488
1995	13	1,354
1998	15	1,617

Source: U.S. Dept. of Commerce, Bureau of the Census, *Statistical Abstract of the United States, 1998* (Washington, D.C.: Government Printing Office, 1998), pp. 723 and 725; and *Current Construction Reports,* Series C20, Housing Starts, Dec. 1998 (Washington, D.C.: Government Printing Office, 1999), p. 7., and *Historical Statistics of the United States to 1970, Part 2* (Washington, D.C.: Government Printing Office, 1975), pp. 369, 641.

the suburbs, over more dense, multi-unit neighborhoods, as found in the cities. But the FHA suburban preference went far beyond a simple matter of geography; FHA administrators actively promoted the idea that housing, and therefore neighborhoods, should be racially and ethnically segregated.

FHA mortgage insurance programs depended on private-sector lending institutions, which made the actual loans. From the beginning, the FHA absorbed the values, policies, and goals of the real estate and banking industries.[83] Indeed, the staff of the FHA was drawn from the ranks of those industries, and it was only logical that the FHA's philosophy would parallel theirs. Thus "FHA's interests went no farther than the safety of the mortgage it secured."[84] Mortgages were typically made available only in "economically sound" areas, where depreciating housing values seemed unlikely.

FHA administrators shared the real estate and banking industry's view that racially segregated neighborhoods were the soundest investments. When it issued its underwriting manual to banks in 1938, one of the guidelines instructed loan officers to steer clear of changing or racially mixed areas:

> Areas surrounding a location are [to be] investigated to determine whether incompatible racial and social groups are present, for the purpose of making a prediction regarding the probability of the location being invaded by such groups. If a neighborhood is to retain stability, it is necessary that properties shall continue to be occupied by the same social and racial classes. A change in social or racial occupancy generally contributes to instability and a decline in values.[85]

A revealing glimpse into how sensitive FHA administrators were to the issue of race can be gained by reading the language of a 1933 report submitted to the agency by one of its consultants, Homer Hoyt, who was a well-known sociologist and demographer at the time. He offered his view that land values and the racial composition of a neighborhood were closely linked:

> If the entrance of a colored family into a white neighborhood causes a general exodus of the white people it is reflected in property values. Except in the case of Negroes and Mexicans, however, these racial and national barriers disappear when the individuals of the foreign nationality groups rise in the economic scale or conform to the American standards of living. . . . While the ranking may be scientifically wrong from the standpoint of inherent racial characteristics, it registers an opinion or prejudice that is reflected in land values; it is the ranking of races and nationalities with respect to their beneficial effect upon land values. Those having the most favorable effect come first in the list and those exerting the most detrimental effect appear last:
>
>   1. English, Germans, Scotch, Irish, Scandinavians
>   2. North Italians
>   3. Bohemians or Czechoslovakians
>   4. Poles
>   5. Lithuanians
>   6. Greeks
>   7. Russian Jews of lower class
>   8. South Italians
>   9. Negroes
>   10. Mexicans[86]

FHA administrators advised the developers of residential projects that they should draw up restrictive covenants barring sales to nonwhites before they applied for FHA-insured financing.[87] Banks were made to understand that even "a single house occupied by a black family in an urban neighborhood, even one tucked away on an inconspicuous side street, was enough for the FHA to label a predominantly white neighborhood as unfit for mortgage insurance."[88] Through such policies, the federal government essentially required that new subdivisions be segregated. Thus, federal policy acted as a powerful instrument to establish the social and racial patterns that emerged in urban America in the postwar years.[89] Between 1946 and 1959, less than 2 percent of all the housing financed with the assistance of federal mortgage insurance was purchased by blacks.[90] In the Miami area, only one black family received FHA backing for a home loan between 1934 and 1949, and there is "evidence that he [the man who secured the loan] was not recognized as a black" at the time the transaction took place.[91]

When the U.S. Supreme Court ruled in 1948 that racial covenants attached to property deeds could not be enforced in courts of law, the FHA was forced to change its policies. In 1950, the FHA revised its underwriting manual so that it no longer openly recommended racial segregation or restrictive covenants. However, it did nothing to reverse the effects of its previous policies and took no actions to discourage realtors, developers, or lending institutions from discriminating against blacks. Until the passage of the Housing Act of 1968, it was still legal for realtors and mortgage institutions to discriminate on the basis of race.

THE WEAK POLICIES OF THE POST–CIVIL RIGHTS ERA

The housing and civil rights acts of 1968 and other measures enacted in the 1960s were supposed to reverse decades of discriminatory behavior in the housing industry. Beginning in 1964, President Lyndon Johnson urged Congress to outlaw discrimination in housing. All eyes were focused on the more basic civil rights legislation, however, and in any case, the idea of applying civil rights remedies to housing ran up against the idea that individual property rights ought not be curbed. In both 1966 and 1967, a fair housing bill died in the Senate. Finally, under Title VIII of the Civil Rights Act of 1968,[92] Congress outlawed racial discrimination in housing. Its provisions were quite sweeping, barring discrimination in rentals and sales and in the provision of information about cost and availability, advertising, purchasing, construction and repair, and real estate services and practices. The statute mandated that each of the federal regulatory agencies involved with the real estate industry take affirmative steps to enforce both the spirit and the letter of the law.[93]

There can be little doubt that the 1968 legislation helped to open the suburban housing market to African Americans. Between 1970 and 1980, the number of blacks who lived in suburbs grew by almost 50 percent, an increase of 1.8 million persons.[94] One in ten blacks living in the central cities in 1970 moved to the suburbs during this period, and the percentage of urban blacks living in the suburbs increased from 16 percent to 21 percent.[95] In the 1980s, the trend continued. By the 1990 census, about 25 percent of urban black families lived in the suburbs, while about 85 percent of white families did so.

Blacks who moved to the suburbs tended to have higher incomes than those who stayed behind.[96] Suburbanization undoubtedly expanded housing choice for blacks, but those who moved to the suburbs in the 1970s and 1980s remained about as segregated from whites as they were before.[97] Blacks moved mostly into older inner-ring suburbs, where they displaced white residents, much as they had previously in central cities.[98] These older suburbs tended to have many of the same problems as central-city neighborhoods. In general, the suburbs to which blacks moved had lower tax bases, higher debts, poorer municipal services, lower socioeconomic status, and higher population densities than did suburbs that were mostly white.[99]

Most suburban whites continued to have little contact with suburban blacks. In the mid-1980s, 86 percent of suburban whites lived in suburbs with a black population of less than 1 percent.[100] Even those suburbs that were racially mixed tended to be highly segregated internally, and it appeared that racial segregation intensified during the 1980s.[101] Why was the racial segregation characteristic of the cities being replicated in the suburbs? Research indicated that discrimination, not social class or income, determined residential location.[102] Socioeconomic differentials between blacks and whites accounted for less than 15 percent of the segregation among suburbs in 1980.[103] Research conducted in the St. Louis area indicated that in the 1980s, nonracial factors such as housing cost and economic factors seemed to be less important in explaining patterns of residential segregation than in any previous decade,[104] and this pattern appeared to continue into the 1990s.[105]

Racial discrimination in housing continued despite the fact that legislation had outlawed it. An important reason for this is that the enforcement provisions of the 1968 legislation were weak. Rather than being granted positive responsibilities for identifying discrimination, the Department of Housing and Urban Development (HUD) as limited to receiving complaints initiated by individual citizens. By thus assuming a passive rather than an active enforcement role, it was easy for HUD to avoid controversy by treating each case as an isolated occurrence rather than as part of a pattern. For citizens, the time and red tape involved in initiating a complaint was daunting, and thus all through the 1970s the volume of complaints processed by HUD remained low. Interestingly, enforcement improved somewhat under a Republican president, Ronald Reagan, when HUD took steps to publicize the remedies available under the 1968 civil rights legislation. Partially as a result, the number of complaints received by HUD rose sharply in the 1980s. Still, most citizens bypassed HUD and state and local civil rights agencies and went directly to the courts.[106] By focusing on individual remedies rather than on large-scale efforts to enforce compliance, the governmental role in fair housing enforcement remained small and inconsequential.

Other efforts by the federal government to eliminate housing discrimination also benefited blacks, but in small, limited ways. The Equal Credit Opportunity Act of 1974, the Mortgage Disclosure Act of 1975, and the Community Reinvestment Act of 1977 (CRA)[107] were intended to ensure that blacks receive equal consideration for home loans and that banks stop redlining areas where blacks lived. (Redlining derives its name from the red line drawn on maps to designate neighborhoods considered poor investment risks.) In the past, banks would simply refuse to make home loans in certain areas regardless of the qualifications of individual loan applicants. Since the 1977 legislation, banks have been subjected to repeated protests and a substantial amount of litigation from community groups challenging apparent redlining practices. Rather than engage in extensive litigation and respond to investigations by federal regulators, banks generally have been willing to enter into negotiations with community groups. According to one estimate, by 1991 approximately $18 billion in urban reinvestment commitments had been negotiated in more than seventy cities across the country.[108] Just as it would be premature to conclude that all redlining has stopped, however, it would be inaccurate to assume that all individual loan applications are judged strictly on their merits. A 1992 study by the Federal Reserve Bank of Boston found that minorities were roughly 60 percent more likely to be turned down for a mortgage, even after controlling for thirty-eight factors affecting creditworthiness, such as credit history and total debt.[109]

To break down the patterns of residential segregation that exist in urban areas, the federal government would have to implement housing policies with the strength and effect of the policies that were once used to promote segregation. Such policies would change the dynamics of the housing market. Rather than merely regulating lending institutions, for instance, the government could, conceivably, become a primary lender. It could also, in principle, seek reparations and damages from landlords and homeowners who violate antidiscrimination laws. It could challenge local zoning laws that have the effect of maintaining segregated housing patterns. No such policies would be politically feasible, but without them it is likely that the effects of decades of national policies that helped create racially segregated neighborhoods will persist.

THE SUBURBAN BIAS IN NATIONAL TRANSPORTATION POLICIES

As we have seen, housing and urban renewal policies sponsored by the federal government have powerfully shaped the racial and socioeconomic segregation that exists in America's urban areas. National transportation policies also encouraged suburban growth and central-city decline. In a few years and at great expense, the U.S. government ensured the triumph of the automobile over mass transit. In doing so, the poor were left stranded in the central cities, ever more distant from suburban jobs, and with few affordable ways to get to them. "Automobility" enabled Americans to implement Henry Ford's solution to urban problems: "We shall solve the problems of the city by leaving the city."[110] Only in the last decade have the policies favoring the automobile been somewhat modified, but so far they are having little effect.

Americans depend on the automobile for urban travel more than people in any other nation. Though other advanced industrial nations such as Germany,

Britain, and Japan embraced the automobile, they also maintained modern systems of mass transit as workable alternatives. In West Germany, for example, between 1950 and 1974, at the same time that automobile travel increased fifteen times, public transit use more than doubled.[111] In the United States, by contrast, between 1950 and 1977, as the volume of automobile traffic on urban roads more than tripled, urban mass transit ridership declined by over half, and it has not rebounded since. Except for New York City and some of the urban corridor along the East Coast, public transit accounts for much less than 10 percent of commuting trips in most metropolitan areas of the United States.[112] Most metropolitan areas now have a one-dimensional urban transportation system.

In the early period of the automobile, cars were built much faster than highways. Between 1910 and 1920, the number of cars increased 1,600 percent, but the miles of paved roads rose by only 82 percent.[113] Mass production methods reduced the cost of automobiles, but highways were expensive, and there was conflict over who would pay for them. The method of paying for them that was finally agreed to was a tax on gasoline, and by 1929, all forty-eight states had enacted gasoline taxes (such taxes are still the main source of highway funds in the United States). Over time, the National Highway Users Conference, which is made up of 2,800 lobbying groups, has pressured successfully for the creation of trust funds earmarked for highways.[114] By 1974, forty-six of the fifty states had established highway trust funds, thus guaranteeing a steady source of revenue for highway construction, free from the uncertainties of the political process.[115] In addition, local taxes have paid for the feeder roads and local streets that make car travel so convenient.

Highway subsidies were pushed through by a powerful coalition led by the nation's largest auto, oil, and tire companies. The beginning of this coalition dates to June 28, 1932, when Alfred P. Sloan Jr., president of General Motors, called together representatives from several companies to form the National Highway Users Conference. The purpose of the conference, which was chaired by Sloan until 1948, was to unite the petroleum-related industries against the railroads and the urban transit (streetcar) companies.

While the conference lobbied for highway legislation, General Motors, Standard Oil of California, and Firestone Tire Company set out to buy up electric streetcar lines and replace them with buses. GM took the lead in this effort in 1932 when it formed the United Cities Motor Transit Company as a subsidiary. United Cities bought electric streetcar companies, tore up the tracks, replaced the trolleys with buses, and then sold the bus companies to firms that agreed to use only GM products. The first cities to successfully convert to buses were Kalamazoo and Saginaw, Michigan, and Springfield, Ohio. Many others soon followed, and "in each case, General Motors successfully motorized the city, turned the management over to other interests and liquidated its investment."[116]

GM established two semi-independent holding companies that could be used to pool funds contributed by petroleum-based corporations. The GM-created Omnibus Corporation and the National City Lines systematically dismantled streetcar companies in the nation's largest cities, including New York, Philadelphia, Baltimore, Salt Lake City, and Los Angeles. By 1949, through

National City Lines, buses had replaced streetcars in forty-five cities. Most of the new bus systems operated under contractual agreements stipulating that only gasoline or diesel fuel could be used in any of their vehicles. This ensured that the systems could not change back to electric trolleys in the future.[117]

In 1949, GM was convicted in federal court, along with Standard Oil and Firestone, of conspiring to eliminate electric transportation and monopolize the sale of buses and parts. The judge administered a slap on the wrist, levying a fine of $5,000 on the company and convicting one of its executives and fining him the sum of $1. Even before this symbolic gesture, the damage to mass transit had already been inflicted. By 1955, Roger M. Keyes, GM's executive in charge of bus sales, pronounced the effort a success: "The motor coach has supplanted the interurban systems and has for all practical purposes eliminated the trolley."[118] Only 5,000 streetcars were still in service, compared to 40,000 in 1936, when National City Lines began its assault on the electric railways.

The dismantling of streetcar systems accelerated a process that might have unfolded anyway, but at a slower pace, and with some streetcar systems left intact. The automobile became favored by the middle classes because of the freedom of movement it brought with it. It emancipated women who felt trapped in the suburbs while their husbands were at work. And it gave commuters a new-found freedom to run multiple errands in one trip, listen to music, and avoid mingling with people in anonymous circumstances. Freeways spread rapidly because of several factors, including collusion among auto interests, public policy, and consumer desires.

As its title implies, the 1956 National Defense Highway Act was justified partly on military grounds—two of its stated purposes were to aid the movement of troops and supplies and to help evacuate American cities in case of a nuclear attack. The main rationale, however, was that freeways would stimulate the economy by creating a national system of superhighways linking all the major metropolitan areas in the nation. Within urban areas, the new expressways were expected to solve the growing problem of traffic congestion. A committee appointed by President Eisenhower asserted that suburbs were superior to cities and recommended that the new freeway system should be used to decentralize American urban areas.[119] That is exactly what the new freeways eventually did.

The 1956 legislation placed federal gasoline taxes and new excise taxes on tires and heavy vehicles into a Federal Highway Trust Fund. Congress established a grant-in-aid formula of a 90 percent federal and a 10 percent state share for construction. The federal government agreed to distribute the funds for the 42,500-mile system on the basis of need. Since costs in built-up urban areas were greater, urban areas would get the most funds.

In the years leading up to the legislation, urban planners debated with highway engineers about how a national highway system should be built. Urban planners wanted to design highways in the context of larger efforts to shape regional development and revitalize declining central cities. Highway engineers, on the other hand, believed that the new interstate system should be designed with one goal in mind: to move people and goods in the most efficient manner from point A to point B. This meant, in effect, that freeways would go directly from the suburbs to the central cities and that whatever got in the way would have to go. The engineers got their way. The 1956 act was written so that the funds allocated by the federal government would be administered by state highway departments. As one historian put it, "Since federal and state road engineers controlled the program, they had few incentives to include urban renewal, social regeneration, and broader transportation objectives in the programming."[120] When highways were built through urban areas, state highway planners chose routes without reference to effects on existing neighborhoods.

It is interesting to note the difference between how federal funds were spent on housing and highways. Public housing was built by local public authorities, and local governments were given the power to veto any projects planned for their jurisdiction.[121] By contrast, interstate highways were built by state highway departments, which were given the power of eminent domain to force private owners to sell their property. Local governments could not refuse to participate in the program. Moreover, most city governments favored the program; they thought the new highways would help revitalize central cities by making it easier for suburban residents to commute to jobs in the cities. They could hardly have been more wrong.

Laying wide swaths of concrete had different effects in crowded cities than in the open countryside. As the highway builder Robert Moses said in a speech before the National Highway Users Conference in 1964, "You can draw any kind of picture you like on a clean slate . . . but when you operate in an overbuilt metropolis, you have to hack your way with a meat axe."[122] The meat axe approach turned out to be the method Moses used to build his highways, displacing 250,000 people in the New York City area alone.[123] Since the highway engineers wanted to cause the least disruption to private commercial land values, highways were routed through neighborhoods, especially those with the cheapest housing occupied by poor people and minorities.[124] The program was justified not only as highway building but also as slum clearance. According to one estimate, the uncompensated loss to city residents who were displaced averaged 20 to 30 percent of one year's income.[125]

The way the interstate highways were rammed through neighborhoods left a damaging imprint that lingers even today. The highways took land off the tax rolls, but the most enduring impact was that some neighborhoods became so isolated that they could not avoid deterioration, and downtown areas were cut off from their waterfronts. In St. Louis, Interstate 70 divides the Mississippi River waterfront from the downtown, a separation that has made downtown revitalization difficult—a problem that is repeated in cities across the nation. By separating the South Bronx from the rest of the city, the Cross-Bronx Expressway in New York helped turn the South Bronx into an infamous ghetto. Scholars estimate that the unsightliness of the Fitzgerald Expressway in Boston reduced surrounding property values by about $300 million.[126]

In response to the meat axe approach, "freeway revolts" began to proliferate.[127] One of the first successes came in 1959, when San Franciscans successfully prevented the completion of the Embarcadero Freeway. If their protest had failed, a freeway would today run along the shores of the San Francisco Bay, making the development of such tourist attractions as Ghirardelli Square and the Wharf almost impossible. Protests forced highway planners to become more sensitive to aesthetic and social considerations, but not before irreversible harm had been done to hundreds of urban neighborhoods and waterfronts.

By the 1980s, the final price tag for building the interstate system exceeded $100 billion. While highway building received huge subsidies year in and year out, urban mass transit was starved. Unlike Europe, where gasoline taxes had always been used to help support mass transit, federal gas taxes in the United States could not be allocated for that purpose until 1975. Funding for urban mass transit gradually increased after that, but remained small. Senator Gaylord Nelson of Wisconsin estimated that up to the 1980s, 75 percent of government expenditures for transportation in the United States in the postwar period had been spent on highways and roads, but only 1 percent went for urban mass transit (most of the rest was spent for railroads and shipping).[128] The inadequate state of mass transit discourages most people from trying it. Except in the New York region, where 30 percent or more of workers commuted by mass transit, for the United States as a whole in 1996 only 4.2 percent of workers used mass transit in 1996—a decline from a 5.4 percentage in 1985. In most metropolitan regions, less than 5 percent of workers use mass transit.[129]

For a brief period, the new highways seemed to benefit both the suburbs and downtown areas. Suburban land values climbed, and at the same time some central business districts went through a minor retail and office boom. Before long, however, it became clear that freeways had the principal effect of making it easier for commuters to move farther and farther out. At the same time that city officials were using urban renewal to raze slums in a desperate attempt to make the city attractive to businesses and the middle class, the interstate highway program was making it easier for both businesses and the white middle class to leave. The freeway system, which evolved into a standard pattern of inner- and outer-ring belts with intersecting spokes from the center, made the development of low-density metropolitan areas possible.

In the 1990s, concerns about urban air pollution and long commuting patterns finally emerged on the national policy agenda. In 1992, Congress passed the Intermodal Surface Transportation Efficiency Act (ISTEA, commonly referred to as "ice tea").[130] The significance of ISTEA is that it took substantial authority over interstate highway funds from politically insulated state transportation departments, which had always been dominated by highway engineers, and put decisions about urban transportations systems into the hands of Metropolitan Planning Organizations (MPOs). Governed by delegates representing municipal governments within urban regions, MPOs assumed authority over funding categories designed to reduce auto congestion and improve air quality.

The ISTEA legislation encouraged regional transportation planning by "flexing" federal highway funds, a process that allowed a portion of motor vehicle taxes to be spent on mass transit and even bicycle and pedestrian uses, if local transportation planners chose to. Between fiscal year 1992 and fiscal year 1999, $33.8 billion was available for transfer from transportation programs to transit projects, but local planners decided to transfer only 12.5 percent, or $4.2 billion, of this amount. Some states, such as New York, Massachusetts, California, and Oregon, transferred more than one-third of highway funds available to them to transit use, while others transferred little or none.[131] In 1998, highway-related projects took 75 percent of transportation funds in the United States,[132] a figure virtually identical to the proportion twenty years before.

The precedent set for local flexibility was carried over in the 1998 Transportation Equity Act for the 21st Century (TEA 21), which replaced ISTEA. Under this legislation, highway builders were required to submit studies of the air quality effects for major new federally funded projects. As urban areas face increasing traffic congestion and air pollution in the years ahead, it is certain that some of them will allocate more funds for new developments in mass transit, clean fuels, modernized buses, and electronic toll devices. Larger metropolitan areas will tend to use their funds flexibly in response to local political pressure and because they already have built relatively large mass transit systems.

THE DAMAGING EFFECTS OF NATIONAL URBAN POLICY

Taken at face value, the national programs to clear slums and to build low-cost housing in inner cities should have helped impoverished city residents the most. Slum clearance and public housing were always defended as socially beneficial to slum residents. The promise was that instead of living in dilapidated, unsafe properties, the poor would have the opportunity to move into safe and adequate housing constructed by the government. The politics of urban renewal and public housing programs, however, undercut their announced social objectives. For blacks, these programs turned into a cruel hoax. Local politicians and businesses used slum clearance to protect the property values of downtown business districts. Slum clearance became a means of moving blacks from potentially valuable real estate. What made such practices so damaging is that the amount of housing lost to the bulldozer vastly exceeded the number of public housing units ever built. Even worse, public housing projects soon were transformed into high-rise slums that segregated blacks even more than before.

The federal government's urban policies interacted in complex ways to shape the development of metropolitan areas. The FHA/VA programs made it difficult for blacks to leave the city and find adequate housing but helped affluent white families to buy in the suburbs, and the new expressways made it possible for them to commute. If they were poor, blacks could find safe and adequate housing only by moving into public housing. Demand always exceeded supply; for the poor families who did not move into housing projects, the big challenge was to keep one step ahead of the bulldozer. For those who outlasted the waiting lists to get into the projects, the reward must have seemed puny indeed. Forced to crowd into dense clusters of high-rise buildings constructed on land cleared of slum housing, "the projects" often became the worst of slums. For many white Americans, public housing became a cultural symbol for blacks on welfare.

Ironically, racist stereotypes were also encouraged when middle-class blacks tried to break out of slums. Shut off from the new housing in the suburbs, middle-class black families inherited the housing left by whites fleeing the cities. In the typical scenario, they displaced whites who lived in areas near all-black neighborhoods or bought into neighborhoods targeted by realtors for blockbusting. Because this process was so often repeated, the white middle class developed the habit of associating declining property values with an "invasion" by blacks. By reducing the supply of inner-city housing, clearance projects increased the pressure on the existing housing stock at the margins of all-black areas.

One way to understand the effect of this dynamic is to imagine the difference it might have made if middle-class blacks had been as free as the white middle class to leapfrog to suburban housing tracts. No doubt a high degree of racial segregation would have continued to exist. Even if it had, however, some black homeowners would have been able to (1) find affordable and desirable housing by buying new homes, instead of moving into neighborhoods already occupied by whites, and (2) benefit from the dynamics of the housing market, just as white homeowners did. With this dynamic in operation, the presence of blacks in a neighborhood would not have become so automatically equated, in the white imagination, with dilapidated housing or with declining property values.

The FHA/VA and interstate highway programs were as expensive as they were influential; over the several decades of their operation, each of them involved more than $100 billion in federal commitments (the value of the insurance covering the FHA/VA loans, on the one hand, and the direct federal expenditures on highways, on the other). It is difficult to imagine that policies of this magnitude would ever be implemented for the purpose of reducing the racial segregation of urban areas. And thus the consequences of past policies linger.

NOTES

1. John H. Mollenkopf, "The Post-War Politics of Urban Development," in William K. Tabb and Larry Sawers, eds., *Marxism and the Metropolis: New Perspectives on Urban Political Economy* (New York: Oxford University Press, 1978), p. 140.
2. For two sources making a similar argument, see Peter Dreier, John Mollenkopf, and Todd Swanstrom, *Place Matters: Metropolitics for the Twenty-first Century* (Lawrence: University Press of Kansas, 2001), pp. 107–110 and 117–120; and Thad Williamson, David Imbroscio, and Gar Alperovitz, *Making a Place for Community: Local Democracy in a Global Era* (New York: Routledge, 2002), pp. 74–75.
3. Bureau of the Census, *Household Economic Studies: Household Net Worth and Asset Ownership, 1995*, pp. 70–71. Michael A. Davern and Patricia J. Fisher, February 2001 (Washington, D.C.: U.S. Bureau of the Census).
4. Melvin Oliver and Thomas Shapiro, *Black Wealth/White Wealth: A New Perspective on Racial Inequality* (New York: Routledge, 1997), pp. 85–87.
5. Joint Resolution 52–22, 52d Cong. (1892); refer also to U.S. Congress, House, *Your Congress and American Housing—The Actions of Congress on Housing*, 82d Cong., 2d sess., 1952, H. Doc. 82–532, p. 1.
6. Public Law 65–102, 65th Cong. (1918); refer also to Congressional Quarterly Service, *Housing a Nation* (Washington, D.C.: Congressional Quarterly Service, 1966), p. 18; and Edith and Elmer Wood, *Recent Trends in American Housing* (New York: Macmillan, 1931), p. 79.

7. Congressional Quarterly Service, *Housing a Nation*, pp. v, xiii.

8. Public Laws 65–149 and 65–164, 65th Cong. (1918); refer also to Twentieth Century Fund, *Housing for Defense* (New York: Twentieth Century Fund, 1940), pp. 156–157; Congressional Quarterly Service, *Housing a Nation*, p. 18.

9. Refer to the Emergency Relief and Reconstruction Act, Public Law 72–302, 72d Cong. (1932).

10. The only other loan made under this authorization was $155,000 for rural housing in Ford County, Kansas.

11. Edwin L. Scanton, "Public Housing Trends in New York City" (Ph.D. diss., Graduate School of Banking, Rutgers University, 1952), p. 5.

12. Public Law 73–67, 72d Cong. (1933).

13. From a statement by Harold L. Ickes, Secretary of Interior and Public Works Administrator, quoted in Bert Swanson, "The Public Policy of Urban Renewal: Its Goals, Trends, and Conditions in New York City" (paper delivered at the American Political Science Association Meeting, New York, September 1963), p. 10.

14. *U.S. v. Certain Lands in City of Louisville*, Jefferson County, Ky., et al., 78 F.2d 64 (1935); *U.S. v. Certain Lands in City of Detroit* et al., 12 F.Supp. 345 (1935).

15. Refer to Glen H. Boyer, *Housing: A Factual Analysis* (New York: Macmillan, 1958), p. 247.

16. Richard D. Bingham, *Public Housing and Urban Renewal: An Analysis of Federal-Local Relations*, Praeger Special Studies in U.S. Economics, Social, and Political Issues (New York: Praeger, 1975), p. 30.

17. Nathaniel S. Keith, *Politics and the Housing Crisis Since 1930* (New York: Universe Books, 1973), p. 29.

18. Public Law 75–412, 75th Cong. (1937). Also found in U.S. Congress, House Committee on Banking and Currency, *Basic Laws and Authorizations on Urban Housing*, 91st Cong., 1st sess., 1969, p. 225.

19. Roscoe Martin, "The Expended Partnership," in *The New Urban Politics: Cities and the Federal Government*, ed. Douglas Fox (Pacific Palisades, Calif.: Goodyear, 1972), p. 51.

20. Keith, *Politics and the Housing Crisis*, p. 33.

21. Speech delivered before the Fourth Annual Meeting of the National Public Housing Conference, New York, December 1935, cited in ibid., pp. 32–33.

22. The restriction limiting participation to low-income families, seen from a comparative perspective, is a root cause of the failure of public housing in America. See Arnold J. Heidenheimer, Hugh Heclo, and Carolyn Teich Adams, *Comparative Public Policy: The Politics of Social Choice in Europe and America* (New York: St. Martin's Press, 1975), pp. 69–96.

23. Public Law 76–671, 76th Cong. (1940), relating to defense housing needs; Public Law 80–301, 80th Cong. (1946), suspended cost limitations for some low-income housing projects.

24. U.S. Housing and Home Finance Agency, *Fourteenth Annual Report* (Washington, D.C.: Government Printing Office, 1961), p. 380.

25. U.S. Congress, Senate Special Committee on Post-War Economic Policy and Planning, *Housing and Urban Development: Hearings Pursuant to S. Res. 102*, Senate, 79th Cong., 1st sess., 1945, pp. 1228–1237.

26. U.S. Congress, Senate Committee on Banking and Currency, *General Housing Act of 1945: Hearings*, 79th Cong., 1st sess., 1945, pp. 837–838.

27. U.S. Congress, Senate Committee on Banking and Currency, *General Housing Act of 1945*, p. 754.

28. Mark Gelfand, *A Nation of Cities: The Federal Government and Urban America, 1933–1965*, Urban Life in America Series (New York: Oxford University Press, 1975), p. 14.

29. Leonard Freedman, *Public Housing: The Politics of Poverty* (New York: Holt, Rinehart and Winston, 1969), pp. 58–75; Keith, *Politics and the Housing Crisis*, pp. 35–39.

30. International Union, United Automobile, Aircraft, and Agricultural Implement Workers of America, *Memorandum on Post War Urban Housing* (Detroit: International Union, United Automobile, Aircraft, and Agricultural Implement Workers of America, 1944), p. 94.
31. Wilson W. Wyatt, quoted in Congressional Quarterly Service, *Housing a Nation*, p. 6.
32. See Keith, *Politics and the Housing Crisis*, pp. 41–100.
33. Housing Act of 1949, Public Law 81–171, Preamble, sec. 2, 81st Cong. (1949).
34. Martin Meyerson and Edward C. Banfield, *Politics, Planning, and the Public Interest* (New York: Free Press, 1955).
35. Freedman, *Public Housing*, p. 55.
36. Robert H. Salisbury, "The New Convergence of Power in Urban Politics," *Journal of Politics* 26 (November 1964): 775–797.
37. Mollenkopf, "The Post-War Politics of Urban Development," p. 138.
38. Quoted in Institute of Housing, "Proceedings" (University College, Washington University, St. Louis, March 21–22, 1952, Mimeograph), p. 18. For studies of the coalition in other cities, see Harold Kaplan, *Urban Renewal Politics: Slum Clearance in Newark* (New York: Columbia University Press, 1963); Meyerson and Banfield, *Politics, Planning and the Public Interest*; Peter H. Rossi and Robert A. Dentler, *The Politics of Urban Renewal—The Chicago Findings* (New York: Free Press, 1961). Refer also to Jewel Bellush and Murray Hausknecht, "Entrepreneurs and Urban Renewal: The New Mean of Power," *Journal of the American Planning Institute* 32 (September 1961); George S. Duggar, "The Relation of Local Government Structure to Urban Renewal," in *Urban Renewal: People, Politics and Planning*, ed. Jewel Bellush and Murray Hausknecht (Garden City, N.Y.: Doubleday, Anchor Books, 1967), pp. 179–187, 200–208, as reprinted from *Law and Contemporary Problems* 26 (Winter 1961); Herbert Kay, "The Third Force in Urban Renewal," *Fortune*, October 1964.
39. Quoted in Robert A. Dahl, *Who Governs: Democracy and Power in an American City* (New Haven, Conn.: Yale University Press, 1961), p. 136. For another insightful example of the use of urban renewal by political entrepreneurs, see Jewel Bellush and Murray Hausknecht, "Urban Renewal and the Reformer," in *Urban Renewal: People, Politics and Planning*, ed. Jewel Bellush and Murray Hausknecht (Garden City, N.Y.: Doubleday, Anchor Books, 1967), pp. 189–197.
40. Gelfand, *A Nation of Cities*, p. 161.
41. Mollenkopf, "The Post-War Politics of Urban Development," p. 140.
42. Ibid., p. 138.
43. Williamson, Imbroscio, and Alperovitz, *Making a Place for Community*, p. 76.
44. Herbert J. Gans, *The Urban Villagers: Group and Class in the Life of Italian-Americans* (New York: Free Press, 1962), chap. 13.
45. John H. Mollenkopf, "On the Causes and Consequences of Neighborhood Political Mobilization" (paper delivered at the annual meeting of the American Political Science Association, New Orleans, September 4–8, 1973).
46. Quoted in Clarence N. Stone, *Economic Growth and Neighborhood Discontent: System Bias in the Urban Renewal Program of Atlanta* (Chapel Hill: University of North Carolina Press, 1976), pp. 48–49.
47. See Chester Hartman et al., *Yerba Buena: Land Grab and Community Resistance in San Francisco* (San Francisco: Glide, 1974). The following material on the Yerba Buena controversy draws on this excellent book. In most cases, citations are limited to quotations or specific data.
48. Ibid., p. 31.
49. Ibid., p. 19.
50. Ibid., p. 190.
51. Ibid., p. 128.

52. Arthur I. Blaustein and Geoffrey Faux, *The Star-Spangled Hustle,* foreword by Ronald V. Dellums (Garden City, N.Y.: Doubleday, Anchor Books, 1973), p. 71.

53. See Martin Anderson, *The Federal Bulldozer: A Critical Analysis of Urban Renewal, 1949–1962* (Cambridge, Mass.: MIT Press, 1964), p. 65; compare Rossi and Dentler, *The Politics of Urban Renewal,* p. 224.

54. Chester Hartman, "The Housing of Relocated Families," in *Urban Renewal: The Record and the Controversy,* ed. James Q. Wilson (Cambridge, Mass.: MIT Press, 1966), p. 322, as reprinted from *Journal of the American Institute of Planners* 30 (November 1964): 266–286.

55. Anderson, *The Federal Bulldozer,* p. 65.

56. Mollenkopf, "The Post-War Politics of Urban Development," p. 140.

57. Anderson, *The Federal Bulldozer,* pp. 65–66; see also Bellush and Hausknecht, "Urban Renewal and the Reformer," p. 13.

58. Anderson, *The Federal Bulldozer,* p. 105.

59. Freedman, *Public Housing,* p. 140.

60. Arnold J. Heidenheimer, Hugh Heclo, and Carolyn Teich Adams, *Comparative Public Policy: The Politics of Social Choice in America, Europe, and Japan,* 3rd ed. (New York: St. Martin's Press, 1990), chap. 4.

61. Freedman, *Public Housing,* p. 105. The points in the discussion of public housing that follow borrow from Freedman's treatment at pp. 105–122.

62. Lawrence M. Friedman, *Government and Slum Housing: A Century of Frustration* (Chicago: Rand McNally, 1968), p. 121.

63. Freedman, *Public Housing,* p. 111.

64. Friedman, *Government and Slum Housing,* p. 123.

65. James Baldwin, *Nobody Knows My Name* (New York: Dial Press, 1961), p. 63, quoted in Freedman, *Public Housing,* p. 117.

66. Friedman, *Government and Slum Housing,* p. 121.

67. Lee Rainwater, *Behind Ghetto Walls: Black Families in a Federal Slum* (Chicago: Aldine, 1970).

68. National Commission on Urban Problems, *Building the American City* (New York: Praeger, 1969), p. 153. This commission, appointed by the president, was established in January 1967 and headed by former Illinois senator and longtime urban policy advocate Paul H. Douglas.

69. Ibid. pp. 164–165.

70. Housing and Urban Development Act of 1968, Public Law 90–448, 90th Cong. (1968).

71. John C. Weicher, *Urban Renewal: National Program for Local Problems,* Evaluative Studies Series (Washington, D.C.: American Enterprise Institute for Public Policy Research, 1972), p. 6, citing unpublished HUD statistics: 538,044 housing units had been demolished as a result of urban renewal activities through 1971.

72. U.S. Department of Housing and Urban Development, *1974 Statistical Yearbook of the U.S. Department of Housing and Urban Development* (Washington, D.C.: Government Printing Office, 1976), p. 104.

73. Barry Checkoway, "Large Builders, Federal Housing Programs, and Postwar Suburbanization," in *Marxism and the Metropolis: New Perspectives in Political Economy,* ed. William K. Tabb and Larry Sawers (New York: Oxford University Press), p. 156.

74. Nicolas Lemann, *The Promised Land: The Great Migration and How It Changed America* (New York: Vintage Books, 1991), p. 6.

75. Stephen David and Paul Peterson, eds., *Urban Politics and Public Policy: The City in Crisis* (New York: Praeger, 1973), p. 94.

76. Charles Abrams, *The Future of Housing* (New York: HarperCollins, 1946), p. 213.

77. Bureau of National Affairs, *The Housing and Development Reporter* (Washington, D.C.: Bureau of National Affairs, 1976).

78. Ibid.

79. Calculated from data in Congressional Quarterly Service, *Housing a Nation*, p. 6.

80. U.S. Department of Housing and Urban Development, *1974 Statistical Yearbook of the Department of Housing and Urban Development*, pp. 116–117.

81. U.S. Bureau of the Census, *Historical Statistics of the United States, Colonial Times to 1970*, pt. 1, Bicentennial ed. (Washington, D.C.: Government Printing Office, 1975), p. 646.

82. Kenneth T. Jackson, *Crabgrass Frontier: The Suburbanization of the United States* (New York: Oxford University Press, 1985), p. 205.

83. For a discussion of this phenomenon, see Murray Edelman, *The Symbolic Uses of Politics*, 7th ed. (Champaign: University of Illinois Press, 1976), pp. 44–76. We are indebted to Jeffrey Gilbert for several of the ideas contained in this section.

84. Michael Stone, "Reconstructing American Housing" (unpublished manuscript), quoted in Chester W. Hartman, *Housing and Social Policy*, Prentice-Hall Series in Social Policy (Englewood Cliffs, N.J.: Prentice-Hall, 1975), p. 30.

85. Quoted in Brian J. L. Berry, *The Open Housing Question: Race and Housing in Chicago, 1966–1976* (Cambridge, Mass.: Balinger, 1979), p. 9.

86. Quoted in Ibid., pp. 9, 11.

87. Luigi M. Laurenti, "Theories of Race and Property Value," in *Urban Analysis: Readings in Housing and Urban Development*, ed. Alfred N. Page and Warren R. Seyfried (Glenview, Ill.: Scott Foresman, 1970), p. 274.

88. Richard Moe and Carter Wilkie, *Changing Places* (New York: Henry Holt, 1997), p. 48.

89. Charles Abrams, quoted in Norman N. Bradburn, Seymour Sudman, and Galen L. Gockel, *Side by Side: Integrated Neighborhoods in America* (Chicago: Quadrangle Books, 1971), p. 104.

90. Gelfand, *A Nation of Cities*, p. 221.

91. Nathan Glazer and David McEntire, eds., *Housing and Minority Groups* (Berkeley: University of California Press, 1960), p. 140.

92. Public Law 90–284, 90th Cong. (1968), Title VIII ("Fair Housing"), sec. 805.

93. D.C. Public Interest Research Group (DCPIRG), Institute for Self-Reliance, and Institute for Policy Studies, *Redlining: Mortgage Disinvestment in the District of Columbia* (Washington, D.C.: DCPIRG, Institute for Local Self-Reliance, and Institute for Policy Studies, 1975), p. 3.

94. U.S. Department of Housing and Urban Development, *1974 Statistical Yearbook of the Department of Housing and Urban Development*, pp. 116–117.

95. Thomas A. Clark, "The Suburbanization Process and Residential Segregation," in *Divided Neighborhoods: Changing Patterns of Racial Segregation*, ed. Gary A. Tobin (Newbury Park, Calif.: Sage, 1987), p. 115; Larry Long and Diane Deare, "The Suburbanization of Blacks," *American Demographics* 3 (1981), cited in Douglas S. Massey and Nancy A. Denton, "Suburbanization and Segregation in U.S. Metropolitan Areas," *American Journal of Sociology* 3 (November 1988): 592–626.

96. Jackson, *Crabgrass Frontier*, p. 205.

97. John R. Logan and Harvey L. Molotch, *Urban Fortunes: The Political Economy of Place* (Berkeley: University of California Press, 1987), p. 195.

98. Clark, "The Suburbanization Process and Residential Segregation," pp. 115–137.

99. Massey and Denton, "Suburbanization and Segregation in U.S. Metropolitan Areas," pp. 592–626.

100. Logan and Molotch, *Urban Fortunes*, p. 194.

101. Douglas S. Massey and Mitchell L. Eggers, "The Spatial Concentration of Affluence and Poverty During the 1970s," *Urban Affairs Quarterly* 29, no. 2 (December). See also S. Roberts, "Shifts in 80's Failed to Ease Segregation," *New York Times*, July 15, 1992, pp. B1–B3.

102. John F. Kain, "Housing Market Discrimination and Black Suburbanization in the 1980's," in *Divided Neighborhoods: Changing Patterns of Racial Segregation*, ed. Gary A. Tobin (Newbury Park, Calif.: Sage, 1987), p. 68.

103. John Farley, *Segregated City, Segregated Suburbs: Are They the Products of Black-White Socioeconomic Differentials?* (Edwardsville: Southern Illinois University, 1983), cited in Joe T. Darden, "Choosing Neighbors and Neighborhoods: The Role of Race in Housing Preference," in *Divided Neighborhoods: Changing Patterns of Racial Segregation*, ed. Gary A. Tobin (Newbury Park, Calif.: Sage, 1987), p. 16.

104. John F. Farley, "Race Still Matters: The Minimal Role of Income and Housing Cost as Causes of Housing Segregation in St. Louis, 1990," *Urban Affairs Review* 31, no. 2 (November 1995), pp. 244–254.

105. Public Policy Research Centers, University of Missouri-St. Louis, *Analysis of Impediments to Fair Housing: St. Louis County* (St. Louis: Author, 1995).

106. William E. Nelson and Michael S. Bailey, "The Weakening of State Participation in Civil Rights Enforcement," in *Public Policy Across States and Communities*, ed. Dennis R. Judd (Greenwich, Conn.: JAI Press, 1985), p. 160.

107. Public Law 94–200, 94th Cong. (1975), Title III, and Public Law 95–128, 95th Cong. (1977), Title VIII.

108. Calvin Bradford, *Community Reinvestment Agreement Library* (Des Plaines, Ill.: Community Reinvestment Associates, 1992), as cited in *From Redlining to Reinvestment: Community Responses to Urban Disinvestment*, ed. Gregory D. Squires (Philadelphia: Temple University Press, 1992), p. 2.

109. Mitchell Zuckoff, "Study Shows Racial Bias in Lending," *Boston Globe,* October 9, 1992.

110. Henry Ford, quoted in J. Allen Whitt and Glenn Yago, "Corporate Strategies and the Decline of Transit in U.S. Cities," *Urban Affairs Quarterly* 21, no. 1 (September 1985): 61.

111. James A. Dunn Jr., *Miles to Go: European and American Transportation Policies* (Cambridge, Mass.: MIT Press, 1981), p. 59.

112. John R. Meyer and Jose A. Gomez-Ibanez, *Auto Transit and Cities* (Cambridge, Mass.: Harvard University Press, 1981), pp. 23, 28, 34.

113. Dunn, *Miles to Go,* p. 116.

114. Whitt and Yago, "Corporate Strategies," p. 52.

115. Dunn, *Miles to Go,* p. 116. Many policy analysts question whether earmarked gasoline taxes pay for the full costs of highways, including the costs of air and noise pollution and the expenses associated with traffic accidents. See Meyer and Gomez-Ibanez, *Auto Transit and Cities;* and Glenn Yago, *The Decline of Transit* (New York: Cambridge University Press, 1984), p. 195.

116. Bradford C. Snell, "American Ground Transport," in *The Urban Scene*, 2nd ed., ed. Joe R. Feagin (New York: Random House, 1979), p. 247.

117. Ibid., p. 248.

118. Quoted in ibid., p. 249.

119. Alan Lupo, Frank Colcord, and Edmund P. Fowler, *Rites of Way: The Politics of Transportation in Boston and the U.S. City* (Boston: Little, Brown, 1971), p. 184.

120. Mark Rose, *Interstate Express Highway Politics, 1941–1956* (Lawrence: The Regents Press of Kansas, 1979), p. 97.

121. Local participation agreement is required before public housing can be built in a jurisdiction. Suburban governments simply refused to negotiate such agreements and therefore excluded all conventional public housing from their locality.

122. Quoted in Helen Leavitt, *Superhighway—Superhoax* (Garden City, N.Y.: Doubleday, 1970), p. 53.

123. Robert A. Caro, *The Power Broker: Robert Moses and the Fall of New York* (New York: Random House, 1974), p. 19.
124. For example, between 1951 and 1974, 89 percent of the 10,000 households displaced by public projects in Baltimore were black. See Anthony Downs, *Urban Problems and Prospects* (Chicago: Marsham, 1970), pp. 204–205.
125. Ibid., p. 223.
126. Meyer and Gomez-Ibanez, *Auto Transit and Cities*, p. 177.
127. By 1970, there were 400 struggles underway by community groups to oppose highway construction. Harry C. Boyte, *The Backyard Revolution: Understanding the New Citizen Movement* (Philadelphia: Temple University Press, 1980), p. 11.
128. Jackson, *Crabgrass Frontier*, p. 250.
129. U.S. Bureau of the Census, *Statistical Abstract of the United States*, table no. 644, Employment Status of Civilian Population: 1950 to 1997, September 30, 1998; and table no. 1055, Passenger Transit Industry—Summary, 1985 to 1986, October 2, 1998.
130. This account of ISTEA relies upon Paul G. Lewis, "The Politics of Structure in Transportation Policy: Resuscitating Metropolitan Planning Organizations Under ISTEA" (paper delivered at the Annual Meeting of the Urban Affairs Association, Toronto, Canada, April 17, 1997).
131. Pietro S. Nivola, *Laws of the Landscape: How Policies Shape Cities in Europe and America* (Washington, D.C.: Brookings Institution, 1999), p. 15.
132. Ibid.

THE RISE AND FALL
OF NATIONAL
URBAN POLICY

THE POLITICS OF NATIONAL URBAN POLICY

In the 1960s, the problems of racial segregation, discrimination, and concentrated poverty burst onto the nation's political agenda as the main ingredients of an "urban crisis." The National Commission on Urban Problems (1958), the National Commission on Civil Disorders (1967), the President's Task Force on Suburban Problems (1967), President Nixon's Commission on Population Growth and the American Future (1972), and a host of state and city task forces decried the segregation of blacks and the poor in ghetto areas of the central cities. To a considerable extent, the national Democratic Party staked its future on solving the problems of race and poverty. The results of the social and urban policies of the 1960s were mixed, but by the mid-1970s there was a growing perception that many of the programs had failed.

From 1969 to 1976, when Republican presidents Richard Nixon and Gerald Ford occupied the White House, many of the grant programs sponsored by the Democrats in the 1960s came under attack. Rather than trying to eliminate them, however, Republicans focused on giving state and local governments broad discretion in spending the money. These reforms were justified as attempts to streamline government and make federal programs more efficient. Spending for programs, however, continued to rise. By the end of the 1970s, Republicans abandoned their efforts to reform federal urban programs and turned instead to a new objective: eliminating them altogether. Ronald Reagan's presidential victory in the 1980 election signaled the beginning of the end for urban programs. Between 1981 and 1986, most of the urban programs inherited from previous presidential administrations disappeared.

For decades, the social programs of the Great Society served as useful targets for politicians on the campaign trail. After the Los Angeles riots in 1992, President George Bush's press secretary, Marlin Fitzwater, declared that the social welfare programs of the 1960s and 1970s were partly to blame.[1] When

164

asked to name the specific programs he had in mind, he replied, "I don't have a list with me," but went on to add, "the basic structures of these communities were formulated in the '60s and '70s on the basis of the social welfare efforts that didn't work." Trying to blame the riots on the Great Society programs struck historian Arthur Schlesinger Jr. as "pathetic." "What can they be smoking over at the White House these days?" he asked.[2]

Whatever it was, it seemed to be extremely addicting. In the first presidential debate of the 1992 campaign, President Bush repeatedly invoked the well-worn slogan "tax and spend." Democratic candidate Bill Clinton retorted, "President Bush is running against Lyndon Johnson, Jimmy Carter, everybody but me in this campaign." In 1992, for the first time in a long time, it was not a winning strategy for the Republicans. Nevertheless, President Bill Clinton did not attempt to revive urban policy. By the 1996 presidential election, neither Republicans nor Democrats spoke about helping the cities or the people living within them. Instead, the talk was about welfare reform, crime, immigration, and balancing the federal budget. Even with the growing budget surpluses of the time, neither candidate in the 2000 presidential election had much to say about the cities. In this chapter, we explain why urban policy attracted so much attention in the 1960s and 1970s and why it fell so far off the agenda after that.

THE DEMOCRATS AND THE CITIES

When President Kennedy was sworn in on January 20, 1961, his administration was already committed to helping the cities. Even before his campaign, Kennedy had concluded that the problem of the cities was "the great unspoken issue in the 1960 election."[3] During the campaign, the Democrats talked about doing something about the urban crisis, while the Republicans tried to avoid such issues. "If you ever let them campaign only on domestic issues," confided presidential nominee Richard M. Nixon to his aides, "they'll beat us."[4] President Kennedy "emerged as an eloquent spokesman for a new political generation. In presidential message after message Kennedy spelled out in more detail than the Congress or the country could easily digest the most complete programs of domestic reforms in a quarter century."[5]

The Kennedy Administration mapped out an ambitious agenda. Widespread poverty, racial segregation, juvenile delinquency and crime, bad schools, and a host of other social problems were discovered in the 1960s only in the sense that they were no longer "out of sight, out of mind." They had existed for a long time and were no worse and little different by the advent of the Kennedy Administration than they had been under presidents Roosevelt, Truman, and Eisenhower. What made them seem worse was their greater visibility. Martin Luther King Jr. understood the task of creating visibility during the civil rights demonstrations in 1963. "I saw no way," he later commented, "of dealing with things without bringing the indignation to the attention of the nation."[6]

King turned the civil rights issue into a national crisis in Birmingham, Alabama, in the summer of 1963. What started in Birmingham spread across

OUT TAKE

RACIAL DIVISIONS EVENTUALLY DOOMED URBAN PROGRAMS

Urban policy was essentially invented during the New Deal. The big-city vote was decisive in every one of Franklin Delano Roosevelt's four presidential election campaigns. The urban vote continued to be essential to the Democrats for decades. Time after time, overwhelming Democratic majorities in the big cities balanced out Republican pluralities in the suburbs and small towns, providing the margin of victory in key states holding large blocs of electoral votes. The Democrats would have lost the presidency in 1940, 1944, and 1948 without the overwhelming margins delivered in twelve big cities in the nation.[7] The urban electorate was essential to John F. Kennedy's victory in the close election of 1960. Kennedy beat Nixon by 112,000 votes, a margin of less than one-tenth of 1 percent, but he carried twenty-seven out of the thirty-nine largest cities in the nation.[8] In 1964, Lyndon Johnson won by an unprecedented landslide, with the cities topping the national Democratic margins by 10 percent or more.

But the 1964 landslide masked a development that would soon undermine the Democrats' ability to win presidential elections. The issue of race was tearing apart the coalition the Democrats had fashioned in the 1930s. Johnson, the Democratic candidate, lost throughout the Deep South. The Republican standard-bearer, Barry Goldwater, received 87 percent of the popular vote in Mississippi, almost 70 percent in Alabama, and substantially more than 50 percent in Louisiana, Georgia, and South Carolina. After 1964, Republican candidates began to win elections in the South for the first time since the carpetbagger governments imposed on southern states after the Civil War.

In 1968, the Republicans capitalized on resentment provoked by the successes of the civil rights movement. The Democratic presidential candidate, Hubert Humphrey, carried only one southern state, Texas. Across the South, he won just 31 percent of the vote, running behind both Republican Richard Nixon (34.5 percent) and Alabama governor and third-party candidate George Wallace (34.6 percent), who ran as an avowed segregationist. In 1968, the Nixon campaign adopted law and order as its main theme. This had been Goldwater's campaign slogan too, but he had handled it crudely and ineptly. Goldwater's television ads tried to convey an impression that America's cities were in ruins by showing scenes of blacks rioting. In the scenes meant to portray Goldwater's vision of the American past he would like to restore, blacks were shown picking cotton.[9] The spot ads aired by Nixon four years later were less blatant, though they were not subtle, either. One of his television spots showed scenes of urban riots, with a Nixon voice-over calling for "some honest talk about the problem of order."[10] But at least blacks were not shown in a rendition of a bucolic agricultural past.

The message worked in the North as well as the South. Working-class whites in semiskilled and unskilled occupations gave Humphrey only 38 percent of their votes, less than two-thirds the 61 percent proportion cast for John Kennedy in 1960. Black voters, on the other hand, abandoned the Republicans. Nixon won 32 percent of the black vote in 1960, but his share fell to 12 percent in 1968.[11] One of the president's closest advisers, John Erlichman, told civil rights administrators that "blacks are not where the votes are, so why antagonize the people who can be helpful to us politically?"[12]

As the 1968 election made clear, it was impossible to divorce the issue of race from social welfare and urban programs. This had become obvious as early as the 1930s, when southern Democrats in Congress often expressed their concern that New Deal programs might be used to upset traditional racial relationships in the South. In the 1940s and 1950s, they fought to make sure that the public housing programs would not be used to promote racial integration. As long as the programs advanced by Democratic liberals in the North could be divorced from racial politics, southern Democrats were willing to go along. The possibility of doing so ended with the civil rights and social programs of the 1960s.

The Great Society became identified as a constellation of programs that primarily benefited inner-city blacks. The truth is that very few programs had this character; funds for Head Start and the War on Poverty, for example, were spread broadly across the country, to urban and rural areas alike, and social programs such as Medicare and Medicaid benefited a wide variety of people. But other programs did not enjoy such support. Even before the Republicans won the presidency in 1980, most urban programs were in trouble. President Ronald Reagan effectively ended national efforts to help the cities in the 1980s. They are not likely to be revived because the balance of power in national politics has shifted decisively to the suburbs and the Sunbelt.

the South and even filtered into northern cities. During the summer, there were 13,786 arrests of demonstrators in seventy-five cities of the eleven major southern states.[13] In the ten weeks that followed nationally publicized police attacks on demonstrators in Birmingham, the Justice Department counted 758 demonstrations across the nation. It quickly became clear that the administration could no longer avoid dealing with civil rights. The brutal treatment of civil rights demonstrators throughout the South was being televised in the living rooms of millions of American homes. By mid-June, 127 civil rights bills had been introduced in the House of Representatives. The Kennedy Administration, like it or not, was being drawn into the nation's most significant and divisive internal conflict since the Civil War.

The political pressures applied by the civil rights movement were reinforced by the influence of the black electorate. As John C. Donovan observed in his book *The Politics of Poverty,* "The greatest strength of the Negro communities lies in its voting power, in its numbers, and in their strategic location."[14] In the South, the black population was geographically diffused and systematically denied the right to the vote. When they moved to northern cities, blacks gained the franchise. Their votes were concentrated in the cities of the states holding a majority of the electoral college votes—Illinois, California, Massachusetts, Ohio, Michigan, New Jersey, New York, Texas, and Pennsylvania. Kennedy targeted his campaign on these key states, and the 68 percent plurality that black voters gave him was crucial to his razor-thin victories in Illinois, Ohio, and other states. In 1956, Adlai Stevenson, the liberal Democratic candidate from Illinois, had received 61 percent of the black vote.[15] If Kennedy had not done better, he would have lost the election: "It is difficult to see how Illinois, New Jersey, Michigan, South Carolina, or Delaware (with 74 electoral votes) could have been won had the Republican-Democratic split of the Negro wards and precincts remained as it was, unchanged from the Eisenhower charm of 1956."[16]

On June 11, 1963, Kennedy overruled his advisers and announced that he would propose a civil rights bill. When Kennedy was assassinated on November 22, the bill had just reached the House Rules Committee. The assassination created an emotionally charged atmosphere that the new president, Lyndon Baines Johnson, adroitly exploited. Opinion polls indicated overwhelming public support for civil rights legislation. Seizing the moment, Johnson added new provisions to the legislation and harried Congress into acting quickly. When Republicans joined with northern Democrats to move the bill out of the House Rules Committee, the bill was sent to the floor, where it passed by a vote of 290 to 130. On June 6, 1964, the Senate mustered the necessary two-thirds vote to overcome a filibuster mounted by southerners, and the legislation passed.

The Civil Rights Act of 1964 was far-reaching. It outlawed discrimination in public accommodations, effectively striking down the South's Jim Crow laws, which denied blacks equal access to bus stations, restaurants, lunch counters, theaters, sports arenas, gasoline stations, motels, hotels, and lodging houses. It outlawed racial discrimination in the hiring, firing, training, and promoting of workers. It barred discrimination in the administration of federal grants. A year later, Congress passed the Voting Rights Act, which not only outlawed literacy tests and other discriminatory voting restrictions but also provided that federal registrars could replace local registrars in counties where there had been a history of discrimination against black voters.

Taking advantage of the post-assassination atmosphere, President Johnson also pressed for a program to redress economic inequalities.[17] Kennedy's advisers had persuaded him that the time had come for his administration to devise a program to attack poverty and unemployment. In June 1963, Kennedy had told Walter Heller, the chairman of his Council of Economic Advisors, to appoint a task force of officials who would be responsible for proposing a program to attack poverty. Although Kennedy's commitment to a program was almost certain by the time of his assassination, it was not clear how hard he would have fought for it.

President Johnson was told about the proposed antipoverty program only two days after assuming office, but he quickly responded, "That's my kind of program. It will help people. I want you to move full speed ahead."[18] The idea of an ambitious, highly visible program appealed to Johnson's desire to be perceived as a second Roosevelt, as a president who would go down in history as the one who completed the social agenda left unfinished in the 1930s. In his first State of the Union address, on January 10, 1964, President Johnson announced that he would seek a "total effort" to end poverty in the United States. Using a grandiose military analogy, he said, "This Administration here and now declares unconditional war on poverty in America, and I urge this Congress and all Americans to join me in that effort."[19] When Johnson signed the Economic

Opportunity Act on August 8, he had two big legislative victories, the civil rights act and his "war on poverty," to carry into the presidential campaign.

The 1964 campaign provided the setting for an unusually contentious national debate over the federal government's role and responsibilities. The Republican nominee, Barry Goldwater, was one of the few nonsoutherners to vote against the civil rights act in the Senate. He attacked the welfare programs funded through the Social Security Act of 1935 and even questioned the immensely popular old-age insurance program established through that legislation. The Republican Party's platform warned that "individual freedom retreats under the mounting assault of expanding centralized power."[20] Lyndon Johnson, by contrast, called for a Great Society that would eliminate poverty and treat other social ills through federal action on civil rights, the cities, health care, welfare, education, and employment.

Johnson won the election by a landslide, receiving 61 percent of the popular vote and picking up 486 electoral college votes to Goldwater's 53. The president's coattails were long; Democrats commanded a 289 to 146 majority in the House to go along with a 67 to 33 majority in the Senate. The Democrats' overwhelming victory set the stage for a period of legislative activism not seen since Roosevelt's fabled One Hundred Days in 1933. Between 1964 and 1966, Congress authorized 219 new programs, which included some of the most important and enduring social initiatives of the 1960s. In 1965, Congress approved Medicare for the elderly and Medicaid for welfare recipients. The Elementary and Secondary Education Act provided federal grants to schools. Food stamps, an experimental program tried during the Kennedy years, became permanent in 1966. New and expanded educational and job-training assistance was made available for the mentally and physically handicapped. The public housing and urban renewal programs were expanded, and a new "model cities" program to treat the problems of cities was initiated. In 1966, Congress also created a new cabinet-level department, the Department of Housing and Urban Development (HUD), to administer urban programs.

The rapid rise in the number of federal programs in the 1960s and 1970s (and the decline thereafter) can be seen by an examination of the graph in Figure 7.1. Spending on regional and community development climbed steeply and steadily from 1962 until 1980, from $2.6 billion (in constant 2001 dollars; the actual figure that year was $445 million) to $19.8 billion in 1980 (2001 dollars; $9.2 billion in actual dollars). Local governments became increasingly dependent upon intergovernmental transfers from federal and state governments. In 1950, grants from states and from the federal government accounted for only 10 percent of the revenues making up local budgets, but this proportion rose to over 26 percent of municipal revenues by 1978. In the 1980s, however, sharp cuts in federal grants reduced the cities' reliance on intergovernmental transfers. Federal funding for regional and community development was cut in half in constant 2001 dollars from 1980 to 1990 (see Figure 7.1) and continued to fall in the 1990s. By the end of the 1990s, cities received only about 7 percent of their income from intergovernmental revenues.

Figure 7.1   **Federal Spending on Regional and Community Development, 1962–2002 (in 2001 dollars)**

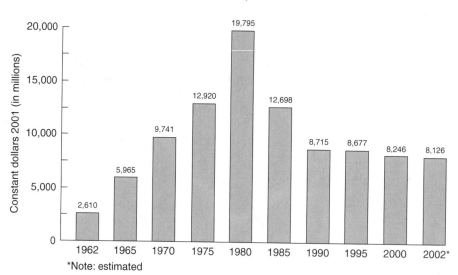

*Note: estimated

Source: Budget of the United State Government, Fiscal Year 2003: Historical Tables, Table 3.2, Economic Report of the President, Table B-60. Excludes spending on disaster relief.

The explosion in federal spending in the 1960s and 1970s was accompanied by an attempt to achieve a large number of national purposes. Not since the closing of the frontier in the 1870s had the federal government attempted so forcefully to set forth a direction for the nation. The Louisiana Purchase of 1803, a succession of township and homestead acts, generous land grants to railroad companies, and an aggressive military policy toward the Indians supported the federal government's intention to open up the West in the nineteenth century.[21] In the 1960s, the president and Congress mapped out a national agenda of comparable ambition. This time, the national government set out to eliminate poverty, erase racial discrimination, provide equal opportunity in education and jobs, and revitalize cities and communities.

The national emphasis on equality and social justice was reflected in especially clear terms in the case of the Civil Rights Act of 1964, when the federal government served notice that its new civil rights statutes would override state and local racial practices. The preambles to the grant programs of Kennedy's New Frontier and Johnson's Great Society articulated a variety of national goals. For example, from the Manpower Development and Training Act of 1962:

> It is in the national interest that current and prospective manpower shortages be identified and that persons who can be qualified for these positions through education and training be sought out and trained, *in order that the nation may meet the staffing requirements of the struggle for freedom.*[22]

Or the Economic Opportunity Act of 1964:

> The United States can achieve its full economic and social potential as a nation only if every individual has the opportunity to contribute the full extent of his capabilities and to participate in the workings of our society. *It is, therefore, the policy of the United States* to eliminate the paradox of poverty in the midst of plenty in this nation.[23]

And the Demonstration Cities and Metropolitan Development Act of 1966 (the so-called Model Cities legislation):

> The Congress hereby finds and declares that *improving the quality of urban life is the most critical domestic problem facing the United States.*[24]

Imagine these kinds of statements of intention introducing hundreds of pieces of legislation, ranging from rent supplements to federal school aid to crime control, and the complexity of the new system of grants becomes readily apparent. Hardly an economic or a social problem escaped attention, and each program specified its own complicated methods of implementation. Recipient institutions were subjected to complex rules and close scrutiny. After all, it makes no sense to fund a national priority unless the money is going to be used carefully, according to prescribed guidelines and standards.[25]

The Great Society

The War on Poverty and Model Cities programs attracted a great deal of attention because they were sold with grandiose promises about what they would accomplish. In 1964, when Lyndon Johnson proposed the War on Poverty, he announced that his objective was "total victory."[26] Such a promise could not possibly be fulfilled no matter how well the program might be implemented. As it turned out, the War on Poverty became a lightning rod for controversy, as did the Model Cities program, which was implemented through the Demonstration Cities Act of 1966. Under the terms of the War on Poverty, community action agencies were instructed to operate with the "maximum feasible participation" of the poor. Likewise, Model Cities agencies were supposed to galvanize participation by local residents. City Hall and other agencies of local government were cut out of the loop. The idea was to create new institutions in the cities capable of mobilizing the energies of people outside the established power structure. An early program guide distributed by the Office of Economic Opportunity said that to qualify for funding, local antipoverty programs should involve the poor from the very first "in planning, policy-making, and operation."[27]

These programs were, in effect, a means of fomenting a revolution in local politics. According to two scholars, Frances Fox Piven and Richard A. Cloward, many of the Great Society programs were formulated to preserve and strengthen the Democratic party's electoral advantage in the industrialized states holding the largest blocs of votes in the Electoral College.[28] Rather than work through local politicians who had repeatedly shown an unwillingness to mobilize the votes of inner-city blacks, federal administrators tried to work directly with organizations and leaders in black communities. The expectation was that blacks would vote Democratic in return.

A multitude of new agencies was established to receive and spend federal dollars. Of all of the community action funds spent by the Office of Economic Opportunity by 1968, only 25 percent were given to public agencies. The remainder went to organizations such as universities, churches, civil rights groups, settlement houses, family services agencies, United Way programs, and newly established nonprofit groups.[29] Likewise, only 10 percent of the funds distributed through programs administered by the Department of Health, Education and Welfare were administered by state and local governments.[30]

A handful of programs received a massive amount of media attention when political activists associated with them became embroiled in political fights with mayors and local government officials. In Syracuse, San Francisco, and the state of Mississippi, local administrators of antipoverty programs led protest actions against mayors, welfare departments, and school boards, demanding the implementation of programs that responded to complaints from the black community. Though such protests happened in only a few places, local authorities were upset when they saw federal monies flowing into their jurisdictions to groups and organizations that regularly opposed City Hall. Such organizations encouraged complaints about all sorts of things—police brutality, the hiring of teachers, welfare policies, public housing maintenance; the list could be endless.

Despite such controversies, the War on Poverty and the Model Cities programs continued to receive congressional support mainly because funds flowed into a large number of states and congressional districts. Thus, politicians of both parties were able to take credit for bringing federal spending to their states and districts. This was hardly accidental. To broaden the base of support in Congress, the Johnson Administration abandoned its original intention to restrict the antipoverty effort to a few "demonstration" projects. In the first year, 650 projects were funded, but by 1967 the number reached 1,100. The same thing happened with the Model Cities program. Like the War on Poverty, Model Cities was promoted with overblown rhetoric; it was supposed to involve an unprecedented "concentration and coordination of Federal, State, and local public and private efforts" in a few target areas.[31] Initially, the number of cities that would receive money for "demonstration" programs was supposed to be as low as five.[32] By the time powerful congressional leaders were accommodated, the number of cities had gone up to seventy-five, and a year later another seventy-five cities were added in a second round of funding.[33] The effect was to spread the federal dollars thin and dilute the impact of each of the programs.

The combination of political controversy, overblown promises, and limited accomplishments became enduring and damaging legacies of the Great Society. Conservative critics have contended that the social programs of the 1960s and 1970s not only failed to eliminate poverty but also made it more intractable by providing incentives for people not to work and support a family.[34] Over the years, such claims took on the status of a conventional wisdom, despite the fact that they were mostly wrong. The poverty rate fell by exactly half after the social programs of the 1960s were enacted, from 22.2 percent of the population in 1960 to an all-time low of 11.1 percent by 1973.[35] In the 1980s, when expenditures on programs for the poor were slashed, the poverty rate rose steadily, and by 1992 it had rebounded almost to the pre-1960s level.[36]

Evaluations of specific federal programs to attack urban problems show mixed results. Often the programs were overly complex and administrators ran into severe implementation problems.[37] But some programs worked. Perhaps the best example is Head Start, a federal program designed to enhance the skills of poor children before they enter school. One study found that children who participated in Head Start were 45 percent less likely to be held back in school than were similar children not enrolled in the program. This produced a substantial savings for local school districts.[38] Medicare and Medicaid improved health care substantially for the elderly and the poor. In 1963, 19 percent of poor persons had never visited a doctor; this fell to only 8 percent by 1970. From 1965 to 1975, the infant mortality rate of the poor fell by 33 percent.[39] Because of such successes, most of the poverty programs became sufficiently popular that they endured despite complaints from conservatives. Two programs—Community Action and Job Corps—took most of the political heat. The first was ended in 1974; the second barely survived as a small program until the 1980s.

THE REPUBLICANS AND THE NEW FEDERALISM

Though the years 1965 and 1966 generally are considered the high-water mark for national urban programs, spending continued to rise for several years through Democratic and Republican administrations alike. From 1969 through 1976, when Republicans held the presidency, aid to state and local governments climbed from $20 billion to $59 billion, staying well ahead of inflation.[40] Funding continued to rise because a broad base of support had been established. Cities had become heavily dependent on federal dollars. Thus, senators and members of Congress from urban districts, and governors, mayors, and other public leaders with ties to cities, wanted the flow of funds to continue. Powerful interest groups rallied behind their favored programs. In addition, both houses of Congress continued to be controlled by the Democratic Party. In this circumstance, and after a failed attempt to kill the War on Poverty programs, President Nixon set out to reform rather than to eliminate urban programs.

Rather than attempting to kill urban programs outright, presidents Nixon and Ford sought to shift urban aid from categorical grants, which applied complex federal rules specifying how federal funds could be spent, to block grants that gave state and local governments broad discretion in deciding how to use the money. Between 1972 and 1978, the proportion of federal grants-in-aid distributed as block grants to states and local governments rose sharply from just 2.8 percent to 34.5 percent.[41] Block grants—so called because they bundled several programs into a "block" requiring only a single application—gave the Republicans the opportunity to rewrite legislation so that funds would flow less to the central cities and more to smaller cities and suburbs, where Republican voters lived.

As soon as he became president, Richard Nixon signaled his desire to change how federal programs were administered. He spoke of the grant programs as producing a "gathering of the reins of power in Washington," which he saw as "a radical departure from the vision of federal-state relations the nation's founders had in mind." He proposed a New Federalism, meant to restore "a rightful balance between the state capital and the national capital."[42] This turned out to be a rather modest summary of a theme he was to return to many times, perhaps most concisely in an October 21, 1972, radio address on "The Philosophy of Government":

> Do we want to turn more power over to bureaucrats in Washington in the hope that they will do what is best for all the people? Or do we want to return more power to the people and to their state and local governments so that people can decide what is best for themselves? It is time that good, decent people stopped letting themselves be bulldozed by anybody who presumes to be the self-righteous moral judge of our society. In the next four years, as in the past four, I will continue to direct the flow of power away from Washington and back to the people.[43]

A revenue-sharing program was the first major initiative of the New Federalism. Under a strict interpretation of revenue sharing, it meant that the federal government would literally share a proportion of revenues coming into the federal treasury with states and localities. The president's proposal, submitted in January 1971, did not go that far, but it came close; state and local governments would automatically receive federal grants, with no strings attached.

The Nixon Administration's revenue-sharing proposal received backing from both Republican and Democratic state and local officials. The support for the program was centered in a group of organizations, known as the Big Seven, that represented state and local government officials. The members of this coalition were the National League of Cities (NLC), the U.S. Conference of Mayors (USCM), the National Governors' Conference, the National Legislative Conference, the Council of State Governments, the National Association of Counties, and the International City Management Association (ICMA). City managers had long defined themselves as trained professionals who rejected political activities as beyond their purview. In the fight for revenue sharing, however, they broke with a fifty-year tradition of legislative neutrality.[44]

The Democratic Party was deeply split over revenue sharing. Some wanted to protect their hard-won social and urban programs, and they suspected revenue sharing of being the entering wedge for dismantling their favored policies. On the other hand, Democratic mayors from the big cities strongly supported the proposal. They welcomed the prospect of new dollars that they could spend as they wished. Moreover, the fiscal condition of the cities, where revenues chronically lagged behind expenditures, was sufficiently pressing that no mayor could afford to oppose any proposal that would bring federal dollars. Though sympathetic to the cities' plight, Democrats in Congress resisted the pressure to approve revenue sharing. With the 1972 presidential election only a year away, the Democratic legislative leadership did not want to give Nixon any type of domestic victory. Big-city mayors such as Pittsburgh's Peter Flaherty and Cleveland's Carl Stokes considered this attitude an "ill-advised . . . partisan reflex"[45] to what they considered a nonpartisan issue of urban need.

The tension between the party's congressional leadership and the mayors came to a head in a March 1971 private meeting of the House leadership and the U.S. Conference of Mayors' Legislative Action Committee:

> As one of those in attendance recalls it, New York's Mayor John V. Lindsay had just gotten up to speak, when Majority Leader Hale Boggs (D-La.) suddenly slammed his fist on the desk and shouted: "You don't need to make any points. Revenue sharing is dead. I'll see that it never passes. So let's get on to something else." Flabbergasted, Lindsay slid back into his seat. There was a moment of embarrassed silence—and then a rolling southern drawl rang out from the back of the room. "Hale," said New Orleans Mayor Moon Landrieu, "that's the rudest treatment I have ever witnessed, and I think you better talk about revenue sharing and you better listen. Because, Hale, if you don't start thinking about helping the cities, I want you to know that you'll never be welcome in the city of New Orleans again." Now it was Boggs' turn to be flabbergasted.[46]

In the aftermath of this heated exchange, the congressional leadership began to reassess its position. After compromises were reached on the tricky issue of how to divide the money among the various levels of government (states, municipalities, counties, and townships), revenue sharing finally passed both houses of Congress and was signed by President Nixon in 1972.

Revenue sharing gave local officials extraordinary latitude in deciding how to spend federal money. Unlike the grant-in-aid programs of the 1960s, federal rules were minimal and virtually unenforceable. Because of the lack of detailed federal oversight, revenue-sharing dollars were intermingled with other monies that flowed into the treasuries of the more than 39,000 state, county, township, and municipal governments across the nation. As a consequence, they could not be traced beyond the reports filed with the Treasury Department by local officials. Revenue-sharing monies constituted a largely unrestricted, though small, supplement to the tax revenues of state and local governments. In 1974, the $4.5 billion apportioned among 35,077 local governments accounted for an average of 3.1 percent of their revenues for that year.[47] Revenue sharing was used to cover ordinary services already provided by the recipient governments; basically, it allowed them to avoid increasing taxes.

Financially strapped big cities were under the greatest pressure to use revenue-sharing funds just to keep things going.[48] Big cities spent nearly all of their revenue-sharing dollars on day-to-day operations and maintenance.[49] Only months after the first checks were sent out by the Revenue Sharing Office, congressional Democrats began to complain about the manner in which the money was being spent.[50] Representative Shirley Chisholm of New York voiced concern "that the program failed to aid the disadvantaged and minority groups."[51] Other members of Congress likewise complained that revenue-sharing funds were not going to people who needed them the most.[52]

Despite such complaints, however, revenue sharing was extended in 1976. As a concession to liberals, a citizen participation rule was added that required public hearings before the money could be spent.[53] Again, it was the unrelenting political pressure applied by the Big Seven, with big-city mayors taking the lead, that prodded Congress to act. The U.S. Conference of Mayors adopted a resolution "supporting reenactment of the general revenue sharing program and promising to make renewal a key local issue in the Congressional campaigns."[54]

The 1976 extension kept funding at the same level, but because of inflation, the actual amount of funding, measured in constant dollars, dropped by 17 percent between 1972 and 1979.[55] In 1980, Congress amended the revenue-sharing legislation to eliminate the states as recipients. Through the first half of the 1980s, revenue sharing constituted about 1.5 percent of municipal budgets. Even at that level, it soon came under criticism from President Reagan, who expressed the view that it simply encouraged state and local governments to spend more money. Conservative Republicans wanted to cut government spending at all levels, so revenue sharing had to go. It was dropped at the end of fiscal year 1986.

The Housing and Community Development Act

The Community Development Block Grant (CDBG) program, enacted in 1974, is the only significant survivor of the major urban policies enacted in the pre-Reagan era. Although Democrats and Republicans often skirmished over details, the program consistently enjoyed bipartisan support, probably because it offered something for everyone. Liberals liked it because it obligated local governments to fight poverty and urban blight; conservatives liked it because two of its objectives, as stated in the original legislation, were "increased private investment and streamlining of all levels of government programming."[56] To its advocates, it was a huge improvement over the grant programs it replaced because it reduce federal oversight and paperwork.

The Housing and Community Development Act of 1974 (CDA) was signed into law by President Gerald Ford in August 1974 and took effect in January 1975. Seven major categorical grant programs (for water and sewerage systems, neighborhood facilities, land acquisitions, code enforcement, neighborhood development, urban renewal, and Model Cities) were folded into one Community Development Block Grant (CDBG). Though cities automatically qualified for the program if they met a specified formula, they were required to submit an application that described how the money would be used and were required to submit quarterly reports to the Department of Housing and Urban Development (HUD).

Of the $8.4 billion authorized by Congress for the first three years, 80 percent was to be distributed to cities of at least 50,000 population within Standard Metropolitan Statistical Areas; thus, all central cities and some larger suburbs qualified. The formula for distributing money to the various entitlement communities (so called because they were "entitled" to a share of funds if they fit the formula) took into account the population of the city, its poverty level, and its percent of overcrowded housing.

Unlike for general revenue sharing, cities were required to submit an annual application for CDBG funds even though they were automatically eligible. The annual applications asked for statistics and statements so that federal administrators could trace the use of the funds. Entitlement cities also were required to submit a three-year development plan that, among other things, projected "long-range community objectives"(which had to include a housing assistance plan for the poor and elderly), respected equal opportunity and environmental protection guidelines, and, most notably, gave "maximum feasible priority" to low- and moderate-income areas.[57] In addition to the pool of entitlement funds, about 20 percent of the total money authorized for the CDBG program was awarded on a competitive basis and in accordance with detailed applications and performance standards and review procedures.[58]

President Ford had expressed strong opposition to any detailed review of applications by HUD, and thus the Ford Administration did not monitor how cities spent the money. By the end of the program's first year, Secretary Carla Hills reported that HUD had reduced the average review period from two years for the programs that the CDA replaced to forty-nine days, and that applications averaged 50 pages, compared with an average of 1,400 pages for the old urban renewal applications alone.[59]

The lack of HUD oversight became an issue as soon as Democrat Jimmy Carter became president. In its first annual report on the program, issued early in 1976, HUD stated that 71 percent of all community development funds were allocated to low- and moderate-income priority areas.[60] A year later, in its second annual report (and the first issued under Carter), HUD revised its calculation and found that the percentage of funds being spent in low- and moderate-income areas (areas in which the median income was 80 percent or less of the metropolitan average) averaged only 44 percent.[61]

Evidence indicated that southern cities, in particular, were allocating far more money to affluent areas than was intended by Congress. According to the Southern Regional Council, "the very mixed achievements of southern cities had shown that local diversions from national purpose are not just occasional abuses, but rather form a pattern inherent in the implementation of the Act."[62] That community development funds would be spent in affluent areas was hardly a surprising turn of events, since local political elites exerted a controlling voice in the allocation process. In most local communities, poorer residents had little influence. As a result of this circumstance, Little Rock, Arkansas, for example, spent $150,000 of the city's block grant funds to construct a tennis court in an affluent section of town. When questioned about this use of funds, the director of the local Department of Human Resources unpersuasively claimed that "ninety-nine percent of this money is going to low and moderate income areas." But he revealingly continued: "You cannot divorce politics from that much money. We remember the needs of the people who vote because they hold us accountable. Poor people don't vote."[63]

One strategy that local communities employed to make it appear that funds were flowing to low- and moderate-income priority areas was to draw their funding district boundaries in such a way as to include affluent and less affluent people within the same program areas. Gulfport, Mississippi, went even further when it declared the entire city to be one big "renewal" area, thus making it impossible to determine who benefited from particular projects. The city built a new central fire station with the money, claiming, "When you expand fire protection, everybody in every census tract benefits from lower insurance rates," including, ostensibly, the primary target population of the legislation, the low- and moderate-income residents.[64]

Whatever gimmick or tortured logic a city might employ, the outcome was that federal guidelines were generally ignored. Analyses of a number of individual cities demonstrated higher-than-expected CDBG allocations in more affluent areas. A study by the Brookings Institution examined the distribution of the block grants funds in sixty-two cities and found that only 29 percent of the monies were spent in neighborhoods that had lower-than-median family incomes.[65] The Carter Administration began to crack down on some communities that flagrantly ignored the congressional intent. In April 1978, HUD issued new regulations that required communities to target 75 percent of their CDBG funds to benefit low- and moderate-income areas.[66] HUD's new policy resulted in significant increases in the proportion of money flowing to such areas.[67]

Midway through Carter's term, HUD's goal of targeting funds so that they would reach neighborhoods in need came into conflict with a new approach. New regulations issued by HUD required cities to designate Neighborhood Strategy Areas where public funds could be used to attract private investment. Though federal administrators rarely admitted it, they were now following a "triage" strategy suggested by a consultant, Anthony Downs. Downs proposed that federal money could be used more wisely if it were distributed strategically, like the triage method used to treat wounded French soldiers during World War I.[68] Medical personnel classified the wounded into three groups: (1) those who were so badly wounded that they could not be saved, to whom painkillers were given; (2) those who would die without treatment but would probably live with it, to whom maximum treatment was given; and (3) those who would survive with minimal medical care, to whom treatment was given when time and resources allowed. Based on the triage concept, Downs recommended that areas within cities be divided into three categories: deteriorated, transitional (or deteriorating), and healthy. Pouring money into deteriorated neighborhoods, he said, would be a waste of money because they were too far gone to be salvaged. Transitional neighborhoods would benefit the most from aid because with some visible public improvements, they might attract private investment.[69] Healthy neighborhoods would survive just fine without aid. If distributed on such a basis, the impact of federal money could be maximized. Urban consultant Roger Starr took the triage analogy even further, arguing that public services should be pulled out of blighted areas entirely so that resources, both federal and local, could be concentrated in neighborhoods considered still viable.[70]

Local governments generally denied that they used the triage strategy. To admit that such a policy was being followed would surely incite protests from people living in the neighborhoods being written off as hopeless. It is clear, however, that the triage approach was used in a great many cities. In a 1974 report to the city planning commission, a St. Louis consulting firm recommended the city reduce services and discourage investment in severely blighted areas and allocate most of its resources to neighborhoods it defined as declined but salvageable.[71] Another researcher showed that a similar triage approach underpinned the "Chicago 21" plan for redevelopment of the Loop.[72] Community development funds in Denver were also distributed in conformity with a triage strategy. According to two Denver researchers, it would be surprising indeed if this were not the case in other cities, considering the guidelines established by the federal government.[73]

In implementing the CDBG program, the Carter Administration tried to pursue two contradictory goals. On the one hand, it tried to enforce the legislative intent that CDBG dollars should go primarily to low- and moderate-income areas. On the other hand, it urged cities to emphasize strategies to stimulate private investment. It soon became apparent that the administration was retreating from any emphasis at all on social, as opposed to economic development, goals. Instead, according to HUD secretary Patricia R. Harris, "The specific intent of action programs will be to stimulate new and increased private investment while establishing private sector confidence that will protect current investment."[74] The new priority placed on leveraging private investment was hammered home on March 27, 1978, when the White House issued a document entitled "New Partnership to Conserve America's Communities."[75] The first section of the document emphasized the goal of economic development: "The loss of private sector activity, and of middle-income households, has eroded the tax base of many urban areas."[76] The new emphasis appealed to conservatives who had previously opposed the program, and helped ensure its long-term survival.

PRESIDENT CARTER AND THE DEMOCRATS' LAST HURRAH

As a Democratic president, Jimmy Carter could have been expected to respond favorably to the cities of the northern industrial states. Voters in these cities had remained faithful to the Democrats for decades, and they helped give Carter his margin of victory in several states in the 1976 presidential election. Accordingly, the administration tried to develop policies that would shore up support among urban voters. The president persuaded Congress to pass an amendment to the revenue-sharing program that added an "excess unemployment" factor to the distribution formula.[77] Cities with high unemployment levels received all the money. He successfully sought increases in CDBG funding and significantly amended the program in 1978 to help the big cities. Large increases were legislated for Comprehensive Employment Training Act (CETA) programs, which gave money to local training centers and to local governments to put people to work repairing parks and public facilities. Despite these accomplishments, however, by the time Carter left office he seemed to be abandoning urban policy altogether.

Soon after Carter assumed office, his administration began efforts to amend the Community Development Act, with the objective of favoring older industrial cities experiencing fiscal and social stress. By the end of 1975 there was growing concern, particularly among the representatives of big cities, that older cities in fiscal and social stress were destined to receive a declining share of CDBG funds over time. From a level of nearly 83 percent of the community development monies allocated in fiscal year 1975, the Illinois Bureau of the Budget projected that only 60 percent would go to older cities of the North by 1980.[78]

By 1980, Newark, New Jersey, would lose more than 52 percent of the block grant allocation that it had in 1975, Philadelphia nearly 45 percent, Detroit 22 percent, and Rochester, New York, almost 70 percent. The "lost" money would be largely reallocated to the growing cities of the Sunbelt. Dallas would receive a huge 549 percent increase in its CDBG block grant by 1980, Fort Lauderdale 536 percent, and Phoenix 727 percent.[79]

Why was this happening? It turned out that the formula for distributing CDBG funds, as adopted in the 1974 legislation, was unintentionally biased against the declining older cities. Money was distributed on the basis of a formula that assigned equal weights for a city's population and the extent of overcrowded housing, plus a double weight for the city's level of poverty. The older cities were going to receive less CDBG money over time simply because they were rapidly losing population. Sunbelt cities, by contrast, would qualify for more money every year because they were growing. The other factors in the formula could not overcome the funding losses from declining population, since levels of poverty in southern and southwestern cities ran at or above the national average and the extent of housing overcrowding did not vary enough from city to city.

Several groups initiated efforts to persuade Congress to revise the formula. The group of representatives who made up the Northeast-Midwest Congressional Coalition in the House lined up behind a new formula that would assign a 20 percent weight to the degree of population *loss* in a city, a 30 percent weight to the city's poverty level, and a 50 percent weight to the *age of the city's housing stock* (defined as the percentage of housing built before 1939). Obviously, two of these factors applied only to older cities: They were losing population, and most of their housing had been built before 1939. This formula gave maximum advantage to the Frostbelt cities, and HUD selected it as its recommended replacement for the 1974 formula precisely for that reason.[80]

As soon as the legislation to revise the formula was introduced, a bitter feud broke out between representatives from the Northeast and Midwest and the congressional delegations from southern and western states. One of two California representatives who introduced an amendment to retain the old formula put the matter succinctly: "The real issue here is: Do we want to address poverty or do we want to address old houses. . . . Poor people live throughout the United States, they are not entirely contained within older cities."[81] The Southern Growth Policies Board, an organization representing state officials and businesses in the South, mounted a well-organized lobbying campaign against the revision.[82]

Ultimately, the new formula won in a vote that divided along regional, not party, lines: Representatives from the East and Midwest voted 215 to 8 in favor, while those from the South and West voted 132 to 18 against. The legislation that passed the house in May 1977 dramatically increased the community development entitlement funds flowing to the distressed cities of the North. Under the HUD-sponsored amendments, New York City stood to receive a 50 percent increase in its entitlement for 1978 and about a 42 percent increase ($100 million) in 1980.[83] Several older cities expected to double their entitlements. To win enough support in Congress, Sunbelt cities were offered a guarantee that they would not lose money. To make this possible, overall CDBG funding was increased and a "dual formula" was devised whereby cities could select the original 1974 formula or the new one, depending on which one they preferred.

To provide additional assistance to distressed cities, in 1978 Congress approved the Urban Development Action Grants (UDAG) program. Unlike the entitlement CDBG grants, these funds required applications to accomplish particular projects, and they were explicitly designed to leverage private investments. Over the years, UDAG grants were used to build festival malls such as Union Station in St. Louis and Harborplace in Baltimore; to expand convention centers; to build public infrastructure (such as improved streets, new lighting, landscaping, and fountains) that might leverage private investment; to repair historic buildings; and to support neighborhood improvements. In July 1977, the community development amendments and the UDAG grants were approved by Congress and sent to the White House for President Carter's signature. As a result of the new legislation, cities in the Northeast received an average 77 percent increase in fiscal year 1980. Cities in the Midwest received 66 percent more in funding. By contrast, cities of the South were held to an 8 percent increase and cities in the West to a 14 percent increase.[84]

The Democrats' bias toward older cities already had been revealed when Congress passed the Anti-Recession Fiscal Assistance Act over President Ford's veto in July 1976. The program distributed aid to cities with particularly high unemployment rates and was designed as an emergency measure to help distressed cities avert layoffs, maintain service levels, and avoid tax increases. It was scheduled to end on September 30, 1977, by which time, it was hoped, the recession's impact on these cities would have run its course. But in 1977, the Carter Administration recommended that the act be extended and funds increased. In the Intergovernmental Anti-Recession Act of 1977, $2.25 billion was added and antirecession assistance to city governments was extended to September 30, 1978.[85] These programs were heavily weighted in favor of distressed cities. Five cities—New York, Philadelphia, Detroit, Chicago, and Los Angeles—received 13 percent of the Anti-Recession Fiscal Assistance funds. (Together these cities made up 8 percent of the U.S. population.[86]) By far, the smallest allocations went to Sunbelt cities. Dallas, for example, received 4 cents per capita through the program and Houston $1.56; in contrast, Newark's allocation amounted to $39.34 per capita.[87]

The various antirecession and public employment programs reflected the political priorities of a Democratic president and a Democratic Congress. Between fiscal years 1972 and 1975, federal grants to eight Frostbelt cities increased by an average of 62 percent, while grants to nine Sunbelt cities rose by 238 percent. This happened because revenue sharing and CDBG grants went to cities on the basis of a formula rather than through an application showing "need." Between 1975 and 1978, however, grants went up faster in the Frostbelt cities (133 percent) than in the Sunbelt cities (83 percent).[88] The federal grants to distressed cities were extremely important to their financial well-being. In 1977, because of new federal funds, revenues in twenty-seven of the largest cities exceeded expenditures by 3.2 percent. By contrast, these cities had accumulated an average per-city debt of $28 million in 1975 and $151 million in 1976.[89]

On March 28, 1978, President Carter announced, with great fanfare, a comprehensive new urban policy. Asserting that "the deterioration of urban life in the United States is one of the most complex and deeply rooted problems of our age," the president stated that "the federal government has the clear duty to lead the effort to reverse that deterioration."[90] The centerpiece of the president's proposal was a national development bank, which would be authorized to guarantee loans to businesses in depressed urban and rural areas; in addition, the administration wanted to offer tax credits for businesses hiring ghetto youths, a labor-intensive public works program, and more money for housing rehabilitation. The amount of additional money requested was relatively modest (about $4.4 billion), but this did not deter the president from promising a "new Partnership involving all levels of government, the private sector and neighborhood and voluntary organizations."[91]

Carter's ringing call for a comprehensive urban policy raised hopes in city halls, but it turned into an abject political failure. The only major legislative proposal that was enacted into law was the Targeted Employment Tax Credit. The timing was bad for any new legislative initiative.[92] In 1978, California voters passed Proposition 13, which sharply reduced local property taxes. The gathering strength of a tax revolt across the nation helped shape a mood of fiscal conservatism in Congress and a go-slow approach in the White House.[93] Perhaps sensing a changing political climate, Carter did an about-face in the last two years of his term, turning his attention away from urban policy toward the problems of the national economy and the cost and availability of energy. A sharp decline in manufacturing jobs and an acceleration in foreign investment by American companies, together with an increase in imports, became the leading domestic issues of the 1980 presidential campaign.

After Carter's election in 1976, Mayor Kenneth A. Gibson of Newark had spoken for many Democratic mayors when he remarked that "we have every reason to believe that this is the beginning of a new relationship between the White House and the nation's mayors."[94] The new relationship, however, proved to be short-lived. Even if Carter had won the 1980 presidential race, it is doubtful that any significant urban programs would have emerged in a second term.

REPUBLICANS AND THE END OF FEDERAL ASSISTANCE

In a press conference held in October 1981, President Ronald Reagan suggested that the residents of cities where unemployment was high should "vote with their feet" and move to more prosperous areas of the country.[95] His remark ignited an instant political controversy, but, in fact, it was consistent with the recommendations of a presidential commission appointed by his predecessor, Jimmy Carter. In a report issued only a few weeks after Reagan took office, the Presidential Commission on the National Agenda for the Eighties urged that the national government stop helping cities. The commission emphasized that federal policies should be used to promote national economic growth, but that these policies should be neutral about where that growth occurred:

> It may be in the best interest of the nation to commit itself to the promotion of location-ally neutral economic and social policies rather than spatially sensitive urban policies that either explicitly or inadvertently seek to preserve cities in their historical roles.[96]

The commission reasoned that economic processes affecting older cities were irreversible:

> The economy of the United States, like that of many of the older industrial societies, has for years now been undergoing a critical transition from being geographically-based to being deconcentrated, decentralized, and service-based. In the process, many cities of the old industrial heartland . . . are losing their status as thriving industrial capitals. . . .
>
> The historical dominance of more central cities will be diminished as certain production, residential, commercial, and cultural functions disperse to places beyond them.[97]

Recommending that the federal government let the process of decay in some areas and growth in others take its natural course, the commission noted that cities adapt and change in response to economic and social forces. This process of adaptation, said the commission, should be facilitated, not altered, by governmental policy:

> Ultimately, the federal government's concern for national economic vitality should take precedence over the competition for advantage among communities and regions.[98]
>
> To attempt to restrict or reverse the processes of change—for whatever noble intentions—is to deny the benefits that the future may hold for us as a nation.[99]

The recommendations by Carter's commission and the policies subsequently pursued by the Reagan Administration constituted a revolutionary change in philosophy: For the first time since national urban policy was first enacted in the 1930s, the judgment was made that individual cities were not valuable cultural, social, or economic entities except to the degree to which they contributed to a healthy national economy. Three University of Delaware researchers characterized the new policy as "a form of Social Darwinism applied to cities."[100] Cities would survive if they could manage to regenerate their local economies. Otherwise, they would be allowed to wither away.

The Reagan Administration set about sharply reducing federal urban aid, proclaiming that "the private market is more efficient than federal program administrators in allocating dollars."[101] Cities were instructed to improve their ability to compete in a struggle for survival in which "state and local governments will find it is in their interests to concentrate on increasing their attractiveness to potential investors, residents, and visitors."[102] Thus, urban policy was built on the assumption that free enterprise would provide a bounty of jobs, incomes, and neighborhood renewal, and that such local prosperity would make federal programs unnecessary. The Community Development Block Grant (CDBG) and Urban Development Action Grant (UDAG) programs won a reprieve from being drastically reduced in the 1983 budget, and so did revenue sharing. Budget Director David Stockman wanted to kill these programs altogether; he had previously attempted to write them out of the budget in 1981. But the administration, bending to the weakened but still viable urban lobby—represented principally by governors and mayors, quite a few of them Republican—backed off. The groups making up the urban lobby came away relieved that the budget cuts were less drastic than they had feared. Only two years later, however, the administration was able to eliminate most urban programs.

Urban programs gave way to a new priority: tax cuts. On February 18, 1981, President Reagan proposed a massive tax cut to stimulate the economy. This package, which would reduce federal revenues by $54 billion in 1982 alone, called for a 10 percent reduction each year for three years for all individual taxpayers, plus accelerated depreciation of capital assets and other liberalized tax write-offs for corporations. Congress was at first cool to the idea, but it soon became apparent to Democratic lawmakers that they could improve their own reelection prospects if they offered "improvements" to the legislation that would be appealing to corporate campaign contributors and individual constituents. By the time individual legislators had outbid one another to satisfy their own constituency groups, the revenue losses from the package were so staggering that some White House advisers wanted to kill the bill.[103] Reagan, however, wanted it passed and he lobbied hard for it, even going on television to appeal for expressions of popular support.

Reagan signed the Economic Recovery Tax Act of 1981 on August 13, 1981, asserting that it was "a turnaround of almost a half a century of . . . excessive growth in government bureaucracy, government spending, government taxing."[104] In its final version the act reduced individual tax rates by 25 percent over three years and also substantially reduced business tax liability. The revenue losses were huge. In just the first two years, $128 billion in revenue was lost to the federal treasury, and the total losses by 1987 amounted to more than $1 trillion.[105] The 1981 tax cuts, in combination with massive increases in military spending, created huge budget deficits into the late 1990s.

The Tax Reform Act of 1986 added to the effects of the legislation adopted five years earlier by further slashing federal revenues and sharply reducing the capacity of governments at all levels to collect increased revenues in step with an improving economy. Most Americans had the impression that the main purpose of the 1986 legislation was to simplify a maddeningly complex tax code, but this promise was never fulfilled. Instead, Congress merely replaced the several tax rates in the code to three basic levels: 15 percent, 28 percent, and 32 percent. The top tax rate was reduced and all three were indexed to inflation, so that over time taxpayers would not slide into a higher tax bracket unless their incomes rose faster than the inflation rate. There were two dramatic effects. First, the new law almost eliminated the feature of the tax code that had historically allowed the federal government to collect increased taxes whenever incomes went up, either in real terms or through inflation. This change had the effect of institutionalizing the tax cuts adopted in 1981 by making it difficult for federal revenues to rise, even in a good economy, to reduce budget deficits. Only cuts in expenditures or increases in tax rates could accomplish that.

The second effect of the Tax Reform Act was that tax rates fell only modestly or not at all for most taxpayers, but they were cut drastically for the rich. In subsequent years, a perception that tax burdens fell unfairly on the middle class helped fuel a tax revolt. George Bush won the presidency in 1988 partly with the promise, "Read my lips: no new taxes." As a follow-up, the administration cut spending for programs for education, housing, health, and welfare.

President Reagan's cuts were the first reductions of consequence in grants-in-aid expenditures since the 1940s. Broad entitlement programs with middle-class recipients, such as the old-age and survivors' benefits funded through the Social Security Act of 1935, veterans' benefits, and Medicare, were affected only marginally. By contrast, deep cuts and new eligibility restrictions were imposed on public assistance programs for the poor. Medicaid, which was available through the states to welfare recipients, was subjected to tighter eligibility requirements, but Medicaid outlays soared anyway because of rising medical costs. Enrollment in Aid to Families with Dependent Children (AFDC) fell by half a million. A million people lost food stamps. It became harder to get unemployment benefits; whereas 75 percent of the unemployed received benefits during the recession of 1975, only 45 percent were able to qualify during the 1982–1983 recession.[106]

The countercyclical urban aid programs inherited from the 1980s (the Anti-Recession Fiscal Assistance Act of 1976 and the Intergovernmental Anti-Recession Act of 1977) were eliminated early in the Reagan Administration. Several other programs were also killed off by the end of Reagan's first term, including revenue sharing and federally assisted local public works. The Urban Development Action Grants were cut in 1986, though a trickle of money continued to flow in the administrative pipeline for several years (the total spending fell from an annual level of between $400 million and $500 million for the first ten years of the program [fiscal years 1978 to 1987] to $200 million in fiscal 1988 and dried up to a nominal $3 million by fiscal 1994).[107] Other budget cuts also affected the cities. Most subsidies for the construction of public housing were eliminated. Only 10,000 new units a year were authorized after 1983, compared with the 111,600 new or rehabilitated units authorized for 1981.[108] Among urban programs, the only real survivor of the Reagan cuts was the Community Development Block Grant program. CBDG spending fell from $4 billion in the 1981 fiscal year to $2.8 billion in fiscal 1990 before rebounding somewhat to $3.1 billion in fiscal 1992, the year the Democrats reclaimed the White House. Under President Clinton, CDBG spending rose modestly to $4.6 billion by the 1996 fiscal year,[109] and to $5.1 billion by Clinton's last budget, the 2001 fiscal year (in constant dollars, the program stayed at about the same level of funding). Under President George W. Bush, the level of funding was slated to fall to $4.7 billion by fiscal year 2003.[110]

Cities also lost intergovernmental funding because many of the remaining federal programs that had gone to local governments were given over to the states. In 1982, President Reagan persuaded Congress to consolidate seventy-six grant programs into nine block grants in health, social services, education, and community development. In the process, overall funding was reduced by 20 percent. Because the states tended to spread funds broadly across a great many jurisdictions and to give little priority to distressed communities, the cities were "one of the clearest losers of federal funds" under these block grants.[111] A 1982 study by the Senate Joint Economic Committee showed that distressed cities were losing a larger absolute amount and a higher percentage of federal aid than the cities that were better off.[112]

President Reagan also attempted to use the tax code to make it more difficult for states and localities to make up for lost grant funds. When the tax rates were reduced to three levels as a result of the 1986 Tax Reform Act, most states similarly revised their state income tax laws; this change was irresistible, since most state tax forms had been modeled on the federal forms. Thus, most states automatically reduced their taxes when the federal government did. The cities' ability to borrow was also affected. One of the provisions of the 1986 law was a state-by-state cap on the volume and purposes of tax-exempt municipal bonds. By the early 1990s, the effects of federal cutbacks and tax code changes had reverberated throughout the intergovernmental system. State and local governments found themselves deeply in debt, forcing them to slash funding for schools, higher education, and other programs.

Urban Enterprise Zones

Right from the beginning, the Reagan Administration had set out to dismantle federal programs designed to help the cities, and in eight years it largely succeeded. During those same years, however, the administration tried to reap political benefits by proposing (though never enthusiastically backing) urban policies that could be labeled "Republican." These policies were founded on the principle that cities should make themselves more attractive to capital investment by cutting taxes and offering incentives to spur local economic growth.

President Reagan promised to push for passage of urban enterprise zones legislation during a special session of Congress in November and December of 1982. In the press of other business, however, the legislation was not even discussed. Finally, on March 7, 1983, the president sent the proposed Urban Enterprise Zone Act to Congress, claiming that the legislation represented a sharp break from past policy:

> Enterprise zones are a fresh approach for promoting economic growth in the inner cities. The old approach relied on heavy government subsidies and central planning. A prime example was the model cities program in the 1960s, which concentrated government programs, subsidies and regulations in distressed urban areas. The enterprise zone approach is to remove government barriers, bring individuals to create, produce and earn their own wages and profits.[113]

No matter what claims the president made, the legislation was not a "fresh approach" but a logical extension of past policies. Since the latter years of the Carter administration, federal policy had stressed the role of government in subsidizing private investment. Throughout the Reagan years, the enterprise zones idea surfaced from time to time, but it was never pushed by the administration. After George Bush's election to the presidency in 1988, the idea continued to receive an occasional nudge from the president or from HUD, but it did not surface as a meaningful item on the president's legislative agenda until after the Los Angeles riot of April 29–May 3, 1992.

Measured by the number of deaths (53), injuries (2,383), property damage (over $700 million), and the response required to reestablish order, the Los Angeles riot was the country's worst episode of civil disorder in the twentieth century.[114] Many people thought that the riot could be used as an opportunity to call attention to the problems of urban America. Two weeks after the riots, 150,000 people descended on Washington for a Save Our Cities/Save Our Children rally. As the crisis atmosphere faded, however, urban issues got lost in election-year politics. Democratic candidate Bill Clinton initially blamed the riots on "twelve years of denial and neglect" by presidents Bush and Reagan, but fearing that he might be accused of advocating new spending programs, Clinton soon muted his criticisms.[115] On Monday, May 5, Bush's press spokesman, Marlin Fitzwater, said the Great Society's programs of the 1960s were to blame for the rioting. Nevertheless, in an attempt to look like he was responding positively, President Bush proposed an emergency aid package. In June, Congress passed $1.3 billion in emergency aid that allocated $500 million for summer jobs, $382 million for loans to businesses damaged or destroyed in the riot areas, and some flood relief for the city of Chicago.

Through the summer and early fall of 1992, Congress worked on a larger, permanent urban aid bill. A version was finally approved by the House on October 6 and the Senate on October 8. The legislation would have created twenty-five urban and twenty-five rural enterprise zones and financed so-called weed and seed programs that combined enhanced law enforcement with job training and education programs. The bulk of the legislation, however, was made up of an array of items that had nothing to do with cities, including liberalized (tax-free) retirement accounts for upper-income people and a provision for the repeal of luxury taxes on yachts, furs, jewels, and planes (Democrats backed this amendment as enthusiastically as Republicans). It was estimated that of the $30 billion that the bill would cost over five years, about $6 billion would be used to help depressed areas in cities.[116] By the time the legislation was passed and sent to the White House for President Bush's signature, the election was over. Bush vetoed it, claiming it was contaminated by pork-barrel amendments.

POLITICAL REALITY AND URBAN POLICY

In the campaigns of 1980 and 1984, the Republicans virtually wrote off the African American vote. Richard Wirthlin, Ronald Reagan's campaign strategist, advised before the 1980 election that the "Reagan for President 1980 campaign must convert into Reagan votes the disappointment felt by Southern white and rural voters."[117] Reagan won only 10 percent of the black vote in 1980 and slightly less in 1984. In 1984, however, three out of four southern whites supported him. The Reagan White House actively worked to undo civil rights guarantees, slashing the budgets of civil rights enforcement units and slowing or stopping enforcement.[118]

In the 1988 presidential election, the Republican candidate, George Bush, was also able to successfully use race to mobilize voters. Republicans ran an attack ad that featured a police photograph of Willie Horton, who had raped a woman in Maryland and stabbed her fiancé while on a weekend pass from a Massachusetts prison. The Democratic candidate, Michael Dukakis, had been the governor of Massachusetts at the time. According to Bush's campaign director, Lee Atwater, the fact that Willie Horton was black was the key element explaining the ad's emotional impact.

In 1992, with voters and the media sensitized to racial manipulation, direct racial appeals by the Bush campaign probably would have backfired. Instead, attacks on cities served as a code language for race and welfare-state liberalism. In one of the opening salvos of the campaign, Vice President Dan Quayle attacked New York City by saying, "The liberal vision of a happy, productive and content welfare state hasn't even worked on 22 square miles of the most valuable real estate in the world."[119] A later Quayle attack prompted a *New York Post* headline: "City to Dan Quayle: DON'T DIS' US!"[120] An editorial in the *New York Times* called Quayle's attacks an attempt to make New York City "The Willie Horton of 1992."[121]

As a self-styled "new Democrat" who wanted to project an image as a friend of the "forgotten middle class," Clinton could hardly be expected to place aid to cities or to the poor on the front burner. The Clinton campaign decided to concentrate on appealing to the white suburban middle class and to assume that inner-city voters would support him anyway because they had no place else to go. Clinton's electoral strategy succeeded in making him the first Democrat to be elected to two full terms since Franklin D. Roosevelt.

The logic behind Clinton's suburban strategy was compelling. By the 1990 census, 48 percent of the nation's population lived in suburbs. Because they tended to turn out for elections at a relatively high rate, it seemed certain that they would cast a majority of the votes in the 1992 election.[122] In addition, a large proportion of suburban voters were so-called Reagan Democrats, blue-collar and middle-class voters who had abandoned the party to vote Republican in the three previous presidential elections. They were heavily concentrated in the older suburbs in key states such as New Jersey, Michigan, and California, which could deliver the big blocs of electoral college votes coveted by every presidential candidate. To bring them back to the fold, Clinton wanted to avoid identifying himself with policies that were targeted to cities, and especially to blacks.

In developing this strategy, Clinton followed the advice of a well-known African American sociologist, William Julius Wilson, whose 1987 book, *The Truly Disadvantaged*, warned against race-specific policies. Wilson, who was a friend and adviser of the president, recommended a "hidden agenda" in which inner-city minorities might be helped "by emphasizing programs to which the more advantaged groups of all races and classes can positively relate."[123] In an interview before the election, Wilson praised Clinton's programs "intended for all low- to moderate-income groups, not just minorities."[124]

Clinton ended up developing what two scholars called a "stealth urban policy" composed of programs that were not specifically targeted to cities but that would help them.[125] In their campaign book, *Putting People First,* Bill Clinton and Al Gore advocated so-called cross-cutting policies designed to help both the middle class and the disadvantaged. Clinton's highly successful campaign bus tours avoided the inner cities and provided the media with ample opportunities to photograph the candidate against small town and rural backdrops. After winning the nomination, Clinton did attend a meeting of the United States Conference of Mayors (USCM) and lent his support to a public works initiative. Clinton stressed, however, that the primary goal was to stimulate the economy and that aiding cities would be a secondary effect.

Clinton succeeded in winning back many of the white suburban voters who had deserted the party in 1980. Even so, he still lost the overall white vote by a 39 percent to 41 percent margin. He carried huge pluralities in the cities, coming out of New York City, for example, with almost a million-vote lead. His ability to capture 82 percent of the African American vote was crucial to his victory.

Clinton began his presidency with the intention of rewarding the cities that had voted lopsidedly for him. To accomplish this, he put together a $19.5 billion economic stimulus bill that included $4.4 billion for public works (mostly in cities), $2.5 billion for community development grants, and $735 million for inner-city schools and jobs. Led by minority leader Bob Dole (R.-Kansas), Senate Republicans filibustered the bill, refusing to let it come up for a vote. Lacking the sixty votes necessary to end the filibuster, the Democrats were forced to back down. Eventually, all that was passed was a $4 billion extension of unemployment benefits for the chronically unemployed.[126]

The only significant new urban initiative of the Clinton Administration was the Empowerment Zones/Enterprise Communities (EZ/EC) program, which was included as Title XIII of the Omnibus Budget Reconciliation Act of 1993. Though pushed since the early 1980s by both Democrats and Republicans, the idea of enterprise zones tended to appeal to conservatives and Republicans more because it was based on the strategy of cutting taxes and regulations in inner cities, with the intention of stimulating investment in depressed neighborhoods. The Clinton Administration adopted this free-market approach, then grafted onto it some Democratic programs for education, job training, and child care. The result was a hybrid, with the federal government acting as a catalyst to bring together the public, private, and nonprofit sectors in the cause of inner-city revitalization.

The EZ/EC program was composed of four basic components:

1. *Tax incentives:* Within designated Empowerment Zones, employers were eligible for up to $3,000 in tax credits for each new hire. The program also included accelerated depreciation of business property and tax-exempt bond financing for businesses in a zone.
2. *Targeted spending:* Areas chosen as Empowerment Zones were eligible for up to $100 million in flexible grant money to assist zone residents for services such as education, job training, and child care.
3. *Strategic planning:* In order to win designation, cities were required to come up with comprehensive strategies for revitalization that took advantage of the particular "strengths" of the chosen communities.

4. *Partnerships:* The planning process was supposed to be "bottom up," involving the residents of the community. This was to be facilitated by a Community Coordinating Board composed of representatives from government, the private sector, and community groups.

The winning communities were announced on December 21, 1994. Six cities were designated as full Empowerment Zones: Atlanta, Baltimore, Chicago, Detroit, New York, and Philadelphia/Camden. Los Angeles and Cleveland were designated as Supplemental Empowerment Zones, with somewhat less than the full complement of resources. Ultimately, thirty-one Empowerment and Supplemental Empowerment Zones were created, and seventy-four additional distressed areas (thirty-three in rural areas) also won grants, but these were small in comparison to the full-fledged Empowerment Zones.

The philosophy underlying the Empowerment Zones program proved attractive to members of both parties because it emphasized private investment and a decentralized administrative style. Still, Republicans could not call the program their own, so the Republican-dominated Congresses that came in after 1994 failed to appropriate the full amount promised for the program. Even if it had, the program would have remained small, with only about $3.8 billion in grants and tax incentives available over a ten-year period, to be spread over 105 urban and rural areas. In an annual federal budget of more than $1 trillion, the EZ/EC program was a drop in the bucket.

In 1999, President Clinton announced his "New Markets Initiative," which essentially built on the Empowerment Zones program. Perhaps to demonstrate an election-year interest in the urban poor, in the spring of 2000, Republicans reached an agreement with the president to create forty "renewal communities" and nine additional empowerment zones at a cost of $5 to $7 billion over five years (mostly in estimated taxes lost to the treasury). Republicans exacted two concessions dear to their hearts. Though they had not been able to eliminate capital gains taxes generally, they were able to do so for the renewal communities and empowerment zones. Religious groups were also authorized to receive grants to provide drug counseling.[127]

But empowerment zones were the exception to the rule. The midterm 1994 elections dealt a blow to those who had hoped for more generous urban and social welfare policies. Led by house speaker Newt Gingrich and his Contract with America (labeled Contract on America by detractors), the Republicans won control of both houses of Congress for the first time in forty years. The Republicans were openly hostile to what remained of federal urban programs. Speaker Gingrich called for the complete elimination of the Department of Housing and Urban Development, asserting that "You could abolish HUD tomorrow morning and improve life in most of America." He was blunt about why HUD was being singled out for especially harsh treatment: Its "weak constituency," he said, "makes it a prime candidate for cuts."[128]

In a desperate attempt to stave off disaster, HUD Secretary Henry Cisneros proposed to "reinvent" his department in ways satisfying to conservatives. Announced a month and a half after the 1994 election, HUD's *Reinvention*

Blueprint called for consolidating HUD's sixty programs into three flexible block grants that would be administered by cities and states, and it proposed converting all public housing aid to vouchers, which would allow recipients to find housing wherever private landlords would take them. Reinventing HUD became the centerpiece of Clinton's National Urban Policy Report, which was issued in July 1995.[129]

The long-term decline in public housing and urban programs predated the Clinton Administration, but having a Democrat in the White House again did not bring about a revival. In the Reagan and Bush years, HUD experienced the largest cuts of any cabinet-level department in the federal government. HUD budget authority (what Congress authorizes it to spend) fell from 7.5 percent of the total federal budget in 1978 to 1.3 percent by 1990. During the Clinton Administration, annual HUD spending recovered slightly, but this only enabled HUD to meet past commitments for housing subsidies. Four programs of special interest to city governments, General Revenue Sharing, Urban Development Action Grants, Local Public Works, and Antirecession Fiscal Assistance, were zeroed out—eliminated entirely.

The welfare reform bill Clinton signed in August 1996 also hurt the cities. Ending the sixty-one-year federal entitlement to welfare, the Personal Responsibility Act of 1996 converted Aid to Families with Dependent Children to a block grant run by the states. In addition to a 64 percent decline in welfare spending from 1990 to 1998, food stamps and community services programs were cut sharply. Three programs—child nutrition, supplemental (infant) feeding, and housing assistance—increased somewhat because they were linked to welfare reform efforts. Medicaid costs went up substantially (by 146 percent), but the big winner was justice assistance, which skyrocketed 1,250 percent in less than a decade! Though some of this money went to cities, most was used by states to build prisons. Obviously, crime control trumped any other social purpose.

As shown by Figure 7.2, at the same time that spending for programs benefiting low- and moderate-income people fell, federal assistance to homeowners rose steadily. The federal government permits people who own their own home to deduct from their income taxes what they spend for mortgage interest and property taxes. Monthly rent payments pay for mortgage interest and property taxes for landlords, but renters get no tax breaks. Total homeowner deductions increased from $34 billion in 1978 to $99.9 billion by 1999, almost a 300 percent increase. Homeowner tax deductions are tilted toward higher-income taxpayers; in 1994 almost half (44 percent) of the value of these subsidies went to the top 5 percent of households, those with incomes over $100,000. In 1996, the wealthiest 20 percent of American households received 82 percent of homeowner tax breaks; by contrast, the bottom 60 percent received less than 4 percent of the subsidy.[130] Housing subsidies work as a powerful urban policy transferring federal aid to affluent suburban homeowners at the expense of lower-income rental households.

The trend in housing expenditures must be understood as only one of a series of policies designed to increase government assistance to wealthy

Figure 7.2   **Federal Spending for Housing, 1978–1997,
in Billions of Constant 1996 Dollars**

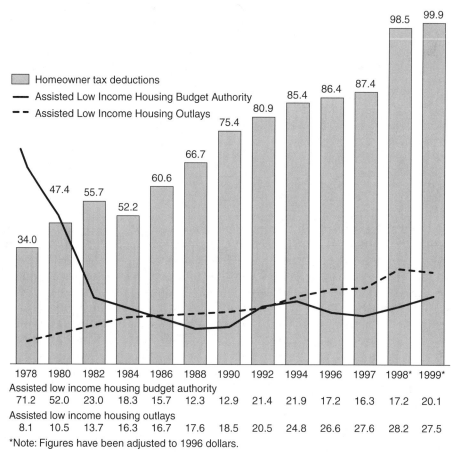

	1978	1980	1982	1984	1986	1988	1990	1992	1994	1996	1997	1998*	1999*
Assisted low income housing budget authority	71.2	52.0	23.0	18.3	15.7	12.3	12.9	21.4	21.9	17.2	16.3	17.2	20.1
Assisted low income housing outlays	8.1	10.5	13.7	16.3	16.7	17.6	18.5	20.5	24.8	26.6	27.6	28.2	27.5

*Note: Figures have been adjusted to 1996 dollars.

Source: National Low Income Housing Coalition, *Housing at a Snail's Pace* (Washington, D.C.: NLIHC 1996), p. 5.

households and reduce aid to the poor. The tax write-offs for mortgage interest, reduced rates on capital gains tax, and capital gains exclusion on home sales (both resulting from the Tax Reduction Act of 2001) will total $146.6 billion in fiscal year 2003. (There are, of course, dozens of other programs that give tax breaks.) By contrast, a combination of the five principal programs giving tax breaks to low-income Americans (earned-income tax credit, tax credits for college tuition, work opportunity tax credits, exclusion of public assistance benefits, and welfare-to-work tax credits) will add up to $39.5 billion in fiscal 2003.[131] As in the past, government programs tend to benefit the well-off disproportionately, in spite of well-worn myths to the contrary.

THE POLITICAL INVISIBILITY OF THE CITIES

Abandoning urban policy made political sense for Republicans and Democrats alike. In the case of the Republicans, party leaders had long sought to capitalize on white suburbanites' disaffection from the Democratic-sponsored civil rights and antipoverty policies of the 1960s. What is more interesting is the way that the past friend of the cities, the Democratic Party, has shied away from urban issues. In 1968, the Democrats used the word *city* twenty-threee times in the party platform adopted at their presidential nominating convention. It did not appear even once in the 1988 platform. The substitute term, which signaled a recognition of the political importance of the suburbs, was *hometown America*. In 1992 and 1996, Clinton avoided identification with policies targeted to cities and concentrated his appeals on the suburban middle class. Notably, in the 2000 campaign, Democratic candidate Al Gore mentioned urban sprawl as a significant national issue. By the new century, urban policy no longer referred to central cities but to urban regions.

The near-invisibility of cities in national politics by the twenty-first century can be explained by a simple fact: By then, central-city voters accounted for a very small percentage of the national electorate. The central cities of the thirty-two largest metropolitan areas reached a high-water mark of 27 percent of the electorate in 1944, but by 1992 they accounted for just 14 percent of the national vote[132] and 12 percent by the 2000 election. As shown in Figure 7.3, the share of their states' vote cast by their largest central cities have fallen steadily for half a century in New York, Illinois, Pennsylvania, Michigan, and Massachusetts.[133] In 1940, New York City voters represented 51 percent of the statewide electorate, but by the 1996 presidential election their proportion of the statewide vote had fallen to 31 percent. Chicago claimed 47 percent of the Illinois presidential vote in 1948 but only 21 percent by 1996.

Cities also lost representation in the U.S. House of Representatives. Between 1963 and 1994, the number of congressional districts with a majority of the population coming from central cities fell from 94 to 84; in the same period, the number of districts with a majority of suburban voters increased from 94 to 214. In 1994, after the Republicans took control of the House, the proportion of leadership positions held by representatives from districts with a sizable proportion of central-city voters fell precipitously, from 30 percent to 10 percent.[134] Similar trends reduced the power of central cities in state governments as well.[135] The number of states with suburban electoral majorities increased from three in 1980 to fourteen in 1990, and will surely increase even more when seats are reapportioned as a result of the 2000 census.

It is generally assumed that the suburbs now hold the key to winning national elections. Suburban votes were critical to the presidential victories of presidents Reagan and Bush; Ronald Reagan won huge landslides in 1980 and 1984 even though he only carried about a third of the central-city vote. In the 1988 election, suburban voters gave George Bush such a comfortable cushion that he could have carried almost all of the northern industrial states without a single vote from the big cities in those states. By contrast, the central-city

Figure 7.3   **City Proportion of Actual State Electorate, 1952–1996**

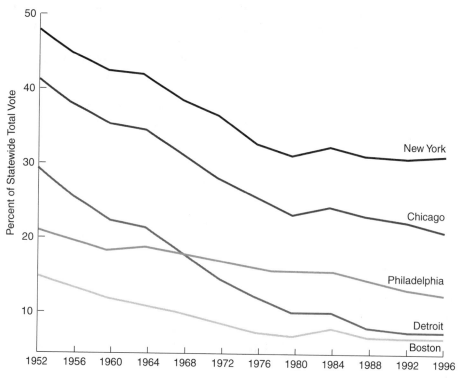

Source: Richard Scammon, *America Votes* (various issues); U.S. Bureau of the Census, *Census of Population and Housing,* various years; and reports of actual city votes from county boards of elections (and newspapers for 1996 election). Data compiled by Richard Sauerzopf.

electorate was an important part of Clinton's winning coalition in 1992 and 1996. In 1992, New York City provided Clinton with 92 percent of his nearly one-million statewide vote margin, and Clinton lost to Bush in suburban Long Island (Nassau and Suffolk counties). In 1996, Clinton did even better in the cities, winning 67 percent of the vote in Milwaukee, 74 percent in Boston, 76 percent in St. Louis and New York, and 80 percent in Chicago. Clinton came out of New York City with over a million-vote margin.

Although President Clinton owed a great deal to central-city voters for his two election victories, he did not make urban issues a priority. During his presidency, federal spending for the cities continued to fall. Clearly, Clinton felt that he could take his urban base for granted; city voters had no other place to go. This strategy did impose a potential cost on the Democrats, however; as the federal government turned away from the cities, voter turnout in them went into a steep slide. Indeed, in the past half-century, 40 percent of the loss in the proportion of votes cast in the thirty-two largest cities can be traced to falling turnout and not to shrinking population.

Figure 7.4   **Relative Propensity to Vote, 1944–1992**

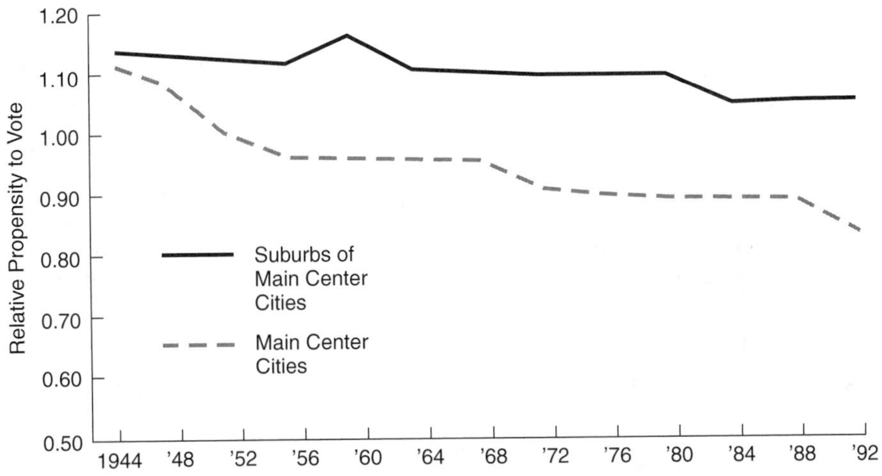

Source: Peter F. Nardulli, Jon K. Dalager, and Donald E. Greco, "Voter Turnout in President Elections: An Historical View and Some Speculation," *PS: Political Science and Politics* (September 1996): 486.

As shown in Figure 7.4, the voter turnout for the presidential election of 1944 was almost the same for the central-city and suburban electorates, and both groups turned out at a greater rate than the national average (an average turnout rate would appear as 1.0 in Figure 7.4). Suburban turnout declined only slightly since then, but turnout by city voters fell sharply. By 1992, voting in the large central cities had fallen 18 percent below the national average. In 1996, the turnout rate in New York City was only 33 percent, compared to 44 percent for the state of New York as a whole.

Any statistics contrasting the voting behavior of city and suburban residents requires a strict—and somewhat artificial—distinction between cities and suburbs. The suburban voting thesis assumes that suburbanites constitute a unified constituency, with interests that are different from those of central-city residents. In fact, however, suburbs are extremely varied; older, inner-ring suburbs have more in common with their central cities than with wealthy suburbs on the fringe. Inner-ring suburbs suffer from declining job bases, high rates of poverty, high crime, declining tax bases, and fiscal stress. Inner-ring suburbs such as Harvey, Illinois; Compton, California; and East Cleveland, Ohio, resemble their central cities more than they resemble wealthy outer suburbs. But even if the inner-ring suburban voters were to make common cause with their cousins in the central cities, it is unlikely that a new round of urban policies would be forthcoming. And even if federal budget surpluses had continued to be generated, it is hard to imagine that urban policies would ever again occupy a significant place on the national policy agenda. Those days are over.

NOTES

1. Quoted in Bob Adams, "The Great Society Programs of the '60s and '70s Under Attack," *St. Louis Post-Dispatch,* May 10, 1992, p. 1B.
2. Quoted in "Schlesinger Accepts Award, Attacks Bush," *St. Louis Post-Dispatch,* May 10, 1992, p. 13C.
3. Reported in the *New York Times,* December 1, 1959, p. 27, quoted in Mark I. Gelfand, *A Nation of Cities: The Federal Government and Urban America,* Urban Life in America Series (New York: Oxford University Press, 1975), p. 295. See also John F. Kennedy, "The Great Unspoken Issue," *Proceedings, American Municipal Congress 1959* (Washington, D.C.: American Municipal League, n.d.), pp. 23–28; and John F. Kennedy, "The Shame of the States," *New York Times Magazine,* May 18, 1958.
4. Quoted in Theodore H. White, *The Making of the President, 1960* (New York: Atheneum, 1961), p. 206. Nixon's strategy, which White contends was no strategy at all, was a "national" one, in which he committed himself to visit all fifty states; Kennedy, on the other hand, used an urban strategy centered on the industrial states with large blocs of electoral votes (see pp. 267–352).
5. John C. Donovan, *The Politics of Poverty,* 2nd. ed. (New York: Bobbs-Merrill, Pegasus, 1973), p. 19.
6. Quoted in White, *The Making of the President,* p. 165.
7. Ibid., p. 1201.
8. John Mollenkopf, *The Contested City* (Princeton, N.J.: Princeton University Press, 1983), p. 83.
9. Kathleen Hall Jamieson, *Packaging the Presidency: A History and Criticism of Presidential Campaign Advertising* (New York: Oxford University Press, 1984), pp. 202–203.
10. Joseph McGinniss, *Selling the President, 1968* (New York: Trident Press, 1969).
11. Numan V. Barley and Hugh D. Graham, *Southern Politics and the Second Reconstruction* (Baltimore: Johns Hopkins University Press, 1975), pp. 126–127; Everett Carl Ladd Jr., "The Shifting Party Coalitions, 1932–1976," in *Emerging Coalitions in American Politics,* ed. Seymour Martin Lipset (San Francisco: Institute for Contemporary Studies, 1978), p. 98; and A. James Reichley, *Conservatives in an Age of Change: The Nixon and Ford Administrations* (Washington, D.C.: Brookings Institution, 1981), p. 145.
12. Quoted in Reichley, *Conservatives in an Age of Change,* p. 186. For a general discussion, see David B. Robertson and Dennis R. Judd, *The Development of American Public Policy: The Structure of Policy Restraint* (Glenview, Ill.: Scott Foresman, 1989), pp. 190–197.
13. Donovan, *The Politics of Poverty,* p. 225.
14. Ibid., p. 104.
15. Nelson W. Polsby and Aaron Wildavsky, *Presidential Elections: Contemporary Strategies of American Electoral Politics,* 7th ed. (New York: Free Press, 1988). The statistics given are for "nonwhite" voters.
16. White, *The Making of the President,* p. 354.
17. For good recent summary accounts, see ibid.; also James A. Morone, *The Democratic Wish: Popular Participation and the Limits of American Government* (New York: Basic Books, 1990), chap. 6.
18. Quoted in Richard Blumenthal, "The Bureaucracy: Antipoverty and the Community Action Programs," in *American Political Institutions and Public Policy,* ed. Allan P. Sindler (Boston: Little, Brown, 1969), p. 149.
19. *Message of the President to Congress,* reprinted in *Congressional Quarterly Weekly Report* 32, no. 2 (January 11, 1964).
20. *Congress and the Nation, 1945–1964* (Washington, D.C.: Congressional Quarterly Service, 1965), p. 1379.
21. Refer to Daniel J. Elazar, *The American Partnership: Intergovernmental Cooperation in the Nineteenth Century United States* (Chicago: University of Chicago Press, 1962).

22. Manpower Development and Training Act of 1962, Public Law 87-415, 87th Cong. (1962); emphasis added.
23. Economic Opportunity Act of 1964, Public Law 88-452, 88th Cong. (1964); emphasis added.
24. Demonstration Cities and Metropolitan Development Act of 1966, Public Law 89-754, 89th Cong. (1966); emphasis added.
25. See James L. Sundquist and David W. Davis, *Making Federalism Work: A Study of Program Coordination at the Community Level* (Washington, D.C.: Brookings Institution, 1969), pp. 3–5.
26. Lyndon B. Johnson, "Total Victory Over Poverty," Message to Congress, March 15, 1964, reprinted in *The Failure of American Liberalism: After the Great Society,* ed. Marvin E. Gettleman and David Mermelstein (New York: Vintage Books, 1970), p. 181.
27. U.S. Office of Economic Opportunity, *Community Action Program Guide* (Washington, D.C.: Government Printing Office, 1965).
28. Frances Fox Piven and Richard A. Cloward, *Regulating the Poor: The Functions of Public Welfare* (New York: Pantheon, 1971).
29. Ibid., p. 295.
30. U.S. Advisory Commission on Intergovernmental Relations, *Fiscal Balance in the American Federal System,* vol. 1 (Washington, D.C.: Government Printing Office, 1967), p. 169.
31. Demonstration Cities and Metropolitan Development Act of 1966, Public Law 89-754.
32. R. Douglas Arnold, *Congress and the Bureaucracy: A Theory of Influence* (New Haven, Conn.,: Yale University Press, 1979), p. 160.
33. Ibid., p. 168.
34. See George Gilder, *Wealth and Poverty* (New York: Basic Books, 1981); and Charles Murray, *Losing Ground: American Social Policy, 1950–1980* (New York: Basic Books, 1984).
35. U.S. Department of Commerce, Bureau of the Census, *Statistical Abstract of the United States, 1980* (Washington, D.C.: Government Printing Office, 1980), p. 464.
36. John E. Schwarz, *America's Hidden Success: A Reassessment of Public Policy from Kennedy to Reagan,* rev. ed. (New York: Norton, 1988), p. 24.
37. Jeffrey L. Pressman and Aaron Wildvasky, *How Great Expectations in Washington Are Dashed in Oakland: Or, Why It's Amazing That Federal Programs Work at All,* 3rd ed. (Berkeley: University of California Press, 1984).
38. Irving Lazar, *Summary: The Persistence of Preschool Effects,* Community Services Laboratory, New York State University College of Human Ecology at Cornell University, October 1977, quoted in Schwarz, *America's Hidden Success,* pp. 217–218.
39. Schwarz, *America's Hidden Success,* pp. 38–39.
40. U.S. Office of Management and Budget, *Special Analyses: Budget of the United States Government: Fiscal Year 1981* (Washington, D.C.: Government Printing Office, 1982), p. 254.
41. U.S. Office of Management and Budget, *Special Analyses, Budget of the United States Government: Fiscal Year 1978* (Washington, D.C.: Government Printing Office, 1979), p. 276.
42. Reagan, *The New Federalism* (New York: Oxford University Press, 1972), p. 97.
43. Quoted in Timothy B. Clark, John K. Iglehart, and William Lilley III, "New Federalism 1: Return of Power to States and Cities Looms as Theme of Nixon's Second-Term Domestic Policy," *National Journal,* December 16, 1972, p. 1911.
44. Timothy Conlan, *New Federalism: Intergovernmental Reform from Nixon to Reagan* (Washington, D.C.: Brookings Institution, 1988), pp. 4, 45. For discussions of the politics of the legislation, see also Paul R. Dommel, *The Politics of Revenue Sharing* (Bloomington and London: Indiana University Press, 1974); and Richard P. Nathan, Allen D. Manvel, Susannah E. Caulkins et al., *Monitoring Revenue Sharing* (Washington, D.C.: Brookings Institution, 1975).
45. *Washington Post,* March 22, 1971, cited in Richard E. Thompson, *Revenue Sharing: A New Era in Federalism* (Washington, D.C.: Revenue Sharing Advisory Service, 1973), p. 69.

46. *Newsweek,* May 24, 1971, p. 94.

47. U.S. Department of the Treasury, Office of Revenue Sharing, *Reported Uses of General Revenue Sharing Funds, 1974–1975: A Tabulation and Analysis of Data from Actual Use,* Report 5 (Washington, D.C.: Government Printing Office, 1966), p. 5.

48. U.S. Department of the Treasury, Office of Revenue Sharing, *Revenue Sharing: The First Actual Use Reports,* by David A. Caputo and Richard L. Cole (Washington, D.C.: Government Printing Office, 1974), pp. 10, 12, 29.

49. Ibid., p. 25.

50. For a discussion of this topic, see Richard P. Nathan, Charles F. Adams Jr. et al., with the assistance of Andre Juneau and James W. Fossett, *Revenue Sharing: The Second Round* (Washington, D.C.: Brookings Institution, 1977), pp. 1–23.

51. *Congressional Record,* February 20, 1973, p. 746, cited in ibid., p. 2.

52. For example, see *Congressional Record,* February 22, 1973, p. 987; and *Congressional Record,* March 1, 1973, p. 1160.

53. Advisory Commission on Intergovernmental Relations (ACIR), *Citizen Participation in the American Federal System* (Washington, D.C.: ACIR, 1979), p. 18.

54. Office of Revenue Sharing, *Revenue Sharing Bulletin,* (Washington, D.C.: Government Printing Office), July 1973, p. 2.

55. Nathan, Adams et al., *Revenue Sharing,* p. 171.

56. Housing and Community Development Act of 1974, sec. 101.

57. Housing and Community Development Act of 1974, sec. 104(a).

58. Most of the funds were allocated to entitlement cities with populations of 50,000 or more, SMSA central cities, and certain urban counties. Jurisdictions that participated in the previous categorical programs folded into the Housing and Community Development Act also received "hold-harmless" grants under which their level of funding could not decline for a three-year period. About 20 percent of the monies were distributed without regard to the entitlement formulas. These funds represent the competitive portion of the program.

59. "New Directions Cited in First Annual Block Grant Reports," *Housing and Development Reporter,* January 12, 1976, p. 761.

60. U.S. Department of Housing and Urban Development, *Community Development Block Grant Program,* (Washington, D.C.: Government Printing Office), p. 38.

61. Reported in *Housing and Development Reporter,* January 10, 1977, p. 684.

62. *Report of the Southern Regional Council in Housing and Development Reporter,* April 5, 1976, p. 1051.

63. Interview by Sharon Cribbs (investigator for the Southern Governmental Monitoring Project) with Nathaniel Hill, Director, Department of Human Resources, Little Rock, Arkansas (Summer 1975), quoted in Southern Governmental Monitoring Project, *A Time for Accounting: The Housing and Community Development Act in the South: A Monitoring Report,* by Raymond Brown with Ann Coil and Carol Rose (Atlanta: Southern Regional Council, 1976), p. 53.

64. Ibid., p. 51.

65. For a review of the Brookings report and other studies, see Carl E. Van Horn, "Decentralized Policy Delivery" (paper delivered at the Workshop on Policy Analysis in State and Local Government, State University of New York, Stonybrook, May 22–24, 1977); and Carl E. Van Horn, *Policy Implementation in the Federal System* (Lexington, Mass.: Lexington Books, 1979).

66. *Code of Federal Regulations,* Title 24, Part 570 (Washington, D.C.: U.S. Government Printing Office, April 1, 1978), pp. 36–157.

67. Cited in Michael J. Rich, *Federal Policymaking and the Poor: National Goals, Local Choices, and Distributional Outcomes* (Princeton, N.J.: Princeton University Press, 1993), p. 41.

68. Anthony Downs, *Recommendation for Community Development Planning,* monograph based on a study for HUD (Chicago: Real Estate Research Corporation, 1975).

69. See M. Leanne Lachman, "Planning for Community Development: A Proposed Approach," *Journal of Housing* 32, no. 2 (February 1975): 58.

70. Roger Starr, "Making New York Smaller," in *Revitalizing the Northeast,* ed. George Stern-lieb and James W. Hughes (New Brunswick, N.J.: Rutgers University Press, 1978).

71. Jerome Pratter, "How Cities Can Grow Old Gracefully," *House Committee on Banking, Finance, and Urban Affairs Report* (Washington, D.C.: Government Printing Office, 1978).

72. James L. Greer, "Urban Planning and Redevelopment in Chicago: The Political Economy of the Chicago 21 Plan" (paper delivered at the Annual Meeting of the Midwest Political Science Association, Chicago, April 19–21, 1979).

73. Alvin H. Mushkatel and Howard Lasus, "Geographic Targeting of Community Development Funds in Denver: Who Benefits?" (paper delivered at the Annual Meeting of the Western Social Science Association, Albuquerque, N.M., April 23–26, 1980).

74. Quoted in Robert L. Joller, "HUD Secretary Quiets Critics," *St. Louis Post-Dispatch,* April 18, 1977, p. 38.

75. Reprinted in Roy Bahl, ed., *The Fiscal Outlook for Cities: Implications of a National Urban Policy* (Syracuse, N.Y.: Syracuse University Press, 1978), pp. 111–127.

76. Ibid., p. 112.

77. Ann R. Markusen and David Wilmoth, "The Political Economy of National Urban Policy in the U.S.A.: 1976–81," *Canadian Journal of Regional Science* (Summer 1982): 145–163.

78. State of Illinois, Bureau of the Budget, Federal Relations Unit, *Equity in Federal Funding: A First Step* (Springfield: State of Illinois, Bureau of the Budget, 1976), p. 2.

79. Rochelle L. Stansfield, "Federalism Report: Government Seeks the Right Formula for Community Development Funds," *National Journal,* February 12, 1977, p. 242.

80. Ann R. Markusen, "The Urban Impact Analysis: A Critical Forecast," in *The Urban Impact of Federal Policies,* ed. Norman Glickman (Baltimore: Johns Hopkins University Press, 1979); see also discussion by Ann R. Markusen, Annalee Saxenian, and Marc A. Weiss, "Who Benefits from Intergovernmental Transfers?" in *Cities Under Stress: The Fiscal Crises of Urban America,* ed. Robert W. Burchell and David Listokin (New Brunswick, N.J.: Center for Urban Research, 1981), p. 656; and Stansfield, "Federalism Report."

81. Quoted in Rich, *Federal Policymaking and the Poor,* p. 78.

82. See Stansfield, "Federalism Report"; and Joel Havemann, Rochelle L. Stansfield, and Neal R. Pierce, "Federal Spending: The North's Loss Is the Sunbelt's Gain," *National Journal,* June 1976, p. 1031.

83. Robert Reinhold, "More Aid on Way for Older Cities," *St. Louis Post-Dispatch,* May 9, 1977, p. 3C, reprinted from the *New York Times.*

84. Calculated from Richard DeLeon and Richard LeGates, "Beyond Cybernetic Federalism in Community Development," *Urban Law Annual* 15 (1978): 31; see also Paul R. Dommel, "Block Grants for Community Development: Decentralized Decision-Making," in *Fiscal Crisis in American Cities: The Federal Response,* ed. L. Kenneth Hubbell (Cambridge, Mass.: Ballinger, 1979), pp. 236–241.

85. John P. Ross, "Countercyclical Revenue Sharing," in *Fiscal Crisis in American Cities: The Federal Response,* ed. L. Kenneth Hubbell (Cambridge, Mass.: Ballinger, 1979), pp. 256–261.

86. Ibid., p. 266.

87. Ibid., pp. 266–267.

88. Dommel, "Block Grants for Community Development," p. 254.

89. U.S. Department of Housing and Urban Development, "The Urban Fiscal Crisis: Fact or Fantasy (A Reply)," in *Cities Under Stress: The Fiscal Crises of Urban America,* ed. Robert W. Burchell and David Listokin (New Brunswick, N.J.: Center for Urban Research, 1981), p. 151.

90. Quoted in Robert Reihold, "President Proposes a Broad New Policy for Urban Recovery," *New York Times,* March 28, 1978.

91. "Excerpts from the President's Message to Congress Outlining His Urban Policy," *New York Times,* March 28, 1978.

92. F. J. James, "President Carter's Comprehensive National Urban Policy: Achievements and Lessons Learned," *Environment and Planning C: Government and Policy* 8 (199): 34.

93. Markusen and Wilmoth, "The Political Economy of National Urban Policy," p. 15.

94. "Washington Update: Administration Officials, Mayors Have Love Fest," *National Journal,* January 29, 1977, p. 189.

95. *New York Times,* October 23, 1981.

96. President's Commission for a National Agenda for the Eighties, *A National Agenda for the Eighties* (Washington, D.C.: Government Printing Office, 1980), p. 66.

97. Ibid., pp. 66–67.

98. Ibid., p. 4.

99. Ibid., p. 66.

100. Timothy K. Barnekov, Daniel Rich, and Robert Warren, "The New Privatism, Federalism, and the Future of Urban Governance: National Urban Policy in the 1980s," *Journal of Urban Affairs* 3, no. 4 (Fall 1981): 3.

101. U.S. Department of Housing and Urban Development, *The President's National Urban Policy Report* (Washington, D.C.: Government Printing Office, 1982), pp. 2, 23.

102. Ibid., p. 14.

103. Conlan, *New Federalism,* p. 137.

104. Ibid., p. 135.

105. Ibid., p. 138.

106. Robertson and Judd, *The Development of American Public Policy,* p. 233.

107. U.S. Office of Management and Budget, *Budget of the United States Government, Historical Tables, Fiscal Year 1996* (Washington, D.C.: Government Printing Office, 1996), table 12.3.

108. Henry J. Aaron and Associates, "Nondefense Programs," in *Setting National Priorities: The 1983 Budget,* ed. Joseph A. Pechman (Washington, D.C.: Brookings Institution, 1982), p. 119.

109. U.S. Office of Management and Budget, *Budget of the United States Government, Historical Tables, Fiscal Year 1996,* table 12.3.

110. The Budget of the United States Government, *Fiscal Year 2003: Appendix,* p. 485.

111. George E. Peterson et al., *The Reagan Block Grants: What Have We Learned* (Washington, D.C.: Urban Institute, 1986), p. 21.

112. U.S. Congress, Joint Economic Committee, *Emergency Interim Survey: Fiscal Condition of Forty-eight Large Cities* (Washington, D.C.: Government Printing Office, 1982), p. 6.

113. White House press release, March 7, 1983.

114. James H. Johnson Jr., Cloyzelle K. Jones, Walter C. Farrell Jr., and Melvin L. Oliver, "The Los Angeles Rebellion: A Retrospective View," *Economic Development Quarterly* 6, no. 4 (November 1992): 356–372.

115. Robert Pear, "Clinton, in Attack on President, Ties Riots to 'Neglect,'" *New York Times,* May 6, 1992, p. 1.

116. Clifford Krauss, "Congress Passes Aid to Cities," *New York Times,* June 9, 1992, p. A20.

117. Quoted in Theodore H. White, *America in Search of Itself: The Making of the President, 1956–1980* (New York: Harper and Row, 1982), p. 381.

118. D. Lee Bawden and John L. Palmer, "Social Policy: Challenging the Welfare State," in *The Reagan Record,* ed. John L. Palmer and Isabel V. Sawhill (Cambridge, Mass.: Ballinger, 1992), p. 200.

119. Quoted in Robert Pear, "Quayle Criticizes New York as Proof of Welfare's Ills," *New York Times,* February 28, 1992, p. 1.

120. *New York Post,* April 28, 1992, p. 1.

121. "The Willie Horton of 1992," *New York Times,* March 3, 1992, p. 3.

122. William Schneider, "The Suburban Century Begins," *Atlantic Monthly,* July 1992, pp. 33–44.

123. William Julius Wilson, *The Truly Disadvantaged: The Inner City, the Underclass, and Public Policy* (Chicago: University of Chicago Press, 1987), p. 155.

124. "A Visit with Bill Clinton," *Atlantic Monthly,* October 1992; and William Julius Wilson, "The Right Message," *New York Times,* March 17, 1992.

125. Bernard H. Ross and Myron A. Levine, *Urban Politics: Power in Metropolitan America,* 5th ed. (Itasca, Ill.: F. E. Peacock, 1996), p. 434.
126. Adam Clymer, "G.O.P. Senators Prevail, Sinking Clinton's Economic Stimulus Bill," *New York Times,* April 22, 1993, p. 1.
127. Deirdre Shesgreen, "Anti-poverty Plan Pushed by Talent Win Bipartisan Support at White House," *St. Louis Post-Dispatch,* April 24, 2000, p. A8.
128. Quoted in Kenneth J. Cooper, "Gingrich Pledges a Major Package of Spending Cuts Early Next Year," *Washington Post,* December 13, 1994, p. 1.
129. U.S. Department of Housing and Urban Development, *Empowerment: A New Covenant with America's Communities* (Rockville, Md.: HUD USER, July 1995).
130. National Law Income Housing Coalition, *Housing at a Snail's Pace: The Federal Housing Budget: 1978–1987* (Washington, D.C.: NLIHC, 1996), p. 75.
131. Figures compiled by Thad Williamson, David Imbroscio, and Gar Alperovitz, *Making a Place for Community: Local Democracy in a Global Era* (New York: Routledge, 2002), pp. 131–13; original data from United States Budget, 2003.
132. Peter F. Nardulli, Jon K. Dalager, and Donald E. Greco, "Voter Turnout in U.S. Presidential Elections: An Historical View and Some Speculation," *PS: Political Science and Politics* (September 1996): 484.
133. Calculations are from Richard Sauerzopf and Todd Swanstrom, "The Urban Electorate in Presidential Elections, 1920–1992: Challenging the Conventional Wisdom" (paper delivered at the Annual Meeting of the Urban Affairs Association, Indianapolis, Indiana, April 22–25, 1993). Updated by authors.
134. Hal Wolman and Lisa Marckini, "Changes in Central City Representation and Influence in Congress" (paper prepared for delivery at the Annual Meeting of the Urban Affairs Association, Toronto, Canada, April 17, 1997). See also Demetrios Caraley, "Washington Abandons the Cities," *Political Science Quarterly* 107, no. 1 (1992): 20.
135. 146 Margaret Weir, "Central Cities' Loss of Power in State Politics," *Cityscape: A Journal of Policy Development and Research* 2, no. 2 (May 1996): 23–40.

CHAPTER
8

THE RISE
OF THE SUNBELT

THE CONCEPT OF THE SUNBELT

The term *Sunbelt* was popularized in the mid-1970s, and it quickly became almost indispensable in everyday discourse about national development and politics. Even though the geographic boundaries of the Sunbelt are rather vague in most people's minds, the term conveys a distinctly positive image of a part of the country that is prosperous and growing: "When a person hears the term on radio or on television, or reads it in a magazine or book, or sees it in the telephone book or on a firm's letterhead, it is likely to conjure up an image of growing cities and booming economies in Southern or Southwestern cities with pleasant climates."[1] It would be possible to regard the term as merely a "rhetorical ruse," as one scholar called it,[2] or a "public relations coup," as the president of a corporation helping other companies move to the Sunbelt labeled it,[3] were it not for the fact that the long-term population growth in the region has resulted in a fundamental realignment of political power in the nation. Since John F. Kennedy, all of the winning presidential candidates have come from the South or West.[4] Over the past half-century, the reapportionment that follows each decennial census has shifted the balance of power in Congress decisively toward the congressional delegations that represent southern and western states. Without doubt, this realignment of power helps account for the decline in federal aid to the cities since the late 1970s and the shift toward conservative social policies.

Kevin Phillips, the chief political analyst for the 1968 Republican presidential campaign, is generally credited as the person who coined the term *Sunbelt*. In his book, *The Emerging Republican Majority*, published in 1969, Phillips asserted that the United States was going through an electoral realignment that was transforming the Republican Party into the nation's majority party. The basis of this national political realignment, he said, was the movement of millions of

Americans out of the old industrial cities of the North to the suburbs and to the South and West. Phillips sometimes lumped the South and the West into an area he called the Sunbelt, though he never actually defined its boundaries; indeed, of forty-seven maps in his book, none portrays such a region.[5]

Phillips's prediction that regionalism would become an ascendant influence in national politics turned out to be correct. In 1973, an embargo on the sale of oil by the Arab oil-producing nations drove the world price of oil sharply upward. The economies of oil-producing states such as Texas, Louisiana, Oklahoma, and Colorado boomed, and new jobs were created throughout the southern and western states. At the same time, energy-dependent industries and consumers in the northern states were hit hard. In 1974 and 1975, northern states went through an economic depression that saw hundreds of thousands of layoffs in industrial jobs. By the spring of 1975, New York City was facing bankruptcy and had to ask the federal government for loan guarantees. President Gerald Ford initially refused to help.[6] Congressional legislative battles began to reflect sharply divided regional politics pitting a prosperous South and West against a declining North.

In this atmosphere, *Power Shift,* a book published by Kirkpatrick Sale in 1975, quickly became a national best-seller.[7] Sale wrote that the states of the South and West—a region he called the Southern Rim—were gaining national political power at the expense of the older industrial states. Trying to find a way to report on the political issues raised by the new regional antagonisms, the media revived Phillips's notion of the Sunbelt, and the term soon came into common use. In February 1976, the *New York Times* published a five-part series documenting the demographic and political trends favoring the Sunbelt. In May, *Business Week* devoted its feature article to "The Second War Between the States."[8] The regional war became one of the hot topics helping to sell newspapers and magazines in 1976 and 1977.

Though the concept of the Sunbelt has entered the everyday language of Americans (the term has been included in dictionaries since the late 1970s), the precise boundaries of the region are hard to pin down. In a letter to a scholar researching the politics of the Sunbelt, Kevin Phillips defined it as the "territory stretching from the eastern Carolina lowlands down around (and excluding) Appalachia, picking up only the Greater Memphis area of Tennessee, omitting the Ozarks and moving west to Oklahoma, thence virtually due west," possibly also including Colorado.[9] It is understandable that Phillips would want to draw his boundaries to exclude pockets of poverty in the border states, but his description is extremely imprecise. For our purposes in this chapter, we adopt Sale's definition, as shown in Figure 8.1. Sale's Sunbelt encompasses the entire portion of the United States below the thirty-seventh parallel, extending across the country from North Carolina to the West Coast, including southern California and part of southern Nevada.[10] (For statistical purposes, we will include all of California and Nevada.) Thus there are fifteen states in the Sunbelt. The fourteen states of the Northeast and the upper Midwest constitute what is sometimes called the *Frostbelt.*

Figure 8.1   The American Sunbelt and Frostbelt

Source: Adapted from Richard M. Bernard and Bradley R. Rice, eds., *Sunbelt Cities: Politics and Growth Since World War II* (Austin: University of Texas Press, 1985), p. 7.

A significant number of scholars are troubled by the concept of the Sunbelt. For one thing, the huge area encompassed by Sale's definition is far from uniformly prosperous. The most rapid economic and population growth has occurred in Florida, parts of Texas, Arizona, southern Nevada, and southern California. Rural areas all across the Sunbelt and many urban areas of the South have remained untouched by the prosperity that is proclaimed as the Sunbelt's principal defining feature, a fact that led two scholars to note that the Sunbelt "has collapsed into only a few 'sunspots.'"[11]

A second problem with the Sunbelt concept is that it assumes that the South and the Southwest are similar enough that they can be lumped together under a single label. Until its image was refurbished by its inclusion in the prosperous Sunbelt, the South was often thought of as a backward, poverty-ridden, violent region with a peculiar caste system. Most political studies of the South focused on issues of race, the enduring effects of the Civil War and Reconstruction, and the dominance of a single, authoritarian party (until the 1960s, the Republican Party rarely ran candidates in most southern states)—the elements that made up a conservative political culture that had changed little since the Civil War. The main industries that had located in the South were those associated with low-wage labor. In the 1930s, Franklin Roosevelt and the New Deal administrators looked at federal programs as a way to bring economic development to this backward region.[12]

The image of the West, by contrast, tended to be "urban, opulent, energetic, mobile, and individualistic, a region of economic growth and openness to continual change which matched America's self-image."[13] If the image of perpetual sunshine gave the Sunbelt its name, then certainly this image fit the West better than the South. Since Los Angeles was the home of the movie and television industries, America's popular culture became increasingly identified with western images. Los Angeles served as a vision of America's future, with its sprawling suburbs, freeways, shopping centers, and even its smog.

Some observers have claimed that the idea of the Sunbelt was nearly dead and that its brief existence was overplayed anyway. Nicholas Lemann, who edited the *Texas Monthly* in the 1980s, observed that "millions of people were living in the Sunbelt without one of them realizing it. They thought of themselves as Southerners or Texans, or Los Angelenos."[14] The concept of the Sunbelt was regarded with suspicion not only because there were so many differences within it but also because all regions of the United States seemed to be becoming more alike. The old industrial states were becoming less industrial, urban populations were spreading out into suburbs in all parts of the country, and a media-based national culture was replacing regional cultural differences. "Just try to find a town anywhere in the United States without a McDonald's or a television happy-news format featuring an anchorperson with an unidentifiable accent."[15]

Despite the shortcomings of the Sunbelt-Frostbelt dichotomy, it remains useful as a starting point for understanding the historic political realignments of the past half-century. Without these realignments, the older cities and their voters would have been able to demand a much larger share of the nation's resources. Programs to treat urban decay, joblessness, and poverty in the cities and to build mass transit systems and other infrastructure would be much more generous than they are.

THE RISE OF THE SUNBELT

For the past half-century, population and economic activities in the United States have been moving away from older urban areas. This population movement contrasts sharply with the historic pattern of national growth. Since the early years of the nineteenth century the industrial cities had acted as magnets, drawing millions of immigrants from abroad and luring migrants from the countryside. The industrial cities were the engines of the nation's economy, and patterns of settlement reflected this fact. In 1950, 65 percent of the nation's metropolitan population lived in or near the industrial belt that reached from Boston and New York in the Northeast across to the Great Lakes and down to St. Louis.[16] More than two-thirds of the manufacturing jobs and ten of the nation's fourteen urban areas of more than one million people were stretched across this industrial zone. Over the next half-century, however, a historic shift in the regional distribution of population occurred.

OUT TAKE

THE SUNBELT'S CONSERVATIVE BENT MAY COME UNDER CHALLENGE

Over time, the Sunbelt was able to flex its muscles in Washington because population equals voters. Politicians could scarcely ignore this reality. The Republicans were strongest in the suburbs, the West, and, after 1964, the South, all of which were booming. Each decennial census was followed by a reapportionment of seats in the House of Representatives, which, together with the two senators from each state, determines the number of Electoral College votes each state casts in a presidential election. As shown by the crossing lines in Figure 8.2, the Sunbelt states increased the number of their congressional representatives and presidential electoral votes every time the country was reapportioned after 1928, but the Frostbelt states lost congressional and electoral votes. The number of representatives from six older industrial cities—Boston, New York, Philadelphia, Baltimore, Detroit, and Chicago—fell from fifty-two in 1923 to only thirty-three by 1983.[17] The 1988 presidential election marked the first time that the fifteen Sunbelt states were able to cast more votes in the Electoral College than were the fourteen Frostbelt states combined, and the gap opened wider as a result of the reapportionments following the 1990 and 2000 censuses.

The rise of the Sunbelt largely accounts for the conservative shift in American politics in the last quarter-century. For decades, corporations moved South and West to escape higher labor costs in the North and to take advantage of a vast pool of low-wage, non-unionized labor in the Sunbelt. Twelve out of fifteen Sunbelt states have right-to-work laws that allow employers to hire workers in a plant even if they refuse to join the plant's union. This helps discourage unionization and to keep wages low.[18] These policies result from a political culture that is highly individualistic and generally hostile to governmental action, unless that action is geared toward helping business and expanding the private economy. Peter Lupsha and William Siembieda sum up the political orientation in the Sunbelt this way: "The critical elements shaping political forms in the Sunbelt were the values of privatism, individualism, religious fundamentalism, fiscal conservatism, laissez faire, and a view of good government as good business."[19] Due in part to the rising influence of Sunbelt politicians in both parties who promoted such values, the nation's political culture has been fundamentally changed since the early 1980s.

But large-scale social forces may be changing the Sunbelt and its politics. Blacks have been moving back into the South from northern states, and millions of immigrants have been moving into southern metropolitan regions and into smaller towns. The new demographic realities have brought about a shifting political landscape. An example of the changes occurred on December 20, 2002, when Senate Majority Leader Trent Lott was forced to resign his post because of remarks made two weeks earlier at the 100th birthday party of Senator Strom Thurmond. Lott, a Republican senator from Mississippi, had praised Thurmond for running for the presidency in 1948 on a platform promising to preserve racial segregation: "I want to say this about my state. When Strom Thurmond ran for president, we voted for him. We're proud of it. And if the rest of the country had followed our lead, we wouldn't have had these problems over all these years either."[20] President Bush and Republican leaders were anxious to show that the new party embraced all ethnic and racial groups. Lott's quick exit showed how immigration is beginning to change politics not only in the South but also in the nation.

Figure 8.2   **Electoral Votes and Congressional Representation:
Sunbelt and Frostbelt States, 1928–1992**

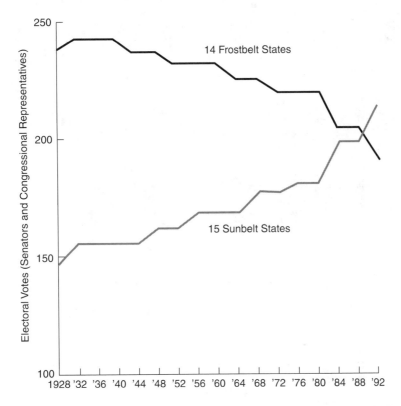

Source: U.S. Bureau of the Census, *Historical Statistics of the United States, Colonial Times to 1970,*
Bicentennial edition, pt. 1 (Washington, D.C.: Government Printing Office, 1975), p. 1015; U.S. Bureau
of the Census, *Statistical Abstract of the United States, 1989* (Washington, D.C.: Government Printing
Office, 1989), p. 241; and Felicity Barringer, "Census Bureau Places Population at 249.6 Million,"
New York Times, December 27, 1990.

In the five decades between 1940 and 1990, the population of the fifteen
Sunbelt states increased 163 percent (to 103,868,000), compared to a population
gain in the fourteen Frostbelt states of 48 percent (to 92,818,000).[21] Over this
half-century, the fastest-growing states were Nevada (+50 percent), Arizona
(+35 percent), Florida (+33 percent), and California (+26 percent). The only
Frostbelt state to show a significant gain was New Hampshire (+20.5 percent),
which was attracting commuters from elsewhere in the Northeast urban corridor.[22] As shown in Figure 8.3, these trends continued through the 1990s. Every
state with a growth rate faster than 13.2 percent for the decade (the national
average) was located in the West or in the Sunbelt, with the addition of Virginia. Three of the states that gained more than 25 percent in population—

Figure 8.3 **Population Growth in States, 1990–2000**

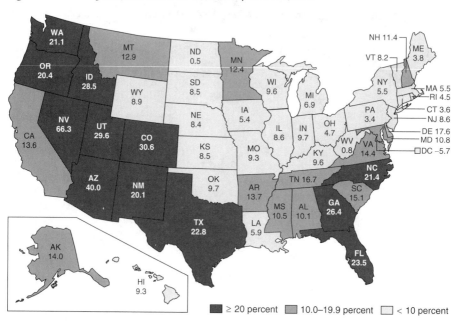

Source: U.S. Census Bureau, Statistical Abstract of the United States, 2001 (Washington, D.C.: U.S. Cenus Bureau), p. 7.

Colorado, Utah, and Idaho—were located outside the Sunbelt, as were two other rapidly growing states, Oregon and Washington.

Most metropolitan areas in the Sunbelt have grown so rapidly since World War II that it has been difficult to build infrastructure fast enough. Table 8.1 shows growth rates for selected Sunbelt and Frostbelt cities. All of the seven Sunbelt metropolitan areas shown in Table 8.1 grew rapidly from 1950 to 2000, in many cases by more than 40 percent per decade before growth rates slowed in the 1990s. Phoenix had a population of 107,000 in 1950 but grew to a metropolitan region of more than 3 million people in half a century. Las Vegas was transformed from a nondescript gambling town of 24,000 in 1950 to a major metropolis (and entertainment city) of 1.4 million by 2000. Several cities in Florida (such as Fort Meyers, Cape Coral, Ocala, Sarasota, and Naples) attracted large number of retirees. But others, such as Boise, Idaho; Austin, Texas; and Provo, Utah, boomed because of an influx of high-tech industries.

The six Frostbelt metropolitan areas listed in Table 8.1 experienced a different fate. Until the late 1960s, the Chicago, Detroit, and St. Louis metropolitan areas continued to prosper as industrial centers, but the bottom fell out during the deindustrialization of the 1970s and 1980s. Modest growth in the 1950s and 1960s was followed by stagnation or population losses. Many manufacturing

Table 8.1 **Population Growth of Selected Metropolitan Areas of 1 Million or More, 1950–1997**

	Percent Increase in Population				
Metropolitan Area (Ranked by Growth in 1970s)	1950– 1960	1960– 1970	1970– 1980	1980– 1990	1990– 1997
Sunbelt and West					
Las Vegas	123	115	69	61	48
Phoenix	100	46	55	40	27
Houston	52	40	45	21	15
Denver-Boulder	52	32	31	44	17
San Diego	85.5	32	37	34	9
Miami	89	36	28	20	5.5
Los Angeles–Long Beach	45.5	16	6	18.5	3
Frostbelt					
Chicago	20	12	2	0.2	5
Detroit	28	12	–2	–2	5
St. Louis	20	12	–2	3	3
New York City	12	8	–4.5	3	1
Boston	7.5	6	–5	6.5	2.5
Pittsburgh	9	20	–5	–7	–1

Source: U.S. Bureau of the Census, *1970 Census of Population,* vol. 1, *Characteristics of the Population,* pt. A (Washington, D.C.: Government Printing Office, 1973), p. 171, table 32; *1980 Census of the Population, Supplementary Reports, Standard Metropolitan Statistical Areas and Standard Consolidated Statistical Areas,* p. 3, table 1; U.S. Bureau of the Census, *State and Metropolitan Area Data Book: 1991* (Washington, D.C.: Government Printing Office, 1991), table A; U.S. Bureau of the Census, *Standard Metropolitan Area Data Book: 1997–98* (Washington, D.C.: Government Printing Office, 1999), table B-1, pp. 60–65.

firms picked up and moved to cheaper sites in the Sunbelt, where labor unions were weak, or abroad. Older metropolitan areas began to revive their economies by the 1990s by attracting service or other high-growth industries. The Pittsburgh region slowed its rate of population loss in the 1990s, and Detroit and Chicago showed some growth after two troubled decades.

The older central cities did much worse than metropolitan-wide growth rates seemed to indicate. In the 1970s, as deindustrialization reached its high point, St. Louis lost 27 percent of its population, but its suburbs grew by more than 6 percent. This was a profile shared by all of the older cities in the industrial belt; for example, Chicago's population fell by 11 percent, Detroit's by 20.5 percent, Cleveland's by 24 percent, but the suburbs grew in each of these metropolitan areas. Most of these cities continued to lose population in the 1990s, but at a slower rate, though New York, Chicago, and a few others arrested their population declines.

In the Sunbelt, most central cities grew in step with their metropolitan regions. One reason that Sunbelt central cities did quite well was that many of them were newer and less built up than the older cities in the North. Another is that they were usually not as isolated within their metropolitan areas as those in the Frostbelt. David Rusk has categorized cities according to their degree of "elasticity"—their ability to grow either by filling in undeveloped land or by annexing new territory. Of the fifty-two metropolitan areas of more than 200,000 population that Rusk rated as having "high" or "hyper" elasticity in 1990, forty-nine were located in the Sunbelt. No Frostbelt city was ranked in these categories.[23]

Older central cities all over the nation found it impossible to change their boundaries, mostly because they had become surrounded by independent suburban municipalities long ago, and suburban governments were able to prevent annexation or merger attempts. Even in the Sunbelt, older cities fit this profile; Atlanta, for instance, lost 14 percent of its population during the 1970s, but its regional population grew by 46 percent. Denver likewise lost population (–4.5 percent) while its suburbs grew (+60 percent). By contrast, newer cities have been able to annex territory to keep themselves from becoming surrounded by independent suburbs. Oklahoma City, for example, grew from about 51 square miles in 1950 to 636 square miles by 1970. Much of its territory is semirural land waiting for new housing tracts. Phoenix expanded from just 17 square miles in 1950 to 469 square miles by 1996.[24] Most Sunbelt cities added substantial territory in the 1950s and 1960s and at least some additional territory since then.[25]

WHY THE SUNBELT BOOMED

The movement of people to the Sunbelt has been matched by a redistribution of the nation's economic resources. In recent decades, job growth has heavily favored the South and West. Table 8.2 shows that in 1960, 58 percent of the nation's workforce was located in the Northeast and Midwest. The West was relatively underdeveloped, with only 15 percent of U.S. employment. But by 1980s, the share of jobs located in the Northeast and Midwest had slipped to 49 percent, and by 2000 it was down to 43 percent. Big gains occurred in the South and West, which together accounted for 56 percent of U.S. employment by 2000 (21 percent in the West). The number of jobs in the South rose by 39.5 percent from 1960 to 1980 and by even more, 42 percent, from 1980 to 2000. Meanwhile, the West experienced a 25.5 percent job growth from 1960 to 1980 and a 26 percent growth over the next twenty years. The rate of growth outside the Sunbelt was much slower.

The reasons for the economic success of the Sunbelt are many and complex. Economic and technological factors played a major role.[26] The urban infrastructure of the older Frostbelt cities was geared to the high-density patterns of production and consumption characteristic of the industrial period. Sunbelt cities had an advantage because they could start afresh to build infrastructure suited to the postindustrial economy. The building of a freeway network throughout the nation provided the foundation for a national economy that favored the decentralization of economic activities. The adoption of air conditioning made the Sunbelt

Table 8.2 **Comparison of Regional* Shares of U.S. Employment and Shares of U.S. Job Growth 1960–2000 (in Percentages)**

	Share of U.S. Employment			Share of Job Growth	
	1960	**1980**	**2000**	**1960–1980**	**1980–2000**
Northeast	29	23	21	13.5	12
Midwest	29	26	25	21.5	20
South	27	32	34	39.5	42
West	15	19	20	25.5	26

*Regions defined according to the Bureau of the Census definition; North Central changed to Midwest in 1989.

Sources: Adapted from *Statistical Abstract of the United States, 1973* using 1960 and 1970 census data, page 227; *U.S. Statistical Abstract of the United States, 2001,* using 1990 and 2000 census data; *Statistical Abstract of the United States, 1996,* using 1980 census data.

more attractive both for living and for white-collar work.[27] The materials used in manufacturing shifted from heavy metals such as iron and steel to lighter materials such as aluminum and plastic, and the newer manufacturing plants could be located on relatively cheap, easily available land in Sunbelt metropolitan areas. Most importantly, the source of energy for industry and for homes shifted from Frostbelt coal to Sunbelt oil. Oil jumped from meeting less than half of the nation's energy needs in 1940 to almost 78 percent by 1975. By the mid-1970s, coal met no more than 17 percent of the nation's energy needs.[28]

Changing demographics and lifestyles favored the Sunbelt as well. Increased leisure time and more emphasis on recreation lured people to warmer climates. After World War II, tourism became a major component of the national economy. Major recreational and tourist facilities developed in Florida and California (homes of Disney theme parks) and in New Orleans and Las Vegas. Whole communities, such as Lake Havasu, Arizona, arose to serve the needs of an expanding class of retired people who preferred Sunbelt lifestyles and the lower cost of living found there.

Demographic and economic trends do not, however, fully explain the Sunbelt boom. Governmental policies played a pivotal role. The national policies that favored the Sunbelt were adopted mainly because the political balance of power in the nation had shifted along with jobs and population. The crucial role of governments can be appreciated by looking at the experience of other advanced industrial countries that have their own "sunbelts": in Britain, employment has shifted from the industrial north to the south of England, where a high-technology economy has emerged along the M-4 motorway between London and Bristol; in Germany, economic growth has shifted from the traditional centers of industry in the Ruhr and Saar regions to new centers of high-technology engineering and electronics in the southern states of Hesse, Baden-Württemberg, and Bavaria. However, no European country has experienced the extraordinary degree of redistribution of population and production that the United States has undergone in the last half-century.

Populations have moved around less in Europe partly because the European countries have enacted explicit regional development policies designed to counteract uneven development. Britain adopted regional policies in the 1930s to restrain the growth of London and to aid the economies of the industrial north to employ laid-off miners and industrial workers. Britain's regional policies were supported by both Labour and Conservative governments, until the accession of Margaret Thatcher in 1979.[29] Support for regional development policies was even stronger in continental Europe, where programs to move jobs to declining regions were inaugurated in Italy (1950), West Germany (1951), the Netherlands (1951), Ireland (1952), France (mid-1950s), Denmark (1958), and Belgium (1959).[30] The effects of these policies are difficult to evaluate, but in a country like France, which made regional development policy an integral part of national economic planning, there is little doubt that national planners wielding construction controls and powerful incentives were able to disperse jobs and population from Paris to "growth poles" in languishing regions.

The United States has always lagged far behind European social democracies in enacting national growth policies. Some regional development policies were begun in the 1960s (such as the Appalachian Regional Commission in 1962), but these policies did nothing but provide some federal assistance for local economic development efforts. Overall, the United States has never enacted comprehensive regional development policies; "Indeed, in treating the geographical distribution of economic activity and population as a matter of market forces, rather than national planning . . . the United States stands alone among advanced democratic countries."[31]

Though regional development planning has been absent in the United States, public spending has exerted a powerful impact. In particular, the Pentagon budget has induced military-dependent sectors to migrate to the Sunbelt. No other major industrialized nation used military spending so forcefully to relocate economic activity from one region to another.[32] The Great Depression ended in the United States when government spending for military procurement climbed sharply in 1940 in response to the stunning success of the Nazi blitzkrieg in Europe. As military contracting soared, the War Production Board made a policy decision to spread out defense installations and productive capacity to make bombing and a potential invasion more difficult. The South and West possessed the advantage of favorable weather for aircraft training facilities. Overall, it is estimated that 60 percent of the $74 billion wartime expenditures went into the fifteen states of the Sunbelt at a time when those states contained less than 40 percent of the national population.[33]

The metropolitan areas of the South experienced the most rapid growth of any region. World War II pulled the rural poor into the cities in search of relatively well-paid industrial employment, which contributed to the rapid urbanization of the South. The beginning of a decades-long process began in the three years between 1940 and 1943, when the population of the metropolitan counties of the South grew by 4 percent and those of the West by 3 percent. By contrast, the metropolitan counties in the upper Midwest grew by only 2 percent and the northeastern metropolitan areas contracted by 0.6 percent.[34]

Some cities, most of them located in the South and West, experienced phenomenal growth when people migrated in search of jobs in defense plants. Between April 1940 and October 1941, 150,000 people poured into Los Angeles, increasing the city's population by about a third. During the war years, San Diego grew by 27 percent and Wichita, Kansas, by 20 percent.[35] The wartime boom taxed the housing stock, infrastructure, and public services in these cities to the breaking point.

Near the end of World War II, war production began to shift from heavy industry (tanks and guns) to high-tech weaponry such as missiles, jet airplanes, and sophisticated communications systems. During the Cold War, military spending remained high, and most of it went to the Sunbelt. One study showed a "definite regional shift" from the Northeast to the Sunbelt between 1950 and 1976 in the awarding of defense contracts.[36] During that period, the number of defense employees in the nation increased by more than 35 percent but fell by 3 percent in the sixteen northeastern and upper midwestern states.[37] By 1975, the defense budget contributed only 4 percent to personal incomes in the Northeast, compared to 9 percent in the Sunbelt.[38]

Defense spending shifted to the Sunbelt not just because the region was an efficient location for some kinds of military production. For a long time, Democratic senators and representatives from the South were so secure in their seats because of uncontested one-party elections that they were able to control key committees in Congress through the seniority system. The southerners used their powerful positions as committee chairs to steer defense spending and major infrastructure investments, such as dams and water projects, to their states and districts. Perhaps the best example is Mendell Rivers, who represented Charleston, South Carolina, for forty years, from 1930 to 1970. As chair of the powerful House Armed Services Committee, Rivers succeeded in getting the federal government to build in his hometown "an Army depot, a Marine Corps air base, a Marine boot camp, two Navy hospitals, a Navy shipyard, a Navy base, a Navy supply center, a Navy weapons center, a Navy submarine base, a Polaris missile base, two Air Force bases, and a federal housing development."[39] Because senators and representatives from more pluralistic and diverse Frostbelt districts usually served fewer terms in Congress before being defeated for reelection, they were not able to accumulate comparable seniority and congressional clout.[40]

Other federal spending programs also disproportionately benefited the Sunbelt. Extensive federal subsidies for highways favored Sunbelt growth over the Frostbelt, which relied more heavily on railroads and mass transit. Federal grants for new sewer and water systems and for large dams and water projects tended to favor the Sunbelt. Of course, some federal spending programs, such as public employment programs and social welfare spending, were biased toward the older industrial cities. The difference is that federal spending oriented to the Frostbelt often came in the form of infusions of urban aid or welfare grants that did little to create sustained economic development. By contrast, federal spending in the Sunbelt created permanent federal payrolls and infrastructure to support whole new industries, such as microelectronics. One of the most important ingredients of economic growth is a skilled labor force. The military actively recruited highly trained white-collar workers, engineers, and scientists to areas near Sunbelt military installations. "Every year the Department of Defense pays a number of companies a large sum of money to move college-educated (often at the public expense) engineers and scientists from the Midwest and other regions to the Southwest."[41]

Besides spending, provisions in the federal tax code benefited the Sunbelt over the Frostbelt. In 1954, accelerated depreciation allowances deducted from corporate income taxes provided tax breaks for constructing new commercial and industrial structures but not for rehabilitating old buildings. Accelerated depreciation thus speeded up the flow of capital out of older industrial cities to suburban and Sunbelt locations.[42] Between 1954 and 1980, this subsidy was worth $30 billion in reduced taxes. The Investment Tax Credit, introduced by President Kennedy in 1962, granted a dollar-for-dollar reduction in corporate taxes for investments in new plant and equipment. Thus, the federal tax code encouraged companies to abandon older plants in the Frostbelt and build new plants in the Sunbelt. Between 1962 and 1981, this subsidy was worth $90 billion,[43] and in 1982 alone it was worth $20 billion.[44] A study conducted in the early 1980s of nine tax subsidies that promoted the mobility of investment (such as accelerated depreciation allowances on old plant and equipment and allowances for new equipment) found that they were worth more than twice the total budget of the U.S. Department of Housing and Urban Development.[45]

Regional inequities in federal policy spawned the formation of regional lobbying groups. In June 1976, the Coalition of Northeast Governors was organized, and in September 1976, congressional representatives from sixteen states formed the Northeast-Midwest Economic Advancement Coalition (today called the Northeast-Midwest Institute). To counter the lobbying of the Frostbelt politicians, the Southern Growth Policy Board, which had been formed in 1971, stepped up its efforts.[46] Regional disparities in federal spending narrowed somewhat between 1975 and 1979,[47] but Ronald Reagan's election in 1980 decisively shifted the momentum.[48] Once in office, Reagan sharply cut programs targeted to older central cities.[49] Between 1980 and 1987, grant programs of special importance to cities, such as mass transit, public housing, social welfare, and job training, were cut by 47 percent.[50] At the same time, his administration increased defense and highway programs that disproportionately benefited the Sunbelt.

The federal budget became a way to redistribute national resources from other regions of the country, in the process rewarding the constituencies that favored Republicans the most. Between 1983 and 1998, the citizens of just two states, New York and New Jersey, paid $500 billion more into the federal treasury than was returned in benefits.[51] In 1997, the citizens of nine southern and border states paid $45 billion less in federal taxes than those states received back, while in the same year, eight northern states paid an $82 billion surplus into the federal treasury. Put simply, northern taxpayers helped pay for much of the economic prosperity of the Sunbelt.

THE NEW POLITICS OF SUNBELT CITIES

The politics of the Sunbelt cities has historically been different from politics in the old industrial cities. Before World War II, many Sunbelt cities were dominated by entrenched political machines, but unlike machines in northern cities, immigrants played less of a role than local businesses. Outsiders were not welcome; what the members of these political alliances wanted most of all was to protect local culture against change. Tampa, Florida, and San Antonio, Texas, for example, were governed by machine politicians until well after World War II. New Orleans was run by a long-time machine, the Regular Democratic Organization, until de Lesseps S. Morrison was elected mayor in 1946.[52]

These machines were ill-prepared for the rapid growth set in motion by the defense buildup during World War II. After the war, a new generation of political activists appeared on the scene. In city after city, "G.I. revolts" sprang up in which "bright young candidates marched against corrupt or inept city hall cliques under the banner of progress."[53] Coalitions of white-collar professionals, business leaders, and growth-oriented city managers and bureaucrats came together to form business-dominated reform governments committed to building new infrastructure and pursuing growth.

This wave of reform changed urban politics throughout the Sunbelt, especially in southwestern cities. Between 1945 and 1955, San Antonio, Houston, Dallas, Oklahoma City, Albuquerque, Phoenix, and San Jose all adopted significant reforms, usually installing nonpartisan city-manager systems with at-large electoral arrangements.[54] These movements, led by such organizations as the Phoenix Charter Government Committee, the Albuquerque Citizens Committee, and San Antonio's Good Government League, were led by middle- and upper-class Anglo professionals and business leaders.

San Antonio produced a typical example of the Sunbelt version of municipal reform. In 1949, A. C. "Jack" White won the mayoralty with the support of good government reformers and the business community. It was not until 1951, however, that reformers put aside their disagreements and voted in a council-manager charter. Subsequently, the Good Government League began endorsing candidates. From 1955 to 1971, seventy-seven out of San Antonio's eighty-one city council members were recruited and endorsed by the league. The Good Government League became the functional equivalent of a political party, a "sort of upper-middle class political machine, officing not in Tammany Hall, but in a savings and loan association, whose electoral wonders are impressive to behold."[55]

The Good Government League succeeded in passing a series of bond referenda to finance infrastructure improvements to facilitate San Antonio's growth; for example, by 1986 the league had built a massive 98-mile freeway system within the city limits. It also sponsored urban-renewal clearance and revitalization of the central business district and facilitated the construction of the HemisFair tourism and shopping project on 149 acres southeast of the Alamo. The HemisFair was a classic example of civic boosterism, with local government providing subsidies to a project that was largely planned and operated by the private sector.[56]

Over the years, whites used various methods, both legal and extralegal, to keep African Americans and Latinos from voting. One of the most effective devices was the white primary, which kept blacks from casting ballots in the Democratic primaries used to nominate the party's candidates. In the southern states, where Democratic candidates ran unopposed, this was tantamount to disenfranchisement. In 1944, the U.S. Supreme Court struck down the white primary as a violation of the Fifteenth Amendment of the Constitution.[57]

Other methods continued to be used to dilute the electoral influence of blacks and Latinos. Many cities used at-large election districts to ensure that minority neighborhoods would be outvoted in the citywide totals. The 1965 Voting Rights Act, however, gave federal judges the power to strike down voting systems when they found that they systematically reduced minority representation. In 1975, the act was extended to Latinos. Both Houston and Dallas were forced to modify their at-large systems by adopting wards that would maximize representation for blacks and Latinos. Likewise, Los Angeles was forced to redraw its ward boundaries. Minority voters helped pass new city charters that provided for ward-based representation in San Antonio, Fort Worth, Albuquerque, San Francisco, Atlanta, Richmond, and several other cities.[58]

These measures helped the growing number of African Americans and Latinos flex their political muscle. By 1990, blacks and Latinos made up majority of the population in many cities in Florida and in a belt stretching from Texas to California, with Latinos outnumbering blacks about two to one. In Miami, more than 90 percent of the population was minority, compared to 60 percent in Los Angeles, Houston, and San Antonio. Minorities constituted more than 50 percent in most Sunbelt cities with populations of more than 500,000. Minority populations continued to grow in the central cities during the 1990s, but the dramatic new development was that minority populations in the suburbs virtually exploded.

Minority populations in the suburbs of Sunbelt metropolitan areas increased rapidly in the 1990s—by more than 18 percent in the Fort Lauderdale area and by more than 11 percent in the Oakland, Las Vegas, Atlanta, San Jose, Houston, Orange County (California), Miami, and Dallas areas, among others.[59] As a result of three decades of immigration, by the year 2000 minorities made up at least 40 percent of the population of the suburbs in twenty metropolitan areas in the Sunbelt. Table 8.3 shows that the urban areas with the highest proportions of minorities in the suburbs are located in the Sunbelt; by contrast, nearly all of those with few minorities in the suburbs are located in Frostbelt urban areas. In middle-sized urban areas in the industrial belt—anchored by such cities as Scranton, Allentown, and Harrisburg, Pennsylvania; Youngstown, Akron, Toledo, and Columbus, Ohio; and Buffalo, Albany, and Rochester, New York—very few minorities live in the suburbs. The impression that northern cities are more troubled by racial diversity and conflict than those in the South and West is wrong. The fact that Sunbelt metropolitan areas have become host to millions of new immigrants will bring profound political changes in the years ahead, for the Sunbelt and for the nation as a whole.

The number of African American and Latinos winning public office has kept pace with the population changes. Nationwide, the number of black

Table 8.3 **Suburban Minority Populations in Metro Areas***
with Population over 500,000 (census of 2000)

| Rank | Highest Suburban Minority Percent | | Lowest Minority Suburban Percent | |
	Metro Area	Percent	Metro Area	Percent
1	McAllen, TX	92	Scranton, PA	3
2	El Paso, TX	90	Fort Wayne, IN	4
3	Honolulu, HI	79	Knoxville, TN	5
4	Miami, FL	78.5	Syracuse, NY	5
5	Los Angeles, CA	69	Youngstown, PA	5.5
6	Jersey City, NJ	62.5	Indianapolis, IN	6
7	Albuquerque, NM	56	Akron, OH	6
8	Fresno, CA	55	Milwaukee, WI	6
9	Riverside, CA	53	Buffalo, NY	6
10	Bakersfield, CA	51.5	Albany, NY	6
11	Oakland, CA	48	Allentown, PA	6
12	Ventura, CA	45	Toledo, OH	7

*Several of the metropolitan areas list two or more central cities. In this table, they are identified only by the name of the first central city, as listed in alphabetical order by the census bureau.

Source: Adapted from William Frey, *Melting Pot Suburbs: A Census 2000 Study of Suburban Diversity,* Table 1 (Washington, D.C.: Center on Urban and Metropolitan Policy, The Brookings Institution, June 2001), p. 5.

elected officials increased from 1,469 in February, 1970, to 9,040 in January, 2000.[60] African Americans were elected mayors in some of the largest Sunbelt cities, including Los Angeles, New Orleans, Atlanta, and Birmingham, as well as in suburban and nonmetropolitan cities and counties. With about 20,000 Latino immigrants gaining citizenship and the right to vote each year, Latino gains have been especially dramatic. Nationwide, the number of Latino public officials increased from 3,147 in September, 1985, to 5,205 in September, 2000.[61] Latinos were elected mayor in Miami, Denver, San Antonio, and many smaller cities.

The incorporation of minorities into the politics of Sunbelt cities has brought about significant policy changes. Atlanta has been governed by black mayors since 1973. The majority of the city council and of the school board is black, and blacks hold a majority of the key appointed and civil-service positions in the city government. Under the city's first African American mayor, Maynard Jackson, the African American proportion of the police department rose from 19 percent to 35 percent in only four years, and complaints about police brutality fell.[62] The city established twenty-four neighborhood councils, each with professional staff, so neighborhoods could influence city planning and development decisions. A preferential program begun under Jackson's first term raised the percentage of minority firms holding city contracts from one-tenth of 1 percent to 35 percent by 1988.[63]

The gains for blacks in municipal employment and contracting in Atlanta have been sustained over time. Similar gains have been achieved Birmingham, Alabama, and New Orleans, which have had black mayors since 1979 and 1977 respectively. In both cities, minority contracting programs have raised minority participation significantly, and community organizations have become active. In both cities, police brutality, a major concern to blacks, has become less important as a policy issue.[64]

Latinos have experienced political gains as well. In Miami, Latinos have become the most important electoral constituency because they are the largest population group and have become successful economically. In the 1990s, Latinos succeeded in overturning at-large election systems that disadvantaged them in Miami and surrounding counties. As a result, Latinos have been able to win public offices at all levels, and Latinos and blacks have become well represented on boards and commissions and in public employment.[65] Similarly, blacks and Latinos have become incorporated into the political system of Denver (a city with many Sunbelt characteristics). In 1983, with the election of Frederico Pena, Denver became the first city without a Latino majority to elect a Latino mayor (at the time, 18 percent of Denver's population was Latino). After Pena's two terms, Wellington Webb became the city's first black mayor at a time when blacks made up 11 percent of the city's population. Latinos and blacks have become well represented on the city council and on city boards and commissions, in public employment, and on the civilian police board.[66]

REGIONAL CONVERGENCE AND NATIONAL POLITICS

A number of scholars have predicted a Sunbelt/Frostbelt economic and political convergence.[67] Economic forces are diversifying the economies as well as changing the demographic profiles of cities all over the nation. In the Frostbelt, corporate white-collar employment, services, and tourism have become increasingly important to urban regions and to downtown economies. Frostbelt metropolitan regions are less heavily blue-collar and union than in the past, and central cities in the North have been attracting a significant proportion of affluent households. At the same time, many of the characteristics traditionally associated with older industrial cities—rapid immigration, concentrated poverty, and racial and ethnic conflict—have come to the cities of the Sunbelt. Cities all over the country are now multiracial and multiethnic.

Reflecting this convergence in politics, the public policies of cities are becoming more alike. Older industrial cities of all sizes have moved aggressively to become more "entrepreneurial" in their pursuit of business investment.[68] Accordingly, many of them have shifted resources away from social services and toward developmental programs that subsidize investment.[69] Large volumes of public money have been invested in facilities such as sports stadiums, convention centers, and redevelopment districts.[70] By investing in high-tech and corporate services and developing an infrastructure to support tourism and recreation, Frostbelt cities have become more like the cities of the Sunbelt.

The regional differences in voting behavior and party identification may be disappearing as well. In the past, the Sunbelt favored the Republican Party and pulled the country in a conservative direction. Recent research shows, however, that Democrats may be gaining in metropolitan areas both North and South, and in suburbs as well as central cities.[71] This trend is fueled, in part, by immigration; African Americans, Latinos, and Asians, when combined, are about 75 percent Democratic. They now constitute more than 20 percent of the U.S. population and a much higher percentage in several Sunbelt states and metropolitan areas. White-collar professionals, who are heavily concentrated in suburbs and, increasingly, in rapidly growing central cities with high-tech sectors, made up 21 percent of the electorate in 2000. They tend to be moderate on social issues and to support environmental protection, civil rights, and women's rights, and their numbers are rapidly growing throughout the Sunbelt. Notably, 54 percent of voters in the fastest-growing fifty counties in the nation—nearly all located in the Sunbelt—supported Al Gore in the 2000 election. Two scholars argue that these trends sum up to an "emerging Democratic majority" in national politics.[72] Whether or not that prognosis turns out to be accurate (it did not seem to apply to the 2002 congressional elections), the distinctive regional politics of the United States may disappear in the next few years.

NOTES

1. Bradley R. Rice, "Searching for the Sunbelt," in *Searching for the Sunbelt: Historical Perspectives on a Region,* ed. Raymond A. Mohl (Knoxville: University of Tennessee Press, 1990), p. 217.
2. David R. Goldfield, *Cotton Fields and Skyscrapers: Southern City and Region, 1706–1980* (Baton Rouge: Louisiana State University Press, 1982), p. 192, cited in Rice, "Searching for the Sunbelt," p. 218.
3. Sam Allis, "Regions," *Wall Street Journal,* April 14, 1981, cited in Rice, "Searching for the Sunbelt," p. 218.
4. The shift in regional political power is dramatically exhibited in the career of Lyndon Baines Johnson. Johnson, who was first elected a senator from Texas in 1952, knew that his political career depended upon hewing close to the conservative policies favored by the oilmen who controlled that state's politics. His presidential ambitions were checked by that same source of power, however, because any candidate from the South was regarded as a politically viable only in the region. This made him a good balance as John F. Kennedy's running mate in 1960. He broke the mold by winning the 1964 presidential election. See Robert A. Caro, *The Years of Lyndon Johnson: Master of the Senate* (New York: Knopf, 2002).
5. Kevin P. Phillips, *The Emerging Republican Majority* (New Rochelle, N.Y.: Arlington House, 1969).
6. Prompting the famous headline, "Ford to City: Drop Dead!" *New York Daily News,* October 29, 1975, p. 1.
7. Kirkpatrick Sale, *Power Shift: The Rise of the Southern Rim and Its Challenge to the Eastern Establishment* (New York: Random House, 1975).
8. "The Second War Between the States," *Business Week,* May 17, 1976.
9. Carl Abbott, *The New Urban America: Growth and Politics in Sunbelt Cities* (Chapel Hill: University of North Carolina Press, 1987), p. 6.
10. Sale, *Power Shift,* p. 11.

11. Bernard Weinstein and Harold Gross, interview quoted in Abbott, *The New Urban America*, p. 4.

12. Bruce J. Schulman, *From Cotton Belt to Sunbelt: Federal Policy, Economic Development, and the Transformation of the South, 1938–1980* (New York: Oxford University Press, 1991), chap. 2.

13. Abbott, *The New Urban America*, p. 22.

14. Quoted in David R. Goldfield and Howard N. Rabinowitz, "The Vanishing Sunbelt," in *Searching for the Sunbelt*, ed. Mohl, p. 224.

15. Ibid., p. 231.

16. William H. Frey, "Metropolitan America: Beyond the Transition," *Population Bulletin* 45, no. 2 (July 1990): 14.

17. R. Cohen, "Task for Politicians: Keeping Up with the Votes," *National Journal* (1981): 2037, cited in Robert B. Bradley, "The Changing Political Realities for National Urban Policy in the Eighties," in *Transition to the 21st Century: Prospects and Policies for Economic and Urban-Regional Transformation*, ed. Donald A. Hicks and Norman J. Glickman (Greenwich, Conn.: JAI Press, 1983).

18. Robert Goodman, *The Last Entrepreneurs: America's Regional Wars for Jobs and Dollars* (New York: Simon and Schuster, 1979), p. 42. None of the fourteen Frostbelt states has a right-to-work law.

19. Peter A. Lupsha and William J. Siembieda, "The Poverty of Public Services in the Land of Plenty: An Analysis and Interpretation," in *The Rise of the Sunbelt Cities*, ed. David C. Perry and Alfred J. Watkins (Beverly Hills, Calif.: Sage, 1977), p. 185.

20. Deirdre Shesgreen, "In Lott Fiasco, GOP Could Face Defining Moment," *St. Louis Post-Dispatch*, December 22, 2002, pp. 1, A15.

21. U.S. Bureau of the Census, *Statistical Abstract of the United States*, 1980, 101st ed. (Washington, D.C.: Government Printing Office, 1981), p. 10; U.S. Bureau of the Census, *Statistical Abstract of the United States*, 1992, 112th ed. (Washington, D.C.: Government Printing Office, 1992), p. 22.

22. U.S. Bureau of the Census, *Statistical Abstract of the United States*, 1992, p. 22.

23. David Rusk, *Cities Without Suburbs* (Washington, D.C.: Woodrow Wilson Center Press, 1993).

24. Timothy Egan, "Urban Sprawl Strains Western States," *New York Times*, December 29, 1996, p. 6.

25. Rusk, *Cities Without Suburbs*.

26. For a thorough analysis of the growth of the Sunbelt that emphasizes economic and technological factors, see John D. Kasarda, "The Implications of Contemporary Redistribution Trends for National Urban Policy," *Social Science Quarterly* 61, no. 3 (December 1980): 373–400.

27. Raymond Arsenault, "The End of the Long Hot Summer: The Air Conditioner and Southern Culture," in *Searching for the Sunbelt*, ed. Mohl, pp. 176–211.

28. Kirkpatrick Sale, "Six Pillars of the Southern Rim," in *The Fiscal Crisis of American Cities*, ed. Roger E. Alcaly and David Mermelstein (New York: Random House, Vintage Books, 1977), p. 174.

29. For a brief discussion of British regional policies, see James L. Sundquist, *Dispersing Population: What America Can Learn from Europe* (Washington, D.C.: Brookings Institution, 1975), chap. 2.

30. David Pinder, *Regional Economic Development and Policy: Theory and Practice in the European Community* (London: Allen and Unwin, 1983), pp. 13–14.

31. Sundquist, *Dispersing Population*, p. 241.

32. Ann R. Markusen, *Regions: The Economics and Politics of Territory* (Totowa, N.J.: Rowman and Littlefield, 1987), p. 113.

33. Sale, "Six Pillars of the Southern Rim," p. 170.

34. Funigiello, *The Challenge to Urban Liberalism, Federal-City Relations During World War II* (Knoxville: University of Tennessee Press, 1978) p. 12–13.

35. Abbott, *The New Urban America*, p. 103.
36. Maureen McBreen, "Regional Trends in Federal Defense Expenditures: 1950–76," in *Selected Essays on Patterns of Regional Change: The Changes, the Federal Role, and the Federal Response*, submitted by Senator Henry Bellmon to the Senate Committee on Appropriations (Washington, D.C.: Government Printing Office, 1977), p. 527.
37. A report issued by the Northeast-Midwest Economic Advancement Coalition, cited in Edward C. Burks, "16 Northeast and Midwest States Find Inequities in Defense Outlays," *New York Times*, September 22, 1977.
38. Richard S. Morris, *Bum Rap on America's Cities: The Real Causes of Urban Decline* (Englewood Cliffs, N.J.: Prentice-Hall, 1978), pp. 148–149.
39. Sale, *Power Shift*, p. 149.
40. Since the early 1970s, exceptions to the seniority rule have been permitted by both parties, and the power of committee chairs has been reduced.
41. Ann R. Markusen, "Regional Planning and Policy: An Essay on the American Exception," Working Paper No. 9 (Brunswick, NJ: Center for Urban Policy Research, Rutgers University, July 1989).
42. See George Peterson, "Federal Tax Policy and Urban Development," in *Central City Economic Development*, ed. Benjamin Chinitz (Cambridge, Mass.: Abt Books, 1979), pp. 67–78.
43. Michael I. Luger, "Federal Tax Incentives as Industrial and Urban Policy," in *Sunbelt/Snowbelt: Urban Development and Regional Restructuring*, ed. Larry Sawers and William K. Tabb (New York: Oxford University Press, 1984), pp. 204–205.
44. John F. Witte, "The Growth and Distribution of Tax Expenditures," in *The Distributional Impacts of Public Policies*, ed. Sheldon H. Danziger and Kent E. Portney (New York: St. Martin's Press, 1988), p. 179.
45. Peter Marcuse, "The Targeted Crisis: On the Ideology of the Urban Fiscal Crisis and Its Causes," *International Journal of Urban and Regional Research* 5, no. 3 (1981): 339.
46. See Markusen, *Regions,* chap. 8. The Southern Growth Policy Board relinquished its federal monitoring activities to the Congressional Sunbelt Council in January 1981.
47. "Neutral Federal Policies Are Reducing Frostbelt-Sunbelt Spending Imbalances," *National Journal*, February 7, 1981, pp. 233–236.
48. For evidence on the Sunbelt bias of direct federal military expenditures during the Reagan Administration, see the data compiled in the *New York Times*, December 20, 1983, cited in Michael Peter Smith, *City, State, and Market: The Political Economy of Urban Society* (New York: Blackwell, 1988), p. 57.
49. Harold Wolman, "The Reagan Urban Policy and Its Impacts," *Urban Affairs Quarterly* 21, no. 3 (March 1986): 311–336.
50. Peggy L. Cuciti, "A Nonurban Policy: Recent Public Policy Shifts Affecting Cities," in *The Future of National Urban Policy*, ed. Marshall Kaplan and Franklin James (Durham, N.C.: Duke University Press, 1990), p. 243.
51. Thad Williamson, David Imroscio, and Gar Alparovitz, *Making a Place for Community: Local Democracy in a Global Era* (New York: Routledge, 2002), p. 56.
52. See Gary Mormino, "Tampa: From Hell Hole to the Good Life," in *Sunbelt Cities: Politics and Growth Since World War II*, ed. Richard M. Bernard and Bradley R. Rice (Austin: University of Texas Press, 1983), pp. 138–161; and Abbott, *The New Urban America.*
53. Abbott, *The New Urban America*, p. 247.
54. Amy Bridges, "Politics and Growth in Sunbelt Cities," in *Searching for the Sunbelt*, ed. Mohl, p. 2.
55. Robert L. Lineberry, *Equality and Urban Policy: The Distribution of Municipal Public Services* (Beverly Hills, Calif.: Sage, 1977), pp. 55–56, quoting Abbott, *The New Urban America*, p. 139.
56. Our account of San Antonio's business-dominated reform movement relies on Abbott, *The New Urban America.*
57. *Smith v. Allwright*, 321 U.S. 649 (1944). See the discussion in V. O. Key, *Politics, Parties, and Pressure Groups*, 5th ed. (New York: Crowell, 1964), p. 607.

58. Abbott, *The New Urban America*, p. 217.

59. William Frey, *Melting Pot Suburbs: A Census 2000 Study of Suburban Diversity*, (Washington, D.C.: Center for Urban and Metropolitan Policy, The Brookings Institution, June 2001), p. 8.

60. Joint Center for Political and Economic Studies, "Black Elected Officials: A Statistical Summary, Annual" (Washington, D.C.: Author, April 2001), p. 250; http://www.jointcenter.org/databank/graphs/99beo.pdf.

61. Ibid., citing original source as National Roster of Latino Elected Officials (Washington, D.C., National Association of Hispanic Elected and Appointed Officials, annual).

62. Michael Leo Owens and Michael J. Rich, "Is Strong Incorporation Enough? Black Empowerment and the Fate of Atlanta's Low-Income Blacks," in Rufus P. Browning, Dale Rogers Marshall, and David H. Tabb, *Racial Politics in American Cities*, 3rd ed. (New York: Longman, 2003), pp. 209–210.

63. Timothy Bates and Darrell Wiliams, "Preferential Procurement Programs and Minority-Owned Business," *Journal of Urban Affairs* 17, no. 1 (1995): 1.

64. Huey L. Perry, "The Evolution and Impact of Biracial Coalition and Black Mayors in Birmingham and New Orleans," in Browning, Marshall, and Tabb, *Racial Politics*, pp. 228–254.

65. Christopher L. Warren and Dario V. Moreno, "Power Without a Program: Hispanic Incorporation in Miami," in Browning, Marshall, and Tabb, *Racial Politics*, pp. 281–306.

66. Rodney E. Hero and Susan E. Clarke, "Latinos, Blacks, and Multiethnic Politics in Denver: Realigning Power and Influence in the Struggle for Equality," in Browning, Marshall, and Tabb, *Racial Politics*, pp. 309–330.

67. Theodore J. Lowi, "The State of Cities in the Second Republic," *Fiscal Retrenchment and Urban Policy*, ed. J. P. Blair and D. Nachmias (Beverly Hills: Sage, 1979), pp. 43–54; John H. Mollenkopf, *The Contested City* (Princeton, NJ: Princeton University Press; 1983); Paul Kantor, *The Dependent City Revisited: The Political Economy of Urban Development and Social Policy* (Boulder, Colo.: Westview Press, 1995).

68. Peter K. Eisinger, *The Rise of the Entrepreneurial State: State and Local Economic Development Policy in the United States* (Madison: University of Wisconsin Press, 1988).

69. For evidence of this shift, see Kenneth K. Wong, *City Choices: Education and Housing* (Albany: State University of New York Press, 1990), p. 16.

70. Dennis R. Judd, ed., *The Infrastructure of Play: Building the Tourist City* (Armonk, N.Y.: M.E. Sharpe, 2003).

71. John B. Judis and Ruy Teixeira, *The Emerging Democratic Majority* (New York: Scribner/A Lisa Drew Book, 2002).

72. Ibid.

PART III

CITY POLITICS AS A MICROCOSM OF AMERICAN SOCIETY

The organization and governance of its metropolitan regions reveal the nation's response to the problems and tensions of a complex society. In the twentieth century, America's urban areas seemed to stand as a microcosm for the nation. Issues of racial division came to be represented in a sharp divide between cities and suburbs. As millions of blacks left the South for the promised land in the north, the white middle class headed for the suburbs. Increasingly, suburban politics became devoted to strategies of exclusion and secession. The concentration of the urban poor into segregated inner-city neighborhoods created a bogeyman used to frighten the white middle class. Lurid stories about crime and violence in inner-city neighborhoods became a staple for the ten o'clock news. Increasingly, walled enclaves seemed to proliferate.

By late century, however, the divided metropolis was changing into a complex mosaic. New immigrants, first Latinos and Asians, then people from all over the globe, moved to the suburbs as well as to the cities. The old pattern has begun to break down, replaced by a new reality that is more complex and less predictable. The suburbs are becoming home to the affluent and the poor alike,

223

to native-born and immigrant, and to every racial and ethnic group. At the same time, affluent empty-nesters and young professionals are moving back downtown. Central cities are once again becoming hotspots for culture, nightlife, and fun.

The breakup of the old urban pattern does not guarantee that the racial and ethnic segregation that has long characterized urban America will become a thing of the past. The new mosaic may reinforce a tendency for affluent urban residents to escape to fortified enclaves. But it may also redefine American society in unexpected ways. The United States is thoroughly urban; what happens to its cities reverberates throughout the nation's politics and culture.

THE FRACTURED
METROPOLIS

THE ROOTS OF THE URBAN CRISIS

In the twentieth century, the divide between the central cities and the suburbs became a defining feature of America's political consciousness. All through the century, the cities continued to serve as magnets for people escaping oppression and poverty and searching for jobs and opportunity. Before and again after the Great Depression, blacks left the South by the millions and poured into the cities of the North, Mexicans moved into cities of the Southwest, and poverty-stricken white families fled depressed rural areas. By the 1950s, it became painfully obvious that the cities were beset with serious economic and social crises. In the years since the prosperity of the 1920s, the physical condition of inner-city business districts and residential neighborhoods had deteriorated. After World War II, millions of newcomers poured into the cities. Mexican immigration once again picked up. Hundreds of thousands of impoverished white families also were on the move, escaping the grinding poverty of Appalachia and other pockets of rural poverty. But African Americans initiated one of the most momentous population movements of the twentieth century, and perhaps of any time. Between 1940 and 1970, five million blacks moved from the South to northern cities.

At the same time that these groups were making their way to the cities, white middle-class families fled the cities to low-density, single-family homes in suburban subdivisions. In the 1920s, for the first time in the nation's history, suburban populations grew at a faster rate than the central cities.[1] After World War II, the floodgates were opened. By the 1970 census, for the first time, more Americans lived in suburbs than lived either in cities or in small towns and rural areas. During the 1980s and 1990s, population continued to sprawl in ever-widening suburban arcs around the core cities.

The movements into and out of the cities created a nearly unbridgeable social chasm. Americans became accustomed to thinking in dichotomies—city/suburban, black/white, ghetto/subdivision, poor/affluent—and these habits of thought consistently cast cities in a dismal light.[2] By the 1970s, a nightly menu of lurid stories of murder, mayhem, and drugs became the way that local news stations kept their ratings up. For suburbanites, crime became a signifier of the inner city and the people who lived there.[3]

By the late twentieth century, the divide between the cities and the suburbs began to give way to the fractured metropolis. Since the mid-1960s, the United States has been experiencing one of the heaviest periods of immigration in the nation's history. Asians and Latinos now constitute a substantial and growing proportion of the residents of America's cities. The political consequences of this development have been far-reaching. For decades, the urban crisis was defined as the segregation between blacks in the central cities and whites in the suburbs. What is different now is that the tensions of urban society have come to the suburbs; they no longer are located primarily in central cities. In the twenty-first century, the suburb/city dichotomy may become a thing of the past, possibly to be replaced by metropolitan areas fractured into a mosaic of interethnic antagonisms.

THE MOVEMENT TO THE CENTRAL CITIES

Three periods of migration and immigration created the crisis of segregation, race, and poverty that characterized America's cities in the twentieth century (see Table 9.1).[4] The first wave crested in the two decades before the Great Depression. Between 1910 and 1930, 700,000 Mexicans moved into Texas, New Mexico, Arizona, and California, and more than a million blacks left the southern states for Chicago, Detroit, Cleveland, New York City, Pittsburgh, Philadelphia, and other cities of the industrial Midwest and Northeast. The second, bigger wave washed over the cities during World War II and did not ebb until the late 1960s. From 1940 to 1970, up to five million blacks and 700,000 Mexicans moved into America's inner cities. During this same period, more than a million and a half impoverished whites also streamed into the cities, though their migration received little attention.

Between 1910 and 1926, Mexicans were driven into the southwestern states by the bloody and protracted violence of the Mexican Revolution. Although the revolution released millions of peasants from their feudal relationship with landholders, it left many of them without the means to sustain an independent livelihood. Bloody confrontations between the Mexican government and landowners drove the newly liberated peasants into Texas, Arizona, and California. During World War II and its aftermath, employment opportunities in the southwestern states induced still more Mexicans to cross the border. By 1970, 5.5 million Mexican Americans lived in the American Southwest, the great majority in towns and cities.[5] Latino immigrants from several other Latin American countries streamed into the southwestern states in even larger numbers in the 1980s and 1990s, pushed by political repression and poverty and pulled by the availability of jobs.

The decline of the coal industry in the southern Appalachian Mountains and the Cumberland plateau of Virginia, West Virginia, and Kentucky prompted a

Table 9.1 Rural to Urban Migrant Streams in Twentieth-Century America

Migrant Group	Principal Migration Period	Approximate Number of Migrants[a]	Origin	Destination
Appalachian whites	1940–1970	1,600,000	Southern Appalachian Mountains (Kentucky and West Virginia)	North central states
Mexicans	1910–1930	700,000	*Mesa Central* primarily, also *Mesa del Norte*	Texas and southwestern states
	1950–1970	700,000	*Mesa Central* primarily, also *Mesa del Norte*	Texas and California
Blacks	1910–1930	1,250,000[b]	Mississippi delta, Michigan, Atlantic coastal plain	Illinois, Ohio, black belt, New York, and Pennsylvania
	1940–1970	5,000,000[b]	Mississippi delta, black belt, Atlantic coastal plain	Cities every- where

[a]These figures are approximate. The data for the Mexican migration, for example, are obscured by contract labor, two-way migration, and illegal entrants.

[b]U.S. Bureau of the Census, *Historical Statistics of the United States: Colonial Times to 1970* (Washington, D.C.: Government Printing Office). Greenberg's original table lists 1 million blacks, 1910–1930, and 3.5 million blacks, 1940–1965.

Source: Adapted from Stanley B. Greenberg, *Politics and Poverty: Modernization and Response in Five Poor Neighborhoods* (New York: Wiley, 1974), p. 19.

massive movement of desperately poor rural white families from the 1930s to the 1960s. The exodus reached such proportions after World War II that some counties in Appalachia were almost depopulated in just a few years. In his moving book, *Night Comes to the Cumberlands*, Harry Caudill describes the grinding poverty that forced families and entire communities to pick up and leave their marginal farm plots and shabby towns. Many of the families that were forced to leave could trace their roots in Appalachia several generations back. An entire genre of country music—bluegrass—was inspired by homesickness for the hills and hollows left behind. In the 1950s alone, a quarter of the population deserted the Cumberland plateau, settling in cities and towns of Kentucky, Tennessee, Maryland, Virginia, and the industrial belt of the upper Midwest.[6] Joining them were a steady stream of impoverished white families who were leaving the border areas of southern Illinois, Kentucky, and Arkansas. Regardless of where they actually came from, the new migrants were derisively called Hoosiers, Okies, and Arkies. Like the epithets flung at African Americans, such labels were a way of keeping them apart.

OUT TAKE

THE RACIAL DIVIDE IS MOVING TO THE SUBURBS

In the wake of urban riots in 1965 and 1966, a series of presidential commissions gave expression to the rising concern that the extreme racial segregation of cities and suburbs had developed into a national urban crisis. The National Commission on Civil Disorders of 1967 (called the Kerner Commission after its chairman, Illinois governor Otto B. Kerner), warned of "two nations, one black, one white—separate and unequal."[7] The commission might just as well have said "two nations: one city, one suburban."

The segregation of blacks and whites has now has been supplanted by a new reality: America has become a multiracial and multiethnic society. Since the 1980s, immigration flows have exceeded even the zenith of immigration of one hundred years ago. The new immigrants are coming from everywhere on the globe, and some of them are skipping the cities entirely. During the 1990s, for example, two parallel streams moved to Orange County, California, just outside Los Angeles: highly educated professionals and foreign-born immigrants. The two streams could hardly have been more different; high-income families making more than $150,000 per year jumped by 184 percent in the county, but at the same time the number of foreign-born immigrants increased by 48 percent.[8] Commenting on these trends, a noted demographer said that the county could go into two directions, either a "mostly gated-community-type mentality," or "Immigrants start integrating into middle-class areas, so you have a blended suburbia."[9]

If the racial and ethnic groups that live in metropolitan America were to become genuinely integrated, it would constitute an extraordinary rupture from the past. Throughout the nation's history, native-born Americans have always been nervous about newcomers, and they have generally responded by trying to keep them out, preserving their own control over political institutions, or escaping to separate neighborhoods or to the suburbs. The tendency toward separation seems to be occurring again. In the 1990s, Asians and Latinos have settled in the suburbs in large numbers. Perhaps a result, a rising proportion of both groups now live in ethnic enclaves that are more separated from whites than before.[10] But these patterns are not written in cement. If the newcomers become incorporated into the politics of cities and of the nation, the past need not serve as prologue.

The movement of African Americans from the southern states to northern cities that lasted for more than sixty years constituted "one of the largest and most rapid mass internal movements of people in history—perhaps the greatest not caused by the immediate threat of execution or starvation."[11] From 1910 to 1920, 450,000 blacks moved out of the South, followed by another 750,000 in the 1920s.[12] In the twenty years between 1910 and 1930, about one million blacks—one-tenth of all blacks living in the South—moved to cities in the Northeast and Midwest. In just twenty years, the black population living outside the South shot up by 134 percent, and the proportion of the nation's black population residing in the South dropped from 89 percent to 79 percent.[13] The northward movement was slowed by the depression of the 1930s, but it gained even more momentum during and after World War II. Between 1940 and 1970, an estimated five million blacks left the South.

Table 9.2 **Growth of Black Population in Several Cities, 1910–1930**

City	1910	1920	1930	Percent Increase 1910–1930	Percent Increase 1910	Percent of Total Population 1930
New York	91,709	152,467	327,706	257.3	2	5
Chicago	44,103	109,458	233,903	429.3	2	7
Philadelphia	84,459	134,229	219,599	160.0	5.5	11
St. Louis	43,960	69,854	93,580	112.9	6	11
Cleveland	8,448	34,451	71,889	751.0	1.5	8

Source: U.S. Bureau of the Census, *Negroes in the United States, 1920–1932* (Washington, D.C.: Government Printing Office, 1935), p. 55.

Like the European immigrants who preceded them, African Americans were pushed by crisis and pulled by opportunity. Poverty and unemployment in the South provided the push, jobs in the North the pull. Beginning in southern Texas in the late 1890s and sweeping eastward through Georgia by 1921, boll weevil infestations wiped out cotton crops, forcing black sharecroppers off the land. During the same period, an abrupt decline in European immigration occasioned by World War I, combined with the rapid expansion of armaments industries, produced labor shortages in the northern industrial cities.

Almost all the African Americans leaving the South left poverty-stricken rural areas and settled into densely packed neighborhoods in northern cities. Only 10 percent of the nation's African Americans lived in cities of 100,000 or more in 1910; this percentage increased to 16 percent in 1920 and to 24 percent by 1930.[14] The biggest cities lured most of the migrants. The proportion of blacks living in cities smaller than 100,000 declined from 1910 to 1930, but the proportion increased substantially in cities of over 100,000.[15] Thus the Great Migration, as it came to be labeled by historians, had two principal components: Blacks were becoming northern, and they were becoming urban. In several of the largest cities, black populations multiplied by three times or more in the two decades from 1910 to 1930 (see Table 9.2).

African Americans made up more than 2 percent of the population in only a handful of northern cities in 1910. By 1930, however, they accounted for 18 percent of the population of Gary, Indiana, and in East St. Louis, Illinois, with its stockyards, rail yards, and heavy industry, blacks made up 16 percent of the population. In big cities, percentages by 1930 ranged from almost 5 percent in New York City to just over 11 percent in St. Louis and Philadelphia (these proportions had roughly doubled in twenty years). African Americans became concentrated in well-defined ghettos. In north Harlem in New York City, about one-third (36 percent) of the population was black in 1920, but this proportion increased to 81 percent by the time the 1930 census was taken.[16]

There were many reasons for the migration to northern cities, but the basic factors were employment opportunities, the grinding poverty of southern agricultural life, and dissatisfaction with the racial caste system in the South. The North was a "promised land" that offered an escape from the violent racism of the South and the opportunity for economic advancement. With the onset of the Great Depression of the 1930s, which brought destitution and unemployment to northern cities as well as to the South, the migration from the farms to the cities slowed abruptly and did not pick up again until after World War II.

Southern blacks began to stream North as a means of escaping the shackles of the southern system of race relations. The migration northward had already commenced when, in May 1917, the publisher of the *Chicago Defender* launched "The Great Northern Drive" to persuade blacks to move. Founded in 1905, by World War I the *Defender* already had reached a circulation of 100,000, and it was read avidly by blacks throughout the South. The *Defender*'s editorials exhorted blacks to come north to the land of opportunity, where they could find employment and, if not equality, at least an escape from harassment and violence. Its columns of job advertisements added substance to the "promised land" vision. At the same time, the *Defender* attacked conditions in the South. Lynchings and incidents of discrimination were regularly highlighted in lurid detail. Moving out of the South was portrayed as a way to advance the cause of racial equality for all blacks.[17]

The *Defender* was only one of many voices encouraging blacks to leave the South. Those who had already moved wrote letters to relatives and friends describing their new life in glowing terms. Despite job and housing discrimination in the North, they found conditions preferable to those they had left behind. Throughout the South, blacks lived under a cloud of terror. From 1882 to 1930, there were 1,663 lynchings in the five states of the Cotton Belt alone—Alabama, Georgia, Louisiana, Mississippi, and South Carolina—and 1,299 blacks were legally executed.[18] In the ten southern states, more than 2,500 blacks—an average of about one black person per week—were lynched between 1880 and 1930.[19] The legal systems of the southern states were so completely rigged that the difference between lynching and legalized murder by police and the courts was not much more than a technicality. Blacks who failed to obey the racial caste system, even inadvertently, could expect immediate retribution in the form of beatings or worse. Failing to step off the sidewalk, forgetting to say "sir" or "ma'am," or looking a white person in the eye could be cause for violent retribution. Lynchings frequently descended into orgies of depravity, the victims slowly tortured to death with blowtorches or other devices, and the mobs carrying off clothing and body parts as souvenirs.[20]

The opportunities for leaving such conditions improved in proportion to the labor shortages in northern factories. After war broke out in Europe in 1914, factory owners found themselves with lucrative armaments contracts but too few workers. They sent labor agents into the South with free train tickets in hand, which could be exchanged for a labor agreement. By the spring of 1916, the Great Migration began in earnest.

Southern white employers and planters took steps to prevent the exodus of their cheap labor. Magazines, newspapers, and business organizations decried the movement, as in this October 5, 1916, editorial in the Memphis *Commercial Appeal:*

> The enormous demand for labor and the changing conditions brought about by the boll weevil in certain parts of the South have caused an exodus of negroes which may be serious. Great colonies of negroes have gone north to work in factories, in packing houses and on the railroads. . . .
>
> The South needs every able-bodied negro that is now south of the line, and every negro who remains south of the line will in the end do better than he will do in the North. . . .
>
> The negroes who are in the South should be encouraged to remain there, and those white people who are in the boll weevil territory should make every sacrifice to keep their negro labor until there can be adjustments to the new and quickly prosperous conditions that will later exist.[21]

States and communities went to considerable lengths to discourage migration. Jacksonville, Florida, passed an ordinance in 1916 levying heavy fines on unlicensed labor agents from the North. Macon, Georgia, made it impossible for labor agents to get licenses and then outlawed unlicensed agents. The mayor of Atlanta talked to blacks about how "dreadfully cold" the northern winters were.[22] In some communities, police were sent to railroad stations to harass blacks near the stations, keep them from boarding trains, or even drive them off the trains.

But the promised land beckoned, and the exodus continued. What the new arrivals found was opportunity—but not equal opportunity—and persistent discrimination. Whenever blacks attempted to move into white neighborhoods, they were harassed or violently assaulted. In the workplace, they were the last hired and the first fired. They were kept in the most menial occupations. Job opportunities were limited not only by employers but even more so by labor unions, which generally prohibited blacks from membership. Because the North was more heavily unionized than the South, there were actually fewer opportunities in some occupations, especially for skilled laborers.[23] In both union and non-union shops, white workers often refused to work alongside blacks. To avoid trouble, employers assigned blacks to the least desirable jobs.

Blacks found it difficult to adjust to urban life. Hardly any of them had previously lived in a city. Many had never even participated directly in the cash economy. Sharecroppers had often worked under contracts that contained provisions that they buy only from the planters' stores and then with scrip and credit rather than cash. Some of them had never seen U.S. currency. As was the case with previous immigrant groups, they were often cheated and overcharged.

These conditions, when amplified by the intense segregation into dilapidated, overcrowded ghettos, led to astonishing levels of social pathology. The arrest rate for blacks in Detroit in 1926 was four times that for whites. Blacks constituted 31 percent of the nation's prison population in 1923, though they made up only 9 percent of the total population. The death rate in Harlem between 1923 and 1927 was 42 percent higher than in New York City as a whole, despite the fact that Harlem's population was much younger than the overall city population. Harlem's infant mortality rate was 111 per 1,000 births, compared with the city's rate of 64 per 1,000. Tuberculosis, heart disease, and other illnesses also far exceeded the rates for the city's general population.[24]

Blacks moving into northern cities were often surprised when they encountered hostility, racism, and discrimination nearly as bad as in the South. Restaurants and stores refused to serve them; banks typically refused them loans. Cemeteries, parks, bathing beaches, and other facilities were put off limits or divided into "white" and "colored" sections. Many dentists, doctors, and hospitals refused to treat blacks. Worse, the violence that had plagued them in the South followed them everywhere they went. On July 2, 1917, thirty-nine blacks and five whites died in a race riot in East St. Louis, Illinois.[25] In the infamous "Red Summer" of 1919, more than twenty cities experienced race riots, all of them involving attacks by white mobs on blacks. Chicago's riot of that summer started when a young black man inadvertently swam across the strip of water separating the beach designated "For Coloreds Only" from the beach reserved for whites only. A white crowd stoned the boy to death and then terrorized blacks throughout the city for days. From July 1, 1917, to March 1, 1921, Chicago experienced fifty-eight racial bombings.[26] Unemployed blacks were forced out of Buffalo by city police in 1920. That same year, in perhaps the worst mass murder of blacks in U.S. history, more than 300 blacks were killed by white mobs in Tulsa, Oklahoma—an incident covered up for almost eighty years.[27] In 1925, blacks who attempted to move into white neighborhoods in Detroit were terrorized by cross burnings, vandalism, and mob violence.

In all cities, restrictive covenants were attached to property deeds to keep blacks from buying into white neighborhoods. Deeds with these restrictions were filed in the office of the county clerk or the register of deeds and were enforced by the courts. Chicago, with more than 11 square miles covered by restricted deeds in 1944, was typical of northern cities.[28] Neighborhood improvement associations were formed in new subdivisions and, by legal prosecution and social persuasion, forced homeowners to accept and abide by restrictive covenants.

Though the migration to the North slowed to a crawl during the Great Depression, the movement picked up momentum again during and after World War II. As before, factory jobs pulled blacks into northern cities, and conditions in the South provided a push. The mechanization of southern agriculture, in particular the widespread adoption of the mechanized cotton picker, threw hundreds of thousands of sharecroppers and farm laborers out of work. From Texas, Louisiana, and Arkansas, blacks streamed into cities of the West, especially in California; from the middle South, they moved to St. Louis, Chicago, Detroit, Cleveland, and other cities of the Midwest; and from Mississippi and eastward in the Deep South, they moved to Washington, D.C., New York, Boston, and other cities in the East. In 1940, 77 percent of the nation's blacks still lived in the southern states (compared with 87 percent in 1910). By 1950, only 60 percent lived in the South, and in the next two decades the South's share declined to 56 percent (1960) and to 53 percent (1970).[29] Nearly all the northward-bound migrants ended up in cities. By the 1970 census, 90 percent of all the blacks who lived outside metropolitan areas in the United States were located in the South.

As blacks continued to move to the cities, the pressure on existing housing stock intensified. White families began to flee, first in areas close to the ghettos, and later from most older neighborhoods. By the mid-1960s, the "white flight" had become a generalized panic. As a result of the twin migrations—blacks streaming into the cities, whites moving to the suburbs—the racial characteristics of central cities changed quickly.

Table 9.3 shows that the racial divide between cities and suburbs that began to appear in 1950 became a chasm over the next two decades. In 1940, blacks constituted more than 10 percent of the population in only four of twelve big cities that became magnets for black migrants after World War II; on average, the proportion was 9 percent in these cities. But by the census of 1970, blacks accounted for more than 72 percent of the population of Washington, D.C., 47 percent in Baltimore, 44 percent in Detroit, 39 percent in Cleveland, and 41 percent in St. Louis. In many

Table 9.3 **Percentage of Blacks in Central Cities and Suburban Rings in Twelve Selected SMSAs, 1940, 1970, 2000**[a]

	Central City			Suburban Ring		
	1940	1970	2000	1940	1970	2000
New York	6	23	29.5	5	6	10
Los Angeles–Long Beach	6	21	12	2	7	6
Chicago	8	34	37	2	4	11
Philadelphia	13	34	45	7	7	12
Detroit	9	44	83	3	4	9
San Francisco–Oakland	5	33	12	4	9	6
Boston	3	18	28	1	2	3.5
Pittsburgh	9	27	28	4	4	5
St. Louis	13	41	52	7	8	13
Washington, D.C.	28.5	72	61	14	9	23
Cleveland	10	39	52	1	1	11
Baltimore	19	47	65	12	6	14.5
All 12 SMSAs	9	31	33.5	4	6	10

[a]Except for St. Louis, Baltimore, and Washington, D.C., figures for 1990 refer to the Consolidated Metropolitan Statistical Areas (CMSAs), which are not strictly comparable to earlier years. For 2000, additional central cities are included for some urban areas: Oakland for San Francisco–Oakland; Bridgeport, Conn., Newark, Jersey City, and New Haven for New York. As of 2000, Washington, D.C. and Baltimore were considered as central cities of a single metropolitan area, but they are kept separate to facilitate accurate comparisons with earlier censuses. Camden has also been deleted as a separate central city for the Philadelphia region. Calculated from U.S. Bureau of the Census, Census of 2000 (www.census.gov).

[b]This figure includes data from the Nassau-Suffolk SMSA, which was deleted from the New York City SMSA in 1971. They are included to maintain comparability across time periods.

Source: Data for 1940 and 1970 adapted from Leo F. Schnore, Carolyn D. André, and Harry Sharp, "Black Surburbanization, 1930–1970," in *The Changing Face of the Suburbs,* ed. Barry Schwartz (Chicago: University of Chicago Press, 1976), p. 80. Reprinted by permission. The figures here were transposed to yield data on black percentages.

cities in the north, the percentages were lower, but the psychology was generally the same. The suburbs remained mostly white. In none of the metropolitan areas shown in Table 9.3 did blacks make up as much as 10 percent of the suburban population in 1970, and in most cases the proportions were much lower. Blacks who did live in the suburbs were segregated into their own enclaves.

The movement to the North ended in the 1970s. Indeed, a reverse migration of blacks back to the South began, and in the 1990s black migration to the South totaled 579,000.[30] Most of the population increases among inner-city blacks after 1970 could be traced to natural increase rather than to migration. Though the racial gap between cities and suburbs seemed firmly fixed by then, in fact new developments began to unfold. In the 1970s, a significant number of blacks began moving to the suburbs for the first time, a trend that has continued in subsequent decades.[31] In both central cities and suburbs, the middle-class gentrification of poor neighborhoods and the immigration of Asians, Latinos, and other groups made metropolitan areas multiethnic rather than biracial. The African American proportion of the population of a few cities—New York, Philadelphia, Detroit, Boston, St. Louis, Cleveland, and Baltimore—increased significantly between 1970 and 2000 but actually fell in three cities that received significant Asian and Latino immigration—Los Angeles, San Francisco, and Washington, D.C. By the turn of the century, urban politics was biracial only in some urban areas of the old industrial belt in the North.

THE URBAN CRISIS

Beginning in the 1960s, "the urban crisis" became a shorthand phrase used to refer to the racial divisions in America's urban areas. The phrase conjured up images of "the black ghetto" juxtaposed with another kind of image: affluent whites living the American Dream in the suburbs. Although the residential patterns were, in reality, somewhat more complex, the image accurately captured a deeper truth: that America had become deeply divided on issues of race and that racial conflict had become the single most important issue in national politics.

The postwar movement of millions of poverty-stricken, mostly rural blacks to the central cities inevitably created intractable social problems. Blacks were not only crowded into inner-city slums; their plight was aggravated by the constant influx of new arrivals, by the ever-present threat of the urban-renewal bulldozer, and their high rate of poverty. A large proportion of blacks lived in neighborhoods in which almost everyone was poor. Ironically, the problem of concentrated poverty became even worse when the housing opportunities for middle-class blacks improved in the 1970s. As more affluent blacks left the ghetto, the poverty level of many neighborhoods rose sharply. In 1970, the census bureau classified more than one-fourth (27 percent) of the census tracts in the hundred largest cities in the nation as "poverty" tracts, where at least 20 percent of the residents were poor. Of these, 6 percent were classified as "extreme poverty" tracts in which at least 40 percent of residents were poor. In the next two decades, poverty became ever more concentrated, so that by the 1990 census the percentage of poverty tracts had increased to 39 percent of all census tracts in these cities, and the proportion of extreme poverty tracts had more than doubled, to 14 percent.[32] In 2000, the poverty rate in central cities was more than double the poverty rate in the suburbs.[33]

An analysis of sixty metropolitan areas found that in 1980 blacks were twice as segregated as Latinos and Asians.[34] Over the next decade, the concentration of poor blacks into poverty census tracts intensified.[35] When the 1990 census was taken, 71 percent of low-income, black, central-city residents lived in poverty neighborhoods, compared with 40 percent of low-income, white, central-city residents.[36] Low-income whites were often able to escape the ghetto and move into working-class or even middle-class neighborhoods, but low-income blacks found it very difficult or impossible to find affordable housing outside racially segregated areas. The intense segregation of the poor interacted with the segregation of minorities to create a hypersegregation of the minority poor.[37]

The concentration of poverty exacerbates the negative effects already experienced by the poor. One of the most important effects is that most of the children living in high-poverty areas attend racially segregated schools. In 1996, about 8 percent of U.S. schools had 90 percent or higher enrollment of African American and Latino students, and nearly all of them were located in central cities. In most of these schools, half or more of the students came from families in poverty. By contrast, only 8 percent of the students in schools with 10 percent or less black and Latino enrollment lived in poverty.[38]

In the 1980s, the sociologist William Julius Wilson coined the term *underclass* to refer to people who were concentrated in poverty areas and who were chronically out of work and out of the social mainstream.[39] The media, politicians, and social scientists quickly appropriated the term, using it to refer loosely to "a constellation of behaviors or conditions, including being poor and living in the inner city, being chronically unemployed, on welfare, homeless, residing in a single-parent family (especially with illegitimate children), having a criminal record, or using drugs (especially crack cocaine)."[40] Though this list clearly included behaviors that might be exhibited throughout society or by poor people regardless of where they lived, the term was normally used to refer to African Americans exclusively. Frequently, the underclass was defined so broadly that it included blacks not living in poverty areas at all but who allegedly exhibited a single characteristic (such as unemployment or single parenthood) that was thought of as "underclass." Basically, the underclass concept became a way of speaking about race without actually admitting that race was the topic of conversation.[41]

Perhaps because the underclass concept has been used so loosely and inaccurately, most scholars have now abandoned it, though it continues to be used in popular discourse, almost as a slang term. Wilson stopped using the term and began instead to refer to the harmful effects that result from concentrating the poor together as "concentration effects" when discussing the high incidence of unemployment, high rates of family breakdown, poor health, substance abuse, deteriorating housing, homelessness, and crime in some poverty neighborhoods.[42] More recently, he has called the effects of concentrated poverty "the new urban poverty," and his main focus has turned to the high proportion of unemployed males in particular areas: "poor, segregated neighborhoods in which a substantial majority of individual adults are either unemployed or have dropped out of the labor force altogether."[43] According to Wilson, most of the negative social behaviors of blacks who live in the "new urban poverty" can be traced to unemployment.[44]

A substantial proportion of residents in high-poverty urban areas have become disconnected from the economy. In 1980, for example, the unemployment rate in high-poverty areas was 30 percent, but this statistic counted only people who were looking for work and could not find it.[45] Wilson found that in fifteen high-poverty black areas in Chicago, just 37 percent of adults held jobs during a typical week in 1990.[46] According to Wilson, persistent joblessness in Chicago's African American areas can be traced to a steep decline of manufacturing jobs over the past thirty years. In the past, African Americans held a disproportionate share of blue-collar jobs, and even though their employment in the service sector has risen sharply, full-employment wages have declined by 25 to 30 percent.[47] Even for the available service jobs, educational requirements have gone up, and the arrival of new immigrants has intensified competition for the jobs that do not require a formal education. Finally, a large proportion of desirable jobs are located in the suburbs. Since public transportation is expensive and inconvenient (especially for working parents), it is doubly difficult for those living in inner-city areas to find work.[48] The experience in Chicago would presumably apply to virtually all large urban areas in the United States.

According to Wilson, joblessness is more closely associated with social disorganization than is poverty itself. Without work, a necessary structure for daily life is eroded, and the activities that replace work often undermine family life.[49] Certainly it is easy to show that poverty areas suffer from unusually high levels of violent crime, drug use, family disorganization, poor health, and other problems. It is also the case that people living in such areas have little access to quality schools and services such as child-care centers, family counselors, and treatment programs.

Poverty is closely correlated with family structure. In 1993, families headed by divorced women made 40 percent as much as households headed by a husband and a wife.[50] Households headed by women who had never been married, however, made only 21 percent as much, and *two-thirds* of all children in such families lived in poverty (compared to one-tenth for married-couple families).[51] Since the mid-1970s, middle-class families have been able to maintain high living standards because there are typically two wage earners. For both the poor and the nonpoor, family income is negatively affected when there is only one female earner. This is because women, on average, make less than men in the same jobs; in addition, many of the jobs that are traditionally held by females, pay less than those dominated by men. Increasingly, women in poverty who once collected welfare so that they could stay home to take care of their children are forced (by welfare reform) to work in low-paying seasonal jobs. Adolescents in single-parent households are subjected to less supervision, which undoubtedly contributes to high-school dropout rates, criminal behavior, and the prevalence of gangs.

Health and health care in inner-city poverty areas have deteriorated since the late 1970s. Chronic illnesses and contagious diseases are common. The poor lack health insurance and often do not have access to even the most basic health care. In 1990, the United States had among the highest infant mortality rates in the industrialized world.[52] While the overall national rate was about 10 deaths for every 1,000 live births in the late 1980s, the rate for inner-city poverty neighborhoods approached that of Third World countries. In 1988–1989, for example, the infant mortality rate in Central Harlem was 23 per 1,000 births, about the same as in Malaysia.[53] The interaction between health and poverty is equally obvious in the case of the AIDS epidemic. AIDS is primarily an urban disease. Ten metropolitan areas with one-eighth of the nation's population had five-eighths of the nation's caseload in 1988, and these were concentrated in poverty areas.[54]

Substance abuse is still another pervasive problem in poverty neighborhoods. Crack began to devastate inner-city poverty neighborhoods in the mid-1980s. The murder rate among young black males tripled between 1984 and 1991, in part because of crack cocaine use.[55] Young men in well-armed gangs fought one another to control the lucrative business. The connection between crack and violence went beyond the gangs, however. Because crack was so addictive, users would do almost anything to get another fix. Burglary, car theft, and robbery helped support the habit. Women who became crack addicts often turned to prostitution to support their habit; casual sex in crack houses became a major factor in the AIDS epidemic. By the early 1990s, thousands of babies had been born addicted to crack, costing the nation an estimated $2.5 billion annually.[56]

Violent crime soared in American cities in the late 1980s and early 1990s.[57] In 1990, New York City set a record with 2,262 murders, yet its per-capita homicide rate ranked it only slightly above average for the country's twenty-five largest cities.[58] Violent death reached pandemic proportions among young black and Latino males in inner-city areas. Citing the fact that homicide was the leading cause of death for black males aged 15 to 24 in 1990, the federal Centers for Disease Control stated that the casualty rate was approaching that of war. According to a study in the *New England Journal of Medicine,* young men in Harlem, primarily because of high homicide rates, were less likely to survive to the age of 40 than their counterparts in Bangladesh.[59] A survey of schoolchildren in Chicago found that an astonishing 24 percent of them had personally witnessed a murder.[60]

In the 1990s, rates of violent crime went into a steep, and surprising, decline. For the nation as a whole, violent crime per 100,000 persons fell by 17 percent from 1990 to 1997 (after an increase of 20 percent from 1987 to 1990), and the murder rate fell by 28 percent (after a 13 percent increase).[61] The drop in crime was even more dramatic in big cities than elsewhere; homicide rates, for example, fell by 75 percent in New York City from 1990 to 1998 (from more than 2,200 to just over 600).[62] The falling crime rates improved the quality of life for ghetto residents but did not, of course, change the fact that they still faced inadequate health care, housing, and other problems.

In the 1980s, the central cities began to make a comeback. One consequence of this development is that they have become sharply divided between minorities living in areas of concentrated poverty and gentrified neighborhoods in and near downtowns. Some healthy neighborhoods occupied by the working class seemed doubly threatened by the poor on the one hand and the gentrifying middle class on the other.

In the 1990s, a downtown revival took effect in central cities, driven by the construction of office towers and of tourist/entertainment districts. Equally important, the suburbs began opening up to minorities and to the poor. Considered against the long shadow cast on the cities by nearly a century of flight by the white middle class, this was indeed a monumental development, and one that can be appreciated fully only be tracing the history of suburban development in America.

THE SUBURBAN MOVEMENTS

In the twentieth century, Americans learned to think in dualist images that sharply contrasted the cities from the suburbs. Images of poverty and slums seemed to symbolize the inner cities, while the suburbs tended to evoke images of tranquil subdivisions with cul-de-sacs and expanses of lawn. These images became deeply rooted in the social consciousness of Americans, and they are still nurtured and kept alive by a drumbeat of overwrought negative images of the inner city.

Despite a steadily falling rate of violent crime, the nation's obsession with crime and violence has persisted, and despite all evidence, crime continues to be identified mainly with the inner cities and their residents. Local media rely heavily on sensationalized accounts of crime and violence to maintain their ratings. Approximately 20 percent of front-page news stories and local news broadcasts focus on violent crime.[63] Live footage of crime scenes is a must for local news stations. The format is extremely standardized. A reporter typically stands at a crime scene in front of a minicam. The talking head soon gives way to a video collage of a bloodstained street or sidewalk, shocked spectators, and perhaps grief-stricken friends and relatives. The reporter often ends his or her monolog with a "running total for the number of murders committed for the year and compares the toll to last year's. Like body counts from the war in Vietnam, the numbers are more important for the emotions they arouse than the information they convey."[64] By the late twentieth century, the discourse about the inner cities and the urban underclass had become "our . . . national morality play," a performance made up of sensationalized and exaggerated narratives of good and evil.[65] The "evil" was located in the cities, the "good" in the suburbs.

By the late twentieth century, some people thought that central cities had become obsolete and that the suburbs would be better off without them. In 1991, *Newsweek* magazine ran a story entitled "Are Cities Obsolete?" quoting an expert in urban land use as saying, "The basic problem is that cities are no longer functional. . . .We don't need them anymore."[66] Polls conducted by the *New York Times* showed that residents of the suburban counties outside of New York City no longer felt significantly connected to the city. The percentage of respondents who said that events in the city had "hardly any impact" on their daily lives increased from 39 percent in 1978 to 51 percent by 1991.[67] The implication of this view is that those who had seceded from the cities by moving to the suburbs had deserted a sinking ship whose fate was of little concern to them.

Suburban development in the United States passed through four distinct stages: (1) the railroad and streetcar suburbs of the nineteenth and early twentieth centuries, (2) the automobile suburbs of the 1920s, (3) the bedroom suburbs of the 1940s through the 1960s, and (4) the multiethnic suburbs and the rise of residential enclaves. In the first three of these periods, a sorting-out process occurred that lowered population densities in urban areas and increased the separation of people of different incomes, family characteristics, and ethnic and racial backgrounds. Even though suburbs varied tremendously in housing conditions, the income, racial, and ethnic characteristics of residents, and the competency of their local governments, in the United States the move to the suburbs became associated with the powerful idea of escaping the problems and conflicts of the central cities.

In the fourth stage of suburban development, the differences between central cities and the suburbs are blurring. Suburbs are undergoing changes that, in the past, were associated with older cities. Many of the newcomers in the latest surge of immigration are moving directly to suburbs without making a stop in the inner cities. Large numbers of ethnic and racial minorities are moving to the suburbs, and a significant movement of poor people is also occurring. Underfunded, low-achieving schools, crime, gangs, and other problems have come to the suburbs (and have been there for some time, in some places) at the same time that older neighborhoods in many cities are gentrifying. The central cities may remain as symbols of what affluent suburbanites want to escape from for some time, but the real world will fit those images less and less accurately.

The Railroad and Streetcar Suburbs: 1815–1918

The American habit of wanting to escape the cities can be traced not only to the conditions in the crowded cities of the nineteenth century but also to a deeply ingrained antiurban bias that dates to the nation's founding. Thomas Jefferson is well known for his suspicion of city life. "The mobs of great cities," he wrote, "add just so much to the support of pure government, as sores do to the strength of the human body."[68] In the 1830s and 1840s, the tendency to dislike cities was given specific form by the Romantic movement, which idealized nature and advocated a balance between humanity and nature that was, Romantic writers argued, being destroyed by cities and technology. Even so, wealthy people tended to live near the center. Homes were rarely located more than a mile or two from places of work, and almost everyone walked. Outlying areas farther from work and the waterfront were mostly reserved for the lower orders of society.[69]

As soon as new forms of transportation made it possible, members of the upper and upper-middle classes began to escape the congestion of downtown.

In 1814, Robert Fulton began the first steam ferry service between Manhattan and Brooklyn, providing a chance for those who could afford it to live apart from the dirt and din of Manhattan. Brooklyn thus became the first commuter suburb.[70] The nineteenth century witnessed a succession of transportation improvements that made it possible for more upper- and upper-middle-class people to escape: the steam ferry, the omnibus, the commuter railroad, the horsecar, the elevated railroad, the cable car, and the electric trolley. With each improvement, the numbers of people living in suburbs increased.

Railroads were best used for travel between cities and not for commuting, but they did enable a small elite to live in pristine isolation from the problems of industrial society. In a pattern repeated in every stage of urban history, transportation improvements were planned not so much for moving people as for capturing the increased land values that resulted from opening up new suburban land for development. Some railroads lost money on day-to-day operations, but that did not prevent railroad entrepreneurs from amassing fabulous fortunes through suburban land speculation.[71] Commuter tickets on railroads were far too expensive for ordinary workers; thus the railroad suburbs that prospered in the mid-nineteenth century were restricted to the wealthiest classes. In many ways, the early railroad suburbs, like Chestnut Hill outside Philadelphia, Bronxville outside New York, and Forest Park outside Chicago, became the epitome of the suburban ideal. Winding lanes, in contrast to the grid-patterned streets of cities, made these suburbs look like "scattered buildings in a park," the homes integrated with nature, with no hint of the grimy factory on which this suburban wealth was based.[72]

Horse-drawn streetcars became widespread after 1850, providing less expensive transportation for urban residents and expanding the commuting distance for workers up to three miles from downtown.[73] The electric trolley began to revolutionize urban transportation in the 1890s. It was the breakthrough that caused a sudden jump in the rate of suburbanization, and trolleys continued to run until the 1960s, many decades after autos had made their entrance. By tripling the radius of cities, the trolley increased the amount of land that could be developed for residential use by 900 percent. Its introduction was followed by a near frenzy of speculation in land.

Henry E. Huntington was one of the most astute of the rail entrepreneurs to profit from land speculation, and layed the foundation for the extreme urban sprawl that would eventually come to characterize southern California. The son of one of the founders of the Southern Pacific Railroad, Huntington failed in his bid to take over that railroad in the 1890s and turned his considerable wealth toward developing a local rail system in the Los Angeles area. In 1901, he formed the Pacific Electric Railway Company. Recognizing that the first few years of intra-urban transit were bound to be unprofitable, Huntington bought up huge tracts of land in the western San Gabriel Valley through which his rail lines would be built. When conditions were ripe, he subdivided and sold the land at huge profits. By 1911, he was able to make a deal with the president of the Southern Pacific that essentially gave him monopoly control over local rail transit in the Los Angeles area. By 1921, his Pacific Electric system was carrying more than 250,000 passengers daily on more than 1,000 miles of track, and Huntington was fabulously wealthy.[74]

The electric streetcar quickened suburban development. Still, no one thought that the suburbs constituted a threat to the cities. Overcrowding, not emptying out, created most of the problems for the industrial cities. Between 1900 and 1920, for example, New York City grew by 2.2 million people, compared to a population increase of just 190,000 in its surrounding area. By 1920, New York City's population was 5.6 million people; 379,000 people lived in its suburban ring. Likewise, in other urban areas the vast majority of people living in urban areas still lived in the core cities.

Industrial and manufacturing facilities remained near water and rail transportation links in the city centers. Between 1904 and 1914, St. Louis lost some industry to its suburbs (its share of industrial employment fell from 95 to 90 percent of the area's manufacturing establishments), as did Baltimore (96 to 93 percent) and Philadelphia (91 to 87 percent), but these cities were the exception rather than the rule.[75] The industrial cities overwhelmingly dominated the economies of their urban areas. Men left the suburbs in the morning to commute to their jobs downtown, and at night they returned home. Railroad and streetcar suburbs prospered, but they were still wholly dependent on the economy in the urban center.

The Automobile Suburbs: 1918–1945

The automobile ultimately came to be regarded as an expression of American values of privacy and individualism. When it was first introduced in the late nineteenth century, it was mainly an expensive plaything for the rich. Henry Ford changed that. In 1908, Ford introduced the Model T, a car for the masses that was dependable and easy to operate. Through the introduction of the moving assembly line in 1913, Ford was able to reduce the cost of a Model T from $950 in 1910 to $290 in 1924. Car ownership skyrocketed. American car production increased from 63,000 automobiles in 1908 to 550,000 by 1914. After World War I, car production really took off, reaching 2.27 million in 1922 and 4.45 million in 1929.[76] The construction of adequate roads lagged seriously behind car ownership, but this problem was eventually solved when automobile owners successfully pressed for massive state and federal funding, mainly through gasoline taxes.

The automobile provided the opportunity for the rapidly expanding upper-middle class to move to the suburbs. Whereas streetcar suburbs had sprung up along the rail lines like the spokes on a wheel, the automobile made it possible to develop the areas in between. Vast new tracts of land were opened to land speculation and suburban development, and the upper-middle class invested much of its newfound wealth in suburban real estate. Total national wealth doubled in the ten years from 1912 to 1922, and from 1915 to 1925 average hourly wages climbed from 32 to 70 cents.[77] The value of residential land and improvements doubled in the 1920s.[78]

As shown in Table 9.4, even before the automobile, the suburbs of several big cities grew at a much faster pace than the core cities. Between 1900 and 1910, New York City's population increased by 39 percent, but its suburbs grew by 61 percent. In the same decade, Chicago's and St. Louis's suburbs skyrocketed, by 88 percent and 91 percent. As more people took to the streetcars, the trend continued; between 1910 and 1920, the suburbs of Los Angeles grew by 108 percent and Cleveland's by an astonishing 140 percent.

Though streetcars continued to carry commuters to the suburbs until the 1950s, middle-class prosperity and the automobile conspired to push suburban development to new levels. In the prosperous decade of the 1920s, suburbs outpaced the cities. The cities of Boston, St. Louis, and Cleveland grew more slowly than ever in their history, but their suburbs boomed, both in total population and rate of growth. For the first time in the nation's history, in most urban areas the total population increases in the suburbs exceeded the growth in the cities.

The truck and the automobile began to change well-established economic patterns. The proportion of factory employment in central cities declined in every city of more than 100,000 residents between 1920 and 1930, and this trend was likely to continue because the new assembly-line production techniques required lots of land rather than vertical buildings, and this land was in the suburbs. However, all through the affluent 1920s, office construction and retailing in central business districts boomed. Almost all white-collar people worked and shopped in the old downtowns. Downtown office space tripled in the 1920s, and employment continued to soar in most central cities.[79]

The Great Depression slowed suburban development, but it even more drastically applied the brake to central-city population growth. The depression signaled the twilight of the city-building era. As the data in Table 9.4 reveal, Boston, St. Louis, and Cleveland all lost population in the 1930s. So did Philadelphia,

Table 9.4 **Metropolitan Area Population, 1900–1940**
(Increases in Population Expressed as Percent
Growth and Number of People Added)

Districts	1900–1910 Central City	1900–1910 Outside Central City	1910–1920 Central City	1910–1920 Outside Central City	1920–1930 Central City	1920–1930 Outside Central City	1930–1940 Central City	1930–1940 Outside Central City
Boston	20%	23%	9%	21%	4%	21%	21%	3%
Chicago	29	88	23	79	25	74	0.6	10
Cleveland	46	46.5	40	140	12	126	−1	13
Los Angeles	206	553	81	108	115	158	−3	30
New York City[a]	39	61	18	35	23	67	8	18
St. Louis	19	91	12.5	26	7	71	−1	16
Mean for all metro districts (nation)	34	38	25	32	21	47	4	14

[a]Includes growth of population in New York City proper and in satellite areas of New York State. New Jersey population is excluded.

Source: U.S. Bureau of the Census, *The Growth of Metropolitan Districts in the United States, 1900–1940*, by Warren S. Thompson (Washington, D.C.: Government Printing Office, 1947), especially table 2.

Kansas City, and the New Jersey cities—Elizabeth, Paterson, Jersey City, and Newark. San Francisco, which had grown by 27 percent in the 1920s, was no bigger by the census of 1940 than it had been in 1930. A great many small manufacturing cities of New England and the Midwest lost population—Akron and Youngstown, Ohio; Albany, Schenectady, and Troy, New York; Joplin, Missouri; and New Bedford, Massachusetts.

The depression affected the suburbs as well as the cities, since most upper-middle- and middle-class people lacked the means to buy a new suburban home. The growth rate of New York's suburbs fell from 67 percent in the 1920s to only 18 percent in the 1930s. In the same decade, Chicago's suburban expansion slowed from 74 percent to 10 percent, Cleveland's from 126 percent to 13 percent, and Los Angeles's from 158 percent to 30 percent. All through the 1930s, the effects of the depression lingered. With the coming of World War II, materials needed for housing construction were commandeered for the war effort. As a result, suburban growth came to a temporary standstill.

The Bedroom Suburbs: 1946–1970s

The slowdown in housing construction during a depression and a war would have caused a serious housing shortage all by itself, but the postwar baby boom made the situation worse. After reaching a low point during the Great Depression, the birthrate began to rise in 1943 and then took off in the postwar years, when 16 million GIs returned to civilian life.[80] By 1947, 6 million families were doubling up with relatives or friends because they could not find a home of their own.[81] The housing industry geared up to meet the demand, pushing single-family housing starts from only 114,000 in 1944 to 1,692,000 by 1950.[82] Virtually all of this new construction took place in the suburbs.

Utilizing mass production methods and sophisticated marketing techniques, big companies began to dominate the housing industry. Big corporations accounted for only 5 percent of all houses built in 1938, but they increased their share of the market to 24 percent by 1949. A decade later, they produced 64 percent of all new homes.[83] These builders concentrated overwhelmingly on the suburbs. Their preferred method was to buy tracts of land on the outskirts of cities and to create entire new subdivisions by bulldozing everything to an even surface and constructing houses quickly using standardized production techniques.

In earlier decades, suburban development had been mainly an upper- and middle-class phenomenon, but now it filtered down to include working-class families. For most families, owning their own home in the suburbs became a better economic bargain than trying to stay in their old neighborhoods. Federally insured home loans, cheap energy, and new efficient building technologies made it less expensive to build a new house in the suburbs than to rehabilitate a home or rent an apartment in the city. The home ownership rate increased from 43.6 percent in 1940 to 62.9 percent by 1970.[84]

The population of the suburbs exploded. The data in Table 9.5 demonstrate the magnitude of the population movements in the sixty years between 1940 and 2000. In the 1940s, the core cities grew by just over 6 million people, a 14 percent rate of growth. The suburbs surrounding these cities, by contrast, grew by 9 million

Table 9.5 **Metropolitan Area Population, 1940–1990 (Increases in Population Expressed as Percent Growth)**

Urban Areas	1940–1950		1950–1960		1960–1970		1970–1980		1980–1990		1990–2000
	Central City	Outside Central City	Central City	Outside Central City	Central City	Outside Central City	Central City	Outside Central City	Central City	Outside Central City	Population Change, Central City
Boston	4%	11.5%	-13%	18%	-8%	11%	-12%	-3%	2%	3.5%	-3%
Chicago	7	3	-2	71.5	-5	35	-11	14	-7	7	0.6
Cleveland	4	42	-4	67	-14	27	-24	0.4	-12	0	-1
Los Angeles	31	70	26	67	14	20	5	1	17	19	4
New York City	6	23	-1	75	1.5	26	-10	0.4[a]	3.5	0.6[a]	1
St. Louis	5	34	-12.5	51	-17	28.5	-27	6	-12	7	-16
Mean for all SMSAs (nation)	14	36	11	49	6	27	0	18	2	12	

[a]Nassau and Suffolk counties were deleted from the New York City SMSA in 1971. They have been included here for purposes of comparability. The actual Outside Central City figure for the revised New York City SMSA is 21.4%.

Source: U.S. Department of Commerce, Bureau of the Census, *Census of Population, 1950, vol. 1, Number of Inhabitants, pt. 1* (Washington, D.C.: Government Printing Office, 1952), p. 69, table 17; *Census of Population, 1970, vol. 1, Characteristics of the Population, pt. A*, p. 180, table 34; *Census of Population, 1980*, suppl. reports, *Standard Metropolitan Statistical Areas and Standard Consolidated Statistical Areas*, p. 2, table B; p. 6, table 1; p. 49, table 3; *State and Metropolitan Areas Data Book, 1991*, table D.

people, a 36 percent increase. But suburban development proceeded much faster than these statistics suggest because all the suburban subdivisions were built after 1946, when wartime conditions finally ended.

The end of war was like removing the cork from a champagne bottle. Across the entire nation, the suburban growth rate in the 1950s was 49 percent. In this Leave-It-to-Beaver decade, suburban populations increased by 19 million, but the core cities grew by only 6 million. The big cities in the industrial belt that stretched from New England through the Great Lakes states actually lost population; Boston retrenched by 13 percent, St. Louis by 12.5 percent, Cleveland by 4 percent. Only in the South and West, where cities benefited from a population movement from northern states, was the story different. Sunbelt cities prospered, and also had the option to annex more land. Phoenix annexed so much land that its suburbs actually shrank in population, and Los Angeles was likewise able to change its boundaries. In the North, that option was unavailable because cities were already hemmed in by a solid ring of suburbs.

In the 1960s, the nation's central cities grew an average of 6 percent, but this statistic hid huge variations. Cities in other regions grew, but those in the manufacturing belt suffered massive population losses; St. Louis lost 17 percent; Cleveland, 14 percent; and Boston, 8 percent. In the same decade, the nation's suburbs added 16 million more people—a total of 35 million in two decades! For several cities, the bleeding continued right to the end of the century. St. Louis lost 27 percent of its population in the 1970s, 12 percent in the 1980s, and 16 percent in the 1990s. In 1950, when it started its long slide, it held 857,000 people, but by century's end only 335,000 people—12 percent of the region's population—lived in the city. Similar trajectories were traced by Pittsburgh, Cleveland, Detroit, and other cities across the industrial belt. And in a new development, as shown in Table 9.5, after the 1960s even the suburbs of these cities grew slowly, or even retrenched. What had begun as decline of the cities at the urban core had turned into a regional problem.

The suburbs of the 1950s and 1960s were by no means all cut from the same cloth. There were working-class, blue-collar subdivisions, a few isolated areas populated by blacks, and, of course, enclaves of the wealthy. However, most suburban homes of that period were built for white, middle-class families. Individual suburbs tended to be remarkably uniform, with row after endless row of houses that looked as if they had been produced by a cookie cutter. Suburbia came to be portrayed in the popular media as a place of lookalike streets and people, where bored couples with small children spent their free time watching television and picking crabgrass out of their lawns, where the men commuted to office jobs leaving behind frustrated housewives to care for the children in culturally sterile environments. This image of suburbia was captured in three best-selling novels published during the period: *The Man in the Gray Flannel Suit* (1955), *The Crack in the Picture Window* (1956), and *The Split Level Trap* (1960). Though the cultural images of suburbia undoubtedly traded on stereotypes, they struck a responsive chord.[85]

Leaders of central cities were increasingly alarmed that the suburbs represented a threat to the vitality and even viability of the urban core. It was not only that the suburbs were growing faster than the cities; they were also pulling affluent white families out of them, leaving behind a segregated population made up of blacks, the poor, and other minorities. Increasingly, suburbanization was understood in racial terms; the phrase "white flight" started to be heard, suggesting that suburbanization was motivated in part by racism, a suggestion for which there is abundant evidence.[86] The riots of the mid-1960s heightened the fears connected to race. In 1967, when the National Commission on Civil Disorders called attention to the stark dichotomy between the cities and suburbs, the suburbs had become far removed from life in the central cities. Many people living in the suburbs regarded the inner cities as reservations for blacks, and many blacks had become completely estranged from the rest of America.[87]

Multiethnic Suburbs and the Rise of Residential Enclaves: 1970s–The Present

In recent decades, the suburbs have gradually been transformed from wholly dependent satellites of cities, places where people lived but not where they worked, to increasingly self-sufficient enclaves. Though suburban development historically had been primarily a residential movement, since at least 1948 jobs have decentralized even faster than population.[88] Retailing moved out at a slower pace than did manufacturing and wholesaling because retailing is directly dependent on a nearby critical mass of buyers. By the early 1960s, however, such a critical mass had been established, and before long regional shopping malls began to spring up to cater to the shopping and entertainment needs of suburban consumers.[89] Suburbanites no longer needed to go downtown, and a historic link between cities and suburbs was severed. Downtown retailing went into a tailspin from which it has never fully recovered.

The suburbanization of manufacturing employment was made possible by technical innovations that freed factories from a dependence on rail connections. Electrification made single-story plants on suburban land more economical than multistory buildings that housed belt-driven machinery powered by water or steam. In addition, manufacturers left cities because they viewed them as hotbeds of union organizing and unrest.[90] Through accelerated depreciation of assets, which allowed manufacturers to take tax deductions when they abandoned inner-city factories, and investment tax credits, which allowed manufacturers to take tax credits for new plant and equipment, the federal government subsidized the flight of industrial jobs to the suburbs (and Sunbelt).[91] By 1970, a majority of the manufacturing jobs in metropolitan areas were located in the suburbs.

The service sector was the last to suburbanize. Central business districts offered advantages to firms desiring face-to-face relations with clients and benefiting from the concentration of business services in downtowns. Advances in communications, however, made proximity less of an advantage than before. Routine service employment, the so-called back-office functions such as copying and secretarial services, were the first to leave expensive downtown office space. In 1975, for the first time, the amount of office construction in the suburbs exceeded the volume of office construction in central cities. Higher-level and higher-paid corporate services, on the other hand, such as legal assistance, corporate consulting, accounting services, and investment services, continued to locate in the downtowns of large cities, partly for prestige reasons. Although many corporations were still headquartered in central cities, many had moved out to the suburbs, in whole or in part. Some suburbs had developed into edge cities, complete with their own office complexes that duplicated many of the characteristics of central business districts.

The effect of these developments was that the suburbs became more independent of their core cities than in the past. Cross-commuting became common; by 1980, twice as many people commuted from suburb to suburb as commuted from suburb to central city.[92] The historic urban form, in which a city is surrounded by dependent suburbs, began to break down and be replaced by the "polynucleated metropolis," characterized by several nodes of concentrated land use that combine residential, retail, recreational, light industry, and service firms. The new urban form has sometimes been called *exurbanization* or even *counterurbanization*,[93] plus a variety of odd and often confusing labels such as "urban villages, technohubs, suburban downtowns, suburban activity centers, major diversified centers, urban cores, galactic city, pepperoni-pizza cities, a city of realms, superburbia, disurb, service cities, perimeter cities, and even peripheral centers."[94] What these edge cities have in common is that they are today springing up as places where jobs, housing, light industry, retail malls, and recreation are concentrated, usually near freeway interchanges or airports.

As more and more people emptied out of the cities, the suburbs became much more diverse than they had been at any time in the past. Condominiums, townhouses, and apartment complexes became as common as the single-family subdivisions that had defined suburban life in the 1950s and 1960s. Developers were especially keen to appeal to the fastest-growing segments of the American population: young singles, childless couples, and the elderly. As the suburbs became more diverse, many of them also became "urbanized" in the sense that they began to exhibit the problems long associated with central cities. Just as importantly, suburban families were subject to the same societal changes as families everywhere else. The decline of the traditional nuclear family, for example, affected all income, racial, and ethnic groups. Though a higher proportion of black families in inner-city poverty areas were headed by a single parent, after the 1960s the rate of increase for out-of-wedlock births was greatest among white families. Between 1980 and 1992, out-of-wedlock births for whites rose by 94 percent, but by just 9 percent for blacks.[95] Day-care and after-school services were erratically available in the United States, even in affluent suburbs. Latchkey children existed in families at all income levels.

Though crack cocaine use had not hit middle-class families as hard as it had poor families in inner cities, by the 1980s, if not before, substance abuse had become a major problem in even the most affluent suburbs, with alcohol, marijuana, and powder cocaine being the drugs of choice. And though crime was clearly higher in central cities, it had been rising faster in many suburban areas than anywhere else.[96] The residents of Green Valley, Nevada, a gated community of more than 20,000 affluent residents on the outskirts of Las Vegas, learned that problems have a habit of following people wherever they go. In the early

1990s, a rash of crimes was committed within the community, all by affluent residents, demonstrating that crimes of rape, child molestation, burglary, teenage gang fights, and even murder are not the exclusive province of the poor. Even the president of the Green Valley Community Association was arrested for burglary. One resident commented, "People are coming here from all over the place and bringing their problems with them."[97]

In the 1990s, many suburban residential areas became narrowly defined enclaves of like-minded people who were trying to sever all contact with central cities and even with nearby neighborhoods.[98] Some gated communities built in the 1980s and 1990s seem like fortresses built to keep the menacing hordes at bay. The emphasis on security in some of these developments is akin to a state of war. Leisure World, a California retirement community, is surrounded by 6-foot walls topped with barbed wire. Quayside, a planned community in Florida, blends the atmosphere of a Norman Rockwell small town of the 1920s with the latest in high-tech security; laser beams sweep the perimeter, computers check the coded entry cards of the residents and store exits and entries from the property in a permanent data file, and television cameras continuously monitor the living and recreation areas. Such trappings of security constantly remind the inhabitants that the world beyond their walls is dangerous, so that "'being inside' becomes a powerful symbol for being protected, buttressed, coddled, while 'being outside' evokes exposure, isolation, and vulnerability."[99]

In southern California, fortress enclaves have become a ubiquitous feature of suburban development. In search of high-tech security, architects for the rich "are borrowing design features from overseas embassies and military command posts," building hardened walls, secret passages and doors, and installing a dazzling array of sophisticated electronic surveillance devices.[100] There is such a heavy demand for gated communities in the Los Angeles suburbs that they are quickly replacing all other kinds of development. Enclave suburb against enclave suburb—as the suburbs become more diverse, this may be replacing the city-suburban divide.

THE NEW IMMIGRANTS

Immigration is changing the face of urban America. In some ways, the ethnic enclaves in many American cities seem little different from their counterparts in the immigrants' countries of origin. Koreatown in Los Angeles is a thriving enclave of immigrant businesses that advertise their wares in brightly colored signs in both English words and Korean characters. Along Calle Ocho (S.W. 8th Street) in Miami, the heart of Little Havana, there is the ever-present smell of Cuban-style coffee and cigars. Bolsa Avenue in Westminster (Orange County), California, called the Vietnamese capital of America, is lined with restaurants selling Asian food. In New York City, Manhattan's Chinatown grew so fast that it burst its seams and spread across the East River into Flushing in the borough of Queens. This new Chinatown is a magnet for Asian tourists and has become known for the variety of its Chinese restaurants.

The number of immigrants entering the United States has increased steadily since 1950, and during this period the sources of immigration have shifted from Europe to Asia, Latin America, and the Caribbean. As shown in Table 9.6, in the decade of the 1950s, Europe was the largest source of immigrations (57 percent). Just 22.5 percent came from the Western hemisphere south of the United States, and 6 percent came from Asia. The composition of immigrant flows changed dramatically in the ensuing decades, however. The proportion of immigrants from Europe fell sharply, decade by decade, to less than 10 percent of immigrants in the 1980s before rebounding to about 14 percent by 1996 because of immigration from Russia and from the formerly Communist countries of eastern Europe. Asian immigrants shot up from 6 percent to more than 38 percent of immigrants in the 1980s and still accounted for more than 30 percent up to 1996. Immigrants from other Western hemisphere countries (referred to as Hispanics by the U.S. census bureau but as Latinos in many sources) increased in every decade; in 1996, they constituted nearly half of all immigrants.

The volume of immigration to the United States in the 1990s was the largest in the nation's history, exceeding even the immigrant flood tide from 1900 to 1910, with the decade of the 1980s close behind. The proportion of immigrants in the population was far less than in the late nineteenth and early twentieth centuries, but a larger number of immigrants lived in the United States by 1990—17 million—than in any previous period in the nation's history.[101]

The immigration laws in effect from the 1920s to the mid-1960s reflected fears that foreigners might overwhelm the country. The National Origins Immigration Act of 1924 allowed 2 percent of the base population of foreign-born nationality

Table 9.6 Immigrants by Place of Origin, 1951–1996

Year	Percent of Total Immigration					Total Number (Thousands)
	Europe	Asia[a]	Canada	Other Western Hemisphere[b]	All Other[c]	
1951–1960	57	6	11	22.5	3	2,515.5
1961–1970	37	13	9	39	2	3,321.7
1971–1980	18	36	3	40	3	4,493.3
1981–1990	10	38	2	47	3	7,338.1
1991–1996	14	32	1.5	49	4	6,146.3

[a]Cambodia, China, Taiwan, Hong Kong, India, Iran, Israel, Japan, Korea, Philippines, Thailand, Vietnam, and "other Asia."
[b]Mexico, Caribbean, Central America, South America.
[c]Africa, Australia, New Zealand.

Source: U.S. Department of Justice, Immigration and Naturalization Service, *Statistical Yearbook of the Immigration and Naturalization Service, 1989* (Washington, D.C.: Government Printing Office, 1990), pp. 2–5; and U.S. Bureau of the Cenus, The Official Statistics, *Statistical Abstracts of the United States,* 1998, September 25, 1998.

groups, as recorded in the census of 1890, to immigrate into the United States. This quota accomplished its intended goal of drastically reducing immigration by all groups except those from northern Europe. Immigration by Slavs, Jews, Italians, Greeks, and other supposedly "inferior" peoples, most of whom entered the country after 1890, was cut by more than 90 percent.

By the 1960s, such a blatantly biased (and racist) formula became difficult to justify. In the Hart-Cellar Act of 1965, Congress essentially put immigrants from all countries on an equal footing and granted a high priority to family reunification. Expanded by special provisions for political refugees from socialist and communist countries, immigration soared well beyond expectations, and the ethnic composition of the immigrants changed rapidly. After the 1960s, between 80 and 85 percent of the new immigrants to the United States came from the Caribbean, Central and South America, and Asia, with Asians accounting for about 46 percent of the total.[102]

The flow of immigrants from the Caribbean, Latin America, Central America, and South America reveals a complex mixture of languages, cultures, and nationalities. The census category is *Hispanic*, though the term *Latinos* (favored here) is also widely employed. The census bureau has found it difficult to accurately identify ethnic categories in New Mexico (where 42 percent of the population is officially classified as Hispanic) because many families are descended from American citizens who lived in the region before white settlers arrived; as a consequence, even if they were citizens of Mexico (with its pre-1946 boundaries), they cannot accurately be classified as coming from Latin America. The complexity of recent immigrant flows is illustrated by the fact that a significant proportion of immigrants from the Caribbean are black, which thoroughly confuses census categories. In 2000, nearly 8 percent of blacks in the United States were foreign-born, with the figure over 20 percent in New York, Florida, and New Jersey. Most of these came from the Caribbean.[103]

Historically, most immigrants settled in central cities, moving into neighborhoods already occupied by the same group. In 1987, less than 7 percent of legal immigrants settled in nonurban areas, and more than half of them moved into just ten metropolitan areas in the United States. As shown in Figure 9.1, the racial and ethnic composition of the immigration flow differs considerably from one urban area to another. In the metropolitan San Francisco area, Chinese and Filipinos were the two leading immigrant groups in 2001, followed by Mexicans, Indians, and Nicaraguans. Most of the new immigrants to Miami in the same year, however, came from the Caribbean and Latin America; more than one-third came from Cuba alone. Mexican immigrants led the list in Los Angeles and Houston, but other groups were also changing these cities. In Los Angeles, Mexicans, Salvadorans, Filipinos, and Chinese were among the top five arriving groups. In Houston, Mexicans, Salvadorans, Vietnamese, and Indians were arriving in significant numbers. Immigrants from the Dominican Republic were the most numerous in New York City, followed by Chinese, Jamaicans, and Haitians. Washington, D.C., attracted large numbers of Salvadorans, plus Indians, Chinese, Pakistanis, and Filipinos. Mexicans led all groups in Chicago. However, a significant number of Indians, Poles, Filipinos, and Chinese also were arriving.

Figure 9.1   **Immigrant Flows to Seven U.S. Metropolitan Areas (One Year), Fiscal Year 2001**

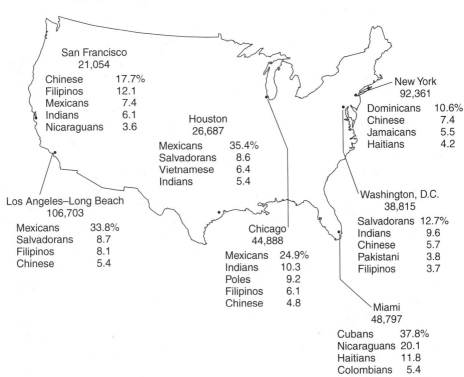

San Francisco 21,054	
Chinese	17.7%
Filipinos	12.1
Mexicans	7.4
Indians	6.1
Nicaraguans	3.6

Houston 26,687	
Mexicans	35.4%
Salvadorans	8.6
Vietnamese	6.4
Indians	5.4

New York 92,361	
Dominicans	10.6%
Chinese	7.4
Jamaicans	5.5
Haitians	4.2

Los Angeles–Long Beach 106,703	
Mexicans	33.8%
Salvadorans	8.7
Filipinos	8.1
Chinese	5.4

Chicago 44,888	
Mexicans	24.9%
Indians	10.3
Poles	9.2
Filipinos	6.1
Chinese	4.8

Washington, D.C. 38,815	
Salvadorans	12.7%
Indians	9.6
Chinese	5.7
Pakistani	3.8
Filipinos	3.7

Miami 48,797	
Cubans	37.8%
Nicaraguans	20.1
Haitians	11.8
Colombians	5.4

Composition of legally admitted immigrant flows to seven major Metropolitan statistical areas, fiscal year 2001.

Notes: "Chinese" includes migrants from mainland China only.

Source: U.S. Justice Department, Immigration and Naturalization Service, *Immigrants, Fiscal Year 2001* (Washington, D.C.: Government Printing Service, 2001), pp. 58–60.

In the 1990s, the patterns of settlement within the United States became more and more complex and unpredictable. Many of the recent immigrants have been bypassing the cities entirely and moving directly into suburbs or into nonmetropolitan cities and towns. By 2000, 58 percent of Asians and 49 percent of Latinos lived in suburbs, and the proportions were much higher in many Sunbelt metropolitan areas.[104] Some rural areas have been changed almost overnight, as immigrants moved near large employers of low-skilled labor, such as meatpacking plants, poultry operations, and agribusinesses devoted to raising livestock or processing agricultural products.

The movement of large numbers of Somalis to Minnesota in the 1990s illustrates the unpredictability of the immigrant flows and the degree to which immigration has become truly internationalized, with people coming from all parts of the world. In 1992, there were only a couple of Somali families in Minnesota, but by the census of 2000 there were officially 11,164 Somali individuals living in the state, 8,933 of them in the Minneapolis–St. Paul metropolitan area.[105] No other urban area in the United States seems to have been as attractive to Somalis. The reasons are obscure; perhaps Somalis came to Minnesota because it is a quiet urban center, and Somali immigrants were fleeing from war; they may also have been attracted by the availability of jobs, educational opportunities, and relatively good social services. It is equally plausible that Somalis favored Minnesota because a few hundred were brought there in 1993 by refugee settlement agencies, and more recent immigrants wanted to live close to other Somalis. The lesson is clear: Once an immigrant community exists, it is likely to act as a magnet for others, permanently changing the places they move to.

Immigrants have also been bypassing central cities and heading directly to the suburbs. Throughout the 1990s, for example, immigrants from an impressive number of countries moved to the suburbs of Long Island: Japanese, Koreans, Vietnamese, Indians, Pakistanis, and Iranians from Asia; and Guatemalans, Cubans, Haitians, and Salvadorans from the Caribbean and Latin America. Most of these immigrants were poor and unaccustomed to American culture, which caused anxiety among the current residents.[106] One of the complaints was that the newcomers did not conform to the suburban norm of retreating into the shelter of home (presumably with the television as a constant companion). Instead, men gathered on street corners and played music until all hours of the night. This brought street life to the suburbs for the first time but annoyed the residents who drove by. As one resident complained, "Suburbia does not like the idea of people congregating fifteen to twenty of them on suburban street corners, sitting on top of their cars blaring their big radios."[107] Immigrants also sent their children to the local schools, thus breaching the most sacred ground held by those residents who had moved to Long Island to escape signs of the city.[108]

In 1998, about 69 percent of the nation's 26 million Latinos lived in five southwestern states, plus Florida. California, with 10.1 million Latinos in 1998, had 33 percent of the nation's Latino population; the second state, Texas, with 5.8 million Latinos, had 19 percent.[109] Approximately 80 percent of the Latinos in the southwestern states came originally from Mexico, compared to 60 percent for the United States as a whole. But the destination of Latino immigration in the 1990s showed that these patterns are changing. The largest percentage increases in Latino population in the 1990s were in North Carolina (a 394 percent increase), Georgia (300 percent), Tennessee (278 percent), and South Carolina (211 percent).

Recently, Latinos have been moving to cities of all sizes and small towns and rural areas in almost every region of the nation, reflecting the fact that employers seeking low-skill workers are now as likely to be located outside as within metropolitan areas. For example, Beardstown, Illinois, located in downstate Illinois near the Mississippi River, has been transformed in recent years from a sleepy hamlet to a town bustling with Mexican immigrants, who have been attracted by the jobs in a nearby meat-processing plant. Because most of the new immigrants arrived unable to speak English, schools, churches, hospitals, and local businesses have suddenly been forced to adapt by employing translators and providing new programs.[110] But for the first time in decades, a renewed prosperity has come to the local economy.

In the 1980s, Asians were the fastest-growing ethnic group, with the metropolitan areas of Los Angeles, San Francisco, and New York having the largest Asian communities. The number of immigrants coming from Asia in the 1980s almost equaled the number from all countries of the Western Hemisphere south of the U.S. border. In the 1990s, Asian immigration slowed while Latino immigration increased sharply.[111] Latino populations are increasing at a much faster rate than non-Latino whites and African Americans, and some researchers predict that Latinos will equal African Americans in national population by the year 2003.

Table 9.7 shows the minority share of the population for the nation's fourteen most diverse metropolitan areas in 2000 (for areas of more than 500,000). In all the central cities, half or more of the population is minority, and in all but four of the suburban areas, minority populations exceeded 40 percent. In the 1990s, minority population gains in the suburbs outpaced the rate of increase for

Table 9.7 City and Suburban Minority shares, 2000 (in percentages) Metropolitan Areas with Populations over 500,000

| Metro Area | City | Suburban | Share of Suburban Population | | |
			Latino	Black	Asian
Los Angeles	69	69	45	8	14
New York	65	32	13	12	4
Chicago	65	26	11	8.5	5
Washington	61	40.5	8.5	22	7
Houston	68	40	23	10	5
Dallas	62	31	15	9	4
Riverside	51	53	38	7	4
Phoenix	37	30	21	3	2
Orange County	70	40	22	1	14
San Diego	50	40	27	4	6
Oakland	67	48	19	8	17
Miami	82	78.5	56	19.5	1.5
Newark	86	34	11	17	4.5
San Francisco	56	43	19	3	17

Source: Adapted from William H. Frey, "Melting Pot Suburbs: A Census 2000 Study of Suburban Diversity" (Washington, D.C.: Center on Urban and Metropolitan Policy, The Brookings Institution, June 2001), p. 14.

the central cities in eleven of these areas (the increases are not shown in the table). By 2000, these suburban areas had become very diverse. In the Washington, D.C., and Newark areas, blacks clearly outnumbered Latinos, but the differences were much smaller in the New York and Chicago areas. In the other metropolitan regions—all in the Sunbelt—Latinos constituted the largest minority group by far. Asians constituted less than 10 percent in all areas except the California metropolitan areas of Los Angeles, Orange County, Oakland, and San Francisco.

The economic well-being of each immigrant group is closely related to the conditions faced by the group before the move to the United States. Adverse economic conditions and political repression have pushed most of the new immigrants to American shores. Economic opportunity in the United States exerted the necessary pull. The minimum wage in the United States, for example, was approximately six times the prevailing wage in Mexico in 1990, where wages were higher than in most other Latin American countries.[112] Though many immigrants worked in poorly paid jobs, quite a few came into the United States to work in professional and technical occupations. Indeed, the proportion of immigrants with professional and technical backgrounds who worked in this country in 1990 consistently exceeded the average for U.S. workers as a whole.[113]

For the most part, Asian immigrants have done well, quickly achieving educational credentials and succeeding at small businesses.[114] Latinos, as a group, have lagged behind the general United States population on all indicators of economic well-being. The median income for Hispanic families in 2000 was $33,447, which was 73 percent of the $45,904 average earnings for non-Hispanic white families but above the average earnings of black families ($30,439).[115] Latinos lagged far behind on educational attainment; nearly 85 percent of all whites had completed high school in 2000, compared with 57 percent of Hispanics and 78.5 percent of blacks. Only 10.6 percent of Hispanics had earned a college degree by the 2000 census, but 26 percent of whites and 16.5 percent of blacks had done so.[116]

The relative lack of educational qualifications, plus a measure of discrimination, have meant that Latinos have also occupied lower rungs on the job ladder. Even though Hispanics held 10.7 percent of all jobs in 2000, they held just 5 percent of managerial professional jobs.[117] As of March 2000, the unemployment rate for Hispanics was 5.5 percent, about the same as for blacks (5.4 percent) but much higher than for whites (3 percent).[118] What these numbers show is that only a small proportion of people of Hispanic descent have entered the middle class in income, education, and occupational status.

Since the early 1970s, Hispanics made only slight gains in family income compared with non-Hispanic whites. The ratio of Hispanic family income to non-Hispanic white family income dropped slightly from 75.5 percent in 1972 to 73 percent by 2000. During the same period, black family income rose from a ratio of 58 percent to 66 percent of white family income.[119] Because of these gains, blacks closed the income gap between themselves and Hispanics considerably, from a 77 percent ratio in 1972 to 91 percent of Hispanic family income by 2000.[120]

Tensions among ethnic groups have become evident from time to time in recent years. Riots erupted in black neighborhoods in Cuban-dominated Miami four times in the 1980s, beginning with the Liberty City disorders in May 1980. Each of the riots was associated with the killing of a black man by Latino or non-Latino white police officers.[121] Rioting erupted in Washington, D.C., when a black female police officer attempted to arrest some Latino men and when a Salvadoran immigrant was shot by police. Ethnic tensions reached a breaking point in Brooklyn in 1991–1992, culminating in a boycott by the African American community of a Korean greengrocer and violent street confrontations between African Americans and Hasidic Jews. In the 1992 Los Angeles riots, 30 percent of the approximately 4,000 businesses destroyed were Latino-owned,[122] but Korean-owned businesses were especially singled out by looters and arsonists.[123]

Illegal immigration has intensified the competition for jobs among African Americans and the new immigrants. Undocumented aliens are willing to take (or are coerced into taking) jobs paying less than the minimum wage, and they often end up in sweatshops, meat-processing plants, or in agricultural jobs working under abysmal conditions. Frequently led across the border by professional smugglers, called *coyotes* for their predatory habits, illegal aliens remain at the bottom of U.S. society. Because they live in constant fear of detection by the Immigration and Naturalization Service (INS), they are in no position to bargain with employers.

To deal with the problem of illegal immigrants, Congress enacted the Immigration Reform and Control Act (IRCA) in 1986, which established stiff penalties for employers who knowingly hired illegal aliens. At the same time, the law made it possible for illegals who had already entered the country to achieve citizenship by registering with the INS. After passage of the IRCA, approximately 2.5 million formerly illegal aliens attained legal status by 1990,[124] and the INS stepped up efforts to find employers who violated the law. One of the unintended effects of the 1986 reform is that many employers began to discriminate against anyone who looked or sounded like they came from anywhere south of the U.S. border.[125] However, this effect may have been temporary; the benefits of hiring illegal aliens clearly outweighed the risks of getting caught.

In 1990, Congress again reformed the immigration laws by adopting legislation that increased the number of legal immigrants allowed into the country by 40 percent. The law more than doubled the number of visas granted to immigrants with job skills needed in the United States, and it allowed the highest percentage of European-origin groups into the country since Hart-Cellar.[126] In the mid-1990s, the United States was admitting more legal immigrants than all the rest of the nations of the world combined.[127] Immigration issues were important in the presidential election of 1996 because of the presence of two independent candidates, Pat Buchanan and Ross Perot, who advocated more restrictive immigration laws. Under the Personal Responsibility Act of 1996, which reformed welfare, legal immigrants were denied welfare benefits, including food stamps and Medicaid—a provision that was, however, rescinded in 1997.

THE METROPOLITAN FUTURE: SEGREGATION OR ASSIMILATION?

The racial, ethnic, and class divisions of American society are expressed in its urban landscapes. Ever since the early days of the republic, ethnic and social groups have tended to fragment into separate communities. Residence became a primary indicator of social status. The squabbles among neighborhoods of the nineteenth century segued into conflicts between cities and suburbs in the twentieth. Political separation in the form of independent suburban municipalities became a way for the privileged to keep the rest of urban society at bay. When race became a central feature of political life in the 1950s, the suburbs became even more defensive of their separate status.

In this new century, America's urban areas sometimes seem on the verge of fracturing into defended fortresses and enclaves, with central cities competing with suburbs, the suburbs with one another, and private gated communities trying to keep out those who live outside the walls. The tendency to flee from problems rather than try to confront and solve them has now taken on a seemingly irresistible momentum. In their search for security and comfort, people try to insulate themselves from potential harm. "The more vulnerable we feel, the more we fragment into small living units and working units, or whatever it takes to create the feeling of insulation and safety and home."[128] If urban residents continue to segregate themselves from one another, the divided metropolis of the twentieth century will seamlessly become the fractured society of the twenty-first.

NOTES

1. Population growth on the outskirts probably exceeded population growth in the center before the 1920s. However, before 1920, annexation of suburban land by central cities obscured the statistical trend. See John D. Kasarda and George V. Redfearn, "Differential Patterns of City and Suburban Growth in the United States," *Journal of Urban History* 2, no. 1 (November 1975): 53.
2. Robert A. Beauregard, *Voices of Decline: The Postwar Fate of U.S. Cities* (Cambridge, Mass.: Blackwell, 1993).
3. Dennis Judd, "Urban Violence and Enclave Politics: Crime as Text, Race as Subtext," in *Managing Divided Cities*, ed. Seamus Dunn (Keele, Staffordshire, U.K.: Ryburn Publishing, Keele University Press, 1994), pp. 160–175.
4. A brief but excellent account of these movements may be found in Stanley B. Greenberg, *Politics and Poverty: Modernization and Response in Five Poor Neighborhoods* (New York: Wiley, 1974), pp. 15–27.
5. See Greenberg, *Politics and Poverty*, pp. 15– 27; Leo Grebler, Joan W. Moore, and Ralph C. Guzman, *The Mexican-American People* (New York: Free Press, 1970), p. 113.
6. Harry M. Caudill, *Night Comes to the Cumberlands* (Boston: Little, Brown, 1962).
7. *Report of the National Advisory Commission on Civil Disorders* (New York: Bantam Books, 1968), p. 1.
8. Jim Hinch and Ronald Campbell, "Gated Enclaves One Future for Orange County," *Orange County Register*, May 15, 2002 (www.ocregister.com).
9. Ibid., quoting William Frey, a demographer in the Milken Institute of Los Angeles.
10. John R. Logan, "The New Ethnic Enclaves in America's Suburbs," a report by the Lewis Mumford Center for Comparative Urban and Regional Research (Albany, N.Y.: 2002), pp. 1–2.

11. Nicholas Lemann, *The Promised Land: The Great Migration and How It Changed America* (New York: Vintage Books, 1991), p. 6.

12. Stewart E. Tolnay and E. M. Beck, "Rethinking the Role of Racial Violence in the Great Migration," in *Black Exodus: The Great Migration from the American South,* ed. Afrerdteen Harrison (Jackson: University Press of Mississippi, 1991), p. 20.

13. Robert B. Grant, ed., *The Black Man Comes to the City: A Documentary Account from the Great Migration to the Great Depression, 1915–1930* (Chicago: Nelson-Hall, 1972), p. 27; see pp. 16–30 for a complete set of statistics on black migration from 1890 to 1930. These data are used throughout this section.

14. Ibid., p. 22.

15. Ibid., p. 23.

16. Winfred P. Nathan, *Health Conditions in North Harlem, 1923–1927,* Social Research Series No. 2 (New York: National Tuberculosis Association, 1932), pp. 44–45, excerpted in Grant, *The Black Man Comes to the City,* pp. 59– 61.

17. *Chicago Defender,* reprinted in Grant, *The Black Man Comes to the City,* pp. 31–40.

18. Tolnay and Beck, "Rethinking the Role of Racial Violence," p. 27.

19. Philip Dray, *At the Hands of Persons Unknown: The Lynching of Black America* (New York: Random House, 2002).

20. A collective amnesia has erased much of this past from America's consciousness. A recent book of photographs from the period is shocking, but an effective antidote to cultural denial. See James Allen, *Without Sanctuary: Lynching Photography in America* (Sante Fe, N.M.: Twin Palms Publishers, 2000).

22. *Chicago Defender,* August 12, 1916, reprinted in Grant, *The Black Man Comes to the City,* p. 45.

23. Herbert Northrup, *Organized Labor and the Negro* (New York: Kraus Reprint, 1971).

24. These statistics are from several sources excerpted in Grant, *The Black Man Comes to the City,* pp. 58–61.

25. See Elliott M. Rudwick, *Race Riot at East St. Louis, July 2, 1917* (Carbondale: Southern Illinois Press, 1964) for a discussion of this event.

26. Chicago Commission on Race Relations, *The Negro in Chicago: A Study of Race Relations and a Race Riot* (Chicago: University of Chicago Press, 1922), p. 122.

27. Tom Kenworthy, "Okla. Starts to Face up to '21 Massacre," *USA Today,* February 18, 2000, p. 4A.

28. Grant, *The Black Man Comes to the City,* p. 71.

29. U.S. Department of Commerce, Bureau of the Census, *Census of Population 1970: General Social and Economic Characteristics* (Washington, D.C.: Government Printing Office, 1972), pp. 448–449, table 3.

30. William H. Frey, "Census 2000 Shows Large Black Return to the South, Reinforcing the Region's 'White-Black' Demographic Profile," U.S. Bureau of the Census, PSC Research Report No. 02-473, May 2001.

31. U.S. Census Bureau, *1990 to 1998 Annual Time Series of Population Estimates by Age, Race, Sex and Hispanic Origin,* January 2000 (Website: www.census.gov/population/estimates/countypop.html).

32. John Kasarda, "Inner-City Concentrated Poverty and Neighborhood Distress: 1970 to 1990," *Housing Policy Debate* 4, no. 3 (1993): 253–302.

33. Poverty in the United States: 2000 (Joseph Dalaker, September 2001), Current Population Reports, pp. 60–214 (Washington, D.C.: U.S. Bureau of the Census).

34. Douglas S. Massey and Nancy Denton, "Trends in the Residential Segregation of Blacks, Hispanics, and Asians: 1970–1980," *American Sociological Review* 52 (1987): 802–825.

35. Ibid.; see also Douglas Massey and Mitchell Eggers, "The Ecology of Inequality: Minorities and the Concentration of Poverty, 1970–1980," *American Journal of Sociology* 95 (March 1990): 1153–1189; Douglas Massey, "American Apartheid: Segregation and the Making of the Underclass," *American Journal of Sociology* (June 1990): 329–357; William Julius Wilson, *The Truly Disadvantaged: The Inner City, the Underclass, and Public Policy* (Chicago: University

of Chicago Press, 1987); William Julius Wilson, *When Work Disappears: The World of the New Urban Poor* (New York: Knopf, 1996).

36. William W. Goldsmith and Edward J. Blakely, *Separate Societies: Poverty and Inequality in U.S. Cities* (Philadelphia: Temple University Press, 1992), p. 48.

37. Douglas Massey and Nancy Denton, *American Apartheid: Segregation and the Making of the Underclass* (Cambridge, Mass.: Harvard University Press, 1993), pp. 74–78.

38. Myron Orfield, *American Metro Politics: The New Suburban Reality* (Washington, D.C.: The Brookings Institution, 2002).

39. Wilson, *The Truly Disadvantaged.*

40. Michaela di Leonardo, "White Lies/Black Myths: Rape, Race, and the Black Underclass," *The Village Voice,* September 22, 1992, p. 31.

41. Norman Fainstein, "Race, Class, and Segregation: Discourses About African-Americans," *International Journal of Urban and Regional Research* 17, no. 3 (1993): 384–403.

42. Wilson, *The Truly Disadvantaged.*

43. Wilson, *When Work Disappears,* p. 19.

44. Ibid.

45. Goldsmith and Blakely, *Separate Societies,* pp. 51–52.

46. Wilson, *When Work Disappears,* p. 51.

47. Ibid., p. 31.

48. For further information on the mismatch between the geographic location of inner-city blacks and available jobs, see John Kasarda, "Urban Change and Minority Opportunities," in *The New Urban Reality,* ed. Paul E. Peterson (Washington, D.C.: Brookings Institution, 1985), pp. 33–67; and John D. Kasarda, "Urban Employment Change and Minority Skills Mismatch," in *Creating Jobs, Creating Workers: Economic Development and Employment in Metropolitan Chicago,* ed. Lawrence B. Joseph (Chicago: Center for Urban Research and Policy Studies, 1990), pp. 65–89.

49. Wilson, *When Work Disappears,* pp. 25–88.

50. Ibid., p. 92.

51. Ibid., p. 93.

52. Lisa W. Foderaro, "In Harlem, Children Reflect the Ravages U.N. Seeks to Relieve," *New York Times,* September 30, 1990, p. 1.

53. Walter J. Jones and James E. Johnson, "AIDS: The Urban Policymaking Challenge," *Journal of Urban Affairs* 11, no. 1 (1989): 85.

54. *Confronting AIDS: Update 1988* (Washington, D.C.: National Academy Press, 1988), p. 52.

55. Joel A. Devine and James D. Wright, *The Greatest of Evils: Urban Poverty and the American Underclass,* (New York: Aldine De Gruyter, 1993) p. 167.

56. Michael deCourcy Hinds, "Number of Killings Soars in Big Cities Across U.S.," *New York Times,* July 18, 1990, p. 1.

57. Robert D. McFadden, "New York Leads Cities in Robbery Rate, but Drops in Murders," *New York Times,* August 11, 1991, p. 1.

58. See James Diego Vigil, *Barrio Gangs: Street Life and Identity in Southern California* (Austin: University of Texas Press, 1988).

59. Ronald Kotulak, "Study Finds Inner-City Kids Live with Violence," *Chicago Tribune,* September 28, 1990, p. 1.

60. Jonathan Kozol, *Rachel and Her Children: Homeless Families in America* (New York: Crown, 1988), p. 9.

61. U.S. Bureau of the Census, *Statistical Abstract of the United States,* table 342, Crimes and Crime Rates, by Type of Offense: 1987 to 1997; U.S. Federal Bureau of Investigation, *Crime in the United States Annual* (Washington, D.C.: Government Printing Office, 1998).

62. Sophie Body-Gendrot, *The Social Control of Cities? A Comparative Perspective* (Malden, Mass., and Oxford, U.K.: Blackwell, 2000), p. 116.

63. Margaret T. Gordon and Claudette Guzan Artwick, "Urban Images in the Mass Media" (research proposal, Urban University Research Consortium, June 17, 1991), p. 2.

64. Robert Suro, "Crime and Its Amplified Echoes Are Rearranging People's Lives," *New York Times,* February 9, 1992, p. 1.

65. di Leonardo, "White Lies/Black Myths," p. 31.

66. Quoted in Tom Morgenthau and John McCormack, "Are Cities Obsolete?" *Newsweek,* September 9, 1991, p. 42.

67. Elizabeth Kolbert, "Region Around New York Sees Ties to City Faltering," *New York Times,* December 1, 1991; William Blaberson, "For Many in the New York Region, the City Is Ignored and Irrelevant," *New York Times,* January 2, 1992.

68. Quoted in James A. Clapp, ed., *The City: A Dictionary of Quotable Thoughts on Cities and Urban Life* (New Brunswick, N.J.: Center for Urban Policy Research, Rutgers University, 1984), p. 129.

69. Kenneth T. Jackson, *Crabgrass Frontier: The Suburbanization of the United States* (New York: Oxford University Press, 1985), chap. 1.

70. Ibid., pp. 25–30. Robert Fishman dates the first true suburb somewhat earlier, in the 1790s in Clapham and other villages outside London; see Robert Fishman, *Bourgeois Utopias: The Rise and Fall of Suburbia* (New York: Basic Books, 1987) p. 53

71. For accounts of railroad suburbs and land speculation, see Jackson, *Crabgrass Frontier,* chap. 5; Fishman, *Bourgeois Utopias,* chap. 5; and Harry C. Binford, *The First Suburbs: Residential Communities on the Boston Periphery, 1815–1860* (Chicago: University of Chicago Press, 1985).

72. The phrase "scattered buildings in a park" is Lewis Mumford's; see his *The City in History: Its Origins, Its Transformations, and Its Prospects* (New York: Harcourt, Brace and World, 1961), p. 489.

73. Peter O. Muller, *Contemporary Suburban America* (Englewood Cliffs, N.J.: Prentice-Hall, 1981), p. 28.

74. Our account of Huntington relies on Robert M. Fogelson, *The Fragmented Metropolis: Los Angeles, 1850–1930* (New York: Cambridge, 1967), pp. 89–92; Jackson, *Crabgrass Frontier,* p. 122; and Fishman, *Bourgeois Utopias,* pp. 159–160.

75. Gary A. Tobin, "Suburbanization and the Development of Motor Transportation: Transportation Technology and the Suburbanization Process," in *The Changing Face of the Suburbs,* ed. Barry Schwartz (Chicago: University of Chicago Press, 1976), p. 100. See also U.S. Bureau of the Census, *Industrial Districts: 1905, Manufactures and Population,* Bulletin 101 (Washington, D.C.: Government Printing Office, 1909), pp. 9–80; and U.S. Bureau of the Census, *Census of Manufactures: 1914,* vol. 1, *Reports by States with Statistics for Principal Cities and Metropolitan Districts* (Washington, D.C.: Government Printing Office, 1918), pp. 564, 787, 1292.

76. These data are cited in Tobin, "Suburbanization and the Development of Motor Transportation," pp. 102, 103, and are also available in National Industrial Conference Board (NICB), *The Economic Almanac 1956: A Handbook of Useful Facts About Business, Labor and Government in the United States and Other Areas* (New York: Crowell for the Conference Board, 1956).

77. Tobin, "Suburbanization and the Development of Motor Transportation," pp. 102, 103.

78. Ibid.

79. Jackson, *Crabgrass Frontier,* pp. 174, 184.

80. The birthrate (the number of live births per 1,000 population) increased from 18.4 in 1936 to 26.6 in 1947. U.S. Bureau of the Census, *Historical Statistics of the United States, Colonial Times to 1970,* Bicentennial edition, pt. 2 (Washington, D.C.: Government Printing Office, 1975), p. 49.

81. Jackson, *Crabgrass Frontier,* p. 232.

82. Ibid., p. 233.

83. Barry Checkoway, "Large Builders, Federal Housing Programs, and Postwar Suburbanization," in *Marxism and the Metropolis: New Perspectives in Political Economy,* 2nd ed. William K. Tabb and Larry Sawers (New York: Oxford University Press, 1984), pp. 155–156.

84. U.S. Bureau of the Census, *Historical Statistics of the United States, Colonial Times to 1970,* Bicentennial edition, pt. 1 (Washington, D.C.: Government Printing Office, 1975), p. 646.

85. For criticisms of the 1950s stereotype of suburbia, see Bennett M. Berger, *Working-Class Suburb: A Study of Auto Workers in Suburbia* (Berkeley: University of California Press, 1968); and Herbert J. Gans, *The Levittowners: Ways of Life and Politics in a New Suburban Community* (New York: Pantheon, 1967).

86. Thomas M. Guterbock, "The Push Hypothesis: Minority Presence, Crime, and Urban Deconcentration," in *The Changing Face of the Suburbs,* ed. Barry Schwartz (Chicago: University of Chicago Press, 1976), p. 26.

87. National Advisory Commission on Civil Disorders, *Report of the National Advisory Commission on Civil Disorders* (New York: Bantam Books, 1968), p. 1.

88. James Heilbrun, *Urban Economics and Public Policy,* 2nd ed. (New York: St. Martin's Press, 1981), p. 48.

89. Muller, *Contemporary Suburban America,* p. 123.

90. David M. Gordon, "Capitalist Development and the History of American Cities," in *Marxism and the Metropolis: New Perspectives in Urban Political Economy,* 2nd ed., ed. William K. Tabb and Larry Sawers (New York: Oxford University Press, 1984), p. 41.

91. George E. Peterson, "Federal Tax Policy and Urban Development," in *Central City Economic Development,* ed. Benjamin Chinitz (Cambridge, Mass.: Abt Books, 1979), pp. 67–78.

92. Robert Cervero, "Unlocking Suburban Gridlock," *Journal of the American Planning Association* 52:4 (Autumn 1986): 389.

93. Brian J. L. Berry, *The Open Housing Question: Race and Housing in Chicago, 1966–1976* (Cambridge, Mass.: Ballinger, 1979).

94. Joel Garreau, *Edge City: Life on the New Frontier* (Garden City, N.Y.: Doubleday, 1991), p. 6.

95. Wilson, *When Work Disappears,* p. 88.

96. Josh Barbanel, "From L. I. Teller Machines to Gas Stations, Suburban Robberies Are on the Rise," *New York Times,* February 18, 1992, p. 1.

97. David Guterson, "No Place Like Home: On the Manicured Streets of a Master-Planned Community," *Harper's,* November 1992, p. 63.

98. Muller, *Contemporary Suburban America,* p. 180.

99. Trevor Boddy, "Underground and Overhead: Building the Analogous City," in *Variations on a Theme Park: The New American City and the End of Public Space,* ed. Michael Sorkin (New York: Noonday Press, 1992), p. 139.

100. Mike Davis, "Fortress Los Angeles: The Militarization of Urban Space," in *Variations on a Theme Park: The New American City and the End of Public Space,* ed. Michael Sorkin (New York: Noonday Press, 1992), p. 173.

101. "Immigration Reform: Recent Trends and Legislative Responses," *The Urban Institute Policy and Research Report* (Winter/Spring 1991): 12.

102. Louis Winnick, *New People in Old Neighborhoods* (New York: Russell Sage Foundation, 1990), p. xvi.

103. Frey, U.S. Bureau of the Census.

104. Logan, "The New Ethnic Enclaves," p. 2; William H. Frey, "Melting Pot Suburbs: A Census 2000 Study of Suburban Diversity" (Washington, D.C.: Center for Urban and Metropolitan Policy, The Brookings Institution, June 2001).

105. Leslie Medrano Lordes, "Minnesota Leads in Somali Residents," *Minneapolis Star Tribune,* September 18, 2002, p. 3.

106. Rosalyn Baxandall and Elizabeth Ewen, *Picture Windows: How the Suburbs Happened* (New York: Basic Books, 2000).

107. Ibid., p. 240.

108. Ibid., p. 241.

109. U.S. Bureau of the Census, *1990 to 1998 Annual Time Series of State Population Estimates by Race and Hispanic Origin* (Washington, D.C.: Government Printing Office, 1999).

110. James P. Miller, "Culture Change in a Small Town," *Chicago Tribune*, Janury 6, 2003, sec. 4, pp. 1, 4.
111. U.S. Bureau of the Census, *1990 to 1998 Annual Time Series of Population Estimates by Age, Race, Sex, and Hispanic Origin*, January 2000 (Website: www.census.gov/population/estimates/countypop.html).
112. Alejandro Portes and Ruben Rumbaut, *Immigrant America: A Portrait* (Berkeley: University of California Press, 1990), p. 10.
113. Ibid.
114. See Min Zhou, *Chinatown: The Socioeconomic Potential of an Urban Enclave* (Philadelphia: Temple University Press, 1992).
115. U.S. Bureau of the Census, *Statistical Abstract of the United States: 2001* (Washington, D.C.: Government Printing Office), p. 140.
116. Ibid., p. 139.
117. Ibid., p. 380.
118. Ibid., p. 389.
119. U.S. Bureau of the Census, *Current Population Reports: Money Income in the United States: 1995* (Washington, D.C.: Government Printing Office, 1996), Report No. P60-193.
120. U.S. Bureau of the Census, *Current Population Reports: Money Income in the United States: 2000* (Washington, D.C.: Government Printing Office, 2002) Report No. P60-213, pp. 18, 19.
121. Christopher L. Warren, John G. Corbett, and John F. Stack, Jr., "Hispanic Ascendancy and Tripartite Politics in Miami," in *Racial Politics in American Cities*, ed. Rufus P. Browning, Dale Rogers Marshall, and David H. Tabb (New York: Longman, 1990), p. 166.
122. Jack Miles, "Blacks vs. Brown," *Atlantic*, October 1992, pp. 41–68. See also Mike Davis, "In L.A., Burning All Illusions," *Nation*, June 1, 1992, pp. 743–746.
123. Tim Rutten, "A New Kind of Riot," *New York Review of Books*, June 11, 1992, pp. 52–54.
124. "Immigration Reform," p. 13.
125. Reported in Charles Kamasaki and Paul Yzaguirre, "Black-Hispanic Tensions: One Perspective" (paper delivered at the Annual Meeting of the American Political Science Association, Washington, D.C., August 29–September 1, 1991), p. 5. See also Stephen Castles and Mark J. Miller, *The Age of Migration: International Population Movements in the Modern World* (New York: Guilford Press, 1993).
126. Robert Pear, "Major Immigration Bill Is Sent to Bush," *New York Times*, October 29, 1990, p. A1; see also Castles and Miller, *The Age of Migration*, p. 249.
127. Rodman D. Griffin, "Illegal Immigration," CQ Researcher 2, no. 16 (April 24, 1992), p. 364.
128. Richard Louv, *America II: The Book That Captures Americans in the Act of Creating the Future* (New York: Penguin Books, 1983), p. 34.

CHAPTER
10

THE POLITICS OF SECESSION

CARVING UP THE METROPOLIS

What distinguishes the urban pattern in the United States most clearly from that of other Western nations is the fragmentation of metropolitan areas into a multitude of separate governments. In Europe and in most other nations, there are fewer suburbs (because cities tend to encompass a large part of their metropolitan areas), and national and regional governments provide crucial services. In contrast, American suburbs are autonomous governmental units that make taxation, spending, and land use decisions independently of one another. Throughout the twentieth century, local governments have proliferated outside the older central cities. In 2002, there were 87,849 local governments in the United States.[1] The "degree of governmental fragmentation in the United States is unique among the urban-industrial societies."[2]

The ability to so easily escape the cities nurtured an "enclave consciousness" that encouraged affluent people to withdraw from the rest of the urban community.[3] Even before the suburbanization of the twentieth century, the better-off native-born Americans tried to separate themselves from recently arrived immigrants. Residence became a primary indicator of social status. The habit of creating social status by residence bred fears that status would be compromised if "undesirable" racial and ethnic groups invaded the "better" neighborhoods. The squabbles among neighborhoods in the nineteenth century were replaced by conflicts between central cities and suburbs and among suburbs in the twentieth century. Political separation in the form of independent suburban municipalities became a way for the privileged to protect their wealth and status by walling themselves off in their own enclaves. When racial animosities became a defining feature of the political and social life of metropolitan areas in the twentieth century, the suburbs became even more defensive of their separate status.

The escape from the cities proved advantageous for the new suburban residents. They benefited from federal policies that subsidized their home loans and built their freeways. Those living in suburbs with high property values and plenty of business investment have been able to pay lower taxes but at the same time enjoy higher levels of public services than the residents of poorer municipalities. Because most suburbs could be selective about who and what they let in, the central city inherited the responsibilities and problems the suburbs did not choose to support, including especially services supplied to poor people.[4] At the same time, suburban residents could continue to use the cultural facilities and the infrastructure of the central city when it suited them. It was a wonderful bargain, though over time suburban residents came to regard it as their right.

The bargain worked as long as minorities, new immigrants, and the poor remained clustered in older, decayed neighborhoods in central cities and in nearby older suburbs. But the old pattern is beginning to disappear. Recently, the differences between older central cities and their surrounding suburbs have been becoming less sharply drawn. In many American cities, affluent residents have been moving downtown, and some suburbs have attracted poor people and waves of new immigrants. As a consequence, the fragmentation of metropolitan areas is spawning a new politics that pits suburb against suburb as much as suburb against city.

THE MOTIVE TO SEPARATE FROM THE CITIES

For wealthy people who fled the industrial cities at the beginning of the twentieth century, political separation promised an escape from the alleged corruption, anarchy, and immorality of the political machines and their immigrant constituents. Those who fought for the incorporation of suburban towns from late nineteenth-century Boston, for example, based their cause on "the ideal of small town life: the simple informal community, the town meeting, the maintenance of the traditions of rural New England. They held out to their constituents the idea of the suburban town as a refuge from the pressures of the new industrial metropolis." Suburban life could be free from "Boston's waves of incoming poor immigrants."[5]

At the edges of all the big cities, municipalities proceeded rapidly to incorporate from the 1890s to the Great Depression. In 1890, Cook County, whose principal city is Chicago, had 55 governments; by 1920 it had 109. Similarly, the number of general-purpose governments in the New York City area grew from 127 in 1900 to 204 by 1920. There were 91 incorporated municipalities in the Pittsburgh area in 1890 but 107 in 1920.[6] During the 1920s, new suburbs were created by the score.

In the first three decades of the century, popular literature exuded an intellectual and sentimental reaction against the city. Cities had few defenders and a host of critics. Academic writers promoted the idea that "our great cities, as those who have studied them have learned, are full of junk, much of it human."[7] A Boston University professor called city life "a self-chosen enslavement" and indicated

OUT TAKE — ATTEMPTS TO FORCE INTEGRATION HAVE FAILED

Federal courts have been unwilling to use the U.S. Constitution to break down the walls of suburban exclusion. This has left the states as the main avenue of redress for those who want to challenge local zoning laws. Since a large proportion of state legislators answer to suburban voters, it is unlikely that state laws will be changed to limit what local governments can do. Therefore, any challenges to zoning would have to go through the courts, but the New Jersey experience shows that this strategy also falls short. Given the racial hostilities in the United States, there may be no effective way to use government to bring about racial integration.

In 1970, Mount Laurel, New Jersey, located not far from Camden and Philadelphia, was a mostly rural community. The area contained a small African American community that had been there since before the Civil War. Quakers had made Mount Laurel a sanctuary for runaway slaves on the Underground Railroad, and their descendants still resided in the area. Many of them lived in small shacks and converted chicken coops, and when these were condemned by the city of Mount Laurel, the residents feared that they would be forced to move to the slums of Camden. They formed an action committee and applied for federal funds to build a subsidized housing project. In 1970, the committee's proposal was turned down by the local planning and zoning board.

The residents then turned to the courts. They found three idealistic lawyers working for the Camden Region Legal Services who agreed to pursue a case to strike down Mount Laurel's zoning laws, which allowed only single-family homes and specified large lots, large building sizes (a minimum of four bedrooms), and substantial setbacks from the street. In 1972, a trial court found that Mount Laurel's zoning laws violated language in the New Jersey Constitution that guaranteed equal protection of the law for all persons. Further, the court ruled that not only Mount Laurel but all of New Jersey's 567 municipalities had an obligation to provide land uses that would meet regional housing needs. The U.S. Supreme Court subsequently refused to hear an appeal of this decision.

The Mount Laurel decision meant that suburbs were obligated to allow low-income housing, but they were not required to provide the resources for it. If low-income housing was not profitable, builders would not construct it. It is hardly surprising that little low-income housing was built, even in the communities whose zoning laws had been declared invalid by the courts. In 1982, the new Chief Justice of the New Jersey Supreme Court, Robert N. Wilentz, heard six cases showing that the city of Mount Laurel was ignoring the original trial court's decision.[8] He combined the six cases into one proceeding, and in 1983 the court issued a pathbreaking, unanimous decision, widely known as Mount Laurel II. The court noted that the town of Mount Laurel had made no real attempt to comply with the original judicial directive; it had simply rezoned 33 of its 14,176 acres, and none of the 515 low-income housing units required to meet the court's decision had been built.[9]

In order to speed compliance with its original decision, Mount Laurel II required that municipalities not only rezone land for low-income housing but also make low-income housing attractive to developers through such devices as tax incentives and subsidies. Second, to encourage builders to pursue lawsuits against exclusionary zoning, the court established "builder's remedies," which allowed developers of low- and moderate-income housing to sue cities that tried to keep them out.

As a result of Mount Laurel II, New Jersey's suburban municipalities were besieged with lawsuits, and politicians were increasingly pressured to do something about it. Republican Governor Thomas H. Kean, who won office in 1981, came out strongly against what he called an "undesirable intrusion on the home rule principle." In a 1984 interview, Kean stated, "I don't believe that every municipality has got to be a carbon copy of another. That's a socialistic country, a Communistic country, a dictatorship."[10] Kean advocated an amendment to the New Jersey Constitution that would place local zoning policy beyond review by state courts. Meanwhile, on July 2, 1985, he signed the Fair Share Housing Act, which was designed to move exclusionary zoning cases (at the time more than a hundred were pending) out of the courts and into arbitration before a nine-member Council on Affordable Housing (COAH), which was appointed by the governor.[11] Cities and towns were given a grace period to achieve their "fair share" housing goals.

In actuality, most communities were let off the hook completely. Municipalities were allowed, for example, to allot up to 25 percent of their "fair share" to the elderly, and any city was allowed to transfer up to 50 percent of its fair share obligation to another city in the region (if the receiving city approved), along with the funds to help the receiving town pay for the housing. Older central cities were put in the position of competing against one another for subsidies from suburbs so they could obtain funds to meet the pressing housing needs of their low-income residents. What had begun as an effort to open up the suburbs ended up doing exactly the opposite.

Despite all of the political thunder and lightning, the payoff from the long, drawn-out Mount Laurel process was meager. The New Jersey Supreme Court estimated that the state needed 277,808 units to meet the Mount Laurel guidelines. By May 1990, less than 3 percent of that number—8,000 housing units—had been built,[12] and most of these were moderate-income, not low-income, units. In the town of Mount Laurel, by the late 1980s only twelve families had moved into low-cost mobile homes, twelve more had put down deposits on similar units, and twenty low-cost subsidized condominiums had been completed. This was the grand total of low-income housing after seventeen years of litigation and political controversy.[13]

The New Jersey case illustrates the difficulty of changing local land-use practices by using the courts when a political consensus is lacking. Mount Laurel represents the clash between two deeply held American values: equal protection of the law and local home rule. Americans are reluctant to support policies that force local governments to give up their autonomy. In an era when the federal government has cut housing subsidies drastically, even if local zoning laws could be successfully challenged, it is doubtful that much low-income housing would be built in the suburbs. If the New Jersey experience offers a lesson, it is that exclusionary zoning is here to stay.

that "the psychological causes of urban drift are socially most sinister."[14] Cities were thought to nurture every conceivable sort of evil, as evidenced by such titles of sociological research as *The Social Evil in Chicago; Five Hundred Criminal Careers; The City Where Crime Is Play; Family Disorganization; Sex, Freedom and Social Control;* and *The Ghetto.*[15]

A back-to-nature movement, built on a romanticized version of rural and semirural environments, swept the country. Boy Scouts, Campfire Girls, Woodcraft Indians, and other organizations sought to expose children to the healthy influence of nature study. Children's literature was filled with stories of adventure in "natural" settings. Adults, too, were thought to be purified and rejuvenated by visits to the countryside. Bird-watching and nature photography became major pastimes. Tourism to national parks boomed, especially after automobiles became more widely available to the middle classes.

Inevitably, the yearning for nature became linked to suburban images. Wealthy urban residents had no intention of giving up the amenities and advantages of urban life. Instead, they attempted a fusion of both worlds—the urban and the rural—in the suburbs. Magazines and newspapers of the day were filled with articles on the advantages of suburban life as an amalgam of city conveniences and rural charm. In 1902, one magazine writer claimed that suburban living could "offer the best of chances for individualism and social cooperation."[16] The next year, *Cosmopolitan* carried an article hailing the "new era" of suburban living:

> The woeful inadequacy of facilities of communication and transportation which formerly rendered every suburbanite a martyr to his faith have, in great measure, been remedied; and moreover, residents in the environs have now reached the happy point where they consider as necessities the innumerable modern conveniences of the city house which were little short of luxuries in the suburban residence of yesterday.[17]

Advertisements for suburban property just after the turn of the century stressed the presence of springs, orchards, and forests; activities such as bathing, fishing, and shooting; the healthfulness of the environment; and houses that had such modern conveniences as hot water, gas lighting, and telephones.[18] "A Country Home with All City Comforts," promised one advertisement, alongside another that talked of crops of oats and hay, orchards, trees and shrubbery, fruit trees, and other accompaniments of the rural environment.[19] Most of the advertisements carried drawings or photographs of wide expanses of lawn, trees, and meticulously tended gardens.

The shaping of a suburban ideal was closely linked to efforts to form suburban governments that were independent of the core cities. Political separation from the industrial cities, however, was not always easy. Local governments are not mentioned in the U.S. Constitution; legally, they are creatures of the states. In the early part of the nineteenth century, the incorporation of a local government was viewed as a privilege bestowed by state legislatures. In their fights to persuade state legislators to allow them to incorporate their own governments, people who had moved beyond the limits of the industrial cities claimed that smaller governments were closer to the people and were therefore the best possible expressions of democracy.[20]

Gradually, over the nineteenth century, state legislatures made it so much easier for suburbanites to incorporate new towns and cities that incorporation shifted from a privilege to a right.[21] Through general incorporation laws, any group of suburbanites who had migrated beyond the boundaries of the city could, if a majority of them approved, form a separate local government. "By the early twentieth century suburbanites had begun carving up the metropolis, and the states had handed them the knife."[22] By 1930, every state legislature in the country had adopted liberalized incorporation laws that put the decision of whether suburbanites would or would not be annexed by the central city firmly into the hands of those who had already fled the city.

Through much of the nineteenth century, even though many people who moved beyond city boundaries had the option to create new suburbs, they usually sought annexation rather than separation. Some chose annexation in order to receive public services that otherwise were hard to get; others were coerced into joining by the city. Los Angeles, for example, used its monopoly over water supply to force consolidation on neighboring communities, including Hollywood, Venice, Lordsburg, Sawtelle, Watts, Eagle Rock, Hyde Park, Tujunga, and Barnes City. After the Metropolitan Water District was formed in 1927, however, Los Angeles lost its monopoly over water, and the courts ruled it could no longer force its thirsty neighbors to agree to annexation.[23] Subsequently, Los Angeles, now the archetype of the fragmented metropolis, led the way in the proliferation of suburban governments through the Lakewood Plan, which enabled suburbs to avoid the need to consolidate by contracting to have services provided cheaply by county government.[24] In other urban areas, special districts enabled suburbanites to receive services without being annexed.

Suburbanites sought to form separate governments not only to gain control over their own services but also to enforce ethnic and racial segregation. At the turn of the century, residents of Oak Park on the border of Chicago feared that the Slavic population might spill over from neighboring Austin. Their motive for incorporating, according to one author, was that "Slavic persons with little aversion for alcohol were rapidly settling the Austin area, and the native American Protestant population of Oak Park feared the immoral influences that might accompany these foreigners."[25] Between 1899 and 1902, Austin joined the City of Chicago, but Oak Park formed a separate suburban government.

On occasion, simple economic self-interest supplied a sufficient motive to incorporate a new suburb. E. J. "Lucky" Baldwin was a notorious gambler and entrepreneur in California in the early twentieth century. He got his nickname by making a fortune gambling on mining stocks,[26] and he was the defendant in a number of seduction and paternity suits that culminated in spectacular trials. Baldwin wanted to build a racetrack, but he knew that he would be opposed by southern California's foes of sin, led by the Anti-Saloon League. Accordingly, Baldwin decided to form his own suburb, called Arcadia. As the name implied, he intended the town to be his personal utopia. He imported his own employees as residents and handed out free watermelons on election day. Not surprisingly, they approved incorporation unanimously and elected a city council composed of Baldwin and his employees. Baldwin realized his dream when Santa Anita raceway opened on December 7, 1907.[27]

Suburban governments sometimes provided industrialists with havens from taxes and regulation. Efforts to incorporate almost always succeeded when they were led by industry.[28] In 1907, meatpacking companies incorporated National City on the northern border of East St. Louis, Illinois, to avoid being taxed by East St. Louis. A few years later, Monsanto Chemical Company created the city of Sauget on East St. Louis's southern border for the same purpose. In the 1950s, a group of industrialists tried to form a separate suburban jurisdiction in Los Angeles County in order to avoid having to pay for the services of a growing suburban population. When they found that the area did not include the 500 residents required for incorporation, they redrew the boundaries to include 169 patients of a mental sanitarium, which put them over the top. Appropriately named "Industry," the new suburb deprived the surrounding municipalities of badly needed tax revenue. In 1977, for example, Industry's tax assessment was $309,970 per capita, compared with only $1,512 per capita in the adjoining city of La Puente.[29]

The people who left the city were free to decide for themselves whether to join the central city or form their own governments, "leaving the parent who had spawned the child helpless in determining their joint future."[30] Abandoned by a growing proportion of their wealthiest residents and economic enterprises over the ensuing decades, the industrial cities lost more and more resources.

HOW DEVELOPERS SHAPED THE SUBURBS

The end of World War II opened the floodgates for suburban development. Loans subsidized through the Federal Housing Authority and the Veterans Administration made it possible for middle-class families to buy homes even if they had few savings—or none at all, in the case of returning veterans. Developers quickly learned how to deal directly with the banks that processed the federally subsidized loans, and thus they became the front-line agents that shaped the development of the suburbs:

> The plain fact is that now as before, the main force in our process of urban development is the private developer. The primacy of the bulldozer in transforming rural land to urban uses, the capacity of the private company to build thousands of homes on quiet rolling hills is a predominant fact of American urban life.[31]

What they put in place would not easily be changed.

To a considerable extent, racial and social segregation between cities and suburbs as well as among suburban jurisdictions was fated by the actions of developers who saw it as an effective or even necessary marketing strategy. The suburbs were promoted as ways to achieve instant social status, escape the problems of the cities, and live in a segregated social environment. Thus the suburbs became sharply differentiated from the cities, both in people's minds and in reality. Developers were careful to target a preferred segment of the housing market and to exclude others. The bigger the house and the larger the income of buyers, the more money was to be made. Developers learned these lessons well in the period when millions of people escaped the cities for the suburbs, from the end of World War and in subsequent decades.

Though it is undoubtedly true that many suburban residents moved out of the cities to escape crime, crowding, noise, and the presence of minorities, the families who made the suburban move exercised less choice about it than is commonly supposed. The availability of relatively inexpensive land in outlying areas encouraged real estate developers and builders to promote construction outside the cities. In their attempt to market the new subdivisions, developers virtually invented an iconic image of the American Dream—the suburban house. The suburbs were created first by developers and only second by the choices of buyers. Developers influenced the character of the suburbs by selecting the clientele that could best supply profits—chiefly the middle to upper classes—and by molding the tastes and preferences of these consumers. Realtors, developers, and financial institutions aggressively marketed the suburbs because new housing construction maximized their profitability.[32] To market the houses they built, these entrepreneurs promised not only a home but also an entire way of life. They were not merely the builders of houses; they were "community builders."[33]

One of the first and most influential community builders was Jessie Clyde Nichols. Born on a farm close to Kansas City, Kansas, Nichols attended the University of Kansas and later studied economics at Harvard. In 1900, Nichols took a trip to Europe, where he admired the beauty and grandeur of European cities. He saw no reason why cities in the United States could not be even more majestic than the cities of Europe. In 1905, Nichols began buying up land southwest of downtown Kansas City, where he intended to build and sell top-market residences.

Nichols was different from the typical small-time real estate operator, or "curbstoner," who bought a few small parcels of land on the edge of the city, divided them into lots, and hoped to make a speculative profit. Nichols believed in a scientific approach to land development. In a speech before a real estate convention in 1912, Nichols attracted national attention by criticizing those land developers who went for the fast sale and the quick profit. Instead, he advocated a long-term approach. He shocked his contemporaries by arguing that planning was not only compatible with private profit but could actually increase profits over the long run. As he later put it in a landmark article on suburban shopping centers, "good planning is good business."[34]

Nichols put his principles into practice by developing the Country Club District on the edge of Kansas City, considered by many at the time the most beautiful suburb in the nation. Nichols appealed to his wealthy clientele with extraordinary aesthetics—he modeled the suburb's shopping center, the first in the nation, on the architecture of Seville, Spain. Nichols also applied the latest in household technology, such as piped gas and electric service, in a period when servants were becoming less common. Nichols's suburban houses promised to provide a secure haven far from the stresses and tensions of city life. Husbands could go off to work in the city secure in the knowledge that their wives and children were safe in the idyllic environment of the Country Club District.

To shape his developments far into the future, Nichols devised the self-perpetuating deed restriction, which required owners to follow requirements laid down by the developer.[35] The deed restrictions specified minimum-lot sizes, minimum cost for houses, setbacks from the street, and even the color and style of houses. And the deeds specified that the houses could be bought by and sold to whites only.[36]

Nichols became a prominent national advocate for planned suburban development. He was a leader in the National Association of Real Estate Boards (NAREB), and in 1935 he founded the Urban Land Institute (ULI), which is influential in the housing industry to this day. In his lifetime, he saw the private planning he pioneered become public policy through local subdivision regulations, zoning laws, and federal loan guarantee programs.

Nichols's projects were limited to the upper classes. Privately planned suburban development became affordable to typical middle- and working-class families only after World War II. The Levitt family of Long Island in New York pioneered the production of standardized tract housing offered at the lowest possible price. In the late 1930s, Levitt & Sons succeeded as a medium-sized developer of plain tract housing for upper-middle-class families leaving New York City for Long Island, but the company's big break came during World War II, when it won contracts to build thousands of houses for the U.S. Navy around Norfolk, Virginia. It is here that the Levitts worked on the mass production techniques that revolutionized home building. Within a few years after the war, William J. Levitt, along with his father, Abraham, and his brother, Alfred, became the largest home builder in the United States.

Unlike Nichols, William Levitt drifted into building houses. Caring little for school, Levitt dropped out of New York University after his third year because, as he put it in a *Time* magazine cover story, "I got itchy. I wanted to make money. I wanted a big car and a lot of clothes."[37] In 1936, after he passed through several jobs, Levitt and his father decided to build a house on a Long Island lot they had been unable to sell. They made a profit. From this small beginning, Levitt launched his amazing career.

The Levitts quietly began buying up land from Long Island farmers and producing inexpensive homes by using assembly-line techniques. The basic method was to lay a concrete slab for a foundation, then place on it preassembled walls and a roof. The Levitts broke down the complex process of building a house into twenty-six operations, each of which was assigned to a separate contractor. Since each contractor did the same job over and over again, it was possible to achieve incredible speed.[38] Levitt avoided unions and used piecework incentives to speed the process even more.[39] At the Levitt lumberyard, one man was able to cut parts for ten houses in one day.[40] By 1950, the firm was producing one house every sixteen minutes.[41] By preassembling as many components as possible, Levitt reduced the amount of skilled labor necessary on the job site, and by purchasing directly from the manufacturers, he eliminated middlemen's fees. Overall, Levitt was able to cut costs on each house by about 17 percent, which meant that a typical house could be built for about $6,000 rather than the $7,000 it otherwise would have cost.[42]

Between 1947 and 1951, the Levitts converted 4,000 acres of potato farms in Hempstead, Long Island, into "the biggest private housing project in American history."[43] Ultimately housing 82,000 residents, Levittown, as it came to be known, became a huge success. Because of the huge pent-up demand for inexpensive housing following World War II, in the first years people lined up and camped out for days waiting to purchase one of the homes. The basic Cape Cod model sold for $7,990. With federal guarantees for the loan and no down payment required for veterans, an ex-GI could buy a Levitt house for only $56 a month.[44]

Like Nichols, Levitt believed that tight controls over buyers and their behavior were the best way to guarantee rising real estate values. Restrictive covenants required the grass to be cut each week (if not done, one of Levitt's men would cut it and send a bill) and disallowed fences (but allowed hedges). Laundry could not be hung out on a clothesline. In addition, the covenants barred tenants or homeowners from selling to or even allowing their property to be used by blacks. The standard lease for the first homes in Levittown, in which the tenant had an option to buy, contained this language: "The tenant agrees not to permit the premises to be used or occupied by any person other than members of the Caucasian race. But the employment and maintenance of other than Caucasian domestic servants shall be permitted."[45] Levitt argued that economic realities required him to recognize that "most whites prefer not to live in mixed communities,"[46] but clearly he was motivated by more than mere economics; he evicted two tenants who had allowed black children to play in their homes.[47] In 1960, not a single black family lived in Levittown,[48] and even thirty years later only about one-fourth of 1 percent of its residents were African American.[49]

In the mid-1950s, Levitt decided to build two more Levittowns, one in Pennsylvania and one in New Jersey. Opened in October 1958 and finished in 1965, Levittown, New Jersey, provided several new features. Fearing that an unfavorable image of sterile uniformity would damage sales, the company offered several house styles and floor plans. The idea of mixing styles was offered by William Levitt's wife and implemented by him over the objections of his executives.[50] Levitt did not offer changes from a standardized model to provide more aesthetically pleasing suburban residential areas. His motives were strictly economic; in order to sell houses, he needed to ensure that the houses would continue to be appealing to the aspiring middle class.

Levitt attracted purchasers by other means as well. Long-term financing with low monthly payments was made possible through the firm. He also offered his clientele a preselected community. His firm attempted to exclude people who did not conform to certain middle-class attributes. Prospective customers were screened, for example, by clothing and appearance. All homes were expressly designed for families with young children. Advertisements stressed that it was a planned community with schools, churches, swimming pools, and parks. In all of these respects, the Levitt company carefully selected the residents of its communities.

Levitt's fortunes began to change in 1968, when he sold his development company to the International Telephone and Telegraph Corporation (ITT) for $60 million in ITT stock. The stock, which he used as collateral for loans, plunged in value. Because of a clause in his sales contract, Levitt was forbidden to renew his building activities for ten years, except in cities where ITT had no interest. Levitt invested $20 million in a project in Iran, but the new government took it over after the 1979 revolution. In 1987, at the age of eighty, Levitt was forced to declare bankruptcy and was evicted from his New York City offices.[51]

The careers of Nichols and Levitt demonstrate the power of private developers in shaping the suburbs. Developers were more concerned with molding consumer tastes than anticipating them. Because developers were constrained to specialize, segregation on the basis of incomes and lifestyles was a natural result of subdivision development. These observations hold for contemporary suburbs as well. Whether a developer builds luxury single-family homes, townhouses for young middle-class home buyers, or condominiums for singles, the character of the community that results will have already been determined before the first person moves in. Buyers can choose their environment before they move, but once they have decided where they are going to live, they "are very largely prisoners of that environment with but little opportunity of changing it."[52]

Selling the American Dream

In the two decades after World War II, the suburban home, complete with a patio, barbecue grill, and a tree in the yard, occupied center stage in the American Dream. The suburban house was more than a physical structure; it was also the promised path to success. Most advertisements in the 1950s promised exclusion, social class segregation, and residential status. The idea of escaping the riff-raff of the city was often made explicit. Advertisements also made thinly veiled references to blacks; one developer, for example, urged potential buyers to "get out of the jungle" of the city.[53] But no theme became more well-worn than the appeal to instant success and status:

> Babylon—An early American Waterside Village—Recreated! For the person who has reached that position in life where they desire complete comfort and relaxation. . . . [54]

Birchwood Park, a Long Island suburb, promised that:

> When you settle at East Hempstead you are "on the right side of the tracks" in more ways than one. It's the hub of Long Island's most desirable residential section.

Another developer advertising in the same real estate section labeled one of his home models, "The Cadillac—Split Level Plus. . . . A most worthy addition to the 'Bluebloods of Distinctive Homes.'" For "living on a higher plane," said the builder, "you must get a 'Cadillac'!!"[55] Not to be outdone, another developer warned that his homes were not built for the "man in the street":

> The Cedar Hill Ranch Home, frankly, wasn't designed for the man in the street. There are many homes costing less that ably satisfy his needs. The size and appointments of Cedar Hill were fashioned for the family who considers anything less than the best inadequate. . . . Yes, Cedar Hill was definitely designed for the family accustomed to finer things.[56]

Starting in the late 1960s, some developers began to promote projects designed for clientele groups other than young, family-centered couples. Around many cities, and especially in Florida, Arizona, and southern California, developers began to construct condominiums and apartments for the growing market of retired and older adults. Naturally, suitable images were required to sell these projects. The following are typical:

> Jefferson Village: The first totally-electric condominium community for people 52 or over. Now that the children have moved out, is your house too large for you? Then consider the comfort of living in a full country apartment, provided for by a full staff of electric servants.[57]

Or,

> Retirement: Where you live it determines how you live it. The "second lifetime" of retirement can be a delight or a delusion. It often depends on where you decide to live it.[58]

A dramatic rise in the number of singles and childless couples in 1970s brought about a shift in marketing approaches. Anyone who has seen television ads for beer would surely anticipate that developers would soon turn to sex and companionship as a marketing standby:

> Your move—make it to Woodhollow—pick of the young professionals . . . great word association: Woodhollow and Young Professionals. Lawyers . . . nurses . . . teachers . . . engineers . . . anyone with success in mind.[59]

And,

> . . . for smart young pace setters who like being together . . . for professionals who enjoy being adult and young at the same time. It's Cypress Village, where you share much more in common with your neighbors."[60]

Here, the promise to fulfill "needs" for "a special kind of excitement" seems almost poignant, as if the developer is actually offering a dating service:

> Today's young people are constantly seeking to fill their needs, whether working, playing or relaxing with a special kind of excitement. The Village gives you the opportunity to fill these needs.[61]

But some developers thought all veiled references should be cast to the winds, in favor of a direct approach:

> A play pen for kids. Big Kids. It's our clubhouse. Top of the knoll. Sort of an adult playground. The kind of place you go with that certain someone. It's roomy and comfortable. A lounge for relaxing . . . cocktails and snapping logs in the fireplace. The games we play are rated M.[62]

Changing demographics brought a new look to the suburbs. In the 1950s and 1960s, virtually all suburbs were built for the standard-issue American family. Homebuyers who did not fit that profile were looked on with suspicion. The remaking of the suburbs required a reconsideration of the notion that all attached or multi-unit dwellings were fit for the cities but not for the suburbs.

The makeover required the cooperation of federal policy makers, financial institutions, and developers.

Enforcing Segregation

Through advertising, home styles, and sales and lending practices, builders, realtors, developers, and financial institutions encouraged racial, social class, and age segregation in the suburbs. They did not trust market forces to sort out various groups into distinct communities. The precedents for segregation enforced by law or the practices of the housing industry were established in the early nineteenth century, and by the time these practices were abandoned in the late 1970s, metropolitan land use patterns had become thoroughly segregated. At no time during all this period would it be accurate to say that the free market determined the patterns of residential segregation.

Beginning in the early twentieth century and continuing for half a century, restrictive covenants became the main instrument used by the real estate industry to enforce segregation. When a buyer purchased a house, the deed might come with a printed covenant that restricted its subsequent sale. Typically, blacks were the chief target, although sometimes Jews and "consumptives" (anyone with tuberculosis) might also be named. Restrictive covenants became, in effect, governmental policy when the supreme courts of fourteen states upheld their legality and ruled that they could be enforced in the courts.[63] It is estimated that restrictive covenants applied to homes sold in half of the subdivisions built in the United States before 1948, when the U.S. Supreme Court ruled that they could not be enforced in courts of law.[64]

The National Association of Real Estate Boards (NAREB) was established in 1908 to represent the interests of builders and real estate agents. From the beginning, the association set out to convince potential home buyers that real estate was a good investment. Builders and realtors accepted as a fundamental law of economics the principle that the value of property was connected to the homogeneity of neighborhoods. Based upon this premise, the NAREB "racialized" land use in urban areas by promoting the idea that whites and blacks must be strictly segregated.[65] From 1924 until 1950, Article 34 of the realtors' national code (circulated to realtors everywhere by the National Association of Real Estate Boards) read: "A Realtor should never be instrumental in introducing into a neighborhood a character of property or occupancy, members of any race or nationality, or any individual whose presence will clearly be detrimental to property values in the neighborhood."[66]

In addition, most local real estate boards were guided by written codes of ethics prohibiting members from introducing "detrimental" minorities into white neighborhoods. The textbooks and training materials used in real estate training courses were careful to point out that realtors were ethically bound to promote homogeneous neighborhoods. The leading textbook used in such courses in the 1940s compared some ethnic groups to termites eating away at sound structures:

> The tendency of certain racial and cultural groups to stick together, making it almost impossible to assimilate them in the normal social organism, is too well known to need

much comment. But in some cases the result is less detrimental than in others. The Germans, for example, are a clean and thrifty people. . . . Unfortunately this cannot be said of all the other nations which have sent their immigrants to our country. Some of them have brought standards and customs far below our own levels. . . . Like termites, they undermine the structure of any neighborhood into which they creep.[67]

Any realtor found breaking the code by selling to members of the wrong groups was subject to expulsion from the local real estate board and loss of license. Even brokers who were not affiliated with the national association felt compelled to accept the realtors' guidelines because most of their business depended on referrals.

In 1948, in the case of *Shelly v. Kraemer*, the U.S. Supreme Court ruled that racially restrictive covenants could not be enforced in the courts.[68] Realtors and developers sought a means of continuing their practice through other means. The device that eventually replaced restrictive covenants was the common interest development (CID), wherein residents not only own their own home but also share in the cost and maintenance of services and amenities held "in common" with other residents. After buying a condominium or home in a CID, the "community" of homeowners are legally bound by a variety of covenants, contracts, and restrictions (CC&Rs). Such rules can be used to enforce the homogeneity of neighborhoods even more effectively than restrictive covenants, with one principal exception—they cannot be used to explicitly sort out buyers on the basis of race, ethnicity, or gender.

The number of CIDs, which include cooperative apartments, condominiums, and single-family housing developments, exploded from fewer than 500 in 1964 to 10,000 by 1970 and to 150,000 by 1992, when 32 million Americans lived within them.[69] CIDs were concentrated especially in the Sunbelt, with California, Florida, and Texas leading the way. All through the Sunbelt, retired people moved in big numbers into gated communities. By 2000, it was estimated that 225,000 homeowner associations would be administering CIDs.[70] In many metropolitan areas, they have become so common that new home buyers who do not want to live in one may find their housing options to be severely limited.

In the 1940s and 1950s, developers were able to enforce income and social class segregation in the suburbs by building subdivisions of uniform lot sizes and housing cost. Suburbia was virtually synonymous with low-density tract housing, an equation that reflected the developers' success in marketing the suburbs as an escape from the cities. But by the 1960s, this version of the suburban dream began to yield lower profits. Builders found that the market for single houses constructed on individual lots was diminishing. Huge demographic and income groups, such as retirees and young singles and married couples without children, remained as vast untapped markets.

The constantly rising price of suburban land meant that developers could build lower-priced homes only if they could achieve much higher densities. Accordingly, the housing industry initiated a campaign to market a revised version of the suburban dream that would include row houses and apartment buildings. By the late 1960s, the American Society of Planning Officials, the Urban Land Institute, developers, and the Federal Housing Administration (FHA) became sudden critics of the "gridiron" housing tracts and large-lot, low-density development that they had promoted for so long. The CID idea anchored a campaign to convince local governments and consumers that higher-density development was compatible with the maintenance of property values and exclusion.[71]

For more than half a century, the housing industry peddled the idea that exclusion was synonymous with low-density development. It is interesting how fast the same principle was pressed into service on behalf of high-density development. In a report published in 1963, the Urban Land Institute pointed out that CIDs could achieve exclusion better than any alternative form of development: "Existing as private or semi-private areas they may exclude undesirable elements or trouble-makers drifting in."[72] The FHA agreed to insure loans for condominiums in multi-unit buildings in 1961. Two years later, the FHA released its first manual explicitly encouraging developers to build planned units that would be governed by homeowner associations. In 1964, the FHA and the Urban Land Institute copublished a 400-page volume describing the history of CIDs and setting forth detailed directions on how to establish CC&Rs and the homeowner associations to enforce them.[73]

Developers, mortgage lenders, and the federal government promoted CIDs as a way to stabilize land uses and property values. Since the early 1970s, the two biggest secondary mortgage purchasers, the Federal National Mortgage Association and the Federal Home Loan Corporation, have insisted on formulating and reviewing guidelines for residential associations before purchasing the loans on properties that will be governed by them. In only two decades, the institutional pressures applied by the housing industry and the federal government changed the face of the suburbs.

CIDs are generally referred to as "gated communities." For developers, the construction of physical walls and guard gates allows them to play up themes of security, seclusion, and exclusivity.[74] Developers establish the rules and regulations and set up the homeowners' association even before the first property is sold. In this way, even they are able to promise to buyers that all residents will follow closely prescribed norms of behavior and decorum. The covenants and restrictions enforced by residents' associations may dictate minimum and maximum ages of residents, hours and frequency of visitors, color of paint on a house, style and color of draperies hung in windows, size of pets and number of children (if either is allowed), parking rules, patios and landscaping—the list can be staggering in length and detail. Many CID residents no doubt find such regulations comforting. For others, the restrictions become intolerable, as evidenced by the high number of lawsuits filed against community associations.

Gated communities are planned as remarkably segregated environments. Some of them are developed and marketed to appeal to people on the basis of particular shared interests or life conditions. There are, for example, communities that exist exclusively for retirees, golfers, singles, even nudists. Green Valley, Nevada, a massive gated community just outside Las Vegas, is sectioned not only by different architectural styles, but by the cost and size of houses.[75] Each of these "villages" (as the developer calls them) carries the accoutrements of community: a name (Silver Springs or Valle Verde, for example), a community center, a school, a recreational center, and sometimes a park.[76] The segregation between this private city and the outside world is, in effect, embellished by layers of segregation within.

The new gated communities, like the walled cities of medieval Europe, are constructed to keep out those who are regarded as dangerous and different. The promotional literature promises exclusivity, security, and, very often, an extreme segregation. Here, for example, are two ads from an advertising supplement to the *New York Times Magazine:*

> The new Southwinds Ocean House offers apartments of 3,000 sq. ft. with all the advantages of a single family home. A resident manager and security gate ensure care-free living. You may laze by the pool/gazebo, exercise in the lap pool, or stroll the miles of sandy beaches at your doorstep.[77]

> Sailfish Point is an idyll celebrating your achievements. Its numbers add up to a lifestyle without compromise. . . . Jack Nicklaus designed our par 72 membership only golf course to stimulate and challenge but not intimidate. . . . Yachtsmen delight in our private sea-walled marina. . . . The St. Lucie Inlet puts boaters minutes from deep-sea fishing and blue-water sailing. . . . Natural seclusion and security are augmented by a guarded gate and 24-hour security patrols.[78]

Gated communities enforce a homogeneity that the housing market itself, if left to operate freely, might never achieve.

SUBURBAN GOVERNMENTS AND ZONING

A desire to escape the problems of urban life is not new; it has always been at the heart of urban development and suburbanization in the United States. Affluent citizens of the metropolitan community have never been content to let the market decide where people should live. The powers of local governments have long been used as exclusionary devices. Zoning has been the most frequently used and effective of these exclusionary tools. The history of zoning shows that it was born as an exclusionary instrument, and it became popular because it was a subtle, though effective, method of segregating on the basis of income and race. Through zoning, communities have been able to regulate the uses of land within their jurisdictions, making it difficult or impossible for less affluent people to cross community boundaries.

The nation's first zoning law was enacted in New York City on July 25, 1916. By the end of the 1920s, 768 municipalities with 60 percent of the nation's urban population had enacted zoning ordinances.[79] Quick adoption was made possible when real estate interests discovered what a useful tool zoning could be for protecting valuable land from uses deemed less desirable. As promoters of New York's ordinance explained it to audiences around the nation, "The small homeowner and the little shopkeeper were now protected against destructive uses next door. Land in the lower Fifth Avenue section, which had been a drag on the market when zoning arrived, was now undergoing so successful a residential improvement that rents were on the rise. 'Blighted districts are no longer produced in New York City.'"[80] The main claim made for zoning was that it kept land values high by segregating "better" from "inferior" land uses. In state after state, real estate groups and politicians lobbied for state laws enabling cities to zone their property.

New York City's zoning ordinance arose from the fears that fashionable sections of Fifth Avenue might be invaded by loft buildings from the Garment District on the West Side. Indeed, there was abundant evidence that such an invasion was likely to occur. From 1850 to 1900, New York's population increased from 661,000 to 3,437,000. Such growth rewarded speculators and entrepreneurs who had been discerning enough to predict the path of the city's expansion. But it was bothersome, too, for the upper-class residents who had repeatedly established themselves at the city's periphery, only to be pushed out again by encroaching waves of immigrants and businesses.

By the turn of the century, the upper class had established a mansion district and an exclusive shopping area on upper Fifth Avenue. They felt threatened by the teeming masses only a few blocks away. The Garment District, characterized by tall loft buildings in which thousands of poorly paid immigrant seamstresses and carters worked, threatened to destroy the exclusive shopping district. A way—a legal way—had to be found to protect Fifth Avenue, which was often described (by the rich) as the cultural fulcrum of New York, "a unique place" in "the traditions of this city and in the imagination of its citizens," "probably the most important thoroughfare in this city, perhaps any city in the New World," an area with a "history and associations rich in memories," "the common pride, of all citizens, rich and poor alike, their chief promenading avenue, and their principal shopping thoroughfare."[81] The Fifth Avenue Association, which employed lawyers to invent this kind of rhetoric, pleaded in 1916 that Fifth Avenue was a special area that should be protected from encroachment. Fifty-four years later, the rationale behind zoning had changed little: "We moved out here . . . to escape the city. I don't want the city following me here," explained a Long Island resident.[82]

Between 1913 and 1916, the Fifth Avenue Association, composed of wealthy retail merchants and landowners, lobbied to exclude tall loft buildings from their district. At first they tried to limit the height of buildings, but soon they hit on a more ambitious scheme. In 1916, the Buildings Heights Commission, first appointed in 1913 to investigate the problems of tall buildings in New York City, proposed carving Manhattan into distinct zoned areas to ensure a "place for everything and everything in its place."[83] According to the commission, "the purpose of zoning was to stabilize and protect lawful investment and not to injure assessed valuations or existing uses."[84]

New York's law specified five zones based on different uses and values of land. In the zoning pecking order, residential uses assumed first place, even though commercial and industrial land was often more valuable. Next in the hierarchy were commercial business districts, differentiated on the basis of building height (the higher the buildings, the lower the place in the zoning hierarchy). Warehouses and industries were allotted last place.

New York City officials set out to publicize their law, in part to ensure that it would be widely adopted before courts could challenge its constitutionality. "By the spring of 1918 New York had become a Mecca for pilgrimages of citizens and officials" who wanted to enact a similar ordinance. Within a year after passage of the legislation, more than twenty cities had initiated "one of the most remarkable legislative campaigns in American history."[85] Zoning was literally mass produced; most cities copied the New York ordinance and adopted it with few changes. Zoning soon became the chief weapon used by urban real estate interests to protect land prices. By 1924, the federal government had given zoning its seal of approval. A committee of the Department of Commerce drafted the Standard State Zoning Enabling Act, which served as a model zoning law for all the nation's cities.

In 1926, the U.S. Supreme Court reviewed a case from Ohio, *Village of Euclid v. Ambler Realty Co.*, and in a landmark decision declared that zoning was a proper use of the police power of municipal authority.[86] One interesting facet of the case revealed how zoning would be used in the future. Ambler Realty had purchased property in the village of Euclid in hopes that it would become valuable as commercial property. In 1922, the village zoned Ambler's property as residential, which had the effect of instantly lowering its market value. In bringing suit against the village, Ambler argued that Euclid's zoning law had lowered its property values without due process of law. In its decision, the court set forth a classic statement in defense of restrictive zoning, arguing that the presence of apartment, commercial, and industrial buildings undermined residential neighborhoods. There was an assumed hierarchy of uses, which the Court itself enunciated:

> With particular reference to apartment houses, it is pointed out that the development of detached house sections is greatly retarded by the coming of apartment houses . . . the coming of one apartment house is followed by others, interfering by their height and bulk with the free circulation of air and monopolizing the rays of the sun which otherwise would fall upon the smaller homes, and bringing, as their necessary accompaniments, the disturbing noises incident to increased traffic and business, and the occupation, by means of moving and parked automobiles, of larger portions of the streets, thus detracting from their safety and depriving children of the quiet and open spaces and play, enjoyed by those in more favored localities—until, finally the residential character of the neighborhood and its desirability as a place of detached residences is utterly destroyed.[87]

In its decision, the court ruled that separating residential from other land uses was a legitimate use of the city's police power to promote the order, safety, and well-being of its citizens.

Zoning became popular at the same time that well-to-do suburbs proliferated around the large cities—Beverly Hills, Glendale, and a multitude of other communities outside Los Angeles; Cleveland Heights, Shaker Heights, and Garfield Heights outside Cleveland; and Oak Park, Elmwood Park, and Park Ridge outside Chicago. It is easy to understand why such communities liked the zoning concept. The possibility that the poor might disperse throughout metropolitan areas threatened people living in exclusive neighborhoods, both in central cities and in suburbs. From its inception, zoning became the legal means to ensure what informal social class barriers or the housing market might not have been able to achieve—the exclusion of the inner-city Great Unwashed.

To accomplish this separation, restrictive residential zoning attempted to exclude apartments, to set minimum lot sizes, or to stop new construction altogether. Apartments in the suburbs represented the possibility of class, lifestyle, or racial changes. The residential character of a tree-lined, curved-street subdivision with individual homes set well back seemed to be threatened by apartment buildings. "We don't want this kind of trash in our neighborhood" was an attitude applied even to luxury apartments. Apartments symbolized the coming to suburbia of city problems:

> The apartment in general, and the high-rise apartment in particular, are seen as harbingers of urbanization, and their visibly higher densities appear to undermine the rationale for the development of the suburbs, which includes a reaction against the city and everything for which its stands. This is particularly significant, since the association is strong in suburbia between the visual characteristics of the city and what are perceived to be its social characteristics.[88]

The residents of many suburban communities became deeply concerned when apartment projects were proposed. For example, an executive living in Westport, an exclusive suburb in Connecticut, exclaimed, "Thank god we still have a system that rewards accomplishment, and that we can live in places where we want to live, without having apartments and the scum of the city pushed on us."[89] Most suburbs excluded the building of apartments entirely. In the 1970s, over 99 percent of undeveloped land zoned residential in the New York region excluded apartments.[90] Although this did not mean apartments could not be constructed, it did require apartment builders to secure zoning variances, which maximized the chances for opposition.[91]

Suburban governments also attempted, in effect, to regulate the social class and incomes of people who occupied single-family homes. Subdivision regulations and building codes made developers go through a costly review process that artificially increased the cost of new houses and gave local residents an opportunity to oppose new developments. But the most common device for raising the minimum cost of new construction was (and is) large-lot zoning. Sometimes the regulations requiring large lots also specified minimum floor-space requirements, the use of particular building materials, and minimum street setbacks. These kinds of regulations raised the cost for the home buyer, and thus helped protect an exclusive area.

Large-lot zoning is a device to keep out people with lower incomes. In some upper-class communities, this means keeping out the middle class; in some middle-class communities, it means excluding the working class. A defender of four-acre lot minimums in Greenwich, Connecticut, said that large-lot zoning is "just economics. It's like going into Tiffany and demanding a ring for $12.50. Tiffany doesn't have rings for $12.50. Well, Greenwich is like Tiffany." Large-lot zoning was defended by a New Jersey legislator as a means of making sure "that you can't buy a Cadillac at Chevrolet prices." An official of St. Louis County, where 90,000 acres were zoned for three-acre lots in 1965, indicated that his suburban county welcomed anyone "who had the economic capacity [to enjoy] the quality of life that we think our county represents . . . be they black or white."[92]

Exclusionary zoning often makes room for industrial and commercial investment that will provide more in taxes than it consumes in services. Of course, communities only want certain kinds of industry—industry that does not produce bothersome pollution and traffic. Sy Schulman, a Westchester County (New York) Planning Commissioner, wryly noted that the ideal industry "is a new campus-type headquarters that smells like Chanel No. 5, sounds like a Stradivarius, has the visual attributes of Sophia Loren, employs only executives with no children and produces items that can be transported away in white station wagons once a month."[93] Since the demand for such clean industry exceeds the supply, there is a fierce competition for it. As with other aspects of suburban development, it is the wealthier suburbs that usually win.

THE NATIONAL CHALLENGE TO EXCLUSIONARY ZONING

As a tool for creating and perpetuating exclusion and privilege, zoning went largely unchallenged in the state and federal courts for nearly half a century.[94] In the 1970s, it was challenged in the federal courts on the ground that it violated the equal protection clause of the Fourteenth Amendment to the U.S. Constitution. Zoning survived, but local governments learned that they could not be overly blatant about using it as a tool to preserve racial segregation. Black Jack, Missouri, found this out when the federal courts overturned their city's zoning ordinance after years of litigation.[95]

On June 5, 1970, the Federal Housing Administration (FHA) granted approval to a federally subsidized housing project to be built near the unincorporated Black Jack subdivision in St. Louis County, just north of the city of St. Louis. The project, to be sponsored by St. Mark's United Methodist Church of Florissant and the United Methodist Metro Ministry of St. Louis, was to contain 210 two- and three-story townhouses for middle-income residents. The application for federal funding stated that the project would fill a need in St. Louis County for integrated, moderately priced housing.

On hearing of the proposed project, the residents of the Black Jack area held neighborhood meetings, circulated petitions against the project, and contacted political figures, going so far as to send a delegation to Washington to present petitions to federal officials. They complained that the apartment project would overload their schools, crowd their highways, and threaten the value of their homes. Although cautious about saying so in Washington, the delegates and their constituents were mainly concerned that low-income blacks would move into their community. Before they learned to be wary of reporters, residents freely expressed racist sentiments in their first discussions of the housing project. After attending a Black Jack meeting in 1971, a *St. Louis Post-Dispatch* reporter wrote, "The most common statement we heard during the meeting in Black Jack was, 'We don't want those people, we don't want another Pruitt-Igoe in North St. Louis County.'"[96] Pruitt-Igoe was the nationally infamous public housing project built in St. Louis during the 1950s, noted for its crime, broken windows, and urine-stained hallways.

Black Jack residents perceived that they could keep blacks out if they incorporated their own suburban jurisdiction. As an unincorporated area of St. Louis

County, they were subject to the county's zoning laws, which made 67 acres available for apartment construction within the Black Jack area. In late June 1970, the Black Jack Improvement Association presented petitions to the St. Louis County Council requesting the incorporation of a new city, to be called Black Jack. The proposed boundaries were to include about 2,900 residents, most of them living in recently constructed middle-income housing tracts. On August 6, 1970, incorporation was approved by the county council, thus terminating the county's zoning authority and passing it to the new Black Jack City Council.

The county's decision to allow incorporation reveals much about the fears of Black Jack residents and of suburban residents elsewhere in St. Louis County. The Black Jack Improvement Association lobbied throughout the North County area, linking the fate of Black Jack with that of other communities. Allowing the project to be built, said the association, "could open the door to similar projects being located almost anywhere in the North County area. By stopping this project, you would lessen the chance of one perhaps appearing in your neighborhood."[97] In the face of overwhelming pressure, the county council decided to beat a retreat from a messy situation by approving incorporation, thus washing its hands of the whole issue.

The Black Jack incorporation ignited a national controversy over zoning. In September 1970, the Park View Heights Corporation (the nonprofit housing corporation formed by the original sponsors of the housing project) filed suit in federal court against the new city of Black Jack, alleging that both the city's incorporation and its proposed zoning ordinance constituted an attempt to use its zoning power to circumvent the Civil Rights Acts of 1866 and 1964, the National Housing Act of 1937, and the Fair Housing Act of 1968. In a brief hearing, Judge Roy W. Harper dismissed the suit, and on October 20, 1970, the Black Jack City Council adopted a zoning ordinance that excluded multi-unit residential buildings. Judge Harper's decision was appealed.

In the months following the Black Jack incorporation, it seemed unlikely that its zoning ordinance would be allowed to stand. Lawton, Oklahoma, southwest of Oklahoma City, had attempted to use its zoning ordinance to exclude apartments, but the federal appellate court for its circuit ruled that municipalities could not use zoning to exclude minorities or the poor unless they could show a nondiscriminatory intent concerning land-use objectives.[98] In the case of Black Jack, this would be extremely difficult. In April 1971, another case gave even more hope to proponents of suburban integration. The U.S. Court of Appeals for the Second Circuit rejected an attempt by the city officials of Lackawanna, New York, to block the building of a black housing subdivision in a white neighborhood.[99] Comments in the editorials of the *St. Louis Post-Dispatch* compared the Lackawanna suit favorably with the Black Jack suit: "The unanimous action indicates that local governments will have legal difficulties if they try to zone out Negroes from white areas. The Lackawanna decision clarifies the fact that misuse of political powers to keep out minority groups is unconstitutional."[100]

The Eighth Circuit Court of Appeals reversed Judge Harper's decision in September 1974. Surprisingly, the court threw out the argument that it was the *intent* of the Black Jack zoning ordinance to discriminate against blacks. The court did, however, rule that the ordinance had a discriminatory *effect*. This ruling seemed to pose the possibility that zoning laws all over the United States might be challenged. If zoning could be invalidated in every case where the courts found a discriminatory effect (as opposed to intent), few zoning laws would pass the test. In June 1975, the U.S. Supreme Court refused to review the circuit court's decision, thereby upholding it.

Just two years later, however, the Supreme Court backed away from this constitutional standard. In reviewing the zoning ordinance of Arlington Heights, Illinois, which barred a federally subsidized townhouse project from being built, the Court declared that the impact of zoning laws could not be used as the only argument against them; rather, they had to be shown to have been enacted with the intent to discriminate: "Disproportionate impact is not irrelevant, but it is not the sole touchstone of an invidious racial discrimination."[101] The Supreme Court had already made it much more difficult for litigants to challenge zoning ordinances by requiring them to show a "distinct and palpable injury."[102] By 1977, then, the courts had gotten out of the business of reviewing zoning laws, except in the rare case when a community was careless or overly blatant in applying them against blacks or other minorities.

The courts have consistently held that discrimination on the basis of income or class is not prohibited by the Constitution. If suburbs can show that their zoning laws are designed to protect the tax base and the exclusive residential character of the community, even though these discriminate against poor people, the laws will not be declared unconstitutional. In 1971, for example, the Supreme Court upheld an amendment to the California Constitution, passed in 1950, which required that low-rent housing could not be built without prior approval by a referendum of the voters of the city. While clearly biased against those seeking low-income housing, the Court ruled that discrimination on the basis of income was not unconstitutional under the equal protection clause of the Fourteenth Amendment.[103] In the intervening years, that court ruling has stood the test of time.

THE COSTS OF EXCLUSION

For affluent people, the benefits of residential segregation have been substantial. Those living in suburbs with high property values and plenty of business investment have been able to pay lower taxes but at the same time enjoy higher levels of public services than the residents of poorer municipalities. In the past, central cities were consistently disadvantaged in comparison to suburbs, even though there were substantial differences among the suburbs as well, with the older suburbs bordering the central cities generally being at the bottom. In the past, the central cities became "the receptacle for all the functions the suburbs [did] not care to support."[104] Now that the problems formerly associated with central cities have moved to many suburbs, wealthier suburbs are likely to become even more militant about trying to preserve their privilege.

The differences between the poorest and wealthiest suburbs are much greater than the differences between any central city and its suburbs. African Americans have been systematically disadvantaged because they reside within poorer jurisdictions. A study of Philadelphia's suburbs for the period 1977 to 1982 found that predominantly black suburbs had a per capita tax base that was 30 percent less than the average for white and mixed suburbs; in addition, municipal debt per capita in Philadelphia's black suburbs was almost twice that in mixed and white suburbs. In general, predominantly black suburbs tended to have lower tax bases, higher debts, poorer municipal services, lower socioeconomic status, and higher population densities than suburbs that housed white families.[105] A 1990 study of 374 suburbs in the New York metropolitan area found that blacks and Latinos of the same socioeconomic class as non-Latino whites typically lived in suburbs that had less tax wealth, lower rates of home ownership, and higher property crime rates.[106]

The wealth differences among suburbs translates into fiscal differences as well. In 1997, among the ninety-two municipalities in St. Louis County, Missouri, the mean (average) assessed (not actual) value of homes in the six richest suburbs (measured by household income) was $48,828. None of these suburbs had more than 1 percent black population. In the same year, the thirteen poorest suburbs had average assessed values of less than one-tenth that level; all were overwhelmingly black except one, which had a 40 percent black population.[107] Differences in the ability to raise taxes affects the ability of these municipalities to provide public services and amenities. In Wellston, one of the poorest suburbs, streets are potholed, curbs are missing or broken, and street signs are frequently missing. Clayton, the county seat, provides a stark contrast. It is able to collect taxes not only on homes but also on a booming business district. In the last few years it has replaced cement curbing with granite, maintained landscaped street medians, and paid for a trash service that manually picks up behind all homes. It is not difficult to understand why suburbs like Clayton fought hard several years ago against a proposal to consolidate municipalities in the county.

The differences between suburbs are widening.[108] Since the suburban boom following World War II there have been working-class, middle-class, and upper-class suburbs—for example, Levittown was a middle-class bastion on Long Island, but it remained worlds apart from the wealthier enclaves only a few miles away. In the last few years, many suburbs—especially those built between 1945 and 1970—have been undergoing rapid change. Middle- and working-class suburban homes built during this period tended to be small tract homes or bungalows that lacked the amenities and conveniences expected today.[109] They tend to be located in suburbs with low housing prices and a low level of public services. Though some of these suburbs are close to the central cities, others are sprinkled among more affluent suburbs farther out.[110]

Poor people and recent immigrants find it easier to find housing in older suburbs because of low market demand for less desirable housing. For example, the 1950s-era suburbs of Long Island, including Levittown, are attracting thousands of immigrants from the Middle East, Central and Latin America, and

Asia.[111] Some families crowd illegally into homes, and their children flood into local schools that lack the resources to properly educate them. They are hidden from the larger society in part because they are walled off into municipalities that have few resources—and therefore they are unable to make effective claims on the political system. As one scholar has asked: "Suburbs are now becoming—albeit not always willingly—multiclass, multiethnic, and multiracial. . . . Can older suburbs accommodate these new ethnic groups, or will outmoded, decentralized government structures and prejudice keep them hidden *baja del agua*—underwater?"[112]

Defenders of segregation in metropolitan areas—and there are many—argue that the differences between residential areas merely reflect people's choices.[113] Some have even argued that the fragmentation of urban areas into a multitude of suburbs is a good thing because it creates a "marketplace" of residential choices, so that people can choose a bundle of services and amenities depending upon what they can afford.[114] Such arguments carry great weight in a culture devoted to privatism and the market ideal. Those who would intervene to change the fragmented governmental system of metropolitan areas must fight an uphill battle. Because affluent suburban residents benefit from the present system, they will fight to protect it. When wealthier residents are able to isolate themselves within a governmental jurisdiction, with modest tax efforts they are able to support superior schools and other governmental services that make one area a more desirable place than another. It would be impossible for the fragmentation of governments to persist in metropolitan areas if it worked to the disadvantage of wealthier, politically influential people.

NOTES

1. U.S. Bureau of the Census, Census of Governments, Preliminary Report No. 1, 2002, Table A, p. 5.
2. Kenneth Newton, "American Urban Politics: Social Class, Political Structure, and Public Goods," in *Readings in Urban Politics: Past, Present and Future*, 2nd ed., ed. Harlan Hahn and Charles H. Levine (New York: Longman, 1984).
3. Sidney Plotkin, "Community and Alienation: Enclave Consciousness and Urban Movements," in *Breaking Chains: Social Movements and Collective Action*, vol. 3, *Comparative Urban and Community Research*, ed. Michael Peter Smith (New Brunswick, N.J.: Transaction Publishers, 1991), pp. 5–26.
4. Quoted in Ronald Sullivan, "Jersey's Zoning Laws Are Upset," *New York Times*, March 25, 1975.
5. Sam Bass Warner, *Streetcar Suburbs: The Process of Growth in Boston, 1870–1900* (Cambridge, Mass.: Harvard University Press, 1962), pp. 164–165.
6. Data cited in Robert C. Wood, *Suburbia: Its People and Their Politics* (Boston: Houghton Mifflin, 1958), p. 69, and in National Municipal League, Committee on Metropolitan Government, *The Government of Metropolitan Areas in the United States*, prepared by Paul Studenski with the assistance of the Committee on Metropolitan Government (New York: National Municipal League, 1930), p. 26.
7. Robert Park, Ernest W. Burgess, and Roderick D. McKenzie, *The City* (Chicago: University of Chicago Press, 1925), p. 109.

8. Joseph F. Sullivan, "Restless Seeker for Justice," *New York Times,* January 22, 1983; Anthony DePalma, "N.J. Housing Woes Are All Over the Map," *New York Times,* April 17, 1983.

9. Robert Hanley, "After 7 Years, Town Remains Under Fire for Its Zoning Code," *New York Times,* January 22, 1983.

10. Robert Hanley, "Some Jersey Towns, Yielding to Courts, Let in Modest Homes," *New York Times,* February 29, 1984.

11. 1985 N.J. Sess. Law Serv. 222 (West).

12. Anthony DePalma, "Subsidized Housing Hurt in Ailing Market," *New York Times,* May 15, 1990.

13. Ibid.

14. Quoted in Peter J. Schmitt, *Back to Nature: The Arcadian Myth in Urban America* (New York: Oxford University Press, 1969), p. 180; original quotation found in Ernest Groves, "The Urban Complex," *Sociological Review* 12 (Fall 1920): 74, 76.

15. A more complete list of titles can be found in Schmitt, *Back to Nature,* pp. 180–182.

16. Editorial, (New York) *Independent,* February 27, 1902, p. 52.

17. Weldon Fawcett, "Suburban Life in America," *Cosmopolitan* (July 1903): 309.

18. Advertisement in *Country Life in America* (November 1906): 3.

19. Advertisement in *Country Life in America* (March 1908): 474.

20. See Anwar Syed, *The Political Theory of American Local Government* (Clinton, Mass.: Random House, 1966).

21. Jon C. Teaford, *City and Suburb: The Political Fragmentation of Metropolitan America, 1850–1970* (Baltimore: Johns Hopkins University Press, 1979), p. 6.

22. Ibid., p. 31.

23. Gary J. Miller, *Cities by Contract: The Politics of Municipal Incorporation* (Cambridge, Mass.: MIT Press, 1981), p. 12.

24. Ibid.

25. Teaford, *City and Suburb,* p. 18.

26. C. B. Glasscock, *Lucky Baldwin: The Story of an Unconventional Success* (Indianapolis, Ind.: Bobbs-Merrill, 1933), p. 140.

27. Teaford, *City and Suburb,* pp. 18–19.

28. Charles Hoch, "City Limits: Municipal Boundary Formation and Class Segregation," in *Marxism and the Metropolis: New Perspectives in Urban Political Economy,* 2nd ed., ed. William K. Tabb and Larry Sawers (New York: Oxford University Press, 1984), pp. 101–119.

29. Miller, *Cities by Contract,* pp. 49–50. Another good example of an industrial suburb is Teterboro, New Jersey, which in 1977 had only 24 residents but employed 24,000 nonresidents. Michael N. Danielson and Jameson W. Doig, *New York: The Politics of Urban Regional Development* (Berkeley: University of California Press, 1982), p. 92.

30. Ann R. Markusen, "Class and Urban Social Expenditure: A Marxist Theory of Metropolitan Government," in *Marxism and the Metropolis: New Perspectives in Urban Political Economy,* 2nd ed., ed. William K. Tabb and Larry Sawers (New York: Oxford University Press, 1984), p. 92. The American system contrasts with that of Britain, where the central government retained control over the organization of local government. "English law did not allow every race track promoter, tax evading industrialist, or community of teetotalers to create its own community." Teaford, *City and Suburb,* p. 70.

31. Robert C. Wood, "Suburban Politics and Policies: Retrospect and Prospect," *Publius, The Journal of Federalism* (Winter 1975): 51.

32. See Mark Gottdiener, *Planned Sprawl: Private and Public Interests in Suburbia* (Beverly Hills, Calif.: Sage, 1977).

33. The term is taken from Mark Weiss, *The Rise of the Community Builders* (New York: Columbia University Press, 1987).

34. J. C. Nichols, "The Planning and Control of Outlying Shopping Center," *Journal of Land and Public Utility Economics* 2 (January 1926): 22. By concentrating in one location and using leasing policy to determine store "mix," "Nichols created the idea of the planned

regional shopping center," Kenneth T. Jackson, *Crabgrass Frontier: The Suburbanization of the United States* (New York: Oxford University Press, 1985), p. 258.

35. Gwendolyn Wright, *Building the Dream: A Social History of Housing in America* (Cambridge, Mass.: MIT Press, 1981), p. 202.

36. Mark H. Rose, "'There Is Less Smoke in the District,' J. C. Nichols, Urban Change and Technological Systems," *Journal of the West* (January 1986): 48. Rose adds, "As late as 1917, no more than five Jewish families resided in the district, the result of resales."

37. "Up from the Potato Fields," *Time,* July 3, 1950, p. 70.

38. Ibid.

39. "The Most House for the Money," *Fortune* (October 1952): 156.

40. Jackson, *Crabgrass Frontier,* p. 234.

41. Wright, *Building the Dream,* p. 252.

42. "Up from the Potato Fields," p. 68.

43. Jackson, *Crabgrass Frontier,* p. 234.

44. "Up from the Potato Fields," p. 68.

45. Bruce Lambert, "Levittown Anniversary Stirs Memories of Bias," *New York Times,* December 28, 1997, 14.

46. Quoted in Herbert Gans, *The Levittowners: Ways of Life and Politics in a Suburban Community,* (New York: Pantheon, 1967, p. 372.

47. Lambert, "Levittown Anniversary," p. 14.

48. Jackson, *Crabgrass Frontier,* p. 241.

49. Lambert, "Levittown Anniversary," p. 14.

50. Gans, *The Levittowners,* pp. 8–9.

51. Joe R. Feagin and Robert Parker, *Building American Cities: The Urban Real Estate Game,* 2nd ed. (Englewood Cliffs, N.J.: Prentice-Hall, 1990), p. 211.

52. Robert Goldston, *Suburbia: Civic Denial* (New York: Macmillan, 1970), p. 68.

53. Ibid.

54. *New York Times,* March 22, 1953.

55. Ibid.

56. *New York Times,* October 26, 1952; emphasis in the original.

57. *New York Times,* May 26, 1968.

58. Ibid.

59. *St. Louis Post-Dispatch,* April 16, 1972.

60. *St. Louis Post-Dispatch,* August 18, 1974.

61. *St. Louis Post-Dispatch,* July 5, 1970.

62. Ibid.

63. Kevin Fox Gotham, *Race, Real Estate, and Uneven Development: The Kansas City Experience, 1900-2000* (Albany: State University of New York Press, 2002), p. 38.

64. Ibid.

65. Ibid., pp. 34–37.

66. National Association of Real Estate Boards, *Code of Ethics* (1924), art. 34 (Washington, D.C.: author).

67. Harry Grant Atkinson and L. E. Frailey, *Fundamentals of Real Estate Practice* (Englewood Cliffs, N.J.: Prentice-Hall, 1946), p. 34, quoted in Evan McKenzie, *Privatopia: Homeowner Associations and the Rise of Residential Private Government* (New Haven, Conn.: Yale University Press, 1994), pp. 61–62.

68. *Shelly v. Kraemer,* 334 U.S. 1 (1948). The Court had struck down racial zoning some thirty years earlier in *Buchanan v. Warley,* 245 U.S. 60 (1917).

69. Evan McKenzie, *Privatopia,* p. 11.

70. Ibid.

71. McKenzie, *Privatopia,* pp. 158–164.

72. Ibid., p. 158.

73. Ibid., pp. 163–164.

74. Dennis R. Judd, "The Rise of the New Walled Cities," in Helen Liggett and David C. Perry, ed., *Spatial Practices* (Thousand Oaks, Calif.: Sage, 1995), pp. 144–166.

75. David Guterson, "No Place Like Home: On the Manicured Streets of a Master-planned Community," *Harper's* (November 1992): 55–64.

76. Ibid., pp. 60–61.

77. From a *New York Times* advertising supplement, November 18, 1990, p. 13.

78. Ibid.

79. Seymour I. Toll, *Zoned America* (New York: Grossman, 1969), p. 193.

80. Ibid., p. 197.

81. Ibid., p. 159.

82. Quoted in Michael N. Danielson, *The Politics of Exclusion* (New York: Columbia University Press, 1976), p. 54.

83. Toll, *Zoned America*, p. 183.

84. Ibid., pp. 182–183.

85. Ibid., p. 187.

86. *Police power* refers to the implied powers of government to adopt and enforce laws necessary for preserving and protecting the immediate health and welfare of citizens. The meaning of this is, of course, subject to a wide variety of interpretations.

87. *Village of Euclid v. Ambler Realty Co.*, 272 U.S. 365, 47 S.Ct. 114, 71 L. Ed. 303 (1926).

88. Danielson, *The Politics of Exclusion*, pp. 53–54.

89. "The End of the Exurban Dream," *New York Times*, December 13, 1976.

90. Danielson, *The Politics of Exclusion*, p. 53.

91. Because of the fears concerning apartment developments, the planning process involving their construction was complicated, requiring petitions for zoning variances, public hearings, and lengthy review proceedings. For an excellent account of these complexities, see Daniel R. Mandelker, *The Zoning Dilemma: A Legal Strategy for Urban Change* (Indianapolis, Ind.: Bobbs-Merrill, 1971).

92. Quoted in Danielson, *The Politics of Exclusion*, p. 60.

93. Quoted in Merrill Folson, "Westchester Finds Influx of Business a Worry," *New York Times*, April 18, 1967; cited in Danielson and Doig, *New York*, p. 90.

94. A detailed discussion of the legal status of zoning is not included in this section. For further information, the following sources are especially useful: Danielson, *The Politics of Exclusion*; Richard F. Babcock, *The Zoning Game* (Madison: University of Wisconsin Press, 1969); Richard F. Babcock and Fred P. Bosselman, *Exclusionary Zoning: Land Use Regulation and Housing in the 1970s* (New York: Praeger, 1973); Daniel R. Mandelker, *Managing Our Urban Environment* (Indianapolis, Ind.: Bobbs-Merrill, 1971); Randall W. Scott, ed., *Management and Control of Growth*, vol. 1 (New York: Urban Land Institute, 1975); and David Listokin, ed., *Land Use Controls Present Problems and Future Reform* (New Brunswick, N.J.: Center for Urban Policy Research, Rutgers University, 1975).

95. This account draws on many sources, including articles in the *St. Louis Globe-Democrat* and *St. Louis Post-Dispatch*; Donald F. Kirby, Frank deLeeuw, and William Silverman, *Residential Zoning and Equal Housing Opportunities: A Case Study in Black Jack, Missouri* (Washington, D.C.: Urban Institute, 1972); *Park View Heights Corp. v. City of Black Jack*, 467 F.2d (1972), reversing: 335 F.Supp. 899 (1971); *U.S. v. City of Black Jack*, Civ. Action No. 71; "Confrontation in Black Jack," in *Land-Use Controls Annual* (Chicago: American Society of Planning Officials, 1972); Danielson, *The Politics of Exclusion*.

96. Jack Quigley, *St. Louis Post-Dispatch*, June 15, 1971.

97. Quoted in William K. Reilly, ed., *The Use of Land: A Citizen's Guide for Urban Growth* (New York: Crowell, 1973), p. 90.

98. *Dailey v. City of Lawton*, 425 F.2d 1037 (1970).

99. *Kennedy Park Homes v. City of Lackawanna*, 436 F.2d 108 (1971).

100. Editorial, *St. Louis Post-Dispatch*, April 5, 1971.

101. Quoted in *St. Louis Globe-Democrat*, January 11, 1977.
102. In 1975, the Supreme Court made it more difficult to challenge exclusionary zoning in federal courts by "refusing standing"—dismissing a case on the grounds that the plaintiffs had no right to sue. Those who want to challenge an exclusionary ordinance must prove "distinct and palpable injury"; a suit cannot be based on general injury to those who do not live in the town but want to live there; see *Warth v. Seldin*, 442 U.S. 490, 1975.
103. See *James v. Valtierra*, 91 S.Ct. 133 (1971), and *Shaffer v. Valtierra*, 402 U.S. 137 (1971).
104. Wood, *Suburbia*, p. 106.
105. For citations to this and a substantial quantity of additional literature, see Douglas S. Massey and Nancy A. Denton, "Suburbanization and Segregation in U.S. Metropolitan Areas," *American Journal of Sociology* 94, no. 3 (November 1988): 592–626.
106. John Logan and Richard Alba, "Locational Return to Human Capital," unpublished manuscript, State University of New York at Albany (April 1990).
107. St. Louis County Department of Planning, *2000 Census Data for St. Louis County: General Population Characteristics (A Supplement to the St. Louis County, Missouri, 1998 Fact Book)* (St. Louis, Mo.: St. Louis County Department of Planning, December 2001), pp. 11–12 and 120–122.
108. Peter Dreier, John Mollenkopf, and Todd Swanstrom, *Place Matters: Metropolitics for the Twenty-first Century* (Lawrence: University Press of Kansas, 2001), p. 41.
109. Ibid., pp. 42–43.
110. Ibid.
111. Rosalyn Baxandall and Elizabeth Ewen, *Picture Windows: How the Suburbs Happened* (New York: Perseus Books, 2000), 239.
112. Ibid. p. 250.
113. Dreier, Mollenkopf, and Swanstrom, *Place Matters*, pp. 94–95.
114. For example, Vincent Ostrom, Charles Tiebout, and Roland Warren, "The Organization of Government in Metropolitan Areas," *American Political Science Review* 55 (1961), pp. 835–842; and Mark Schneider, *The Competitive City: The Political Economy of Suburbia* (Pittsburgh: University of Pittsburgh Press, 1989).

CHAPTER
11

URBAN SPRAWL
AND REGIONAL
GOVERNANCE

THE SPRAWLED METROPOLIS

Population movement outward from the urban core is a feature of urban development all over the world. With transportation breakthroughs such as automated rail systems and the automobile, urban areas in the advanced Western countries have been spreading out for at least a century.[1] There are, however, several characteristics that set the experience in the United States apart. Virtually all of America's metropolitan areas contain vast tracts of detached, single-family homes with large yards. No other nation matches the United States in the degree of urban sprawl—even in Canada, for example, which has experienced extensive suburban development, population densities in 1985 were about twice that of American cities.[2]

In the United States, cheap energy and subsidies for automobile use made long commutes affordable. Americans drive farther to work than people in other countries, and commuting distances have steadily increased.[3] In 1996, gas taxes were $2.31 in Great Britain, more than $3 in France, 84 cents in Canada, but only 42 cents in the United States.[4] Nearly all gas taxes collected in the United States were spent on highways and roads, but in Europe a higher share of motorists' taxes were used to support mass transit.[5] Housing policies also supported low-density development in the United States; tax write-offs of interest, real estate deductions on federal income taxes, and other subsidies encouraged homeowners to move frequently and into larger homes.[6] The Tax Reduction Act of 2001 added to these benefits by eliminating taxes on capital gains on homes for all home owners.

The old urban form, which found a big city surrounded by rank on rank of spreading suburbs, has given way to a new urban form in which "the periphery [is] no longer a subordinate dependent of the center and thus no longer a candidate for the prefix *sub*."[7] The age of suburbia has given way to *post-suburbia*, a metropolitan form characterized by many nodes of activity.[8] On any given day, the members of an urban family might commute, shop, and play by going in any conceivable direction from their home. Even at the very edge of an urban area, a new office park or shopping center might spring up, with every service and amenity—even a Starbucks—that may be found everywhere else. In short, the old concepts of center and periphery have lost much of their meaning.

The sprawled metropolis has spawned a set of chronic and sometimes vexing problems. For most suburban residents (the term *postsuburban* is suggestive, but seems awkward, so it will not be used here), traffic congestion and gridlock are the most irritating consequences of sprawl, followed by a concern about the sheer ugliness of uncontrolled development. But there are other problems as well. Air pollution, the loss of open space and farmland, and a host of other environmental consequences have accompanied sprawl. Though it does not generally register on the radar of most suburban residents, the decline and abandonment of older neighborhoods necessarily accompanies the relentless spread to the edge. In most European countries, the urban core has remained healthy precisely because sprawl is kept in check.

In the late 1990s, urban sprawl blossomed as an important issue. Scholars, environmentalists, and advocates of the central cities had been trying to sound the alarm for decades, but mostly they played to a deaf audience. Only rarely did the public seem to care about the incredible pace at which new housing subdivisions gobbled up farmland, forest, and open space. Suburbia, after all, seemed to express the American Dream of prosperity and progress. Critics such as the urban specialist Neal Peirce called Americans "the champion land hogs of history" because the country's urban areas were growing in land area at a rate four to eight times faster than the growth of the national population. The cost of sprawl, he said, was "frightening" because it brought "despair in the inner cities, environmental degradation, undermining of old neighborhoods and suburbs."[9] For a long time, such critics were generally ignored or even greeted with derision, like the deranged prophets carrying signs with the inscription, "The end is near!" Late in the twentieth century, however, several events caused the public to begin to heed some of the alarums.

THE CONCERNS ABOUT SPRAWL

For sprawl to emerge onto the political agenda, large segments of the public had to experience some of its negative effects firsthand and close up. That began to happen when highway congestion increased to the point that the daily commute ceased to be a mere inconvenience and a headache and began to become a nightmare. In November 1999, *USA Today*, in a special report on "National Gridlock," offered up one horror story after another. The average commuter's daily experience seemed to be summed up by a Chicago driver's description of a bottleneck called "the Strangler": "It's not even a traffic jam. It's my enemy. It's my daytime bad dream."[10] In 2001, the knot of off-ramps that made up the Strangler were finally eliminated, but other gridlocked spots were sure to take its place.

OUT TAKE

THE COSTS OF SPRAWL ARE HOTLY DEBATED

The term *urban sprawl* is often used loosely to refer to low-density residential development at the periphery of urban areas. One leading study published in 1974 defined it as residential density of two dwellings per acre, but a late 1980s study and another conducted by the Environmental Protection Agency in the early 1990s defined it as residential density of three dwellings per acre or less.[11] By such a definition, sprawl is rare in Europe and Asia, where land is more scarce than in the United States and where land-use controls are the norm. In such contexts, urban areas may be expanding outward, but not in such a way as to create the social and political dynamic that characterizes sprawl in the United States: low-density development at the edge of metropolitan regions that consumes huge tracts of land and entails the abandonment of older areas at the urban core.

Because densities are generally low in the suburbs, land is gobbled up at a rate all out of proportion to the population growth of urban regions—indeed, sprawl occurs even in metropolitan areas with steady-state or declining populations! For example, though the New York region's population grew by only 5 percent between 1964 and 1989, the amount of developed land increased by 61 percent.[12] Similarly, from 1950 to 1995 the population of the St. Louis region increased by just 35 percent, but the area of developed land exploded by more than 10 times that much, 355 percent.[13] Though there were significant variations among urban regions, most of them continued to sprawl outward all through the 1990s, with no end in sight.[14]

Why does land disappear so fast even in slow-growth urban regions? First, families have become smaller and smaller in recent decades because of the increasing number of single-parent families, childless and unmarried couples, and singles. The decline of the "typical" suburban family requires more dwellings for a given population size and makes many of the single-family houses built only a couple of decades ago obsolete. Second, and despite the declining size of the average family, the size of homes has steadily increased in step with a desire for more luxuries and amenities. And third, when people move within metropolitan areas, they tend to leave high-density neighborhoods nearer the urban core for lower-density subdivisions farther out; only a small percentage move in the other direction. In a study conducted in the early 1990s, more than two-thirds of respondents said that they preferred to live in low-density, single-family neighborhoods than in denser neighborhoods closer to the central city.[15]

Urban sprawl is associated with a wide variety of serious problems. First, it is more expensive to supply most infrastructure—new highways, streets, and bridges; schools; sewer and water systems; street lighting; gas, electric, and telephone hookups; libraries and parks—to low-density areas. A comprehensive review of several studies comparing high with low-density development concluded that infrastructure development was consistently more expensive in low-density areas.[16]

Second, sprawl has brought with it the decline of the central cities and the abandonment of neighborhoods in the cities and older suburbs. The concentration of poverty, racial and ethnic segregation, and physical dilapidation at the urban core contrasts sharply with more affluent, newer suburban housing developments and edge cities. The location of new development imposes social as well as environmental costs. The authors of a detailed study of the public and social costs of building an electrical plant in the central city or suburbs in the Chicago metropolitan area concluded that the suburban plant would bring more traffic congestion, traffic accidents, loss of open space, loss of jobs for low-wage workers, a loss of value for existing homes, and less return for local governments than a central-city plant. In return for these social costs, virtually all the benefits of a suburban location would flow to businesses located there.[17]

Finally, sprawl is associated with numerous environmental problems. Thousands of acres of farmland, wetlands, and open space disappear each year. Runoff from highways, parking lots, and lawns pollutes streams and rivers; auto and truck traffic spews ozone-depleting and greenhouse gases into the atmosphere. Excess energy consumption and air pollution are implicated in global environmental problems. Urban residents in the United States consumed about four times as much gasoline per capita as did urban residents in Europe in 1990.[18] Urban sprawl was the basic reason for this difference. It is instructive to note that in the late 1980s, annual consumption in sprawled-out Houston was 567 gallons per person, compared to 335 gallons in New York City, where high population density facilitated the use of mass transit. (In Manhattan, gasoline consumption was only 90 gallons per person.)[19] In 1999, drivers in the U.S. wasted 6.8 billion gallons of fuel in traffic jams, where they spent approximately 40 percent of their driving time.[20]

The United States consumes an extraordinarily high percentage of the world's energy and produces a disproportionate share of the world's pollution. In 1990, with 5 percent of the world's population, the United States produced an estimated 25 percent of the carbon dioxide emissions in the world,[21] a principal cause of the greenhouse effect. High energy consumption in the United States is not due solely to a prosperous economy. European countries that are as prosperous as the United States consumed far less energy per capita in 1980, even before the latest wave of sprawl.[22] Unplanned urban sprawl and an overwhelming reliance on the automobile and truck are major causes of high energy consumption and air pollution. In 1994, forty-two metropolitan areas failed to meet national ambient air quality standards for ozone.[23]

The evidence that urban sprawl requires a greater amount of energy and other resources, and therefore imposes greater environmental costs than denser development, does not settle the issue. Conservatives defend sprawl as a logical outcome of prosperity and the American Dream, "an expression of the upward mobility and growth in home-ownership generated by our past half-century of economic success."[24] Even when they admit there are costs, they also assert that there are distinct advantages—otherwise, why would so many people move to the suburbs at all?

If commuters think that urban highways have become more crowded in the last few years, they are right. In the 1970s there were 61 yards of roadway per vehicle in the United States, but by 1986 this space had shrunk by more than one-third, to 39 yards.[25] The number of vehicles on the roads has increased dramatically. Trucks by the dozen fill rear-view mirrors because they have substantially eclipsed trains for the movement of goods. The number of licensed drivers jumped 65 percent between 1970 and 1997, but registered vehicles increased even more, by 87 percent. Demographic changes accounted for the higher traffic volumes. Though the U.S. population only rose by 32 percent between 1970 and 1997, the number of women in the workplace jumped by 240 percent.[26] As more women entered the workforce and recreational vehicles joined the family car in the garage, two-and three-car families became the norm.

At the same time, cross-commuting gradually replaced trips to the center. Even by 1980, before sprawl reached its current dimensions, over 40 percent of all work trips were suburb to suburb, and only 20 percent were from suburb to the central city in the average metropolitan region.[27] Reverse commuting—travel by central city residents to jobs in edge cities or elsewhere in the suburbs—also increased.[28] Urban transportation networks are most efficient when they link nodes of dense development. It may be impossible to construct transportation systems at acceptable cost when travelers are criss-crossing everywhere while traffic volume increases, and so gridlock is inevitable.

Traffic engineers define traffic congestion as an average flow below 35 miles per hour. In the decade from 1975 to 1985, the percentage of urban traffic that could thus be classified increased from 41 percent to 56 percent[29]—and this was before the incredible traffic volume of the 1990s. In the fifteen years leading up to 1997, congestion on America's roadways grew by 235 percent. What does this mean for the average commuter? By 1998 a typical suburban motorist could expect to spend almost an hour and a half a day commuting.[30] The percent of time spent in traffic backups increased from 23 percent in 1983 to 40 percent in 1999, and drivers were delayed three times as long at the end of that 16-year period.[31] Can it occasion any surprise that incidents of road rage have become a widespread public concern, prompting many state legislatures to enact road rage legislation?

In the first six months of 2000 and again in 2003, rising gasoline prices made long commutes an even more pressing issue when prices for a gallon of regular unleaded ratcheted to close to two dollars. Though most people preferred to blame such factors as unrest in Venezuela, or regulations requiring cleaner-burning gasoline, they were themselves responsible for creating the mismatch between demand and supply. Because of the growing popularity of four-wheel-drive sport-utility vehicles (SUVs) and light trucks, the average fuel economy of new vehicles had fallen from 26 miles per gallon in 1987 to 24 in 1999, despite dramatic advances in engine fuel-management technology.[32] The reason for the declining average was that sales of small cars had sagged from one-third of all new-car sales in 1985 to less than one-fourth by 1999.[33] In the place of small cars the highways were clogged by $2^{1}/_{2}$-ton SUVs, their four-wheel-drive systems destined never to experience an off-road adventure. Longer commutes combined with poor gas mileage drove up the costs of getting to work. In 2000, some residents of sprawled-out metropolitan areas such as Houston and Atlanta spent more for transportation than for housing.[34]

A growing popular concern about sprawl became evident by the mid-1990s, when sprawl became regarded by many suburban residents as a form of urban blight brought too close to home. When they moved to the suburbs they thought they would find less density and more open space, but over the years many of them have found it impossible to stay ahead of the subdivision bulldozer. Concerns about the effects of sprawl were increasingly expressed as much by conservatives wishing to preserve their quality of life as by liberals wanting to protect the environment.

In May 1995, *Newsweek* magazine devoted a cover story to the problems of urban sprawl in New York, Memphis, Miami, Los Angeles, San Francisco, and Washington, D.C. In all of these regions, said the *Newsweek* reporters, sprawl had created "blighted metropolitan landscapes" of strip malls, traffic, and monotonous sameness. In reference to California, they observed that "No wonder they're so sterile—sterility is designed into them! They wrote about "the new American phenomenon, the suburban slum," with aging tract housing interspersed with strip development.[35]

Four years later, in its July 19, 1999, issue, *Newsweek* featured sprawl again, this time declaring that it had become an urgent public issue, part of a "livability" agenda being promoted by affluent suburban residents, suburban politicians, and Vice President Al Gore. The key elements of this agenda, according to *Newsweek,* included "the triple evils of sprawl: air pollution, traffic congestion, and visual blight."[36] In the fall of 1999, as part of its continuing Challenge to Sprawl Campaign, the Sierra Club released its annual ratings of how effectively the states were regulating sprawl.[37] News stories about the report were carried in national and numerous local newspapers, often as feature stories.

Even the conservative *Wall Street Journal* chimed in when it profiled the battle between community groups and developers in the suburbs surrounding Colorado Springs, Colorado. According to the *Journal*, the conflicts in Colorado Springs merely illustrated similar battles occurring in all of the rapidly growing metropolitan areas of the Rocky Mountain West, such as Denver, Salt Lake City, and Boise. Always an advocate of an unfettered market, the *Journal* nevertheless noted the efforts of Boulder, Colorado to slow growth by the adoption of new regulations.[38] A couple of months later, in January 2000, the *Journal* reported that campaigns against sprawl had inspired a political revolution that was toppling pro-growth politicians.[39] Apparently trying to change public sentiment in its urban area, the *St. Louis Post-Dispatch* ran one of a series of articles on sprawl under the headline, "Urban sprawl Is a Hot Topic." The paper seemed puzzled by the attitude of its readers, observing, "But Missouri's attitude seems to be: What us worry?"[40]

Some politicians joined the media by making sprawl a big issue. In 1999, *Governing,* a magazine widely read by state and local public officials, devoted two issues and several other articles to the topic of urban sprawl.[41] In January 1997, Democratic governor Paris Glendening of Maryland promised to fight for a proposed Smart Growth initiative to curb sprawl, and the next year the Republican governor of New Jersey, Christie Todd Whitman (appointed in 2001 to head the Environmental Protection Agency by President Bush) shepherded an even stronger bill through her legislature. In the latter half of the 1990s, more than half the nation's governors took on issues related to sprawl.

In fact, a growth-control movement had been picking up steam for some time. Leaders of the movement advocated such measures as caps on the pace of new construction, impact fees (imposed on developers as a way of paying some of the public costs of growth), and linkage fees (which require developers to help pay for costs linked to development such as affordable housing, schools, and day care). Growth controls spread rapidly in the 1970s; by 1975, they were in effect in over 300 jurisdictions across the country.[42] Between 1971 and 1986, more than 150 growth control measures appeared on local ballots; 50 measures appeared on ballots in 1986 alone, with three-quarters of them winning.[43] Interestingly, growth controls were pushed hardest in politically conservative areas of southern California. In 1986, over the objections of Mayor Tom Bradley, Los Angeles voters passed Proposition U, which effectively ended most new office construction in residential neighborhoods on the West Side and in the San Fernando Valley.[44] In the same election, voters in Newport Beach in Orange County, a bastion of conservatism, defeated plans for a $400 million mixed-use complex overlooking the harbor. The no-growth forces won even though they were outspent in the campaign by $500,000 to $10,000.[45]

Growth control was especially popular in wealthier cities. Ventura County, California, provides an example of the kinds of controls that were commonly adopted. In November 1998, voters there overwhelmingly approved several local initiatives creating urban growth boundaries, which were designed to limit new development at the edges of the county's cities and towns. The new rules specified that land outside the boundaries of specified cities could not be rezoned for development until 2020. To ensure that their wishes could not be overridden by public officials, these laws even took the power to rezone land protected from development out of the hands of the county's board of supervisors.[46] In the same month, New Jersey voters approved $1 billion to protect about half of the state's undeveloped open land from urban development.[47] More than 2,000 miles away, in November 2002, Nevada voters approved a conservation bond issue to protect open lands from unplanned sprawl. The impetus for the measure came from unbridled growth; in only thirty years the state's population had soared from less than a half-million people to more than two million; by 2000, only 21 percent of Nevada residents were natives. The newcomers were trying to keep the Las Vegas and Reno urban areas from becoming as crowded as the places they had left.[48]

Overall, voters passed 70 percent of the 240 local no-growth measures placed on ballots in 1998.[49] For the first time in history, the sprawl issue was incorporated (though in a minor way) into a national political campaign. In January 1999, Vice President Al Gore announced a proposal (never adopted) by the Clinton Administration to spend $9.5 billion to preserve open space, build roads and public transit, and encourage local communities to plan new schools.[50] At one point, Vice President Gore promised to make urban sprawl a central issue in his campaign. Calling it his "livability agenda," Gore said that the sprawl issue would appeal to people caught in "tidal flows of traffic" who spent too much time trying to get to work and back, at the cost to their family life. According to Gore, "There have been races for governor and mayor all over this country where the voters have made it very clear that this is an issue about which they feel passionately, and I plan in the next 13 months to take this issue to the voters of America."[51] When challenged on the question of whether such a complex issue could be turned into a hot political item, Gore answered, "Give me time." In fact, the issue played no role at all in his presidential campaign. For his part, Republican presidential candidate George W. Bush refused to talk about it, saying that it should be left to state and local governments.[52]

The heightened concern about sprawl does not necessarily mean that effective solutions will be forthcoming. Suburban residents may be troubled by gridlock, the disappearance of open space, and the endless proliferation of new subdivisions, but they are also reluctant to give up dependence on the automobile or loyalty to their local republic-in-miniature. Yet it is clear that urban sprawl cannot be curbed without fundamental changes in public policies and governance arrangements. In light of this contradiction, what, if anything, can be done?

In answering this question, it is useful to consider the three main approaches to the problems of sprawl: Smart Growth, the New Urbanism, and regional governance. Each of these movements offers its own prescriptions. The Smart Growth movement emerged in the 1980s around a collection of proposals designed to achieve "balanced" growth through improved transportation, community, and environmental planning. The New Urbanism movement became formally organized in the 1990s, with a focus upon the design and architectural features necessary to promote livable communities. The third approach evolved from the municipal reform era of the early nineteenth century. As applied to the issue of sprawl, reformers have focused upon the governance of metropolitan regions. For decades, they fought to achieve metropolitanwide governance. They mainly failed to achieve this vision, but cooperation among existing urban governments has become increasingly common.

SMART GROWTH

To a considerable degree, the Smart Growth movement grew from the concerns of wealthier suburban residents who began to worry that the things they most valued about suburban living were being compromised. The leaders of the Smart Growth movement contend that planned development is the answer to urban sprawl: Growth must occur, but it should be balanced growth, or "quality development," that improves blighted areas, promotes environmental quality, lowers energy consumption through better transportation systems and improved urban design, assesses the cost and need for new public infrastructure, and preserves agricultural, rural, and open space.[53]

Although the rhetoric of the Smart Growth movement often stresses that urban development must be seen in a metropolitan perspective, the term is also often used to promote more narrow objectives, namely to promote the kind of development that keeps poorer people or minorities from moving into a community. Thus, at the heart of the Smart Growth movement is a split, though it is rarely acknowledged. On the one hand, citizens' and environmental groups marching under the Smart Growth banner may agree to the assertion, as stated in a study sponsored by the Bank of America, that "we continue to abandon people and investments in older communities as development leap-frogs out to fringe areas to accommodate another generation of low-density living."[54] In fact, however, the fate of older communities is rarely of any concern to affluent suburban residents; they care whether their new communities can avoid the problems associated with urban sprawl and metropolitan growth.

The tensions within the Smart Growth movement can be seen in a controversy that broke out in November 1999 in Loudoun County, Virginia, when developer John Andrews ran into furious opposition to his plans to subdivide a cornfield into 69 one-acre lots. He intended to build an upscale housing development so he anticipated no problems, especially in a county dominated by Republican voters. But in the November elections, a new group calling itself Voters to Stop Sprawl swept all eight seats on the county's Board of Supervisors. Reading the tea leaves, the planning commission of the tiny town of Hamilton, which held zoning jurisdiction over the new development, did the unthinkable. It voted against it.

This revolt of the affluent against the affluent grew its roots in the same fertile soil found on the margins of every metropolitan area in America. Located 16 miles from Washington, D.C., until the 1980s Loudoun County was dotted with farms and horse barns. By the turn of the century, its population had quadrupled, and even though the new residents were prosperous, they brought with them traffic congestion, overcrowded schools, and new subdivisions. Explaining the sudden success of the revolt against sprawl, the newly elected Republican chair of the county board observed, "This wasn't a Republican or a Democrat thing. They [the new county board] did everything out there that the Republican Party should have done, but failed to do."[55]

Even in Loudoun County, Smart Growth carried different meanings. In the part of the county that was already developing, the major issues included the costs of infrastructure and the quality and aesthetics of new development. In the sections of the county that were still mostly rural, the preservation of open space and the character of the landscape dominated the discussion.[56] The issues raised in Loudoun County highlight a central tendency of the Smart Growth movement: a desire by affluent suburbanites to regulate development so that the problems associated with metropolitan development can be kept from their front door.

Despite the fact that Smart Growth appeals so broadly across the political spectrum that it sometimes unites conservatives with environmentalists, its application across the country is extremely uneven and likely to remain so. Unlike European countries, the United States has no national land-use policy— nor is there likely to be one in the future. In 1971, Henry M. Jackson, a Democratic senator from Washington, proposed the Land Use Policy and Planning Assistance Act. It passed the Senate but narrowly failed in the House. Under its provisions, states would have been required to develop statewide plans intended to direct urban development, influence the location of new communities, and protect the environment.[57] Though the legislation was remarkably vague about what the states should do to accomplish these objectives, the federal government would have picked up 90 percent of the tab. But even with this incentive, enough state and local officials lined up against the proposal to kill it.

Despite the failure of the legislation, advocates of land-use planning continued to hope that some urban areas would regulate urban growth. In a 1972 case from Ramapo, New Jersey, that state's high court upheld a town plan that required an eighteen-year planned sequence of development. Developers appealed the decision to the U.S. Supreme Court, but the justices refused to hear the case; in doing so, they established, in effect, that local governments everywhere could regulate development.[58] This principle opened the door to the Smart Growth movement.

Smart Growth goes beyond the municipal and county zoning, building, and subdivision regulations in effect in all urban areas. Planning requirements that add up to the usual definition of Smart Growth are metropolitan in scope and necessarily include such policies as greenbelts and urban development corridors. For example, in Boulder, Colorado, the city and county have taken steps to reduce growth by designating a greenbelt around the city, establishing scenic areas, and refusing to supply public infrastructure or improvements except in areas approved for growth.[59] Montgomery County, Maryland, has designated three corridors that distinguish between existing communities, fringe growth areas, and rural and agricultural areas, and a timed growth plan has been recommended that would control the rate of development in each area.[60] The idea of different corridors or "tiers" has been adopted in several metropolitan areas and is being pushed by the land-use specialists of the American Bar Association.[61]

Urban sprawl is encouraged by the fragmentation of governments in metropolitan areas. To keep property values high, municipalities adopt restrictive zoning requirements and fight with one another for shopping malls, businesses, and high-end residential areas. For any kind of metropolitanwide planning to work, the ability of some municipalities to preserve themselves as islands of affluence must be reduced. The Minnesota legislature has entertained perhaps more proposals than any other state for curbing the tendency toward polarization among jurisdictions. Bills have been considered that would require all municipalities to accept a "fair share" of affordable housing, pool their tax bases, give up local land-use decisions to a regional planning authority, and regionalize critical public services. The Minnesota case is interesting for what it reveals about the political reaction to proposals to regulate growth through such policies.

In 1967, the Minnesota legislature approved the creation of a Metropolitan Council for the Minneapolis urban region. Originally, the council was merely given the authority to review the master plans of local communities, with no authority to penalize local governments that did not cooperate. However, in 1994 a coalition of struggling suburbs joined representatives from Minneapolis and St. Paul in pushing a Metropolitan Reorganization Act through the legislature. The Metropolitan Council for the Twin Cities suddenly became a $600-million regional government that operated sewers and transit and supervised the regional airport.[62] In the same year, the legislature also took a step toward regional land-use planning when it passed the Metropolitan Land Use Reform Act. The legislation did little—it only protected farmers from public assessments and tax increases that often forced them to sell to developers—but it provided a framework for the future. That future has not been realized, however, in large part because of the passions ignited by proposals that might curb the autonomy of local governments and the activities of developers.

In 1993, a fair-share housing bill passed the Minnesota legislature but was vetoed by Republican governor Arne Carlson. In its original form, the legislation would have allowed the Metropolitan Council to penalize local communities that used their zoning and regulatory powers to stop affordable housing (these communities would lose funds from a local revenue-sharing pool and would be barred from using tax abatements or increment financing for development). Even after all the penalties were removed in an attempt to placate the governor and his allies, Carlson still exercised his veto. As it happens, the governor would not have had to take such action after the 1994 elections because Republicans won majority control of the legislature, and this doomed all fair-share housing legislation.

Since the 1970s, cities in the Minneapolis region had participated in a regional tax-sharing pool that required each city to place the taxes gained from an increase in the value of commercial industrial growth into a common pool. This tax-sharing arrangement helped curb beggar-thy-neighbor policies (such as tax abatements) that municipalities typically used to lure shopping centers and other businesses. In 1995, new legislation was introduced that would have pooled all municipal taxes collected on homes valued above $150,000. The legislation was defeated. Another much weaker tax-sharing bill, this one completely voluntary, became the lightning rod for a vicious partisan battle. Jesse "The Body" Ventura, the pro wrestler who became Minnesota's governor in 1996, attacked Myron Orfield, the Democratic state representative who had introduced the legislation. Ventura's rhetoric harkened back to the Communist-hunting days of the 1950s: "Representative Myron 'the Communist' Orfield, his latest wealth-sharing strategy, I mean this guy really needs to go to China. I mean I think he'd be most happy there. . . . Oh Myron, Myron, Myron. You never realized the communists folded for a reason. You didn't figure it out, did you Myron?"[63] The tax-sharing legislation went down to defeat.

Policies meant to reduce inequality between suburbs often provoke vitriolic reactions like Ventura's. Most battles over such policies have been fought at the local level, but in years ahead it seems likely that the battle lines will become hardened into national partisan divisions because measures to control sprawl inevitably involve an expansion of governmental authority. The St. Louis region may be a harbinger of things to come. There, Republicans in suburban St. Charles County have objected to the term *urban sprawl*, and have asserted that they were simply exercising their "urban choice" when they moved to the suburbs. In this formulation, sprawl is equated with freedom.

Because they require metropolitanwide cooperation, urban growth boundaries are rare in the United States—only in Portland, Oregon, does one exist that is enforceable by a regional planning agency—but they constitute the purest expression of the Smart Growth movement. In European nations, urban growth boundaries or greenbelts that preserve land from development exist in most urban areas.[64] In England, greenbelts provide a guarantee that new urban development beyond some cities will be clustered at some distance from the major city, like planets around a star. Without such regulations, European urban areas would still be less sprawled than those in the United States simply because gasoline prices are much higher (in 2000, a gallon of gas cost $5.00 in England and more than $4.00 in France), and mass transit systems are well developed. Even taking these differences into account, however, without land-use controls urban growth would tend to spread aimlessly, as in the United States, rather than in clusters of development.

The Portland, Oregon, metropolitan region has the only European-style growth boundary in the United States. Because it is drawn around a rapidly growing city, the boundary is easy to see both from the air and from the ground—on one side, there are townhouse developments and subdivisions; on the other, cows graze, grapevines leaf out, and wheat fields ripen. The growth boundary came about as a result of legislation passed by the Oregon state legislature in 1973 that required all local governments in the state to prepare a comprehensive land-use plan and submit it to the State Land Conservation and Development Commission for approval. Unlike other metropolitan areas in the state, Portland's urban region spanned several counties. Control over Portland's urban growth boundary was given over to an elected regional government, the Metropolitan Service District, which had been established in 1970. Portlanders soon labeled the new entity Metro, and in 1992 the name was made official when voters gave the entity expanded powers.[65]

In most states and metropolitan areas, an effective urban growth boundary would be unthinkable because business organizations, developers, and local governments possess the power to stop the necessary state legislation. Oregon is the only state to approve a growth boundary. Environmental organizations and farmers supplied critical support for drawing a growth boundary around the state's largest city, Portland. Over time, the coalition supporting Portland's boundary has broadened its appeal with the argument that planned growth actually helps promote local prosperity.[66] After losing three attempts to overturn the growth boundary (in 1976, 1978, and 1982), businesses and developers have learned to accept the boundary because they "know what the rules are."[67]

Since its adoption, growth beyond the boundary tends to occur in clusters, in and around smaller cities and towns within commuting distance of Portland. The subdivisions that normally spread across the landscape at the edges of urban areas are notably absent. The state government's willingness to override municipal governments is the key to preserving this kind of pattern. Historically, municipalities in all states have vigorously resisted attempts to control their land-use decisions, and most state legislatures and administrative agencies have been reluctant to step into the fray. Oregon is exceptional in its attitude that "We've had some problems with them [municipalities] and had to whip them into line."[68]

In most states, the municipal free-for-all will continue for some time to come. Smart Growth will spread only when suburban residents are persuaded that planned growth improves the quality of their lives. Smart Growth advocates claim that planned growth would lower the cost of urban infrastructure, improve the physical environment of the suburbs, and bring economic prosperity to central cities and urban regions. In most urban areas, suburban residents will, in all probability, be persuaded only slowly. To assess the prospects for such a change of mind, it may be useful to ask: How strong is the evidence?

Several studies have shown that the costs of public infrastructure are higher when urban development is left unregulated.[69] When infrastructure such as highways, sewers, water lines, and utilities are supplied in areas with low-density development, costs are much higher than in high-density areas. Infrastructure costs are also driven up when the existing public facilities in older areas are abandoned. A Smart Growth advocate has pointed out that in the twenty years between 1970 and 1990, a Maryland county spent $500 million to close sixty schools while opening sixty more, just to keep the schools located in areas where people had moved. He also cited a study estimating that by 2020, Maryland residents would spend $10 billion on new roads, sewers, and water systems in newly developed areas. From this evidence, he concluded that regional planning was necessary to stop the twin processes of abandonment and new investment.[70]

For most suburban residents, the argument that sprawl drives up the cost of infrastructure is not likely to carry much weight, especially since those costs are widely distributed, hard to measure, and paid, in large part, by the states and the federal government. Because financing is so complex, it is difficult to document the often asserted argument that people in older areas help subsidize the cost of new development.[71] It is even less likely that suburban residents will suddenly be struck with remorse by the thought that by moving out, they have contributed to the decay of older cities and neighborhoods. It is possible, however, that suburban residents may pay some attention if an effective case can be made that decay at the urban center threatens the economic viability of the regions they live within. Accordingly, this argument has gained much currency in debates over urban sprawl.

Recently, some analysts have turned the familiar refrain that sprawl brings "despair to the inner cities"[72] on its head by claiming that it may ultimately bring despair to the suburbs as well. Of thirteen studies conducted between 1989 and 1996, all but one showed that central-city economic performance was associated with the economic performance of suburbs and of metropolitan areas; in addition, studies showed a relationship between greater interjurisdictional inequality and regional economic performance.[73] However, no connection was shown between the degree of concentrated poverty within metropolitan areas and the economic health of suburbs.

Aside from the rather technical nature of such studies, it is hard to imagine that most suburban residents will buy into abstract arguments about how their own fate is linked to that of their poorer neighbors. Self-interest tends to be immediate—a lower tax bill, a better school, rising property values—but concern for others tends to be more abstract. For this reason, as the Minnesota case illustrates, attempts to implement fair-share housing and tax equalization are likely to become intensely partisan issues wherever they are proposed. But some measures will prove more popular. The revolt against uncontrolled growth in Loudoun County, Virginia, was prompted by a concern that unchecked development was ruining the environment that people had moved to the suburbs to enjoy. Perhaps it is the sheer ugliness of sprawl that provokes intense reaction from affluent suburban residents—a feeling that paradise is being lost. For them, a recent movement called the New Urbanism may seem very appealing.

THE NEW URBANISM

Advocates of the New Urbanism promote Smart Growth principles such as regional land-use planning, but their passion is mainly focused on the question of how design and architecture can be used to revive local community and reduce reliance on the automobile. Thus: "individual architectural projects should be seamlessly linked to their surroundings"; "the economic health and harmonious evolution of neighborhoods, districts, and corridors can be improved through graphic design codes"; and "civic buildings and public gathering places require important sites to reinforce community identity and the culture of democracy."[74]

The New Urbanism is energized by a diagnosis of a terrible disease—"blighted metropolitan landscapes," "banal places with the souls of shopping malls, affording nowhere to mingle except traffic jams, nowhere to walk except in the health club."[75] The proposed antidote is made up of transportation networks designed to reduce reliance on the automobile and carefully designed urban environments with harmonious streetscapes and pleasing design features (such as buildings with dormers, gables, and porticos) that integrate home, business, recreation, and community life. By fostering a sense of community in the suburbs, advocates of the New Urbanism hope to calm the restlessness that makes people constantly move on to the next subdivision in their search for a suburban Eden.

The alleged disease of the American suburb has long been the subject of commentary. The writer James Howard Kunstler begins his book *The Geography of Nowhere* with this vivid summary:

> Eighty percent of everything ever built in America has been built in the last fifty years, and most of it is depressing, brutal, ugly, unhealthy, and spiritually degrading—the jive-plastic commuter tract home wastelands, the Potemkin village shopping plazas with their vast parking lagoons, the Lego-block hotel complexes, the 'gourmet mansardic' junk-food joints, the Orwellian office 'parks' featuring buildings sheathed in the same reflective glass as the sunglasses worn by chain-gang guards, the particle-board garden apartments rising up in every little meadow and cornfield, the freeway loops around every big and little city with their clusters of discount merchandise marts, the whole destructive, wasteful, toxic, agoraphobia-inducing spectacle that politicians call 'growth.'"[76]

In Kunstler's account, suburban residents have learned to live "in places where nothing relates to anything else," a landscape in which daily activities—home, work, shopping, recreation—are pulled apart into large-scale, segregated developments accessible only by automobiles: "The houses are all in their respective income pods, the shopping is miles away from the houses," and schools, malls, and office parks are also set apart, together with their seas of cars glistening on massive parking lots.[77] This version of suburbia might present the image and possibility of open space, but in actuality (in this narrative) human beings are forced to sit in their cars, gridlocked, or find themselves in the embrace of a gated community, school, or shopping mall.

Like clear-cutting a forest, a parking lot, mall, or a housing subdivision can be most efficiently built by means of industrial methods; the first step is a bulldozer that removes everything for the sake of progress. Such methods link efficiency and wastefulness in an intimate dance. Urged on by advertising, constant changes in product lines and styles, and the proliferation of disposable packaging, "most consumer goods are destined for a one-night stand."[78] Applied to land and places, such a consumer habit has far-reaching social consequences— "cycling of people through places," a mobility and rootlessness that replaces community with the hope of renewal that comes from moving, "a kind of magic that keeps expectations high."[79] If the new place disappoints, the answer will be found in another move, and still another one after that.

Can suburban environments be designed to discourage this constant restlessness? For advocates of the New Urbanism, the answers are to be found in better design. *Newsweek* distilled the lessons of the New Urbanism into a fifteen-item list: give up big lawns ("the goal of making a walkable community is defeated when houses are spread out on huge lots"), bring back the corner store ("It should still be possible to provide some of the necessities of life within walking distance of many people"), make the streets skinny ("Force cars to slow down"), drop the cul-de-sac ("streets . . . can follow predictable routes and interconnect"), draw boundaries ("imagine how Los Angeles would look today if it had done this [adopt an urban growth boundary] 20 years ago"), hide the garage ("the blank and desolate face of a garage door"), mix housing types ("in Harbor Town . . . the leading recreational activity would be chatting with neighbors"), plant trees curbside ("a canopy over the roadway"), put new life into old malls ("the land they occupy can . . . become the nucleus of a real neighborhood"), plan for mass transit ("Is there any way to get Americans out of their cars and into buses and trains?"), link work to home ("If companies don't want to be downtown, they should . . . integrate their offices—or factories, for that matter—into communities"), make a town center ("a plaza, square or green that is a geographical reference point and a focus of civic life"), shrink parking lots ("Only in the United States does the humblest copy-shop or pizzeria boast as much space for cars as the average city hall"), turn down the lights ("why not use . . . smaller lamps that cast a gentler glow and let you see the stars?"), and think green ("before lawn meets lawn and asphalt meets asphalt, covering the land in a seamless carpet of sprawl").[80]

The problem with a list such as *Newsweek*'s is that it mixes nostalgia for a past that probably never existed with some complex policies and distills them into empty homilies about community and family. The list begs the question of whether suburban residents actually care about community, as opposed to some of its quaint architectural signifiers. As it turns out, however, the *Newsweek* article captures the central tendencies of the New Urbanism, which are to mix sensible planning suggestions with far-fetched social goals.

The Congress for the New Urbanism, organized in 1994, announces in its founding charter that it "views divestment in central cities, the spread of place-less sprawl, increasing separation by race and income, environmental deterioration, loss of agricultural lands and wilderness, and the erosion of society's built heritage as one interrelated community-building challenge."[81] Though the congress goes to some pains to point out that "we recognize that physical solutions by themselves will not solve social and economic problems," the approach of the New Urbanism is almost entirely oriented to the physical redesign of urban space. The twenty-seven principles endorsed by the congress emphasize "the neighborhood, the district, and the corridor as the essential elements of development." These principles stand in opposition to the style of urban development that has relied on the bulldozing of vast spaces for single uses such as subdivisions, shopping centers, and office parks. Such segmentation has created an urban pattern that favors cars over human beings, forcing people to spend time on the highway that might be spent at home or in a community setting.

Three advocates of the New Urbanism have distilled these precepts into a simple refrain:

> *No more housing subdivisions!*
> *No more shopping centers!*
> *No more office parks!*
> *No more highways!*
> *Neighborhoods or nothing!*[82]

In place of monotonous subdivisions of lookalike houses, "the goal of the New Urbanism is to promote diverse and livable communities with a greater variety of housing types, land uses, and building densities—in other words, to develop and maintain a melting pot of neighborhood homes serving a wide range of household family sizes, cultures, and incomes."[83]

To replace the shopping centers, the New Urbanists urge the building of pedestrian-friendly shopping areas on streets and squares, within walking distance of nearby residences. Office parks are to be banned because they segregate work from home and shopping; like shopping centers, they entail the proliferation of huge parking lots and maximize reliance on the automobile.[84] The New Urbanists recognize that "automobiles are a fact of modern life," but they urge that the grid of high-speed streets and highways that intersect urban areas be replaced by highway corridors clearly separated from neighborhoods. Within neighborhoods, they want to slow traffic by narrowing streets and creating traffic circles and other "traffic calming" devices. They also promote the idea that bicycle paths and sidewalks should be built along all streets, and that mass transit must be made convenient.[85]

The environments envisioned by the New Urbanists would be delightful places to live; people would be walking and bicycling to a café or restaurant, stopping to visit with their neighbors, walking to work. Unfortunately, such environments are unlikely to be realized in any complete form. For residents to be able to walk and bicycle to shop, work, and play, densities would have to be as high as those achieved in the densely populated downtowns of major cities. Such densities cannot be achieved without high-rise living. However, all New Urbanist developments are composed of low-density townhouses or single-family homes, guaranteeing that the spatial integration of activities sought by the New Urbanism cannot be achieved except when a housing project is inserted into a densely packed city. This goes against the grain of the New Urbanism, which markets itself as an antidote to sprawl and amorphous suburban development.

Suburban residents may be tired of freeway congestion and gridlock, and they may sometimes revolt against the ugliness of large-scale development—especially when it is in their backyard—but the New Urbanism is likely to become little more than a recipe for design features that developers can use to market their developments. Just outside Disney World near Orlando, Florida, the Disney Corporation has built Celebration, a gated community built according to the principles of the New Urbanism. All houses have front porches, a touch from the past designed to encourage people to visit with their neighbors (though, as it happens, it is too hot in Florida for this to work). The houses also have other design features meant to signify a happy, wholesome suburban life—gables, elaborate trim, picket fences. One suspects that Celebration is much like the Frontier Village or Main Street in Disneyland—"authentic reproductions" based on an idealized version of the real thing. If affluent home buyers come to prefer the design features of the New Urbanism, developers will be happy to accommodate them. Many of the architectural touches of the New Urbanism—stone and copper facades, porches, elaborate door lintels and balconies—cost money, and thus they serve as markers more of social class than of community. They add to the real-estate markup.

To serve as an effective remedy for urban sprawl, the New Urbanism must gain support from a coalition of political interests capable of achieving regional planning. Only in that manner can goals of improved transportation networks, mixed-use housing, and social equity be accomplished. In the Minneapolis region, a coalition comprising representatives of the central city, inner-ring suburbs, and affluent suburbs wishing to rein in developers came together in the 1970s behind the cause of regional governance. Though regional reform has not been accomplished in Minneapolis, this alliance has succeeded in implementing a modest tax-sharing plan, the regionalization of some services, and the creation of a Metropolitan Council capable of carrying out some planning.[86] If it stays together, this alliance will probably win important victories in tax and school-district equalization, and it may eventually achieve regional planning with enforceable land-use controls. Without such coalitions, the New Urbanism cannot hope to change the face of the suburbs. The task is formidable. Are suburban residents ready to give up their single-family homes, lawns, and multiple cars? Do they really care about community? Are they willing to share tax bases or support other measures to reduce disparities within urban regions? Judging from history, the answers to these questions are not likely to be positive.

REFORMING METROPOLITAN GOVERNANCE

The advocates of metropolitan reform have long fought to eliminate the governmental fragmentation of metropolitan areas. In their view, few problems of the suburbs or of the central cities can be solved in the absence of regional governments. Though nearly all of the efforts to achieve metropolitan government have failed, in recent decades cooperative arrangements among suburban governments have been forged to improve service delivery in the suburbs. These modest governmental arrangements preserve local political autonomy, but they make it possible for one of the main characteristics of sprawl—the proliferation of governments—to be partially overcome.

A single regional government would, in principle, be able to represent the many voices that make up the metropolis. At the same time, such a government could plan transportation systems, balance investment in older communities and in new infrastructure, impose land-use and environmental controls, and provide efficient services in an equitable fashion to all urban residents. In fact, however, urban areas are made up of a multitude of governments with widely varying taxation levels that provide services ranging from the excellent to the abysmal. These governments compete fiercely with one another for a piece of the economic pie; one result is that regional planning is sacrificed.

Convinced that such a state of affairs is inefficient and inequitable, for many decades reformers focused their energies on the goal of eliminating the governmental fragmentation of urban areas. Time after time they have met with failure, despite the fact that the benefits sounded (to their own ears, at least) irresistible. The reformers of the metropolis were cut from the same cloth, and indeed they were often the same people, as the municipal reformers who fought behind the banners of efficiency and economy in government. And their remedies were similar. They maintained that a single government should exercise all public authority within each metropolitan area. They believed that only a few of its officials should be elected, with a sharp distinction drawn between politics and public administration.[87] The proliferation of municipalities within urban regions could be compared to the wards in cities—to the reformer, wards were nothing but hotbeds of parochial politics, with their representatives lacking the capacity or the perspective to attend to the overall problems of the city. Likewise, they said, the multitude of governments in urban regions made it impossible to achieve efficiency and economy. Thus, writing in 1912, one reformer said: "Here [in metropolitan Boston] are thirty-eight towns and cities as intimately related to everything that concerns daily life as the wards of an American city, but with no power or means . . . of constructing, or improving public works or of taking public action that is for the metropolitan district as a whole."[88]

Nearly twenty years later, an influential reformer picked up the same themes when he described what he saw as the parochialism and chaos arising from the fragmentation of local government: "They [the many governments] tend to divert attention of the inhabitants from the fact that they are members of one large community and lead them to act as members of separate units. They result in great variation in municipal regulations . . . and in standards of services, in sectional treatment of problems which are essentially metropolitan."[89] The reformers pressing for single-government urban regions agreed on the solution: "Only a government with community-wide jurisdiction can plan and provide the services, physical facilities, guidance, and controls necessary to relate functional plans with real plans. None of the metropolitan areas has such a government today."[90]

The reformers were convinced that truth and virtue were on their side. Such confidence fueled the bitter disappointment they felt when voters repeatedly rejected their proposals in metropolitan areas all across the country, campaign after campaign, decade after decade. Between 1921 and 1979, reformers went to voters eighty-three times in an attempt to gain approval of city-county consolidations. They succeeded only seventeen times, and only two of those successes came in metropolitan areas of 250,000 or more (Nashville–Davidson County, Tennessee, 1962, and Jacksonville–Duval County, Mississippi, 1967). (The consolidation of Indianapolis with Marion County in 1969 was imposed by the state legislature and not by a popular referendum.)[91] Many other reform attempts were made to consolidate governments by creating two-tier systems (a metropolitan district with specific service responsibilities, but with municipalities and counties continuing to possess important powers). The most notable success came with the creation of Metropolitan Dade County (Miami) in 1957. Under this reform, the county assumed many of the responsibilities (such as fire and police protection, traffic control, parks and recreation, health and welfare programs, air pollution control, and some other activities) formerly assumed by municipal governments.

Most of the ambitious schemes to impose metropolitan governments went down in flames because both suburban and central-city voters wanted to preserve their control over local powers and services. The experience in the St. Louis metropolitan area was typical, except there the reformers tried, and failed, more times than anywhere else: in 1926, 1930, 1959, 1962, 1989, and 1990. In 1926, the voters in St. Louis County defeated a proposal to consolidate the city of St. Louis with the county. Four years later, the county's voters vetoed a somewhat less ambitious proposal that would have placed the city and county under a regional government, except for a few services and public functions.[92] In 1959, the reformers gave it another try. This time they proposed a Greater St. Louis City-County District that would have assumed responsibility for forging a regional plan and for promoting economic development, managing regional mass transit and traffic control on major streets and highways, administering all sewage facilities, and supervising all police training, communications, and civil defense. Municipalities would have been left with the responsibility of regulating local street traffic and providing police and fire protection and garbage pickup. Local officials in the county reacted with a furious campaign of opposition, and voters soundly defeated the plan.[93] But even before tempers cooled from this attempt, reformers were at it again. This time, in 1962, the "borough plan" would have placed the city and county under a single government and divided the county into twenty-two boroughs, each exercising some limited powers. This plan would have eliminated all existing municipalities. The plan was defeated by a 4-to-1 landslide, an even more lopsided margin than in 1959.

In 1989, an elected Board of Freeholders placed a consolidation plan before the voters of St. Louis County (language in the Missouri Constitution empowered such a board of "freeholders"—property owners—to make such proposals). In addition to reducing the number of municipalities in the county from ninety to thirty-seven, the plan would have transferred most land-use, zoning, and building inspections to the county and also created a county commission to oversee fire and emergency services. It quickly became obvious that opposition to reform had not died in the nearly three decades that had passed since the previous reform try. An acrimonious campaign ensued, and both sides readied for the scheduled June 20, 1989, vote. Before election day, however, the U.S. Supreme Court declared the Board of Freeholders illegal because it denied equal protection of the law to non–property holders.[94]

The successive generations of reformers in St. Louis showed remarkable resolve because they felt that righteousness and truth was on their side. It was not difficult for them to demonstrate that tax burdens and service levels varied wildly among municipalities. It was also easy to show that the city of St. Louis was in economic decline and had been since the 1920s. Patterns of racial and social-class segregation between the city and county, and between cities within the county, was a defining feature of the St. Louis region, and the zoning ordinances of the many municipalities demonstrably helped establish and preserve such segregation. But such evidence could not overcome the deep attachment people felt to their local communities.

Some of the things the reformers saw as problems—such as varying taxing levels and service provisions—others saw as solutions. Most suburban residents had long felt this way, and in the 1980s they began to find support for their point of view in academic quarters. In September 1988, just a few months before the vote on the freeholders' plan, the influential Advisory Commission on Intergovernmental Relations proclaimed that urban residents benefited when they were given the ability to shop around for different bundles of taxes, services, and amenities offered by municipalities.[95] This and similar studies undermined the metropolitan reform movement. It became possible for the defenders of local autonomy to cite scholarly approval for the view that they were doing nothing but exercising their free choice to live wherever they wished rather than appearing to defend parochial self-interests.

Though suburban residents resisted regional governance, they embraced cooperative arrangements when, as a practical matter, it seemed in their interest to do so. Cooperative agreements exist among local governments almost everywhere in the United States. These agreements have typically arisen when an urban county has agreed to collect taxes to provide services for small municipalities. They have also evolved as interlocal agreements among two or more governments as a way of providing common services or sharing tax collection and assessments, data processing, and the like. For the most part they are mundane, boring, everyday administrative undertakings—the exact opposite of the bitterly contested fights over metropolitan reform.

Some examples of cooperation within metropolitan areas reveal both the accomplishments and the limitations of piecemeal reform. In the 1940s, voters agreed to a new charter for St. Louis County (then the principal suburban county in the St. Louis region) that allowed the county to expand its service and administrative responsibilities. The county soon adopted a building code, and in the next few years it began to conduct electrical inspections of new construction in unincorporated areas; it also contracted with municipalities for this service. By 1964, the county was running thirty-two parks and an extensive library system. Following a charter revision in 1954, the county formed its own police department. Over the years, the county police have contracted with numerous cities for police enforcement. In 1971, voters approved another charter amendment, this one giving the county control over waste disposal and authorizing it to set minimum training and educational standards for firefighters. Today, the county also administers 911 emergency services, runs a system of health clinics, builds roads and coordinates transportation, and operates a system of jails and courts.[96]

Similarly, urban counties elsewhere have taken on new responsibilities. By the mid-1980s, DuPage County, west of Chicago, ran an extensive parks system and coordinated municipal services for those cities that volunteered to participate. Through a regional planning commission, it provided planning expertise and advice to cities and applied for federal grants on behalf of municipalities and special districts.[97] Oakland County, Michigan, north of Detroit, also slowly expanded its responsibilities, finally running an airport, providing contracted services to municipalities, and running a public library system and emergency services. Over time it has become, in effect, a regional government that coordinates public works projects.[98] By the early 1970s, Orange County, California, had evolved into an administrative structure sufficient to provoke repeated protests from local officials. Like other urban counties, it had grown less through big reform than by a gradual accumulation of responsibilities.

Cooperative agreements can sometimes segue into more ambitious reforms. In January 2003, Louisville, Kentucky, and its surrounding county, Jefferson County, merged into a single metropolitan government—the first merger of its size since the Indianapolis and Marion County merger in 1969. But voters were persuaded to vote for the merger, in part, because they already had become accustomed to a cooperative agreement to run a joint water and sewer authority, park, zoo, library systems, and a consolidated metropolitan school district. Officials from other urban areas have already come visiting to see if they can emulate Louisville's example.[99]

Urban areas have also been able to overcome many of the effects of governmental fragmentation through special districts. In 2002, there were 87,900 local governments in the United States; of these, fewer than one in four—19,431— were municipalities.[100] The fastest-growing form of local government is the special district—an authority granted taxing and spending powers so that it can undertake designated responsibilities such as administering sewer systems, running toll tunnels and bridges, and providing mass transit services. Special districts are generally run more like private corporations than like governments, and most of them are virtually invisible.[101] Most of them come into existence to supply services to new developments (they are often organized, in fact, by developers for the purpose of providing public services to new subdivisions, malls, or other developments), but others are truly metropolitan in scope.

Urban counties, interlocal agreements, and special districts have facilitated improved service delivery while preserving municipal autonomy. Without them, governmental fragmentation would give rise to irresolvable problems; precisely because they exist, fragmentation can be sustained. But the proliferation of intergovernmental agreements and special districts creates an incredible level of complexity that undermines democratic governance. They are generally out of the public eye and are run like private corporations that are not responsible to voters.[102] Rather than acting as an antidote to sprawl, they facilitate it by providing a flexible means by which developers and urban residents can obtain the public infrastructure and services for new development at the urban edge.

WHITHER SPRAWL?

Americans are wedded to the ideals of local government and suspicious of any attempts to interfere in the workings of the marketplace. The culture of privatism favors individual actions over community and cooperation. Even so, history shows that when problems seem serious enough, urban residents are willing to support governmental action. In principle, a comprehensive consolidation of governments would seem to be the most obvious, and perhaps the only, effective way to solve the problems of sprawled-out metropolitan areas.

But municipalities tend to guard their land-use authority jealously—and of course, this is precisely the power that must be regionalized if urban sprawl is to be reined in. Except for Portland, Oregon, no regional body in the United States holds the authority to regularly countermand local land-use regulations. Because resistance to regional land-use planning has been so difficult to overcome, states and regions have opted instead for land-trust programs that replace regulations with attempts to preserve farmland and open space. From 1988 to 1998, 4.7 million acres of open space were protected from development, an increase of 135 percent. Several states have attempted to curb sprawl by buying up open space. In 1998, voters in New Jersey agreed to spend $98 million in state and local taxes and issue $1 billion in bonds to protect land from the developers. In the same year, the Florida legislature established a $3 billion bond program and Illinois committed $160 million for the acquisition of open space. New York's governor launched a task force to study ways to favor redevelopment over new development, and Connecticut's governor set a goal of tripling the amount of land preserved from sprawl.[103] In May 2000, Congress authorized $42 billion to be spent over fifteen years to preserve land from development.[104]

Does such activity signal an antisprawl revolution? New Jersey's experience with land trusts suggests otherwise. In 1998, Governor Christie Todd Whitman announced that New Jersey's program—with its goal of acquiring more than one million acres of open space—could serve as a national model. But in the end, New Jersey was reluctant to place environmental concerns ahead of economic development. In 2000, when Merrill Lynch announced that it would leave the state unless it was granted permission to build in a rural area, politicians quickly caved. An assistant in the governor's policy office explained, "They wanted a suburban-style campus, so it was either here or Pennsylvania."[105] Even in the unlikely event that politics elsewhere might be different, land trusts can do little more than preserve islands of open space in the stream of development.

Suburban residents are caught in a bind, and the way out is likely to be painful. On the one hand, they are fed up with gridlock and the bulldozer. On the other, they are keen to preserve the privileges guaranteed by municipal autonomy. If they forsake local control for the goal of curbing urban sprawl, they may find an affordable housing project sprouting up in the next block, or may discover that some of their tax dollars are being used to help support cities with lower tax bases. So far, suburban residents have not had any trouble in choosing between the alternatives.

NOTES

1. For a comparative analysis of suburban development in advanced industrial countries, see Donald N. Rothblatt and Daniel J. Garr, *Surburbia: An International Assessment* (New York: St. Martin's Press, 1986); and Christopher M. Law, *The Uncertain Future of the Urban Core* (London: Routledge, 1988).
2. Barry Edmonton, Michael A. Goldberg, and John Mercer, "Urban Form in Canada and the United States: An Examination of Urban Density Gradients," *Urban Studies* 22 (1985): 213.
3. According to the 1980 census, the typical American worker traveled 9.2 miles and expended 22 minutes each way in reaching his or her place of employment, at an annual cost of more than $1,270 per employee. See Kenneth T. Jackson, *Crabgrass Frontier: The Suburbanization of the United States* (New York: Oxford University Press, 1985), p. 10. Between 1970 and 1990, commuting distances increased in the United States by 50 percent. See Matthew L. Wald, "How Dreams of Clean Air Get Stuck in Traffic," *New York Times,* March 11, 1990, p. 1.
4. Pietro S. Nivola, *Laws of the Landscape: How Policies Shape Cities in Europe and America* (Washington, D.C.: Brookings Institution, 1999), pp. 13–14.
5. Ibid., p. 15.
6. Peter Dreier, John Mollenkopf, and Todd Swanstrom, *Place Matters: Metropolitics for the Twenty-first Century* (Lawrence: University Press of Kansas, 2001), pp. 110–111.
7. Jon C. Teaford, *Post-Suburbia: Government and Politics in the Edge Cities* (Baltimore: The Johns Hopkins University Press, 1997), p. 1.
8. Ibid.
9. Neal Peirce, "The Senselessness of Urban Sprawl," *National Journal,* September 25, 1993, p. 2326.
10. Scott Bowles, "National Gridlock," *USA Today,* November 23, 1999, p. 2A.
11. Office of Technology Assessment, Congress of the United States, *The Technological Reshaping of Metropolitan America,* OTA-ETI-643 (Washington, D.C.: Government Printing Office, 1995).
12. Anthony Downs, *The Costs of Sprawl: Environmental and Economic Costs of Alternative Development Patterns of Metropolitan America* (Washington, D.C.: Real Estate Research Corporation, 1974), p. 2.
13. Neal Peirce and Curtis Johnson, "St. Louis: Exploded Galaxy?," *St. Louis Post-Dispatch,* March 16, 1997, p. 6B.

14. Russ Lopez and H. Patricia Hynes, "Sprawl in the 1990s: Measurement, Distribution, and Trends," *Urban Affairs Review* 38, no. 3 (January 2003): 325–352.
15. Office of Technology Assessment, *Technological Reshaping*, chap. 8.
16. Robert Burchell et al., *The Costs of Sprawl Revisited* (Washington, D.C.: National Academy Press, 1998). See also Office of Technology Assessment, *Technological Reshaping*, chap. 8.
17. Joseph Persky and Wim Wiewel, *When Corporations Leave Town* (Detroit: Wayne State University Press, 2000).
18. Wald, "How Dreams of Clean Air Get Stuck in Traffic."
19. Peter G. Newman and Jeffrey R. Kenworthy, "Gasoline Consumption and Cities," *Journal of the American Planning Association* (Winter 1989): 26–27.
20. Rogers Worthington, "Burning Gas, Not Miles," *Chicago Tribune*, May 8, 2001, pp. 1, 12.
21. Craig R. Whitney, "Scientists Warn of Dangers in a Warming Earth," *New York Times*, May 26, 1990.
22. James A. Dunn, Jr., *Miles to Go: European and American Transportation Policies* (Cambridge, Mass.: MIT Press, 1981), p. 150.
23. U.S. Bureau of the Census, *Statistical Abstract of the United States* (Washington, D.C.: Government Printing Office, 1996), p. 235.
24. Fred Siegel, quoted in Dreier, Mollenkopf, and Swanstrom, *Place Matters*, pp. 94–95, citing "The Sunny Side of Sprawl," *New Democrat* 11, no. 2 (March-April 1999): pp. 20–21.
25. Wald, "How Dreams of Clean Air Get Stuck in Traffic."
26. Bowles, "National Gridlock," p. 2A.
27. Robert Cervero, "Unlocking Suburban Gridlock," *Journal of the American Planning Association* (August 1986): 389.
28. H. V. Savitch and Ronald K. Vogel, *Regional Politics: America in a Post-City Age* (Thousand Oaks, Calif.: Sage, 1996), p. 18.
29. J. A. Lindsey, "Urban Freeway Congestion: Quantification of the Problem and Effectiveness of Potential Solutions," *ITE Journal* 57 (1987): 27–32, cited in Robert Cervero, "Jobs-Housing Balancing and Regional Mobility," *Journal of the American Planning Association* 55, no. 2, (Spring 1989): 136.
30. U.S. Department of Housing and Development, *The State of Our Cities* (Washington, D.C.: Government Printing Office, 1999), p. iv.
31. Worthington, "Burning Gas, Not Miles," p. 12.
32. Keith Bradsher, "With Sport Utility Vehicles More Popular, Overall Automobile Fuel Economy Continues to Fall," *New York Times*, October 5, 1999, p. A17.
33. Warren Brown, "We Like to Think Big," *Washington Post National Weekly Edition*, March 1, 2000, p. 19.
34. Janet Frankston, "Suburban Sprawl's Sticker Shock," *Chicago Tribune*, January 5, 2003, Section 16, pp. 1–2.
35. Jerry Adler, "Bye, Bye Suburban Dream," Vol. 125, issue 20, *Newsweek*, May 15, 1995, pp. 40–45.
36. Daniel Pederson, Vern E. Smith, and Jerry Adler, "Sprawling, Sprawling . . . ", *Newsweek*, July 19, 1999, pp. 23–27.
37. Ibid.
38. Vicki Lee Parker, "Western Cities Grapple with Rapid Growth," *Wall Street Journal*, September 22, 1999, p. B16.
39. John J. Fialka, "Campaign Against Sprawl Overruns a County in Virginia, and Soon Perhaps Much of Nation," *Wall Street Journal*, January 4, 2000, p. A24.
40. Bill Lambrecht, "Urban Sprawl Is a Hot Topic," *St. Louis Post-Dispatch*, February 7, 1999, p. A6.
41. *Governing: The Magazine of States and Localities*, January 1999 and August 1999 issues.
42. D'vera Cohn, "Big Is No Longer Beautiful for Many U.S. Communities," *Santa Barbara News-Press*, March 4, 1979, cited in John R. Logan and Harvey L. Molotch, *Urban Fortunes: The Political Economy of Place* (Berkeley: University of California Press, 1987), p. 159.

43. Mark Baldassare, "Suburban Support for No-Growth Policies: Implications for the Growth Revolt," *Journal of Urban Affairs* 12, no. 2 (1990): 198.

44. Robert Reinhold, "Growth in Los Angeles Poses Threat to Bradley," *New York Times*, September 22, 1987.

45. Charles Lockwood and Christopher B. Leinberger, "Los Angeles Comes of Age," *Atlantic Monthly* (January 1988): 48.

46. William Booth, "For Voters, the Target Is Sprawl," *Washington Post National*, December 7, 1998, pp. 30–31.

47. Ibid., p. 31.

48. Martin Griffith, "Alarmed by Growth, Nevadans go 'Green'," *Chicago Tribune*, December 19, 2002, p. 39.

49. Sierra Club, *Solving Sprawl: The Sierra Club Rates the States* (Washington, D.C.: Sierra Club, 1999), p. 2.

50. Terence Samuel, "Gore Pushes a Plan to Help Curb Problems Related to Urban Sprawl," *St. Louis Post-Dispatch*, January 12, 1999, p. A8.

51. Terence Samuel, "Al Gore Makes Sprawl Central to His Campaign," *St. Louis Post-Dispatch*, www.postnet.com, October 12, 1999.

52. Fialka, "Campaign Against Sprawl," p. A24.

53. Robert H. Freilich, *From Sprawl to Smart Growth: Successful Legal, Planning, and Environmental Systems* (Washington, D.C.: American Bar Association, 1999), p. 323.

54. Bank of America, "Beyond Sprawl: New Patterns of Growth to Fit the New California," http://seafirst.com/community/comm_env_urban1.html.

55. Fialka, "Campaign Against Sprawl," p. A24.

56. Ibid.

57. Jayne E. Daly, "A Glimpse of the Past, A Vision for the Future: Senator Henry M. Jackson and National Land Use Legislation," *Urban Law* 28, no. 1 (1996). www.law.pace.edu/landuse/senator_jackson.html

58. For a full description of the case and its importance, see Freilich, *From Sprawl to Smart Growth*, p. 323.

59. Ibid., pp. 195–196.

60. Ibid., pp. 131–132.

61. Ibid.

62. Myron Orfield, *Metropolitics: A Regional Agenda for Community and Stability* (Washington, D.C.: Brookings Institution Press, and Cambridge, Mass.: Lincoln Institute of Land Policy, 1997), p. 13.

63. Quoted in ibid., p. 149.

64. Arnold J. Heidenheimer, Hugh Heclo, and Carolyn Teich Adams, *Comparative Public Policy: The Politics of Choice in Europe and America*, 2nd ed. (New York: St. Martin's Press, 1993), chap. 8.

65. Paul G. Lewis, *Shaping Suburbia: How Political Institutions Organize Urban Development* (Pittsburgh: University of Pittsburgh Press, 1996), pp. 105–107.

66. Christopher Leo, "Regional Growth Management Regime: The Case of Portland, Oregon", *Journal of Urban Affairs* 20, no. 4 (1998): 363–394.

67. Lewis, *Shaping Suburbia*, p. 115.

68. John DeGrove, *Land, Growth, and Politics* (Chicago: APA Planners' Press, 1984), pp. 249–250.

69. For a comprehensive review, see Office of Technology Assessment, *Technological Reshaping*, chap. 8.

70. Edward T. McMahon, "Stopping Sprawl by Growing Smarter," *Planning Commissioners Journal* 26, (Spring 1997): 4–7.

71. Office of Technology Assessment, *Technological Reshaping*.

72. Neal Peirce, "St. Louis: Exploded Galaxy?," *St. Louis Post-Dispatch*, March 16, 1997, p. 6B.

73. Rosalind Greenstein and Wim Wiewel eds., *Urban-Suburban Interdependencies* (Cambridge, Mass.: Lincoln Institute of Land Policy, 2000), pp. 25–28.

74. Congress for the New Urbanism, *Charter of the New Urbanism* (New York, McGraw-Hill, 2000).

75. Adler, "Bye, Bye Suburban Dream."

76. James Howard Kunstler, *The Geography of Nowhere* (New York: Touchstone, 1993) p. 10.

77. Ibid., p. 118.

78. John A. Jakle and David Wilson, *Derelict Landscapes: The Wasting of America's Built Environment* (Savage, Md: Rowman and Littlefield, 1992), p. 182.

79. Ibid., p. 40.

80. Adler, "Bye, Bye Suburban Dream."

81. Congress for the New Urbanism, *Charter of the New Urbanism*.

82. Andres Duany, Elizabeth Plater-Zyberk, and Jeff Speck, *Suburban Nation: The Rise of Sprawl and the Decline of the American Dream* (New York: North Point Press, 2000), p. 243.

83. Marc A. Weiss, in Congress for the New Urbanism, *Charter of the New Urbanism*, p. 91.

84. Elizabeth Moule, in ibid., pp. 105–108.

85. Douglas Farr, in ibid., pp.141–146.

86. Orfield, *Metropolitics*, pp. 1–14, 74–103.

87. G. Ross Stephens and Nelson Wikstrom, *Metropolitan Government and Governance: Theoretical Perspectives, Empirical Analysis, and the Future* (New York: Oxford University Press, 2000), pp. 31–32.

88. Quoted in ibid., p. 33.

89. Paul Studenski, *The Government of Metropolitan Areas in the United States* (New York: National Municipal League, 1930), p. 29.

90. Victor Jones, "Local Government Organization in Metropolitan Areas: Its Relation to Urban Redevelopment," in Coleman Woodbury, ed., *The Future of Cities and Urban Redevelopment* (Chicago: University of Chicago Press, 1953), pp. 604–605.

91. Vincent Marando, "City-County Consolidation: Reform, Regionalism, Referenda, and Requiem," *Western Political Quarterly* 32, no. 4 (December 1979): 409–422.

92. Teaford, *Post-Suburbia*, p. 110.

93. Ibid., pp. 110–112.

94. Ibid., p. 195.

95. Ibid., p. 194.

96. Ibid., pp. 136–138.

97. Ibid., pp. 145–146.

98. Ibid., p. 152.

99. Alan Greenblatt, "Anatomy of a Merger," *Governing*, 16, no. 3 (December 2002): 2025.

100. U.S. Census Bureau, Census of Governments, GC02-1P (Washington, D.C.: Government Printing Office, 2002).

101. Nancy Burns, *The Formation of American Local Governments: Private Values in Public Institutions* (New York: Oxford University Press, 1994).

102. Gerald E. Frug, "Beyond Regional Government," *Harvard Law Review* 115, no. 7 (May 2002): 1785.

103. Terence Samuel, "Suburban Communities Grab Up Land to Keep Developers at Bay," *St. Louis Post-Dispatch*, May 14, 2000, p. A8.

104. Ibid.

105. Iver Peterson, "In New Jersey, Sprawl Keeps Outflanking Its Foes," *New York Times*, March 17, 2000, pp. A1, A19.

CITY FINANCES
AND THE DYNAMICS
OF GROWTH

WHY CITY BUDGETS ARE POLITICAL

What cities do with their considerable fiscal resources is generally a matter of little debate; nothing can put a person asleep faster than reading a city budget. Everyday services such as police protection, maintenance of water and sewer pipes, and flowers in the park are virtually hidden from view because they are ubiquitous and expected. But occasionally cities do things that hit a nerve. Proposals to raise property taxes, subsidize a stadium, or build public housing tend to provoke opposition because it appears to some that the costs and benefits are not being spread out fairly. Despite their snooze value, city budgets are important political documents because they represent a constant struggle over who should pay for and who should receive services and programs.

A leading scholar of urban politics, Paul Peterson, has proposed that city budgets should not be political. In his view, there are two things that cities can do that benefit all citizens equally—promote local economic growth and provide everyday services. Under no circumstances, he says, should cities engage in policies that redistribute from the wealthy and middle-class to poorer citizens. His reasoning is that "economic or market standing" is fundamentally important to cities, and that cities should do nothing that might compromise the possibility of achieving economic success.[1] Because cities compete for investors and middle-class homeowners who bring wealth to a city, city officials must be careful not to drive them away. Therefore, according to this logic, the primary task of local political leadership is to keep the city competitive.

This kind of argument often provokes disagreement among scholars and in public debates.[2] When public officials ask voters to approve public financing for stadiums, for example, letters to the editor often express the view that the money should be spent on low-income housing, homeless shelters, or other social needs.[3] But Peterson maintains that policies that redistribute services and resources from taxpayers to poorer citizens tend to be controversial because they are perceived as unfair. They backfire because those who pay for such policies become motivated to escape the costs by leaving the city and moving to an environment they consider more beneficial. According to Peterson, only well-off cities can afford redistributive policies; "The great irony of redistribution at the local level is that it occurs most where the poor are relatively scarce"[4] because poorer cities can least afford to drive any source of wealth away.

Whatever disagreements there might be about Peterson's argument, the political leaders of cities act as if they agree with it. Cities are constrained to emphasize economic development because of the place they occupy in the American intergovernmental system, which forces them to compete with other cities, and because of the powerful role that investors play in the ability of cities to borrow and spend. Cities are expected to provide a high level of services and also to promote local prosperity, yet they cannot run year-to-year deficits and they are limited in the ways they can raise revenues. In an attempt to get out of this straightjacket, in recent years more and more of the big development projects have been offloaded to special authorities that are not accountable to the public. This is a far-reaching development in municipal finance and policy making that may be undermining democracy at the local level.

CITIES IN THE INTERGOVERNMENTAL SYSTEM

What cities do is crucially important to the health and welfare of citizens. In most other Western nations, much of the basic infrastructure and many of the services provided to citizens originate from central governments. In 1984, for example, when intergovernmental transfers provided only about 20 percent of local revenues in the United States, they provided 40 percent in Japan, 54 percent in Britain, and 80 percent in the Netherlands.[5] Most West European city governments do not have to rely on private lenders to raise money for capital projects; those are generally financed by national governments. The U.S. arrangement is peculiar: "By not providing capital resources to subnational governments from the central government, the United States stands apart from almost every other advanced capitalist state, even other federal states."[6]

Even so, cities in the United States are expected to do more than cities almost anywhere else, despite the fact that their capacity to pay for these activities is limited in a variety of ways. Unlike the federal government, cities cannot run deficits year after year and then cover them by going deeper and deeper into debt. City governments in ninety-nine out of the hundred largest cities in the country are, by law, required to balance their budgets.[7] One consequence is that cities cannot easily adjust to swings in the economic pendulum or to adverse social and demographic trends. (They cannot, therefore, spend their way out of a recession, as the national government can theoretically do.) Their place in the U.S. intergovernmental system basically limits their freedom to maneuver.

Municipal governments are located at the bottom of a three-tiered federal system of governance. At the top, the federal government enjoys the greatest freedom to impose taxes and go into debt. At its discretion, it may make states and cities implement policies that are costly (such as drunk driving, education testing, and antipollution laws), but it does not necessarily provide the money for "unfunded mandates." The federal government has access to the best, most flexible sources of revenue: the personal income tax, payroll taxes (for social security), and corporate income taxes. States are next in line. They also collect personal income taxes (but at a lower rate), and also impose sales and receipts taxes. A large share of their revenues also comes from intergovernmental transfers from the federal government—funds to help pay for such things as welfare, medical and social services, pollution control measures, and transportation infrastructure. Intergovernmental transfers are here to stay basically because members of Congress succeed in their careers by delivering programs for the folks back home (which is called *pork barrel funding* if it is in somebody else's state).

Cities also rely upon a continuous flow of intergovernmental revenues, a small amount from the federal government (for such things as pollution control and law enforcement) but most of it from the states or passed through the states from the federal government (especially important are road construction and maintenance, corrections, and public safety). They also rely upon property taxes, sales taxes, and user charges (such as admission fees to parking facilities, museums and zoos, and special attractions). But it is difficult to find a pattern that fits all cities. Big cities generally derive only a small proportion of their revenues from property taxes, while smaller cities may rely on them as their principal source of funds. A few states allow their cities to collect sales taxes, but most do not. A few cities collect earnings taxes, but most do not (or are not allowed to). The one thing that all cities have in common is the fact that they operate under state laws that dictate how they may raise money.

Local governments may be at the bottom in powers, but not in resources or responsibilities. As shown in Table 12.1, in 1997 local governments employed 12 million workers, with the largest employers being school districts, municipalities, and counties. This was more than four times the 2.7 million civilian workers employed by the federal government and more than six times as many federal workers when postal workers and civilian military personnel are excluded. Local governments also employed more than twice as many workers as the states. The federal government collected nearly $2 trillion in revenue, more than twice as much as the states and three times as much as local governments, and spending patterns (not shown) closely followed these differences. One notable fact is that although local governments collect less revenue and spend less money, they employ far more workers than any other level of government. This is because the services provided by local governments, such as education, police, fire, and sanitation, are extremely labor intensive.

The states impose limitations on how local governments may finance their operations. But there is another strict limitation as well: All local governments must constantly calculate whether their level of taxation is so high that it might drive investors and residents into other jurisdictions. Thus, property taxes

Table 12.1 Federal, State, Local Government Employment and Revenues

Employment (in thousands)

Federal (civilian) (FY 2001)	2,710
Federal less U.S. Postal Service and Department of Defense	1,191
State (FY 1997)	4,733
Local (FY 1997)	12,000
Counties	2,425
Municipalities (cities, towns, and boroughs)	2,755
Townships	455
School districts	5,675
Special districts	691

Revenues (own-source) (in billions of dollars) (FY 1999)

Federal	1,946
State	899
Local (including school and special districts)	625

Note: The revenue figures do not include intergovernmental transfers or borrowing.

Source: All data: *Statistical Abstract of the United States, 2002,* various fiscal years. Federal employment: No. 475, Federal Civilian Employment by Branch and Agency: 1990 to 2001 (data for FY 2001). State and Local employment: No. 441, Governmental Employment and Payrolls: 1980 to 2000 (data for FY1997). Federal revenues: No. 449, Federal Budget—Receipts, Outlays, and Debt: 1960 to 2002 (estimated FY 2002). State and local revenues: No. 417, State and Local Governments—Revenue and Expenditures by Function: 1999 (FY 1999).

cannot creep up past a certain level, and the cities that are allowed by their states to impose earnings or corporate income taxes must consider whether these might injure the local business climate. The constant worry about how local finances and policies will affect local economic performance is actually created by the U.S. intergovernmental system. The ability of a city to collect revenues is directly related to local economic conditions. If property values are falling, so will property tax collections; if retail sales are down, sales taxes fall; if fewer people use facilities in the city, user fees will drop.

The budgetary policies of the federal or state government filter down to local governments. In December 2002, in the midst of a recession, projected state budget deficits reached levels not seen since World War II or, in some cases, since the Great Depression of the 1930s. Because the deficits had reached 13 to 18 percent of state expenditures, states took steps to slash spending. Since a substantial portion of state spending flows to local governments—for education, pollution control, infrastructure such as roads, bridges, water and sewer lines, health clinics, etc.—the cities expected to receive less aid than before. Compounding the problem, the federal government also began to withhold funds. Previously, for example, the White House had promised to send money to cities to assist in the enhanced security costs associated with homeland security and had also promised to defray some of the costs borne by school districts for new educational testing requirements imposed by Congress. Neither was forthcoming. Not only do local governments have less access to the best sources of revenue, they also sometimes are left holding the bag.

CITY REVENUES

The sources for the revenues that cities collect are dictated by two basic considerations: what state laws allow, and what the local officials feel they can impose without harming their ability to compete for investors and middle-class residents.[8] Because state and city officials tend to agree on the latter, states tend to approve taxes that do not threaten local economic performance. Nearly all cities are allowed by their states to impose property taxes, probably because this tax has such a long history. Most of them are also allowed to charge user fees for such facilities as public parking, museums and zoos, ice rinks, and swimming pools, and in the same spirit, most cities are permitted to collect taxes that target visitors, such as hotel/motel and entertainment taxes. Twenty-eight states allow their cities to impose taxes on retail sales, but only 8 percent of cities (most of them in Ohio and Pennsylvania) are able to impose income taxes.[9]

Historically, the property tax was the principal source of revenue used by local governments. The most important and widely used form of property tax is the ad valorem real property tax, a levy imposed as a percent of the value of land and its improvements. From colonial times through the early years of the republic, real property was taken to be the best indicator of both wealth and the ability to pay taxes. Indeed, this was generally true. Most of the wealth of the era was tied to the land, and fortunes were made in land speculation. A person's wealth was roughly proportional to landholdings. The real property tax, therefore, was relied on to finance state and local governmental services.[10]

Taxation of personal (or nonreal) property—that is, assets other than real estate and improvements—evolved steadily as the cities became more complex. As trade and manufacturing grew in importance, more and more wealth became represented in bank accounts, merchandise, patent rights, machinery, capital stock, and corporate assets. Cities (and states) began to levy taxes on such sources of wealth in order to maintain a reliable relationship between individual tax burdens and personal wealth. Such assets were often hard to find and assess, however. Because of this, although the numbers of people with significant personal assets mushroomed after the Civil War, the proportion of the property tax attributable to personal property actually fell.[11]

Because they are distasteful to residents and businesses, in recent years property taxes have steadily fallen as a proportion of revenues collected by cities. In 1902, personal and real property taxes accounted for 73 percent of all municipal revenues, with license and franchise fees accounting for most of the rest. These taxes continued to provide approximately three-fourths of all local receipts until the late 1930s and early 1940s, when the proportion began to decline in favor of other revenue sources, especially new municipal sales and income taxes.[12] By 1962, property taxes accounted for barely 50 percent of municipal revenues in the seventy-two largest metropolitan areas (even though the property tax continued to generate almost all the revenue for school districts). By fiscal 1975, property taxes accounted for little more than a third (35 percent) of the revenues in the largest metropolitan areas, despite a 130 percent increase in the average per capita levy since the early 1960s.[13]

Other sources of revenue had increased much faster than property taxes, including especially intergovernmental aid, sales taxes, user fees, and special charges for such entertainment costs as hotels, motels, and rental cars. Because of this trend, by 1996 reliance on the property tax had dropped to 19 percent for cities over 400,000 in population. In some big cities, property taxes accounted for less than 10 percent of the budget. Property taxes have remained more important for other local governments than for cities. In 1990–1991, school districts raised 97.4 percent of their tax revenues (not counting state aid) from the property tax.[14]

Only in rapidly growing cities of the Sunbelt has the property tax been used as an important source of revenue growth since the 1960s. This has been possible because of the sharply escalating value of property in those cities. In Phoenix, the value of taxable property rose 251 percent from 1965 to 1973; in Newark it increased only 2 percent and in Detroit 14 percent during the same period.[15] But stagnant property values in the industrial cities were only part of the problem. Antiquated assessment procedures in many cities failed to keep the assessed valuations of property in line with their market values in periods of inflation.[16]

The property tax has a number of weaknesses, which has prompted cities to search for alternatives. One weakness is the high proportion of tax-exempt property. According to one study, almost one-third of all real property in the United States is subject to some kind of exemption.[17] In 1982, in just twenty-three states and the District of Columbia, there was $15 billion in exempt property for religious institutions, $22 billion for educational institutions, $15 billion for charitable institutions, and $128 billion for government property.[18] In recent decades, the proportion of tax-exempt property has increased. Many cities have provided tax relief for the homes owned by the aged or the poor ("circuit breaker" laws). States and cities have tried to attract or retain businesses and investors by forgiving or reducing their property taxes. Many states have exempted various forms of business property, such as machines and inventory, from taxation without consulting local governments.[19]

The burden of tax-exempt property falls most heavily on those cities that are least able to afford it because cities have twice as much exempt property located in them as their surrounding suburbs.[20] In 1985, more than 51 percent of the real property in Boston was tax exempt, up from 41 percent in 1972.[21] A 1983 article traced a 3.2-mile route through Boston where a walker would not set foot on a single parcel of taxable property.[22] Cities must provide services for these properties, including police and fire protection, but the owners pay no taxes. The situation in New York so incensed one taxpayer that he sued the city tax commission over the "subsidy of religion," going all the way to the U.S. Supreme Court before finally losing the case.[23]

Another weakness of the property tax as a revenue generator for central cities is that it does not touch suburban commuters and visitors who work and play in the city but do not live there. Commuters cost cities money. Researchers have found that cities with higher proportions of suburban commuters "must spend more per capita on crime protection, traffic control, parking, parks, and other general services to keep up with the flow of people into and through the central city."[24] Sales taxes and user fees have been the answer. Twenty-eight states allow their cities to impose sales taxes, which adds up to nearly 58 percent of cities of over 50,000 population.[25]

One method cities have used to deal with this problem is to levy earnings taxes to be paid by anyone working in the city. Although Charleston, South Carolina, is reported to have levied a tax on income prior to the Civil War, the modern municipal income tax movement began in Philadelphia in 1939. That levy, a flat-rate payroll tax on all earnings of persons who lived or worked in the city, was adopted to relieve financial pressures during the Great Depression. The big advantage of the income tax is that it enables cities to tax nonresident commuters. Research demonstrates that the export ratio (proportion of taxes paid by nonresidents) is higher for local income taxes than for sales taxes or property taxes.[26] In 2002, it was levied by about 8 percent of municipalities of 50,000 or more.[27] Nearly all cities in Ohio, Pennsylvania, and Kentucky could impose it, plus the larger cities in some other states, such as New York City, Kansas City, and St. Louis.[28] More cities would probably use it, but few states allow them to, and there is a nagging fear that it makes cities less competitive in their metropolitan regions.

The revenue source that saved the cities during the 1960s, allowing them to expand both the level and scope of services, was intergovernmental aid. At that time, the federal government established a direct partnership with city governments that helped relieve their fiscal stress. Between 1965 and 1974, intergovernmental transfers to all cities rose 370 percent, more than twice the 153 percent increase in municipal expenditures.[29] As shown in Figure 12.1, in 1978 direct federal aid to cities peaked at 26 percent of cities' own-source revenue. Federal aid began to decline during the Carter Administration, and the bottom fell out in the 1980s. By 1992, federal aid bottomed out at 6.5 percent of city revenues. Subsequently it climbed again to 6.4 percent by 1997. Most of the new aid was allocated for law enforcement activities.

The Reagan Administration effectively ended the special relationship that had been forged between the federal government and cities in the 1960s. Overall, nine grants-in-aid programs of special importance to urban governments were cut 47 percent between 1980 and 1987. General revenue sharing for cities was eliminated in 1986, and the Community Development Block Grant was reduced by 20 percent between 1980 and 1987. Moreover, the targeting of federal grants shifted from distressed to relatively prosperous urban areas.[30] Few cities emerged unscathed, but the most distressed cities lost the most. Direct federal aid to Chicago fell from $472 million in 1981 to $151 million in 1986.

Figure 12.1   **Direct Aid to Cities as a Percentage of
Own-Source Revenue, 1965–1997**

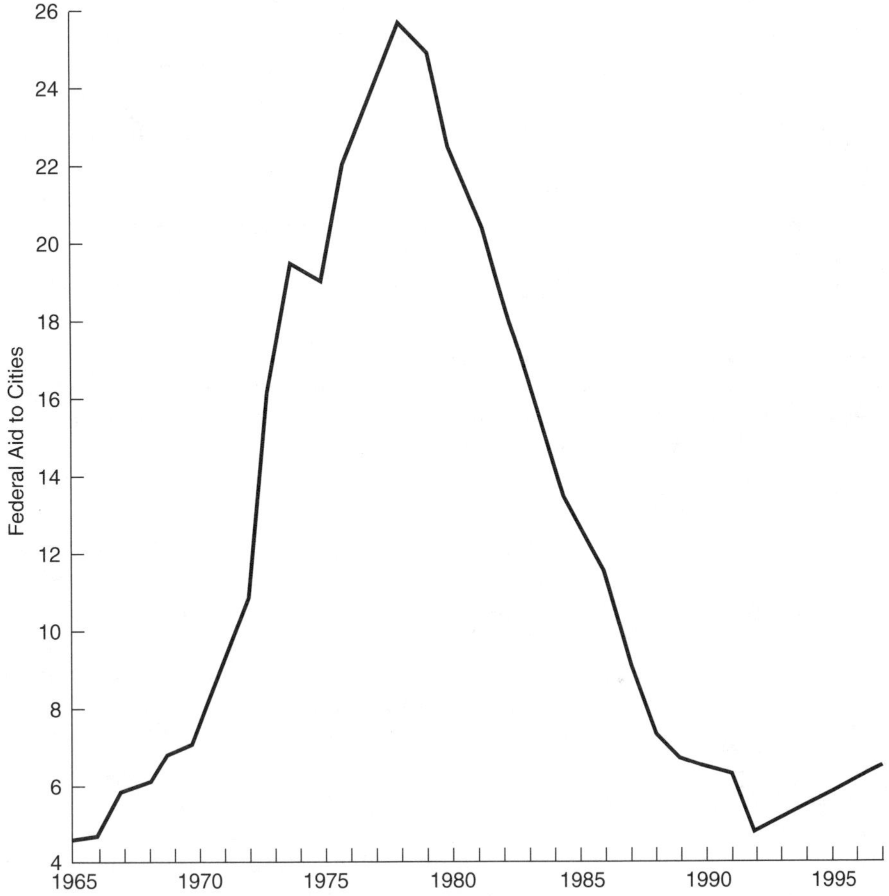

Source: Helen F. Ladd and John Yinger, *America's Ailing Cities: Fiscal Health and the Design of Urban Policy,* updated ed. (Baltimore: Johns Hopkins University Press, 1989), p. 270. Updated using U.S. Bureau of the Census, Census of Governments, Vol. 4, *Government Finances of Municipal and Townships Governments* (Report GC 97), September 2000.

Baltimore's grant volume fell from $220 million to $124 million, Indianapolis's from $125 million to $65 million. Detroit lost $305 million, falling from $456 million in 1981 to $151 million by 1986.[31]

Although federal assistance grew at a faster rate than state government aid in the 1960s and 1970s, more intergovernmental assistance still came from the states. In 1974, cities as a whole received nearly $2 in state revenue for each $1 in federal revenue. By 1980, the ratio of state to federal dollars had declined to $1.47 in state funding for each federal dollar.[32] In the 1980s, some state governments, such as New York, Florida, and Oklahoma, stepped in aggressively to compensate for the federal cuts, but others, such as California, responded minimally.[33] In any case, no state stepped in to completely replace the federal programs.

Not surprisingly, cities responded to cuts in aid from higher levels of government by raising taxes. Between 1980 and 1993, city governments' tax revenues increased 152 percent, but many city governments still had trouble balancing their budgets.[34] Moreover, many found it difficult to respond to cuts in grants by increasing taxes, for they had not escaped the taxpayers' revolts started in the 1970s. During that period, at least fourteen state legislatures enacted laws that limited property tax rates or spending by local governments.[35] Even more far-reaching, however, were the citizen initiatives. The first well-publicized of these was Proposition 13 in California, which was passed by popular referendum in June 1978. From March to November 1978, sixteen states held initiatives or referenda to limit taxes or spending, though not all were binding on public officials.[36] Thirteen of the citizen initiatives passed. More such proposals were approved after 1978. Consequently, even though cities faced severe fiscal problems, their budgetary options were drastically constricted.

Cities imposed an expanding variety of user fees in lieu of new taxes. In 1991, 73 percent of cities increased user fees and 40 percent adopted new user fees for at least one city service.[37] Fees for parking, museums, botanical gardens, zoos, aquariums, and planetariums, ice rinks, and swimming pools were increased, and many of the institutions and programs supporting these services were expected to be self-supporting. In many cities, garbage collection became a private service for which each household pays instead of being a public service paid for out of general tax revenues. User fees and sales taxes take a larger proportion of income for low-income households than for better-off households. To the degree that these taxes have replaced property and income taxes, therefore, the municipal tax structure has become steadily more regressive.[38]

In response to mounting budget deficits in 2003, states and cities all over the nation redoubled their efforts to raise revenues by imposing new fees or hiking those already on the books. New York's mayor, Michael Bloomberg, a Republican, increased fees by $139 million, but also proposed lowering the city's income tax rate. Literally dozens of fees were involved, including a 33 percent increase in subway and bus fares, a 7 percent jump in tuition for public colleges, increases in parking fines, and higher fees to obtain a marriage license and birth certificates or to place a cell phone call from within the city. Fees had already been hiked for the use of public tennis courts and baseball diamonds. In California, a long list of new fees increased the costs of college tuition, car licenses, hunting and fishing licenses, admission to museums and parks, and even tuberculosis (a proposed $50 fee for anyone testing negative and $400 for positive). By raising money through fees rather than taxes, the cost for services used most by poor and working-class people, such as mass transit and public college and community-college education, has increased sharply. At the same time, less regressive forms of taxation (which is what fees are, in reality) have remained steady or even dropped.[39]

The reliance on sales taxes and user fees has made the municipal tax structure extremely sensitive to variations in the economy. The new sources of revenue helped cities take advantage of the economic boom of 1997–2000. At the end of fiscal year 2001 (which ended in July 2001, only weeks before the September 11th terrorist attacks), cities had accumulated ending balances—that is, surpluses—of 19 percent of expenditures, the highest ever recorded in annual budget surveys conducted since 1985 by the National League of Cities.[40] Many cities were able to fund capital projects from these surpluses rather than borrowing money.[41]

The terrorist attacks of September 11, 2001, changed the cities' economic fortunes very quickly. Travel and tourism plummeted, along with the stock market and retail sales. By March 2002, sales taxes had declined to 97 percent of earlier estimates, but income and tourist taxes had fallen to 90 percent.[42] Cities were squeezed between falling revenues and sharp increases in costs for law enforcement and security. As a result, they began making deep cuts in expenditures.

CITY EXPENDITURES

Collectively, local governments in the United States spend huge sums of money. In fiscal year 1999, for example, they spent $938.6 billion; cities accounted for about one-third of this total. The leading municipal budget by far was New York City's, an astonishing $54.1 billion. The next two largest cities, Chicago and Los Angeles, spent $8.1 billion and $5.5 billion respectively.[43]

City expenditures are driven by powerful forces that are largely beyond the control of local officials and voters. City governments are not sovereign entities. Higher levels of government (state and federal) allocate responsibilities—generally called *mandates*—to city governments within the intergovernmental system. Equally important, no matter how dire their budgetary situation may be, cities must provide a minimum level of services necessary for maintaining the physical well-being of city residents and the viability of a city: public health, police and fire protection, education, water distribution, sewage collection, parks, highways, museums, and libraries.

The relative distribution of municipal expenditures among various services and responsibilities for a year typical of the mid-1990s is shown in Table 12.2. In 1996, America's six cities of over one million population devoted a combined 34 percent of their expenditures for "social" programs such as education, community development and housing, public welfare, and health and hospitals. Most cities, even most big cities, do not run the schools within their boundaries; normally, education is financed through independent school districts. The exceptions include some older cities, such as New York, Boston, San Francisco, and Baltimore, that built schools before it had become the usual practice to finance education through special districts, although Chicago has also recently taken over its schools.

Except for education, many of the social services provided by cities would be considered by most people as redistributive in nature, in the sense that they disproportionately benefit lower-income residents. However, failure to treat the

Table 12.2   **Direct Expenditures for Selected Services, Urban Governments[a], in 1996 (In Percentages)**

	Cities of 1,000,000 Population	Cities of 999,999 to 400,000 Population
Expenditures		
Education	12%	9%
Community development and housing	4	3
Public welfare	11	5
Health and hospitals	7	7
Police protection	8	9
Corrections	2	2
Fire protection	3	4.5
Highways	3	4
Parks and recreation	2	5
Sewerage and solid waste	6	7.5
Governmental administration	3	5
General public buildings	0.1	0
Interest on debt	5	7
Other[b]	33	33

[a]38 Cities with estimated populations in 1996 of 400,000 or more.

[b]Includes all expenditures relating to outstanding debt, utilities, and pension systems.

Source: U.S. Bureau of the Census, *Statistical Abstract of the United States, 1999* (Washington , D.C.: Government Printing Office, 1999), pp. 334–335, tables 530–531.

problems of the poor can reverberate through the urban community and affect everyone. Public hospitals and health clinics, for example, are used mostly by people without health insurance. In the absence of public health facilities, many families would quickly become reduced to desperation and penury in an attempt to find health services. Considered on it own merits, this would be a social disaster, but in addition, rates of communicable and contagious diseases such as tuberculosis and AIDS would spread more quickly.

Homelessness is another social problem that most cities attempt to treat with a more complex and compassionate manner than mere law enforcement. Virtually all large cities have a population of homeless people wandering downtown streets. Law enforcement can manage but cannot solve the problem. In January 2003, Chicago's mayor, Richard M. Daley, announced an effort to end homelessness in the city by 2013 by closing homeless shelters and using the money to fund permanent housing and social services. The mayor's proposal, which was drafted by nonprofit organizations working with city administrators, was motivated, in part, by the expense and intractability of the problem. It cost $1,200 a month to provide temporary shelter for a family of three—money that could, instead, be devoted to rental of permanent housing and social services.[44]

Public health services are a major expense in the budgets of large cities, and one they dare not abandon. Cities and counties engage in restaurant inspections and move quickly when cases of food poisoning break out. Health clinics offer free flu shots and screening for diseases. There are constant reminders of the importance of such services. In the summer of 2002, an epidemic of the West Nile virus, which is carried by birds, spread throughout the Midwest, with a heavy outbreak in Illinois. The state of Illinois and Chicago authorities moved fast in an attempt to track the disease. Local governments throughout the Chicago area sprayed ponds and rivers where mosquitoes might breed, and plans were in place to initiate an aggressive campaign of eradication at the start of the mosquito-breeding season in the spring of 2003.

Though smaller cities spend about the same proportion on health and hospitals, they spend less on other social services. Big cities take on more responsibilities for a variety of reasons: Their citizens demand more and better services (for example, well-trained police officers and firefighters), they pay higher salaries to their public employees, and they experience the high service costs made necessary by high-density populations, aging buildings and infrastructure, and high rates of poverty and unemployment. Because they take on more, they spend more; on average, the cities with populations exceeding one million people spend about twice as much for each citizen as the average U.S. city, and many times more than most small cities.

City expenditures rose sharply in the second half of the twentieth century, not only in total amount but also relative to the economy as a whole, increasing from 5 percent of the gross national product (GNP) in 1949–1950 to a high of 9 percent in 1975–1976. But after the recession of 1974–1975, the brakes were applied to municipal budgets. The six biggest cities lost almost 10 percent in spending power from 1975 to 1980, when inflation is taken into account. After adjusting for inflation, cities of all sizes, on the average, did not increase spending at all over the same years. Since 1980, spending has declined slightly (after adjustment for inflation) for cities of all sizes.

The ability of cities to maintain expenditure levels is closely related to local economic vitality. As shown in Table 12.3, some cities in the Frostbelt were forced to make deep cuts in their budgets in the twenty-year period from 1975 to 1996. Measured in constant 1996 dollars (to account for inflation), Baltimore's budget shrank by 36 percent, Cleveland's by 16 percent, and St. Louis's by 27 percent. Of the Frostbelt cities shown in Table 12.3, only New York and Chicago were able to increase their budgets. The contrast with Sunbelt cities is striking. Of the five shown, four increased their budgets substantially; indeed, Phoenix more than doubled its spending. It is true that the populations of several Frostbelt cities fell during this period at the same time that Sunbelt cities grew rapidly. However, city expenditures are not related one to one with population; if anything, older cities bear a bigger burden because of old infrastructure and serious social problems.

Table 12.3 **Total Expenditures for Selected Large Cities, 1975–1996 (in Millions of 1996 Dollars***a***)**

	Fiscal Year 1975 Expenditures	Fiscal Year 1996 Expenditures	Percent Change 1975–1996	Percent Change 1991–1996
Frostbelt Cities				
Baltimore	$2,811	$1,802	–36	00
Chicago	2,880	3,890	35	12
Cleveland	764	644	–16	02
New York	34,292	38,753	13	02
St. Louis	670	487	–27	–14
Sunbelt Cities				
Dallas	614	1,197	95	32
Denver	934	1,716	84	48
New Orleans	661	652	0	–15
Phoenix	567	1,221	115	06
San Jose	376	790	100	05

*a*Adjustments for inflation are calculated using GNP Price Index for state and local government purchases, U.S. Bureau of Economic Analysis, *Survey of Current Business, Dec. 1999*, p. 141, Table 3.

Sources: U.S. Bureau of the Census, *City Government Finances: 1975–76*, GF 76, No. 4 (Washington, D.C.: Government Printing Office, 1977), table 5; U.S. Bureau of the Census, *Statistical Abstract of the United States, 1995*, table 493, (Washington, D.C.: Government Printing Office, 1995) and U.S. Bureau of the Census, *Statistical Abstract of the United States, 1999* (Washington, D.C.: Government Printing Office, 1999), p. 335, table 531.

The economic vitality of cities varies tremendously, and the differences are particularly sharp between central cities and their suburbs. In a 1960 sample of sixty-two cities, the per capita income of central-city residents was 105 percent that of people living in the suburbs; in other words, people living in central cities earned, on the average, slightly more than suburban residents. Clearly, many affluent people still lived in the cities, even after more than a decade of suburban flight. By 1989, the income ratio had fallen drastically; by then, city residents made just 84 percent as much as the residents of suburbs. In 1989, the poverty rate in central cities was 18 percent, but in the metropolitan areas outside central cities it was only 8 percent.[45]

High rates of poverty boost the cost and the need for city services. Central cities and older suburbs, therefore, are particularly vulnerable to fiscal stress. Poverty and unemployment are basically national problems, but they are concentrated in central cities and older suburbs, a result of historical patterns of population immigration and of exclusionary policies that keep poor people out of wealthier suburban jurisdictions. The governments of central cities and older suburbs are in no position to reduce poverty and unemployment, but they are disproportionately saddled with these problems.

Poverty boosts public spending not only for welfare and social services but also for a broad range of other services. Central-city governments spend money on lead paint poisoning prevention (a problem prevalent in older homes), rat control, and housing demolition. Courts have ordered cities to provide shelter for the homeless at significant expense to local governments. In 1987, for example, New York City, as required by court order, spent $274 million to provide emergency shelter to its homeless population.[46] Poverty also drives up the cost of many services. Street cleanliness is more difficult to maintain in ghetto neighborhoods, where the streets are used heavily for recreation but infrequently repaired. Costs of fire protection are higher than elsewhere because of deteriorating housing, the high density of building, old and outdated wiring, and a concentration of flammable materials.

Almost all older cities have experienced significant population losses due to the flight of the middle class to the suburbs. As a city's population falls, the cost of providing infrastructure and basic services, such as police and fire, does not decline correspondingly.[47] Cities still have the same sewer and water lines—often old and in need of frequent repair—and the same miles of streets to plow and patrol. Once the middle class has fled, however, there are fewer taxpayers to pay for these services, and the taxpayers who are left make less taxable income and own less valuable property than those in surrounding jurisdictions.

Another factor that drives up the cost of city services is the panoply of expensive mandates forced on cities by higher levels of government. Cities are not mentioned in the U.S. Constitution; legally, city governments are the creatures of state legislatures. Though many cities have home rule charters that allow them to govern themselves internally within broad guidelines, municipal corporations are not fully sovereign. The scope of a city's service responsibilities is beyond its control. State and federal governments can, and frequently do, order cities to provide particular services or meet minimum standards of service provision. Rarely do the cities receive more money to cover the costs of the mandated standards and services.

Beginning in the mid-1960s, unfunded federal mandates imposed on cities have proliferated. In the case of concurrent powers shared by the federal and state governments, Congress has the power to preempt (override) state and local laws. According to the Supremacy Clause (Article VI) of the Constitution, when there is a conflict between a national law and a state (or local) law, the national law prevails. After 1965, Congress frequently used its powers of preemption to force city governments to address pressing problems without members of Congress having to take the politically unpopular action of appropriating money. Thus Congress has been able to take credit for solving problems while foisting the costs of these solutions onto lower levels of government.

The Supreme Court upheld federal preemption in the 1985 Garcia decision.[48] In Garcia, the Court upheld the constitutionality of the 1974 amendments to the Fair Labor Standards Act, which applied minimum-wage and overtime pay provisions to public transit workers in San Antonio. This decision made it clear that state and local governments are not protected from federal preemption statutes by the Tenth Amendment (which reserves powers not granted to the federal government to the states). Their only protection comes from political

pressures they can put on Congress. In 1986, the U.S. Department of Labor estimated that the cost to state and local governments of complying with the new
labor standards exceeded $1.1 billion.[49]

Federal mandates to preserve environmental quality have been enormously
expensive. The Clean Air Act of 1990, for example, required one hundred cities
to install antipollution devices on their garbage incinerators at an estimated
average cost of $20 million per incinerator.[50] The U.S. Environmental Protection
Agency estimated that the total cost of environmental mandates for local governments increased from $7.7 billion in 1972 to $19.2 billion in 1987.

In March 1995, Congress passed, and President Clinton signed, the
Unfunded Mandates Reform Act, which required Congress to weigh the costs
and benefits of new rules costing over $50 million and to help pay the costs if
state and local governments were forced to implement them, but this legislation
came rather late in the day for most cities. In any case, it has been ignored. In
2002, President Bush promised to help pick up the increased cost of security
borne by cities because of the war on terrorism. As of April 2003, no aid was
forthcoming, and the amount proposed was considered inadequate by local officials. In 2002, the federal government began requiring school districts to administer standardized tests as a condition of receiving federal aid—but no money
was appropriated to cover the costs.

A variety of economic and political forces beyond the control of local officials impact local-government expenditures. Economic downturns, concentrated
poverty, unfunded mandates, and terrorist threats impose unpredictable costs.
As observed by one fiscal expert,

> A city's fiscal health . . . depends on economic, social, and institutional factors that
> are largely outside the city's control. Poor fiscal health is not caused by poor man-
> agement, corruption, or profligate spending, and a city government's ability to alter
> the city's fiscal health is severely limited.[51]

CITIES FOR SALE: THE MUNICIPAL BOND MARKET

If cities had always relied on taxation alone, they would never have been able to
build the permanent infrastructure on which all city life depends. From the mid-
nineteenth century to the present, cities have issued municipal bonds to private
investors as a way of borrowing money.[52] Cities are authorized by state legislation to issue long-term bonds to pay for capital improvements, such as schools,
highways, bridges, and hospitals, that will benefit city residents over a long
period. Cities in most states can borrow short term, using tax anticipation notes
(TANS) repaid in 30 to 120 days, to cover temporary budget shortages or to time
their entry into the long-term bond market. Unlike the federal government,
cities cannot use bond funds to cover long-term operating deficits.

Given the continuing need to build and maintain public infrastructure,
access to the municipal bond market is essential for the well-being of cities.
Cities are directly dependent on the willingness of private-sector individuals

OUT TAKE

INVESTORS HAVE A LOT TO SAY ABOUT URBAN POLICY

A good way to understand how the municipal bond market, banks, and investors influence the choices that cities can make can be seen in the case of New York City's fiscal crisis of 1975. The financial institutions that helped bail it out of that crisis essentially assumed control of its finances and therefore many of its political options. The New York case raises a fundamental question: Do investors or citizens control the budgetary and policy priorities of cities?

Many of New York's fiscal problems can be traced to economic changes beyond its control. In the two decades between 1960 and 1980, New York's population fell by 9 percent, and the nonwhite percentage of the total population increased from 15 percent to 39 percent.[53] In the ten-year period from 1967 to 1977, New York lost 287,000 manufacturing jobs.[54] One study rated cities according to "standardized fiscal health," which was measured as the difference between a city's revenue-raising capacity and its expenditure needs based on economic and social trends. In 1972, out of seventy-one cities, New York ranked dead last.[55]

In an attempt to balance the books, New York's officials engaged in creative accounting. One method of making each year's budget appear balanced when it actually was not was to count projected revenue instead of actual revenue received. The flaw in this method was that not all revenue was collectible even in the distant future. From 1970 to 1976, between $2 billion and $3 billion in city taxes, fees, and fines went uncollected, $1 billion in 1976 alone. Between 1970 and 1975, the delinquency rate for real property taxes rose from 4 percent to 7 percent, totaling $571 million by June 30, 1975.[56] By treating all taxes, fees, and fines as collectible and therefore as projected income, millions of dollars were added, on paper, to the revenue side of the ledger.

Other techniques moved funds around and put off the day of reckoning. Outstanding bills and the last payday of the year were advanced into the next fiscal year. Some current operating expenses, such as planning and engineering operations, were dumped into the capital expenditures budget, which was supported by long-term bonds. In 1975–1976 alone, $600 million was thus transferred to long-term debt.[57] Contributions to the city's pension funds were delayed and underfinanced.[58] Present expenses were shifted into future years by calling borrowed funds "income" and issuing Revenue Anticipation Notes (RANs) and Tax Anticipation Notes (TANs), which were short-term bonds that were to be paid off by future revenues. Short-term debt grew by over 400 percent in ten years.

The politicians and accountants could not have resorted to such clever shell games without the cooperation and even enthusiastic encouragement of bankers and lenders. The bankers were making an enormous amount of money underwriting and marketing New York's securities. Between 1965 and 1975, New York issued nearly $58 billion in bonds. Of this total, $48.5 billion was in short-term, high-interest notes used to roll over the accumulating deficit and rectify the cash flow problems of the city. Bankers and brokers made commissions on every bond sale and were able to promote the bonds to investors because of the high interest rates they carried.

continued on next page

The banks and bond brokers were direct participants in the financial processes of the city through the Bond Council and the Comptroller's Technical Debt Advisory Committee. The latter body, which was composed of both public officials and bankers, existed to advise the city on its borrowing strategy. It implicitly endorsed the city's practices by approving the continuous stream of bonds. William E. Simon, one of the nation's biggest bond brokers, was a member of the committee in 1971 and 1972. As a senior partner in the firm of Salomon Brothers, he "was personally in charge of Salomon's [substantial] municipal and governmental bond sales."[59] One participant in the committee's meetings remarked that "all Simon and some of the other bankers wanted to do was sell bonds, make their profits, and look the other way."[60] This was the same William E. Simon who, as President Gerald Ford's Secretary of the Treasury, advocated a policy of punitive measures against New York when the city asked for a federal loan to avoid default on its debts in 1975. His own culpability in New York's problems did not deter him from observing, when the city asked for help, "We're going to sell New York to the Shah of Iran. It's a hell of an investment."[61]

The deteriorating national economy in the mid-1970s and the troubles of many private businesses (such as the failure of the retail chain W. T. Grant, which left banks holding $640 million in debts[62]) led banks to reevaluate their holdings. New York's bonds were doubly threatening. Not only were they deemed marginal but also, should the city default, the banks could not avoid a possible bankruptcy action that might result in a write-down in the value of the bonds. A rapid write-down would translate into huge losses for the banks[63] and would reverberate through the national and world economies. A near panic about the financial viability of the city ensued.

As described in a report issued by a committee of the New York State legislature, the banks scrambled to save their own profits at the city's expense:

> They began to rapidly and quietly (and perhaps improperly and illegally) unload their New York City bonds and thus saturated the market. You recall, they claimed the market was saturated and hence they could not sell their bonds. This seems to be untrue. In fact it appears that Chase [Manhattan Bank] unloaded two billion dollars' worth of bonds in a very short time!
>
> . . . Here is where the problem gets sticky for the banks. They had knowledge of the problems ahead, but they kept this knowledge to themselves while unloading their portfolios on others. They created the panic by their heavy sales.[64]

New York City's fiscal crisis came to a head in May 1975, when the banks refused to market the city's securities. To resolve the crisis, the state legislature of New York, in response to pressure from the city's banking and business elite, established the Municipal Assistance Corporation (MAC) and the Emergency Financial Control Board (EFCB), both of which essentially took control of city government away from the city's elected officials. Members of the financial community firmly controlled both agencies and through them wielded the power to review annual budgets and borrowing requests.

The bankers were still not satisfied. To get the taxpayers to ensure the safety of their investments, they asked the federal government to guarantee MAC bonds issued to cover the city's debts. Initially, President Ford refused to consider any special aid for New York, prompting a *New York Daily News* headline, "FORD TO CITY: DROP

DEAD" (October 29, 1975). Eventually, the Ford Administration did support a modified bailout bill that enabled the city to borrow funds at 1 percent above the U.S. Treasury borrowing rate. Summing up the federal bailout, one scholar remarked, "Not only did the federal government make money on New York's fiscal crisis but the 'aid' package to the city was actually much less than the Chrysler Corporation bailout [of 1975] and aid given to many Third World nations."[65]

The fiscal retrenchment that followed the crisis had a profound impact on New York City. Immediately, 25,000 city workers were fired, with African American and Latino workers disproportionately losing their jobs. Between 1975 and 1980, city expenditures fell by 21 percent (in constant dollars).[66] Municipal services declined in quantity and quality. Within a year of the crisis, the century-old tradition of free tuition at the City University ended. Subway fares were increased three times in the next six years.[67] As New York gradually regained access to the bond market, tax subsidies for economic development were accorded highest priority and social services were pared.[68] Poor people bore most of the burdens of retrenchment.[69]

The fiscal crisis became the most important issue in the 1977 mayoral campaign. Led by Mayor Edward Koch (1978 to 1989), New York formed a "fiscal crisis" regime in which priorities shifted from city services to tax breaks and other incentives for corporate investors and real estate developers, under the theory that such incentives were necessary to lure investment. Koch effectively used the threat of another fiscal crisis to limit demands for public spending.[70] These measures were far less important than an uptick in the national economy in resolving the city's fiscal crisis. Beginning in 1977, New York enjoyed a decade-long economic boom that enabled the city to balance its budget once again. Between 1978 and 1987, the city's economy gained over 300,000 jobs and tax revenues soared.[71] With another economic downturn that began in 1989, the city found itself, once again, on the brink of fiscal crisis. Despite a healthy national economy, Mayor Giuliani's preliminary budget for 1989 projected a $1.9 billion deficit.[72]

The chronic nature of New York's fiscal crisis revealed how vulnerable the city was to events beyond its control. The city's problems were also structural, in the sense that it administered services it could not easily abandon. New York had costly responsibilities in welfare, health care, education (including an expensive city university system), public hospitals, public housing, and mass transit. In 1968, the state of New York created the Metropolitan Transit Authority (MTA) to coordinate mass transit policy for the city and seven suburban counties, but the city still carried a substantial financial burden for mass transit.[73] In most cases, the city could do little to reduce these services because it was New York State that determined the city's responsibilities. For example, New York City paid 23 percent of the Medicaid bill for recipients in the city.[74]

The degree to which New York's fiscal problems are structural has become even clearer in the wake of the terrorist attack on the World Trade Centers on September 11, 2001. This tragic event, when combined with a lingering recession, has been devastating for the city, costing $7 billion and precipitating a sharp downturn in tourism. Although the federal government has promised to help the city rebuild, the promised funds have not all materialized, and no assistance was offered to compensate the city for lost revenues or help pay for added service or social costs stemming from the disaster.

and institutions to buy their bonds. The municipal bond market is a significant sector of the economy. Borrowings typically represent 20 to 25 percent of all state and local spending. In 1995, cities and towns issued $28 billion in new long-term debt, with total debt outstanding by all local governments amounting to $626 billion.[75]

The most important fact about municipal bonds is that they are tax-exempt. Because the interest income derived from municipal bonds is not subject to taxation, investors are willing to buy municipal bonds at a lower interest rate than they would pay for corporate bonds. In effect, the federal government provides cities with a subsidy by exempting municipal bonds from taxation. In 1988, the Supreme Court ruled that state and local governments had no constitutional right to borrow at tax-exempt rates; Congress has the power to take away this subsidy to state and local governments.[76]

Municipal bonds are purchased by commercial banks, casualty insurance companies, pension funds, and, increasingly, wealthy individual investors, who find the federal tax exemption especially attractive.[77] The federal subsidy to cities through the bond market is relatively inefficient because only part of it, in the form of lower interest rates paid to investors, goes to cities. The rest of the federal subsidy is siphoned off to investors who avoid paying federal taxes by buying the tax-exempt municipal bonds. Legislation has been proposed, but never passed, to allow municipalities to float bonds at normal interest rates in exchange for a direct subsidy by the federal government.[78] In this way, the subsidy would go entirely to cities and not, indirectly, to investors.

Cities issue two types of long-term bonds: general obligation bonds and revenue bonds. General obligation bonds pledge the "full faith and credit" of the city's taxing powers behind the bonds, generally require approval by voters or a representative body, and are used to build public infrastructure like bridges and parks. Revenue bonds are not guaranteed by the issuing government and therefore do not require voter or legislative approval; anticipated future revenues from the facilities that are constructed with the bond monies are committed to pay back the bonds. Revenue bonds are usually issued by public authorities set up by local governments. Run by appointed boards, authorities are free from democratic controls.[79] However, when revenues are not sufficient to pay bond premiums (and they often are not), local governments generally must make up the difference. Sports stadiums (such as the Superdome in New Orleans) often lose millions of dollars a year, and taxpayers pay these debts.

By the mid-1990s, state and local governments had established between 6,000 and 7,000 authorities,[80] and in 1995 alone, these authorities issued $75.3 billion in new long-term debt.[81] Almost any facility that can charge user fees—sports stadiums, convention centers, museums, aquariums—is financed through revenue bonds. Local government borrowing through revenue bonds has risen sharply since the 1970s. Until the 1970s, general obligation bonds represented about 60 percent of outstanding local long-term debt.[82] By 1985, however, nonguaranteed revenue-bond debt represented 63 percent of all outstanding debt issued by city governments and their dependent agencies.[83]

Revenue bonds permit cities to use their tax-exempt borrowing privileges to support private programs and activities. In the late 1970s, cities began issuing mortgage revenue bonds to subsidize interest rates for middle-income home buyers, although in 1980 Congress restricted this practice with the passage of the Mortgage Subsidy Act. In an attempt to stimulate economic growth, in the 1970s and 1980s cities increasingly issued industrial revenue bonds to subsidize a broad assortment of businesses, including K-Mart, McDonalds, liquor stores, and law offices. Critics charged that the tax-exempt borrowing was being used for private purposes that did not serve any public interest. Examples of flagrant abuses abounded. Chester County, Pennsylvania, for example, issued revenue bonds for an adult bookstore and topless go-go bar in downtown Philadelphia. Congress, noting the hemorrhage of federal tax revenues, restricted the use of revenue bonds by passing the Tax Equity and Fiscal Responsibility Act of 1982 and the Deficit Reduction Act of 1984.[84] The Tax Reform Act of 1986 placed state-by-state limits on what it termed governmentally subsidized "private-activity bonds."[85]

Besides being used for questionable private purposes, municipal bonds have been subject to a number of other abuses. Some local governments have borrowed money in the tax-exempt market and then put that money into risky investments, hoping to make substantial profits. Unwilling to raise taxes, Orange County, California, attempted to maintain services by putting the proceeds of bond sales into risky investments called *derivatives* that were essentially gambling on the direction of interest rates. When interest rates plunged, Orange County lost $1.6 billion. In April 1994, Orange County became the largest local government in history to file for federal bankruptcy protection under Chapter 9. More than 180 other governments lost money in similar high-risk investment pools.

In recent years, the municipal bond market has been rocked by charges that bond underwriters, in order to obtain lucrative government bond business, kicked back profits to public officials in the form of campaign contributions.[86] In April 1994, the Securities and Exchange Commission (SEC) enacted Rule G–37, which barred campaign contributions by municipal bankers. To get around this ban, municipal finance companies provided funding for lavish receptions at the 1996 Democratic and Republican conventions where bond underwriters could mingle with top state and local officials. At the Republican convention in San Diego, this included golf and tennis parties, a fishing expedition, and a luncheon honoring House Speaker Newt Gingrich.[87] A 1996 lawsuit alleged that bond underwriters overcharged municipalities for escrow accounts by as much as $1 billion.[88] Such abuses have led to repeated demands that the municipal bond industry be more closely regulated.[89]

A city's cost of borrowing is basically determined by its bond rating. A bond rating purports to represent the relative credit quality of the issuing municipality and thus determines the rate of interest a city must pay. A high rating means a lower interest rate, on the theory that there is less risk for the investor. When a city's bond rating is lowered due to fiscal problems, a bond may be more difficult to sell, and the additional interest paid over the amortized life of the bond can amount to millions of dollars.

Bond ratings are published by several national rating firms, including Moody's Investors Service, Standard and Poor's Corporation, and Fitch's Investor Service. Cities pay to have their bonds rated, but they have no choice but to seek a rating if they want to be able to market their bonds. Although the purpose of the rating is to assess risk, in fact municipal bond ratings are totally unrelated to the likelihood of default. (Default may not mean that the loan was not repaid; a payment may simply not have not been paid on time.) The discrepancy in the interest rates between the highest and lowest investment grade bonds is inexplicable on the basis of relative risk.[90] From 1929 to 1933, when 77 percent of all municipal defaults of the twentieth century occurred, the highest-rated bonds recorded the highest incidence of default.[91]

Major cities simply do not fail to pay their debts. True, from the first recorded default in 1838 (Mobile, Alabama) through 1969 there were more than 6,000 recorded bond defaults by local governments. Fewer than a third of these, however, involved incorporated municipalities (cities); most of the rest were special districts that provided particular services such as irrigation. Seventy-five percent of all such failures occurred between 1930 and 1939. Less than 10 percent occurred after the depression.[92] During the worst period for municipal bonds, 1929 through 1937, only 8 percent of all cities and 19.9 percent of their bonded debt were ever in default.[93] Almost all of the debts were eventually paid.

From World War II through early 1970, a total of 431 state and local units defaulted on their obligations. The total principal involved was $450 million, approximately 0.4 percent of the outstanding state and local debt. Three special authorities, the West Virginia Turnpike Commission, the Calumet Skyway Toll Bridge, and the Chesapeake Bay Bridge and Tunnel Commission, accounted for over 74 percent of this amount (virtually all local governments are considered municipal in the bond market). Only two of twenty-four major default situations ($1 million or more) were related to general obligation bonds.[94] Of 114 defaults by cities during the 1960s, almost all were temporary or technical defaults. Only thirty-four involved general obligation bonds, and in all these cases the cities had populations under 5,000 and the amount in default was less than $1 million.[95]

An analysis of cases filed in federal district courts between 1938 and 1971 reveals that nine cities took advantage of federal municipal bankruptcy legislation. With one exception (Saluda, North Carolina), all the cases came from small, rather obscure cities in Texas (Ranger, Talco, Benevides) or Florida (Manatee, Medley, Center Hill, Webster, Wanchula). Only in the case of Benevides (population 2,500) were general obligation bonds of post–World War II origin involved. In all other cases, the defaulted debt was of prewar origin, related to revenue bonds, or unrelated to bonds altogether.[96]

In the rare cases when a city defaulted on its obligations, it has invariably involved only a technical failure to pay on time, and the failure has been temporary. Bondholders have always recovered their money. On December 15, 1978, Cleveland became the first major city to default, even in a technical sense, since 1933. On that day, the city failed to make payments on $14 million in short-term notes; the city renewed payments a few months later and officially ended default in 1980.[97] There would appear to be little justification for the differential rating of city bonds, especially to give business to rating services and make money for investors.

THE POWERFUL FISCAL ROLE OF SPECIAL AUTHORITIES

An inspection of city budgets can uncover only a portion—perhaps not even the most important portion—of the policy priorities of urban governments. City governments tend to provide basic services—what Paul Peterson has called allocational services. These services, such as police, fire, and trash collection, are used by all citizens.[98] They tend to be noncontroversial and are often almost invisible because they are taken for granted as a part of daily life. But it is obvious that much bigger projects are being undertaken in cities. If most of these projects cannot be found in city budgets, then where are they?

The biggest undertakings—those that seem to be (or are rhetorically) devoted to improving the economic performance of cities—are financed and administered by special authorities that operate independently of city governments. A complete understanding of the policy priorities of urban governments can only be gained by examining the multitude of authorities that have taken responsibility for transportation infrastructure (highways, roads, bridges, tunnels, mass transit, airports, seaports, harbors), water supply, wastewater management, solid waste disposal, and host of institutions involved in urban development. In addition to these traditional activities, special authorities by the dozen finance and manage tourism and entertainment facilities (such as convention centers, sports stadiums, museums, and urban entertainment districts). Even though these authorities constitute much of the institutional fabric of urban government, citizens are often unaware that they even exist. Except for occasional controversies, they tend to operate quietly. Paul Peterson believes that this is a good thing:

> Operating like private firms, these independent authorities see little point in public discussion. Because it is in the city's interest to develop self-financing projects that enhance the productivity of the community, there can be no place for the contentious group conflict that may characterize another policy arena.[99]

People may disagree about whether such authorities should operate outside the constraints of public accountability, but Peterson's description of how they operate is accurate. They are not democratic.

Special authorities have operated regional transportation systems since the 1930s. The Port of New York Authority and the Triborough Bridge and Tunnel Authority, created in the 1930s, became the model for similar regional port and transportation authorities from coast to coast. These institutions amassed huge budgets by collecting tolls and taxes on roads, tunnels, and bridges. In the New York–New Jersey region, the Triborough Authority, under the direction of Robert Moses, cleared vast swaths through urban neighborhoods, built parks, and shaped the growth of the metropolitan region through the location of key infrastructure. Moses acted as a virtual czar of development for three decades, from the 1930s to the 1960s, until his accumulation of vast power was challenged by political activists protesting his dictatorial brand of urban development. Robert Caro's monumental book, *The Power Broker*, stands as a classic study of how excessive power can overwhelm democratic governance, often to the detriment of sound urban development and simple justice for people living in the path of the bulldozer.[100]

In recent decades, huge fiscal resources have been poured into the physical reconstruction of older downtowns and in the building of an infrastructure of tourism and entertainment. Mass volumes of public money have been involved in this effort; for example, more than $2 billion was spent annually in the first half of the 1990s on sports facilities and convention centers alone.[101] In addition, billions of public dollars have been spent on urban entertainment and cultural districts, renovated waterfronts, aquariums, marketplaces, festival malls, and the other accoutrements of the tourism/entertainment complex. Municipal governments could not possibly have raised such resources, though they have been essential to the task. Cities have been involved in complicated deal-making, offering to provide public infrastructure and amenities, to rezone or assemble parcels of land through the power of eminent domain, to reduce or forgive taxes, or to subsidize private development.[102] But the latter role—the fiscal one—has more often been assumed by new public/private authorities created for the purpose.

Beginning in the 1980s, a generation of visionary mayors accepted the fact that they would have to find ways to regenerate their own economies. These "messiah mayors" preached a gospel of self-help for cities in desperate need of new ideas and directions. As noted by the historian Jon Teaford, "if nothing else the messiah mayors ... boosted the spirits of many urban dwellers and made them proud of their cities."[103] But much more was involved than cheerleading. These mayors also pioneered in the creation of institutions that could earmark taxes, charge user fees, issue bonds, establish trust funds, and use other mechanisms to finance big undertakings.[104]

The revival of downtown real estate was connected to a change in the methods used by city governments to spur development. The urban renewal and slum clearance programs of the 1950s and 1960s had been based on a massive infusion of federal funds. In the 1970s and 1980s, cities began to experiment with partnerships between the public and private sectors to promote investment in the local economy. They devoted federal block grants to big downtown projects, floated bonds, offered property tax abatements, built utilities tunnels, constructed sewer lines and water mains, and rerouted and resurfaced streets. In these and other ways, cities provided public subsidies to encourage private investment in office towers, malls, and cultural and tourist facilities.

The melding of public subsidies and private dollars took place through newly created incorporated entities that oversaw specific projects—a sports authority to build a stadium, for example, or a public development corporation run like a private corporation, established specifically to receive a combination of public subsidies and private investment funds.[105] As more cities began cutting complex deals with private developers, the dividing line between the public and private sectors became blurred. In exchange for subsidies, some cities took profit-sharing positions in development projects. In the case of Quincy Market, for example, the city of Boston provided $12 million—almost 30 percent of the total cost of the project—and gave the Rouse Corporation a ninety-nine-year lease on the property. In exchange, the city was guaranteed a minimum annual cash payment plus a portion of income from store rents above that minimum.

The main achievement of these mayors was to find ways out of the straightjacket of debt limitations imposed on municipal governments. Their solution was to offload many of the responsibilities of city government onto institutions that could generate their own resources and that could be run like private corporations. These public/private institutions were generally established through enabling legislation passed by state legislatures, and they were run by boards appointed by a governor and mayor, the mayor alone, or some combination of public officials. They were not bound by the rules that frustrated public initiatives by general-purpose governments. They could make decisions without worrying about what voters thought. They could protect their information and books from public scrutiny, but at the same time, since they pursued public objectives, they could act just like governments and generate revenue, receive funds from other governments, and borrow money and sell tax-free bonds.

The sprawling McCormick Place convention center and the renovated Navy Pier entertainment complex in Chicago are administered by the Metropolitan Pier and Exposition Authority, which is governed by a board appointed by the mayor of Chicago and the governor of Illinois. The state of Illinois designates $98 million annually, derived from revenues from taxes (mainly a tax on cigarette sales) to pay off previous bonds for construction and remodeling.[106] Not only has Illinois paid for the world's largest convention center complex (which is undergoing another expansion); in 2000, the Pier and Exposition Authority floated a $108 million tax-exempt bond issue to build and own the Hyatt Regency McCormick Place Hotel.[107]

It is a mistake to describe special authorities as mere mechanisms for financing and administrating large undertakings. They are also political in nature and are always on the lookout for ways to promote their own projects and enhance their fiscal and administrative capacity. In the case of the professional football and baseball stadiums in Baltimore, an agency of the state government, the Maryland Stadium Authority, financed the two stadiums through proceeds from a sports lottery offered through the Maryland State Lottery.[108] The campaign to build the sports stadium was guided by this new agency, which commissioned studies to show a powerfully positive impact on Baltimore's economy. When another state agency followed with its own studies, it reduced the estimated impact, but independent studies sharply contested even these estimates as unrealistic, concluding that stadium development brought virtually no measurable economic benefit.[109]

The political nature of special authorities is illustrated in the case of the Denver Metropolitan Stadium District, which was created in 1990 by the Colorado legislature as a means of pushing forward plans for a new baseball stadium. The bill establishing the district did not contain financing mechanisms, because any that would have been proposed would have ignited controversy. Instead, the task of lining up political support for a new stadium was left to the seven-member Stadium District Board. Securing financing was more a political than a fiscal exercise. In close collaboration with the city of Denver, the board ran an astute campaign that kept voters in the metropolitan counties outside Denver in the dark about whether the stadium might be built close to or within their own jurisdictions. The uncertainties about location carried the day. In August 1990, voters in the six-county district passed a sales tax levy to build the stadium; large majorities in the city and an adjacent county overcame a losing margin elsewhere.[110] Just as many voters had suspected, the fix had been in all along, and the stadium was built in downtown Denver.

Special-purpose authorities have sprung up to administer the many components that make up the tourism/entertainment complex in cities, such as convention centers, festival malls, and urban entertainment districts. Redevelopment corporations also have proliferated, often to administer the funds made available from Tax Increment Finance districts (TIFs), which have become popular instruments for financing urban redevelopment. TIF corporations are able to market bonds to investors based on the taxes that are expected to be collected on land slated for redevelopment. The proceeds from bonds are generally used to make public improvements that will lure private investment.

The proliferation of special-purpose authorities throughout metropolitan areas has removed more and more of the most important public policies from general-purpose municipalities. While municipalities are run democratically— with mayors, city councils, and other elected officials—special-purpose authorities operate out of the public eye. Some of the most expensive and sometimes controversial undertakings have been assigned to special-purpose authorities. Convention centers and stadiums are built with public money, but with little or no public input. An absence of public accountability always raises troubling questions. In the 1950s, urban renewal authorities regularly abused their powers. Transportation authorities rammed highways through urban neighborhoods. In both cases, excessive authority facilitated abuses, which were only curbed when citizens organized protests. Special-purpose authorities today are equally lacking in accountability.

FISCAL FRAGMENTATION

Cities provide essential services and also assume critical social responsibilities. It would be impossible for them to maintain the social peace and abandon all services that might be classified as redistributive. In a nation where nearly 40 percent of citizens lack health insurance, they are frontline providers of health services through public hospitals and clinics, not only for the poor but also for some members of the underinsured middle-class. They also provide essential housing services, even if most of this takes the form of contributing to or maintaining homeless shelters. And nearly all larger cities provide some public welfare, normally emergency aid for people who do not qualify for other benefits. During cold and heat emergencies, cities are expected to assist in providing immediate help. Between July 17 and 20, 1995, the city of Chicago was hit by a heat wave in which temperatures reached 106 degrees. City officials were not only unprepared; they did not feel it was in their purview to respond except through normal emergency services. By the time the heat wave had run its course, the number of excess deaths attributed to the heat wave reached 739. Realizing that a repeat of such a disaster would become a public relations nightmare as well as a social catastrophe, the city subsequently (but quietly) put into place an emergency plan.[111] Cities simply cannot opt out of their social responsibilities.

For the most part, however, what cities do is provide basic public services. These do not cause controversy, and in any case they are sufficiently expensive and labor-intensive that they soak up most of the city's budget. These allocational services are "more or less neutral in their effects" and therefore do not tend to stir up much controversy.[112] City employees may demand better pay and benefits, neighborhoods may squabble over the location of a new school or fight about whose park gets improved first, but these kinds of conflicts occur from time to time in all cities.

Today, the most ambitious undertakings are not located in municipalities at all, but in a panoply of special authorities. Skylines have been transformed in the last thirty years more by governments hidden from view than from governments presided over by democratically elected officials. Likewise, most of the basic infrastructure of urban areas is built by professionals working in institutions that seem more like private corporations than like governments. To understand the fiscal structure of metropolitan areas, it is necessary to look outside municipalities. From that broader perspective, it becomes obvious that developmental politics—a devotion to promoting economic growth—is the highest policy priority in urban America, today as in the past.

NOTES

1. Paul Peterson, *City Limits* (Chicago: The University of Chicago Press, 1981), p. 22.
2. For an example of the disagreement among scholars, see John Logan and Todd Swanstrom, eds., *Beyond the City Limits: Urban Policy and Economic Restructuring in Comparative Perspective* (Philadelphia: Temple University Press, 1990).
3. A quite typical example occurred during the controversy over public funding for a domed stadium for the National Football League's St. Louis Rams, which moved to the city in 1995. The Reverend Larry Rice, a well-known advocate for the poor, organized a campaign against the proposal and even went on a hunger strike, claiming that it was immoral to fund a stadium while so many people in the city were in need. For an account of this controversy, see David Laslo, Claude Louishomme, Donald Phares, and Dennis R. Judd, "Building the Infrastructure of Urban Tourism: The Case of St. Louis," in ed. Dennis R. Judd, *The Infrastructure of Play: Building the Tourist City*, (Armonk, N.Y.: M.E. Sharpe, 2003).
4. Peterson, *City Limits*, p. 64. In addition to policies of development and redistribution, Peterson proposes a third category: allocational policies. These, he says, include such services as police and fire services, which are available to all citizens. Though disagreements may arise over the level of services and how to pay for them, the primary emphasis tends to be placed on efficiency.
5. Arnold J. Heidenheimer, Hugh Heclo, and Carolyn Teich Adams, *Comparative Public Policy: The Politics of Social Choice in America, Europe, and Japan*, 3rd ed. (New York: St. Martin's Press, 1990), p. 278.
6. Thomas H. Boast, "A Political Economy of Urban Capital Finance in the United States" (Ph.D. dissertation, Cornell University, 1977), p. 114.

7. Carol W. Lewis, "Budgetary Balance: The Norm, Concept, and Practice in Large U.S. Cities," *Public Administration Review* 54 (November/December 1994): 517–518.

8. Any summary of revenue sources for all cities is misleading and is therefore not presented in this chapter. Cities simply vary too much for such summaries to be meaningful; earnings taxes can be collected by a few cities, but not most; sales taxes are allowed by twenty-eight states, and so forth.

9. Michael A. Pagano, *City Fiscal Conditions in 2002: A Research Report on America's Cities* (Washington, D.C.: National League of Cities, 2002), p. 3.

10. Refer to Richard T. Ely, *Taxation in American States and Cities* (New York: Crowell, 1888), pp. 109–113; and Sumner Benson, "A History of the General Property Tax," in *The American Property Tax: Its History, Administration, and Economic Impact*, ed. C. G. Benson, S. Benson, H. McClelland, and P. Thompson (Claremont, Calif.: College Press, 1965), p. 24.

11. E. R. A. Seligman, *Essays in Taxation*, 9th ed. (New York: Macmillan, 1923), p. 24.

12. U.S. Bureau of the Census, *Historical Statistics of the United States: Colonial Times to 1970*, Bicentennial ed. pt. 2 (Washington, D.C.: Government Printing Office, 1975), p. 1133.

13. Calculated from the data in U.S. Bureau of the Census, *Local Government Finances in Selected Metropolitan Areas and Large Counties: 1969–70*, GF 70, No. 6 (Washington, D.C.: Government Printing Office, 1970), p. 7; U.S. Bureau of the Census, *Local Government Finances in Selected Metropolitan Areas and Large Counties: 1974–75*, GF 75, No. 6 (Washington, D.C.: Government Printing Office, 1976), p. 7.

14. U.S. Census Bureau, *Statistical Abstract of the United States*, Table 259 (Washington, D.C.: Government Printing Office, 1996) p. 169.

15. George Peterson, "Finance," in *The Urban Predicament*, ed. William Gorham and Nathan Glazer (Washington, D.C.: The Urban Institute, 1976), p. 52.

16. Ibid., p. 53.

17. Alfred Balk, *The Free List—Property Without Taxes* (New York: Russell Sage Foundation, 1971), pp. 10–12.

18. J. Richard Aronson and John L. Hilley, *Financing State and Local Governments*, 4th ed. (Washington, D.C.: Brookings Institution, 1986), p. 136.

19. Helen F. Ladd and John Yinger, *America's Ailing Cities: Fiscal Health and the Design of Urban Policy*, updated ed. (Baltimore: Johns Hopkins University Press, 1989), pp. 129–130, 180. See also Michael Wolkoff, "Municipal Tax Abatement: A Two-Edged Sword," *New York Case Studies in Public Management* 4 (Albany, N.Y.: Rockefeller Institute of Government, 1984).

20. Gregory H. Wassall, *Tax-Exempt Property: A Case Study of Hartford, Connecticut* (Hartford, Conn.: John C. Lincoln Institute, 1974), p. 27.

21. Todd Swanstrom, *Capital Cities: Challenges and Opportunities* (Albany, N.Y.: Rockefeller Institute of Government), p. 17.

22. Michael J. Barrett, "The Out-of-Towners," *Boston Globe Magazine*, August 7, 1983.

23. *Walz v. Tax Commission of the City of New York*, 397 U.S. 664. See also Boris I. Bittker, "Churches, Taxes and the Constitution" *Yale Law Review* 78 (July 1969): 1285–1310.

24. Ladd and Yinger, *America's Ailing Cities*, p. 87.

25. Michael A. Pagano, *City Fiscal Conditions in 2002: A Research Report on America's Cities* (Washington, D.C.: National League of Cities, 2002), p. 3.

26. Ladd and Yinger, *America's Ailing Cities*, p. 54. Surprisingly, local sales taxes have an even worse export ratio than property taxes.

27. Pagano, *City Fiscal Conditions in 2002*, p. 3.

28. Ibid.

29. Eric A. Anderson, "Changing Municipal Finances," *Urban Data Services Reports* 7, no. 12 (Washington, D.C.: International City Manager Association, December 1975), p. 2.

30. Peggy L. Cuciti, "A Nonurban Policy: Recent Public Policy Shifts Affecting Cities," in *The Future of National Urban Policy*, ed. Marshall Kaplan and Franklin James (Durham, N.C.: Duke University Press, 1990), pp. 243–244. See also Hal Wolman, "The Reagan Urban Policy and Its Impacts," *Urban Affairs Quarterly* 21, no. 3 (1986): 311–335.

31. Richard L. Cole, Delbert A. Taebel, and Rodney V. Hissong, "America's Cities and the 1980s: The Legacy of the Reagan Years," *Journal of Urban Affairs* 12, no. 4 (1990): 348.

32. U.S. Advisory Commission on Intergovernmental Relations, Significant Features of Fiscal Federalism 1980–81, (Washington, D.C.: Author, 1981), p. 59.

33. Richard P. Nathan and Fred C. Doolittle, *Reagan and the States* (Princeton, N.J.: Princeton University Press, 1987), p. 19.

34. U.S. Census Bureau, *Statistical Abstract of the United States, 1996,* Table 497 (Washington, D.C.: Government Printing Office, 1996), p. 315.

35. John L. Mikesell, "The Season of Tax Revolt," in *Fiscal Retrenchment and Urban Policy,* ed. John P. Blair and David Nachmias (Beverly Hills, Calif.: Sage, 1979), p. 109.

36. Ibid.

37. Michael A. Pagano, *City Fiscal Conditions in 1991: A Research Report of the National League of Cities* (Washington, D.C.: National League of Cities, 1991), p. 24.

38. Cole, Taebel, and Hissong, "America's Cities and the 1980s," p. 352.

39. Michael Powell and Christine Haughney, "Wary of Taxes, Officials Boost Fees; Tactic Hurts Poor and Working Class, Critics Say," *Washington Post,* April 7, 2003, p. A3.

40. Pagano, *City Fiscal Conditions in 2002,* p. 18. See also Michael A. Pagano, "Municipal Capital Spending During the 'Boom,'" *Public Budgeting and Finance* 22, no. 2 (Summer 2002), pp. 1–20.

41. Ibid.

42. Ibid., p. 20.

43. U.S. Bureau of the Census, *Statistical Abstract of the United States, 2002,* (Washington, D.C.: Government Printing Office, 2002), Table 438, "City Governments—Expenditure and Debt for Largest Cities, 1999."

44. Gary Washburn, "City Maps Long-term Homeless Program," *Chicago Tribune,* January 22, 2003, p. 3.

45. Larry C. Ledebur and William R. Barnes, *City Distress: Metropolitan Disparities and Economic Growth* (Washington, D.C.: National League of Cities, 1991), pp. 2, 6. Figures based on the eighty-five largest metropolitan areas.

46. Jonathan Kozol, *Rachel and Her Children: Homeless Families in America* (New York: Crown, 1988), p. 14.

47. Roy Bahl, Jorge Martinez, and Loren Williams. "The Fiscal Conditions of U.S. Cities at the Beginning of the 1990s," Urban Institute Conference on Big City Governance and Fiscal Choices, Los Angeles, June 1991. pp. 5–6.

48. *Garcia v. San Antonio Metropolitan Transit Authority,* 469 U.S. 528 (1985).

49. Employment Standards Administration, *Minimum Wage and Maximum Hours Standards Under the Fair Labor Standards Act* (Washington, D.C.: U.S. Environmental Protection Agency, 1986), pp. 110–111; U.S. Congress, House Committee on Education and Labor, *Report to Accompany H.R. 3530,* 99th Cong., 1st sess., 1985. H. Rept. 99–331, p. 30; both cited in Joseph F. Zimmerman, "Federally Induced State and Local Governmental Costs" (paper delivered at the Annual Meeting of the American Political Science Association, Washington, D.C., August 29–September 1, 1991), p. 14.

50. Todd Sloane, "Clean Air Act Likely to Burn Many Municipalities," *City and State,* November 19, 1990, p. 2, cited in Zimmerman, "Federally Induced State and Local Government Costs," p. 12.

51. Ladd and Yinger, *America's Ailing Cities,* p. 291.

52. Bonds issued not only by cities but also by states and all local governments are referred to as municipal bonds, a cause of endless confusion.

53. U.S. Bureau of the Census figures as compiled by Ester R. Fuchs, *Mayors and Money: Fiscal Policy in New York and Chicago* (Chicago: University of Chicago Press, 1992), pp. 22–23. For our comparison of New York and Chicago, we rely heavily on Fuchs's insightful account.

54. U.S. Bureau of the Census, *Census of Manufacturing,* selected years (Washington, D.C.: Government Printing Office, 1950 and 1981), as compiled by John D. Kasarda, "Urban

Change and Minority Opportunities," in *The New Urban Reality*, ed. Paul Peterson (Washington, D.C.: Brookings Institution, 1985), p. 44.

55. Ladd and Yinger, *America's Ailing Cities*, p. 121.

56. Jack Newfield and Paul DuBrul, *The Abuse of Power: The Permanent Government and the Fall of New York* (New York: Viking, 1977), p. 31.

57. Fred Ferretti, *The Year the Big Apple Went Bust* (New York: Putnam, 1976), p. 46.

58. George E. Peterson, "Finance," in *The Urban Predicament*, p. 65.

59. Ferretti, *The Year the Big Apple Went Bust*, p. 45.

60. Roger E. Alcaly and Helen Bodian, "New York's Fiscal Crisis and the Economy," in *The Fiscal Crisis of American Cities*, ed. Roger E. Alcaly and David Mermelstein (New York: Random House, 1977), p. 288.

61. Quoted in Ferretti, *The Year the Big Apple Went Bust*, p. 6.

62. Alcaly and Bodian, "New York's Fiscal Crisis and the Economy," p. 53.

63. Edward J. Kane, "Why 'Bad Paper' Worries Economic Policies," *Bulletin of Business Research* (July 1975), cited in ibid., pp 53–54.

64. From a confidential memorandum from William Haddad, director of the Office of Legislative Oversight and Analysis, to George Cincotta, chairman of the New York Assembly Banking Committee, July 7, 1976; quoted in Newfield and DuBrul, *The Abuse of Power*, p. 42.

65. Ester Fuchs, *Mayors and Money: Fiscal Policy in New York and Chicago* (Chicago: University of Chicago Press, 1992), p. 91.

66. Raymond D. Horton and Mary McCormick, "Services," in *Setting Municipal Priorities, 1981*, ed. Charles Brecher and Raymond D. Horton (Montclair, N.J.: Allanheld Osmun, 1980), p. 89.

67. Martin Shefter, *Political Crisis/Fiscal Crisis: The Collapse and Revival of New York City* (New York: Basic Books, 1985), p. 135.

68. Charles Brecher and Raymond D. Horton, "Retrenchment and Recovery: American Cities and the New York Experience," *Public Administration Review* 45 (March–April 1985): 270.

69. Shefter, *Political Crisis/Fiscal Crisis*, p. 148.

70. Fuchs, *Mayors and Money*, p. 10.

71. Robert F. Wagner Jr., *New York Ascendant: The Report of the Commission on the Year 2000* (New York: HarperCollins, 1987), p. 1.

72. Clifford J. Levy, "Mayor Rebuts Criticism of Budget Plan," *New York Times*, February 1, 1997, p. 1.

73. Fuchs, *Mayors and Money*, p. 205.

74. Wagner, *New York Ascendant*, pp. 93–94.

75. U.S. Bureau of the Census, *Statistical Abstract of the United States, 1996*, p. 304. Amounts are estimates subject to sampling variation.

76. *South Carolina v. Baker*, 108 S.Ct. 1935 (1988).

77. Alberta Sbragia, "Finance Capital and the City," in *Cities in Stress: A New Look at the Urban Crisis*, ed. M. Gottdiener (Beverly Hills, Calif.: Sage, 1986), p. 210.

78. See Robert Huefner, *Taxable Alternatives to Municipal Bonds*, Research Report No. 53 (Boston: Federal Reserve Bank of Boston, 1972); and *Building a Broader Market: Report of the Twentieth Century Fund Task Force on the Municipal Bond Market*, with a background paper by Ronald W. Forbes and John E. Peterson (New York: McGraw-Hill, 1976).

79. For insightful discussions of the powerful role of local authorities, see Ann Marie Hauck Walsh, *The Public's Business: The Politics and Practices of Government Corporations* (Cambridge, Mass.: MIT Press, 1978); and Alberta M. Sbragia, *Debt Wish: Entrepreneurial Cities, U.S. Federalism, and Economic Development* (Pittsburgh: University of Pittsburgh Press, 1996).

80. Sbragia, *Debt Wish*, p. 144.

81. U.S. Bureau of the Census, *Statistical Abstract of the United States, 1996*, p. 304.

82. Elaine B. Sharp, "The Politics and Economics of the New City Debt," *American Political Science Review* 80, no. 4 (December 1986): 1271–1288.

83. U.S. Bureau of the Census, *Statistical Abstract of the United States,* (Washington, D.C.: Government Printing Office, 1992), p. 285.

84. Thomas A. Pascarella and Richard D. Raymond, "Buying Bonds for Business: An Evaluation of the Industrial Revenue Bond Program," *Urban Affairs Quarterly* 18 (September 1982): 73–89.

85. Daphne A. Kenyon and Dennis Zimmerman, "Private-Activity Bonds and the Volume Cap in 1990," *Intergovernmental Perspective* 17, no. 3 (Summer 1991): 35–37.

86. For citations on municipal bond corruption, see Sbragia, *Debt Wish,* pp. 224–225.

87. Leslie Wayne, "Ban on Political Contributions Considered for Bond Lawyers," *New York Times,* August 5, 1996, Section D, p. 2.

88. Peter Truell, "Municipal Bond Dealers Face Scrutiny," *New York Times,* December 17, 1996, Section D, p. 1. Michael R. Lissack, "A Giant Shell Game Snares Taxpayers," *Albany Times Union,* August 1, 1996, p. A11.

89. "Shine the Light on Muni Deals," *Business Week,* August 26, 1996.

90. Thomas Geis, "Municipal Credit and Bond Rating System" (paper delivered at the Municipal Officers Association Meeting, Denver, May 31, 1972), pp. 5–6.

91. Ibid.

92. U.S. Advisory Commission on Intergovernmental Relations, *City Financial Emergencies* (Washington, D.C: Government Printing Office, 1971), p. 10.

93. Ibid., p. 12.

94. Ibid., p. 16.

95. Ibid., p. 17.

96. Ibid., pp. 81–82.

97. Todd Swanstrom, *The Crisis of Growth Politics: Cleveland, Kucinich, and the Challenge of Urban Populism* (Philadelphia: Temple University Press, 1985), chap. 7.

98. Peterson, *City Limits,* pp. 150–166.

99. Ibid., p. 134.

100. Robert A. Caro, *The Power Broker: Robert Moses and the Fall of New York* (New York: Knopf, 1974).

101. Peter Eisenger, "The Politics of Bread and Circuses," *Urban Affairs Review* 35, no. 3 (January 2000): 316–333.

102. For a detailed account of these complex processes, see Bernard J. Frieden and Lynne B. Sagalyn, *Downtown Inc.* (Cambridge, Mass: MIT Press, 1989).

103. Jon Teaford, *The Rough Road to Renaissance: Urban Revitalization in America, 1940–1985* (Baltimore: Johns Hopkins University Press, 1990), p. 307.

104. James Leigland, "Public Infrastructure and Special Purposed Governments: Who Pays and How?", *Building the Public City: The Politics, Governance, and Finance of Public Infrastructure* ed. David C. Perry, (Thousands Oaks, Calif: Sage, 1995), p. 139.

105. These arrangements are described in Peter K. Eisenger, *The Rise of the Entrepreneurial State: State and Local Economic Development Policy in the United States* (Madison: University of Wisconsin Press, 1988).

106. State of Illinois, Compliance Audit Report (1998 and 1999). http://www.state.il.us/auditor.

107. William Fulton, "Paying the Bill," *Governing* 15, no. 11 (August 2002): 60.

108. Donald F. Norris, "If We Build It, They Will Come! Tourism-Based Economic Development in Baltimore," in Judd, *The Infrastructure of Play,* p. 162.

109. Ibid., p. 151.

110. Susan E. Clarke and Martin Saiz, "From Waterhole to World City: Place Luck and Public Agendas in Denver," in Judd, *The Infrastructure of Play,* pp. 183–184.

111. Eric Klinenberg, *Heat Wave: A Social Autopsy of Disaster in Chicago* (Chicago: University of Chicago Press, 2002), p. 9.

112. Peterson, *City Limits,* p. 41.

CHAPTER

13

REVIVING THE CENTRAL CITIES

AN URBAN RENAISSANCE

At the beginning of the twenty-first century, it became clear that central cities were on the rebound. Downtown business districts and entertainment/tourist districts drew people from throughout metropolitan areas and elsewhere. City neighborhoods also seemed to be undergoing a renaissance. An informal *New York Times* survey of nine cities (Boston, Chicago, Houston, Los Angeles, Miami, New York, San Antonio, San Diego, and Washington, D.C.) conducted in 2000 found that as crime rates dropped, businesses and new residents began pouring into neighborhoods previously considered off limits. Displacement of poorer residents was no doubt occurring, but the quality of life for long-term residents had also improved.[1]

Recently, most American central cities experienced at least some degree of gentrification—the movement of young professionals and businesspeople into downtown neighborhoods. In some cities, there was a massive displacement of the poor and aged from older residential areas. From 1990 to 2000, downtown populations increased in eighteen of twenty-four cities studied by the Fannie Mae Foundation and the Brookings Institution.[2] As shown by Table 13.1, the cities were located in all regions of the nation and included older industrial as well as Sunbelt cities. Some cities (such as Atlanta, Baltimore, Boston, Chicago, Los Angeles, and Philadelphia) built upon a downtown population base that was already substantial, while others (such as Denver, Des Moines, Detroit, Lexington, Norfolk, and Phoenix) attracted new residents to downtown populations that were quite small. In all cases, the increases signaled a significant new development for American cities: the decades-long abandonment of the urban core seemed to be coming to an end.

The movement to downtowns was driven by affluent young professionals, "the singles, the mingles and the jingles."[3] White populations in the twenty-four downtowns increased by 7.5 percent in the 1990s, a faster population growth than for blacks (6 percent) and Latinos (4.8 percent). By contrast, in neighbor-

346

Table 13.1 **Downtowns That Grew in the 1990s (Selected Cities)**

City	1990 Downtown	2000 Downtown	Change	Change %
Atlanta	19,763	24,731	4,968	25
Baltimore	28,597	30,067	1,470	5
Boston	75,823	79,251	3,428	4.5
Chicago	27,760	42,039	14,279	51
Cleveland	7,261	9,599	2,338	32
Colorado Springs	13.412	14,377	965	7
Denver	2,794	4,230	1,436	51
Detroit	5,970	6,141	171	3
Houston	7,029	11,882	4,853	69
Los Angeles	34,655	36,630	1,975	6
Memphis	7,606	8,994	1,388	18
Milwaukee	10,973	11,243	270	2.5
Norfolk, Va.	2,390	2,881	491	20.5
Philadelphia	74,655	78,349	3,694	5
Portland, Ore.	9,528	12,902	3,374	35
San Diego	15,417	17,894	2,477	16
Seattle	9,824	16,443	6,619	67

Source: Adapted from Rebecca R. Sohmer and Robert E. Long, *Downtown Rebound* (Washington, D.C.: Brookings Institution, Fannie Mae Foundation, 2001), pp. 2–3.

hoods outside downtown areas, white populations fell by 10.5 percent, while black populations held almost steady (growing by 2.4 percent) and Latino populations virtually exploded (growing by 43 percent).[4] If these trends continue, the American urban pattern will begin to resemble the experience in other countries, where affluent people have long claimed the most valuable real estate in the center of the historic city.

The revival of downtowns can be traced to two major developments. First, downtowns are becoming the centers of businesses connected to a "new economy" centered around electronic trade and commerce, telecommunications, finance, marketing, and corporate services. Second, tourism/entertainment, culture, and urban amenities are becoming clustered in and near downtown areas. Jobs are connected to amenities; the new downtown residents want to commute less but also prefer to live in an urban environment with nightlife and excitement. With their historic architecture, public monuments, redeveloped waterfronts, and older neighborhoods, cities are uniquely positioned to provide an exciting urban culture. For the first time in half a century, cities seem to be indispensable to their metropolitan regions.

THE DECLINE AND RECOVERY OF DOWNTOWN

The distribution of economic activities in the nation has changed fundamentally over the past hundred years. In the late nineteenth and early twentieth centuries, cities prospered as centers of manufacturing production. Railroad connections made it possible to transport raw materials into industrial cities and ship the finished products to markets around the world. Large factories, by employing the new energy sources of steam and electricity, reaped the benefits of economies of scale as the new techniques of mass production were perfected. These factories required thousands of workers. As the center of the nation's economic production, cities, with their concentrations of immigrant workers, burst at the seams. But in the 1920s, American cities began to lose their status as centers of goods production, wholesale trade, and retail sales. By the 1970s, a large proportion of manufacturing, retail, and wholesale activities had moved to the suburbs, along with much of the middle-class population. The older industrial cities seemed to be sliding into irreversible decline.

The events of the 1970s ushered a new tongue-twister into the language, *deindustrialization.* Technological advances in production processes, such as the use of robots for assembly, made it possible to produce goods with far fewer workers than in the past. Between 1970 and 1988, though the volume of production increased, the nation's manufacturing employment remained stable at 19 million jobs. Over the same period, however, the number of service jobs increased rapidly. There were two distinct tiers of service employment. The upper tier included jobs in business and financial services (white-collar professionals such as lawyers, accountants, investment brokers, and computer and communications specialists). The lower tier was composed of employment in food, retail, and personal services (such as those provided in restaurants, stores, laundromats, and barbershops). From 1975 to 1990, 30 million new jobs were created in service industries, so that by the end of the 1980s, 84 million people were employed in services, as compared to 25 million in goods production.[5] Almost 80 percent of employment growth in the 1980s came in the form of service jobs.[6]

These changes thoroughly restructured urban economies. As shown by Table 13.2, in seven northeastern and midwestern metropolitan areas, the percentage of jobs in the manufacturing sector fell from 30 to 12.5 percent in the 27 years from 1970 to 1997. The largest gains came in services, which grew from 18 percent of local employment to 36 percent over the same period. Though it remained a relatively small proportion of the economy in many cities, the only other sector to show an increase in jobs in these cities was finance, insurance, and real estate, which grew from 6 percent to 10 percent.

Deindustrialization also occurred because factories left urban regions; indeed, many left the United States entirely. Manufacturers also moved out of older metropolitan areas to such places as the Caribbean, Latin America, and Asia, where wages were much lower and environmental regulations were lax.[7] Within metropolitan areas, a spatial restructuring was taking place. Manufacturing, retailing, and wholesaling activities moved out of the central cities to the suburbs. The development of highways and truck transportation enabled factories to move to the

Table 13.2 **Change in Job Categories in Seven Northeastern and Midwestern Metropolitan Areas, 1970–1997**

	Percent Employed in Each Category					
	1970	1975	1982	1986	1991	1997
Manufacturing	30	26	22	18.5	16	12.5
Transportation, communications, and public utilities	6	6	6	6	6	5
Wholesale and retail trade	21	22	22	22.5	22	20
Finance, insurance, and real estate	6	7	7	9	9	10
Services	18	21	25	27	31	36
Government	14	15	14.5	13	13.5	11

Source: U.S. Department of Labor, Bureau of Labor Statistics, *Earnings and Employment* (Washington, D.C.: Government Printing Office, 1970, 1975, 1982, 1986, 1991, and 1997).

periphery of metropolitan areas and beyond, especially to locations with convenient connections to interstate highways. Modern mass production requires large amounts of inexpensive land for one-story, assembly-line production methods. With the range of commuting made possible by the automobile, factories could locate at a distance from residential centers and still be accessible to workers.

Until the 1950s, cities were the centers of retail and wholesale trade. The large downtown department stores offered the best selection and prices, and middle-class shoppers took mass transit downtown to shop. Downtown shopping was killed in the 1950s by suburbanization and the automobile. By the 1960s, suburban shopping centers had begun to eclipse central business districts. With big parking lots and freeway interchanges nearby, the shopping centers and their later incarnation, the malls, were more convenient for shoppers, who had by now completely abandoned mass transit for the automobile.

In 1956, the first enclosed, climate-controlled mall, Southdale, was opened in the Minneapolis suburb of Edina. By making shopping comfortable all year round, it was an instant success.[8] Mall owners created a leisurely atmosphere conducive to consumption, including common hours for stores, directories and uniform signs, and benches and landscaping. By comparison, downtown shopping seemed chaotic and inconvenient, and sometimes even menacing. By 1974, 15,000 shopping centers had captured more than 44 percent of the nation's retail sales.[9] Downtown department stores began to close for good. Hudson's, a longtime landmark in downtown Detroit, finally closed its doors in 1981.[10]

By the mid-1970s, civic leaders reluctantly came to the conclusion that central cities could not compete head to head with suburbs for manufacturing, retailing, and wholesaling. Something new was needed. A generation of "messiah mayors" preaching a gospel of self-help for their downtowns led the way in experimenting with new methods of development to promote investment in office towers, malls, and tourist and entertainment facilities.[11] Cities provided direct subsidies or promised public improvements such as new roads, landscaping, and pedestrian malls; special authorities were created to finance and administer sports stadiums, convention centers, and redeveloped waterfronts; cities even became partners in building malls and entertainment districts—anything to entice developers downtown.

A downtown renaissance began to take shape; corporate offices, hotels, convention centers, sports stadiums, concert halls, and new museums formed new skylines. By the mid-1980s every mayor's downtown "trophy collection" included at least one luxury hotel (preferably one with a multistory atrium), a new sports stadium (usually domed), a downtown shopping mall, a redeveloped waterfront, and a new convention center.[12] These facilities were the infrastructure necessary for downtowns to become centers of corporate white-collar employment, entertainment, culture, and a burgeoning tourism and convention trade.

The economic sectors that led the revitalization of downtown comprised the components a new globalized economy that revolved around high-level corporate services, telecommunications, and technology. Globalization has been facilitated by the reorganization of corporations. Since the 1980s, corporations have been growing larger through mergers and buyouts. Large firms are able to coordinate activities on a global scale—the movement of capital investment, the location of factories, and the distribution and marketing of products. The innovations required by modern corporations in product design, advertising, the adoption of new technologies, and corporate organization is made possible by frequent coordination among highly specialized professionals, most of whom do not work within the corporation itself. As a consequence, corporations prefer to locate in close proximity to other firms.

The management and control functions of corporations are disproportionately centralized in a network of cities that occupy strategic places in a global economy. In many cities across the United States, downtowns have been revitalized for the simple reason that many business concerns find it advantageous to be located next to one another. Especially (but not exclusively) in larger cities, high-level professional operations and information industries have become clustered into "strategic nodes with a hyperconcentration of activities"[13] supporting layer on layer of highly educated, technologically sophisticated professionals offering specialized services—corporate managers, management consultants, legal experts, accountants, computer specialists, financial analysts, media and public relations consultants, and the like. Such jobs are essential for keeping a metropolitan area competitive in the global marketplace; in 1990, central cities in the United States contributed $23 billion more in services to the world economy than they took in.[14] The clustering of highly skilled workers in downtown office buildings explains why the earnings of workers in central cities are higher than the average earnings of those who work in the suburbs.[15]

The skyscrapers that sprout from the downtowns of American cities are the physical manifestation of the clustering of economic activities in central cities. From the 1920s to the 1950s, few office towers were built in downtowns. But between 1950 and 1984, over 40 percent of the nation's gain in office employment and construction was concentrated in the downtowns of the thirty largest urban areas.[16] During the 1980s, cities even increased their share—a significant feat given the simultaneous boom in suburban office construction.[17] In subsequent years, corporations have clustered both in downtowns and in edge cities or office parks located in the suburbs. However, downtown areas have continued to attract firms that benefit most from intense concentration.

Corporate headquarters cluster most densely in a few global cities such as New York, Paris, London, Chicago, Los Angeles, Miami, Hong Kong, Sydney, and Tokyo.[18] Sitting atop the new urban hierarchy created by globalization, these cities house corporations that manage production and distribution networks around the world. For example, the largest corporations, especially international banks, stock and commodity exchanges, and media empires, are located in global cities. Second-level cities, such as Montreal and Hamburg, may lay claim to a few international firms, but for the most part they house national and regional corporate systems. Further down the hierarchy, medium-sized cities such as Atlanta, Cleveland, and St. Louis are mainly the hubs of regional corporate networks. Down the pyramid further still are cities that depend upon quite specialized activities such as an auto plant (Smyrna, Tennessee), a cluster of electronics software firms (San Jose, California), or a meatpacking plant (Beardstown, Illinois). The more specialized a city's economy, the more subject it is to sudden economic changes; conversely, the more complex a city's economy and the more thoroughly it is tied into the global economy, the more control it has in shaping its economic future.[19]

The highly specialized, well-paid professionals who flocked into downtown areas drove up the cost of housing, sometimes to fantastic levels, and they supported amenities such as expensive restaurants, exclusive shopping districts, and the arts. By the end of the 1990s, the successful downtowns offered a unique "urban culture," a special mix of job opportunities and amenities that could not be found anywhere else: restaurants, blues and jazz clubs, art galleries, theaters and performance halls, and also the elements necessary for an exciting nightlife, such as bars, dance clubs, after-hours clubs, and coffee shops.[20] In "happening" cities, the narrative of decline began to be replaced by a narrative of revival.

THE DEVELOPMENT OF TOURISM AND ENTERTAINMENT

In recent decades, cities have become increasingly focused on promoting tourism, entertainment, and culture. These sectors are especially attractive because it is generally assumed that tourists spend money without taking anything out of the local economy. Tourism frequently has been described as "the industry without a smokestack." As a consequence, there is keen competition among cities for a share of the nation's tourist and entertainment business. To remake themselves into places that tourists want to visit, cities have invested heavily in tourism facilities and the reconstruction of downtown environments. Indeed, the rebuilding of downtown areas to make them friendly for visitors

OUT TAKE BALTIMORE'S REVITALIZATION IS DEBATED

B altimore provides an excellent illustration of central-city revitalization through the development of tourism and entertainment.
Writing in *Fortune* magazine in 1977, journalist Gurney Breckenfield praised the
close collaboration between government and business in Baltimore: "Their [public
and private sector] strategy, established at the outset, has been to convert the
heart of the city into a culturally rich, architecturally exciting magnet where both
affluent and middle-class families will choose to work, shop, and live."[21] Called the
"Cinderella city of the 1980s,"[22] Baltimore is one of the nation's best-known examples of a downtown development strategy that emphasizes tourism and entertainment. Because of its size and proximity to New York City and Washington, D.C.,
Baltimore was not likely to attract a concentration of global corporations, so it
focused singularly upon tourism and entertainment.

Downtown redevelopment in Baltimore is closely identified with an extraordinary politician, William Donald Schaefer. As the leader of a coalition of government
and business, Schaefer served as the energizing force behind redevelopment in Baltimore during his four terms as mayor from 1971 to 1987. After spending nineteen
years on the city council, Schaefer understood the limitations of city government,
even in a city with a strong-mayor form of government. As soon as he was elected
mayor, he devised an aggressive strategy for revitalizing Baltimore's waterfront.

Schaefer's predecessors had already set out to bring new life to a 33-acre
wedge of the old downtown known as Charles Center. The Charles Center project
was moving forward, but the revitalized area was small and hemmed in by deteriorated neighborhoods on three sides and the dilapidated harbor on the other.
Schaefer decided to undertake something much bigger and more dramatic—the
Inner Harbor project. In an earlier time, the harbor had been a thriving center of
commerce, but by the 1960s it was an eyesore composed of rotting, rat-infested
piers, abandoned buildings, and desolate parking lots, perched on a harbor that
smelled, in H. L. Mencken's words, "like a million polecats."[23] The audacious idea
was to transform this blighted mess into a national tourist attraction.

Wanting to redevelop the downtown and the harbor as fast as possible, Schaefer devised a strategy that circumvented the slow-moving bureaucratic and democratic processes of city government at the same time that he won the confidence of
corporate investors. Schaefer relied on a network of twenty-four quasi-public development corporations (which grew to more than thirty by 2002) that contracted
with the city government to direct and implement the redevelopment efforts.
Charles Center–Inner Harbor Management, Inc. (CCIHM) was at the center of this
network of quasi-public corporations. The city contracted with CCIHM to plan and
implement the Inner Harbor project. Several specialized development corporations
were established to implement parts of the plan, such as housing. Though they
contracted for public projects and received public funds (and thus could be called
quasi-public), as private entities the development corporations were able to pay
higher salaries than public agencies, and they could circumvent public regulations
concerning such requirements as competitive bidding and affirmative action. Proponents viewed them as an "apolitical means for improving the city's development potential by infusing speed, flexibility, and technical expertise into the
policy-making process."[24]

The linchpin of the Inner Harbor plan was Harborplace, anchored by two block-long, translucent pavilions enclosing a festival mall designed by the famous developer James Rouse. Rouse intended to create "a warm and human place, with diversity of choice, full of festival and delight."[25] Completed in 1980, Harborplace succeeded beyond anyone's expectations, attracting 18 million visitors the first year, earning $42 million, and creating 2,300 jobs. In 1981, the National Aquarium was completed, giving the Inner Harbor a distinct and highly visible tourist attraction. By 1992 more than 15 million visitors had toured the aquarium's exhibits, including a 64-foot glass pyramid housing a reproduction of a South American rain forest.[26]

The success of the Charles Center and of the Inner Harbor development unleashed a surge of private investment in downtown Baltimore. Between 1980 and 1986, the number of visitors and the amount of money they spent tripled; to accommodate the increased demand, the number of hotel rooms also tripled. The city's manpower programs succeeded in placing 1,300 persons in jobs at Harborplace in just six years,[27] and more than 40 percent of the Harborplace workforce was drawn from minorities.[28] By 1990, the Charles Center and Inner Harbor projects had created an estimated 30,000 new jobs directly and indirectly.[29] A study in 1998 estimated that visitors to Baltimore spent $847 million in one year, which supported a visitor-related payroll of $266 million and generated $81 million in state and local taxes.[30]

Inner Harbor was a big political winner for Schaefer. The press hailed him as "The Best Mayor in America."[31] In November 1986, after serving for nearly four terms, Schaefer rode the wave of positive publicity about Baltimore's renaissance into the Maryland governor's mansion. But the drumbeat of positive press about Baltimore's downtown revival overlooked the conditions in the city's deteriorating neighborhoods. Kurt Schmoke, who succeeded Schaefer as Baltimore's first black mayor in 1987, observed, "If you were revisiting Baltimore today after a 20-year absence, you would find us much prettier and much poorer."[32]

It seemed that there were "two Baltimores,"[33] one inhabited by suburban workers and visitors, the other by poor people who lived in slums. The hemorrhaging of the city's population continued, falling by 135,000 people from 1980 to 2000, to 651,000. Meanwhile, the suburbs grew by 250,000 in the 1990s alone. Relative to the suburbs, the city's job situation also worsened. In 1950, 79 percent of the region's jobs were located in the city, but this proportion fell to 33 percent by 2000. The per capita income of Baltimore's residents continued to fall behind the suburbs; in 1950, the city's residents made slightly more than the residents of surrounding suburbs, but by 2000 they made half as much ($27,713 compared to $55,404). During the 1980s, property values stabilized in the city, but then continued a steep long-term decline, both in absolute terms and relative to the suburbs.[34] All this happened while the number of people living downtown increased in the 1990s, showing the narrow scope of the city's revitalization.[35]

How can the apparent paradox of the stunning success of Baltimore's development strategy and the declining conditions in nearby neighborhoods be explained? The Baltimore experience seems to confirm findings in other studies showing that downtown revitalization has been largely irrelevant to the success of small businesses and the creation of jobs for inner-city residents.[36] This raises important questions about Baltimore's version of downtown revitalization: Have public dollars been

continued on next page

wisely spent? Is development that focuses upon the downtown misguided and unfair? Who benefits?

There are opposing answers to these questions. There is widespread agreement that the redevelopment of its downtown has not turned Baltimore around.[37] According to one critic, an equally bad result is that the glitter of Inner Harbor obscures the problems in the rest of the city:

> . . . a serious social danger attaches to creating an island of affluence and power in the midst of a sea of impoverishment, disempowerment, and decay. Like the city fair, the Inner Harbor functions as a sophisticated mask. It invites us to participate in a spectacle, to enjoy a festive circus that celebrates the coming together of people and commodities. Like any mask, it can beguile and distract in engaging ways, but at some point we want to know what lies behind it. If the mask cracks or is violently torn off, the terrible face of Baltimore's impoverishment may appear.[38]

But there is an opposing view. Tangible benefits have accrued because of Baltimore's strategy, including the creation of jobs, an increasing tax base (but not enough to offset losses in other parts of the city), and the physical reconstruction of an important part of the city. Private investment has been attracted, and the "face, the streetscape, and the skyline of the Inner Harbor and nearby neighborhoods have been dramatically transformed."[39] Without the downtown redevelopment, nothing else would have been happening in the rest of Baltimore anyway. Finally, no city is in a position to overcome the large-scale social factors that have brought about the move to the suburbs and the decay of the inner cities.[40]

Because the benefits of downtown development are not spread equally, it is certain that the debate will continue.

has been so massive that it can be compared to the building of the industrial city a century ago, when cities invested in mass transit systems, paved streets, sewer and water systems, and parks. The only other period of city-building on such a scale occurred in the 1950s and 1960s, with the urban renewal clearance projects.[41] In the latest phase, cities have built an expensive infrastructure essential to tourism and entertainment. Any city that does not have the full complement of facilities is at a disadvantage.

In Chicago, as in many cities, the leading industry is now tourism and entertainment. The number of tourists increased from 32 million in 1993 to 43 million in 1997, a product of indefatigable promotion and a huge investment in the infrastructure of tourism.[42] Chicago has built the world's largest convention center, an entertainment district on an old pier (Navy Pier), and has one of the world's most beautiful park systems, which runs for miles along the Lake Michigan lakefront. The city is host to several extraordinary museums and other attractions (such as the John G. Shedd Aquarium and the Adler Planetarium), maintains elaborate floral and garden displays along Michigan Avenue and on many other streets, and hosts dozens of events each year in the parks. Grant Park, which stretches between the downtown Loop and Lake Michigan, is the most visited park in the United States, attracting more visitors than even the Grand Canyon.[43] Chicago has a complex economy, but it would be in trouble without tourism.

In older cities, tourist entertainment venues have often been constructed on sites that were once devoted to manufacturing, warehousing, retailing, or harbor activities. These developments try to project a contrived, nostalgic, and idealized version of city life, and they do so by utilizing architectural features that define the historic city. For instance, South Street Seaport in New York strives to create an ambience evoked by "authentic reproductions" of a working harbor[44]— in effect, an urban miniversion of Disneyland (in Anaheim, California), with its Main Street, U.S.A., and Frontier Village. The examples abound: the Wharf and Ghirardelli Square in San Francisco, and the renovated Union Stations everywhere (while the actual train stations are out of sight and sound).

The facilities and amenities devoted to leisure activities and tourism are often clustered within a well-defined space separated from the rest of the city. Where crime, poverty, and urban decay make parts of a city inhospitable to visitors, specialized areas may become tourist reservations. Greektown, a two-square-block renovated district in downtown Detroit anchored by an enclosed mall, is an island of renewal in a sea of decay. Such areas are, in effect, tourist "bubbles" that "envelope the traveler so that he/she only moves inside secured, protected and normalized environments."[45] Some of the facilities that make up the tourist bubble include convention centers, sports stadiums, festival malls and urban entertainment districts, and gaming casinos.[46] Recently, however, reduced crime rates have encouraged cities to nurture the development of an active street life and urban culture that spills beyond the tourist enclaves. Where they succeed, the cities become, as in the past, the true center of their metropolitan regions, the home of activities, culture, and a lifestyle that cannot be imitated anywhere else.[47]

Convention Centers

Until the 1960s, few cities had built the huge convention centers that are so prevalent in and near downtown areas today. For the most part, town halls doubled as assembly facilities, if any were needed. In the 1920s, some cities built the first generation of meetings and exhibition halls; St. Louis, for example, built the St. Louis Arena in 1929 to accommodate an agricultural exhibit. During the Great Depression, the federal government, through the Public Works Administration, financed large public assembly and exhibition facilities in a number of cities. This generation of halls often contained one or more auditoriums as well as exhibition space under one roof, and in many cities these structures were not replaced until the 1980s or 1990s. These all-purpose facilities were expensive to operate and virtually always lost money, but they had the effect of attracting, and even helping to create, an array of traveling shows and exhibitions. The benefits to the local economy and to their own fortunes were soon comprehended by civic boosters, who then pushed for larger and better facilities.

In the 1950s, a few cities began constructing a second generation of meeting halls in the form of convention centers built specifically for professional meetings and trade shows. The proliferation of convention centers began in the 1960s and accelerated in the 1970s as air travel, growing affluence, and greater specialization in the job market gave rise to more meetings, exhibitions, and consumer shows (such as autos, boats, and electronics), and conventions. In the 1980s, cities began a virtual arms race for the convention trade, with even small towns joining the competition. By July 1998, 409 convention centers with exhibition space were operating in U.S. cities, and more than 70 percent of them had opened since 1970.[48] And in just four years, from 1998 to 2002, the amount of space increased by another 13 percent, with fourteen new facilities opening between August 2001 and July 2002.[49] A decline in travel and in the number of meetings brought about the terrorist attacks on the World Trade Center on September 11, 2001, caused some concern, but the convention-center wars show no signs of abating.

All convention centers require annual subsidies for the payment of construction bonds and for operating costs, but escalating construction, maintenance, and promotion costs have not deterred cities from investing in larger and more elaborate convention facilities. Much is at stake. In 2002, there were nearly 23,000 associations and 6.5 million total private business establishments in the United States.[50] The 23,000-plus associations in the nation spent $32 billion for meetings in 1992, and corporations spent an additional $29 billion on off-premises meetings and conventions.[51] Tourism-related organizations alone had 1.4 million members in 1998, and the meetings industry produced $81 billion in economic output.[52] The average attendance at new exhibitions nearly quadrupled from 1990 to 1997.[53] Although only from 4 to 5 percent of meetings are held in convention centers,[54] the size of the meetings and convention business has been large enough to prompt hundreds of cities to build or expand their existing convention centers. In 2000, forty-one convention centers were being built or renovated, and sixty-six were slated for expansion or renovation.[55]

The convention business is extraordinarily competitive. Except for the top couple of cities, it is doubtful that any city captures (or can capture) as much as 5 percent of the national market, and only the top ten are likely to capture as much as 2 percent.[56] As the number of cities competing for conventions increases, it becomes difficult for a particular city to increase its share of the nation's convention business. There is also a great deal of volatility because more cities are aggressively marketing themselves and the number and size of facilities is constantly increasing. From 1981 to 1992, New York City fell from first to seventh place in its share of meetings booked, and Anaheim dropped from seventh to eighteenth place, but during the same period Orlando, Florida, shot up from twenty-seventh to second place. Changes do not occur only over the long term; as shown in Table 13.3, Orlando slipped from second place in 1990 to fifth place in 1991, then rebounded to second place in 1992.

The construction of a convention facility may provide a foundation, but obviously a lot of other factors determine a city's ability to successfully compete for meetings. In Orlando's case, obviously, Disney World is the entire story. For other cities, such a singular magnet is rarely, if ever, available. Convention centers do not exist in isolation from the cities they are located within. Large cities, with their abundance of entertainment, cultural, and commercial attractions, remain the primary drawing cards for national and international conventions.

Table 13.3 **Top U.S. Cities Booked, 1990–1992**

City[a]	1992 Rank	1991 Rank	1990 Rank
Chicago	1	1	1
Orlando	2	5	2
Dallas	3	2	3
Atlanta	4	3	6
Los Angeles	5	4	5
San Diego	5	7	9
New York	7	8	6
Boston	8	9	8
New Orleans	9	14	14
Phoenix	10	12	13
San Francisco	10	6	4
Houston	12	10	10
Las Vegas	13	13	10
Washington, D.C.	14	11	18
Nashville	15	—	—
Denver	16	16	18
Philadelphia	17	20	15
Anaheim	18	14	31
Miami	18	—	—
St. Louis	18	—	—

[a]Duplicate rankings indicate ties.

Source: Successful Meetings magazine, July 1993, p. 62.

By the 1980s, virtually every major city in the United States had formed a convention and visitors bureau, and throughout that decade these increased rapidly in size. Convention bureaus construct lists of international, national, regional, and local associations that regularly sponsor or organize conventions. The bureaus send them promotional literature and frequently attend the meetings of these organizations, where they may stage rather elaborate promotional presentations or exhibits. Cities often invite representatives of the tourist industry and of important business and professional groups for a complimentary visit. In November 1975, for instance, the St. Louis Convention and Visitors Bureau hosted representatives of 227 associations for a weekend tour in an effort to promote the city's new convention center, which was then under construction.[57]

The intense competition among cities makes it possible for groups of professional and trade associations to drive a hard bargain. The biggest associations already assume that they can persuade cities to give them convention space rent-free, and the bargaining position of these organizations will only improve over time. In 1993, the Future Farmers of America (FFA), a youth organization that had traditionally met in Kansas City, demanded that the city give it cash subsidies, lower hotel rates, and other incentives. Since their annual convention brought 28,000 visitors to the city, the city's Convention and Visitors Bureau chair thought it was worth spending "whatever it takes" to keep the group from going elsewhere.[58] Such an approach will become more common as groups become more adept at playing cities off against one another. (Ultimately, Kansas City lost the FFA.)

Sports Stadiums

Civic boosters consider professional sports franchises pivotal to the economic revitalization of central cities and often have used sports facilities as an anchor for development.[59] Cities compete vigorously for sports teams by helping finance the construction of stadiums and allowing owners to keep parking and concession fees and other revenues. Because teams sometimes move or can threaten to, sports cartels and team owners find it easy to persuade cities to meet their demands. Studies consistently show that sports stadiums do not bring measurable benefits to local economies and that some may even have a negative effect by replacing some local spending with expenditures that exit the local economy quickly.[60]

But these facts do not deter civic leaders from making often desperate efforts to get or keep professional teams. Sports teams have long been central to the civic and cultural life of American cities. Oddly, the assumption that a team expresses a city's essence, spirit, and sense of community has not been much eroded since teams became highly mobile. Part of the reason for this is that local boosters consider professional sports teams an absolutely essential signifier of "big league" status. Sports teams carry a substantial emotional charge, so that their worth is rarely, if ever, calculated in simple economic terms. Through the national and international publicity accompanying network broadcasts of games and playoffs, professional sports teams are a powerful vehicle for conveying a city's image.

Professional sports is a big business. In 2002, there were 122 North American franchises in four major sports (baseball, football, basketball, and hockey) worth more than $30 billion. Major league baseball franchises were valued from a low of $108 million for the Montreal Expos and $127 million for the Minnesota Twins (two teams targeted by the commissioner of baseball for closure) to $730 million for the New York Yankees (with an average value of $286 million). National Football League (NFL) teams ranged in value from $374 million for the Arizona Cardinals to $845 million for the Washington Redskins. Some National Basketball Association (NBA) franchises could be bought for smaller sums; the Charlotte Hornets, for example, were valued at a mere $135 million. However, the New York Knicks were valued at $392 million and the Los Angeles Lakers, the most valuable professional basketball team, was valued at $403 million. Professional hockey teams went for less, making it possible for someone with an extra $100 million to $200 million lying around to bid for a team.[61] In Denver, Colorado, the four major professional sports have teams valued at a total of $1.3 billion, which comes out to more than $500 per person in the metropolitan area.[62]

Sports teams are profitable, despite the claims of owners and the leagues that many of them lose money. In 2002, baseball commissioner Bud Selig testi-fied to Congress that Major League Baseball generated an operating loss of $200 million that year, but *Forbes* magazine produced figures showing a $75 million profit.[63] The escalation of team values all through the previous decade made it a dubious claim that baseball owners lost money. The lucrative media contracts for most baseball teams also made the claim suspect.[64]

For decades, professional sports teams were so closely identified with their cities of origin that moving would have been unthinkable. In baseball, this link was first broken in 1953, when the Boston Braves relocated to Milwaukee. The baseball franchise relocation game began in earnest in 1957, when owner Walter O'Malley moved the Brooklyn Dodgers to Los Angeles. At first, O'Malley wanted public assistance to build a new stadium in New York, but he was thwarted by Robert Moses, who controlled the public authorities in the New York region. To lure the Dodgers out of New York, Los Angeles agreed to reno-vate its minor league stadium at Chavez Ravine and give the stadium to O'Mal-ley. As the clincher, they offered him 300 acres of downtown Los Angeles real estate. O'Malley jumped at the chance to add to his personal fortune.[65]

It did not take long for other owners to follow O'Malley's lead. Threats to move became potent weapons for prying more subsidies out of cities. Between 1953 and 1982, there were seventy-eight franchise relocations in the four major professional sports: eleven in baseball, forty in basketball, fourteen in hockey, and thirteen in football.[66] In just six years, from 1980 to 1986, more than half the cities with major league sports franchises were confronted with demands for increased subsidies, with relocation an implied if not always explicit threat hanging over negotiations.[67] From 1980 to June 1992, an incredible amount of activity involved baseball and football teams. During this period, twenty cities sought baseball teams and twenty-four cities tried to attract football teams, an interesting statistic considering that there were, at that time, a total of twenty-eight major league base-ball and twenty-eight professional football franchises (two new expansion football franchises were added in 1993, with several cities competing for them). Eleven cities had completed or were building stadiums, and twenty-eight more consid-ered building or had plans to build stadiums. As shown in Table 13.4, new sports facilities were completed in the downtowns of thirty North American cities from 1990 to 2002. These were often the high-profile flagship projects of more compre-hensive efforts at downtown development.[68] This impressive list includes cities from coast to coast and three cities in Canada. Approximately fifty minor league and collegiate sports facilities also were completed in the 1990s.[69]

Except for baseball, where teams move less frequently, moves have become an ever-present possibility for many cities, in part because they pay off for the owners. In the 1990s, for example, the Quebec Nordiques (a hockey team) moved from a small market to Denver, Colorado, and renamed them-selves the Avalanche. In 1995, in their first season, they won the Stanley Cup for the first time. In 1996, when the NFL Cleveland Browns became the Baltimore

Table 13.4 **North American Cities with New Downtown Sports Facilities, 1990-2002**

Atlanta	Detroit	St. Louis
Baltimore	Houston	St. Paul
Boston	Indianapolis	Salt Lake City
Buffalo	Los Angeles	San Francisco
Charlotte	Miami	San Jose
Cincinnati	Montreal	Seattle
Cleveland	Nashville	Tampa
Columbus	New Orleans	Toronto
Dallas	Phoenix	Vancouver
Denver	Pittsburgh	Washington, D.C.

Source: Tim Chapin, "Beyond the Entrepreneurial City: Municipal Capitalism in San Diego," *Journal of Urban Affairs* 24, no. 5, p. 568.

Ravens, they signed a stadium deal that increased revenues substantially enough to allow them to pay big signing bonuses to key players. In 2001, they won the Super Bowl. Perhaps even more dramatically, the perennially losing Rams left Los Angeles (actually Anaheim) for St. Louis in 1995. An extraordinary stadium deal was the lure, and after four more losing seasons, the team won Super Bowl XXXIV in 2000.[70]

Because cities are desperate to get and keep a professional sports team, owners realize that public subsidies are theirs for the asking. From 1953 to 1986, sixty-seven of the ninety-four stadiums used by professional sports teams were publicly owned.[71] Beginning in the early 1980s, the two most important new revenue sources for sports teams came from network broadcasting and local and state subsidies.[72] By the end of the 1980s, it had become a rare exception when an owner agreed to build a stadium with private dollars. Owners came to expect other subsidies as well, in the form of guaranteed attendance minimums, the construction of luxury boxes, and control of stadium merchandising.

As teams became more and more footloose, cities found themselves at a disadvantage. In an attempt to improve their poor bargaining positions, some cities built stadiums even when they did not have teams. In the 1980s, Indianapolis built a football stadium, then persuaded the owner of the Baltimore Colts, Robert Irsay, to move. After the Maryland legislature passed an eminent domain law to make it possible for Baltimore to seize the Colts for public use, Irsay moved the team in the middle of the night.

St. Petersburg, Florida, built a $139 million domed stadium in 1988 in the hopes of attracting a major-league baseball team. Called "heaven's waiting room," boosters justified the Florida Suncoast Dome as a way of changing the city's image as a conservative retirement community.[73] For years, the stadium remained the site of tractor pulls and concerts. In the 1990s, St. Petersburg tried to lure several major league baseball teams, including the Seattle Mariners, the

San Francisco Giants, and a National League expansion team. When Florida won a baseball team in 1991, it was awarded to Miami. In October 1993, an expansion team of the NFL was awarded to Jacksonville; St. Petersburg's stadium was purpose-built for baseball and would not have been suitable for football. St. Louis, which also put in a bid for one of the NFL expansion teams, lost out. St. Louis undertook the construction of a domed stadium anyway, many months before the negotiations that eventually brought the Los Angeles Rams to the city in 1995.

Stadiums require generous land, infrastructure, and direct public subsidies because almost all of them (but not usually the teams playing in them) lose money. Annual operating deficits are generally considerable; the New Orleans Superdome lost about $3 million a year during the 1980s, for example, compared to the annual $1 million loss for the Pontiac, Michigan, Silverdome. In its first year, the Florida Suncoast Dome lost $1.3 million, plus $7.7 million in debt payments.[74] Modern domed stadiums cost so much to build that they cannot conceivably schedule enough events or charge enough for them to avoid operating deficits. Toronto ended up paying $400 million for its domed stadium, while Baltimore spent $200 million for its new open stadium. St. Louis's domed stadium, completed in 1995, cost $301 million.[75] All require annual subsidies.

It is undoubtedly true, as civic boosters argue, that the most important benefits of a major sports franchise are intangible and therefore impossible to measure solely in economic terms. However, as teams become more mobile and owners ask for more, such arguments may be wearing thin. In December 1996, the owners of the Seattle Mariners baseball team put the team up for sale, even though the city had earlier bought land and made plans to construct a new ballpark. Just a few months earlier, Seattle's football team, the Seahawks, had threatened to leave town, and it too demanded a new stadium. Together, the two stadiums were estimated to cost $760 million. A group called Citizens for More Important Things initiated a campaign opposing public subsidies behind the slogan "Just say no to welfare for the wealthy." Though the owners of the teams in Seattle got their stadiums, "just say no" campaigns have sprung up in other cities.

In St. Louis, the Cardinals launched an effort in 2000 to persuade the state legislature and the city to build a new stadium to replace the thirty-six-year-old Busch Stadium (which had been constructed with private funds). After going to the legislature three times and coming back emptyhanded, the Cardinals began an effort to piece together a package combining private funding and public subsidies from the city and other sources. Already the city's voters had passed a referendum requiring a vote on any public funding proposal of more than $1 million for stadiums. On the day before the new law was to take effect, the Land Clearance and Redevelopment Authority, whose board members and chief administrator are appointed by the mayor of St. Louis, approved the elimination of a 5 percent tax that had always been assessed on the team's ticket sales. Over a thirty-year period, this would provide a subsidy of $240 million for the new stadium (which would finance $135 million in bonds, the rest to be paid in interest). St. Louis County was also expected to commit $45 million and the state of Missouri $40 million in public infrastructure.[76] In addition, the Cardinals set out to raise $275 million in private financing, which would make the stadium only the second Major League Baseball team in the last three decades to build a stadium primarily with private funds (the other stadium is Pacific Bell Park in San Francisco).[77] Clearly, the political climate had changed since the early 1990s, when the state, county, and city financed a new football stadium for the Rams.

Ticket prices have increased sharply to help pay for the new stadiums, and as a consequence, professional sports attendance has become more class-stratified. For example, the new Cardinals stadium in St. Louis will have twice the number of club seats as in the old Busch Stadium, and prices were sure to increase (in 2003, they already cost $155). There will be fewer luxury boxes, but they will cost more. All other ticket prices will rise as well. Virtually all new stadiums have incorporated a larger number of premium and luxury seats as a means of increasing revenues.[78]

Festival Malls

Enclosed malls have become a principal weapon used by cities in the competition for recreational shopping and tourism. Cities typically have subsidized the construction of downtown malls heavily. To support mall development, they have devoted Community Development Block Grant and Urban Development Action Grant funds, floated bonds to finance site acquisition and loans to developers, offered property tax abatements, created tax increment districts, built utilities tunnels, constructed sewer lines and water mains, and rerouted and repaved streets. Civic leaders are eager to support mall development because it promises to bring a special form of "entertainment" retailing downtown. Boston's early success set the tone for such expectations.

On August 26, 1976, Boston's mayor, Kevin White, presided over opening-day ceremonies for Quincy Market in downtown Boston. The brainchild of developer James Rouse, who made a fortune developing suburban shopping malls, Quincy Market was housed in three 150-year-old market buildings that were creatively renovated, at a cost of more than $40 million, into a collection of boutiques, gourmet food shops, and restaurants.[79] Few expected Quincy Market—located as it was, in the center of a declining central city with inadequate parking and no big-ticket items to sell—to succeed. Indeed, six weeks before opening day, the retail complex was less than 50 percent leased. In order to hide the empty stores, Rouse came up with the idea of leasing pushcarts to artists and craftspeople for $50 a day, plus a percentage of the sales.

By eleven o'clock on opening day, only a modest crowd had gathered for the ceremonies. After the speeches were over, Mayor White cut the ribbon, and developer Rouse and a company of kilted highland bagpipers led the crowd inside for a champagne reception. At lunchtime, the crowd swelled as curious workers poured out of nearby office buildings. By midafternoon, it was clear that opening day would be a huge success, with police estimating the crowd at 100,000.

People never stopped coming to Quincy Market. In its second year of operation, the market drew 12 million visitors—more than Disneyland that year. Newspapers reported the market's "instant acceptance" by the public, which delighted in the colorful sights, sounds, and smells of the food and imaginatively displayed merchandise and the festival air created by a liberal sprinkling of pushcarts, magicians, acrobats, and puppeteers. The banks that financed the project were originally highly skeptical; they calculated that Quincy Market would have to produce retail sales comparable to the most successful suburban shopping malls ($150 per square foot) to justify its unusually high development costs. Quincy Market shocked the experts by producing sales of $233 per square foot in its first year, with the pushcarts doing best of all. The opening of Quincy Market was hailed by the media as a sign of an urban renaissance. It seemed to disprove the conventional wisdom that the downtowns of American cities were doomed to obsolescence and decline.

Malls are important not only because they can help reverse the long-term decline of downtown retailing but also because they are a means of creating defended space in the midst of urban crime and decay. Malls built by the developers John Portman and James Rouse and their imitators have become such common features of American downtowns that it is hard to recall how recently they have been constructed. The malls increasingly engulf and centralize activities that were formerly spread through the urban community at large. Such complexes are easily criticized as "fortified cells of affluence,"[80] but there can be little doubt that as locations for tourism and entertainment, these spaces are extremely successful.

Since opening his first mall in Boston, Rouse has designed festival malls for cities all across the country. What made Rouse's developments so distinctive and newsworthy was the artful combining of play and shopping. His formula was to create a carnival atmosphere, accomplished through a mixture of specialty shops, clothing stores, restaurants, and food stands, with musicians, jugglers, acrobats, and mimes to entertain shoppers. There soon were Rouse malls at the Gallery of Market Street East in Philadelphia, Grand Avenue in Milwaukee, Pike Street Market in Seattle, Horton Plaza in San Diego, Trolley Square in Salt Lake City, Union Station in St. Louis, Harborplace in Baltimore, South Street Seaport in New York, and on and on.

Many of the enclosed malls began modestly and then accreted block by block over many years, with tubes and skyways connecting the various components. In Minneapolis, a sprawling mall complex has grown by eating away the interiors of the downtown buildings, leaving their historic facades intact. In Kansas City, the Crown Center inexorably spread from its beginnings as a luxury hotel; by the mid-1990s, it occupied several city blocks. In Montreal and Dallas, veritable underground cities have been formed through a network of tunnels. The mall's assault on Atlanta has been much more direct; the huge Peachtree complex has been built on the rubble of the historic downtown.

Because they are an aspect of leisure and tourism, the kinds of malls built in downtown areas do not revitalize retailing in the city center per se. Rather, they rely on a style of shopping that is most effectively promoted within a controlled environment. The malls' mix of gift and souvenir shops, specialty food stores, bars, and fast-food or franchise restaurants mimic tourist villages such as Jackson Hole, Wyoming, and Estes Park, Colorado. Malls give developers control over a contiguous space sufficient to accomplish a totally planned combination of shopping and entertainment. In the West Edmonton Mall in Alberta, Canada, for example, leisure facilities take up about 10 percent of the total floor space, but their presence is essential to an ambience of leisure that permeates the entire mall.[81] The West Edmonton Mall copies Disney World in the theming of particular areas, such as (for example) an imitation Parisian street, Bourbon Street in New Orleans, Hollywood, and Polynesia. The combination of shopping and leisure in this way encourages a "shop 'til you drop" approach to buying.

Bubble Cities and Entertainment Complexes

Sprawling indoor complexes connected by pedestrian bridges and tubes have proliferated in American cities. Architect John Portman pioneered such "bubble cities" when he opened the Peachtree Plaza in downtown Atlanta in 1967. The Peachtree complex dates back to the original cylindrical towers that distinguished Portman's first atrium hotel, which opened in downtown Atlanta in 1967. It was an instant hit with architectural critics, the media, and the public. The hotel lobbies and vaulted atriums that made up the complex were dazzling, filled with flowing water and pools, ascending ranks of balconies vanishing toward a skylight, corridors rigged with lights and mirrors, glass elevators outlined in lights.

By the late 1980s, Peachtree Plaza had swallowed up Atlanta's historic downtown. Sixteen buildings clustered around the aluminum cylinder that housed the Marriott Hotel, anchoring a constantly expanding, enclosed downtown business district. Atlanta moved indoors, its city streets left almost deserted, especially at night. Shops, hotels and their lobbies, offices, food courts, and atriums are connected by a maze of escalators, skytubes, and arcades forming glassed-in skyways that isolate inhabitants from the streets below. Pedestrians can gain access to the center only through a few grand porticos, usually the entrance to a hotel lobby. The effect is to sharply separate the city-within-a-city from the public street outside.

Portman later built several other complexes, lesser in scale but aspiring to a similar grandeur, in several other cities—the Renaissance Center in Detroit, the Hyatt at Embarcadero Center in San Francisco, the Bonaventure Hotel in Los Angeles, and the Marriott Marquis in Times Square, New York City. In most cities, the Portman-like complexes do not swallow up an entire downtown. However, urban entertainment complexes have sprung up that enclose a large amount of space and house several related activities. These complexes commonly house one or more malls, but they also spread out to portions of the surrounding city. Because they offer a way to build a defended space even in a seemingly hostile environment, entertainment centers provide even the most dilapidated cities with a strategy for revitalizing the city center.

New York City's Times Square and San Francisco's Yerba Buena Center both anchor urban entertainment centers, but such centers have sprung up elsewhere as well, usually in historic areas and often in connection with revitalized waterfronts. Contained within these districts are restaurants, coffeehouses, sports bars, jazz clubs, dinner theaters, and other entertainment venues, plus an array of corporate retail tenants offering an assortment of clothes, shoes, electronic goods, jewelry, and so forth.[82]

Malls, themed shopping-leisure environments, and urban entertainment centers are turning downtowns into places of specialized consumption. In these environments, out-of-town visitors mingle with local residents because in them, local consumers are prompted to act as if they are, in effect, in a dreamscape far removed from the city outside. The similarity between Disney theme parks and these environments is not accidental. Thirteen years before James Rouse built Quincy Market, he asserted that Walt Disney was the most influential urban planner ever. And so he was. Malls and entertainment complexes establish the atmosphere and the context that potentially makes every city, whatever its past function or present condition, a tourist attraction.

Casino Gaming

Until the 1980s, there were few casinos in any major city in the world, but in less than two decades, casino gaming has spread rapidly. Since the mid-1980s, gaming casinos have become established as a component of tourism promotion in many cities throughout the world—notably in Adelaide, Perth, Sydney, and Brisbane; in Montreal, Winnipeg, and Windsor; in Christchurch and Auckland; in Amsterdam and Rotterdam; and in several cities on the Mediterranean, such as Athens, Istanbul, and Cairo.[83] In the United States, Atlantic City, New Jersey, broke Nevada's monopoly in 1978, but it took until 1992 for New Orleans to open the first casino in a major U.S. city. Within a year, Kansas City and St. Louis, Missouri, joined the list. However, the spread of gaming across the country has been much slower than most observers had expected, and it has not yet become a standard element in the economic development strategy of most cities. Driven by the desire to find new ways to promote local growth, many mayors will try to add casinos to their trophy collection, but only some of them will succeed.

Historically, Nevada served as the casino gambling mecca for most of the United States, making it possible for the state to keep its property taxes low and to avoid a state income tax. In 1967, New Jersey adopted a lottery, and in 1978, Atlantic City, New Jersey, broke Nevada's monopoly on casino gaming. All through the 1970s and 1980s, states adopted lotteries either through legislative action or referenda; by 1994, thirty-eight states ran lotteries. Following the spread of state lotteries, gambling became legitimated as a source of tax revenues. By 1996, twenty-six states allowed or had approved casino gaming in some form, but most gaming occurred on Indian-owned land.[84] As a means of promoting economic development on Indian reservations, in 1988 Congress passed the Indian Gaming Regulatory Act. The legislation permitted tribes to negotiate with states to run gaming operations and required the states to negotiate with the tribes that wanted to open casinos. Since then, casinos have been opened on Indian lands in twenty-two states.

In 1990, Iowa became the first state to approve riverboat gaming. After the opening of the first boat in Iowa in April 1991, six riverboats generated $12 million in state income taxes within eight months, prompting neighboring states to begin steps to join the competition.[85] In 1992, riverboats began operating in Illinois, two near St. Louis (one in East St. Louis, Illinois, directly across from St. Louis and the Gateway Arch). Mississippi began operating boats in 1993. Missouri, Louisiana, and Indiana all approved riverboat gaming soon after, with operations beginning in 1994.[86]

Despite the promises proffered by the industry and the eagerness of public officials to get a piece of the action, the initial euphoria about gambling melted away. Though the majority of Americans have come to accept gambling as a legitimate activity over the past thirty years,[87] a Harris Poll conducted in 1992 still found that 51 percent of the public opposed casino gaming in their own state, and 56 percent opposed it in their own communities.[88] The media find gambling a convenient topic, much like crime, for "controversy" and "analysis." For example, in its April 1, 1996, issue *Time* magazine carried a feature story that documented a national backlash against gaming. Proposals to allow gaming typically are accompanied by a considerable amount of controversy. In 1992, Colorado voters soundly defeated a constitutional amendment that would have allowed gaming to spread past the three communities named in an earlier referendum. In Missouri, three contentious voter referendums were required before the industry, with strong support from public officials, was able to secure approval for full casino operations.

Three issues are often raised by opponents of casino gambling. Though concerns about its social and moral effects once came mainly from religious groups, a diverse array of people have now raised that alarm. Substantial research has demonstrated that teenagers have about twice the rate of addiction to gambling as do adults and that lotteries have contributed to the problem.[89] Perhaps as part of a public relations effort, the industry has acknowledged that there are gambling addicts, and it finances research on the problem (providing the financing, for example, for the National Council on Problem Gambling). In 1996, the Missouri Gaming Commission, with industry support, proposed legislation that would allow gambling addicts to put themselves on a list that would bar them from entering any of the state's casinos.[90]

The second argument is that gaming does not deliver on its promised economic benefits because casinos cannibalize other businesses by locating restaurants, bars, and shops on premises, thereby drawing business away from local enterprises. Research is also accumulating that demonstrates a spending substitution effect whereby gamblers spend less on goods and services to make up for what they lose on the lotteries and in the casinos.[91]

A third often-discussed issue is the concern that the gaming industry brings with it crime, organized crime, and political corruption. Virtually all efforts to legalize casino gambling are accompanied by well-publicized reports of political corruption. For instance, in 1994, the governor of the state of Missouri asked the members of the St. Louis Election Board to resign because all of them had financial ties to gaming companies. In Louisiana, the relationship between gambling and politicians seemed even closer, a circumstance that prompted a segment on ABC's *60 Minutes*. A grand jury investigating the gaming industry in 1994 found that friends and relatives of Governor Edwin Edwards had been paid large amounts of money for consulting, legal advice, and as "returns" on investments. Governor Edwards, a notorious gambler for years, liked to host high-stakes poker games in the governor's mansion.

Industry projections of the potential contributions of gaming to local treasuries often make it appear that gaming would constitute a magic elixir for ailing central city economies. Despite this promise, casino gaming is likely to spread somewhat more slowly than was anticipated only a few years ago. In 1996, ten state legislatures refused to pass laws to legalize casinos or slot machines,[92] and Congress passed legislation to initiate a two-year study of gaming. When completed in 1999, the study urged states and localities to be cautious about pursuing gaming. Faced with fiscal crisis, however, local officials will still be lured by the potential of gaming to raise much-needed public revenues. In 2002, the mayor of Chicago, Richard M. Daley, mentioned the possibility that Chicago might seek approval for a casino license. Because such a facility might help close the city's multimillion budget deficit, Rod Blagojavich, the state's new governor inaugerated in January 2003, began to backtrack on statements made during his campaign that he would oppose such a move. To plug their budget gaps, state and local officials elsewhere are also likely to take another look at gaming.

Street Life and Urban Culture

In cities where physical dilapidation and crime discourage visitors, the marketing of tourism has resulted in the production of defended enclaves where tourists feel protected within a safe cocoon. But when crime rates began to fall in the early 1990s and downtown office construction and gentrification took off, street life and urban culture became the objects of fascination and consumption for visitors. In cities such as Boston, San Francisco, Chicago, New York City, and Portland, Oregon, visitors wandered and mingled freely with local residents. In fact, except in convention centers, it became harder to distinguish visitors from everyone else. The "localization of leisure turned cities into entertainment destinations not only for out-of-town visitors but also for suburban commuters and the growing number of affluent downtown residents."[93] Increasingly, local residents acted "like tourists in their own cities."[94]

A leading urban scholar, Richard Florida, has identified the rise of "the creative class" to explain the recent emphasis on tourism and entertainment. This class, which is composed of highly educated professionals with rarified intellectual, analytic, artistic, and creative skills, frequently regard lifestyle as more important than a particular job in choosing a place to live.[95] The members of this class demand social interaction, culture, nightlife, diversity, and authenticity, which became defined as "historic buildings, established neighborhoods, a unique music scene or specific cultural attributes. It comes from the mix—from urban grit alongside renovated buildings, from the commingling of young and old, long-time neighborhood characters and yuppies, fashion models and 'bag ladies.'"[96] Florida indicates that the creative class tends to reject the "canned experiences" associated with tourist enclaves. Instead, the creative class has become the basis for a new political movement that demands a high level of urban amenities, both public and private, in the downtowns and neighborhoods they frequent.[97] The result is a revival of the city center after decades of decline.

THE NEW DOWNTOWN ECONOMIES

The three elements making up the downtown renaissance include a cluster of corporate towers, an infrastructure of tourism and entertainment, and neighborhood gentrification. Mirroring the tendency of suburban residents to separate themselves into enclaves, many of the affluent workers and residents of inner cities have retreated into protected spaces.[98] Projects like the Peachtree Center in Atlanta, Renaissance Center in Detroit, Water Tower Place in Chicago, and the IDS Center in Minneapolis bring recreation, shopping, and work into enclosed environments. These multiuse structures make it possible for suburban residents to drive into the city, park in an underground garage, work in an attached office tower, shop in a mall connected by skyways, and perhaps attend a ball game in a domed stadium or attend a concert—all without setting foot on a city street. But in most cities, a combination of street life and entertainment venues attracts visitors from the suburbs and from out of town.

Critics often note that many of the facilities of tourism and entertainment do not pay for themselves. Public officials and civic boosters do not, on the whole, care much if they do. This apparently cavalier attitude toward taxpayers' money can be explained by noting the general irrelevance—to city officials and civic boosters—of cost-benefit analyses of tourism infrastructure. The attitudes of public officials toward development projects have "little do with the . . . profitability . . . of a project" and far more to do with the vision officials share about the overall direction a city is taking.[99] The intense interurban competition dictates that cities must compete, to do so they must be as generous as their competitors in providing subsidies, and they must try to adopt every new variation that comes along. The competition imposes a logic of its own that is hard to resist.

Public officials may be proceeding on the basis of blind faith, but they feel they have little choice. It is true that abject, even humiliating failure is possible, as the attempt by Flint, Michigan, to become a tourist city makes clear. In the 1970s, after the closing of its General Motors plant devastated the local economy, public officials in Flint launched an effort at regeneration behind the motto "Our New Spark Will Surprise You." The city committed $13 million in subsidies to the construction of a luxury hotel, the Hyatt Regency. Within a year, it closed its doors. Approximately $100 million in public money was used to build AutoWorld, a museum that contained, among other items, the "world's largest car engine" and a scale model that portrayed downtown Flint in its more prosperous days. AutoWorld closed within six months. Still more public subsidies were committed to the construction of the doomed Water Street Pavilion, a theme park/festival market built by the renowned mall developer James Rouse.

But few, if any, mayors would find it useful to be deterred by Flint's fiasco, which was wryly recorded in the popular movie *Roger and Me*.[100]

Virtually all cities of consequential size must take some steps to promote tourism, recreation, and culture. Now that the basic infrastructure is in place in many cities, public support for the arts and culture has become common. Every one of the nation's fifty largest cities provides public support for the arts. Some smaller cities are also offering subsidies. From the big cities (New York, with the Kennedy and Lincoln Centers and more recently, the Ford Center on 42nd Street) to villages (Riverhead, a hamlet outside New York, which is building an arts and historic district), from the downtowns in need of a boost (Newark, with its $180 million New Jersey Center, opened in October 1997), to the already prosperous (San Francisco, with a newly renovated opera house and several other performance halls), the development of local culture has become a leading formula for urban revival.[101] The text for a major exhibit in 1998 sponsored by the National Building Museum in Washington, D.C., noted that culture has replaced both the urban renewal bulldozer and the preservation movements that followed in its destructive wake as the main focus for downtown revitalization.

Collectively, cities of all sizes support an almost unimaginable variety of events that carry the signature of local culture and community. Jazz and blues festivals, strawberry and garlic festivals, jumping frogs and gold rush days, rodeos and fireworks—such activities help define and sometimes knit together local communities.[102] These activities usually take place in or near the new tourism/entertainment infrastructure (in smaller towns, this may mean at local parks, bandstands, waterfronts, or baseball diamonds). Every city must go through debates about how much of the public purse should be devoted to these activities. But few cities can afford to forego public subsidies altogether.

NOTES

1. New York Times News Service, "City Neighborhoods Are Undergoing a Renaissance as Crime Rates Drop," *St. Louis Post-Dispatch*, May 29, 2000, p. A-12.
2. Rebecca R. Sohmer and Robert E. Long, *Downtown Rebound* (Washington, D.C.: Fannie Mae Foundation and Brookings Institution), pp. 1–4.
3. Ibid.
4. Ibid.
5. U.S. Bureau of the Census, *Statistical Abstract of the United States, 1992*, 112th ed. (Washington, D.C.: Government Printing Office, 1992), p. 397.
6. Robert B. Reich, *The Work of Nations* (New York: Random House, Vintage Books, 1991), p. 86.
7. Barry Bluestone and Bennett Harrison, *The Deindustrialization of America* (New York: Basic Books, 1982).
8. Ibid., p. 65.
9. Ibid., p. 69.
10. Kenneth T. Jackson, *Crabgrass Frontier: The Suburbanization of the United States* (New York: Oxford University Press, 1985), p. 261.
11. Jon C. Teaford, *The Rough Road to Renaissance: Urban Revitalization in America, 1940–1985* (Baltimore: Johns Hopkins University Press, 1990), p. 307.
12. Bernard J. Frieden and Lynn B. Sagalyn, *Downtown, Inc.: How America Builds Cities* (Cambridge, Mass.: MIT Press, 1989), p. 43.

13. Sassen, *Cities in a World Economy* (Thousand Oaks, CA: Pine Forge Press, 2001).

14. Joseph Persky, Elliot Sclar, and Wim Wiewel, *Does America Need Cities?* (Washington, D.C.: Economic Policy Institute, 1991), p. 4.

15. "In a sample of fourteen large metropolitan areas, the wages of central city jobs in 1987 averaged 20 percent higher than those of suburban jobs." Ibid., p. 12. In the 1990s, the per capita income of central cities increased relative to the suburbs, reversing a long-term decline. See Peter Dreier, John Mollenkopf, and Todd Swanstrom, *Place Matters: Metropolitics for the Twenty-first Century* (Lawrence: University Press of Kansas, 2001), p. 40.

16. Alexander Ganz, "Where Has the Urban Crisis Gone?," *Urban Affairs Quarterly* 20, no. 4 (June 1985): 456.

17. Frieden and Sagalyn, *Downtown, Inc.*, pp. 256–266.

18. The concept of the global city is somewhat imprecise. Some scholars would question whether Chicago, Miami, and Los Angeles are global cities in the same sense as New York, London, and Tokyo, which clearly contain a much denser concentration of financial and media firms and corporations with true international reach. The two books to consult regarding this debate are Saskia Sassen, *The Global City: New York, London, Tokyo*, 2nd ed. (Princeton, N.J.: Princeton University Press, 2001), and Janet L. Abu-Lughod, *New York, Los Angeles, Chicago: America's Global Cities* (Minneapolis: University of Minnesota Press, 1999).

19. Norman J. Glickman, "Cities and the International Division of Labor," in The Capitalist City, ed. Michael Peter Smith and Joe R. Feagin (Cambridge, MA: Basil Blackwell 1987), pp. 66–86.

20. Richard Florida, *The Rise of the Creative Class and How It's Transforming Work, Leisure, Community and Everyday Life* (New York: Basic Books, 2002), p. 225.

21. Gurney Breckenfield, "It's Up to the Cities to Save Themselves," *Fortune*, March 1977, p. 196.

22. Neal R. Peirce, Robert Guskind, and John Gardner, "Politics Is Not the Only Thing That Is Changing America's Big Cities," *National Journal* 22 (November 26, 1983): 2480.

23. Quoted in Tony Hiss, "Annals of Place: Reinventing Baltimore," *New Yorker*, April 29, 1991, p. 62.

24. Robert P. Stoker, "Baltimore: The Self-Evaluating City?" in *The Politics of Urban Development*, ed. Clarence N. Stone and Heywood T. Sanders (Lawrence: University Press of Kansas, 1987), p. 248.

25. Quoted in "He Digs Downtown," *Time*, August 24, 1981, p. 42.

26. Christopher Corbett, "What's Doing in Baltimore," *New York Times*, February 23, 1992.

27. Bernard L. Berkowitz, "Rejoinder to Downtown Redevelopment as an Urban Growth Strategy: A Critical Appraisal of the Baltimore Renaissance," *Journal of Urban Affairs* 9, no. 2 (1987): 129.

28. "He Digs Downtown," p. 47.

29. Donald F. Norris, "If We Build It, They Will Come! Tourism-Based Economic Development in Baltimore," in *The Infrastructure of Play*, ed. Dennis R. Judd (Armonk, N.Y.: M.E. Sharpe, 2003), pp. 150.

30. Ibid., p. 151.

31. Richard Ben Cramer, "Can the Best Mayor Win?" *Esquire*, October 1984, p. 58.

32. Quoted in Hiss, "Annals of Place," p. 41.

33. Richard C. Hula, "The Two Baltimores," in Dennis Judd and Michael Parkinson, *Leadership and Urban Regeneration: Cities in North America and Europe* (Thousand Oaks, Calif: Sage, 1990).

34. Norris, "If We Build It," pp. 140–141.

35. Haya El Nasser, "Downtown Makes Cities Winners," p. 3A.

36. Marc V. Levine, "Downtown Development an Urban Growth Strategy," *Journal of Urban Affairs* 9, no. 2 (1987), p. 116.

37. Ibid.; Hula, "The Two Baltimores"; and David Harvey, *Spaces of Capital: Towards a Critical Geography* (New York; Routledge, 2001).

38. Harvey, *Spaces of Capital*, pp. 143–144.

39. Norris, "If We Build It," p. 144.

40. Ibid., p. 143.

41. Norman Fainstein, Susan S. Fainstein, Richard Child Hill, Dennis Judd, and Michael Peter Smith, *Restructuring the City: The Political Economy of Urban Redevelopment* (New York: Longman, 1983).

42. Terry Nichols Clark, Richard Lloyd, Kenneth K. Wong, and Pushpam Jain, "Amenities Drive Urban Growth," *Journal of Urban Affairs* 24, no. 5 (1993): 504.

43. Ibid, p. 505.

44. Christine Boyer, "Cities for Sale: Merchandising History at South Street Seaport," in *Variations on a Theme Park: The New American City and the End of Public Space*, ed. Michael Sorkin (New York: Hill and Wang, 1992), pp. 189–190.

45. G. J. Ashworth and J. E. Tunbridge, *The Tourist-Historic City* (London and New York: Belhaven Press, 1990), p. 153.

46. See also Dennis R. Judd, "Constructing the Tourist Bubble," in *The Tourist City*, ed. Dennis R. Judd and Susan S. Fainstein (New Haven: Yale University Press, 1999).

47. For an expanded discussion, see Dennis R. Judd, in "Visitors and the Spatial Ecology of the City," *Cities and Visitors*, ed. Lily M. Hoffman, Susan S. Fainstein, and Dennis R. Judd (Blackwell, 2003), pp. 22–38.

48. David H. Laslo, *Proliferating Convention Centers: The Political Economy of Regenerating Cities and the St. Louis Convention Center Expansion*, Ph.D. dissertation, University of Missouri–St. Louis, May 1999.

49. Tradeshow Week. Major Exhibit Hall Directory. 25th edition (August 2002), p. 15.

50. *Encyclopedia of Associations*, 38th ed. National Organizations of the United States. Volumes 1–3 (New York: Author, 2002).

51. George G. Fenich, "The Dollars and Sense of Convention Centers" (Ph.D. dissertation, Rutgers University, 1992), p. 34.

52. Laslo, *Proliferating Convention Centers*, p. 67.

53. *Tradeshow Week Data Book, 1998* (New York: Bill Communications, 1998), p. 6.

54. "State of the Industry 1993," *Successful Meetings*, (July 1993): 32–33.

55. *Convene Magazine* website http://www.pcma.org/convene, accessed April 2000.

56. Even in 1981, when the competition was much less fierce than now, New York, then the top convention city, captured 10.6 percent of the market, followed by Chicago, which captured 6.7 percent, and Atlanta, at 4.4 percent. The city ranked tenth in meetings with exhibitions (Boston) captured 2.3 percent, and the city ranked fifteenth (Houston) captured 1.5 percent. See *Successful Meetings*, Convention and Exhibit Market Profile, July 1983, p. 62.

57. *Sunday Magazine, St. Louis Globe Democrat*, November 9, 1975, p. 8.

58. Lawrence Tabak, "Wild About Convention Centers," *The Atlantic*, April 1994, pp. 28–34.

59. Robyne S. Turner and Mark S. Rosentraub, "Tourism, Sports and the Centrality of Cities," *Journal of Urban Affairs* 24, no. 5 (2003): 489.

60. By now the evidence is overwhelming and the studies are numerous. Some leading studies are: Robert A. Baade, "Professional Sports as Catalysts for Metropolitan Economic Development," *Journal of Urban Affairs* 18 (1996): 1–17; Mark Rosentraub, David Swinderll, M. Przybylski, and D.R. Mullins, "Sports and Downtown Development Strategy: If You Build It, Will Jobs Come? *Journal of Urban Affairs* 16 (1994): 211–239; John Zipp, "The Economic Impact of the Baseball Strike of 1994," *Urban Affairs Review* 32, no. 2 (November 1996): 157–185; Dan Coates and B. Humphries, "The Growth Effects of Sports Franchises, Stadia, and Arenas," *Journal of Policy Analysis and Management* 18, no. 4 (1999): 601–624; Robert Noll and A. Zimbalist, eds., *Sports, Jobs, and Taxes: The Economic Impact of Sports Teams and Stadiums* (Washington, D.C.: Brookings Institution Press, 1997); and Phillip A. Miller, "The Economic Impact of Sports Stadium Construction: The Case of the Construction Industry in St. Louis, MO," *Journal of Urban Affairs* 24, no. 2 (2002): 159–173. Some smaller teams have been able to turn minor-league teams into more profitable

investments for the public by resorting to public ownership (see Joseph W. Meder and J. Wesley Leckrone, "Hardball; Local Government's Foray into Sports Franchise Ownership," *Journal of Urban Affairs* 24, no. 3 (2002), pp. 353–368). This option is not open with the major sports because the sports cartels are able to exclude all teams that do not meet their regulations, which includes private ownership.

61. Kurt Badenhausen, Cecily Fluke, Lesley Kump, and Michael K. Ozanian, "Double Play," April 15, 2002; Forbes.com.

62. Davide Dukcevich, "America's Most Valuable Fans," *Forbes*, February 1, 2002; Forbes.com.

63. Michael Ozanian, "Is Baseball Really Broke?" *Forbes*, April 3, 2002; Forbes.com.

64. Infoplease.com; keywords Sports—Business/Ballparks/Arenas. Comparisons among the professional sports are difficult to make. The National Football League has a fully nationalized media arrangement with teams sharing in revenues (which has promoted equity among the teams). By contrast, major league baseball teams sign their own contracts with mostly local or regional media outlets, with limited revenue sharing among the teams. Thus, in 2002 Major League Baseball's four-year media contract was estimated at almost $1.8 million, but this figure is a tiny proportion of all media revenues collected by the individual teams.

65. Neil J. Sullivan, *The Dodgers Move West* (New York: Oxford University Press, 1987).

66. Arthur T. Johnson, "The Sports Franchise Relocation Issue and Public Policy Responses," in *Government and Sport: The Public Policy Issues,* ed. Arthur T. Johnson and James H. Frey (Totowa, N.J.: Rowman and Allanheld, 1985), p. 232.

67. Arthur T. Johnson, "Economic and Policy Implications of Hosting Sports Franchises: Some Lessons from Baltimore," *Urban Affairs Quarterly* 21, no. 3 (March 1986): 411.

68. Tim Chapin, "Beyond the Entrepreneurial City: Municipal Capitalism in San Diego," *Journal of Urban Affairs* 24, no. 5 (1993): 567–568.

69. F. Jossi, "Take Me Out to the Ballgame," *Planning* 64, no. 5 (1998): 4–9.

70. Jacob Luft, "Relocation Celebrations: NFL, NHL Franchises Find Success in New Cities" (January 26, 2001); CNNSI.com-Statitudes: NFL, NHL teams benefit from moving on.

71. Robert A. Baade and Robert E. Dye, "Sports Stadiums and Area Development: A Critical Review," *Economic Development Quarterly* 2 (1988): 265–275; Robert A. Baade, "Professional Sports and Economic Development," *Journal of Urban Affairs* 18, no. 1 (1996): 1–18.

72. Charles C. Eichner, *Playing the Field: Why Sports Teams Move and Cities Fight to Keep Them* (Baltimore: Johns Hopkins University Press, 1993), pp. 12–13.

73. Ronald Smothers, "No Hits, No Runs, One Error: The Dome," *New York Times,* June 15, 1991.

74. Eichner, *Playing the Field*, p. 67.

75. Donald Phares and Mark S. Rosentraub, "Reviving the Glory of Days Past: St. Louis's Blitz to Save Its Image, Identity, and Teams," in Mark S. Rosentraub, *Major League Losers: The Real Cost of Sports and Who's Paying for It* (New York: Basic Books, 1997).

76. Heather Cole, "Cardinals, City Sing Stadium Deal," *St. Louis Business Journal*, November 8, 2002, p. 1.

77. Christopher Carry and Doug Moore, "Lamping Reflects New Confidence on Stadium," *St. Louis Post-Dispatch*, November 23, 2002, pp. C1, C7.

78. Ibid., p. C7.

79. This account of Quincy Market is based on Frieden and Sagalyn, *Downtown, Inc.*, and Teaford, *The Rough Road to Renaissance.*

80. Mike Davis, "Fortress Los Angeles: The Militarization of Urban Space," in *Variations on a Theme Park,* ed. Michael Sorkin, (New York: The Noonday Press, 1992) p. 155.

81. Myriam Jansen-Verbeke, "Leisure+Shopping=Tourism Product Mix," in *Marketing Tourism Places,* ed. Gregory Ashworth and Brian Goodall (London and New York: Routledge, 1990), p. 132.

82. The Urban Land Institute, *Developing Urban Entertainment Centers* (Washington, D.C.: Urban Land Institute, 1998).

83. William R. Eadington, "The Emergence of Casino Gaming as a Major Factor in Tourism Markets: Policy Issues and Considerations," in *Change in Tourism: People, Places, Processes,* ed. Richard Butler and Douglas Pearce (London and New York: Routledge, 1995), pp. 159–186.

84. Ibid., p. 4.

85. Fred Faust, "It Wasn't in the Cards," *St. Louis Post-Dispatch,* April 10, 1994, pp. 1–5E.

86. *Company Analysis* (New York: Donaldson, Lufkin and Jenrette Securities Corporation, June 23, 1993), p. 12.

87. Ibid., p. 6.

88. Robert Goodman, *Legalized Gambling as a Strategy For Economic Development* (Northampton, Mass.: United States Gambling Study), p. 34.

89. Ibid., pp. 91–94.

90. William C. Lhotka, "Gambling Addict? State May Let You Deal Yourself Out," *St. Louis Post-Dispatch,* June 11, 1996, p. 6A.

91. Sabina Dietrick, Robert A. Beauregard, and Cheryl Zarlenga Kerchis, "Riverboat Gambling, Tourism and Economic Development," in *The Tourist City,* ed. Dennis Judd and Susan S. Fainstein (New Haven: Yale University Press, 1999); Goodman, *Legalized Gambling,* pp. 51–57; Margot Hornblower, "No Dice: The Backlash Against Gambling," *Time,* April 1, 1996, pp. 29–33.

92. Ellen Perlman, "The Gambling Glut," *Governing: The Magazine of States and Localities* 9, no. 8 (May 1996): 49–56.

93. John Hannigan, *Fantasy City: Pleasure and Profit in the Postmodern Metropolis* (New York: Routledge, 1998).

94. Richard Lloyd, "Neo-Bohemia: Art and Neighborhood Redevelopment in Chicago," *Journal of Urban Affairs* 24, no. 5 (2002): 517–532.

95. Florida, *The Rise of the Creative Class,* p. 224.

96. Ibid., p. 228.

97. Clark, Lloyd, Wong, and Jain, "Amenities Drive Urban Growth," pp. 493–516.

98. Dennis R. Judd, "Enclosure, Community, and Public Life," *Research in Community Sociology* 6 (1996): 217–236; see also Dennis R. Judd, "The Rise of the New Walled Cities," in *Spatial Practices,* ed. Helen Liggett and David C. Perry (Thousand Oaks, Calif.: Sage, 1995), pp. 144–166.

99. Michael A. Pagano and Ann Bowman, *Cityscapes and Capital: The Politics of Urban Development* (Baltimore: Johns Hopkins University Press, 1995), p. 74.

100. Michael Moore, *Roger and Me.* A Dog Eat Dog Films Production. (Warner Bros. Pictures 1989).

101. Bruce Weber, "Cities Are Fostering the Arts as a Way to Save Downtown," *New York Times,* November 18, 1997, p. A1.

102. Dennis R. Judd, William Winter, William Barnes, and Emily Stern, *Tourism and Entertainment as a Local Economic Development Strategy: The Report of a NLC Survey* (Washington, D.C.: National League of Cities: A Research Report, 2000), p. 8.

CHAPTER
14

THE CHALLENGE OF GOVERNANCE

A DELICATE BALANCING ACT

Racial and ethnic conflicts have long served as the fault lines in the politics of America's cities. The successive waves of foreign immigration in the nineteenth and early twentieth centuries were followed by massive internal migrations. In recent decades, the flow of foreign immigration has again accelerated. As in earlier periods, immigrants have settled in the cities and, as a result, the cities have become places where an intense power struggle is taking place between the newly arrived immigrants, African Americans, and middle- and upper-income residents. In such a context, governance becomes an urgent and difficult task. Can city governments keep the peace among the contending groups?

It should be noted that the peace has not always been preserved. The history of American cities is peppered with violent clashes between racial and ethnic groups. White mobs attacked blacks in New York City in 1863, East St. Louis in 1917, Chicago in 1919, and Tulsa in 1920. Blacks rioted in Detroit in 1944 and again in the 1960s. More recent social disorders—Liberty City in Miami, 1980; Washington, D.C., 1991; and Crown Heights in Brooklyn, 1991—revealed that racial tensions have persisted. The most serious riot of the twentieth century occurred in Los Angeles in 1992, with 53 people dead, 2,383 injuries, 16,291 arrests, over 5,500 fires, and over $700 million in property damage. Unlike previous riots, it was multiethnic, involving blacks, Latinos, and Asians.[1] In subsequent years, it might have seemed that racial and ethnic tensions had subsided, but in April 2000 fears of rioting ran rampant in Miami the day after federal agents seized Elian Gonzalez from relatives in Miami and returned him to his father in Cuba. Cuban American leaders called for calm, fearful that rioting might break out. This incident revealed that the social fabric is held together by tenuous bonds in America's cities.

Maintaining social order without the use of force is the challenge of urban *governance.* City governments are designed as mechanisms not only for providing services but also for managing social and political tensions. They do this—ideally—by incorporating into the democratic process the various political interests that make up a city. The legitimacy of local government requires that citizens perceive it as sufficiently representative and responsive to their needs. If citizens become convinced that their participation makes no difference, they will demonstrate their alienation from the political system by withholding their vote, refusing to participate in the civic life of organizational politics, and—occasionally—by resorting to violence to vent their frustrations.

Cities are contested arenas within which groups jostle for political influence and advantage. In recent decades, the struggles for power have given rise to two distinct and potentially conflicting political movements. The first, the fight for political incorporation, drew its strength from the conviction that particular groups and sectors of society had been denied adequate representation at all levels of the political system in America. The fight for incorporation originated in neighborhood protests of the 1950s against urban renewal and highway building. Neighborhood organizations began to articulate a variety of issues, and their continued existence was assured by the civil rights movement and the federal programs of the 1960s. The War on Poverty, Model Cities, and other programs contained citizen participation requirements. Soon federal funds flowed into neighborhood organizations or equivalent institutions such as community action and Model Cities agencies.

The result was a profound transformation in city politics. The civil rights and community organizing activities helped mobilize the black electorate. Within a few years, African American mayors and other public officials were taking the reins of city governments. Neighborhood organizations and community action agencies were transformed into community development corporations (CDCs). CDCs are major service providers in virtually all large cities today, and in some cities they play a major political role as well.

A second movement emerged in the 1980s as a reaction by business leaders and white working-class and middle-class voters to crime, disorder, and liberal social policies. Conservative mayors promised to cut taxes by holding down spending. To bring order to the streets, they promised to get tough with criminals, panhandlers, and the homeless. Further, they promised to use local government to restart the engine of private investment. This three-part agenda appealed to a broad alliance of voters, but it brought with it the danger that racial and ethnic antagonisms might be reignited.

In fact, however, there has been a remarkable degree of convergence between these two seemingly antagonistic political movements. Unlike their counterparts at the national level, urban conservatives, in recognition of the complex makeup of their constituencies, have generally taken moderate positions on such explosive social issues as affirmative-action hiring and multicultural curriculums in the schools; and minority mayors have generally been as aggressive as their conservative counterparts in pursuing economic growth and downtown development. In this chapter, we trace the trajectory of each of these movements and explain why they are tending toward convergence.

OUT TAKE

HAVE THE BENEFITS OF MINORITY INFLUENCE IN CITIES BEEN ENOUGH?

Many mayors walk a political tightrope. On the one hand, they feel it necessary to provide tax breaks and other incentives to business and affluent residents that may help generate jobs and aid the local economy. On the other hand, poor people and minorities are located disproportionately in cities, and there are pressures to respond to the serious social problems there. As a consequence, some city officials have to search for economic growth strategies that will keep voters satisfied without alienating key downtown businesses and investors. As cities have become multiethnic rather than biracial, the job has become harder.

The first blacks elected as mayors of major American cities—Richard Hatcher in Gary, Indiana, and Carl Stokes in Cleveland (both elected in 1967)—successfully pushed for more spending for health, education, housing, and job training programs, and for increases in federal grants.[2] Studies showed that in the next several years, cities with black mayors and council members had a higher proportion of social welfare expenditures.[3] These findings seemed to apply to Latino officeholders as well. A study that measured the degree of incorporation of blacks and Latinos into the politics of ten California cities in the early 1980s found that "Political incorporation was responsible for dramatic changes in bureaucratic decision rules in many policy areas" such as local-government hiring and contracting procedures. The study also found that incorporation increased voter turnout and the mobilization of new leaders.[4] Significant gains were achieved in integrating municipal labor forces, school administrators, and teachers, and neighborhood programs were initiated in many cities. Old racial barriers fell. Many observers interpreted these findings as a sign that more progress was yet to come, including initiatives in neighborhoods and social programs that might bring broad benefits to disadvantaged minorities.

Such expectations seem to have been dashed. Coleman Young and Andrew Young presided over conventional, downtown-growth politics in Detroit and Atlanta. Wilson Goode campaigned for the mayoralty of Philadelphia in 1983 on a platform that promised to streamline city bureaucracies, build a convention center, improve the port, and promote economic development.[5] A comprehensive study in 1983 found that black urban officials expressed attitudes and followed policies not distinctly different from white urban leaders regarding levels of city taxation and indebtedness.[6]

In the intervening years, blacks and Latinos have been elected to office in cities of all sizes and in all parts of the nation. As Latino and Asian populations increased, the biracial politics of an earlier time has given way to a complex multiethnic politics. To assemble winning electoral coalitions, it has become necessary to downplay racial issues and find issues that cut across many groups. Issues have changed as well; like whites, minority groups are stratified along class lines. Middle-class blacks, Asians, and Latinos are more open to moderate and conservative ideas than in the past. As a consequence, the gains of the first generation of minority mayors have been preserved, but demands on behalf of the poor have been moderated.

Has minority incorporation into the political system paid off? From one perspective, office holding itself is "symbolic but terribly important."[7] In addition to the symbolic benefits of incorporation, the material benefits have also been substantial; the gains in public employment have not only contributed to middle-class economic progress but also to significant changes in police behavior in minority communities.[8] But another frequently expressed view is that minority incorporation should have been economically beneficial not only for the minority middle-class but also for the poor. Perhaps this kind of expectation is unrealistic: "The painful truth is that many of the forces shaping the conditions under which the mass of low-income minority people live are not under the control of city governments."[9]

THE RISE OF THE NEIGHBORHOOD ORGANIZING MOVEMENT

Between 1956 and 1972, nearly 4 million people were displaced in cities as a result of two federal programs: urban renewal and interstate highways. Up to one-fifth of the entire population of New Haven, Connecticut, was displaced by public projects over roughly the same period.[10] The uncompensated costs equaled 20 or 30 percent of the annual income of families forced to move, a fact that prompted a noted researcher to call it "an injustice on a massive scale."[11] Of course, the costs of displacement were borne not only by individuals; the social networks and community ties making up the neighborhoods torn apart by clearance were irretrievably broken.

With inner-city neighborhoods bearing huge uncompensated costs for these projects, it is hardly surprising that residents began to organize to defend themselves. For the most part, the victims of renewal and clearance found elections an unsatisfactory means of bringing about change. Most city officials accepted the idea that what was good for downtown was good for the city, and they generally succeeded in bringing middle-class voters around to their point of view. Moreover, urban renewal authorities were run by boards dominated by politicians and civic elites, while expressways were being rammed through densely settled urban areas by state highway departments whose engineers regarded local protests with contempt. In New Haven, Mayor Richard Lee (1954–1967) led an executive-centered coalition that, following long-standing plans of business, succeeded in getting more urban renewal money per capita than any city in the country except the nation's capital.[12] The minority community's need for low- and moderate-income replacement housing was largely ignored. Quite the opposite. Urban renewal destroyed more housing than it built in New Haven, resulting in a net loss of 5,636 units by 1972.[13] A similar pattern was replicated in cities across the country.

Neighborhood organizers learned about protest tactics from the civil rights movement, but the community organizing movement also produced its own leaders and teachers. Saul Alinsky, a neighborhood organizer in Chicago, is generally considered the father of the community organizing movement in the United States. In the late 1940s, Alinsky began organizing in the Back of the Yards, a sprawling area of mostly one- and two-story working-class flats made famous early in the century by Upton Sinclair's novel *The Jungle*. Alinsky had a forceful personality, and he was not afraid of antagonizing people. Corporations hired detectives to tail him everywhere he went, and the Oakland, Illinois, city council once passed a resolution barring him from entering the city. In the end, however, it was not Alinsky's personality that irritated the powers-that-be so much as his organizational methods, recognized as effective even by his opponents. Through traveling seminars, demonstrations, and a number of influential books, Alinsky helped train an entire generation of organizers. As Heather Booth, a national leader in the community organizing movement, put it, "Alinsky is to community organizing as Freud is to psychoanalysis."[14]

Alinsky's method of community organizing can be summarized in three basic principles:

1. *Empowerment*: The goal of organizing is power; the best way to improve American democracy is to empower the powerless, starting where they live in their communities.
2. *Nonideological pragmatism*: Organizers should not impose their values or ideologies but should start with the concrete interests and issues of the community; organizers should be catalysts for empowerment, uniting all the institutions and leaders of the community.
3. *Conflict tactics*: For people without money or political influence, the end justifies the means; any tactics are justified so long as they bring about victories.

Controversy followed from Alinsky's dictum that the best tactics are those that confront the powerful and force them to react—resulting in either a victory or, if the establishment counterattacks, an escalation that stirs the pot even more. "A People's organization is a conflict group," Alinsky said.[15]

Alinsky-style community organizing against urban renewal and highway projects began in the 1950s. The Embarcadero and Central Freeway projects in San Francisco were stopped in their tracks by well-organized groups. In the 1960s, community organizers won significant victories against urban renewal authorities in several cities. In San Francisco, for example, a community organization that had asked Alinsky for advice mobilized people to sit down in front of bulldozers; it finally won a lawsuit requiring the city to come up with an acceptable relocation program.[16] Changes in federal relocation guidelines also reflected the numerous protests across the country. By 1970, 400 communities were fighting against highway plans.[17]

In his 1964 State of the Union Message, President Lyndon Johnson called for an "unconditional war on poverty," and that summer Congress passed the Economic Opportunity Act, which authorized the establishment of community action agencies (CAAs) funded by the federal government and "developed, conducted, and administered with the maximum feasible participation of residents of the areas and members of the groups served."[18] Two years later, Congress approved the Model Cities program, which also contained requirements for citizen participation; in subsequent years, similar requirements were inserted into other urban programs. These federal programs gave a tremendous boost to community organizing, especially in inner-city minority communities.

The concept of community action, as implemented in the War on Poverty, was inspired by Alinsky-style community organizing.[19] Community action provided a way for federal administrators to bypass local Democratic Party organizations, which had long ignored the needs of African American communities. By giving grants directly to community action agencies, the federal government could build direct ties with African American voters, thus improving the electoral prospects for the Democratic presidential ticket.[20]

Within a year and a half of the passage of the Economic Opportunity Act, more than a thousand CAAs were operating in cities around the country. Most of the CAAs received and administered federal funds quietly. About 10 percent of them went further, however, when their staffs organized against such institutions as local housing agencies, welfare offices, school boards, and mayors' offices. These activities nurtured activists and encouraged new neighborhood organizations to form. One study of Cincinnati found a high correlation between War on Poverty involvement in neighborhoods and the development of neighborhood organizations. The Neighborhood Services program, launched in 1967, even paid the salaries of part-time staff working for community organizations. During the first two years of the War on Poverty, twenty new neighborhood organizations formed in Cincinnati, twice as many as there had been in the previous decade.[21] Thus, the War on Poverty aided community organizing in low-income neighborhoods, which previously had lacked the financial resources and connections to organize themselves.

Mayors were incensed by these activities and angry that the federal government was funding their political opponents. "I have a very definite feeling," said San Francisco's mayor John Shelley, "that this program is headed in a direction we don't want . . . it has the potential for setting up a great political organization. Not mine. Because I have had nothing to say about it."[22] The mayors responded by pressuring Congress to give them more control over the program. In 1967, Congress passed an amendment to the appropriations bill for community action agencies that stipulated that all future grants be routed through state or local governments. The amendment also gave public officials the right to appoint the members of CAAs and lifted the requirement that all board members had to come from the community served by the CAA.

Though this amendment gave City Hall leverage over the community action agencies and, indirectly, over the nonprofit organizations and neighborhood organizations receiving funds from the CAAs, there was no turning back the clock. The complexion of city politics had already changed too much. Even though local elected officials were able to reassert some influence over many of the federal programs flowing into the cities, community groups continued to flex their muscles. Many federal programs still allocated funds directly to such groups. Federal, state, and local governments contracted with community groups to provide social services such as job training, day care, and housing.

Saul Alinsky and some Alinsky-style groups, such as the National People's Action, charged that such programs were turning community organizations into mere service providers and diverting them from advocacy and protest.[23] They had a point. Many organizers were drawn into government employment, and after acquiring professional titles and good incomes, they generally moved out of low-income neighborhoods. Poverty pimps, they were derisively called.

Other community organizers, however, began to recognize the limits of protest, especially as it became more and more difficult to maintain the fevered pitch of excitement required to sustain confrontational politics. One of the most effective national coalitions, ACORN (Associated Community Organizations for Reform Now), was founded in 1970 in Little Rock, Arkansas. ACORN claimed 50,000 dues-paying members in twenty-six states by 1982, and it increasingly became involved in local electoral activities. Other national community coalitions such as Citizen Action and Mass Fair Share also pushed an electoral strategy.

Even Saul Alinsky's organization, the Industrial Areas Foundation (IAF), began to move into electoral politics by the end of the 1970s. Following a less confrontational approach than when it was run by Alinsky, the IAF began to emphasize networking and coalition building. In Texas, the IAF sponsored voter registration projects and get-out-the-vote efforts to help pass bond referendums for improvements in IAF neighborhoods. In the 1980s, the IAF organization in San Antonio, Communities Organized for Public Service (COPS), became one of the most powerful community organizations in the country. As one IAF organizer boasted, COPS is "now part of the power structure in San Antonio."[24]

The impact of the community organizing movement reverberated through city politics. Neighborhood organizations became a permanent feature of local politics in cities large and small. These organizations administered important programs and services and organized to keep social issues on the political agenda. They were essential for recruiting new political leadership and helped prepare the way for the first generation of African American mayors.

THE INCORPORATION OF BLACKS AND LATINOS INTO CITY POLITICS

Before the civil rights movement succeeded in mobilizing the African American electorate, few blacks held public office in the United States. Until 1967, not a single African American had ever been elected mayor of a major American city. In that year, Richard Hatcher was elected mayor of Gary, Indiana, and Carl Stokes became the mayor of Cleveland. In the intervening years, the number of black mayors of major cities (over 50,000 population) increased steadily, reaching twenty-eight by 1988 and thirty-eight five years later.[25] The number of African American elected officials in the United States increased from 1,469 in 1970 to 9,040 by 2000 (see Figure 14.1). The vast majority of these officials were elected to positions in local governments, with large numbers in education, the judicial system, and law enforcement.

With the election of Kurt Schmoke as the first black mayor of Baltimore in 1987, every city of more than 100,000 people that had a majority black population had elected an African American mayor. At different points in the 1980s, African American candidates won the mayor's office in four of the five largest cities in the country, even though African American voters were in the minority in those cities (David Dinkins in New York, Tom Bradley in Los Angeles, Harold Washington in Chicago, and Wilson Goode in Philadelphia), and in the 1990s African Americans won in several cities where they constituted a minority of voters, including St. Louis, Denver, Kansas City, and Seattle.

Figure 14.1   **Black Elected Officials,* 1970–2000, and Latino Elected Officials,† 1985–2000**

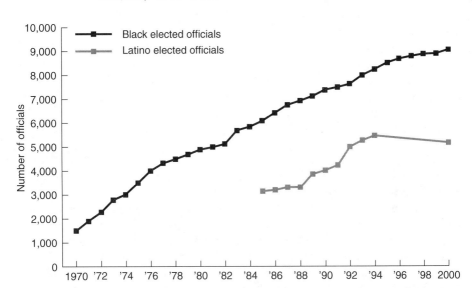

*Includes Congress
†Does not include Congress

Source: Citing data from the Joint Center for Political and Economic Studies, *Black Elected Officials: A Statistical Summary, annual* (Washington, D.C.: p. 250, table No. 399); and the National Association of Latino Elected and Appointed Officials (Washington, D.C. National Roster of Hispanic Elected Officials, annual).

The biracial nature of politics in American cities changed rapidly beginning in the 1980s, when Latinos began entering political office in large numbers. As shown in Figure 14.1, the number of Latino elected officials at all government levels in the United States grew from 3,147 in 1985 to 5,459 in 1994 before dropping off slightly to 5,205 in 2000.[26] Latino mayors won office in Denver, Miami, San Antonio, and numerous smaller cities. Federico Peña's election in Denver in 1983 was considered a breakthrough because he was the first Latino to be elected mayor of a large American city without a Latino majority. At the time, Latinos constituted just 18 percent of the city's population, with blacks making up another 12 percent.[27] Peña and the former mayor of San Antonio, Henry Cisneros, were appointed to Bill Clinton's cabinet in 1993.

Minority mayors have been forced to negotiate the difficult terrain of coalition politics. In the vast majority of the cases where African Americans or Latinos have become mayors in big cities, their respective groups have not constituted a majority of either the overall population or of the voters. Even in those cases where blacks or Latinos have made up an electoral majority, minority candidates have almost always had to win a significant proportion of the votes cast outside of minority neighborhoods to assemble a winning electoral coalition. Because of this, minority candidates have been forced to walk a fine line. The more they stress such issues as minority hiring and contracting, the more they risk alienating white supporters. Minority mayors have found that whatever the composition of their electoral coalition, they are unable to do very much unless they forge a good working relationship with the one group that can bring about prosperity in the downtown—the business community. But once in office, if they seem to ignore their constituents in the neighborhoods, minority mayors may harm their chances for reelection.

A comparison of electoral politics in the nation's two largest cities, New York and Los Angeles, sheds light on the conditions that can undermine interracial and interethnic coalitions. By 1990, non-Latino whites made up less than half—43 percent—of the population of New York City. Blacks accounted for 25 percent, Latinos 24 percent, and Asians 8 percent.[28] With a large Jewish population (accounting for about half of the non-Latino whites) that was historically sensitive to discrimination and supportive of the civil rights movement, New York City seemed to be an ideal setting for forging a multiracial and multiethnic coalition. In fact, however, this context produced an unstable and fractious politics that first elected a conservative white ethnic politician as mayor (Ed Koch elected and reelected in 1977, 1981, and 1985), then a one-term African American mayor (David Dinkins, 1989), followed by a Republican conservative (Rudolph Giuliani, 1993 and 1997). By contrast, Los Angeles, which is also racially and ethnically diverse, elected an African American mayor, Tom Bradley, in 1973, and then kept him in office for five consecutive terms. Blacks accounted for just 14 percent of the population of Los Angeles in 1990. Much can be learned about the nature of coalition politics by an examination of the Bradley years.

Tom Bradley, the son of Texas sharecroppers, moved to Los Angeles with his family at the age of seven. An exceptional student and athlete, he attended The University of California, Los Angeles, and then took a job with the Los Angeles Police Department. Moving his family to a largely white neighborhood, he organized a new community relations unit on the West Side, where he formed close personal contacts with Jewish merchants and civic leaders. Studying at night, he obtained a law degree and quit the force to practice law. Bradley became active in reform Democratic politics at a time when cooperation was being forged among upwardly mobile African Americans, Jews, and liberals—all of them largely excluded from the regular Democratic Party.

In 1969, the reform Democrats ran Bradley as a mayoral candidate against the conservative incumbent, Sam Yorty. In the racially polarized atmosphere, which was still influenced by the Watts riot of four years before, Yorty won an overwhelming majority of white votes and received particularly strong support from upper-middle-class homeowners in the San Fernando Valley. When he ran against Yorty four years later, Bradley broadened his appeal by expressing his support for policies to stimulate the revitalization of the downtown and by promising to keep taxes low. This time, Bradley was able to pull enough white and Latino votes to defeat Yorty. Bradley's electoral coalition included African Americans of all income levels, higher-income and especially Jewish white liberals, and Latinos. In subsequent elections, Bradley gradually incorporated Asian Americans into his coalition as well. Bradley succeeded largely because he was able to symbolize different things to different people: "Whites saw Bradley as a symbol of racial harmony, while blacks saw him as a symbol of racial assertion."[29]

Bradley's success was predicated on a long history of collaboration between white liberals and the upwardly mobile black middle class. Both groups had been systematically excluded from governance prior to Bradley's victory, and therefore they did not view each other as competitors but as allies in ousting the Yorty regime. After his initial victory, Bradley also reached out to business, making the downtown banks and corporations key elements of his regime. As a result, Bradley always had a massive campaign chest at his command when he ran for reelection.

Many of the conditions that allowed an African American to become the mayor of Los Angeles were absent in New York, despite the fact that blacks were already well entrenched in New York City's government by the mid-1960s.[30] By the time blacks entered New York City's political system, liberals and Jews had already established themselves by successfully electing a liberal Republican, John Lindsay, as mayor for two terms (1966–1973). Though New York's blacks, Jews, and white liberals could clearly cooperate, their leaders viewed one another with suspicion. These tensions came to a head in 1968, when the African American community attempted an experiment in community control in the Ocean Hill–Brownsville schools in Brooklyn. The school board's attempt to transfer nineteen teachers, some of them Jewish, out of the district resulted in a bitter city-wide strike by the teachers' union, which divided blacks and Jews in ways that are still being felt in New York today. The same sort of conflicts and suspicions have characterized the political relationships between African Americans and Latinos, 90 percent of whom identify themselves as white (the other 10 percent mostly come from the Caribbean).[31] Conflicts among these groups allowed Ed Koch to assemble a conservative coalition with Jews and Catholics at its center, which became the basis of his mayoral victories in 1977, 1981, and 1985.[32]

In 1989, New York elected a black mayor, David Dinkins. Having come up through the regular Democratic Party, Dinkins possessed a dignified, nonconfrontational style that was nonthreatening to whites, though without doubt blacks made up the heart of his electoral coalition. In the early stages of the mayoral contest, Koch miscalculated by attacking Jesse Jackson, who had made a run for the presidency the year before, for expressing support for the Palestine Liberation Organization (PLO). Koch commented that Jews "would have to be crazy" to vote for Jackson. An African American newspaper, *Amsterdam News,* replied bitterly by reminding Koch that "he is mayor of the city; not just of New York Jewry."[33] In an atmosphere of growing racial tension, many white voters felt that Dinkins would be better able to keep the peace, and he defeated Koch in the 1989 multicandidate Democratic primary by a 51 to 41 percent margin.

Dinkins lasted one term and was defeated by a self-styled conservative, Rudolph Giuliani, in 1993. Giuliani, a former prosecutor and a Republican, quickly set out to terminate affirmative action programs, slash spending for welfare and housing, cut health services, and beef up the police forces.[34] Crime control became the leitmotif of his administration, and he became nationally prominent for his advocacy of the "broken windows" theory, based on the premise that if small crimes were punished, larger ones would be deterred. While in office, Giulani made it point to snub African American leaders and groups. In 2001, when he was forced to leave office because of term limits, he was succeeded by Republican Mike Bloomberg, who personally spent $99 per vote to narrowly defeat the Democratic candidate.[35]

New York's racial politics became divisive only in part because white voters became concerned about crime and social disorder. The city also had become racially and ethnically diverse to the point that the various groups began to resent any benefits conferred on another group.[36] The Latino population had grown very rapidly since the mid-1960s and felt that blacks had secured a disproportionate share of municipal offices and perks. But even Latinos were divided between West Indians, Dominicans, Puerto Ricans, and Jamaicans. Asian voters also fought for a place in politics. This fractious politics has contributed to racial polarization, improving the prospects for any mayoral candidate who focuses on controlling crime and promoting downtown development—two issues that appeal quite broadly.

White candidates in other cities, most notably Los Angeles, have likewise been able to play a game of divide and conquer; indeed, racial resentments have been the key ingredient in the rise of several conservative mayors. But such cases are not necessarily typical. Overt hostilities are not the norm, and there are many examples of successful coalitions across racial and ethnic lines. Denver provides a good example. Federico Peña became the city's first Mexican American mayor in 1983 by cobbling together a coalition of highly educated white professionals connected to Denver's high-tech economy and Latino and African American voters. Peña stressed downtown and neighborhood development but also initiated affirmative action hiring in all public agencies and appointed a large number of minorities to boards and commissions. His African American successor in 1991, Wellington Webb, embellished Peña's programs by emphasizing infrastructure improvements throughout the city and by establishing a revolving fund for affordable housing.[37] Denver's experience shows that it is possible for minority candidates to emerge from a "unite and govern" rather a "divide and conquer" politics.

The Rewards of Political Incorporation

The ability to elect a mayor is only the first step toward exercising political power. To actually derive substantial benefits, it is also necessary for minorities to seek political incorporation, which can be defined as possessing "an equal or leading role in a dominant coalition that is strongly committed to minority interests."[38] Incorporation entails the ability to influence a city council and the various bureaucracies that deliver important services; otherwise, a mayor can become isolated, unable to deliver on the campaign promises made. In Chicago, for example, Harold Washington, who was mayor from 1983 to 1987, found himself tied down in the so-called council wars during his entire first term. The city council—still dominated by white ethnic politicians left over from the Daley organization—overrode Washington's policy proposals. Department administrators and city workers routinely ignored problems in the African American neighborhoods; instead, they followed orders from aldermen and precinct captains hostile to Washington. Blacks in Chicago had succeeded in electing a mayor, but until Washington's second term, they did not change Chicago's government very much.

To govern effectively and deliver benefits to supporters, a mayor must assemble a broad and comprehensive governing coalition. In American cities, authority is highly fragmented and dispersed.[39] The mayor's office is a center of power, but many other centers of power can act as veto points to frustrate mayoral leadership. In order to produce significant results that can be used to run for reelection, mayors need cooperation from institutions well beyond the city council, including labor unions, the media, independent authorities (such as school boards), the courts, and state and federal officials. To be effective while in office, a mayor must seek support from many sectors.

Downtown business leaders are essential partners or deadly adversaries. In his study of governance in Atlanta, Clarence Stone argued that downtown business exercised a "preemptive power" to shape the city's regime because it possessed the institutional resources that enabled mayors to accomplish important public tasks, like building a new stadium, a rapid transit system, or an airport. The day after he was elected Atlanta's mayor in 1981, Andrew Young, a former top aide to Martin Luther King Jr., confirmed the accuracy of Stone's assessment in a speech before a group of downtown business leaders. "I didn't get elected with your help," Young began, but then quickly added, "I can't govern without you."[40] Mayors must recognize that economic logic requires them to pay close attention to the attitudes of business leaders and investors. This often conflicts with a political logic that tempts them to spread benefits broadly to the major groups that elected them.

Minority mayors and city councils have been successful in rewarding their followers in ways that do not adversely affect the downtown business establishment. Public employment is their most important resource; downtown business does not care, for the most part, if blacks rather than whites pick up their garbage or police their streets. Studies have consistently shown that when blacks are politically incorporated—that is, when they win the mayor's office and infiltrate the institutions of local government—minority employment in city government increases.[41] From 1973 to 1991, under Mayor Bradley in Los Angeles, black, Latino, and Asian American municipal employment increased from 36 to 50 percent. Minorities are often concentrated in lower-level jobs, but in Los Angeles during this period minority representation in top-level city jobs increased as well.[42]

Minority mayors have also frequently enacted preferential procurement programs requiring that a minimum percentage of city contracts be given to minority business enterprises (MBEs). In 1973, at a time when blacks accounted for a majority of Atlanta's population, black-owned firms received only one-tenth of 1 percent of the city's contracts. As a result of a preferential procurement program, by 1988, 35 percent of the city's contracts were awarded to minority firms. Preferential procurement programs have been damaged, however, by evidence that some MBEs have acted as mere fronts for nonminority firms doing most of the work.[43] Moreover, like many affirmative action programs, preferential procurement generally has benefited higher-income and better-educated people within the minority community. Atlanta's first black mayor, Maynard Jackson, boasted that the minority set-asides for Atlanta's airport expansion created twenty-one African American millionaires; however, benefits to the low-income community were more difficult to identify.[44]

The U.S. Supreme Court has made it harder for cities and states to use preferential procurement programs. In *City of Richmond v. J. A. Croson Co.* (1989), the Court ruled that Richmond's program requiring that 30 percent of contracts be set aside for MBEs violated the Equal Protection Clause of the Fourteenth Amendment.[45] In order to withstand the "strict scrutiny" standard of constitutionality, cities must document past discrimination by city government and demonstrate that race-neutral alternatives will not solve the problem. This ruling makes preferential procurement programs difficult but not impossible to implement.[46]

Police reform is another important policy benefit flowing from political incorporation. Police brutality and inadequate police protection have long been two of the most frequently expressed grievances in minority communities around the country. For many years, the police department of Los Angeles was particularly loathed in minority communities. Under the city's governmental structure, the LAPD operated well beyond the influence of elected officials. Appointed by an independent Police Commission, the chief of police had a free hand in running the department. The LAPD had always prided itself on its tough law-and-order approach to law enforcement, and the chief liked to brag about the department's state-of-the-art high-tech weaponry. In Los Angeles, policing relied on helicopters equipped with infrared cameras for night vision and 30-million-candlepower spotlights, called "Nightsuns," that could turn night into day. Street numbers painted on rooftops gave police helicopters a navigable street grid from the air (now replaced by satellite navigation). Synchronization with patrol cars was facilitated by a high-tech communications system conceptualized by Hughes Aircraft and refined by NASA's Jet Propulsion Laboratory.[47] In low-income neighborhoods, this strategy meant that the LAPD acted more like an occupying army than as an instrument for preserving public safety.

From 1978 to 1992, Chief Daryl Gates ran the LAPD as his own personal fiefdom. Under operation HAMMER, patrol officers and elite tactical squads descended on South Central Los Angeles, arresting thousands of minority youths in each sweep. Young men were brought in for a wide range of infractions, from selling drugs to suspected gang activity to charges of loitering and jaywalking. In the absence of other charges, resisting arrest became a favorite police option. By 1990, as many as 50,000 suspects had been arrested in these sweeps, which is astounding considering there were only about 100,000 African American youths in all of Los Angeles.[48] The LAPD had a practice of using a dangerous chokehold to control people in custody. In 1982, after frequent use of the chokehold resulted in a rash of deaths among young black men, Chief Gates made the inflammatory statement that the problem could be traced to the anatomy of blacks rather than to police practices: "We may be finding that in some Blacks when [the carotid chokehold] is applied the veins or arteries do not open up as fast as they do on normal people."[49] The beating of Rodney King, which set off the 1992 riots, came as no surprise to blacks in Los Angeles.

Mayor Bradley, who had the advantage of being a former cop, succeeded in bringing the LAPD under some degree of civilian control, but only after twenty years of fierce political battles. The LAPD's share of the city's budget fell from 23 percent in 1972–1973 to 18 percent in 1987–1988. Between 1980 and 1988, minority representation in the LAPD increased from 20 to 32 percent, but minority representation in leadership positions still lagged. Most importantly, in June 1992, shortly after the riots, the voters approved Proposition F. Strongly supported by Bradley, Proposition F limited the terms of police chiefs and removed their civil service protection. Having campaigned vigorously against Proposition F, Chief Gates resigned and was succeeded by an African American, Willie Williams, who pledged to implement community-based policing.[50]

What the Los Angeles case shows is that even under adverse conditions, when minorities are incorporated into the political system they are able to bring about important changes. In Los Angeles, the black community considered it essential that more African American police officers be hired and that the police department be brought under greater civilian control.[51] Racism and police brutality still occur within integrated police forces, but changing the composition of the force is a first step toward reform.

An increasing number of racial and ethnic groups have recently sought incorporation into city politics. When these groups must cooperate to gain access to the political system, they are often able to put aside their differences and support a candidate. But these alliances are hard to keep together. A study of forty-one cities with at least 10 percent blacks and 10 percent Latinos found that, generally, black and Latino municipal employment was associated with the incorporation of both groups into local political systems. The same research showed, however, that as the African American population increased, the Latino share of municipal employment fell.[52] Tensions arise because it is difficult to satisfy both groups with the limited jobs and other resources available. In New York City, the failure of blacks and Latinos to forge a stable electoral coalition facilitated the election of conservative mayors Ed Koch and Rudolph Giuliani. Similarly, after Bradley retired in Los Angeles, his black and Latino coalition fell apart, which paved the road to the mayor's office for Republican conservative Richard Riordan.

However, the main weakness of the racial and ethnic coalitions has not been their instability but their failure to deliver much-needed social programs. In the 1960s and 1970s, when federal grants were flowing into cities, the first generation of minority mayors were able to fund programs that benefited the poor. Since the withdrawal of federal funds, mayors have found it difficult to find the necessary resources to fund housing, health, jobs, recreation, and other initiatives. In an attempt to improve local economics, black mayors have adopted rather conventional pro-growth policies in the hopes that the benefits will trickle down:

> The black mayors operate on the basis of a simple equation: private economic development in the city produces jobs in the private sector and tax money that may be used for jobs and purchases in the public sector. Through the various affirmative action devices . . . a certain proportion of these jobs and purchases may be channeled to the black community.[53]

But public-sector jobs can supply employment to no more than 6 to 8 percent of the black population of central cities—even assuming that no jobs would go to other groups.[54] In any case, a large proportion of public jobs, minority business contracts, and other benefits have gone to middle- and upper-income people and even to suburban residents.[55]

Minority mayors have often subsidized downtown development as a way to turn their cities around. Tom Bradley provides a good example. Early on, he stressed the need to make Los Angeles a "world class" city. He courted Japanese investors, who poured more than $3 billion into Los Angeles real estate in 1988 alone. Before Bradley, there was almost no downtown in Los Angeles; in 1975, there were only five buildings above thirteen stories. By 1990, there were over fifty such buildings—many of them visible in the dramatic footage that opened the television series *L.A. Law*.[56]

To subsidize downtown growth, Los Angeles created a huge 255-block Tax Increment Finance (TIF) district. The TIF allowed the city to float bonds to provide public improvements and services to stimulate private investment. But because the city was required to use all the additional taxes from the downtown redevelopment to retire the bonds or to support further development, the new taxes could not be used for projects or services elsewhere in the city.[57] The downtown office complex experienced a boom, but the high-level professional jobs generated by corporate investment were taken either by suburban residents or by professionals who moved into gentrified neighborhoods close to the downtown. The overall effect was to displace lower-income residents, drive up the cost of housing, and segment urban space into distinct enclaves.

The 1992 riots laid bare the limitations of Bradley's regime. His policies had mainly aided real estate developers and expanded opportunities for white-collar professionals, including some who were black and Latino. Redevelopment did not benefit the poor. According to the 1990 census, the poverty rate in South Central Los Angeles, where the riots started, was 33 percent. The area was seething with tensions between newly arrived Central American immigrants and long-time African American residents. Competition for housing was fierce. Finally recognizing the depth of the housing crisis, in 1991 Bradley began to push for "linkage" fees that would require developers to allocate funds for low-income housing in exchange for approval of downtown building projects.

As development spread from downtown to the affluent West Side, Bradley began to encounter stiff opposition from environmentalists who objected to increased air pollution and traffic congestion. Unable to keep up with new development, the sewage system broke down in 1987, dumping millions of gallons of raw sewage into Santa Monica Bay. Bradley proposed a cap on new sewer construction to slow the pace of new development. The next year, however, Bradley infuriated environmentalists by reversing his long-standing opposition to oil drilling in the Pacific Palisades, an area on the ocean floor extending several miles out from Los Angeles. Under siege from residents in low- as well as high-income neighborhoods, Bradley chose not to run for a sixth term in 1993.

Most African American mayors have supported a pro-growth, downtown development agenda much like Bradley's.[58] Atlanta's experience shows why. In 1973, Maynard Jackson was elected the first African American mayor of Atlanta with strong support from the black community and from neighborhood activists in both black and white neighborhoods. Jackson came into office with a strong social reform program, explicitly rejecting what he termed "slavish, unquestioning adherence to downtown dicta."[59] What set Jackson apart from previous mayors was that he insisted that business elites "come to City Hall to meet in his office and to ask for his support, rather than simply to inform him of their needs and assume his compliance."[60]

In order to undertake complex projects that he could take credit for when seeking reelection, however, Jackson needed the support of the business community, and, over time, he was pulled toward accommodation with downtown business elites. He supported all the major redevelopment projects favored by downtown business, including construction of the MARTA (Metro Atlanta Rapid Transit Authority) system, which mainly connected downtown to the Atlanta airport. Jackson's successor, civil rights activist Andrew Young, continued Jackson's unqualified support of downtown development. Commenting on his partnership with the business elite, Young said, "Politics doesn't control the world. Money does."[61]

Jackson and Young were able to increase African American public employment, government contracts for minority-owned firms, and African American representation on the police force, but the booming downtown and suburbs did little to help blacks trapped in inner-city low-income neighborhoods. They were left behind.[62] From 1980 to 1985, predominantly white areas in the Atlanta region experienced job growth 14 times greater than predominantly black areas. Between 1970 and 1982, the percentage of central-city households living in poverty doubled. Atlanta's housing and job markets remained highly segregated. After 1980, applications to higher education, especially among Atlanta's black males, fell rapidly. A 1989 study by the *Atlanta Constitution* found that one black man in six had been imprisoned.[63]

Studies in several other cities also found that the economic gains of blacks and Latinos have been marginal or nonexistent.[64] Even in Miami, the one large American city where Latinos have become the core political constituency that dominates virtually all local governmental institutions, public programs favoring poorer citizens have not resulted.[65] To expect these kind of gains is probably unrealistic, however; incorporation of any group cannot result in the overturning of the basic economic arrangements that preserve inequality. As noted by one scholar, "There is no precedent for expecting political participation to produce revolutionary outcomes for any group in American urban politics specifically or American politics in general."[66] But gains have certainly been achieved in access to public office, public employment, access to public contracting, and influence on police conduct. Symbolic gains have been considerable; political incorporation has brought a sense that blacks and Latinos have achieved social parity and respect.

The drive for political incorporation has highlighted the difficulty of forging and maintaining multiethnic coalitions. The expectation that blacks and Latinos would make common cause because both groups are disadvantaged has not been realized. In Denver, despite the fact that Latino and black leaders have forged a good working relationship, a coherent political agenda has not emerged, aside from the benefits that automatically inhere in incorporation itself (such as access to public office and to public employment). Even within the Latino community, "there is little consensus on a Latino political agenda . . . much less one that would reflect the shared concerns of blacks and Latinos over poverty, affordable housing, safety, health care, and neighborhood well-being."[67] *Minority* is a problematic term that papers over significant differences; the challenge is to forge alliances over issues that attract support from across ethnic groups.[68]

In sum, the payoffs for minority political incorporation have been uneven. Minority regimes have been quite successful in altering hiring policies and reining in the police. Minorities have gained access to jobs in public agencies. These are important accomplishments. Studies provide little evidence, however, that the incorporation of blacks and Latinos into political systems has led to significantly different taxing, spending, and service delivery policies. For the most part, African American mayors have not significantly altered development trends favoring downtown areas over the neighborhoods. The incorporation of African Americans and Latinos has had the effect of making people feel better about local politics, however. Survey research shows that blacks living in cities with a black mayor expressed more trust in and paid more attention to political affairs, and participated more in politics.[69] Participation by Latinos has increased in the cities where Latinos have become incorporated into local power structures.[70] Regardless of its objective limitations, minority incorporation has increased the legitimacy of city governments among a substantial portion of the urban population.

NEIGHBORHOOD ORGANIZATIONS AND POLITICAL INCORPORATION

Neighborhood activists have taken the lead in challenging the assumption that cities should focus primarily on local economic growth. Big downtown projects pushed by mayors and business elites—convention centers, sports stadiums, subsidized mall and entertainment districts—are regularly questioned because of the presence of neighborhood organizations. The incorporation of neighborhoods into city politics has created a political dynamic wherein neighborhood organizations and their leaders articulate issues of equity and social justice, while City Hall and downtown business tend to promote an ideology of growth.

Neighborhood organizations have lobbied city governments to decentralize the administration of services and infrastructure. A 1990 survey of 161 cities with populations of over 100,000 people found that 60 percent of them had active systems of neighborhood councils, with 70 percent of these being officially recognized by city government.[71] By the early 1990s, New York City had instituted a system of moderate decentralization wherein fifty-nine community planning boards appointed by elected officials exercised advisory powers over land use and city services.[72] St. Paul has one of the most extensive systems of neighborhood control in the country. Seventeen district councils, each elected by district residents, possessed substantial powers over zoning, the distribution of goods and services, and capital expenditures.[73] The degree to which neighborhood organizations are incorporated into local government structures varies greatly from city to city, but these organizations play some role virtually everywhere. For example, in most cities, a substantial proportion of the federal government's block grant funds flow through neighborhood and nonprofit organizations.

Neighborhood groups have pressed city governments to give high priority to neighborhood revitalization, with a special emphasis on housing. A 1991 survey of 133 cities with populations over 100,000 found that 64 percent had formed housing advocacy coalitions.[74] Partly in response to cuts in federal support for housing in the 1980s, state and city governments began to spend more on housing. Cities also began to use their regulatory powers to increase the supply of low- and moderate-income housing by passing rent control laws, placing moratoriums on the conversion of rental units to more expensive condominiums, and implementing zoning ordinances that require developers to add units in their projects for low- and moderate-income families. Linkage policies that impose fees on downtown developments have also become more common, with the revenue usually being used to build affordable housing.[75]

Community organizations did not take over city governments (and that was rarely their intent), but they did manage to help elect a number of mayors and other public officials. In 1967, Kevin White was elected mayor of Boston in part because of support from neighborhood groups that opposed urban renewal. Once in office, he supported rent control and set up "Little City Halls" around the city to satisfy demands for more community control. Later, White lost neighborhood support when he reversed himself on rent control and supported unbridled downtown growth. In 1972, Neil Goldschmidt won the mayor's office in Portland, Oregon, with key backing from neighborhood activists. A veteran of the civil rights movement before being elected to the Portland City Council, Goldschmidt had worked with Legal Services, which provided legal assistance to antipoverty and community groups. In 1971 and 1972, Goldschmidt cast the only dissenting votes on the city council on major urban renewal projects. As mayor, he formalized neighborhood authority over selected land use decisions, and the city even provided professional staff to neighborhood associations so that they could review planning proposals. Between 1974 and 1979, the number of neighborhood groups in Portland doubled to sixty.[76]

Another early success for the neighborhood movement came in Cincinnati. This was notable because the city's reform-style governmental structure—with a city manager and at-large, nonpartisan elections—seemed to discourage the decentralization of decision making. But in 1971, several neighborhood groups came together to propose a slate of council candidates. Enough members of the slate were elected to make up a majority of the new city council. Whereas the previous Republican council had emphasized downtown development, the new council stressed neighborhood revitalization. Soon Cincinnati instituted neighborhood planning and began providing direct assistance to neighborhood associations.[77] From 1969 to 1979, Hartford, Connecticut, operated under a city council whose members had strong roots in the neighborhoods. During these years, the city negotiated an equity partnership for neighborhood groups in major downtown developments, thus providing these organizations with a steady source of income and a stake in the downtown's success.[78] In 1981, Santa Monicans for Renters' Rights (SMRR) swept the city council elections in Santa Monica, California, and then implemented a strong rent control ordinance that reportedly saved renters $1.1 billion between 1987 and 1997.[79]

Such success stories should not be taken as typical, however. The politics of most cities continued to be focused on downtown development, and in many cities—especially Sunbelt cities like Phoenix, Las Vegas, and Houston— neighborhood groups have had relatively little success in organizing or in shaping city government policies. Commenting on Houston, one study called its neighborhood groups "largely invisible." During the 1970s and 1980s, Houston had only one organization representing poor neighborhoods, the Alinsky-style TMO (The Metropolitan Organization).[80] Though TMO won infrastructure improvements for poor neighborhoods, it failed to stop the Hardy Toll Road that, for the convenience of white suburban commuters, destroyed many units of moderate-income housing.[81] Denounced as radical, TMO has been excluded from the governing regime. Compared with cities like Boston and San Francisco, which have hundreds of community-based nonprofit housing developers, Houston had only five in the early 1990s. In 1988, Houston spent only 10 percent of its Community Development Block Grant (CDBG) on housing, compared to the 75 percent spent in Boston and Santa Monica.

Although neighborhood groups have changed the complexion of politics in many cities, racial, ethnic, and class differences have often divided them. Harold Washington, elected in 1983 as Chicago's first African American mayor behind a strong neighborhood agenda, was crippled by racial conflict during his entire term in office. Neighborhood groups can be parochial and obstructionist. The NIMBY syndrome (Not In My Backyard) often pits middle-income neighborhood groups against low-income people who need subsidized housing, thus splitting neighborhoods along class lines.

Neighborhood groups are often perceived as antibusiness and lacking in a broad program of economic revitalization. The belief that the main purpose of government should be to facilitate the accumulation of private economic wealth is still the dominant ideology not only in cities but in American culture generally. In 1977, Dennis Kucinich was elected mayor of Cleveland with strong support from neighborhood groups. He carried the confrontational approach of Alinsky-style neighborhood groups into the mayor's office, engaging, for example, in a bitter fight with corporations and banks over tax abatements for downtown properties. In retaliation, the banks pushed Cleveland into default by refusing to refinance the city's debt. Perceived as antibusiness, Kucinich was defeated by Republican George Voinovich after only two years in office.[82]

Mayors cannot govern effectively in the face of widespread business opposition. Somehow, they must bridge the chasm between downtown and neighborhood interests. Ray Flynn of Boston was one of the nation's most successful mayors in bridging the gap. First elected in 1983, Flynn left office nine years later to become Ambassador to the Vatican. Growing up in South Boston, Flynn's father was an immigrant longshoreman, and his mother cleaned downtown office buildings. After serving fifteen years on the city council, Flynn mounted a surprisingly strong campaign in the 1983 mayoral race by building on his support from tenants' groups and neighborhood organizations. He stirred up his poor, largely Roman Catholic followers by pitting them against the Yankee blue-bloods and downtown Republicans and promised to implement linkage policies to force developers to help the neighborhoods.

Once in office, Flynn recognized the importance of forging a governing coalition. Largely abandoning the confrontational rhetoric that had gotten him elected, he called for an alliance with business based on a program that would pursue downtown development and neighborhood revitalization at the same time. Boston's booming downtown office market allowed developers to make profits even while paying linkage fees. By walking a tightrope between downtown and the neighborhoods, Flynn was able to accomplish an impressive agenda of reform. He strengthened the city's rent control laws and enacted regulations to limit the conversion of rental units into condominiums. Flynn enacted a housing policy that required developers of projects with ten or more units to set aside 10 percent of the units for low- and moderate-income families. To deal with redlining, Flynn enacted a "linked deposit" policy in which the city would deposit its funds only with banks that demonstrated a commitment to Boston's neighborhoods. The city contributed funds to Boston's nonprofit housing developers and also gave crucial support to one of the most successful comprehensive neighborhood revitalization projects in the country, the so-called Dudley Street Neighborhood Initiative (DSNI). With one-third of the land vacant, DSNI was blocked from assembling desirable parcels by an incredible jigsaw puzzle of private owners. In an unprecedented move, the city gave DSNI, a community-based organization, the power of eminent domain so that it could force owners to sell their properties.[83]

How successful was Flynn in improving the lives of neighborhood residents? By 1993, linkage had raised about $70 million and helped build 10,000 affordable housing units, and by the end of Flynn's second term, community-based housing corporations had built or rehabilitated another 5,000 units. The banks agreed to commit $400 million to a community reinvestment plan for low- and moderate-income neighborhoods. Through Neighborhood Councils and other innovations, the Flynn administration gave residents more power over land-use decisions. Nevertheless, only so much could be accomplished through purely local efforts.[84] Innovative local housing policies could not compensate for cuts in federal housing assistance imposed by the Reagan administration. And there was relatively little the Flynn administration could do about the income inequality arising in Boston from the combination of a booming corporate services sector and a rapidly declining industrial base.

Community Development Corporations

Beginning in the late 1960s, neighborhood organizations across the country began to spin off community development corporations (CDCs) to deliver services and rehabilitate housing in their neighborhoods. CDCs are nonprofit corporations run by boards composed of area residents, formed for the purpose of delivering services and building infrastructure in neighborhoods or in somewhat larger areas. Federal, state, and city governments contract with CDCs to administer services such as job training, day care, homeless shelters, health clinics, and meals-on-wheels. They also administer funds to rehabilitate housing or fix up playgrounds and other neighborhood facilities. To varying degrees, CDCs have become incorporated into local governmental structures, though they exercise considerable autonomy in deciding how to spend the funds they receive. Because they nurture their own constituencies, in many cities they have become influential political organizations.

The CDC movement began in the 1960s as a variation on the community action agencies funded by the federal government (many CDCs evolved from community action agencies). They were supposed to arise from and represent the neighborhoods within which they were located. By seeking funding from many sources, they would establish their independence and thereby be able to represent the neighborhoods. It was expected that, over time, they would evolve into agencies that delivered important social and community services.

The CDC idea was planted when Senator Robert Kennedy toured the Bedford-Stuyvesant section of Brooklyn on a chilly afternoon in 1966. After seeing unemployed men lounging on street corners, children playing without coats in 30-degree cold, and mounds of uncollected garbage, Kennedy attended a meeting with community activists. Angry residents took out their frustrations on the surprised senator. A prominent black politician from the area told Kennedy: "I'm weary of study, Senator. Weary of speeches, weary of promises that aren't kept. . . . The Negro people are angry, Senator."[85] Appalled by the urban decay and the bitterness expressed by the residents, Kennedy vowed to devise a comprehensive strategy that would involve the residents themselves in revitalizing their neighborhood. The result was the Bedford-Stuyvesant Restoration Corporation (BSRC). Public funds were the key to leveraging private investment. The recipient of $33 million in federal dollars between 1968 and 1974, BSRC succeeded in attracting retail stores and rehabilitating thousands of housing units.

By the mid-1970s there were an estimated 200 CDCs in the country, and in the next few years they sprang up almost everywhere. A 1989 survey of 133 cities with populations of more than 100,000 found CDCs active in 95 percent of them.[86] According to a national survey, by 1994 the number of CDCs in the United States had grown to over 2,000.[87] CDCs were much more common on the west coast and in the Northeast than in the South and the mountain states.[88] With a median staff size of seven, most CDCs were quite small, often employing from one to five people. Ninety percent of CDCs were engaged in housing production, 23 percent were involved in business development, and 66 percent were focused on advocacy and community building.[89]

Over the years, a network has evolved to support the work of CDCs. National institutions developed by the Ford Foundation and the Enterprise Foundation (the latter established by the developer James Rouse)[90] market federal Low Income Housing Tax Credits (LIHTCs) to wealthy investors, who are enticed by the tax write-offs. The investments are then bundled together and allocated to CDCs, which rehabilitate housing units and sell them to individual buyers (who generally qualify for below-market interest loans). The LIHTC program has become the main federal support for low-income housing, with nonprofits receiving in 1994 over one-quarter of the subsidies. Foundation support for CDCs expanded from $74 million in 1987 to $179 million in 1991.[91] Housing advocacy coalitions have formed in eighty-five cities as conduits for low-income tax credits, foundation grants, and local, state, and federal housing funds. By pooling funds from many sources, the advocacy coalitions work with CDCs (and sometimes independently) to build affordable housing.

CDCs receive assistance from private banks, which were goaded into helping by the requirements of the Community Reinvestment Act (CRA) of 1977. Congress passed the CRA in response to intense pressure applied by neighborhood groups, which sent activists from cities around the country to pack the halls of Congress. The protesters argued that banks were engaging in redlining—the practice of drawing a red line around certain areas and refusing to grant mortgage loans within those boundaries. The CRA outlaws redlining, specifically stating that "regulated financial institutions have continuing and affirmative obligations to help meet the credit needs of the local communities in which they are chartered."[92] It is almost impossible to define the "affirmative obligations" of banks, and federal regulators have tended to side with the banks, very rarely ruling against them.

Nevertheless, the CRA has given advocacy agencies and CDCs leverage with the banks. Under CRA, a community group can file a formal protest with a relevant federal regulator if it thinks a bank is failing to meet the credit needs of the community. During the time when the protest is under consideration, the bank is forbidden to engage in certain actions, such as buying another bank or opening up a new branch. To avoid such disruptions and to steer clear of negative publicity, banks are usually willing to cut a deal with neighborhood activists. According to one study, by 1992 approximately $18 billion in new investment commitments had been negotiated with private lenders by over 300 neighborhood groups in seventy cities across the country.[93] Much of this money has been used by CDCs to build or rehabilitate housing.

Some CDCs have become significant players in local politics. The New Community Corporation (NCC) of Newark, New Jersey, is one of the country's oldest and most successful CDCs. Formed after the 1968 riots in Newark, by the mid-1990s the NCC had become the city's largest employer, providing jobs for

1,426 people. NCC's job training centers placed 1,100 graduates each year, operated 2,500 housing units, ran seven day care centers enrolling 500 children, and operated a nursing home, a credit union, a domestic violence shelter, a supermarket, and a restaurant. Until the late 1990s, when some corporate offices once again began moving into Newark, the NCC filled the vacuum left by the absence of big employers.

Mayors often find CDCs troublesome, but they must work with them. With the exception of a period of cooperation under Mayor Harold Washington, CDCs in Chicago have been viewed as rivals who might threaten the power and patronage of the Democratic Party's organization. By contrast, Pittsburgh has brought CDCs directly into its governance structure. In most cities, the city council, mayor's office, or an administrative agency of the city government determines how block grants and city funds will be spent, and CDCs compete for a piece of the pie. In Pittsburgh, an unusual arrangement exists in which the Partnership for Neighborhood Development, which is composed of representatives of CDCs, foundations, business, and city government, makes the allocation decisions. As a result, 80 percent of the city's capital budget between 1978 and 1987 went to neighborhoods, compared with only 20 percent at the peak of neighborhood investment in Chicago.[94]

CDCs have steadily increased their capacity, especially in the area of low-income housing. In 1994, for example, they produced an estimated 30,000 to 40,000 units of low- and moderate-income housing. Proponents of CDCs argue that they do more than rehabilitate housing—they rehabilitate communities. At their best, CDCs are expressions of grassroots democracy, run by local residents and not by remote planners in city hall or Washington, D.C. CDCs form grassroots lobbying efforts to press for funding from governments, foundations, and private corporations. The main argument for CDCs is that they knit together the fabric of local community by empowering the residents to solve their own problems.

The problem with the CDC model is that poverty, inequality, and neighborhood decline are brought about by factors well beyond the influence of individual neighborhoods. CDC development is highly uneven in different regions of the country and within cities. Neighborhoods that are well organized are represented by CDCs, but as one would expect, neighborhoods with the highest poverty levels are generally those that are the least organized. Even the most successful CDCs cannot address the root causes of poverty, inequality, and urban decline. Critics maintain that these causes can only be addressed by challenges to the national political system. As CDCs have been pulled into delivering services and developing housing, they have largely given up their advocacy mission.[95] When CDCs rely on corporations, foundations, and governments for funding for their continued existence, they hesitate to confront these same institutions.[96]

Whatever their limitations, CDCs have become an essential part of the institutional fabric in neighborhoods all across the country. They help mobilize citizens, supply critical services, and bring additional public and private resources into communities. CDCs have been able to garner substantial resources from private corporations and foundations, but they are still largely creatures of public funding. A 1992 study of 130 CDCs found that 78 percent received federal funds and that such funding represented about twice the resources derived from any other public or private source.[97] The biggest danger to CDCs is that federal support could be withdrawn at any time.

THE CONSERVATIVE REACTION

In the 1990s, the national conservative movement began to put down roots in local politics, energized in considerable measure by racial, ethnic, and class divisions within the cities. Within a few years, self-styled conservative white mayors replaced prominent African American mayors in several cities. In 1993, Rudolph Giuliani, a white former district attorney, defeated New York's first black mayor, David Dinkins; that same year in Los Angeles, white millionaire financier Richard Riordan defeated Mike Woo, an Asian American who tried unsuccessfully to reconstruct Tom Bradley's coalition. A year earlier, Bret Schundler had become the first Republican in seventy-five years to be elected mayor of Jersey City, New Jersey, and Republican William Goldsmith became mayor of Indianapolis. Elsewhere, African American mayors were defeated by Democrats who advocated distinctly downtown-oriented agendas. Richard M. Daley, the son of Democratic machine boss Richard J. Daley, twice defeated African American opponents, and Edward Rendell replaced Philadelphia's first black mayor, Wilson Goode.

The conservative reaction was provoked by resentments about minority political demands, especially in the areas of affirmative action and busing; opposition by downtown business elites to higher taxes and programs with a social-welfare dimension, such as linkage policies; and widespread anxiety about crime and disorder. The conservative mayors also promised a renewed focus on downtown development and amenities. Coming into office with this mix of issues, conservative mayors faced the challenge of delivering tangible benefits to their core constituencies without at the same time provoking unacceptable levels of racial and ethnic animosity.

The first generation of conservative mayors came into office during a period of high tension. In the wake of the Los Angeles riots of 1992, issues connected to social disorder, drugs, and crime reverberated all through the American political system. By playing on such themes, Republican Rudolph Giuliani was able to overcome a six to one Democratic advantage in party registration in the 1993 mayoral race in New York City. While Giuliani received 78 percent of the white vote, the African American incumbent, David Dinkins, carried 95 percent of the African American vote. Giuliani's campaign slogan, "Taking Back the City," played on a law-and-order themes and racial antagonisms. Latinos played a crucial role in the election. Giuliani had lost by a narrow margin in 1989, when he received 34 percent of the Latino vote. In the 1993 election, Giuliani put a prominent Latino politician, Herman Badillo, on his ticket for the office of City Comptroller. This time, Giuliani got 39 percent of the Latino vote. He also benefited from an unusually high voter turnout in the borough of Staten Island, a turnout stimulated by a ballot initiative calling for secession from New York City. Racial tensions provided the main motivation for the controversial proposal to secede.[98]

Latino voters also supplied the swing vote in the 1993 Los Angeles mayoral race. A Republican, Richard Riordan, carried only 14 percent of the African American vote that year, but he defeated a Democratic candidate, Mike Woo. Riordan won the election by persuading 67 percent of white voters and 43 percent of Latino voters to support him. To achieve the necessary name recognition, Riordan poured $6 million of his own money into the campaign. Riordan had acquired his fortune by financing leveraged buyouts through junk bonds and by speculating in downtown Los Angeles real estate. He had been a frequent contributor to Tom Bradley's campaigns, and by portraying himself as a pragmatic manager "tough enough to turn L.A. around" he was able to win 31 percent of the votes cast by previous Bradley supporters.[99] In April 1997, Riordan won reelection with 61 percent of the vote; he improved his support among Latino voters but lost the black vote by a three-to-one ratio.

The conservative mayors have fought hard to reverse policies perceived as unfairly benefiting blacks. At the time Giuliani was elected, 38 percent of New York City's municipal jobs went to blacks, even though they constituted only 29 percent of the city's population.[100] On taking office, Giuliani repealed the city's affirmative action policies in hiring and contracting, and he began to reduce city payrolls. Within two years, the city's workforce had been trimmed by 17,000 workers.

Concerns about law and order also energized the conservative turn in city politics. Crime became a highly charged symbolic issue, "a shorthand signal, to crucial numbers of white voters, of broader issues of social disorder, tapping powerful ideas about authority, status, morality, self-control, and race."[101] Some voters perceived black mayors as being soft on crime because they sometimes advocated more spending on social services and supported civilian review boards to monitor police conduct.[102] Conservatives vowed to "get tough" with criminals. As a former federal prosecutor, Giuliani was ideally situated to portray himself as a law-and-order candidate.

Giuliani delivered on his promises by cutting budgets for almost every city agency except the police and fire departments. He hired William Bratton as his police commissioner. Bratton instituted three controversial policing strategies. First, officers were allocated to hot spots identified from daily computer mappings of shootings and drug sales. Second, police began to crack down on minor offenses such as drinking in public, urinating on the street, and hassling motorists by demanding money for cleaning their windshields. This strategy was derived from the so-called broken windows theory of urban decline. Stated broadly, the theory suggested that small signs of decay, such as broken windows and trash on empty lots, served as signs that a neighborhood was dangerous and in decline. As applied to crime control, it meant that small offenses would be punished. Third, officers were encouraged to frisk people who were stopped for minor violations, such as playing loud music or drinking in public, in order to get guns off the street.

The new policing strategies appeared to work when New York's crime rate dropped dramatically. The number of murders fell nearly 60 percent, from a high of 2,262 in 1990 to 983 by 1996. Formerly regarded as one of the most dangerous cities in the country, for the first six months of 1996 New York City ranked 144th out of the largest 189 cities in per capita total crime.[103] Though the media attributed the decline to the new policing strategies, in fact the crime rate had begun to drop in the last year of the Dinkins administration, and the decline in the city's crime rate followed a national trend. Nevertheless, Giuliani made the improved crime statistics a major plank in his successful 1997 reelection campaign. In Giuliani's second term, crime continued to fall (again, in parallel with a national trend), so that there were just 672 murders in the city in 2000.[104]

In addition to exploiting racially charged issues, conservative mayors also claimed to possess the magic formula for bringing prosperity to the local economy. The formula was made up of a combination of cuts in spending and aggressive policies to stimulate investment. Conservatives had initially developed their analysis of the urban condition in response to New York City's fiscal crisis of 1975. When the banks refused to underwrite any more of its loans in April of that year, the city suddenly found it impossible to borrow the money it needed to meet payroll obligations and redeem outstanding notes. Conservatives blamed the crisis on a habit of profligate spending. The writer Ken Auletta said that the prominent conservative William F. Buckley had been right when he ran for mayor in 1965. As Auletta put it: "We [in New York City] have conducted a noble experiment in local socialism and income redistribution, one clear result of which has been to redistribute much of our tax base and many jobs right out of the city."[105]

Ed Koch won the mayoral race in 1977 by emphasizing just such an analysis of the causes of New York's fiscal crisis. Soon after entering City Hall, Koch asserted that "the main job of municipal government is to create a climate in which private business can expand in the city to provide jobs and profit. It's not the function of government to create jobs on the public payroll."[106] In subsequent years, Koch provided billions of dollars of incentives for businesses at the same time that he laid off 60,000 city workers. His policies appealed to homeowners in Brooklyn and Queens, who were sick of high taxes, and to real estate developers and to Wall Street firms, who expressed their gratitude in the form of generous campaign contributions.

In the 1990s, conservatives continued to attack their opponents as representatives of special interests whose free-spending policies would bankrupt cities. At the same time, they maintained that all problems could ultimately be solved if the private sector were unleashed. The rhetoric of fiscal crisis became a useful way of withdrawing the city from a variety of programs and services with a social content.[107] Mayor Giuliani cut city payrolls and services, reduced income taxes and property taxes on condominiums and co-ops, and slashed the commercial rent tax and the hotel tax on the grounds that reduced taxes would stimulate private investment. His counterpart across the country, Los Angeles mayor Richard Riordan, took a similar approach. "Economic development is the whole future of the city," Riordan said during his first year in office.[108] Working to reduce the regulatory burden on developers, Riordan pushed generous business subsidies. In one case, he put together a $70 million subsidy package to convince Dreamworks SKG to build its new studio in Los Angeles.[109]

Privatization was another top priority for conservative mayors. As they employed it, the term meant that to reduce costs, city governments should contract out such services as garbage collection and even education (in the form of charter schools). As a way of cutting costs and improving quality, privatization is long-standing and noncontroversial. In the city-building era at the beginning of the twentieth century, all cities contracted for streetcar, telephone, and utilities services, and many also contracted with private firms for water supply. The city of San Francisco contracted out garbage collection to private companies as early as 1932.[110] Partial privatization, which involves contracting out publicly funded services, often saves city governments money. One of the earliest scholarly evaluations concluded that Scottsdale, Arizona, by contracting for fire protection from a private firm, paid about half of what it would have had to pay if it had provided the service itself.[111] A 1982 survey of 1,780 cities found that the average city contracts approximately 26 percent of its services, in whole or part, to private firms.[112]

In the 1980s, however, privatization became a strategy not only to make government more efficient but also to reduce the size and scope of government altogether. E. S. Savas, called the "the godfather of privatization," served as Assistant Secretary of Housing and Urban Development (HUD) in the Reagan administration. In his books, Savas stressed that privatization was a tool not only to make a better government but to make a more limited government— "limited in its size, scope, and power relative to society's other institutions."[113] Savas later became an adviser to the Giuliani administration, which used privatization mainly as a threat to squeeze concessions out of municipal unions.

Among mayors, Indianapolis mayor William Goldsmith became one of the most ardent proponents of privatization. Elected in 1992, during his first eighteen months in office Goldsmith privatized fourteen services, sold off the municipal golf course, and slashed the city payroll from 5,700 to 4,200, giving Indianapolis the lowest number of employees per capita of any of the nation's fifty largest cities.[114] When Goldsmith attempted to contract with neighborhood groups and churches to maintain local parks, however, he found little interest, and his proposal to privatize two troubled public housing projects was vehemently opposed by the residents themselves.[115] Called a "populist Republican," Goldsmith won support by allocating city resources to neighborhood organizations in distressed inner-city neighborhoods, but critics argued that this only crippled the ability of the city to regulate some of its key services.[116]

It is difficult to assess the political significance of the conservative mayors. Cities are still voting overwhelmingly Democratic in national elections, and urban conservatives rarely have majorities on city councils. Moreover, demographic trends do not favor the conservative base in big cities. The conservative mayors recognize that they must appeal across a diverse array of racial and ethnic groups. Accordingly, both Giuliani and Riordan bucked the national Republican agenda and opposed legislation that would deny government benefits to immigrants who had not yet become citizens.

The key to the long-term success of the urban version of the national conservative movement lies in its ability to deliver benefits to its core constituencies— better services and amenities to middle-class voters and a better business climate for corporations. At the same time, other constituencies must remain satisfied enough, or at least not excessively alienated. Economic growth will not solve all problems, and sometimes it foments tensions. Like mayors of all political stripes, conservative mayors find themselves torn between an economic logic that leads them to use public resources to promote economic growth and a political logic that requires them to cultivate broad electoral support.

A CONVERGENCE OF STYLES

Though it may sometimes appear that a vast gulf divides the different groups that make up the urban electorate, in recent years there has been a notable convergence in governance styles. Conservative and liberal mayors alike must emphasize issues of economic growth. For their part, the conservative mayors must also recognize political realities. This means they must avoid taking inflammatory positions on social issues, and it also means that whatever their preferences, they must learn to work with neighborhood leaders and organizations. Mayors must be careful not to rock the boat in those cities where Community Development Corporations have forged close working relationships with city councils and with city planners and administrators. As a consequence, mayors devoted to fiscal austerity and law-and-order policies often preside over city administrations that work actively with neighborhood organizations and CDCs.

The nature of a city's electorate and its political culture powerfully shape a mayor's municipal policy. Except in cities with a divisive political culture or a racially charged atmosphere, mayors tend to be more pragmatic than ideological. Blacks, Latinos, Asians, women, and in some cases, gays have fought for incorporation into local political structures and the rewards that come from that incorporation. Where they have succeeded, the gains are permanent, no matter what label a mayor may wish to campaign under.

NOTES

1. James H. Johnson Jr., Cloyzelle K. Jones, Walter C. Farrell Jr., and Melvin L. Oliver, "The Los Angeles Rebellion: A Retrospective View," *Economic Development Quarterly* 6, no. 4 (November 1992): 356–372.
2. William E. Nelson Jr. and Philip J. Meranto, *Electing Black Mayors: Political Action in the Black Community* (Columbus: Ohio State University Press, 1977); and Charles H. Levine, *Racial Conflict and the American Mayor: Power, Polarization, and Performance* (Lexington, Mass.: D.C. Heath, 1972).
3. Albert K. Karnig and Susan Welch, *Black Representatives and Urban Policy* (Chicago: University of Chicago Press, 1980).
4. Rufus P. Browning, Dale Rogers Marshall, and David H. Tabb, *Protest Is Not Enough: The Struggle of Blacks and Hispanics for Equality in Urban Politics* (Berkeley: University California Press, 1984), p. 252.
5. Thulani Davis, "Black Mayors: Can They Make the Cities Work? *Mother Jones* 9, no. 6 (July 1984): 36.
6. Terry Nicholls Clark and Lorna Crowley Ferguson, *City Money* (New York: Columbia University Press, 1983), pp. 144–148.

7. Rufus P. Browning, Dale Rogers Marshall, and David H. Tabb, *Racial Politics in American Cities*, 3rd ed. (New York: Longman, 2002), p. 374.

8. Ibid., pp. 375–376.

9. Ibid., p. 377.

10. Susan S. Fainstein et al., *Restructuring the City: The Political Economy of Urban Redevelopment*, rev. ed. (New York: Longman, 1986), p. 49.

11. Anthony Downs, *Urban Problems and Prospects* (Chicago: Markham, 1970), chap. 8.

12. Robert Dahl, *Who Governs? Democracy and Power in an American City* (New Haven, Conn.: Yale University Press). Criticizing Dahl, G. William Domhoff presents convincing evidence that urban renewal was initiated by business, not ordinary citizens, in *Who Really Rules? New Haven and Community Power Reexamined* (Santa Monica, Calif.: Goodyear, 1978).

13. Fainstein et al., *Restructuring the City*, p. 47.

14. Quoted in Harry C. Boyte, *The Backyard Revolution: Understanding the New Citizen Movement* (Philadelphia: Temple University Press, 1980), p. 39.

15. Saul D. Alinsky, *Reveille for Radicals* (New York: Vintage Books, 1969), p. 132.

16. Chester Hartman et al., *Yerba Buena: Land Grab and Community Resistance in San Francisco* (San Francisco: Glide, 1974), p. 128.

17. Boyte, *The Backyard Revolution*, p. 11.

18. Economic Opportunity Act of 1964 (P.L. 88–452), title II.

19. The following account of the War on Poverty is taken from Nicholas Lemann, *The Promised Land: The Great Black Migration and How It Changed America* (New York: Alfred A. Knopf, 1991), pp. 109–222.

20. Frances Fox Piven and Richard A. Cloward, *Regulating the Poor: The Functions of Public Welfare*, rev. ed. (New York: Vintage Books, 1993), chap. 9.

21. John Clayton Thomas, *Between Citizen and City: Neighborhood Organizations and Urban Politics in Cincinnati* (Lawrence: University Press of Kansas, 1986), pp. 33, 69.

22. Quoted in Piven and Cloward, *Regulating the Poor*, pp. 271–272.

23. See Saul Alinsky, "The War on Poverty—Political Pornography," *Journal of Social Issues* 21 (January 1965): 42.

24. Quoted in Robert Fisher, *Let the People Decide: Neighborhood Organizing in America*, updated ed. (New York: Twayne, 1994), p. 195.

25. U.S. Bureau of the Census, *Statistical Abstract of the United States: 1995* (Washington, D.C.: U.S. Government Printing Office, 1995), p. 287.

26. National Association of Latino Elected and Appointed Officials (Washington, D.C. National Roster of Hispanic Elected Officials, annual).

27. Rodney E. Hero and Susan E. Clarke, "Latinos, Blacks, and Multiethnic Politics in Denver: Realigning Power and Influence in the Struggle for Democracy," in Browning, Marshall, and Tabb, *Racial Politics in American Cities*, p. 316.

28. John Mollenkopf, *A Phoenix in the Ashes: The Rise and the Fall of the Koch Coalition in New York City Politics* (Princeton, N.J.: Princeton University Press, 1992), p. 12.

29. Raphael J. Sonenshein, *Politics in Black and White: Race and Power in Los Angeles* (Princeton, N.J.: Princeton University Press, 1993), p. 63.

30. Patrick D. Joyce, "A Reversal of Fortunes: Black Empowerment, Political Machines, and City Jobs in New York City and Chicago," *Urban Affairs Review* 32, no. 3 (1997): 291–318.

31. Charles P. Henry, "Urban Politics and Incorporation: The Case of Blacks, Latinos, and Asians in Three Cities," in *Blacks, Latinos, and Asians in Urban America: Status and Prospects for Politics and Activism*, ed. James Jennings (Westport, Conn.: Praeger, 1994), p. 18.

32. Our account of Koch is based on Mollenkopf, *A Phoenix in the Ashes*.

33. Quotes in ibid., pp. 171–172.

34. John Mollenkopf, "New York: Still the Great Anomaly," in Browning, Marshall, and Tabb, *Racial Politics in American Cities*, p. 120.

35. Ibid.

36. Ibid.

37. Hero and Clarke, "Latinos, Blacks and Multiethnic Politics in Denver," p. 317.

38. Rufus P. Browning, Dale Rogers Marshall, and David H. Tabb, "Minority Mobilization in Ten Cities: Failures and Successes," in *Racial Politics in American Cities*, ed. Rufus P. Browning, Dale Rogers Marshall, and David H. Tabb (New York: Longman, 1995), p. 9.

39. Barbara Ferman, *Governing the Ungovernable City: Political Skill, Leadership, and the Modern Mayor* (Philadelphia: Temple University Press, 1985), chap. 1; Clarence N. Stone, *Regime Politics: Governing Atlanta 1946–1988* (Lawrence: University Press of Kansas, 1989), chap. 1. Urban regime theory stresses that cities are not governed by elected officials but by "informal arrangements by which public bodies and private interests function together in order to be able to make and carry out governing decisions." Ibid., p. 6.

40. Quoted in Stone, *Regime Politics*, p. 110.

41. Browning, Marshall, and Tabb, *Protest Is Not Enough*; Peter K. Eisinger, "Black Mayors and the Politics of Racial Economic Advancement," in *Urban Politics: Past, Present, and Future*, 2nd ed., ed. Harlan Hahn and Charles H. Levine (New York: Longman, 1984), pp. 249–260; Kenneth R. Mladenka, "Blacks and Hispanics in Urban Politics," *American Political Science Review* 83, no. 1 (March 1989): 165–191. Mladenka concludes that minority mayors have little impact on policy outcomes, but minority council majorities do.

42. Sonenshein, *Politics in Black and White*, p. 152.

43. Timothy Bates and Darrell Williams, "Preferential Procurement Programs and Minority-Owned Businesses," *Journal of Urban Affairs* 17, no. 1 (1995): 1.

44. Stone, *Regime Politics*, p. 145.

45. *City of Richmond v. J. A. Croson Co.*, 109 S. Ct. 706 (1989).

46. Mitchell F. Rice, "State and Local Government Set-Aside Programs, Disparity Studies, and Minority Business Development in the Post-*Croson* Era," *Journal of Urban Affairs* 15, no. 6 (1993): 529–553.

47. Mike Davis, *City of Quartz: Excavating the Future in Los Angeles* (London: Verso, 1990), pp. 251–253.

48. Ibid., p. 277.

49. Ibid., p. 272.

50. Sonenshein, *Politics in Black and White*, pp. 155–161.

51. Albert Karnig and Susan Welch, *Black Representation and Urban Policy* (Chicago: University of Chicago Press, 1980); Eisinger, "Black Mayors"; Browning, Marshall, and Tabb, *Protest Is Not Enough*; Mladenka, "Blacks and Hispanics in Urban Politics"; Grace Hall Saltzstein, "Black Mayors and Police Policies," *Journal of Politics* 51, no. 3 (August 1989): 525–544.

52. Paula D. McClain and Albert Karnig, "Black and Hispanic Socioeconomic and Political Competition," *American Political Science Review* 84, no. 2 (June 1990): 535–545; Paula D. McClain, "The Changing Dynamics of Urban Politics: Black and Hispanic Municipal Employment—Is There Competition?" *Journal of Politics* 55, no. 2 (May 1993): 399–414.

53. Eisinger, "Black Mayors," p. 257.

54. Ibid., p. 258.

55. William Julius Wilson, *The Truly Disadvantaged: The Inner City, the Underclass, and Public Policy* (Chicago: University of Chicago Press, 1987), p. 115.

56. Ibid., p. 135.

57. Sonenshein, *Politics in Black and White*, p. 168.

58. See Adolph Reed, "The Black Urban Regime: Structural Origins and Constraints," *Comparative Urban and Community Research* 1, no. 1 (1987): 138–189; and "Demobilization in the New Black Political Regime: Ideological Capitulation and Radical Failure in the Postsegregation Era," in *The Bubbling Cauldron: Race, Ethnicity, and the Urban Crisis*, ed. Michael Peter Smith and Joe R. Feagin (Minneapolis: University of Minnesota Press, 1995), pp. 182–208.

59. Maynard Jackson, quoted in Stone, *Regime Politics*, p. 87.

60. Adolph Reed Jr., "A Critique of Neo-Progressivism in Theorizing About Local Development Policy: A Case from Atlanta," in *The Politics of Urban Development*, ed. Clarence N. Stone and Heywood T. Sanders (Lawrence: University Press of Kansas, 1987), p. 206.

61. Quoted in Stone, *Regime Politics*, p. 136.

62. The evaluation of black progress in Atlanta that follows is based on Gary Orfield and Carole Ashkinaze, *The Closing Door: Conservative Policy and Black Opportunity* (Chicago: University of Chicago Press, 1991).

63. Cited in ibid., p. 151.

64. See the detailed case studies of twelve cities in Browning, Marshall, and Tabb, *Racial Politics in American Cities*, 3rd ed. (2002).

65. Christopher L. Warren and Dario V. Moreno, "Power Without a Program: Hispanic Incorporation in Miami," in Browning, Marshall, and Tabb, *Racial Politics in America*, 3rd ed. (2002) pp. 283–284.

66. Perry, in Browning, Marshall, and Tabb, *Racial Politics in America*, 3rd ed. (2002), p. 251.

67. Hero and Clark, p. 327.

68. Raphael Sonenshein, "The Prospects for Multiracial Coalitions: Lessons from America's Three Largest Cities," in Browning, Marshall, and Tabb, *Racial Politics in America*, 3rd ed. (2002), pp. 333–356.

69. Lawrence Bobo and Franklin D. Gilliam Jr., "Race, Sociopolitical Participation, and Black Empowerment," *American Political Science Review* 84, no. 2 (June 1990): 377–393.

70. See Browning, Marshall, and Tabb, *Racial Politics in American Cities*, 3rd ed. (2002).

71. Carmine Scavo, "The Use of Regulative Mechanisms by Large U.S. Cities," *Journal of Urban Affairs* 15, no. 1 (1993): 100.

72. Robert F. Pecorella, *Community Power in a Postreform City* (Armonk, N.Y.: M. E. Sharpe, 1994).

73. Jeffrey M. Berry, Kent E. Portney, and Ken Thomson, *The Rebirth of Urban Democracy* (Washington, D.C.: Brookings Institution, 1993), p. 13.

74. Edward G. Goetz, *Shelter Burden: Local Politics and Progressive Housing Policy* (Philadelphia: Temple University Press, 1993), p. 52.

75. W. Dennis Keating, "Linking Downtown Development with Broader Community Goals: An Analysis of Linkage Policies in Three Cities," *Journal of the American Planning Association* 52, no. 2 (1986): 133–141.

76. Carl Abbott, *Portland: Planning, Politics, and Growth in a Twentieth-Century City* (Lincoln: University of Nebraska Press, 1983), chaps. 8 and 9.

77. Thomas, *Between Citizen and City*, chap. 6.

78. Pierre Clavel, *The Progressive City: Planning and Participation, 1969–1984* (New Brunswick, N.J.: Rutgers University Press, 1986), chap. 2.

79. Stella M. Capek and John I. Gilderbloom, *Community Versus Commodity: Tenants and the American City* (Albany: State University of New York Press, 1992), p. 182.

80. Ibid., p. 212.

81. Joe R. Feagin, *Free Enterprise City: Houston in Political and Economic Perspective* (New Brunswick, N.J.: Rutgers University Press, 1988), pp. 279–280.

82. Todd Swanstrom, *The Crisis of Growth Politics: Cleveland, Kucinich, and the Challenge of Urban Populism* (Philadelphia: Temple University Press, 1985).

83. Peter Medoff and Holly Sklar, *Streets of Hope: The Fall and Rise of an Urban Neighborhood* (Boston: South End Press, 1994).

84. Peter Dreier and W. Dennis Keating, "The Limits of Localism: Progressive Housing Policies in Boston, 1984–1989," *Urban Affairs Quarterly* 26, no. 2 (December 1990): 191–216.

85. Quoted in Jack Newfield, *Robert Kennedy: A Memoir* (New York: E. P. Dutton, 1969), p. 94.

86. Edward G. Goetz, *Shelter Burden: Local Politics and Progressive Housing Policy* (Philadelphia: Temple University Press, 1993), p. 117.

87. National Congress of Community Economic Development, *Tying It All Together: The Comprehensive Achievements of Community-Based Development Organizations* (Washington, D.C.: NCCED, 1995), pp. 1, 2.

88. U.S. Department of Housing and Urban Development, *Status and Prospects of the Nonprofit Housing Sector* (Washington, D.C.: HUD, June 1995), p. 31.

89. NCCED, *Tying It All Together*, p. 9.

90. James Rouse died on April 9, 1996.

91. Reported in HUD, *Status and Prospects*, p. 46.

92. Community Reinvestment Act of 1977, 12 USC 2901.

93. Calvin Bradford, *Community Reinvestment Agreement Library* (Des Plaines, Ill.: Community Reinvestment Associates, 1992); as reported in *From Redlining to Reinvestment: Community Responses to Urban Disinvestment,* ed. Gregory D. Squires (Philadelphia: Temple University Press, 1992), p. 2.

94. Barbara Ferman, *Challenging the Growth Machine: Neighborhood Politics in Chicago and Pittsburgh* (Lawrence: University Press of Kansas, 1996), p. 99.

95. Randy Stoecker, "Empowering Redevelopment: Toward a Different CDC," *Shelterforce* (May/June 1996).

96. Robert Fisher, "Community Organizing in the Conservative '80s and Beyond," *Social Policy* 25, no. 1 (Fall 1994): 11–20.

97. Avis C. Vidal, *Rebuilding Communities: A National Study of Urban Community Development Corporations* (New York: New School for Social Research, 1992), p. 54.

98. Karen M. Kaufmann, "A Tale of Two Cities: The Impact of Intergroup Conflict on Mayoral Voting Behavior in Los Angeles and New York" (paper delivered at the American Political Science Association Meeting, San Francisco, August 29–September 1, 1996), p. 18. Giuliani was reelected by a wide margin in 1997.

99. Ibid., p. 22.

100. Institute for Puerto Rican Policy, *The Giuliani Budget Cuts and People of Color: Disproportionate Employment Impact* (New York: Institute for Puerto Rican Policy, 1994), p. 1; as reported in Michael Leo Owens, "Race, Place, and Government Employment" (paper delivered at the New York State Political Science Association Meeting, Ithaca, New York, March 29–30, 1996), p. 12.

101. Thomas Byrne Edsall and Mary D. Edsall, *Chain Reaction: The Impact of Race, Rights, and Taxes on American Politics* (New York: Norton, 1991), p. 224. Emphasis on the word *signal* removed from the original.

102. Grace Hall Saltzstein, "Black Mayors and Police Policies," *Journal of Politics* 51, no. 3, pp. 525–544.

103. Randy Kennedy, "FBI Reports New York Safer Than Most Cities," *New York Times,* January 6, 1997, Section B, p. 5.

104. University of Virginia Library, Geospatial and Statistical Data Center; fisher.lib.virginia. edu/crime/crimes94.html.

105. Quoted in William E. Simon, *A Time for Truth* (New York: Berkeley Books, 1978), p. 155.

106. Quoted in Martin Shefter, *Political Crisis/Fiscal Crisis: The Collapse and Revival of New York City* (New York: Basic Books, 1985), p. 175.

107. Ester R. Fuchs, *Mayors and Money: Fiscal Policy in New York and Chicago* (Chicago: University of Chicago Press, 1992).

108. Quoted in Laura Mecoy, "Ain't Too Proud to Beg: Is L.A.'s Businessman Mayor Good for L.A. Business?" *Los Angeles* (July 1996).

109. Ibid.

110. David F. Linowes, *Privatization: Toward More Effective Government. Report of the President's Commission on Privatization* (Urbana: University of Illinois Press, 1988), p. 2.

111. Roger S. Ahlbrandt Jr., *Municipal Fire Protection Services: Comparison of Alternative Organizational Forms* (Beverly Hills, Calif.: Sage, 1973).

112. Derived from *Rethinking Local Services: Examining Alternative Service Delivery Approaches* (Washington, D.C.: International City Management Association, 1984), table B; as reported in E. S. Savas, *Privatization: The Key to Better Government* (Chatham, N.J.: Chatham House, 1987), p. 72.

113. Ibid., p. 288.

114. Nancy Hass, "Philadelphia Freedom: How Privatization Has Worked Wonders in the City of Brotherly Love and Beyond," *Financial World* 162, no. 16 (August 3, 1993): 37.

115. William D. Eggers, "Righting City Hall," *National Review* 46, no. 16 (August 29, 1994): 40.

116. Rob Gurwitt, "Indianapolis and the Republican Future," *Governing* 7, no. 5 (February 1994): 24–28.

THE EMERGING
METROPOLIS

The emerging metropolis of the twenty-first century is riddled with an apparent contradiction: the revival of downtown and the opening up of the suburbs. Not long ago, it would have been said that downtown revitalization and the opening of the suburbs to people of all income levels and ethnic backgrounds would have constituted the end of the urban crisis, at least as it came to be defined in the second half of the twentieth century, as a crisis of racial segregation and conflict. Now the impact of these developments seems less certain. In some ways, the more things have changed, the more they have remained the same, and so it will be if the divided metropolis gives way to a metropolis fractured into a thousand pieces.

DOWNTOWN REVIVAL

The revival of downtown is both an economic and a cultural phenomenon. The groves of skyscrapers and clusters of entertainment facilities that have sprouted in recent years house the new economic activities that drive downtown development: finance, telecommunications, corporate and professional offices, tourism and leisure. But the cultural dimension is as important as the economic. The new downtowns reflect the rise of an urban culture that revolves around "quality of life" concerns.[1] It is increasingly difficult to distinguish spaces set aside for tourists from "local" spaces because leisure, entertainment, and cultural activities are consumed as much by local residents as by visitors. The rise of a new urban culture devoted to aesthetic pursuits has remade cities into places that provide the consumption activities of travel right at home. "Residents increasingly act like tourists in their own cities."[2]

A globalized middle-class culture has spread to all developed countries. The characteristics of this new cosmopolitan class can be observed in urban lifestyle magazines that carry the title of the city in question. These magazines are similar from city to city because the target audience is unvarying: an affluent middle class made up disproportionately of empty-nesters and younger singles or childless couples. Each month, columns written by a new breed of lifestyle writers and critics profile restaurants and entertainment spots, wine and cigar bars, shopping opportunities, and the other components of an urbane lifestyle. As a result, similar downtown environments have been reproduced over and over, though the details may differ.

According to Richard Florida, the members of the globalized "creative class" of professionals, intellectuals, and artists demand social interaction, culture, diversity, and authenticity.[3] Florida indicates that the creative class tends to reject "canned experiences": "a chain theme restaurant, a multimedia-circus sports stadium or a prepackaged entertainment-and-tourist district."[4] In short, the new downtowns cannot be, or seem to be, homogeneous enclaves.

But such downtowns are, in fact, enclaves in the most meaningful sense of that term when they are surrounded by areas of concentrated poverty. The revival of downtowns has created within cities extreme divisions between wealth and poverty. The minority poor remain concentrated into ghetto neighborhoods, and housing shortages have become progressively worse. In 2000, for example, a full-time minimum-wage worker could not afford the rent for a typical one-bedroom apartment unit; to do so, this worker would have had to work more than 100 hours per week.[5] In the absence of policies to house the poor, the gentrification of neighborhoods surrounding revived downtowns only exacerbates these problems.

It is important to consider whether affluent urban residents live, work, and play in "Potemkin cities," where a thriving downtown and a tourist bubble hide urban problems, or in "boutique cities" like Seattle and Denver, where highly paid professionals can sustain a critical mass of expensive restaurants, international boutique and clothing stores, and neighborhoods with stratospheric housing prices.[6] The downtowns of large cities are often demarcated and defended from surrounding land uses that might seem threatening.[7] In St. Louis, for example, a huge stadium/convention center complex anchors the north side of the downtown and a baseball stadium and an elevated freeway anchors the south. To the east is a freeway and the grounds of the Gateway Arch. Only the west side is lacking in physical barriers of some sort. For pure defense of downtown corporate enclaves, however, physical walls are more efficient than porous barriers. Atlanta and Detroit have shown the way by moving a large proportion of their downtown office workers into the comprehensive sealed realms of the Peachtree Center and the Renaissance Center. In both these structures, workers drive into parking garages and then enter a city-within-a-city where they can work, shop, eat lunch, and find a variety of diversions after work. They never have to set foot in the rest of the city.

OPENING THE SUBURBS

The last two decades represent the first period in American suburban development in which the suburbs have become open to all income and ethnic groups. Up to this point, the evidence is clear: This new opening has not been accompanied by integration so much as by the proliferation of enclaves. Whether suburbs will become more integrated in the next few years depends mainly upon whether the response to recent immigration is similar to the twentieth-century response to large-scale population movements. We do not know the answer, but there are some clues.

There seems to be a fascination with crime in American culture, as evidenced by the proliferation of crime dramas and televised real-life car chases and drug busts. Local media rely heavily on sensationalized accounts of crime and violence to maintain their ratings. The preoccupation with crime has the effect of increasing social and racial tensions. For all but those urban residents who live in crime-infested areas, there is no direct link between crime rates and the fear of crime. Most people do not have personal experiences with violent crime. Crime is highly segregated, especially along racial lines. Studies have shown that fear of crime is related to the amount of time spent viewing television programs dealing with crime in distant urban settings.[8] Because a local area may not produce a sufficient quantity of sensational crime stories on a daily basis, local news stations often import crime stories from other areas to fill in the gaps. People are sensitive to such coverage. Although people express more fear of crime when the stories are about local crimes,[9] newspaper reports that emphasize random and sensational crimes, whatever their origin, increase the fear of crime.[10]

A preoccupation with crime will inevitably produce a geography of suspicion and fear. Over the past four decades, the material enclosure of urban space in the United States has been proceeding at an accelerating pace. The urban scholar Peter Marcuse has identified three features that distinguish the divided cities of the late twentieth century from the industrial cities inherited from the nineteenth century: (1) an intensified "turf allegiance," (2) sharply defended "turf barricades and turf battles," and (3) "the subsuming of the public interest under the private."[11] The enclosure of urban space represents a secession from the larger society that is inspired by (and inspires) fear of crime and social disorder,[12] and it signals a withdrawal from public space and public life.[13]

Current trends in housing can be regarded as a bellwether of a society that is achieving a remarkably efficient social segregation, even by the standards of the segregated living patterns that have characterized urban America in the past. By 2002, an estimated 50 million Americans lived in common interest developments with private governments, compared to 32 million only one decade before.[14] The gated housing developments that have sprung up in suburbs make a fine-tuned segregation possible that separates people not only along the traditional dimensions of race, ethnicity, and wealth but also on the basis of age and lifestyle. Perhaps gated communities can be regarded merely as the latest expression of a logic of urban growth that has been unfolding for decades. What makes them different from the typical suburb, however, is that they are privatized and walled, and entry is often strictly regulated.

A large proportion of urban residents commute from suburban subdivisions, gated communities, townhouse developments, or high-rise condominium towers to downtown office complexes or suburban office parks; they drive to enclosed malls or mall complexes for shopping and commute to tourist bubbles to enjoy themselves.[15] For many, the urban experience has turned into a series of enclosures, each connected by a transportation corridor. Tourists and visitors who visit central cities now commonly fly into an airport, take a taxi or a light rail to a downtown hotel, and stay within the well-defined tourist area, never seeing or even becoming aware of the larger city around them. To a considerable degree, the geography of America's urban areas is made up of a mosaic of enclaves. Whether this pattern continues to define the cities of the twenty-first century remains to be seen.

NOTES

1. Terry Nichols Clark, Richard Lloyd, Kenneth K. Wong, and Pushpam Jain, "Amenities Drive Urban Growth," *Journal of Urban Affairs* 24, no. 5 (1993): 504.
2. Richard Lloyd, "Grit as Glamour: Neo-Bohemia and Urban Change," University of Chicago (unpublished ms., 2000), p. 21.
3. Richard Florida, *The Rise of the Creative Class* (New York: Basic Books, 2002), p. 228.
4. Ibid., p. 232.
5. National Low Income Housing Coalition, *Out of Reach: The Gap Between Housing Costs and Income of Poor People in the United States* (Washington, D.C.: Author, 1999).
6. Neal R. Peirce, "Business Basic: Rx for All Cities," *Washington Post*, March 5, 1999.
7. Saskia Sassen, *Cities in a World Economy* (Thousand Oaks, Calif: Pine Forge Press, 1994); and Sharon Zukin, *Landscapes of Power: From Detroit to Disney World* (Berkeley: University of California Press, 1991).
8. Linda Heath and John Petraitis, "Television Viewing and Fear of Crime: Where Is the Mean World?" *Basic and Applied Social Psychology* 8 (1987): 91–92.
9. E. Liska and W. Baccaglini, "Feeling Safe by Comparison: Crime in the Newspapers, A Multi-methodological Investigation," *Journal of Personality and Social Psychology* 47, no. 2 1989: 366.
10. Heath and Petraitis, "Television Viewing and Fear of Crime," p. 92.
11. Peter Marcuse, "What's So New About Divided Cities?" *International Journal of Urban and Regional Research* 17, no. 3 (September 1993): 358.
12. Dennis R. Judd, "The Rise of the New Walled Cities," in *Spatial Practices: Critical Explorations in Social/Spatial Theory*, ed. Helen Liggett and David C. Perry (Thousand Oaks, Calif.: Sage, 1995), pp. 144–166.
13. Michael Sorkin, "See You in Disneyland," in *Variations on a Theme Park: The New American City and the End of Space*, ed. Michael Sorkin (New York: Noonday Press, 1992), pp. 205–232.
14. "Homeowner Associations—General Housing," *Realty Times*, June 28, 2002; Evan McKenzie, *Privatopia: Homeowner Associations and the Rise of Residential Private Government* (New Haven, Conn.: Yale University Press, 1994).
15. Dennis R. Judd, "Enclosure, Community, and Public Life," in *Research in Community Sociology: New Communities in a Changing World*, ed. Dan A. Chekki (Greenwich, Conn. and London: JAI Press, 1996), pp. 217–238.